Travellers **S**urvival **K**it

South Africa

JAMES & DEBORAH PENRITH

Published by
VACATION WORK, 9 PARK END STREET, OXFORD

TRAVELLERS SURVIVAL KIT: SOUTH AFRICA

by James and Deborah Penrith

Copyright © Vacation Work 1997

ISBN 1 85458 175 9

Cover Design:
Miller Craig & Cocking Design Partnership

Maps by Andrea Pullen

Chapter headings by Nigel Casseldine

Printed by Unwin Brothers Ltd, Old Woking, Surrey, England

Contents

REGIONS OF SOUTH AFRICA

MAPS

Acknowledgements

In one way or another, many people and organisations have provided the straw for the bricks we made to build this guidebook. We'd like to single out for special thanks Kenny, Shelley, Tamzon and Megan Jacobs, of Johannesburg, for unreserved familial support; Dorien du Plessis, for his varied and at all times unstinting help; Professor Phillip Tobias, director of the Palaeo-Anthropology Research Group at the University of the Witwatersrand, for his kind vetting of material on the field in which he is renowned as a world authority; Bert Woodhouse, president of the Institute for the Study of Man in Africa (Isma), and Neil Lee, for sharing their expertise on San rock art; Dr Andrew Jamieson for casting an expert eye over the medical section; Wilma Swarts, the energetic and professional travel manager at the Automobile Association of South Africa; Rob Filmer of Eco-Access, Johannesburg, for information on travel facilities for the disabled; Wolf Avni, who initiated us into the private lives of brown and rainbow trout; Eric Viedge and Tuan Pickard, who gave first-aid support during successive computer crises; Helmut and Ruth Greiter, who provided the roof over our heads; and Brian Dowding, who, wittingly or unwittingly, tempered the wind to the shorn lambs.

Sources of Information

Information has been culled from a wide variety of sources, foremost among them the Automobile Association of South Africa (AA), the South African Tourist Board (Satour), a selection of the country's more efficient and co-operative publicity organisations, friends, relatives, leading outdoor publications such as *Getaway, Out There,* and *Go,* and specialist journals such as the Botanical Society of South Africa's minutely informative *Veld & Flora,* the bulletins of the Institute for the Study of Man in Africa (Isma), and the South African Archaeological Society's *Digging Stick.*

While every effort has been made to ensure that the information contained in this book is as up-to-date as possible, some details are bound to change within the lifetime of this edition, and readers are strongly advised to check facts and credentials themselves.

The *Travellers Survival Kit: South Africa* will be revised regularly. We are keen to hear comments, criticisms and suggestions from both natives and travellers. Please write to the authors at Vacation Work, 9 Park End St, Oxford OX1 1HJ. Those whose contributions are used will be sent a complimentary copy of the next edition.

Preface

Seasoned travellers say that South Africa is one of world tourism's best-kept secrets. This is bang on the money. For most of the past half century this richly endowed country dominating the African sub-continent has existed in a time warp, sealed off from the rest of the world. Apartheid ('apartness', or separate development) was the misguided political experiment that denied the country contact with the liberal and democratic countries of the Western world, and the socialist and communist countries of the old Eastern Bloc were literally a red rag to the South African bull. Travel — the great leveller — was one of the victims during this long night of political and economic isolation. The result was a decline in tourist numbers but, mercifully, the preservation of enormous tracts of coastline and wilderness areas that might otherwise have long gone the way of, for instance, Hawaii, Spain, Greece and, increasingly, Turkey. It is this untouched quality, coupled with its astonishing wildlife and scenic diversity, that gives this country at the toe of Africa its undoubted lure.

International research shows that travellers are attracted to a country by its ecological resources — its natural beauty and the diversity of its flora and fauna. Eco-tourism is on the rise and South Africa is the eco-tourist's paradise, with five distinct ecological zones, the world's richest and most varied flora, stunning scenery and an abundance of game reserves protecting most of its exceptional bird and animal life. South Africa's terrestrial mammals are among the most spectacular on earth, ranging in size from the tiny pygmy shrew to the giant African elephant, and the country is one of only a handful in Africa where you can see the 'Big Five' (elephant, lion, rhino, leopard and buffalo).

South Africa is a country in transition and the convulsions it is undergoing can be expected in time to subside. What remains unchanged is a warm, sunny climate, a well developed infrastructure, and unlimited opportunities for game and bird-watching, climbing, hiking, whale-watching, white-water rafting, deep-sea fishing, scuba diving, surfing, sailing and a host of other watersports. In addition, there are unique prehistoric, early-man sites, battlefields, winelands, and a wide range of other special interest trails and routes.

We have tried to give a representative selection of places and their attractions to give the taste and flavour of the country. We know from personal experience how delightful it is to be pointed in the right general direction and then discover that odd little country inn, that virtually unknown restaurant, bed and breakfast or campsite undiscovered by everyone and buried in unpublicised, pristine surroundings. Having said all this we don't expect everyone to share our views on what is must-see in South Africa, although tourist statistics naturally endorse the major ones, such as the Kruger National Park, Table Mountain, Cape Town's Victoria and Alfred Waterfront, the Garden Route, the Drakensberg and Sun City. Nor have we set out to write a 'turn left, turn right' compendium of road and route directions. The Automobile Association of South Africa (AA), among others, can provide you with a comprehensive range of route-finders that do this. Our aim is to ensure you have fun and enjoy your visit. Restaurants, like hotels and other accommodation, are listed in up-market, reasonable and budget price brackets.

It is still very much a case of *Ex Africa semper aliquid novi* ('Out of Africa always something new'), especially when it comes to regional dialling codes and telephone numbers. The numbers we've used were correct at the time of writing (May 1997), but double-check them in the telephone directory or through directory enquiries. Postal addresses are less likely to change than street addresses and telephone numbers. South Africa is still catching up with the rest of the electronic world, so not every establishment — especially the smaller, budget-type ones — has a fax machine, and fewer still can be accessed via the Internet. Where these numbers and addresses are available we have given them. Exchange rate fluctuations tend to make the inclusion of prices of limited value, but we have given them where necessary as an indication of the local norm. One thing you can rely on: with the rands you get for your pounds or dollars you know that it's getting cheaper for visitors to South Africa all the time.

James and Deborah Penrith
Johannesburg, July 1997

SOUTH AFRICA AND ITS PEOPLE

South Africa has a respectable historical and geological pedigree. Roughly 135 million years ago a cataclysmic event occurred that was to have far-reaching repercussions for future long-haul flights and travellers with a penchant for vacations with a touch of the primeval. The stupendous land mass that then dominated the planet — Gondwanaland — was racked by titanic convulsions that tore it apart. Over the aeons the massive fragments drifted away from one another to form today's familiar continents. Africa was at the heart of Gondwanaland, and it does not take much imagination to see that most of the world's major continents should still fit neatly around it. Africa still retains evidence of this misty past, and the flora and fauna of South Africa in particular show unmistakeable links with species in places as far apart as South America, India, Australia and Antarctica. South Africa also boasts some of the oldest rocks and geological formations on Earth.

GEOGRAPHY

South Africa sits at Africa's toe, and there is nothing between it and the next big chunk of land to the south but thousands of miles of icy ocean waters. The country is largely a 1200m-high plateau, which covers two-thirds of its surface. This is fringed by a narrow coastal plain along the Indian and Atlantic oceans, with an escarpment sweeping up to the interior and to the semi-desert areas of the Karoo, and the Highveld lying at up to 1700m above sea level. The whole resembles a huge, inverted saucer, its interior a vast plain broken by occasional hills and mountains, with its rim a coastal belt varying from 60km/37 miles in width in the west to more than 200km/124 miles wide in the east. The highest point of the plateau is along its south-eastern edge, where the Drakensberg range rears; there the highest peak is Injasuti, at 3400m. The plateau falls roughly into three regions: the Highveld; the Middleveld, lying at an average of 900m above sea level; and the low-lying bushveld region.

South Africa's total land area covers 1,223,410 sq km (472,236 sq miles), including the Prince Edward Islands (Marion Island and Prince Edward Island), which lie 1920km/1200 miles south-east of Cape Town and halfway to the Antarctic. In size, the Republic is bigger than Texas and California combined, and five times the size of Britain. Most of South Africa is below the Tropic of Capricorn, and it covers about 4% of the entire African continent.

South Africa consists of nine provinces: Gauteng, Mpumalanga, Northern Province, North-West Province, Northern Cape, Free State, KwaZulu-Natal, Eastern Cape and Western Cape. These have only been in existence for a few years, having been formed from the old provinces of Cape, Orange Free State, Transvaal and Natal in the early 1990s.

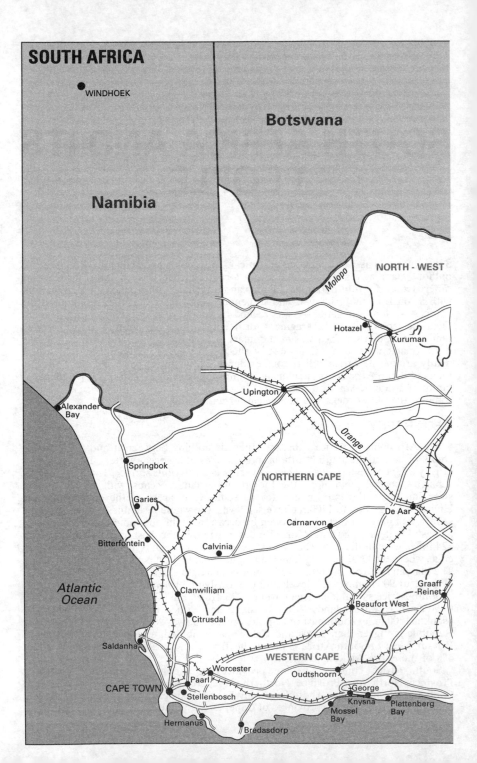

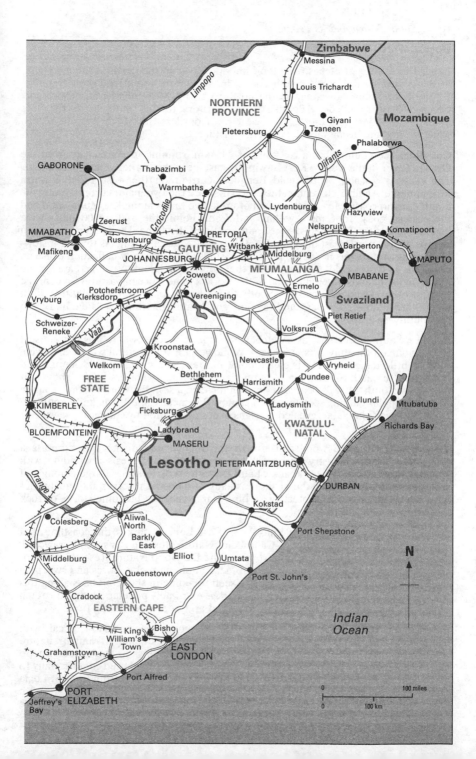

Boundaries

Land. The country stretches from the Limpopo River in the north to Cape Agulhas in the south. To the north, South Africa has common boundaries with Namibia, Botswana and Zimbabwe, and in the north-east with Mozambique and Swaziland. Completely surrounded by South African territory to the south-east is the little mountain kingdom of Lesotho. The west coast borders the South Atlantic Ocean while the Indian Ocean laps the eastern coastline.

Coastline. The country has a coastline of 2954km, running in a great arc from the Orange River in the west to Kosi Bay in the east, near the border with Mozambique. The coast is washed by the cold Benguela current on the west and the warm Mozambique-Agulhas current on the east. These are the two major currents along the South African coast. Moving at a speed of up to five knots along KwaZulu-Natal and the eastern coast to Cape Agulhas and Cape Point, the 160km/100 miles-wide Agulhas meets the Benguela off the southern tip of the Cape. The icy Benguela then sweeps up in a north-west direction from the great Antarctic drift. As this great slow-moving current travels north the prevailing winds and a westerly deflection cause an upwelling of dense, cold, nutrient layers that nourish the plankton and create for the fishing industry and angler alike one of the world's richest ocean pastures. In contrast to most other seaboard countries, South Africa has a coastline unusually free from natural indentations and bays, and the only good natural harbour is Saldanha Bay in the south-west Cape.

Beaches. South Africa has vast stretches of unspoilt beaches where it is not unusual to find yourself the only person in sight. While you must be careful where you swim, there is little danger from a hygienic point of view. The Council for Scientific and Industrial Research (CSIR) conducts regular tests of the water and these show that the sea off South Africa's beaches is among the cleanest in the world. Samples taken from 10 popular bathing spots between Camps Bay, near Cape Town, and Umhlanga Rocks in KwaZulu-Natal revealed no signs of contamination by chemicals, sewage or *Salmonella*.

West Coast. This is a wonderful stretch for anglers and divers and supports a prosperous fishing industry. Inshore there are large kelp forests abounding with limpets, mussels, *perlemoen* (abalone) and crayfish (rock lobster). Large colonies of seals and seabirds breed on the offshore islands, and marine reserves and sanctuaries have been established to protect these bird islands and the breeding stocks of rock lobsters.

South Coast. From the Cape Peninsula to East London this is the coastline that attracts millions of visitors a year. Cape Point Nature Reserve is a special drawcard, and another that is growing in importance is the De Hoop Nature Reserve, north of Cape Agulhas, which has a splendid coastline, combining rocky shores and sweeping sand dunes. Southern right whales can be seen breeding in sheltered bays along this coast. The Tsitsikamma Coastal National Park is extremely popular. This wild stretch of coast is famed for its Otter Hiking Trail and an underwater diving trail.

East Coast. From East London to Kosi Bay, the coast becomes sub-tropical, with mangroves and palms lining the rivers. Dwesa, Hluleka and Mkambati nature reserves protect part of this beautiful coast, providing a stark contrast to neighbouring shores where locals harvest shellfish and seaweed used commercially to make agar. In KwaZulu-Natal, a large area of northern Zululand from Lake St Lucia to Ponta do Ouro on the Mozambique border is protected. This area has South Africa's only coral reefs. Access to beaches here is strictly controlled, as they are breeding grounds for threatened loggerhead and leatherback turtles.

Terrain

South Africa is truly, as the tourist brochures state, 'a world in one country'. It has every type of terrain imaginable, from the bleak sands of the Kalahari in the west through the semi-desert Karoo and rolling prairie grasslands of the central plateau to the lush, sub-tropical valleys and coastal plains of the east; from the thornscrub of the northern bushveld to the verdant winelands and wheatlands of the south. There are no permanent snowfields, but there is an icy alpine belt that sees heavy falls of snow along the topmost ridges and peaks of the Drakensberg (Dragon Mountain) range, whose spine curves under one name or another from the Eastern Cape to the Northern Province, through Lesotho and KwaZulu-Natal, where the mightiest snow-clad peaks of all are found.

The country's climatic variations and its geology combine to make it a stunning mosaic of attractions. The Cape region is renowned for the remarkable wealth of its *fynbos* habitat, which is better known as the Cape Floral Kingdom, of whose 8550 species more than 70% occur nowhere else in the world. Table Mountain alone has a greater diversity of flora than Tasmania, an area 2000 times greater, and the Cape Peninsula has more plant species than the whole of Great Britain.

This *fynbos* region is one of the six accepted floral kingdoms of the world, and is the only kingdom falling entirely within one country. The Cape Floral Kingdom covers about 70,000 sq km/27,345 sq miles of the eastern and southern Cape, an area of winter or year-round rainfall. The name *fynbos* means 'fine bush' and is applied to the large group of evergreen plants with small, fine leaves, such as heather. The striking proteas for which South Africa is well known are part of this floral group, which also produces useful plants such as *rooibos* (red bush) tea and *buchu*, the leaves of which have medicinal properties.

The Cape's west coast and the Namaqualand region of the Northern Cape are another major drawcard. In spring, if there has been enough rain, the landscape here is transformed into a brilliant floral carpet stretching from horizon to horizon. This is a memorable sight and should not be missed if you are visiting South Africa in spring.

The Great Karoo, stretching through parts of the Western Cape and the Northern Cape provinces is an arid but strangely fascinating expanse that covers more than a quarter of South Africa. This is where dinosaurs roamed 150 million years ago and left their bones to fossilise in the sediment of the Stormberg rocks. Much, much later, vast herds of springbok made this their stamping ground, but fell in untold numbers to the rifle and gave way to the fat-tailed sheep of the invading herders and farmers. It is still the domain of sheep renowned throughout South Africa for their fragrant herb-scented mutton and lamb.

The Klein Karoo, or Little Karoo, lies between the 200km/124 miles-long Swartberg range in the north and the coastal Langeberg range in the south. These mountains form a barrier between the ocean and the interior and parch the winds of the moisture that might otherwise fall in the arid Karoo. The area is thinly populated. The only medium-sized towns are Oudsthoorn — centre of a thriving ostrich farming area — and Worcester.

For its size South Africa has remarkably little tree cover. Less than 1% of its surface area is covered by indigenous trees and a further 1% is covered by stands of pines from Europe and America, and gums from Australia, which have been planted to provide timber and pulp. The country once had 4 million hectares of natural forest, but only 300,000 hectares remain. The only forests of any significance are at Knysna and Tsitsikamma, where you can still see forest giants such as yellowwood, ironwood and lemonwood. These forests are a magical world of ferns, lichens and colourful forest birds, such as the Knysna loerie, the Cape parrot and the rameron pigeon. Other reasonably large protected patches of indigenous forest occur in the high-rainfall areas of the eastern escarpment — Magoesbaskloof, Soutpansberg and Blouberg — and in some eastern seaboard areas.

South Africa is a dry country, although the proliferation of garden swimming pools everywhere might lead you to think otherwise. Perennial rivers are found only in a quarter of the country, in the south and south-western Cape and the eastern plateau slopes, and even the flow of these is seasonal and determined by rainfall. There are no natural lakes of any note, and in the entire western interior rivers flow only after infrequent storms.

The country's main and longest artery is the Orange River, which rises in Lesotho and debouches into the Atlantic after a journey of 1400km/870 miles. On the river is one of the world's greatest waterfalls, the Augrabies Falls. In times of flood 405 million litres of chocolate-brown water flow over 19 separate waterfalls every minute and pour down the granite gorge — an awe-inspiring sight. Other important rivers include the Vaal, which is the border between Gauteng and the Free State; the Limpopo, the frontier between South Africa and Zimbabwe; the Tugela, Umzimvubu, Umzimkulu and Pongola, in KwaZulu-Natal; the Sundays and Great Fish rivers in the Eastern Cape; the Berg and Breede, in the Western Cape; Letaba in the Northern Province; Caledon in the eastern Free State; and a number of others in various parts of the country and all named Crocodile or Olifants.

The highest waterfall in South Africa is the Tugela Falls, in the Mont-aux-Sources area of the Drakensberg, which plunges 948m/3010ft in a series of falls. It is the second highest in the world after the Angel Falls in Venezuela, which at 979m is more than twice the height of the Empire State Building.

CLIMATE

Way back in 1891 British aristocrat and MP Lord Randolph Churchill wrote of South Africa that 'to the traveller in search of health, distraction, amusement, sport, beauty of scenery, excellence of climate, I can recommend it as being the region of the world most favoured by nature, either for the residence, or the wanderings of man.'

As South Africa lies in the southern hemisphere, the seasons are the reverse of those in Europe, the USA and other northern hemisphere countries. Midwinter is in June and midsummer in January, which means that while Christmas naturally falls in December, you are likely to be eating your turkey and plum pudding with the sun beating down. The climate is generally sunny and pleasant even in winter. Winters are usually mild, although snow can fall on mountains in the Cape and KwaZulu-Natal. It has even snowed in Johannesburg, although this is a rare occurrence. Frost occurs from April to October in the eastern and southern plateau areas bordering on the Drakensberg escarpment. It is a rarity on the coast. No matter when you visit, you can always find at least one place where the sun is shining. The Western Cape has warm to hot, dry summers and chilly, wet winters; the Highveld areas have hot summer days, often ending with hail and spectacular thunderstorms around tea-time, and frosty, crisp, dry winters. The coastal areas of KwaZulu-Natal and the Eastern Cape are sub-tropical — which means year-round beach weather — with high humidity in summer and balmy winters. Temperatures in winter (April to September) range from below freezing to 20°C/68°F. Average temperatures in summer range from 15°C/60°F to 35°C/96°F. One climatic feature you should be aware of is the Cape Peninsula's notorious skirt-lifter, the gale-force south-easter that blows during the summer months and is known as the Cape Doctor for its presumed cleansing effects. This is the wind that rolls the famous white tablecloth of cloud over the top of Table Mountain. Another climatic oddity is the hot dry wind known as the berg wind, which blows across the western and eastern coastal belts, often presaging widespread bush fires.

South Africa is famed for its sunshine and ranks high in the world as far as hours of sunshine are concerned. In contrast, it gets only half the world's average annual rainfall. The Northern Cape gets the most hours of sunshine and fewest wet days. Average daily temperatures over the year are pretty evenly spread throughout the country at between 21°C/70°F and 27°C/81°F, although it does regularly soar well above 30°C/86°F during the summer in eastern Mpumalanga and the Northern Cape.

Minimum hours of sunshine coincide with the rainy seasons, which are generally in winter in the south and during the summer months in the north. The Cape has an invigorating Mediterranean climate with dry, long, hot summers but plenty of rain in winter. April and May are usually the most pleasant months in South Africa; the rainy season in the summer rainfall region has ended by then and it has not really started in the winter rainfall areas.

Average annual rainfall is only 464mm/18 inches, against a world average of 857mm/34 inches, and overall 65% of the country has an annual rainfall of less than 500mm/20 inches, which is usually regarded as the absolute minimum for successful farming. More than 90% of any downpour evaporates before it reaches the country's 10 main river systems. Wide fluctuations in the average annual rainfall are the rule rather than the exception, and the country is periodically stricken by crippling droughts, which often end in severe flooding. The last two major droughts devastated farming from 1960 to 1966 and from 1981 to 1987.

Generally speaking, summer is beach time, autumn and spring are the best seasons for walking and backpacking, and winter is the time for white-water rafting and canoeing in the Cape, when the rivers are high, and for game-watching in the bushveld when the cover is sparse. The average number of hours of sunshine a day varies from 7.5 to 9.4 compared with 3.8 hours in London, 6.4 in Rome, and 6.9 in New York.

Weather Report. For a 24-hour weather report call:

> Gauteng: 082 234 433 1
> Mpumalanga: 082 234 433 2
> Northern Cape: 082 234 433 3
> Eastern Cape: 082 234 433 4
> Western Cape: 082 234 433 5
> North-West: 082 234 433 6
> Free State: 082 234 433 7
> KwaZulu-Natal: 082 234 433 8
> Northern Province: 082 234 433 9

Temperature. To convert Celsius to Fahrenheit multiply °C by nine, divide by five, and add 32. To convert Fahrenheit to Celsius subtract 32 from °F, multiply by five, and divide by nine.

HISTORY

South Africa's recorded history can correctly be said to have begun with the arrival from the north of the first San people (Bushmen) more than 20,000 years ago. While the ancient pharaohs of Egypt were busy recording their dynasties in weird hieroglyphs, the little hunter-gatherers at the other end of the continent were engraving their versions of their everyday world on handy boulders and rock faces. Unfortunately, they left no Rosetta Stone behind for us to interpret their work, so archaeologists and palaeontologists are still scratching their heads in puzzlement over most of this widespread rock art. Some 2000 years ago the Bushmen were joined by bands of Khoikhoi (Hottentot) herders who gradually displaced them along the coast.

The Coming of the Europeans. What later Eurocentric generations of historians term the country's recorded history dates from tentative and often adventitious forays along the coast in the 15th century by Portuguese mariners searching for a sea route to the riches of India and the east, and later the momentous decision by a group of merchants in the Netherlands to establish a refreshment station — in effect the country's first takeaway — for their ships plying the profitable spice route they wrenched from Portuguese control. It is generally accepted that the first European navigator to sight the distinctive long, table-shaped mountain rearing up 1164m/3696ft at the bottom of Africa was Bartolomeu Dias, who sailed past in 1487, although there has always been sneaking support for the romantic legend recorded by Herodotus that a Phoenician fleet circumnavigated Africa around 600BC and put into Table Bay; the theory that other Arab dhows and Chinese junks voyaged to the foot of Africa also has its supporters.

Dias sailed into Mossel Bay and later landed on an island in Algoa Bay, where he erected a stone cross incised with the arms of Portugal (bits of this cross can be seen in the South African Museum in Cape Town). This island is now called St Croix. On the return voyage to Portugal, Dias rounded the stretch of land he called the Cape of Storms, now better known as the Cape of Good Hope. Later, when Sir Francis Drake, Queen Elizabeth I's great admiral, saw the Cape of Good Hope in his voyage around the world, he wrote: 'This Cape is a most stately thing, and the fairest Cape we saw in the whole circumference of the Earth.'

On April 6 1652, a group of Khoikhoi herdsmen wandering along the shores of Table Bay were astonished to see three sailing ships (*Dromedaris*, *Goede Hoop* and *Reijer*) appear and drop anchor off the place they called *Huigais* ('Stone Place'), present-day Cape Town. They were about to meet Jan van Riebeeck, sent to the Cape of Good Hope with 116 men by the Dutch East India Company (VOC) to establish a victualling station for their passing ships. Neither side imagined that this halfway-house was the first step to subsequent European colonisation, or that the Commander in the fancy lace collar and strange hat would subsequently be revered as the father of the Afrikaner nation, which would fight and struggle with the British for domination of the country for the next three centuries. The arrival of the Europeans was naturally an unhappy event for the Khoikhoi, who realised when the stone Castle of Good Hope, which still stands, was built and farmers settled on their land that the white men intended to stay. Soon the herders would no longer barter with the white community and drove off those attempting to take their livestock by force. As the refreshment station grew the need for labour became urgent and the VOC shipped in slaves from their eastern possessions and elsewhere in Africa. Within a decade the Cape had become a society of racially distinct and unequal groups, and blacks were never numerous or strong enough to break down the social and economic barriers.

The Dutch settlers soon began to move into the interior, first to hunt and barter and then to settle down with their livestock and farm. They moved into a frontier zone already peopled by the Bushmen, and further north and east, by Bantu-speaking pastoralists, and clashes with them marked this period of European expansion in the 17th and 18th centuries. In 1795, the Cape was annexed by Britain and four years later the first of nine bloody frontier wars erupted in the area between the Sundays and Kei rivers. The British responded to these with military might and by encouraging British settlement in the frontier areas of the eastern Cape. Some 4000 settlers eventually arrived at Algoa Bay and dispersed into the interior. These hardy people put their mark permanently on South Africa, rooting their language side by side with Dutch and laying the foundations for agriculture, science, commerce, education, law and communications.

In 1803, it was the turn of the Dutch again to rule the Cape, which they did until 1806 when the British reoccupied the colony after the Battle of Blaauwberg, effectively beginning 155 years of direct British rule of South Africa. In 1833, the British abolished slavery at the Cape. This incensed the Dutch settlers — by now calling themselves Afrikaners — and between 1835 and 1836 they packed their long covered ox-wagons and left the colony for the far north in what is now known as the Great Trek. On the plains of the vast uplands they established *Boer* (farmer) republics in the Orange Free State and the Transvaal. These *Voortrekkers* (pioneers) settled in a rural bliss broken only by periodic skirmishes with the black tribes they had dispossessed, until in one of the fine ironies of history the very *uitlanders* (foreigners) whose irksome rule they had fled from in the Cape arrived in their peaceful republics. A British plan to make the Transvaal part of a territorial federation once again infuriated the Boers and they responded by defeating the British in 1881 at the Battle of Majuba, during the first Anglo-Boer War.

By the turn of the century diamonds had been discovered near the confluence of the Orange and Vaal (drab, or ash-coloured) rivers, and various gold strikes had fuelled the fever, resulting in an influx of often unsavoury diggers from all over the world. Equally unsavoury were many of the thousands who flooded President Paul Kruger's South African Republic in the Transvaal after gold was found and the glittering reef of the Witwatersrand was discovered in 1886. Kruger and his *Volksraad* (Parliament) in Pretoria regarded the tented town that sprang up to become Johannesburg as a Gomorrah on the veld and prophesied trouble. It was not long in coming. The *uitlanders*, prodded by Cecil John Rhodes, pressed Kruger for electoral reform and other concessions, which the *Volksraad* rejected. Various underhand stratagems, including the abortive Jameson Raid in January 1896, made the Boers even more obdurate. The stage was set for the second Anglo-Boer War, which was fought by Boers desperately trying to retain their independence and a biblical lifestyle free from foreign interference, and by the British cynically striving for control of the world's richest goldfields. As they clashed, the black tribes whose age-old land was the battleground looked on.

Anglo-Boer War (1899–1902). The war began in October 1899. After some initial Boer commando successes, quickly reversed after the arrival of the main British force in January 1900, the bitter guerrilla phase of the war started when Boer forces regrouped after the fall of Pretoria and carried on the conflict for two more years, before agreeing terms with the British in May 1902 and signing the Treaty of Vereeniging. In order to entrench their influence in southern Africa the British granted generous terms to the Boers, largely at the expense of blacks who were excluded from the political process. One of the peace treaty's more dubious paragraphs was one shelving 'the question of the native franchise' and leaving them in limbo for the next 90 years. When the war broke out in 1899, South Africa had a black population of nearly 4 million people, and it was inevitable that they would become embroiled in the conflict. The British scorched earth policy meant white and black families alike were left destitute and went into the concentration camps set up by the British to deprive Boer guerrillas in the field of comfort and support.

Separate camps for blacks were established in 1901, mainly as labour depots for the British Army. By May 1902, there were nearly 120,000 blacks in these camps. According to incomplete British records, 14,154 black people — 81% of whom were children — died. British Quaker Emily Hobhouse fought to improve conditions in the camps, with little success. In 1903, the Cape African Native Congress remarked that 'the neglect of the black refugee problem during the war and its aftermath concealed a story of profound misery and inhumanity.'

Near war's end some 147,000 people were confined in 46 camps, by which time British concern had been stirred and the death rate had fallen from an average of 344 per thousand to 69 per thousand. At war's end the total Boer death toll was 24,000. Of these 20,000 were women and children who perished in camps far from the battleground. British deaths totalled 25,000.

Although it was generally considered a 'White Man's War', blacks served on both sides. At the beginning they were used as non-combatants by both sides, the British employing them for the erection of most of the 10,000 blockhouses built across the land. The Boers employed them as unarmed herdsmen and drivers. Later they were used as scouts during guerrilla operations. Only at the end of 1900 were blacks in the service of the British armed for self-defence.

Between 1906 and 1907 Britain granted constitutions to the Transvaal and the Orange Free State, the defeated Boer republics, that gave them absolute political control, and in 1909 the British did not object when the South African National Convention voted for a constitution that made sure political power remained in white hands.

Union of South Africa (1910–1960). The dominant Afrikaner mood after the return of self-government was one of conciliation but this soon changed to a reaction against the imperial connection and in 1914 to opposition to war against Germany. The covert Broederbond emerged shortly after the First World War to shape and direct the future of the Afrikaner people.

When the Second World War broke out in 1939, Afrikaner nationalists tried, but failed, to keep South Africa neutral. General Jan Smuts, who had fought the British during the Anglo-Boer War, now fought for them and took his troops to most of the major theatres of war. Like Winston Churchill in post-war Britain, Smuts was defeated at the polls and in 1948 clergyman Dr DF Malan's National Party (NP) took power and began a rule that was to last nearly 50 years under a succession of leaders, including apartheid's prime architect, Hendrik Verwoerd, John Vorster and PW Botha. As Afrikaner and black nationalism developed and diverged, the National Party devised the rigid system of territorial, social and political segregation known as *apartheid*, which met increasingly with black resistance and hostile world opinion.

Apartheid was intended to create a permanent, white political majority by purging the electoral roll of all non-white peoples and by setting up black independent and self-governing 'homelands' where they could vote and have citizenship. Apartheid was also designed to keep economic power in white hands by directing skilled blacks into these homelands. Black resistance to apartheid reached a turning point in 1960. The government banned both the African National Congress (ANC) and the Pan African Congress (PAC). Mass detentions and repressive measures increased, ushering in an even more dismal era. On 26 March thousands of PAC supporters marched throughout the country to hand in their passbooks at police stations. Hours later 69 blacks lay dead and 180 wounded in Sharpeville after clashes with armed police, and the name of this Transvaal town hit the headlines around the world.

The NP took South Africa out of the Commonwealth as a republic in 1961 (850,450 people voted in favour of republican status, 775,878 against). The ANC went underground and launched its armed wing *Umkhonto weSizwe* ('Spear of the Nation') and accelerated its campaign of violence and sabotage. This resulted in the arrest of Nelson Mandela, the 'Black Pimpernel', and other ANC leaders. Mandela was sentenced to life imprisonment and sent to Robben Island, off Cape Town. While ANC leaders languished in prison or in exile international sanctions and the growing interdependence of black and white in a modern industrial economy were undermining the apartheid structure. In 1976, after it was announced that they would be taught in Afrikaans as well as English, black schoolchildren in Soweto staged a protest march on 16 June that ended with scores dead or wounded. This stiffened the resistance campaign designed to make the black townships, and eventually the country, ungovernable. Further repression failed to restore law and order. With the end of the war in neighbouring Rhodesia the liberation of the rest of Africa rolled to South Africa's borders and the support of newly independent Zimbabwe gave fresh impetus to the black struggle in South Africa. This brought a decade under former State President PW Botha, who set up a tricameral parliamentary system in 1983 that included coloured and Indian representatives, but no blacks, and saw the declaration of states of emergency, increased censorship, hit squads and hot pursuit cross-border raids. It seemed throughout this decade that South Africa was doomed to massive racial conflict. Then the miracle occurred. FW de Klerk and other prominent Afrikaners met to discuss terms with the ANC in 1988 and 1989. The upshot was President de Klerk's unconditional release of Nelson Mandela and the unbanning of the ANC, PAC, and the South African Communist Party in February 1990, actions that stunned the world. All political parties met at the World Trade Centre near Johannesburg between 1991 and 1993 to hammer out a transitional constitution, leading to South Africa's first democratic elections. In December 1993, De Klerk and Mandela were jointly awarded the Nobel Peace Prize. The rest, as they say, is history.

HISTORICAL HIGHLIGHTS

From 20,000 BC Stone Age Bushmen (San) hunter-gatherers migrated along the West Coast into southern Africa, followed by Khoikhoi herders, who arrived at the Cape about 2000 years ago. From AD 200 onwards Bantu-speaking tribes migrating from the north settled in the eastern coastal regions of South Africa.

1488:	Portuguese explorer Bartolomeu Dias lands at the Cape of Good Hope.
1497:	Vasco da Gama discovers sea route to India via the Cape.
1652:	Dutch East India Company establishes refreshment station at the Cape under Jan van Riebeeck on 6 April.
1659:	First wine pressed at the Cape.
1667:	First Malays arrive at the Cape as slaves.
1688–1700:	More than 200 French Huguenots settle in the Cape.
1779:	First of nine frontier wars in the Eastern Cape between white settlers and the Xhosa.
1795:	Britain annexes the Cape.
1803:	Cape Colony reverts to Dutch rule.
1806:	Britain reoccupies the Cape — the beginning of 155 years of direct British rule.
1814:	The Cape is formally ceded to Britain by the Dutch.
1815:	Shaka becomes King of the Zulus.
1820:	British settlers arrive in the Eastern Cape.
1820–30:	Shaka extends kingdom, scattering other black tribes and leaving vast areas depopulated.
1824–25:	First white traders enter Shaka's kingdom and establish Port Natal (later Durban).
1828:	Shaka murdered by half-brothers, Mhlangana and Dingane. Dingane becomes King.
1833:	British abolish slavery in South Africa.
1834–40:	About 15,000 Voortrekkers (Afrikaner pioneers) embark on the Great Trek north to escape British rule.
1836:	Voortrekkers defeat the Ndebele at the Battle of Vegkop.
1838:	Voortrekkers under Andries Pretorius defeat Zulus under Dingane at Blood River, Natal.
1843:	Natal becomes a British colony.
1848:	British sovereignty proclaimed between the Orange and Vaal rivers.
1852:	Voortrekkers establish the Zuid-Afrikaansche Republiek.
1854:	Independent Republic of the Orange Free State founded.
1860:	First Indian migrant labourers arrive in Natal.
1867:	Diamond found at Hopetown, Cape Colony.
1877:	Britain annexes the South African Republic.
1879:	Zulu impis wipe out British force at Isandhlwana. British break the Zulu nation, ruled by Cetshwayo, at Ulundi.

1880–81:	Transvaal claims independence and declares itself a republic. First Anglo-Boer War.
1883:	Paul Kruger becomes president of the South African Republic.
1884:	Cetshwayo dies. His son, Dinizulu, becomes king. John Tengo Jabavu launches the weekly newspaper *Imvo Zabantsundu*.
1886:	Gold found on the Witwatersrand. Birth of Johannesburg.
1893:	Mohandas Ghandi arrives in South Africa.
1897:	Enoch Mankayi Sontonga composes *Nkosi Sikilel' iAfrica* ('God Bless Africa').
1899–1902:	Second Anglo-Boer War.
1904:	Chinese labour imported for Transvaal mines.
1905:	Cullinan diamond, the largest ever found, discovered at the Premier Mine, Transvaal.
1910:	Union of South Africa proclaimed on 31 May.
1912:	Formation of the South African Native National Congress, known after 1923 as the African National Congress (ANC).
1913:	Natives Land Act is passed, limiting land ownership by blacks.
1914:	National Party (NP) founded. South Africa enters First World War on Allied side. Ghandi returns to India.
1918:	Cornelis Langenhoven writes *Die Stem van Suid-Afrika*.
1920:	South African Indian Congress (SAIC) founded.
1921:	Afrikaner Broederbond established. Formation of the South African Communist Party (SACP).
1925:	Blacks removed from Cape electoral roll. Afrikaans replaces Dutch as an official language of the Union.
1927:	Compulsory segregation announced.
1939:	South Africa enters the Second World War on the side of the Allies.
1947:	British royal tour of South Africa.
1948:	National Party under Dr DF Malan wins general election. Acts follow that enforce policy of apartheid, or separate racial development.
1949:	Racially mixed marriages banned by law.
1950:	Population Registration, Group Areas, Immorality, Separate Representation of Voters, and Suppression of Communism Acts passed. Blacks riot in Johannesburg against apartheid.
1952:	ANC launches Defiance Campaign. HF Verwoerd proposes independent black homelands.
1955:	Freedom Charter adopted by Congress of the People.
1956:	Coloured (mixed race) people removed from electoral roll.
1957:	*Die Stem van Suid-Afrika* set to music as South Africa's national anthem.
1958:	Dr Hendrik Verwoerd succeeds JG Strijdom as Prime Minister.
1959:	Formation of the Pan Africanist Congress (PAC).
1960:	'Winds of Change' speech by British Prime Minister Harold Macmillan in the South African Parliament. Anti-pass law protest in Sharpeville leads to death of 69 black demonstrators. ANC and PAC banned.
1961:	South Africa becomes a republic outside the Commonwealth. Currency decimalised. ANC launches armed struggle. Unsuccessful attempt on Verwoerd's life. Albert Luthuli awarded Nobel Peace Prize.
1962:	Nelson Mandela is arrested.
1963:	Police arrest ANC activists. Start of Rivonia treason trial.
1964:	Nelson Mandela, Walter Sisulu and five other ANC activists jailed for life.

1966:   Apartheid's main architect, Hendrik Verwoerd, assassinated in Parliament, succeeded as premier by BJ Vorster.

1967:   World's first human heart transplant performed by Professor Chris Barnard at Groote Schuur Hospital, Cape Town.

1969:   Beginning of Black Consciousness movement. South African Students Organisation established under Steve Biko.

1972:   Black People's Convention (BPC) founded.

1974:   South Africa rejected by the UN General Assembly.

1975:   Mangosuthu Buthelezi revives Zulu cultural movement *Inkatha Yenkululeku Yesizwe*.

1976:   Protest against Afrikaans as the medium of instruction in black schools leads to violence in Soweto. Riots spread to other black areas and a student uprising on 16 June. TV makes its debut in South Africa.

1977:   UN Security Council imposes mandatory arms embargo on South Africa. Black consciousness activist Steve Biko dies in detention.

1978:   BJ Vorster resigns as Prime Minister and is succeeded by PW Botha. Vorster becomes State President. PAC leader Robert Sobukwe dies in detention.

1979:   Azanian People's Organisation (Azapo) formed. Vorster resigns as president.

1983:   A new Constitution provides for a tricameral parliament for whites, coloureds and Indians, but not for blacks. United Democratic Front (UDF) founded.

1984:   PW Botha becomes executive State President. National Union of Mineworkers founded. Archbishop Desmond Tutu receives Nobel Peace Prize.

1985:   Unrest spreads and State of Emergency declared. Congress of Trade Unions (Cosatu) formed.

1986:   Apartheid Acts abolished, including Prohibition of Mixed Marriages Act, Section 16 of the Immorality Act, and the Pass Laws. US Congress imposes sanctions against South Africa.

1989:   Harare Declaration signed, setting out the ANC's pre-negotiating position with the government. PW Botha and Nelson Mandela meet for first time. Botha resigns as State President. NP wins the general election, FW De Klerk becomes State President. Walter Sisulu and seven other long-term political prisoners released.

1990:   De Klerk announces plan to scrap apartheid. ANC, PAC and SACP unbanned. On 11 February Mandela released from prison after 27 years. Zulu organisation *Inkatha* becomes a political party called the Inkatha Freedom Party (IFP). State of Emergency lifted. The Groote Schuur Minute signed, paving way for majority rule. Separate Amenities Act repealed. ANC suspends armed struggle. Amnesty extended to political prisoners.

1991:   Government and the ANC agree on all-party congress to discuss negotiations and constitutional principles. EC lifts trade sanctions. Remaining discriminatory apartheid legislation scrapped. National Peace Accord signed. Mandela becomes President of the ANC. Violence between ANC and IFP spreads. UDF disbands. Declaration of Intent signed at Convention for a Democratic South Africa (Codesa).

1992:   South Africa takes part in Olympic Games. Codesa negotiations scrapped. Last whites-only referendum overwhelmingly in favour of political reform. Record of Understanding signed for a democratically elected interim Government of National Unity (GNU).

1993:	Nelson Mandela and FW de Klerk share Nobel Peace Prize. SACP leader Chris Hani assassinated. Afrikaner Volksfront formed to negotiate self-determination for Afrikaners. Compulsory white national service scrapped. Preparations for South Africa's first democratic elections. US Senate approves lifting of sanctions. UN lifts sanctions. Transitional Constitution providing for non-racial multi-party democracy, three tiers of government and a Bill of Rights in a unitary South Africa accepted. South Africa's new Interim Constitution enacted by Parliament, signalling end of apartheid and birth of new South Africa.
1994:	Seven million people in homelands regain South African citizenship. South Africa's first democratic general election won by ANC. Mandela becomes South Africa's first black president. South Africa joins the Organisation for African Unity (OAU). UN Security Council lifts arms embargo. South Africa rejoins Commonwealth, and reclaims seat in UN General Assembly.
1995:	Constitutional Court states death penalty inconsistent with Interim Constitution. Queen Elizabeth II visits SA on first royal visit since 1947 and bestows Order of Merit on Mandela. South Africa hosts and wins World Cup Rugby Tournament. Third-tier local government elections held in all provinces except KwaZulu-Natal and part of Western Cape. ANC wins 67% of votes. Truth and Reconciliation Commission appointed under Archbishop Tutu.
1996:	De Klerk resigns deputy presidency and pulls National Party out of Government of National Unity (GNU) on 30 June to become official Opposition. Queen Beatrix of the Netherlands arrives on 28 September for first state visit ever by Dutch monarch. Constitutional Court certifies South Africa's final Constitution on 4 December, and on 10 December President Mandela signs it into law.
1997:	Senate disbanded and replaced by National Council of Provinces (NCOP) and final Constitution comes into effect on 3 February.

POLITICAL DEVELOPMENTS

When the treaty ending the second Anglo-Boer War was signed on 31 May 1902 it contained a clause that effectively sowed the seeds for nearly 90 years of black bitterness. This stated that the franchise for black South Africans would be decided after the country had been granted self-government. From then until 1990 Afrikaners and other whites struggled between themselves for power while the hopes and aspirations of the country's majority were sidelined. They were not even articulated until the formation of the South African Native National Congress, the forerunner of the ANC, in 1912. After decades of rule by English-speaking political parties, the National Party (NP) representing the downtrodden Afrikaner came to power in May 1948 and subsequently won all the elections in 1953, 1958, 1961 and 1966. The main aims of the NP were the formation of a republic and the introduction of apartheid. Throughout the years of NP rule English-speaking opposition parties fought against the government's racial policies, but the granite cracked only in 1990 when President FW de Klerk announced that apartheid was to be abandoned. Years of black — and white — resistance, world opprobrium and economic sanctions had done their work.

After extensive and prolonged multi-party negotiations, South Africa got a new constitution in 1993. This was developed to smooth the way for the transition to democracy and provide a foundation for the final constitution. The principles that provided the framework for the 1993 Interim Constitution are those now enshrined as the cornerstones of the final Constitution, which became binding at midnight on 3 February 1997.

The Constitution recognises that all South Africans are entitled to a common citizenship in a sovereign and democratic constitutional state in which there is equality between men and women and people of all races, and all can enjoy and exercise their fundamental rights and freedoms — a major democratic milestone, whose provisions can only be changed by 75% of the members of the National Parliament.

The Constitution contains a Bill of Rights guaranteeing freedom of religion, belief and opinion; freedom of expression; freedom of movement; and equality and equal protection before the law. Separation of powers is an important principle underpinning South Africa's constitutional democracy. This recognises that there are three arms of government that are separate and independent from one another: the legislature, or Parliament; the executive, comprising the President and Cabinet; and the judiciary, consisting of the courts. This ensures that there is a balance of power with no arm of government becoming all-powerful.

South Africans of all races went to the polls together for the first time in the country's history during the period 26 to 29 April 1994 to elect a Government of National Unity (GNU). Each cast two votes, one for the National Assembly and one for a provincial government. Nineteen parties took part in the hustings but only seven of them gained seats in the National Assembly. The African National Congress (ANC) gained 62.65% of the votes, falling just short of the two-thirds majority that would have enabled it to write the country's final Constitution virtually unopposed. The ANC took 252 seats in the National Assembly and in the provincial elections it gained a majority in seven of the nine provinces — Mpumalanga, North-West, Northern Province, Free State, Gauteng, Eastern Cape and Northern Cape. The Western Cape went to the National Party (NP), and KwaZulu-Natal to the Inkatha Freedom Party (IFP). This made these parties the three major political players in the country. The Freedom Front (FF), Democratic Party (DP), Pan African Congress (PAC) and African Christian Democratic Party (ACDP) each polled less than 3% of the vote and took only 23 seats between them. What was interesting was that radical and extreme groups on both sides of the political spectrum fared badly in the elections.

In Cape Town on 9 May 1994 the 400 members of the new National Assembly were sworn in and unanimously elected Nelson Rolihlahla Mandela (popularly known as *Madiba*, or Old Man) as President. Dr Frene Ginwala was elected Speaker, becoming the first woman to hold this office. Mandela officially assumed office on 10 May, when he was sworn in at the Union Buildings in Pretoria. Earlier, Thabo Mbeki and FW de Klerk had been sworn in as Executive Deputy Presidents. De Klerk's tenure was brief, as he pulled the National Party out of the GNU on 30 June 1996 and joined the Opposition benches.

Initially there were widespread fears that the alliance with the South African Communist Party and the labour movement that brought the ANC to power would see a left-leaning government dedicated to the centralised control and nationalisation of assets abandoned and discredited in former communist countries throughout the world. The realities of power, however, and the dawning realisation of South Africa's international role, have brought significant shifts in government policy and moved it nearer to the middle of the road. The first was the ANC's decision to abandon its long-held commitment to nationalisation; instead it has embarked on a programme that will see the privatisation of many state assets. Six months after the ANC took office came the second shift when Mbeki announced major government reforms. As well as a commitment to privatising some state enterprises, there were measures to reduce the size of the civil service and cut government expenditure. A major shift was announced in June 1996, when the finance minister presented a new-look macroeconomic policy that definitively moved the ANC from its left-wing, state-interventionist policies of the 1980s to a centrist, growth-driven approach for the 1990s. That this has happened with at least four cabinet ministers and four deputy ministers members of the South African Communist Party is little short of a political miracle.

The main thrust of the ANC government is to create jobs, raise the standard of living for the formerly disadvantaged (more than 45% live below the poverty line), improve health and education, and remove the last vestiges of discrimination. Paradoxically, to achieve the latter it is promoting 'positive discrimination' (or 'affirmative action') to ensure that black South Africans are employed in all spheres in a ratio more appropriate to the demographics of the country. Affirmative action is defined as 'laws, programmes or activities designed to redress past imbalances and to ameliorate the conditions of individuals and groups who have been disadvantaged on the grounds of race, colour, gender or disability.' This drive is proving more successful in the public service, parastatals and other arms of the state than in the private sector. Another major concern has been to achieve national reconciliation between all race groups and, in some cases, formerly sworn enemies. In November 1995 a Truth and Reconciliation Commission (TRC) was set up under the chairmanship of Archbishop Desmond Tutu to investigate gross human rights violations committed by all parties between 1 March 1960 and 10 May 1994, to recommend reparation for victims, and to receive applications for amnesty and indemnity from the perpetrators.

The regular televised regional sittings of the TRC produced a series of horrifying and agonising disclosures by top echelon members of the former National Party government, the police and the Defence Force, as well as revelations of atrocities committed by members of the ANC, PAC, Inkatha and other organisations involved in the freedom struggle. While all this is searing for the public conscience, it is believed that the nation will be better for this catharsis. Archbishop Tutu says the process should enable all South Africans to come to terms with the past in a spirit of forgiveness, and regards the work of his commission as the only alternative to Nuremberg, on the one hand, and amnesia on the other.

Reconstruction and Development. On 24 May 1994 President Mandela opened Parliament and announced the government's goal of a people-centred society shaped through a Reconstruction and Development Programme (RDP). The RDP was regarded as the most significant statement on South African society since the ANC's Freedom Charter was adopted in 1955. On 15 November 1994 the RDP White Paper was tabled in Parliament and on 23 November 1994 it was Gazetted. The basic aim of the RDP is to mobilise all people and resources towards the building of a democratic, non-racial and non-sexist society.

The RDP lays particular emphasis on the empowerment of women in general, and black, rural women in particular. Special attention is also paid to people with disabilities. The government has moved away from care and welfare to a more developmental approach. Mass participation is seen as essential to the success of the RDP, which is a 25-year plan designed to normalise South Africa and its economy. It envisages at least a million more low-cost houses, more health facilities, better education, 30% of agricultural land to be redistributed among blacks, and 2.5 million more households to get electricity, water and sanitation by the year 2000. Past policies have left about 80% of the black population with no tap water, while 85% of blacks in rural and 31% in urban areas do not have adequate sanitation. In other words, RDP is shorthand for the social and economic upliftment of the under-privileged masses who are the ANC's bedrock support. It is on this ambitious programme that the ANC government will be judged by the masses at the 1999 general election and a delivery crisis is already in the making. The RDP has travelled a rocky road. From being a major cabinet portfolio, it was moved to become the responsibility of Deputy

President Thabo Mbeki, and it is now largely up to the nine provinces themselves to decide what the RDP priorities are in their areas and to get on with them.

Education. With the establishment of a single national Ministry of Education in 1994, the first step was taken to create a new system of education for South Africa. Improving the quality of education for South Africa's 12 million pupils is high on the government agenda and a priority has been the introduction of 10 years of free and compulsory schooling. Under-qualification of the country's more than 300,000 teachers is a major problem. Less than half of the country's black teachers are adequately trained.

There is a strong system of higher education, with 21 universities and 15 technikons teaching nearly 500,000 students. There has been a significant reversal of old black-white student ratios at most of the universities. At the Rand Afrikaans University (RAU) in Johannesburg, for instance, black students now account for 22% of the 21,000-strong student body. Between 1990 and 1996 the number of Afrikaans-speaking students at Pretoria University declined from 83% to 65%. The most dramatic changes have been at the University of the Free State, where black student numbers have increased by 219%, and blacks now make up 30% of the 10,000 student population and account for half of the annual student intake. Traditional favourite seats of learning such as the University of the Witwatersrand (Wits) and the University of Cape Town (UCT) are enrolling increasing numbers of black students; Wits has 17,800 registered students, of whom 8000 are black.

Land. As in other African countries, land ownership is a contentious and emotional issue in South Africa, where grossly distorted usage and ownership left blacks restricted to about 13% of the country's land. While most other Western countries moved away from discriminatory actions and laws after the Second World War, the National Party government increased its racially based laws, and rural black communities that had for generations lived in so-called white areas were dispossessed and relocated. The hardship caused by these forced removals during the 1950s and 1960s was one of the nastier parts of the apartheid process. Today, the political and economic focus is on unravelling the disastrous social engineering of the past half century. Within a year of the 1994 elections, the Restitution of Land Rights Act became law, and it is ironic that its implementation, with its RDP promise of the redistribution of 30% of South Africa's land to black people dispossessed since 1913, is the responsibility of a white cabinet minister.

Defence Force. The South African National Defence Force (SANDF) comprises the Army, Navy, Air Force, and Medical Services. The SANDF that was once at the forefront of actions against the ANC and other liberation movements now has in its ranks the armed forces of the former black homelands of Transkei, Bophuthatswana, Venda and Ciskei and the ANC and PAC military activists it once regarded as terrorists.

To promote national confidence in the military the government has sought to demonstrate that the amalgamation of formerly antagonistic forces is more than simply the absorption of former *Umkhonto weSizwe* ('Spear of the Nation') and Azanian Peoples Liberation Army members into the old South African Defence Force. More than 15,000 ex-MK and Apla members have been integrated in the SANDF, as well as more than 11,000 members of forces from the old homelands. More than 2200 of these are now officers, and 16% of all SANDF officers are black, a percentage that is rapidly increasing. The ANC chose as its first Minister of Defence Joe Modise, who was a member of the MK High Command during the organisation's years of exile and armed struggle. The government plans to reduce defence force numbers to 70,000 by 1999, by which time it should be ready to protect hearth and home and for any UN peace-keeping duties on the African continent.

Foreign Affairs. South Africa's international isolation ended officially on 23 June 1994, when South Africa resumed its seat in the UN General Assembly and the world body removed from its agenda the standing item on the elimination of apartheid that had been there for some three decades. In the same month, South Africa became the 51st member of the British Commonwealth after an absence of 33 years.

South Africa has since reshaped its diplomatic ties. Relations with many countries have been upgraded, new trade links have been established and various restrictions have been lifted. South Africa now has relations at varying levels with more than 160 countries. Foreign policy decisions generally seem to be *ad hoc* and a number of them have caused international consternation. The US in particular, has been ruffled by South Africa's cosying up to such avowed enemies of American interests as Libya, Iran and Cuba.

NATIONAL, PROVINCIAL AND LOCAL STRUCTURES

Parliament is the legislative authority and has the power to make laws for the country in accordance with the Constitution. Cape Town is the legislative capital and Parliament sits here when in session. Pretoria is the administrative capital of the country and Bloemfontein is the judicial capital. Parliament consists of a National Assembly and a National Council of Provinces (NCOP), which replaced the old 90-member Senate at the beginning of 1997. Business is conducted in public. Parliament sits for five years before a new general election is held. The National Assembly comprises 400 members elected by a system of proportional representation. Each political party has a number of seats based on the share of the votes it gained in the general elections. Of the 400 members, 200 are elected on a national list, and 200 on provincial lists. The NCOP consists of 10 representatives for each of the country's nine provinces. Each Provincial Legislature nominates these in proportion to political party support in the province. There is also a legislative mechanism for traditional leaders to advise the government on issues where they have a special interest.

Executive Branch. Chief of state and head of government is Executive President Nelson Mandela and his deputy is Thabo Mbeki. Any political party winning 20% or more of the National Assembly votes in a general election can nominate an executive deputy president. The cabinet comprises 25 ministerial portfolios.

Provincial Government. After the advent of democratic government South Africa's four old provinces of the Cape, Transvaal, Orange Free State and Natal were split into nine provinces. These are Gauteng, Northern Province, North-West Province, Mpumalanga, Northern Cape, Western Cape, Eastern Cape, Free State and KwaZulu-Natal.

Reincorporated into these provinces are the four former independent — but internationally unrecognised — homelands of Bophuthatswana, Ciskei, Transkei and Venda, and the six previously self-governing territories of Gazankulu, Kangwane, KwaNdebele, KwaZulu, Lebowa and Qwa Qwa. Each has its own capital, legislature, prime minister and government. This is proving somewhat unwieldy and often gives rise to a tug-of-war between the provinces and central government over the exact limits of power. In this second-tier system of government each of the provinces has between 30 and 100 members in its legislature, depending on the size of the provincial population. They are elected by proportional representation.

Local Government. This third tier of government, with about 300 local authorities, substructures and councils responsible for much of the country's day-to-day business, is given prime importance in the government's Reconstruction and Development Programme (RDP), as it is the level of democracy closest to the masses and often involves the allocation of resources directly affecting them. Local authorities are expected to embark on programmes to restore, maintain, upgrade and extend services normally expected by households and rate-payers.

THE ECONOMY

Gold has been the bulwark of the South African economy through the fat years and the lean, although its overall importance is reducing due to a fall in both production and the gold price, and the rise in manufacturing's contribution. The total value of the country's economic production is around R382.6 billion, unevenly spread among the nine provinces. Gauteng is the country's powerhouse, responsible for more than a third of all economic output. Three provinces, Gauteng (37.7%), KwaZulu-Natal (14.9%) and the Western Cape (14.1%), generate two-thirds of all South Africa's economic wealth. Contributions from the other six provinces range from 8.1% for Mpumalanga to 2.1% for the thinly populated Northern Cape.

Until the discovery of payable gold in the last century, the country was an agricultural nation and farmers were the backbone, and masters, of the country. The kings of the land were the white mealie (maize) barons whose black labourers tilled boundless fields producing 10 million tons of this staple grain a year. Not so long ago, many farm workers received a ration of wine, a so-called *dop* (tot), as either part or full payment of their wages, particularly in the Cape. The system came to symbolise the relationship of servitude to a master that existed in one form or another throughout South Africa. More enlightened practices have now replaced this and business relationships are beginning that place worker and farmer on an equal footing in joint ownership farming activities.

Black South Africans are also upwardly mobile in other industrial and commercial sectors. From political and trade union springboards they have leaped to prominence in mining, publishing and electronic media, and that old bastion of the privileged, the Johannesburg Stock Exchange (JSE), the 12th largest bourse in the world. More than 630 companies are listed on the JSE and their combined market capitalisation exceeds R1.1 trillion. Of these, 14 listings worth R8 billion are now controlled by black investors, up from a near zero base in 1992.

Mining. South Africa is blessed with most of the world's important minerals, which are found in diverse and extensive geological formations. South Africa has the world's largest reserves of chrome ore (72%), vanadium (45%) and andalusite (about 90%). The deposits of manganese ore in the Northern Cape are the largest proven reserves in the world, and there are also substantial reserves of other industrially important metals and minerals, such as antimony, asbestos, diamonds, coal, fluorspar, iron ore, lead, zinc, phosphates, uranium, vermiculate and zirconium. South Africa is the world's largest producer of gold, which is the country's main source of foreign currency and also its most important export commodity, accounting for about two-thirds of the value of mineral export sales.

South Africa is a world leader in deep-level mining, with some mines operating at 3km/1.9 miles to 4km/2.5 miles below the ground, making gold production costs among the highest in the world. Gold output has been slipping over the past few years, a dismal state of affairs that is being blamed on ageing and costly mines, declining ore grades and low productivity because of widespread labour unrest and a plethora of new public holidays and celebrations. Most of the mining is controlled by a handful of conglomerates, chief among them Anglo American, and the government has initiated moves that will see more blacks involved at both boardroom level in corporate mining and in ownership of small mining enterprises.

Recorded mining history began with copper mining in Namaqualand shortly after the arrival of the Dutch at the Cape in the 17th century. Diamonds were discovered near Kimberley in 1867 and gold on the Witwatersrand in 1886. Some 600,000 workers are employed in the mining industry, 64% of them in gold mining. The most important mining provinces are the North West, principally for platinum group metals and gold, Gauteng and the Free State for gold, and Mpumalanga for coal.

Total coal reserves are estimated at a gigantic 80 thousand million tons. Most of the country's power stations are fuelled by coal (there is a nuclear power station at Koeberg, near Cape Town), but despite this plenitude South Africa has an unusual pattern of energy use. Although it produces 60% of the electricity used in Africa, two-thirds of all South Africans do not have access to electricity and rely instead on wood and other fuels such as coal, paraffin, gas and candles. Historical inequality left 62% of all households without electricity, mainly in the rural areas. Through provider Eskom the government plans to electrify 300,000 homes a year for the next five years and to ensure that 80% of all households in the country have electricity by 2010. This programme is one of the best indicators of planned improvements in black living standards.

Agriculture. Although South Africa is now the continent's biggest and best functioning modern economy, agriculture is still vitally important, not only as the bread basket of the nation as a whole, but also for the millions of black subsistence farmers and their families who have been left by a series of unjust laws with only 13% of the country's 120 million hectares/297 million acres of land. The rest of the arable land is owned by 60,000, mainly white, commercial farmers.

Agriculture contributes about 5% of the gross domestic product (GDP), employs more than 1.2 million farm labourers, and makes the country not only self-sufficient in virtually all major agricultural products, but in good years a net food exporter. Total cultivated area is 15 million hectares/37 million acres, of which about 36% is under maize and 21% under small grains. After maize, wheat is South Africa's most important grain crop and South Africa is the world's 10th largest producer of sunflower seed. Livestock is farmed in most parts and there are dairy farmers throughout the country, with the highest concentrations in the eastern and northern Free State, the KwaZulu-Natal Midlands, the Eastern and Western Cape, the Gauteng metropolitan area and the southern parts of Mpumalanga. Sheep-farming is concentrated in the Northern and Eastern Cape, Free State and Mpumalanga provinces. Intensive poultry and pig industries are located near metropolitan areas such as Gauteng, Durban, Pietermaritzburg, the Cape Peninsula and Port Elizabeth.

Fishing. With a coast of nearly 3000km/1864 miles, South Africa's marine resources are considerable, with three-quarters of the catches coming from the rich fishing grounds off the West Coast, which are among the world's most productive. The West Coast also produces most of the prized rock lobster exported to Europe and the USA every year. The R1.5 billion fishing industry provides jobs for about 28,000 people. The surface area of South Africa's fisheries zone, extending up to 200 nautical miles offshore, is larger than that of the entire country.

Foreign Investment. The economy is not expected to grow at the required 6% a year the government regards as necessary to fill its projections for new jobs and services without substantial foreign investment, and this is slow in materialising. Six months after president Bill Clinton lifted US sanctions against South Africa in November 1993, he announced a $600 million three-year trade, investment and development package to boost the economy of the new South African democracy. Investment of R8 billion since 1994 now makes the USA the largest foreign investor, followed by Germany. The UK is third with investments of R2.3 billion. Other potential investors are dragging their heels because of the country's high crime rate and the government's reluctance to privatise parastatals and antagonise the vociferous left-wing labour unions. They would also like to see a speedy end to South Africa's restrictive foreign exchange controls.

Tourism. Tourism currently plays a relatively small role in the economy. It is estimated that value added tourism in South Africa contributed about 4% of Gross Domestic Product (GDP) in 1995, which is low by any standard. Comparative figures for the US and UK economies were 10.5% and 12.3%, respectively. Even so, tourism is the country's fourth largest earner of foreign exchange, bringing in R10 billion a year. The government is hoping the industry will triple its contribution to national income and at least double its foreign exchange earnings by the year 2000. If tourism could contribute 10% of the GDP as it does in the USA, then the industry would generate about R40 billion a year and create 2 million more jobs. At present the industry directly employs about 480,000 people. More than a million foreign tourists a year — most of them from the UK, followed by Germany, France, the Netherlands and Australia — are currently coming to South Africa, excluding those from other parts of Africa, and the number is expected to double by the year 2000. While there is no doubt that growth is happening, there is no guarantee that it will continue. If it does happen, as hoped, tourism will become the engine of growth for other sectors of the economy.

In its 1996 White Paper on tourism, the government noted that, crime apart, there are other problems impacting negatively on the growth of tourism. One is the limited integration of local black communities in the industry, another is the poor service tourists find at all levels. The culture of poor and mediocre service is so widespread that South Africans often tell visitors with a sort of inverted pride that the country is near the bottom of international lists assessing service levels throughout the world. There is also a need for drastic improvement in the transportation available for moving tourists around once they arrive. In many areas of government, tourism is still seen as something belonging to the past, a plaything of the previously privileged class. Its true wealth-creating potential has still to be grasped. Eco-tourism companies and conservation agencies are promoting black community participation and share-holding in their ventures. These initiatives are, however, still the exception and hotels and other tourism establishments will be expected to play a more active role in reshaping the quality of the total South African experience for visitors from overseas.

THE RAINBOW NATION

South Africa is indeed home to a rainbow nation, made up of an extraordinary variety of ethnic groups, cultures, creeds and languages. The history of this human diversity extends over millennia to the original inhabitants, the Stone Age hunter-gatherers known as Bushmen, or San, who were supplanted by black migrant farmers arriving from the north and by Europeans moving inland from the Cape. The country today is a dynamic, cosmopolitan place with a mix of different racial and cultural groups, including *Nguni* people (Zulu, Swazi, Xhosa), who make up about two-thirds of the entire population; the *Sotho* people (Tswana, Bapedi, South Sotho); the *Venda*; and the *Shangaan-Tsonga*. The most numerous tribes are Zulu, Xhosa, North Sotho, South Sotho and Tswana. Also in the pot-pourri are coloured (mixed race) people, Chinese, Indians, Afrikaners, English-speaking South Africans, and people who have immigrated from the Netherlands, France, Portugal, Italy and other European and Asian countries.

Ethnic Diversity. When the first Europeans landed at the Cape they found two aboriginal races, much alike physically but completely different in language, customs and way of life. The first, who herded cattle and sheep, they called *Hottentots*; the others, who lived by hunting and food gathering, kept no livestock and spoke a language full of clicks and gutturals, the settlers called *Bosjemans* (Bushmen) and this came to be their accepted name (now also San). The Hottentots called themselves Khoikhoi (meaning 'Men of Men') and nomadic herders who lost their livestock became *strandlopers* (beach rangers, or beach combers), whose shell middens are found all along the beaches of the Cape. Surviving true Khoikhoi still live in the Richtersveld, in northern Namaqualand, south of the Orange River.

A few thousand surviving Bushmen still live in remote areas of the Kalahari, self-sufficient and relying on the arid land for all their needs. From desert plants, they get food, building materials, tools, and make musical instruments, bows and arrows. They still practise their extraordinary skills to track, stalk, snare and shoot game. Traces of their peppercorn hair and distinctive physical features can still be discerned among other people of the Northern Cape.

Although Xhosa people today are increasingly opting for urban lifestyles, those who remain on their land in the Eastern Cape cling to their old tribal customs and traditions. Rural families live in groups of huts, known as a kraal, with an enclosure for cattle and a small vegetable plot. In these kraals men live with their families and their married sons and their wives and children. Traditionally the Xhosa are allowed more than one wife, but today only the wealthy follow this custom. Cattle, sheep and goats are important in Xhosa life and ritual. Men count their wealth in cattle, so daughters are valuable assets, as their bride price is paid in livestock. A major grievance among early white settlers was the Xhosa practice of rustling cattle and this, as well as Xhosa resistance to colonial encroachment on tribal lands, led to nine Frontier Wars between the settlers and the Xhosa of the Eastern Cape between 1779 and 1878.

Although most South Sotho people live in Lesotho, there are many in the Qwa Qwa area and other parts of the Free State. Both men and women, winter and summer, dress in brightly coloured blankets. The conical, curiously oriental-looking straw hat worn by men is the national emblem of Lesotho. Marriage customs among the traditional South Sotho people are similar to other ethnic groups, involving the exchange of *lobola*, or bride price, of a specified number of cattle. Marriage between relatives is not frowned on as this keeps wealth within the family.

Coloured people are the racial bridge between white and black, the result of miscegenation between the original inhabitants of the Cape, early white settlers, slaves imported from the East and, later, blacks. The coloured community includes two distinctive groups, the Cape Malays and the Griquas. The 200,000 Malays live mainly in the Malay Quarter of Cape Town, while the Griquas are concentrated in the north-western and north-eastern Cape.

The majority of South Africa's 880,000 Asians are of Indian origin; 10,000 are of Chinese descent. The first Indians were brought to South Africa by the British in 1860 to work as indentured labourers on Natal's sugar plantations. The Chinese first came to work on the mines of the Witwatersrand in 1904.

Population. The population is expected to increase to 65.7 million by the year 2020, by which time 82.4% will live in urban areas compared to today's 61.8%. South Africa's cities will contain 70% of the population by 2020. October 1996 saw the first post-apartheid population census and the first time the country had been counted as a single, unified nation. This was dubbed the third miracle, after the general election in 1994 and local government elections in 1995. For counting an estimated 44 million people, the budget for Census '96 was R365 million, or R8 a person (Australia spent R16 per head on its last census). A fairly precise count of the people is necessary for the government to estimate budgetary and provincial allocations, and to estimate the number of jobs that must be created (half the population is under 24 years old and nearly 40% of the labour force is out of work).

Population growth is a major problem as it is outstripping economic growth and stretching all resources, and steps are being taken by government to curb it through birth control programmes. The rural birth rate is 5.3 children per woman.

Demography. Most people live in the eastern regions of South Africa, where higher rainfall, better soil and rich minerals offer more job opportunities. The highest concentrations of people are in the Johannesburg–Pretoria–Vereeniging area of Gauteng; the Durban–Pinetown–Pietermaritzburg area of KwaZulu-Natal; the south-western Cape area around Cape Town; and the Port Elizabeth–Uitenhage area of the Eastern Cape. More than a third of all South Africans live in these four metropolitan areas. About 80% of all Indians still live in Natal, the majority within a radius of 150km/93 miles of Durban. South African Indians are the largest Indian community in Africa and the West. The Chinese community is concentrated on the Witwatersrand and in Port Elizabeth, where most are engaged in commerce.

Apartheid policies ensured that 42% of South Africa's people lived on 13% of the land in the so-called black homelands. There are about 500 small towns with a total of about 3.3 million people, making up 8% of the country's population. Some of these towns are the economic heartland for about 75% of the country's poor and 80% of the ultra-poor people who live in the rural areas in huts with no basic services.

Women in South Africa. Women have never been rated very highly in traditional African society, where their role has been to bear and raise children, cook, and tend the crops in the field. While this is still the way women are viewed in rural South Africa, their role in the new democratic dispensation has radically changed, and South Africa's final Constitution lays down that no person shall be unfairly discriminated against on the grounds of sex.

Most women in Western societies would regard this as normal, but in the Republic it has been a hard-won battle, though with a male-dominated government with them all the way. In the time the government has been in power it has significantly improved the status of women, with 124 women sitting in Parliament, four in the Cabinet, eight women deputy ministers and five women ambassadors. Port Elizabeth has even got a woman tug-master — the first in South Africa. There is a Commission on Gender Equality, which works with the Human Rights Commission and an Office on the Status of Women in the President's Office to ensure that government continues to pay more than lip-service to its policies concerning women.

A Parliamentary Committee monitors the government's implementation of the UN Convention on the Elimination of all Forms of Discrimination against Women (CEDAW). National Women's Day in South Africa falls on 9 August every year and remembers the time in 1956 when 20,000 women marched to the Union Buildings in Pretoria to protest against the government's plan to extend the apartheid pass laws to include them. The doors of the buildings that were slammed shut against them then are now wide open, and more than a quarter of the MPs who walked into Parliament in 1994 were women, and South Africa now has more women parliamentarians than any other country in Africa. Percentage-wise, it is also way ahead of the UK and the USA, and is surpassed only by Scandinavian countries and the Netherlands.

By ensuring women's equality, the government has found itself in a political minefield. Early in 1997 the Choice on Termination of Pregnancy Act, termed the most advanced in the world, made abortion on demand available to all women, recognising their human right according to the Bill of Rights in the Constitution. This has brought outraged opposition from a wide variety of organisations, including members of the medical profession, and shortly before Parliament's final vote on the new abortion laws the Catholic Church reminded its adherents that under canon law any professing Catholic involved in a deliberate and successful attempt to bring about an abortion would be automatically excommunicated.

Sex in South Africa. A recent sex survey showed that safe sex is less likely in South Africa and AIDS a bigger risk than in any of the other 14 countries checked. Frightening AIDS statistics and a dramatic increase in the number of prostitutes in the cities has put the debate over the decriminalisation of prostitution back in the spotlight. Although no official statistics exist, it is conservatively estimated that about 50,000 prostitutes work in the South African sex industry. Most of them work in

Johannesburg, followed by Durban and Cape Town. Under the Sexual Offences Act of 1957, engaging in any sexual act for reward or living off the earnings of a prostitute, as well as any other manifestation of the profession, is forbidden, but arrests are rare.

Research commissioned by the government into whether prostitution should be legalised shows that most people are against any move in this direction. The most distressing finding is that a third of all South Africa's sex workers are children, reflecting a pattern emerging in the rest of Africa.

In the apartheid days South African men were notorious for their haunting of bars and night clubs in neighbouring black countries, in search of ladies of the night, preferably dark-skinned. Now there is no need for them to travel so far. Since democratisation massage parlours, escort agencies and blatant brothels have sprung up in their thousands throughout the country. The new laws, or lack of them, on pornography have also flooded stores and street corners with hard-core magazines and videos. The odd thing is, there is a distinct lack of interest in these wares, even among those who once furtively smuggled in copies of *Playboy*.

Gay South Africa. Not long ago in South Africa a gay affair meant only a merry party or gathering; now there are regular Gay Pride raves and street marches, an annual Gay and Lesbian Film Festival, a Gay Pride Day in September and a competition to crown Mr Gay SA. An organisation for Les-Bi-Gay Sport, also known as TOGS, is promoting homosexual sporting activities and festivals (the Royal Netherlands Embassy sponsored the 1996 event) and plans to send representatives to various gay sporting events abroad. Local gay publications are backing Johannesburg as the venue for the 2010 Gay Gaymes.

A Gauteng radio station, Radio 702, made South African broadcasting history in February 1997 when it launched the first gay show on a commercial station. The station has initiated the show because it believes at least 10% of its target audience is homosexual. Another radio station, SAfm, dropped its plans for a gay show after a lot of controversy, and Radio Tuks, a community station based on the University of Pretoria campus, launched a gay programme late in 1995, but dropped it after six months because of complaints. All this goes to show that while gay people in South Africa are now able to use the closet as functional space and not as dysfunctional storage, there is still an ambivalent attitude towards them.

The new Constitution enshrines freedom of sexual orientation and gives gays a legal status and protection they have never before enjoyed. This has opened the closet doors for black gays who, more than any other group, suffered abuse and discrimination in their own communities. In Soweto, the sprawling black township near Johannesburg, gay black bars are becoming a feature of social life. As well as cruisers, and those who are straight by day and gay by night — known as 'after-nines' — these also attract AIDS counsellors who pop in to leave condoms among the snacks on the bar counter and chat to gay patrons about their problems. This is a far cry from the traditional fate of black homosexuals, who were thrown into a kraal to be trampled to death by the cattle. In Tswana gays are now known as *kgwete*, which means bold, beautiful and unique, and Zulu gays are called *nkonkoni* (wildebeest), although conservative elders say they are *stabani*, or those with two parts. Militant ANC comrades have decided to call gays 'lady comrades'.

LANGUAGES

South Africa is a linguistic melting pot with 11 official languages. They are English, Afrikaans, North Sotho, South Sotho, Shangaan, Sindebele, Swazi, Tswana, Venda, Xhosa and Zulu. The languages spoken by black South Africans fall into four major linguistic groups: Nguni, Sotho, Venda and Tsonga. Included in the Nguni groups are Xhosa (spoken in the southern and eastern Cape), Zulu (Natal), South Ndebele and

Swazi. English is widely spoken throughout the country (except in some remote rural areas) and is regarded as the country's lingua franca. Afrikaans is the mother tongue of the Afrikaners who make up 15% (6 million) of the population and is widely used by the coloured (mixed race) community, which numbers more than 3 million. A high proportion of other groups — English-speaking whites, black people and Asians — use Afrikaans as a second or third language. French, Italian and German are spoken by staff in many of the hotels and shops in larger centres. There are also substantial Portuguese and Greek polyglot communities. South Africans of Asian origin speak English, although older members of the community still speak Tamil, Telugu, Gujarati, Urdu and Hindustani.

A Pan South African Language Board has been established to promote the official languages, and if you watch TV you will find programmes screened in all of them. A language task group has also been set up to consider how the black languages can be modernised to cope with, for instance, scientific and technological subjects. Afrikaans has lost the prominence it enjoyed during the years of National Party government. The SABC no longer accords it equal treatment with English and the country's new education system means young South Africans can complete their schooling without ever having to read or write a word of Afrikaans. Afrikaans is similar to Flemish, and grew out of the original High Dutch spoken by early settlers. German, Huguenot French, English and a some Malay words and phrases have been absorbed over the past 200 years.

Although Afrikaans has been officially downgraded you will notice that most signs are still in Afrikaans, as well as English. These are some of the ones that you are likely to come across:

Berg	mountain
Dal	dale or glen
Drif	ford
Eiland	island
Gat	hole
Gevaar	danger
Huis	house, home
Kasteel	castle
Kloof	gorge, ravine
Kraal	corral, village
Krans	cliff, precipice
Lughawe	airport
Oord	resort
Plaas	farm, place
Poort	gateway, defile
Pos	post
Punt	point
Rand	ridge, reef
Rivier	river
Stad	city
Stadig	slow
Stasie	station
Veld	field, pasture
Verminder spoed	reduce speed
Vlakte	plain, flats
Vlei	a watery hollow or marsh

If you can get your tongue around them here are some useful phrases. You won't need them, but you are sure to make someone's face light up.

English	Afrikaans	Zulu	Xhosa	Tswana
Good morning	Goeie môre	Sakubona	Molo	Dumela
Good afternoon	Goeie middag	Sakubona	Molo	Dumela
Good evening	Goeinaand	Sakubona	Molo	Dumela
Yes	Ja	Yebo	Ewe	E
No	Nee	Hayi	Hayi	Nya
Please	Asseblief	–	–	–
Thank you	Dankie	Ngiyabonga	Enkosi	Ke e leboga
No thank you	Nee dankie	Hayi, ngiyabonga	Hayi, enkosi	Nya ke a leboga
Goodbye	Totsiens	Sala kahle/ Hamba kahle	Sala kakuhle/ Hamba kakuhle	Sala sentle

South Africanisms. Visitors to South Africa are often bewildered when, after asking when something will be done, they are told, 'just now' and find themselves still waiting hours later. Be warned: 'just now' carries the same indication of urgency as the Spanish *mañana* and means some time in the future; 'now, now' means soon. If you want something immediately use the imperative 'now, now, now'. Other widely used linguistic oddities include *ja-nee*, which translates as yes-no, but equally can mean maybe or sure; *sies* or *siestog*, which is used as an exclamation of disgust; 'shame', an all-purpose word used to express virtually any emotion, from 'shame, what a lovely baba (baby)' to 'shame, she can't spell'; and *lekker*, which is Afrikaans and can mean delicious (taste), nice (weather), sweet (smell) or fine (fellow).

The following are words commonly used in conversation:

Aikona	an emphatic no
Babbalas	hangover
Bakkie	pick-up or utility vehicle
Biltong	dried meat, jerky
Bioscope	cinema, movies
Boer(e)kos	farm food
Boer(e)wors	spiced farm sausage
Braaivleis	barbecue (literally to roast or grill meat)
Clipper	township slang for R100
Dagga	Marijuana
Dop	a shot or tot of spirits
Dorp	small town
Frikkadel	meat ball
Konfyt	jam, preserves
Kreef	crayfish, rock lobster
Mieliepap	maize porridge
Muti	medicine
Oom	uncle, term of respect
Padkos	provisions for a trip
Pasop	watch out
Regmaker	hangover cure
Robot	traffic light
Rondavel	round hut, or cottage
Seker	certainly
Skaam	shy, bashful
Skollie	hooligan
Sosatie	kebab
Stoep	verandah, porch
Stoot (on doors)	push (*druk* — pull)
Tackies	tennis shoes

Tickey box	telephone box or pay-phone
Toyi-toyi	dance performed at black gatherings and in the streets by striking workers
Tula	be quiet
Vasbyt	hang in there
Velskoen	casual country shoes
Voetsek	not a nice way of saying go away
Wag 'n bietjie	wait a minute
Yebo Gogo!	simple greeting, or enthusiastic response to anything at all

Finally, if somebody responds to your questions or your attempts to use the vernacular by saying something that sounds like 'Ah big yaws', it simply means 'I beg your pardon.'

RELIGION

The Constitution recognises and enshrines complete freedom of worship, and it is not unusual to find a mosque, a Catholic church, an Anglican church and a synagogue not far from each other in many towns and cities. This religious co-existence reflects the diversity of the nation's communities, each giving unique expression to different spiritual values.

There are more Christians — about 80% of the total population — than any other religious grouping and most major denominations are represented in the country. There are more than 120,000 Jews, members of either Orthodox or Reform congregations, who are pillars of the commercial community. Their forebears arrived mainly from Poland and Lithuania in the late 1800s. Others came later from Britain and Germany; all found a religious tolerance that had spread with the second occupation of the Cape by the British in 1806. South Africa has always been tolerant of different religious beliefs, although there is an old story that when Johannesburg was being laid out each of the main religious denominations was given four stands on which to build a place of worship. The Jews were given only two stands because — President Paul Kruger is said to have told the rabbi — they believed in only half of the Bible.

Churchmen played a leading role in the anti-apartheid movement from the days of Father Trevor Huddlestone to Beyers Naude, Peter Storey and Nobel Peace Prize Winner Desmond Tutu, who was the first black Archbishop of Cape Town and head of the Anglican Church in southern Africa. On his retirement in September 1996, he was succeeded by Winston Hugh Njongonkulu Ndungane, Bishop of Kimberley and Kuruman, who as a youthful PAC activist served a three-year sentence on Robben Island for furthering the aims of a banned organisation before training for the ministry. The PAC has a churchman as its leader, Bishop Stanley Mogoba, who was head of the Methodist Church in South Africa before taking over the PAC presidency from ousted Clarence Makwethu in December 1996. Like Archbishop Ndungwane, Mogoba was jailed on Robben Island for his PAC activities and spent his time in prison studying theology.

Asians (Indians and Chinese) are either Hindus (68%), Moslems (20%), Christians (10%) or Buddhists. Traditional religious beliefs are still strong among blacks, especially in the rural areas. They share four basic tenets — belief in a creator, veneration of ancestral spirits, the intercession of diviners and mediums, and the animistic conviction that natural elements and objects such as wind, water, trees and rocks possess souls. Among the black population the Methodist Church has the largest number of adherents of all the Christian denominations. Principal Christian groupings are the Dutch Reformed family of churches (3.5 million members); the Anglican Church (Church of the Province of South Africa — 1.3 million members); the Roman Catholic Church (2.5 million); the Methodist Church (2.3 million); and the amorphous groupings of African indigenous churches, which combine charismatic Christianity with elements of traditional belief. There are about 2000 indigenous church groups, most of them in Gauteng and adjoining provinces (Soweto alone has 500), the largest of which is the Zion Christian Church. This has its headquarters at Zion City Moria, near Pietersburg. Most of the indigenous church groups believe in prophet-healers, and their adherents are a common sight at the weekend in their brightly coloured uniforms and robes.

The Dutch Reformed Church (DRC), to which most Afrikaners belong and which preaches a Calvinist Christianity based on strict Old Testament teachings, was long isolated by the majority of the world's Protestant communities for citing biblical writ as a justification for apartheid. The DRC no longer subscribes to this view and its *dominees* (ministers) have publicly apologised to blacks for their church's past stand.

Islam came to South Africa largely as the religion of slaves and political prisoners from the Netherlands' eastern possessions. The significance of this is noticeable in the spirit of resistance that underlies the history of Islam in South Africa, and which characterised the Muslim fight for political freedom from European colonial powers, and in the struggle to protect the basic tenets of their religion. There are about 400,000 practising Muslims in the country, the majority of them among the Asians of KwaZulu-Natal, where there are also 600,000 Hindus, and a large number in the Western Cape, the historical home of the Malay and mixed-descent (coloured) communities.

Among places of worship in Johannesburg are:

Anglican Cathedral, St Mary's	(011) 333-2537
Catholic Cathedral, Christ the King	(011) 402-6342
Church of England, Christ Church	(011) 484-1741
Great Synagogue	(011) 725-5444
Greek Orthodox	(011) 725-4745
Methodist Church	(011) 337-5938
Presbyterian Church	(011) 720-7911
Central Baptist Church	(011) 725-1993
NG Kerk	(011) 402-6438
Gereformeerde Kerk	(011) 403-1245

Consult the press for details of their services here and in other centres.

Generally speaking, South Africa's peoples are religiously oriented and religious beliefs play an important role in public life, although a sizeable minority has no religious affiliation. All the major Christian religious holidays are officially observed and Jewish businesses close on their holy days.

NATIONAL ANTHEMS AND FLAG

South Africa has two national anthems, which are played at all official and sporting occasions. They are *Nkosi Sikelel' iAfrika* ('God Bless Africa') and *Die Stem van Suid-Afrika* ('The Voice of South Africa'). The latter, an Afrikaans poem written in 1918 by Cornelis Langenhoven, was put to music and became South Africa's national anthem in 1957; the former is a hymn written in 1897 by Enoch Mankayi Sontonga, a teacher at the Methodist mission school at Klipspruit, near Johannesburg. The ANC adopted it as its anthem in 1925. Sung over the years at political gatherings, protests and funerals, this inspiring and moving song symbolises hope, unity and commitment to a just society. It is also used as a national anthem by other African countries. Sontonga's grave in Braamfontein Cemetery, Johannesburg, was declared a national monument on Heritage Day (25 September) in 1996.

The motto of South Africa is *Ex Unitate Vires* ('Out of Unity Strength'). The yellowwood is South Africa's national tree; the blue crane is its national bird; and the protea is its national flower, and is now worn as a sporting emblem by teams representing the country (except for the rugby team, which retains the old Springbok emblem at Mandela's express wish).

The Flag. This has two equal-width horizontal bands of red at the top and blue at the bottom, separated by a central green band which splits into a horizontal Y, the arms of which end at the corners of the hoist side. Between them is a solid black triangle separated from the arms by narrow yellow bands; the red and blue bands are separated from the green band and its arms by narrow white stripes. Before 26 April 1994 the national flag was actually four flags in one - three miniature flags of the old Orange Free State, the old Transvaal Republic, and the Union Jack in the centre of the former flag of the Netherlands.

The flag was designed with colours representative of South Africa. The blue symbolises the sky and oceans; green is for the land; red is for the blood shed in the many wars fought throughout the country's history; white stands for peace; gold is for the country's mineral wealth; and black represents the majority of its people.

FURTHER READING

Books on the history of South Africa from anything but a Eurocentric perspective have still to be written. A relatively unloaded version is the simple *Illustrated History of South Africa* (1994, Reader's Digest, R140; £18.65/$30.80). Pivotal books are Thomas Pakenham's *The Boer War* (1996, Abacus, R60) and *Long Walk to Freedom* by Nelson Mandela (1994, Abacus, R56), both dealing in vastly different ways with history-shaping events.

Books on birds and wildlife are numerous and every book shop has at least several metres of them in stock. A handy book for the not-so-knowledgeable game-watcher is *The Safari Companion: A Guide to Watching African Mammals* by Richard Estes (1996, Russell Friedman Books, R125). A classic animal reference book is *Maberly's Mammals of Southern Africa* edited by award-winning wildlife film-maker Richard Goss (Jonathan Ball & AD Donker, R55). The twitcher's standard field guide is *Newman's Birds of Southern Africa* by Kenneth Newman (1996, Southern Book Publishers, R90). Once you have this trio in your pack all you need is Chris and Tilde Stuart's *Guide to Southern African Game and Nature Reserves* (1997, Struik, R109).

If you plan to do any driving or caravanning the best maps and road guides in South Africa are published by the Automobile Association of South Africa and by Struik. Foremost are the *New Southern African Book of the Road* (1995, AA The Motorist Publications, R130), the *Touring Atlas of Southern Africa* by Michael Brett and Alan Mountain (1997, Struik, R145), and Maxwell Leigh's *Touring in South Africa* (1995, Struik, R100).

If you are a walker or backpacker the handiest book to carry is *Hiking Trails of Southern Africa* by Willie and Sandra Olivier (1995, Southern Book Publishers, R95); a weightier read is Jaynee Levy's *Complete Guide to Walks and Trails in Southern Africa* (1994, Struik, R149). For inner space explorers there is Al J Venter's *Diving in Southern Africa* (1995, Central News Agency, R80) and *The Dive Sites of South Africa* by Anton Koornhof (1997, New Holland, R109), which lists not only 180 of the best dives in the country, but includes a number of interesting dives inland in the North-West Province, Gauteng and Mpumalanga.

A good introduction to sites piscatorial is *Flyfishing Venues in Southern Africa*, compiled by Garth Brook (1996, Federation of Southern African Flyfishers, R40), and for an introduction to things vinous there is nothing to beat *South African Wines* by John Platter (1997, John & Erica Platter, R44), a little breast-pocket-size annual that is *the* wine bibber's bible and, like the stuff it so meticulously describes, improves by the year.

PRACTICAL INFORMATION

ACCESS BY LAND

Not too many people arrive overland from Europe these days, but if you are one of the adventurous planning to use this route you should contact the South African Department of Home Affairs before you set out for details of the locations and opening and closing times of the various border posts along the borders with Botswana, Namibia and Zimbabwe. Write to the department at Private Bag X114, Pretoria 0001, Gauteng, tel (012) 314-8911, fax (012) 323-2416.

Temporary entry requirements for vehicles driven into South Africa and other countries in the Southern Africa Common Customs Area (Botswana, Lesotho, Namibia and Swaziland) include triptyques, which, although not compulsory, are recommended. If you cannot meet other importation conditions your triptyque guarantees payment of customs duties and sales tax. Motoring organisations in your home country will advise you on triptyques and carnets.

If you arrive at a South African border post without a triptyque or carnet, customs can demand a deposit to cover normal duties and tax. These duties are high and unless you can pay the necessary deposit your vehicle will be refused entry.

Your vehicle registration certificate or logbook should be handy for customs inspection. You can keep your vehicle in South Africa for a maximum of 12 months from your date of entry. Keep your vehicle in the country longer than this without written permission and you will be liable for customs duties and VAT.

BY RAIL

Spoornet's rail passenger services connect Harare and Bulawayo in Zimbabwe with Pretoria and Johannesburg and also run to and from other neighbouring countries. The Bosvelder train runs from Beit Bridge on the Zimbabwe border to Johannesburg (655km/407 miles); a first-class single costs R134 (£17.85/$29.50). Bulawayo to Johannesburg (1189km/739 miles) costs R235; Harare to Johannesburg (1376km/855 miles) on the *Limpopo* express costs R1376.

BY SEA

Cargo Vessels. The Cape sea route to and from Europe has been famous for centuries. One of the most popular and more pleasant ways of getting to and from South Africa used to be the regular mailship sailings. These came to an end in September 1977, much to the dismay of confirmed sea travellers. Since 1990, Safmarine has been operating four 55,000-ton container ships, known as 'Big Whites' because of their size and colour, between ports in Europe and South Africa. These vessels also carry passengers from Tilbury, England via Le Havre to Cape Town, Port Elizabeth or Durban, and either Durban, Port Elizabeth or Cape Town to Zeebrugge and Tilbury.

This passenger service offers regular sailings in each direction, about seven days apart. This results in some 32 northbound and 32 southbound voyages a year. A total of 10 passengers, in twin-bedded cabins, all with private facilities, can be accommodated on each of Safmarine's four large container vessels. The four vessels being used are the *SA Winterberg, SA Waterberg, SA Helderberg* and *SA Sederberg*.

Southbound fares range from US$1460 to US$1850 per person, sharing a twin cabin, in low season (April to August) and US$1950 to US$2450 per person sharing a twin cabin in high season (September to March). These one-way fares from Tilbury to Cape Town are quoted in US dollars, as is customary with cargo vessels internationally. South African coastal fares are quoted in rands. A return ticket Cape Town–Durban–Cape Town costs R2250–2900 (£300–387/$495–638), depending on the class of cabin occupied. The price of a passage ticket includes accommodation and three meals a day and is exceptional value. These are working cargo liners; Safmarine is not attempting to provide the facilities found on a cruise vessel, although they offer a high standard of comfort and amenities, including a TV and VCR in each cabin, lounge with cocktail bar (drinks duty-free at sea), dining room, swimming pool and sun deck, personal laundry service, a video and reading library, and a passenger steward.

Medical certificates are required for all passengers taking the voyage, as no doctor is carried and the 16-day trip is non-stop. Medical certificates are not required for coastal voyages. Minimum age for passengers is two years; there is no upper limit.

You can book the voyages through any travel agent, or direct with Safmarine. Safmarine's UK representative in Southampton is Captain Richard Hellyer, tel (01703) 334415, fax (01703) 334416. In Cape Town contact Janet van de Vijver or Kim Booysens at (021) 408-6911, fax (021) 408-6370.

Passenger Ships. The *RMS St Helena*, of the St Helena Line, managed by Curnow Shipping Ltd of Porthleven, Cornwall, sails to Cape Town from her home port of Cardiff four times a year and makes nine trips each year from Cape Town for the island of St Helena. Outward-bound voyages from Cardiff to South Africa are scheduled for 23 October 1997, and for 26 February and 14 May in 1998. They return from Cape Town on 20 September in 1997, and on 11 April and 4 July in 1998. Most of these voyages include shuttle service between St Helena and Ascension islands *en route*, and if you are on one of these you will have to spend eight or nine days on St Helena at your own expense. The trips take from three to four weeks, depending on ports of call.

For a room only for two people at the Consulate Hotel in Jamestown, St Helena, you will pay about £48 a day for up to 10 days, with full board £64 a day for two. The Wellington Hotel charges £34 daily per person for full board. There are also a number of self-catering places charging £15 to £20 per person. The St Helena Line can give you a list of these. If you want to stay on board ship during the shuttle period it will cost you another R3080.

Sailing from Cardiff, the 7767-ton *RMS St Helena* calls at Tenerife, in the Canary Islands, Ascension Island and the island of St Helena, famous as Napoleon Bonaparte's place of exile. The ship has stabilisers, modern facilities and air-conditioning to ensure a comfortable voyage and carries up to 128 passengers in cabins ranging from single and two occupancy, to three and four berths. In addition, there are 28 budget berths and one cabin specially designed for wheelchair passengers. A single ticket from Cardiff to Cape Town can cost you from R26,705 for sole use of an outer cabin down to R9730 if you share a four-berth cabin. Return fares are double.

Contact Curnow Shipping Ltd, The Shipyard, Porthleven, Helston, Cornwall, UK, tel (01326) 563434, fax (01326) 564347; or St Helena Line (Pty) Ltd, 2nd Floor, BP Centre, Thibault Square, Cape Town 8001, tel (021) 25-1165, fax (021) 21-7485.

Yachts. Yachties from the north arriving by sea at Cape Town are sailing in the wake of some of the world's most famous mariners. Captain Antonio da Saldanha of Castile arrived in the bay at the foot of a flat-topped mountain in 1503. He named the bay *Agua da Saldanha* and sailed on to India. A century later, Captain van Spillberger sailed his Dutch squadron into the bay and named it *Tafel Baai* (Table Bay). He was followed in 1652 by Jan van Riebeeck in the *Dromedaris*. Captain James Cook, the greatest seaman, explorer, navigator and cartographer the world had ever known, visited Cape Town four times between 1771 and 1776. Another famous visitor was Captain Joshua Slocum, the first man to sail alone round the world. He sailed the *Spray* into Cape Town at Christmas in 1897.

In keeping with this seafaring tradition the Royal Cape Yacht Club (RCYC) keeps an open welcome for visiting yachts and their crews. The maximum length of yacht the club can accommodate is 22m/72ft, with a draft of 4m/13ft. You pay a subscription fee of R79.80 per person for one to three months and another R14 for up to six months. There is also a fee of R200 per person if you live on board over an extended period. You can use all the club's facilities, which are excellent.

BY AIR

Most international tourists fly into Johannesburg, gateway to the rest of the country, although Cape Town and Durban are receiving increasing numbers of direct international flights. Nearly 80 airlines now serve South Africa regularly — there were only 21 in 1990 — and competition for passengers is fierce. This has kept fares extremely low and cut-throat pricing has meant a bonanza for air travellers. There are no direct services to South Africa operated by carriers in the USA, Canada, New Zealand or Scandinavia.

South African Airways (SAA) is the country's national carrier and the largest commercial airline in Africa. It operates 12 weekly flights from London, six from New York, seven from Frankfurt and two from Perth and Sydney. SAA also has regular scheduled flights from and to Bangkok, Mumbai, Dubai, Hong Kong, Singapore, Tokyo, Tel Aviv, Amsterdam, Düsseldorf, Frankfurt, Munich, Paris, Zürich, New York, Miami, Rio de Janeiro, Buenos Aires and Sao Paulo. Flying times between Johannesburg and some major cities are:

Bombay	8 hours 40 minutes
Buenos Aires	11 hours
Frankfurt	11 hours
Hong Kong	13 hours 15 minutes
London	11 hours
Miami	18 hours
Nairobi	4 hours
New York	17 hours 30 minutes
Paris	11 hours
Perth	9 hours 15 minutes
Rio de Janeiro	9 hours
Singapore	10 hours 15 minutes

For SAA frequencies, times and fares check with your nearest SAA office, or with SAA, PO Box 7778, Johannesburg 2000, Gauteng, tel (011) 356-2036, fax (011)

356-2019. SAA International Customer Care line is tel (011) 773-9375, fax (011) 773-9533.
Some of SAA's international passenger offices are:

UK: St Georges House, 61 Conduit Street, London W1R 7FD, tel (44) 171-312-5010, fax (44) 171-312-5008;
USA: 9th Floor, 900 3rd Avenue, New York NY 10022, tel (1) 212-418-3700, fax (1) 212-418-3744; Suite 100, 901 Ponca de Leon Boulevard, Coral Gables, Miami, FL 33123, tel (1) 305-461-3484/5, fax (1) 305-461-3861;
Australia: 9th Floor, 5 Elizabeth Street, Sydney, tel (61) 2-223-4448, fax (61) 2-223-4682; 7th Floor, Exchange House, 68 St Georges Terrace, Perth 6000, tel (61) 9-322-7388, fax (61) 9-324-1724.

SAA Economy Class air fares London to Johannesburg are R9300 (£1240/$2045); New York to Johannesburg R12,160 (£1621/$2675); Frankfurt to Johannesburg R9270; and Sydney/Perth to Johannesburg R11,450. Students qualify for a 50% discount. Seasonal excursions, Pex and Super Pex excursions are also available. For fare quotations tel (011) 356-1133, reservations tel (011) 356-1111. SAA also has money-saving packages known as RSA Costcutters, which include return Economy Class flights from Cape Town, Durban and Port Elizabeth to Johannesburg, one night's bed and breakfast and two day's Imperial car hire on an unlimited mileage basis. You can get details of current offers from any SAA office, or from SAA Costcutters, tel (011) 356-1144.

British Airways (BA) operates 13 flights a week from London to Johannesburg, four flights a week from London to Cape Town and three flights a week from London to Durban. BA is under pressure from competitor Virgin Atlantic and this schedule may change. High-season Super Pex fares are: London to Johannesburg R7770 (£1036), London to Cape Town R8100 (£1080), and London to Durban R7935 (£1058). Student and special discounts are available and should be checked with British Airways when making a booking.
Contact details in South Africa:

Johannesburg: 158 Jan Smuts Avenue, Rosebank, Gauteng, tel (011) 441-8600;
Cape Town: 12th Floor, BP Centre, Thibault Square, tel (021) 25-2970;
Durban: First Floor, Salisbury Centre, 332 Smith Street, tel (031) 304-4741.

Central reservations in London is in Regent Street, tel (0171) 434 4700.
Virgin Atlantic Airways services to Johannesburg from London Heathrow started in October 1996 with three flights a week, and rose to the present six a week in March 1997. Virgin's arrival was a wake-up call for SAA and BA, both of which responded by lowering their fares. Virgin Atlantic operates a two-class system: Upper Class (the airline's business class) and Economy Class, which is segmented into Premium Economy Class (a full fare separate economy cabin) and Economy (all other coach/economy fares). Virgin is a member of 'Access to the Skies', a committee that operates under the auspices of the Royal Association for Disability and Rehabilitation (Radar), and has special facilities for disabled passengers. Check with Virgin for fares and specials:

South Africa: PO Box 411934, Craighall 2024, Gauteng, tel (011) 340-3400, fax (011) 340-3506;
UK: tel (01293) 747747;
USA: tel (800) 862-8621.

Lufthansa operates 11 weekly flights into South Africa — seven non-stop from Frankfurt to Johannesburg, two non-stop from Frankfurt to Cape Town, and two from Frankfurt to Cape Town via Johannesburg.

Reservations: tel (011) 484-4711/7522, fax (011) 484-2992;
Johannesburg International Airport: tel (011) 975-0484, fax (011) 975-5096;

Cape Town International Airport: tel (021) 934-8534, fax (021) 936-5063; *Durban:* tel (031) 305-4262, fax (031) 307-3295.

Central reservations in Germany, tel 01803 803 803.

Lufthansa and SAA are partners, and their frequent flyer programmes are linked. This means that a Lufthansa Miles and More bonus card-holder can accrue air miles and redeem awards on SAA and SA Express. The same applies for an SAA Voyager card holder when flying Lufthansa.

Qantas Airways operates four flights a week. On a Monday: Sydney to Perth to Johannesburg; Tuesday: Sydney to Melbourne to Johannesburg; Thursday: Sydney to Perth to Harare to Johannesburg; and Saturday: Sydney to Perth to Johannesburg. Return economy class fares Sydney to Johannesburg to Sydney are: Low Season (16 January–30 April) A$1984; Shoulder Season (1 May–15 November) A$2299; and High Season (16 November–15 January) A$2824. No special discounts.

> *South Africa:* Johannesburg, tel (011) 884-5300, fax (011) 884-5312; Cape Town, tel (021) 25-2978, fax (021) 21-4759; and Durban, tel (031) 304-4702, fax (031) 304-5133;
> *Australia:* Sydney, tel (61) 2 9691 3636, fax (61) 2 9691 3277.

Competition between airlines flying from London to South Africa is hotting up, with British **charter airlines** Britannia and Caledonian undercutting scheduled services. Britannia Airlines flies once a week from London's Gatwick Airport to Johannesburg and once a week to Cape Town on behalf of tour operator Bluebird Holidays. Caledonian Airways has a weekly flight to Johannesburg, and on to Cape Town.

South Africa has relaxed restrictions on charter airlines, which means that British tour operators can now sell seat-only tickets as well as package holidays, with big savings for holiday-makers. Contact Caledonian Airways and Bluebird Express in Johannesburg, tel (011) 884-1212.

Other Airlines. In addition to those mentioned above, many other airlines offer services to South Africa; further details can be obtained by contacting the offices listed below.

> *Air France* operates six flights a week to Johannesburg, with three of them continuing to Cape Town; special fares available; PO Box 41022, Craighall 2024, Gauteng, tel (011) 880-8040, fax (011) 880-7772; France, 119 Avenue Champs Elysées, Paris 75008, tel (01) 42 99 21 01, central reservations, tel (01) 44 08 22 22;
> *Alitalia* has seven flights a week to Johannesburg; tel (011) 880-9254, fax (011) 880-9277; Italy, reservations on 0939 6 65621, fax 0939 6 65628310;
> *Cathay Pacific Airways* flies from Hong Kong to Johannesburg; economy fares are currently R3990–4520 (£532–603/$878–994); Private Bag X28, Rivonia 2128, Gauteng, tel (011) 807-6618, fax (011) 807-6933;
> *EgyptAir* flies to Johannesburg from Cairo, linking with its flights from major cities in Europe, the USA and Australasia; worth checking out, as its fares are often the lowest on offer, and discounted youth and student fares are available; tel (011) 880 4126/7/8/9, fax (011) 880 4360; Egypt, tel (02) 245 0260/70; UK, tel (171) 734 2864/2395, fax (171) 287 1728; USA, tel (718) 997 7700/1/2/3, fax (212) 315 0967; Australia, tel (02) 232 6677;
> *KLM Royal Dutch Airlines* flies from Amsterdam to Johannesburg and on to Cape Town or Harare, and special fares are available; reservations and information, tel (011) 881-9696, fax (011) 881-9691; The Netherlands, tel 20 4 747 747 (24 hours a day); UK, tel 0181 750 9000; USA, tel 1 800 3 747 747 (toll-free); Australia, tel 008 222 747 (toll-free);
> *Olympic Airways* flies between Athens and Johannesburg; PO Box 47224, Parklands 2121, Gauteng, tel (011) 880-1614, fax (011) 880-7075; UK, tel (0171) 409 2400, fax

(071) 493-0563; USA, tel (212) 838 3600, fax (212) 735 0215; Australia, tel (02) 251 2044/1040, fax (02) 252-2262, toll-free 008 221 663;

Sabena Airlines flies between Johannesburg and Brussels, with economy class fares ranging from R2500 (£333.35/$550) to R4000; 99/133 Carlton Centre, Johannesburg 2001, tel (011) 331-8166/9166.

Singapore Airlines (SIA) flies from Singapore to Johannesburg, Cape Town and Durban, and has connecting flights to Australia and New Zealand; tel (011) 880-8560, web site http://www/singaporeair.com;

Swissair operates flights from Zürich to Cape Town and Harare, via Johannesburg; PO Box 3866, Parktown 2193, tel (011) 484-1986, fax (011) 484-1999; reservation office in Zürich, tel (0848) 800 700, fax (01) 258 34 40, web site http://www.swissair.com.

Help. The Info Africa Passenger Services Centre in the international arrivals hall at Johannesburg International Airport offers a multilingual (more than 25 languages) passenger and public relations service at immigration and passenger arrivals, as well as a national accommodation, transportation, travel and leisure ticketing service, and many more helpful options. Contact Info Africa on (012) 660-0880, e-mail info@ iafrica.com. Info Africa also has the largest travel site on the Internet covering southern Africa (http://www.infoafrica.co.za), with more than 400 pages of information and details of nearly 10,000 companies.

ENTRY REQUIREMENTS

Passports and Visas. You need a valid passport to enter South Africa, but visitors from the EU, the USA, Canada, Australia, New Zealand, Singapore, Switzerland and Japan do not need a visa. Regulations have been relaxed to the extent that normal holiday and business visits and transit stops are allowed without visas for most foreign travellers, but for longer stays, possible settlement and for specific events, such as sporting events, you are given a three-month temporary residence permit. If this does not give you enough time, you can apply for a 90-day extension. It is best to do this in person in Johannesburg or Cape Town at the Department of Home Affairs (open Monday to Friday, 8.30am–3.30pm). Check your status with your travel agent or with the office of the nearest South African representative. If you do need a visa you must get it before you leave, as they are not issued on arrival. Visas are free. You should get a multiple visa if you intend travelling to neighbouring countries during your visit to South Africa. On arrival you might be asked to provide proof that you have enough money to support yourself during your stay; you must also have a valid return or onward ticket endorsed 'Not refundable.' It is an offence to enter or leave South Africa at any place other than a control post where there is an Immigration Officer.

For up-to-date information you can also check with the South African Department of Home Affairs, Private Bag X114, Pretoria 0001, Gauteng, tel (012) 314-8911, fax (012) 323-2416.

Health Requirements. No immunisation is needed to enter South Africa. The only inoculation requirement is a valid international yellow fever vaccination certificate

MALARIA RISK AREAS

High risk
Low risk

Botswana

Namibia

NORTHERN PROVINCE

Tzaneen

Mozambique

Skukuza

PRETORIA
GAUTENG
JOHANNESBURG   MFUMALANGA

NORTH - WEST

Swaziland

Sodwana Bay

FREE STATE

KWAZULU-NATAL

Lesotho

NORTHERN CAPE

DURBAN

Atlantic Ocean

EASTERN CAPE

Indian Ocean

N

WESTERN CAPE

EAST LONDON

CAPE TOWN

PORT ELIZABETH

0   100 miles
0   100 km

from travellers over one year of age who enter within six days of leaving an infected country. If you plan to travel through or disembark in any yellow fever area you should be inoculated against the disease beforehand. Malaria, predominantly in the malignant form *P. falciparum*, exists throughout the year in certain areas of the country. It is endemic in some parts of Mpumalanga, the Northern Province and KwaZulu-Natal. Resistance to chloroquine has been reported. It is recommended that you use chloroquine plus proguanil in risk areas, but consult a doctor or pharmacist about the most suitable prophylactic, or contact the South African Department of Health, Private Bag X828, Pretoria 0001, Gauteng, tel (012) 312-0000, fax (012) 325-5706.

Pets. Dogs and cats from rabies-free countries are allowed in without quarantine, but a Veterinary Health Certificate must accompany the Veterinary Import Permit. You can get these permits from the Director of Animal Health, Private Bag X138, Pretoria 0001, Gauteng, tel (012) 319-7514. For detailed information contact the State Veterinarian, PO Box 168, Cape Town 8000, tel (021) 949-5500; PO Box 920, Durban 4000, tel (031) 32-6731; and PO Box 17, Johannesburg 2000, tel (011) 838-5603.

CUSTOMS AND IMMIGRATION

Immigration. If you arrive by yacht from a foreign port the immigration department regards you as being in transit. If you want to visit the interior or neighbouring countries you must obtain their permission. This is especially important if you visit neighbouring territories, as otherwise you may have difficulty re-entering South Africa. If you stay in South Africa for a year, customs can make you pay import duty and sales tax on your boat. Contact the Immigration Office, 77 Harrison Street, Johannesburg, Gauteng, tel (011) 836-3228.

You will be given a temporary residence permit (TRP) on arrival in South Africa, which you will have to renew at the Department of Home Affairs if you intend staying longer than three months. TRPs are issued on the condition that you do not alter the purpose of your visit after arrival or accept employment without permission from the Director-General of Home Affairs, Private Bag X114, Pretoria 0001, Gauteng, tel (012) 314-8891, fax (012) 323-2416. If you want to take a job during a temporary stay you must first obtain a temporary work permit. Details from any South African mission abroad or the Department of Home Affairs in South Africa.

Customs. After collecting your bags you can choose either the red or the green channel to pass through customs. Where this system is not in operation you should report to a customs officer and declare all the goods in your possession. You can use the green channel only if you have goods that fall within your duty-free allowance: 400 cigarettes, 50 cigars, 250g tobacco, 2 litres of wine, 1 litre spirits, 250ml toilet water, and 50ml perfumery. Any more than this is liable for duty. No duty-free tobacco and alcohol can be brought in by anyone under 18 years of age. There is a long list of prohibited goods, which includes narcotic and habit-forming drugs, fully automatic weapons, poison and other toxic substances, and cigarettes weighing more than 2kg per 1000. Lots of plants and plant products are restricted. Firearms and ammunition for use while hunting in the Republic are released with a temporary police permit.

If you are not sure whether you are carrying dutiable goods you should take the red channel and declare everything in your possession. Personal effects, sporting and recreational equipment brought for your own use must be taken with you when you leave. You may be asked for a cash deposit to cover the duty and tax on expensive articles, such as video cameras. This will be refunded when you leave. If you leave from Cape Town, Durban, Komatipoort, Beit Bridge or Johannesburg International Airport, you should send the duplicate copy of the receipt issued for the deposit to the controller of Customs and Excise at the place of departure at least seven days before you depart, so that customs can have your refund available. VAT paid by visitors on purchases in the Republic is refundable. These regulations apply in all countries belonging to the Southern Africa Common Customs Area. Contact the Department of Customs and Excise, tel (012) 314-9911.

What Money to Take. The favourable exchange rate makes South Africa a relatively cheap holiday destination, especially if you are coming from a sterling, dollar or franc currency area. The rate makes even five-star accommodation reasonably priced, while food and good wine come at absolute bargain prices. It is advisable to carry your money as US dollar or sterling travellers' cheques.

Plastic Cash. Travellers' cheques in major currencies and international credit cards such as American Express, Diners Club, MasterCard, Visa and others are widely accepted in South Africa. You might, however, have difficulty using them in small towns and rural areas, and many small shops do not have the facility to accept them. Petrol (gasoline) and other fuel must be paid for in cash; filling stations do not accept credit cards. Always check to see that your card is acceptable in restaurants *before* you eat. Automatic teller machines (ATMs) are situated outside most banks in towns and cities, and operate 24 hours a day.

Credit card fraud and scams are rife throughout the country, so be careful when using one. A favourite trick is to run two slips over your card, hold one back and trace your signature on to it at a later stage. Often the only way you will know that this has happened is when you get home and see your credit card account. Credit card fraud in South Africa as a percentage of cards held is the highest in the world. A few years ago this fraud represented about 0.01% of the value against a global figure of 0.1%. The fraud level in South Africa is now double the world average. Keep your cards on you all the time; do not leave them in your car or lying around. Report stolen cards immediately.

MasterCard is accepted by 80,000 merchants in South Africa, and allows you to get an emergency cash advance at any institution displaying the MasterCard sign. American Express is accepted at more than 40,000 South African establishments, including all the big chain stores, major hotel groups and most restaurants and resorts. Although Diners Club is traditionally used as a travel and entertainment card, you can also use it at retail chains such as Pick 'n Pay, Woolworths, Checkers and the OK Hyperama.

South Africa has the highest number of compatible ATMs in the world and you can access emergency cash with a Diners Club card, for instance, at 6000 ATMs through Saswitch and MultiNet networks, whose signs and logos appear on the ATMs. First National Bank (FNB), the largest provider and acquirer of Visa and MasterCards, has about 30,000 Speedpoint terminals in southern Africa. Visa has 1.26 million card holders in South Africa.

Rands and Cents. South Africa's currency was decimalised on 1 February 1961, shortly before the country became a republic. On that day South Africa stopped using pounds, shillings and pence, and introduced rands and cents. The monetary unit is the rand (R), which is equal to 100 cents. The international symbol is ZAR. Bank notes are issued in denominations of R200, R100, R50, R20 and R10. Coins are issued for R5, R2, R1, 50c, 20c, 10c, 5c, 2c and 1c. South Africa uses a comma as a decimal point.

The rand has steadily dropped against the US dollar and other major currencies since 1990, when it was R2.58 to the dollar. At the time of writing (June 1997) there were R4.55 to the US dollar, and R7.50 to the pound. It is unlikely that it will change by more than 10% either way in the foreseeable future.

Foreign Exchange. At Johannesburg International Airport you will find a 24-hour currency exchange service, duty-free shops, banks, cocktail bars and restaurants. Travellers' cheques and foreign bank notes of most major currencies can be exchanged at any commercial bank. Most hotels, shops and businesses accept travellers' cheques and foreign currency, although commission varies. International credit cards are widely accepted. American Express offices, Rennies Travel and most hotels have exchange facilities. Check daily fluctuations in foreign exchange rates through the press, radio or TV. In Johannesburg, contact:

    American Express: tel (011) 833-0811, fax (011) 834-3744;
    Diners Club: tel (011) 337-3244, fax (011) 333-4591;
    Thomas Cook Rennies Travel: tel (011) 407-3211, fax (011) 339-1247.

Banks and Banking. Banks can deal with all international transactions and 41 registered banks have more than 4000 branches throughout the country, or one for every 10,000 of the population. Banks are open Monday to Friday, 9am–3.30pm, and

52   *Practical Information*

Saturday 8.30–11am. In country areas banks open weekdays 9am–12.45pm and 2–3.30pm, and on Saturday 8.30–11am. ATMs are available round the clock outside banks in most towns and cities. Banking services at airports are available two hours before and after the arrival and departure times of all international flights.

Major South African commercial banks include Absa, First National, Nedcor and the Standard Bank. Foreign banks with branches in the main cities include Banko Espirito Santo e Comercial de Lisboa, Banque Française du Commerce Exterieur, Credit Suisse, Deutsche Bank, National Bank of Egypt, Standard Chartered Bank and the Swiss Bank Corporation.

Information and Complaints. Information on banking is available from the Association of General Banks, Finance House, PO Box 610380, Marshalltown 2107, Gauteng, and the Council of Southern African Bankers (COSAB), PO Box 61674, Marshalltown 2107, both at tel (011) 838-5833, fax (011) 836-5509.

Bank toll-free hotlines are as follows:

> *Allied:* 0800 123 456
> *Boland Bank:* 0800 111 722
> *Nedbank:* 0800 116 662
> *Saambou Bank:* 0800 139 555
> *Standard Bank:* 0800 121 000
> *Trust Bank, Allied Bank and United Bank:* 0800 111 950
> *United:* 0800 123 456
> *Volkskas:* 0800 123 456

A novel 24-hour service is the Absa Bank Travelphone (0839-011-011), which offers a wide range of information, including road reports, safety hints and tips (how not to get mugged), toll fees, and contact numbers for embassies, consulates and police stations throughout the country. It also includes numbers for taxis, car hire, bus services, scheduled airline flight timetables, accommodation and restaurants. You can also find information on things to do, see, calendar events, entertainment and sports.

If you have a complaint against a bank, discuss it with the branch manager. If you are not satisfied, pursue it with the bank's head office or write to the Banking Ombudsman, PO Box 61674, Marshalltown 2107, Gauteng, tel (011) 838-4978, fax (011) 836-5509.

Currency Restrictions. If you have more than R500 in South African cash in your possession when leaving the country you need a permit to take it out from the South African Reserve Bank, PO Box 427, Pretoria 0001, Gauteng, tel (012) 313-3911, fax (012) 313-3197. For more information or advice you can contact Customs and Excise: Pretoria, tel (012) 314-9911; Cape Town, tel (021) 21-1930; Durban, tel (031) 37-8511; Johannesburg, tel (011) 975-9308.

South Africa has a currency exchange control system to protect the country's foreign reserves, but this is unlikely to be of interest to tourists. Contact the Department of Finance, Private Bag X115, Pretoria 0001, Gauteng, tel (012) 315-5111, fax (012) 323-3262 for details.

Tipping. While tipping is customary, South Africans are not as generous with tips as Americans, the British and other Europeans. Restaurants are allowed to levy a service charge (though not all do), in which case there is no need to tip the waiter. Tips are not compulsory, of course, but simply a token of your appreciation for help and good service. When in doubt, remember that the modern habit of tipping started out meaning 'to ensure promptness', or 'to ensure performance'. If you are not happy with performance, do not tip.

As a guide, tip barmen, waiters and taxi drivers 10%, porters R1 to R2 a bag, petrol pump attendants R2 and hairdressers R5. Tips to guides and coach drivers are usually between R5 and R10 a day. If you do not tip for any reason — dissatisfaction, no small change — you may not get a smile, but at least you won't get the sort of abuse New York taxi drivers reserve for tight-fisted passengers.

BEFORE YOU LEAVE

Health insurance is often one of the last items on your checklist, yet it is one of the most important. People from countries with free or aided health care tend to forget that they may have to pay exorbitant medical fees if they fall ill or have an accident while on holiday. South Africa has no reciprocal health care agreements with other countries for free or reduced cost emergency medical treatment, so before you travel, always arrange adequate health insurance. Talk to your travel agent, insurance company or bank. Some credit and charge cards provide health insurance for travellers. Check that it is adequate for your needs; if not, take out extra cover. If you have an accident while you are driving in South Africa, you may not be covered for medical or hospital expenses. Check this with your insurance company or a motoring organisation before leaving home.

What medical precautions to take will depend not only on the countries you plan to visit but which parts of them, for how long, at what time of the year, and where you will be staying. Camping, for example, presents different potential health problems to staying in an hotel. You can get more information on all these points from your travel agent, the South African Embassy or Consulate, or from a specialist travel clinic. Consult your doctor well in advance of your departure for advice and immunisations. Some of these cannot be given at the same time and some take time to become effective. Immunisation against Hepatitis B, for example, can take six months to give full protection. Tell your doctor where you are going and if you are taking children with you. This is particularly important if they have not had their full course of childhood immunisations. If you need anti-malaria medication your doctor will advise on which is most appropriate. You should start taking the medication a week before departure. If you require prescription medicines while away, check on their availability; if you are doubtful about whether they can be obtained buy sufficient supplies before leaving.

If you want to take any kind of medicine with you — either prescribed or bought over the counter from a pharmacist — make sure you know about any restrictions on taking it out of your own country and into South Africa. Check with the South African Embassy or Consulate.

Carry any medicine in a correctly labelled container, as issued by the pharmacist, or carry a letter from your doctor giving details of the drug prescribed to avoid problems going through customs. Remember that some medicines available over the counter in your own country may be controlled in South Africa. Keep a written record on your person noting any medical condition that affects you, such as angina pectoris, diabetes or haemophilia, and the proper names — not just the trade names — of any medication you are taking. Dental treatment can be expensive in South Africa, so have your teeth checked before you leave home.

When You Return. Plan not just for your holiday but for what to do when you get home. If you received any medicines while away it may not be legal to bring them back. If in doubt, declare them at customs on your return. If you were taking anti-malaria tablets, remember to continue for a month after you return. If you fall ill on your return, do not forget to tell your doctor where you have been while away, and tell your GP if you have been bitten by any animal or exposed to any sexually transmitted diseases. If you had medical treatment while away claim on your insurance as soon as possible.

MEDICAL SERVICES

While health care in South Africa is generally of a high standard — except in remote areas — there is no comprehensive national health scheme and as a visitor you are responsible for your own medical bills. Private medical practitioners are listed in local telephone directories under 'M' for medical, and hospitals are listed under 'H'. Emergency services are available and usually of a high standard, especially at private clinics and hospitals. In emergencies, you can obtain treatment at hospital out-patient departments for a nominal fee.

Health care for the majority of the population of 44 million people is a growing problem, as only 8 million are on any form of medical aid or insurance. About 92% of all in formal employment are members of medical aid schemes, but nearly 40% of the country's labour force is unemployed, and is therefore outside the health care net. The rest of the population is impoverished and cannot afford doctor's bills. To deal with this situation the government deregulated the medical aid industry in 1994 and is supporting private sector moves to introduce other types of scheme, such as a managed health care system that is being undertaken with the help of UK, US and Australian experts.

The State's health services are based on primary health care principles, with the focus on women, children and the poor, with more than 400 regional, community and teaching hospitals, and more than 3000 primary health care clinics. There is a growing number of mobile clinics, including a primary health care train called *Phelophepa* ('good, clean health'), which travels around rural communities, providing them with an eye clinic, a dental and X-ray clinic and a pharmacy. Universal access to a primary health care service ensuring all South Africans free treatment at any publicly financed health care facility is the government's aim. In 1995, free medical care for children under six and pregnant women became available. With its new emphasis on primary health care and plans to extend the service the state's dilemma is that it has neither the resources nor the infrastructure to implement a comprehensive national health strategy. Doctors and other qualified medical staff are leaving the country in increasing numbers for the UK, USA and Australia and the health system is beginning to show stress.

If you should find yourself headed for a private hospital or clinic you can be sure of two things: you will receive the finest care available — and the bill you get might give you a heart attack. If you have a sports-related injury you will find lots of specialist physiotherapists listed in the telephone book, or any sports shop will recommend one. Johannesburg has a Centre for Sports Medicine, which opened in 1995, and is the place for you if you are in Gauteng. It is run by a team of highly qualified personnel. In Cape Town, world-famous sports medico Tim Noakes is Professor of Sports Science in the University's Department of Physiology, tel (021) 650-9111, fax (021) 650-2138, and runs the Sports Science Institute of South Africa, tel (021) 686-7330, fax (021) 686-7530.

Worldnet Africa has a Health Online site (http://africa.cis.co.za/health/health.html) that offers free, 24-hour medical consultations. Worldnet Africa Health Hub says the service combines Internet technology with the need to provide a medical service to all.

Doctors. There are around 8000 dispensing doctors in South Africa. Several hundred Cuban doctors have arrived in the country — with more coming — as part of an agreement reached between South Africa and Cuba in 1996. These cigar-smoking medicos have aroused strong feelings in the local medical profession, whose members are critical of their qualifications and experience. Another difficulty is that the Cubans practise mainly in rural areas, where language problems compound the issue.

Dentists. Nowhere — with the possible exception of the USA — will you spot fewer cavities and ruined teeth than in South Africa. The standard of dentistry practised is excellent. If you need a dentist they appear in the telephone book under 'D'.

Pharmacies. Most medicines can be bought, but if you are on specialised medication take supplies with you to be on the safe side. There are nearly 3000 dispensing pharmacies in South Africa and most remain open until as least 6pm on weekdays (1pm on Saturday) and some until 8pm. You will always be able to find an emergency night pharmacy open and some offer a limited Sunday service. Check with your hotel reception or the Yellow Pages in the local telephone book.

ALTERNATIVE AND TRADITIONAL MEDICINE

Alternative Medicine. Any health store will be able to point you in the direction of virtually any alternative health care service you are likely to want. There are lots of health stores and there are lots of alternative practitioners. Acupuncture is one of the oldest known forms of medicine; it has been practised for more than 6000 years and is becoming increasingly popular in South Africa. You can get information about this from Jimmy Lu (Lu Chien-Ming), Professor in Acupuncture and Chi-Kong (Therapeutic Energies), Honorary Life President of the South African Society of Chinese Traditional Medicine and Acupuncture, 3 Tana Road, Emmarentia 2195, Gauteng, tel (011) 888-3071, or contact Dr Vladimir Bilik, Acupuncture Specialist (University of Moscow), 53 Galway Road, Parkview 2193, Gauteng, tel (011) 646-0152. In health stores, pharmacies and supermarkets throughout the country you will find a wide range of proprietary natural, non-prescription medications. Among the better-known brands are Lennon, Bettaway, Natrodale, Vitaforce, Weleda Homeopathic and Leppin sports products. Lennon consultants offer information and help on their toll-free hotline 0800 118 088 between 9am and 12pm.

Traditional Medicine. Traditional African views of health and illness co-exist with those of Western medicine in South Africa. Not only are physical aspects of the world seen as influencing health, but also spiritual or magical elements. Not surprising, then, that there are an estimated 300,000 traditional healers and herbalists ministering to the physical and spiritual ailments and needs of the majority of black people, even those who are urbanised and Westernised. Whites are also calling on their services in increasing numbers. Though they would deny it, many families have had recourse to either a traditional or faith healer, a *sangoma* (diviner), an *inyanga* (herbalist), an *isanusi*, a homeopath, a fortune-teller or a tarot card reader in a bid to solve personal problems or to rid themselves of physical ailments. Some 70% of families believe the claims of these mystical men and women that they can see into the future, avert calamity, exorcise demons and evil spirits, and communicate with the dead. To most white South Africans all traditional medicine men and women are simply witch-doctors (*inyangamthakathi*; from *inyanga*, doctor, plus *umthakathi*, witch). There is, however, a vast difference between traditional healers and witch-doctors. *Sangomas* or *inyangas* are consulted by people who want to protect themselves against witches and witchcraft *muti* (medicine). Witch-doctors are usually called on only to cast spells, maim, or even kill for those consulting them. Witch-doctors are still frequently linked to ritual murders in which people, especially children, are killed so that their body parts can be used to make *muti* or charms.

In 1996, the Northern Province Council of Churches met in Pietersburg to discuss witchcraft following a report that more than 300 people had lost their lives after being 'sniffed out' as witches. Thousands more had been chased away and lost their property for 'crimes' ranging from turning themselves into bats and birds and other people into zombies, to causing lightning to kill villagers or strike their homes. The church commission found that 'the overwhelming majority of people interviewed in both urban and rural areas still believe in witchcraft', and said this belief continues to be a danger in traditional societies. It is a common story. In Alexandra township, Johannesburg, three teenagers were assaulted by their grandmother who, they said, took them on regular trips on a broomstick to and from their rural village in the Northern Province. In this region, which vies with the Eastern Cape as the poorest of all nine provinces, with a vast unemployed and illiterate population, belief in the unknown is widespread.

One of the important functions of traditional healers is to counter this black magic, and many believe the current breakdown of the social fabric is the result of people no longer adhering to tradition. Though the majority of traditional healers live and practise in rural areas, others are trained nurses, teachers, and even lecturers. Whereas Western-trained doctors tend to concentrate on the disease and its symptoms, traditional healers focus on the people who are ill and treat them in relation to their families and their community. There are even a few white *sangomas* who have felt the ancestral call and given up their jobs to apprentice themselves to black healers. Most *sangomas* are women who have some knowledge of herbal remedies, but specialise in divining the illness and its causes by spiritual communication with the patient's ancestors. Disease is also regarded as a manifestation of discord between patients and the society they live in. Blood-letting, induced vomiting and enemas are often used to cure illness, and while these treatments seem medieval to modern doctors they do fulfil deeply held cultural expectations and psychological needs.

There is a growing school of thought in the conventional medical profession that co-operation with traditional healers could be mutually beneficial. Not only are these healers usually compassionate, wise and non-judgmental counsellors, they also have an enviable knowledge of the natural resources that constitute three-quarters of the plant-derived prescription drugs in common use today. More than 700 indigenous plant species are sold for medicinal purposes in KwaZulu-Natal alone. These are most commonly used by traditional healers in hot and cold infusions, as powders rubbed into incisions in the body, as poultices, lotions, ointments, vapour baths, emetics and enemas. Researchers are investigating the active ingredients of these medicinal plant species as they could be useful in pharmaceutical medicine. Although plants are used as the basis of most traditional medicines, animal and bird parts are also used. As with plants, there is concern that exploitation of these is threatening their existence. Of particular concern is the decline in the number of pythons, pangolins, striped weasels, lizards, and various vultures.

Some South African universities have already introduced traditional healing as a medical school subject to give students an understanding of the importance of using local resources, especially in primary health care. The critical shortage of qualified medical staff means that a huge proportion of the rural population depends on such plant remedies. Some 200 traders are licensed to sell traditional medicine on the Witwatersrand and there are about 12,000 traditional healers using this in Soweto alone. Supplies come from all over southern Africa and as far afield as India, mostly in the form of bark and roots, although leaves, stems, whole plants and bulbs are also sold. If you want to know more about this contact the Professional Herbal Preparation Association of Inyangas in Johannesburg, tel (011) 838-2931.

What used to be disregarded as mumbo-jumbo is achieving respectability in health care circles. Since 1994, a growing number of medical aid schemes have allowed black members to claim for treatment by traditional healers. Others who want to undergo the initiation ceremony to become *sangomas* are now allowed four months' unpaid leave. Traditional healer and best-selling author Credo Mutwa has built a healing village in a valley not far from the cultural village complex at Shamwari Game Lodge, 75km/47 miles from Port Elizabeth. Sangomas are trained here and he says people plagued by illness or demons can be healed by them.

EVERYDAY HEALTH

Treating Water. There are lots of ways to treat water to make it safe to drink. You can use iodine, boil it, chlorinate it — easy, effective and cheap — flocculate it, or filter it. Best of all is to chlorinate it to kill the bugs, flocculate it to settle and clear the water, and then filter it. Old hands in the bush rely on iodine (2% aqueous solution) as an emergency stop-gap to purify water, or at least to render it safe for drinking. Filter the water before adding three teaspoons (15ml/0.5fl oz) iodine to a litre of water and let it stand for 30 minutes before using it. More up-market and reliable are mechanical purification systems such as the Swiss-made Katadyn pocket and mini ceramic filter pumps, available at most outdoor supply shops, or inexpensive chemical aids such as Chlor Floc and Micropur water purification tablets and Watermaker powder sachets. All can produce clean, drinkable water within minutes. Most travellers are unlikely to have to resort to purifying their own water supply, but it's just as well to know the options. The simplest solution in doubtful situations is to carry boiled water.

Toilets. City centres, parks, beaches, cinemas, theatres and amusement centres all have well signposted public toilets. For hygienic reasons, however, your best bet is to use the toilets in hotels, restaurants, shopping malls and filling stations.

Gastric Upsets. 'Montezuma's Revenge' does not only strike in Central America. Tummy bugs and traveller's diarrhoea are common and easy to get in South Africa, especially if you are dehydrated or are not careful about what you eat and drink. Most gastroenteritis is caused by a virus, and symptoms develop within two days. Drink plenty of water and take an anti-diarrhoeal preparation such as Imodium, obtainable from any pharmacist, although the problem should be controlled by dietary measures alone where possible. Most bouts of gastroenteritis settle in between one and three days and a normal diet can then be followed. Fasting for 24 hours is recommended. Avoid spicy foods such as curries and alcohol for a while. South Africans believe fresh paw-paw fruit is good for diarrhoea. As well as having viral causes, diarrhoea is also often the result of food poisoning. This poisoning or infection inflames the digestive tract, or more specifically the lining of the stomach and intestines. It is caused by eating food contaminated by bacteria. The infection will vary, depending on the different kinds of bacteria and the types of food eaten. Be careful of dysenteries; both bacterial and parasitic (amoebic) dysentery can be contracted by eating salads and uncooked vegetables. The onset is generally accompanied by what in South Africa is called 'the trots'. In the bush the general rule is boil it, cook it, peel it, or forget it. Heat is the great steriliser. This restriction does not, of course, apply to the salads, dressings and other cold foods served in hotels and restaurants.

Viral hepatitis is an infection of the liver that can cause jaundice. There are two forms: hepatitis A, sometimes called infectious hepatitis; and hepatitis B. Health authorities in South Africa recommend immunisation against hepatitis A, which is usually caused by contaminated food or water. This disease can also be spread from person to person, since the virus is present in faeces, and travellers to places where sanitation is primitive need to be especially aware of the risk of infection. An injection of normal immunoglobulin (Gamma Globulin) shortly before travelling will reduce risk.

Hepatitis A is the most common vaccine-preventable infection suffered by travellers. Most countries in Africa are affected. While hepatitis A infection is common in South Africa the risk for tourists is low, unless you are exposed to unhygienic conditions. A course of vaccine is recommended for non-immune individuals.

Hepatitis B occurs throughout the world and is spread in the same ways as HIV (the virus that causes AIDS), which is through intimate person-to-person contact, through contaminated blood entering the body, or through the use of inadequately sterilised equipment in medical treatment, tattooing and ear piercing. There is a vaccine that gives good protection against the disease. However, it can take six months to become effective. The best way to prevent infection is to avoid high-risk activities and take a travel kit for use in medical emergencies. New health guidelines for travellers to South Africa are being compiled by the Department of Health. Contact the Director-General, Private Bag X828, Pretoria 0001, Gauteng, tel (021) 351-0000, fax (021) 325-5706.

Sensible Precautions. Many diseases and parasites are contracted by consuming unhygienic food and water. If you are off the beaten track remember always to wash your hands after using the toilet, and certainly before handling food or eating. If you have any doubts about water for drinking, washing food or cleaning your teeth, boil it, sterilise it with disinfectant tablets or use bottled water — preferably carbonated — from sealed containers. Avoid ice unless you are sure it is made from safe water. This includes ice used to keep food cool, as well as ice for drinks. Eat fresh, well cooked food while it is still hot; avoid uncooked food, food that has been kept warm, or food that is likely to have been exposed to flies. Eat only fruit you have peeled or shelled yourself. Avoid unpasteurised milk, or boil it. Fish and shellfish can sometimes be suspect away from the coast and uncooked shellfish, such as oysters, can be a particular hazard. All water in cities is safe to drink.

A variety of diseases is spread by insects. Use insect repellent and cover your arms and legs with appropriate clothing when walking, especially in wooded or grassy areas. Animal bites can start infections that can be serious and sometimes fatal. Be wary of animals, even when they seem tame.

Bathing is fine for cooling off but remember that fatal accidents can easily happen. Adults should watch each other for signs of trouble when swimming, and children should always be supervised by an adult. Young children should never be left unattended near a stretch of water, even a paddling pool. If you are going to dive into water, make sure that it is deep enough. Each year, many people are permanently paralysed as a result of injuries caused by diving into shallow water.

AIDS

Incidence and Awareness. You cannot be infected with the HIV virus through everyday social contact, insect bites, dirty food or crockery, or activities such as kissing, coughing or sneezing. You can get it by having unprotected sex with an infected partner. There is no vaccine for HIV or cure for AIDS. The Department of Health estimates that more than 10% of the population is infected, with some 500 more becoming so every day. Medical procedures requiring injections and/or blood transfusions use products tested to internationally accepted standards and are considered safe. Measures for preventing sexually transmitted diseases are the same as in all other countries; abstention is naturally the best prevention, but if this does not appeal to you remember that many people who are HIV-positive are not aware of it, so always use a condom. Pack an adequate supply of condoms if you think you may need them, as they might not be as easily available or of as good a quality as in other countries.

The spread of HIV is reaching alarming proportions and predictions are that by the year 2005 one-fifth of South Africa's population — men, women and children — could test HIV-positive. The HIV/AIDS epidemic could be more severe in South Africa than in other African countries because of its rapid urbanisation, labour mobility, and a highly developed transport infrastructure. Almost all communities in South Africa's nine provinces are in the epidemic stage, which means prevalence is greater than 1% in the adult population. AIDS, however, is not a notifiable disease, and because of this the number of South Africans with AIDS who have died is really a mystery. The most recent statistics for HIV prevalence show that it is highest among 15 to 29-year-olds, with young women at most risk. Young South Africa is sitting on an AIDS time bomb, with predictions that by the year 2000, a total of 3.7 million people will be HIV-positive and in that year about 200,000 people will die of AIDS-related diseases. At 14.3% KwaZulu-Natal has the highest HIV rate.

If you are HIV-positive or have AIDS do not travel without consulting a doctor or a travel health clinic; low immunity puts you at special risk. See page 219 for contacts in Johannesburg.

HEALTH HAZARDS

Malaria. Along with the rest of Africa, South Africa is regarded as a high risk area for malaria. It is caused by the bite of the female anopheles mosquito, which transmits a microscopic protozoan parasite called *Plasmodium*, of which four species affect humans. The most dangerous is *P. falciparum*, which causes cerebral or malignant malaria. The female mosquito lays eggs in open, stagnant water and as warm weather aids the breeding process it is probably safer to visit malarial areas during the dry, cooler months. Mosquitoes bite mainly once dusk has fallen and then throughout the night. To avoid being bitten sleep under a mosquito net, and liberally spray an insecticide such as Perinel on the net. Make sure the net has no holes and keep it tucked in. Mozzies are the master burglars of the insect world. Spray the room with a knock-down repellent before you climb under the net. Sleeping or awake, rub your face, arms and legs and any other exposed skin with a repellent containing diethyltoluamide (DEET).

Tabard is one of the best known insect repellents in South Africa and comes as a stick, spray and lotion. Other good ones are Mozzi Guard mosquito repellent wipes (in packs of 100) and Moss-guard wet wipes. Pyrethrum repellent coils, which burn slowly through the night, are also popular. The smoke from these asphyxiates insects — and often the user. Always wear light-coloured clothing — long sleeves, long trousers — from dusk onwards. Dark clothing, perfume and after-shave attract mosquitoes. March is normally the peak malaria season in South Africa. Incidence of the disease seems to be increasing and the high-risk belt stretches from Messina in the Northern Province through the Kruger National Park and eastern Mpumalanga to northern KwaZulu-Natal.

Symptoms of all forms of malaria appear seven to 30 days after infection and usually start with vague pains and a general feeling of weariness, most noticeable in the morning. Next come severe headaches, aching joints and muscles, and a feeling of coldness, with shivering in spite of an elevated temperature, which may exceed 40°C/104°F. Prevention is better than cure and it is advisable to start taking anti-malarial medication well before you leave home, as this gives you an opportunity to test any possible side-effects and to substitute something more acceptable if necessary. No prescription is required for most brands. The main thing is to continue with the medication while in the malarial risk area and after you have left. Your doctor or pharmacist will advise you on this.

There is something of a controversy about malarial medication. Mefloquine (Larium) is an effective anti-malarial medication, but it can have some adverse side-effects. Your doctor or pharmacist can tell you about these. Pregnant women and small children should not visit a malarial area at all. Another contra-indication to Larium can be if you are taking beta-blockers for heart ailments or high blood pressure. Chloroquine accompanied by proguanil is a tried and trusted anti-malarial cocktail, although the side-effects can be similar to Larium. Doctors recommend Larium for areas of high malarial risk, such as sub-Saharan Africa, while chloroquine (Plasmoquine, Daramal) with proguanil (Paludrine) is regarded as adequate for malarial areas such as the Kruger Park and the northern regions of KwaZulu-Natal. For more information, get a copy of *A Layman's Guide to Malaria*, by Martine Maurel (Southern Book Publishers, R44.95), or contact the Directorate of Communicable Disease Control in Pretoria at (012) 312-0104.

Yellow Fever. This tops the danger list of contractable diseases in Africa and the mortality rate is high. The scourge of early explorers and settlers in tropical America and Africa, yellow fever is transmitted by a mosquito bite. It results in fever, jaundice (which produces yellowing of the eyes and skin), bleeding from the mucous membranes and dark vomit. South Africa is believed to be free of yellow fever, although mosquitoes that can transmit the virus are present in some areas, especially KwaZulu-Natal's sub-tropical coastal belt. Visitors to or from areas where yellow fever is endemic must, by law, be vaccinated and have a certificate to prove it.

Tick-bite Fever. Tiny blood-sucking parasites cause tick-bite fever. They belong to the order *Acari*, which with 20,000 species is the largest arachnid order after spiders. So it is no wonder they are found all over the place; waiting to leap on to any bit of exposed flesh. They are most prolific in grassy and woodland areas and on shrubs. Once on you they usually head for warm, dark spots, like the underarm and the crotch areas, where they are very difficult to spot. You can get tick-bite fever from the bite of the red-legged tick, the multi-coloured or *bont* tick, as well as from the common dog tick. They are most active in spring and summer, which is when most people are out of doors. If you find one on your skin remove it with your fingers if it is not holding fast, and crush it. If the tick has sunk its fangs into you and will not come off easily, do not pull. Cover it with Vaseline or thick oil to cut off its air supply, then pull it off with tweezers. A glowing cigarette end also works well to loosen them. Wash the bite thoroughly with soap, water and disinfectant. Ticks rarely give you fever if removed within an hour.

The incubation period for tick-bite fever is normally six to seven days after being bitten, but it can be as long as four weeks. Lymph glands nearest the site of the bite become enlarged and tender and you feel feverish, tired and usually get a severe headache. A few days later a rash appears on your face, the soles of your feet and your palms. See a doctor long before this stage if you can. Antibiotics are the answer and can also prevent the development of the other symptoms. Better than antibiotics, of course, is prevention. Clothing sprays and washes can be bought at hardware stores, supermarkets, pharmacies and outdoor sports shops. Bayticol Aerosol Fabric Spray is a product that stays on for two washes and is rainfast. There is also an ozone-friendly aerosol spray. You can also wash your clothes in Peripel 55 repellent, which keeps off other insects as well as ticks.

Bilharzia. This disease is found in South Africa largely in those areas also affected by malaria. It is caused by a microscopic organism found in rivers, streams, dams and lakes — both stagnant and flowing — in the northern and eastern areas of the country. There is no practical way of distinguishing infested from safe water, so all contact with open water should be avoided in these areas. This means no drinking, washing, paddling or swimming in such water, no matter how inviting it appears.

This parasitic disease, also known as schistosomiasis, is caused by a worm that penetrates your skin and can cause damage to your intestines, liver and urinary tract. Symptoms begin with a slight itch where the skin was penetrated, followed a few days later by a rash. The onset of fever and muscle pain occurs after a month and is soon followed by abdominal pain and diarrhoea, or the appearance of blood in the urine, together with a burning sensation when urinating. If not diagnosed and treated, serious and irreversible damage may be done to the bladder, liver and kidneys. If you are accidentally contaminated by suspected water you can reduce the risk of infection by rubbing alcohol or towelling off vigorously. There is no vaccine against bilharzia.

Tuberculosis. The most common communicable diseases in the country are tuberculosis (TB), sexually transmitted diseases (STDs), malaria and measles. There is minimal risk of contracting tuberculosis; for a tourist the risk is probably no greater than in New York City. If you or your family have not been immunised against TB and you are going to stay for more than a month you should discuss the need for BCG immunisation with your doctor at least two months before leaving. Immunisation is not necessary for short visits if you are staying in international-style hotels. Revaccination is not recommended if you were vaccinated as a child.

Poliomyelitis. If you are travelling to countries anywhere in Africa you should be protected against poliomyelitis. If you have never been immunised you should receive a full course of three doses of vaccine. If you were immunised more than 10 years ago you will need a booster dose.

Tetanus. This is a dangerous disease, causing severe and painful muscle spasms. It is caught from bacterial spores getting into your body through even the slightest wound. These spores are found mainly in soil and manure. Tetanus is particularly dangerous where medical facilities are not available for immediate treatment. You should be protected by immunisation, especially if you plan to travel to remote areas. If you were immunised as a child, ask your doctor about a booster. If you were not, you will need a course of three injections.

Typhoid. Typhoid fever results from contaminated food or water. Immunisation against the disease is recommended if you are travelling to places where sanitation is primitive.

Congo Fever. Congo-Crimean haemorrhagic fever is a viral infection transmitted by the bite of an infected tick. Symptoms include the sudden onset of fever, chills, aches and pains, headaches, and severe pain in the arms or legs. A rash may appear and internal bleeding can occur. Treatment is limited and no vaccine is available. This is a rare disease in South Africa, although there was a worrying outbreak in November 1996 in the Oudsthoorn area of the Western Cape. This is believed to have been caused among a dozen workers at an ostrich abattoir by the infected blood of a single bird; one worker died (after the scare, the European Union banned the importation of ostrich meat from South Africa). The fever can be caused by a virus passed on by the *bont* tick, either to humans through a bite, or to animals and birds, which can then infect people who come into contact with their blood or body fluids. It takes only a minuscule amount of blood or fluid to infect you. The mortality rate is around 60% and victims die because their blood does not clot and they bleed to death.

For up to date information on all health issues contact the *Travel Health Clinic* (part of the South African Institute of Medical Research) in Johannesburg, which is on the corner of De Korte and Hospital streets, tel (011) 489-9000, fax (011) 489-9001. For R40 you get up to an hour-long consultation with trained professionals. The Travel Health Clinic also provides medication, any vaccinations needed, mosquito nets and other goodies. *British Airways Clinics* are at the following locations:

Johannesburg: Sunninghill Family Medcare Centre, corner of Edison Crescent and Maxwell Drive, Sunninghill, Sandton, Gauteng. PO Box 573, Sunninghill 2153, Gauteng, tel (011) 807-3132, fax (011) 803-9562;
Cape Town: Room 1027, Fountain Medical Centre, Heerengracht, tel (021) 419-3172, fax (021) 419-3389;
Knysna: On the corner of Queen and Main streets, tel (0445) 826366, fax (0445) 826420.

NATURAL HAZARDS

Sunshine and Sunburn. Too much sunshine can be a hazard to your health, especially in South Africa, where summertime ultraviolet (UV) radiation levels are among the highest in the world. Danger levels of UV radiation are reported during weather forecasts on TV. If you don't want to fry now and pay later, remember that over-exposure to the sun can result in anything from a mild burn to a more severe dose with swelling and blisters. Symptoms of sunstroke are chills, fever, nausea and delirium. Itching and peeling may follow any degree of sunburn and normally begin four to seven days after exposure. Severe sunburn or sunstroke should always be treated by a doctor. Long-term damage caused by suntanning includes premature skin ageing and skin cancer. If you want to work on your tan, avoid the sun between 11am and 3pm — the time the rays are at their strongest — and protect your skin by using a sunscreen that filters out the damaging UV rays.

SPF stands for Sun Protection Factor, and the number indicates the degree of protection a product offers. The higher the number, the better the protection. An SPF of 5 means you can stay in the sun without burning five times as long as you could without any protection. An SPF of 15 means you can spend 15 times as long in the sun. Children and those with sensitive skins or pale complexions need higher SPF protection than adults with darker or less sensitive skins. SPF25 should be used for children and for extremely sun-sensitive skins. Apply the stuff regularly, especially after you have been swimming or exercising. The back of your neck, upper arms and upper legs need special care. T-shirts and long shorts offer better protection than skimpy clothing, and hats are a must, especially for children. Always wear good quality sunglasses.

Protection is necessary even on cloudy or hazy days, and especially at altitude. If you are not used to the sun, tan slowly — 15 minutes for a start — and increase the time by five minutes a day. Protect babies under six months of age with adequate loose clothing and keep them shaded. Apart from burning, you can also get sunstroke (heatstroke) or suffer from heat exhaustion from overexposure to the sun. Never underestimate how sick careless exposure can make you. Avoid strenuous activity during the hottest hours and make sure you drink plenty of non-alcoholic, caffeine-free liquids to make up for the loss of body fluid through sweating. Heatstroke and heat exhaustion are different conditions and are treated differently. The first is a medical emergency. If in doubt, treat for heatstroke, which occurs when high temperatures overwhelm the body's heat-control system. Immediate medical help is necessary. Heat exhaustion is caused by loss of salts and fluid during heavy sweating and can be rectified by drinking fresh fruit juice, which contains the right combination of water and electrolytes to fix you up.

Snakes. Snakes terrify most people, but it is highly unlikely that you will ever come across one in South Africa unless you are visiting a snake park. Of South Africa's 167 or so species of snake fewer than 16 are potentially lethal, and they are usually as wary of you as you are of them. To see a snake in the veld is a rare experience, but if you do, treat it with respect. There are three groups of poisonous snakes in southern Africa: the cobras and the mambas, which are front-fanged; adders, boomslangs and vine snakes, which are back-fanged; and spitting snakes such as the Mozambique spitting cobra and the rinkhals. Of these, the rinkhals, cobras and mambas are probably the most dangerous.

If you are unlucky enough to be bitten, forget all the Boy Scout stories about tourniquets and knife slashes to let the poison out. First of all, if you are uncertain whether or not a snake is poisonous, play safe and assume that it is. The effects of a serious bite are immediate burning pain, followed by swelling (most adders and maybe the spitting cobra), dizziness, and difficulty in swallowing and breathing (most cobras, mambas and the rinkhals). These symptoms do not occur immediately. Snakebite outfits containing antivenom can be bought from leading pharmacies and snake parks, but unless you know what you are doing you can cause even more damage — injecting antivenins is best left to the experts. What you can do is apply a broad, firm pressure bandage over the bitten area immediately and, if possible, the entire limb. Do not use a tourniquet. Lay the victim down and keep them calm; unnecessary movement increases circulation of the venom in the system. Do not give any alcohol and do not cut the bitten area. You can, however, try to suck out any poison if you do it immediately; spit out all fluid. Don't waste time — get the victim to the nearest doctor or hospital. If the snake has been killed, taking it with you as identification can simplify treatment; it may even have been a harmless snake. Snakebite victims are usually kept in hospital for observation for at least 24 hours, and sometimes for up to four days.

Spitting snakes do not actually spit their venom, they eject it up to 2.5m/6.6ft. If this goes in your eyes you should rinse them out immediately with large quantities of water. You can also use any other bland fluid, such as milk, tea, beer or even urine. Left untreated, the venom can cause partial blindness.

The best advice is to leave snakes alone; wear stout shoes or boots (not sandals) and long trousers in the veld; do not walk around without footwear, especially at night; and do not step over logs or large rocks, step on to them first to see whether a snake is coiled up on the other side. The widespread puff-adder is often found lying curled up on the path like this and it is the snake you do not see that bites you. Do not mess with snakes that seem dead as they often sham death. If you do come across a snake stand perfectly still; they do not strike at stationary objects. Then retreat slowly. At the seaside the only dangerous water snake is a yellow and black one. This is the most widely distributed sea snake throughout the Indo-Pacific oceans, and has been found from Table Bay to Zululand. You are not likely to see one in the sea, but they are often washed ashore during heavy storms. If they are still alive they will attack you if you fiddle with them, but there have been no cases of sea snake-bite reported in South Africa this century.

Spiders. There are more than 80,000 species of insects and their relatives — such as scorpions and spiders — in southern Africa, but so far they have not all been scientifically described. If this seems an awful lot of creepy crawlies to nip and bite, take heart: there are only a few you need to know about. It is a good idea to give all shiny brown and black, spherical spiders a wide berth in case they are button spiders, South Africa's answer to North America's nasty black widow. Southern Africa has two species of these, and they can be brown or black. They can be found among rocks and long grass and recognised by their abdominal marking, a red stripe or stripes or a dull red spot above their spinnerets. The brown widow, or hourglass spider, can be mistaken for its relative, but is not so dangerous. Bites are rare as spiders are not aggressive and bite only when you poke them or inadvertently disturb them. South Africa's black widow or button spider is the most dangerous spider in southern Africa, but because it hides away in dry, desert areas it is unlikely you will ever see it, let alone be bitten. Button spiders will only bite if you actually press them against your skin, but the bites of button spiders, violin spiders and a few others do call for immediate first-aid, as with all insect bites and stings. Then get to a doctor as soon as possible.

You can get more detailed information from *Spiders* by Garry Newlands (Struik Pocket Guides, Cape Town), and information on antivenins can be obtained from the South African Institute for Medical Research, PO Box 1038, Johannesburg 2000, Gauteng, tel (011) 489-9000, fax (011) 489-9001.

Scorpions. These are 'living fossils' and their family can be traced back in the geological record at least 400 million years. That does not mean much if one stings you. That requires immediate first-aid, followed by professional medical attention. Scorpions look like little lobsters. There are 175 different species and subspecies scurrying around South Africa, but there are only two kinds you need to know about. The most venomous one is *Parabuthus villosus*. This is one of South Africa's largest and most dangerous, with enough venom to kill a child. This is the one with thin pincers and a thick tail. If you remember nothing else, remember that the baddies are the ones with thin pincers and thick tails. The ones with thick pincers and thin tails are relatively harmless. The venom of scorpions is neurotoxic, that is, it affects your central nervous system. Burning pain, numbness or tingling, nausea, fever, stomach cramps, difficulty in speaking, convulsions, sweating and shock are what you can expect if you are stung by a dangerous scorpion. Lie still with the affected part immobile and lower than your heart. Apply ice wrapped in cloth or a cold compress. Do not apply ice directly to the skin. Seek medical attention immediately.

Bees and Wasps. African bees are notoriously aggressive, and certain types of swarming colony are dangerous to both men and animals. Fortunately, attacks are rare and occur mostly in the remoter areas, but they still kill more people every year in South Africa than snakes. Only the honey bee leaves its sting in the skin. Do not squeeze to remove, as this will force more venom into the puncture. If you can see the sting, carefully remove. Wash all bee stings with soap and water. Relieve pain with calamine lotion or a paste made of baking soda and water. If this is not available, toothpaste is a good stop-gap. Seek a doctor as soon as possible. If you are allergic to bee stings or show any signs of distress, such as rapid swelling or difficulty in breathing, get someone to drive you to a hospital.

There are several thousand species of wasp in South Africa. If it is any consolation, only the females can sting. Treat as for bee stings, although wasps do not leave their stings behind like bees.

Animal and Bird Attacks. Rabies is a contagious viral disease that affects a variety of mammals, and is characterised by abnormal behaviour. Wild animals will often lose their fear of humans, while domestic animals can become aggressive. The virus is carried by a number of animals, particularly dogs. Rabies is endemic in the Northern Province, Mpumalanga, KwaZulu-Natal and the Northern Cape, and there have been outbreaks in all other areas, with the exception of the Western Cape. Rabies attacks the nervous system. Its symptoms include delirium and painful muscle spasms in the throat. Once these symptoms develop in humans, the disease is usually fatal. You contract the disease by being bitten, so be careful not to touch any animals, whether they are wild or apparently tame. If you are bitten, early treatment usually prevents the disease developing. Wash the wound immediately, using soap or detergent. Apply alcohol if possible. Get to the nearest doctor or hospital as soon as you can. You may need a rabies vaccination and the course of injections must be started immediately. Inform the local police. Whether or not you receive treatment, consult your own doctor as soon as you get home.

Baboons and **ostriches** are probably the most dangerous wild animals you will meet in South Africa, although hippos kill more people than any other animal. Baboons are usually looking for food, so move slowly and deliberately if you are carrying any or leave it on the ground. The ostrich is the world's largest living bird and the only one with two toes. It is the fastest creature on two legs, capable of reaching speeds of 60km/h (37.5mph) in just 1.5 to 2 seconds from a standing start. The ostrich can deliver a lethal kick. It kicks forward, never backwards. Do not underestimate the danger of this peculiar bird, especially during the mating season. If attacked, lie face-down flat on the ground and cover your head with your arms. Keep still and the bird will lose interest. There are 90,000 domesticated ostriches in the Oudtshoorn district, where they are raised for their feathers and meat.

Crocodiles have colonised most countries in Africa, but hunting and spreading urbanisation and agriculture have put them under pressure in South Africa. If you are grabbed by one of these scaly monsters while swimming, foolishly, in a river, first-aid is not going to help. Crocs, like elephants, kill two or three people a year throughout the whole of the southern African region. You can see *Crocodylus niloticus* at 28 croc farms throughout the country if you are keen to get up close.

You will probably only ever see **lions** from a game-drive vehicle, sitting close to a ranger with a heavy calibre rifle. Swedish botanist Dr Carl Peter Thunberg, 'the father of Cape botany' who travelled in South Africa between 1772 to 1774, advised: 'On meeting a lion one ought never to run away, but stand still, pluck up courage, and look it stern in the face. If the lion lies still without wagging its tail there is no danger, but if it makes any motion with its tail then it is hungry and you are in great danger.' Thunberg never met a lion, although he was nearly killed by a buffalo.

Old hands say that one sure way to keep wild animals away at night is to urinate around your campsite (a few drops at a time) against rocks, the bottom of trees, and in the grass. Most animals, including lions, respect territories marked in this way and will leave you alone.

SEASHORE HAZARDS

Sharks. You are more likely to be struck by lightning or die from a bee sting than be attacked by a shark in South Africa — but there is always that remote chance. Numbers of shark attacks in South African waters, never high, have been dwindling over the years, probably because of the highly effective protective netting system off the more popular eastern Indian Ocean coast bathing beaches. The Sharks Board in KwaZulu-Natal provides safe bathing at 44 beaches, using 40km/25 miles of netting. An additional netted beach is situated at the Wild Coast Sun Hotel (Eastern Cape) immediately south of the KwaZulu-Natal/Eastern Cape border. There were no shark attacks along this coastline in 1996. One attack on a surfer took place at Jeffrey's Bay, Eastern Cape, in October 1996, but he received only minor injuries. The largest Great White captured off the KwaZulu-Natal coast weighed 892kg/1967lb. In the past there was a relentless and mindless campaign to exterminate sharks and until recently, the only good shark was a dead shark. Now their special niche in the oceanic food chain has been recognised and they are no longer ruthlessly hunted.

Sharks can be relied on for one thing, and that is their unpredictability. They have been known to swim through crowds of bathers in relatively deep water to bite someone standing in knee-deep surf. To be on the safe side, do not swim in dirty water, at dawn or at dusk, and never enter the water, sea or estuary, with a bleeding cut or graze. If you are snorkelling and spear-fishing bleeding fish have an irresistible attraction for hungry sharks, which have the uncanny ability to detect blood in water in infinitesimal amounts at incredible distances.

Some South Africans believe that light-coloured swimsuits catch light and cause inquisitive sharks to investigate, as do rings and pieces of jewellery, and erratic swimming and splashing. On the other hand, divers and surfers in dark wetsuits swimming on the surface have been bitten by sharks, which presumably mistook them for seals, their favourite food. Who knows what goes on in a shark's walnut-sized brain?

The Natal Sharks Board says that the most important factor in surviving a shark attack is for the victim to receive the correct treatment at the beach. Massive shock and loss of blood are the main causes of death in shark attacks. The victim should be got out of the water as quickly as possible and placed on his back on the nearest dry place close to the water's edge. Stop bleeding by pressing a clean pad on the wound. Keep the legs higher than the head to ensure the flow of blood to the heart and brain. Do not give warm drinks or alcohol. The most important thing is to call a doctor or ambulance to the scene, and not to panic.

The Surf Life-saving Association of South Africa says that shark attack is a rare phenomenon and the above advice is far more likely to be of use in helping someone injured in a car crash than in a shark attack. International Shark Attack File figures show that only 8% of shark attacks globally have happened in South African waters, compared to 19% for the USA and 27% for Australia. Maybe Ozzies taste better.

Shark experts say that attacks on humans are investigatory rather than aggressive, but that is little consolation if you are the human being investigated. Most Great Whites in South Africa seem to be concentrated in the south-western Cape with its cool waters and abundance of seals. This makes the region ideal for Great White-watching. It is also a consolation if you plan a swimming or surfing holiday in, say, Natal.

Blue-bottles. Children especially have fun popping the bladders of blue-bottles like bubblegum when these jellyfish are stranded on the beach, but remember that even when they are dead their trailing tentacles can still give nasty, painful stings that can take hours to disappear. Treat blue-bottle stings by applying alcohol, methylated spirits, vinegar, ammonia, or, if you have brought it along for the barbecue, meat tenderiser. If possible, immerse the afflicted part in water as hot as you can bear. Do not listen to anyone who tells you to rub the sting with sea water or wet sand. Local wisdom says that relief can also be obtained by rubbing the sting with paw-paw juice.

Sea Urchins. The spines of sea urchins are usually more irritating than painful, except for the ones you might brush up against in the east coast waters of KwaZulu-Natal, where two varieties have hollow spines carrying quite a potent venom. Although you might get only a small amount of this the pain can be intense. Symptoms include difficulty in breathing, cramps, muscular paralysis, and faintness. Pull the spike out with tweezers and soak the wound in extremely hot water to neutralise the venom. Spines remain particularly painful because they usually break off in your skin. If they do it can take weeks for them to work themselves out. Help them out with the old-fashioned remedy made by mashing up equal portions of green soap and sugar and putting this as a poultice over the punctures. Antibiotics are also recommended to prevent infection.

Stings from any form of sea life can be extremely painful, but rarely result in permanent harm or death. Keep the stung part immobile and lower than your heart. Do not squeeze any sting. Wash well. If there is any sign of shock or you have difficulty breathing, get medical attention. Wash **coral** stings with salt and water and paint with mercurochrome. For other stings soak the area in water that is as hot as you can bear without scalding yourself. Continue this for 30 minutes to an hour if you can while on your way to the doctor. Most divers, incidentally, believe the greatest danger from the sea lies on your plate in the form of fish or seafood poisoning.

FIRST AID HINTS

Carry a first aid kit. A minimum would be a packet of adhesive dressings, some insect repellent, a tube of antiseptic cream and a packet of water sterilisation tablets such as Chlor Floc or Micropur. More ambitiously, you can buy an emergency medical travel kit from a pharmacy or travel clinic containing a variety of sterilised and sealed items, such as syringes, needles and suture materials. This kit should normally be handed to a doctor or nurse for use in a medical emergency, especially in remote areas where there might be a shortage of equipment. A typical kit contains two syringes, five needles, a dental needle, an intravenous cannula, a skin suture with needle, a packet of skin closure strips, alcohol swabs for skin cleansing, a variety of non-stick dressings, and a roll of surgical tape. These kits should be easy to identify by customs officials so that the contents are not exposed until needed. It is also a no-no to carry loose syringes or needles without a letter from a doctor verifying your need for them. You might, for example, be a diabetic, but to the customs man you might be a drug addict.

At the seaside all cuts, grazes and bites should be thoroughly washed and disinfected as soon as possible. Merthiolate is effective for minor cuts, stings and punctures from marine organisms. Meat tenderiser washed into the weals of jellyfish stings with a little water is a tried and tested first-aid remedy. You can also buy an effective spray called Stingose for insect stings and bites. Puncture wounds should be immersed as soon as possible in water as hot as you can bear it. General cuts and scratches from barnacles, rocks, coral and the like should never be left untreated. Wash well with hot water and disinfectant, dry and paint with mercurochrome, which is definitely your best friend at the beach. Failing all this, the juice of the triangular green succulent creeper known as the Hottentot fig or sour fig usually does the trick. This grows on sand dunes all along the South African coast and is easily identified.

Services. The Travelsafe Clinic in Johannesburg has qualified medical doctors with post-graduate qualifications in tropical medicine and hygiene who can provide you with the latest medical information and prophylaxis or treatment for yellow fever, hepatitis (A and B), meningitis (A and C), typhoid, tetanus, polio, cholera, rabies (pre-exposure), malaria and traveller's diarrhoea. General health tips and inoculation information are available to tour groups and also to HIV-positive travellers. Consultation is by appointment only. Contact Dr Isak Joubert, Medical Suite, Epsom Downs Centre, Sloane Street, Bryanston, Johannesburg, Gauteng, tel (011) 807-5534, fax (011) 807-5533.

Worldwide Travel Medical Consultants is a full-time dedicated travel health clinic and consultancy offering up-to-date information on government health requirements, vaccination regulations and recommendations, prophylaxis and treatment of malaria and traveller's diarrhoea. Personalised medical travel kits and specialised travel arrangements for the disabled traveller are available. Offices are at 113 DF Malan Drive, Roosevelt Park, Johannesburg, Gauteng. For an appointment, tel (011) 888-7488/1520 from 8.30am to 5pm on weekdays and 8.30am to midday on Saturdays.

Round-the-clock assistance is offered to travellers by MedicAir, such as worldwide air ambulance transfers, medical escort service, emergency evacuation and medical insurance for people travelling in Africa. Tel (011) 609-8433/453-4337/452-4611, fax (011) 454-3191.

CLOTHING

What to Wear — and When. President Nelson Mandela has set a new fashion with his penchant for colourfully patterned, loose-fitting casual shirts, which he wears even to Parliament without a jacket or tie. While these shirts are now all the rage with swingers and the politically correct, you might not get into a top restaurant, hotel cocktail bar or dining-room wearing one in the evening. South African men, especially the older generation, prefer to sweat over dinner in, if not a dinner jacket, at least in a conservatively styled suit and a collar and tie. Apart from such a rarefied atmosphere, the South African approach to clothing is sensible: if it is hot, wear something light; if it is cold, slip into something warm — preferably a hot toddy. In the hot summer months South Africans dress informally during the day, unless they are business people. When it rains, umbrellas mushroom, but you will rarely see anyone wearing a raincoat. If you are packing for a summer holiday (October to April) clothing should be lightweight with a light jacket or sweater for the evening. Most of the country lies in the summer rainfall region, so a small folding umbrella is useful. Elegantly casual dress is suitable for restaurants and theatre. If you are planning a trip during the winter months, pack warm clothing, especially if you are heading for the Highveld or mountainous regions; people do die of cold and exposure every year. Your umbrella will be needed during Cape winters and KwaZulu-Natal summers. Dress along the coast is more informal than inland and trousers and an open-necked shirt are usually quite acceptable at hotels after dark. This informality does not extend to going into restaurants and bars in a swimsuit.

If you are planning a safari or intend to spend some time in the bush hiking, camping or backpacking, then pack well used walking shoes or boots. Clothing should be in neutral shades of green or khaki and lightweight for daytime activities, long-sleeved and warm for nights. There is still an ambivalent feeling about camouflage and anything military, so do not arrive looking like Rambo.

Clothing Sizes

Men's suits and coats

SA/UK/US	36	38	40	42	44	46	48
Europe	46	48	50	52	54	56	58
Metric (cm)	91	97	102	107	112	117	122

Shirts (collar size)

SA/UK/US (inches)	$14\frac{1}{2}$	15	$15\frac{1}{2}$	16	$16\frac{1}{2}$	17	$17\frac{1}{2}$
Metric (cm)	37	38	$39\frac{1}{2}$	41	42	43	44

Sweaters

	S	M	L	XL
SA/UK/US	34	36–38	40–42	44
Europe	44	46–48	50–52	54

Shoes

SA/UK	4	5	6	7	8	9	10
US men's	5	6	7	8	9	10	11
US women's	$5\frac{1}{2}$	$6\frac{1}{2}$	$7\frac{1}{2}$	$8\frac{1}{2}$	$9\frac{1}{2}$	$10\frac{1}{2}$	$11\frac{1}{2}$
Europe	37	38	39	$40\frac{1}{2}$	42	43	$44\frac{1}{2}$

Womens, dresses, suits and skirts

SA/UK	10	12	14	16	18	20	22
US	8	10	12	14	16	18	20
Europe	38	40	42	44	47	50	52

Blouses and sweaters

SA/UK	34	36	38	40	42	44	46
US	32	34	36	38	40	42	44
Europe	40	42	44	46	48	50	52

Children's Wear

SA/UK	1	2	5	7	9	10	12
US	1	4	6	8	10	13	15
Europe	1	2	5	7	9	10	12

Communications

The first post office in South Africa was a shoe hung up in a tree in Mossel Bay by a Portuguese sailor 13 years after the discovery of the Cape. He left a report about his misfortunes in the shoe in the hope a passing ship would deliver it to Lisbon before the year was out. There are many today who would say that this was the heyday of the South African Post Office in terms of delivery time. For one reason or another, the Post Office seems to have run into insurmountable problems and the best advice we can give you is not to use it for anything except to send postcards and letters whose arrival is not all that important anyway.

MAIL

There are post offices virtually everywhere, nearly 2000 of them throughout the country. They are open from 8.30am to 4.30pm on weekdays (most close between 1pm and 2pm) and from 8am to midday on Saturday. Long queues and inefficient service are not unusual. The names and postcodes of all post offices, postal agencies and mail collection points in South Africa are listed alphabetically in the postcode list available free from any post office. Sometimes the word 'boxes/busse' and not 'streets/strate' appears after the name of a post office in the postcode list; this means that articles can only be addressed to boxes, as no street deliveries are made in the area.

The Post Office has a wide array of services. As well as normal letter and parcel services, there are also registered mail, certified mail, cash-on-delivery (COD), insured parcel, express delivery, Fastmail and Speed services. Surface mail is distributed to 85 countries and received from 67, while airmail is delivered to 56 countries and received from 76. It handles about 8 million postal items every working day, more than a third of them in the Witwatersrand area. Stamps can also be bought at post offices, as well as outlets such as CNA, book stores, supermarkets, pharmacies, corner shops and garage filling stations. Take stamps with you if you are travelling to rural areas such as game reserves, as they might be difficult to find.

Cost of international mail to all countries outside the southern African region:

Letters (per 10g): R1.40	Postcards (each): R1.00
Printed matter (per 10g): R1.35	Small packets (per 100g): R8.00
Aerograms (each): R1.00	

Postage rates for parcels differ from country to country. Parcelplus is the parcel division of the Post Office. Parcels of up to 30kg/66lb are accepted. For information on parcels and services offered at the Post Office, call them toll-free on 0800 117 444. Customer service centre general enquiries, toll-free 0800 11 44 88. To enquire about missing parcels, registered and insured letters call Track and Trace, toll-free 0800 111 502.

Most corporate customers have deserted the Post Office in favour of private parcel courier services. Erratic or non-delivery of parcels are some of the shortcomings of the postal service. The Post Office's 'snail mail' and other poor services has resulted in the mushrooming of alternative services by private enterprise, and one of the most successful is the agile US postal franchise PostNet. If you want to be certain that your outgoing mail is safe and secure and will actually arrive at its destination within a reasonable time then we recommend it. The first PostNet outlet opened in mid-1994 and outlets have been increasing in number ever since, most of them in Gauteng and the Western Cape. It rents mail boxes, forwards mail and parcels, and runs local, national and international courier services, which offer a choice of same day to three-day delivery. You have the option of counter-to-door, door-to-door, and counter-to-counter services.

PostNet also has a service called PostWorld, which you can use to by-pass the SA Post Office and despatch mail to anywhere overseas, at a price competitive to the Post Office's, but vastly more efficient. The smart little PostNet Business Service Centres also provide one-stop shopping for photo-copying, graphic design and printing, word processing, telephones, faxes, e-mail, Internet and cell phone services. PostNet Express outlets are smaller versions of the centres and are found in supermarkets, stationery shops and pharmacies. Letters and parcels (up to 15kg/33lb) are transported by courier to various points around the world. A universal price of R1.95 per 10g is charged. Against the Post Office's R1.40 per 10g you get safer, quicker service, as your mail is couriered in bulk to the destination country and enters the postal system there as first-class mail. Most people are happy to pay a bit more for the security offered. As in other developing countries mail in South Africa can be stolen, and this is a growing problem. There have also been other postal hiccups; postmen have been caught delivering literally tons of mail to a paper company for shredding and recycling.

You can contact PostNet's head office in Johannesburg, tel (011) 805-0395, fax (011) 805-3267, and in Cape Town, tel (021) 75-8925, fax (021) 75-8926.

The Post Office has responded with (expensive) speed services, which offer same-day delivery to major centres in South Africa, overnight delivery from Monday to Friday, and international service to 140 countries, with delivery in one to six working days. Contact toll-free 0800 02 3133.

Poste Restante. Poste restante is available at post offices, but if you want to use this service while travelling you should ensure that nothing valuable or important is sent to you, and make sure you have your passport with you when you go to collect your mail.

Telegrams. These can be sent from any post office or you can telephone 1028 and send them as phonograms. To speed delivery send your telegram or phonogram to the addressee's telephone number. Double rates are charged for phonograms sent on Sundays. Neither phonograms nor telegrams are delivered on Sundays and public holidays, or after midday on Saturdays. The charge for phonograms is debited to the telephone number from which you send it. Enquiries (phonograms only), tel (011) 337-9088.

TELEPHONES

There are still more telephone lines in Manhattan than in all of sub-Saharan Africa. South Africa has about eight telephone lines for every 100 people, but there is less than one line per 100 people in black communities, compared to the 60 per 100 people in white areas. State-owned telecommunications utility Telkom has plans to provide 3 million more telephone lines and 150,000 pay phones, mainly in underprivileged urban and under-serviced rural areas. Currently there are 4.5 million business and residential telephones and 70,000 pay phones. Telephones are fully automatic, with direct dialling to 226 international destinations. Pay phones are found outside post offices, in cafés and in most public places. Use the post office phones if possible, as they are less likely to be vandalised. Different models of wall-mounted public coin phones are in use, and they accept both the old and new coins. Telephone cards are available at post offices, airports, and major shopping centres in R10, R20, R50, R100 and R200 denominations. These can be used to make local, national and international calls. When all the units on the card are used up during a call you can replace it with another without interruption. The local system is not yet linked to satellite, so the cards can be used only in South Africa. Hotels generally charge a premium on telephone calls, which is usually listed at reception or in the bedroom. Most hotels are equipped with fax machines. The international dialling code for South Africa is 27 followed by the area code (minus the first zero) and then the subscriber number. Main telephone area codes are Johannesburg (011), Pretoria (012), Cape Town (021), Durban (031) and Port Elizabeth (041).

Numbers for various telephone services are as follows:

Directory enquiries: 1023 South Africa, 0903 International (free);
Booking of trunk calls: 0020 (free);
Fixed-time calls: 1 0216 (free);
Collect and personal calls, trunk call enquiries, cancellations and complaints: 0020 (free).

Electronic Yellow Pages. This service allows you to get useful information by phone. Dial 1 0118 and the operator will help you to find information about hotels, restaurants, hiring services, and many other classifications.

Callmore Time. Telephone calls made during Telkom's Callmore Time — between 7pm and 7am Monday to Friday, and all weekend from 7pm on Friday until 7am on Monday — give you twice the time for the normal business hours charge. Callmore Time for international calls applies from 8pm to 8am, Monday to Friday, as well as all weekend from 8pm on Friday to 8am on Monday.

Theft of copper-wire cable is becoming a major problem for telephone users. It is not unusual to find entire areas knocked out, usually at the weekend, by this type of theft. One exasperated tourist hotel resorted to an advertisement in a major newspaper saying: 'If you've had difficulty calling us lately, we apologise. Our telephone cables have been stolen four times.'

Telex. There is one international and seven national telex exchanges serving more than 8000 subscribers. Services to about 200 international destinations are available. More than 1500 subscribers are served by five teletext exchanges. This network transmits memory-to-memory at a speed 40 times faster than regular telex transmissions. Telex and teletex enquiries toll-free 0800 12 4500.

Cellular Phones. One of the most common sights on the roads is a driver with a cell phone glued to his or her ear, making one of the 6 million South African cell calls a day – and the most unusual is a driver with both hands on the steering wheel. Since the commercial switch-on in June 1994 of South Africa's cellular network, Vodacom and MTN (Mobile Telephone Network) cell phones have become an R8 billion a year industry and South Africa the fourth fastest growing cell phone market in the world using GSM (Global Systems for Mobile Communications) technology. Between them, network operators Vodacom and MTN cover most of the country and at present growth rates expect to have 2 million users between them by the year 2000. Telkom owns 50% of Vodacom; among its other shareholders is Vodafone UK, the world's largest and most successful cellular network. Vodacom has the largest GSM network outside Europe and among its first subscribers was President Mandela. It offers more value-added services than any other of the 121 GSM networks in 71 countries around the world.

Both Vodacom and MTN offer voice, fax and data transmission facilities at virtually any time and more than 100 emergency services giving instant access to police, fire and rescue services. Vodacom's 147 SOS number, for instance, puts you in touch with a vast range of services, including medical and roadside assistance, access to a 24-hour helpline, information on transport services, accommodation, and access to the poison and hazardous chemicals register. MTN also has an easy booking service. By dialling 131 you get immediate access to Computicket, which enables you to book for an event anywhere in the country.

If you want to bring your own cell phone with you to South Africa contact your service provider before leaving home to have your SIM unbarred for international calls and international roaming. If this is not done, you will be unable to log on to any foreign network or make international calls. Clearance for international roaming and the facility to make international calls are two different things. You can have one without the other. Cell phones should be switched off and not left on standby or slumber mode when flying. The USA does not use the GSM system so American visitors should hire a cell phone on arrival. You can hire an instrument by the day, week and month with no lengthy contract and with a minimum of fuss. Itemised bills for hiring charges and calls are given on completion of the contract period. It costs about R28 a day for one to six days' hire of a cell phone simply to make and receive calls. For one to six days for a cell phone with fax and data capabilities it will cost you about R52 a day. You can hire a SIM card for R10 a day if you have your own instrument. Cost of local calls is R1.14 per unit and national calls are R1.36 per unit. Contact Hirefone toll-free 0800 123 800 or in Cape Town, tel (021) 23-3421; GSM Renta Fone is on the national 24-hour toll-free number 0800 010 920.

Useful Vodacom numbers include:

Emergency calls: 112;   *Customer care:* 111;
International SOS: 147;   *Directory enquiries:* 110.
Cellwatch (stolen cars): 082 2777;

For MTN enquiries: tel (011) 445-6000, fax (011) 444-4930.

Electronic Services. The number of South African homes with a personal computer is small by overseas standards. Only one in every 30 urban South Africans has a PC, compared to one in three in the USA and one in 13 in the UK, but the number is growing as people realise the benefits of tapping into the rest of the world via the Internet. Vodacom has entered the Internet service provider (ISP) arena with Yebo! Internet. The good news is you need no subscription; you pay as you go for as little as 33 cents per minute, charged to whichever telephone line you are using. A single cellular network 082 telephone number is used from anywhere in the country to access the Internet. Telkom is also providing Internet access through its South African Internet Exchange (SAIX). Contact toll-free 0800-22-27-72 or visit their home page on http://www/saix.net

MASS MEDIA

Television. South Africa was a late starter in the TV stakes. The big switch-on happened on 5 January 1976. The South African Broadcasting Corporation (SABC) revamped its television services in 1996 to make them more representative of the country's diverse cultures and it currently has three TV channels, televising programmes in 10 official languages. SABC 3 is the English channel, 1 and 2 transmit in eight African languages, as well as Afrikaans. There are weekly multilingual programmes in German, Portuguese, Italian, Greek and Indian languages.

As well as these offerings from the national broadcaster, there is a subscription television service called M-Net, which is one of the most extensive pay TV networks in the southern hemisphere. M-Net viewership has been steadily increasing since it started broadcasting in October 1986 and now tops 1 million subscribers. M-Net usually offers the best viewing, focusing on movies, sport, sitcoms, mini-series, actuality programmes and children's entertainment. Since its launch, M-Net has scooped a number of exclusive rights to broadcast major sporting events and tournaments and has introduced viewers to some of the great names in world sport. Some 75% of its viewers subscribe specifically for SuperSport programmes. M-Net schedules major rugby, cricket, soccer and golf events on its main channel and nearly 70 other sports get time on satellite channels. M-Net sister company MultiChoice runs South Africa's other pay-TV service. Multichoice offers 27 channels and 48 audio selections with round-the-clock music and news from around the world through its digital satellite hook-up. An estimated 5.2 million families out of 8.5 million households own TVs, a third of them black-and-white sets. Black South Africans are buying about 250,000 new sets a year, and research shows that 85% of all blacks regard TV and radio broadcasts more credible and trustworthy than any other media. White TV ownership is fairly static, although 10% watch less television these days.

From 1997, all viewers face a choice between digital and analogue television if they want to get more channels and more programmes. The SABC's six-channel satellite pay-TV service AstraSat will compete with the established MultiChoice, with its attractive bouquet of 27 channels. Where MultiChoice uses digital technology, expensive but used worldwide, AstraSat is going the old-fashioned analogue route because it is cheaper and will enable it to reach more people in the black community. Eventually, with other smaller broadcasters, such as the Christian channel Uplink and the world's most popular music channel MTV, there will be 19 channels to choose from with an analogue system and 34 channels to surf with digital.

SABC TV programmes are carried daily in newspapers or for the entire week in Saturday and Sunday newspaper magazine sections. M-Net programmes are also published. All programmes are in English unless coded: A – Afrikaans; M – multilingual; N – Ndebele; So – Sotho; SP – Sepedi; ST – Setswana; TS – Tsonga; V – Venda; X – Xhosa; Z – Zulu.

SM indicates English-language simulcast on Radio 2000 and R means a repeat programme. As the programmes can change at the last minute without notice TV schedule updates can be obtained by contacting the SABC at tel (011) 330-9797, (011) 330-9744. For M-Net contact tel (011) 329-5555, fax (011) 329-5420.

Radio. In South Africa radio has a bigger audience than print and TV combined. More than three-quarters of the population listens to radio, which is often their only link with the outside world. Listeners' licences were abolished in 1982 to encourage more people to tune in. Regular radio broadcasts began in Johannesburg, Cape Town and Durban in 1924 and until 1994 the monolithic SABC, whose headquarters and main transmitting stations are at Auckland Park, Johannesburg, controlled the country's radio services. In 1994, the Independent Broadcasting Authority (IBA) opened up the airwaves to community radio stations countrywide broadcasting programmes in all 11 official languages. In 1996, the SABC sold off six regional stations, favouring consortiums with strong black representation, even where their bids were among the lowest. This has given South Africa a total of 14 private commercial radio stations. These stations must provide at least 30 minutes of news a day and if they play music for more than 15% of their airtime, 20% of it must be of South African origin. The six regional radio stations are 94.7FM Highveld (Johannesburg), Radio Jacaranda (Pretoria), East Coast (Durban), Radio Oranje (Bloemfontein), Radio Algoa (Port Elizabeth), and the Western Cape's KFM. It is estimated that by 1999 the country will have 32 commercial radio stations, 18 public radio stations and more than 100 community stations and at least 27 public broadcasters.

The SABC has refocused 10 of its remaining 16 radio stations. Nine African language stations have been given listener-friendly names such as 'Your true friend', 'Your best friend' and 'Honour, dignity and respect', to reflect the culture of their listeners. The former Afrikaans language station, Afrikaans Stereo, is now Radio Sonder Grense (radio without boundaries). The remaining SABC radio stations are Radio 2000, national music stations Radio Metro, SAfm, and 5FM, and regional stations Radio Lotus, for Indian listeners, and Good Hope FM. Radio 702 is an independent commercial station broadcasting to the Gauteng area and is a leading phone-in chat show station, and Radio Today, covering Greater Johannesburg, has nostalgic music and drama for the over-40s.

The growth of community radio stations (there are more than 60) has brought some interesting changes. In rural KwaZulu-Natal Radio Kwezi, for example, records local choirs for broadcast to their listeners and teaches adult literacy live on air. There are classical, jazz and pop stations, a station owned by two Ndebele kings, another that runs job searches, and an 'eco'-station, as well as township, campus, Christian and Muslim stations broadcasting in most of the official languages, as well as in Indian, Chinese, Portuguese, Greek and German. Most of the community stations get their bulletins from the same source, Network Radio Services, to keep down costs, so the news broadcasts always sound the same. The SABC compiles its news through its own local and overseas editorial staff and various local and international agencies.

SABC contact numbers:

Johannesburg, tel (011) 714-2112, fax (011) 714-5281;
Cape Town, tel (021) 434-1155, fax (021) 439-0395;
Pretoria, tel (012) 841-0285, fax (012) 804-1184.

The Independent Broadcasting Authority can be reached on: tel (011) 447-6180, fax (011) 447-6187.

For eco-buffs travelling in or near the Kruger National Park Radio Safari 94.4FM's programmes promote environmental awareness among visitors and neighbouring residents alike, spreading the word in six different languages. Radio Safari 94.4FM's target audience includes about 3500 daily visitors to the national park and 1.9 million people living close by.

Newspapers. More than any other industry in South Africa, the newspaper publishing business is going through a dramatic shake-up as empowered blacks move to take control of previously all-white media groups. Until 1994 the English-language press was dominated by mining giant Anglo American, which controlled Times Media Limited (TML), largely a morning and financial publication group, and Argus Newspapers, historically the evening newspaper conglomerate. On the eve of the 1994 election Independent Newspapers bought the Argus Group. In October 1996, the National Empowerment Consortium (NEC), a grouping of 50 black businesses and trade unions, gained control of Johnnic, one of the country's largest industrial conglomerates, in South Africa's largest black empowerment deal. This marked a major step in the drive of black South Africans to turn their political victory into an economic triumph. This also gave NEC control of TML, and 21% of the newspaper *The Sowetan* to New Africa Investments Limited (Nail), which is part of the NEC. Other ownership changes are in the pipeline that will make black groups significant players in printing and publishing.

There are more than 30 dailies and weeklies and about 100 regional or country newspapers. Most country newspapers are weekly bilingual tabloids serving particular towns. More than 700 newspapers, periodicals and journals are published regularly in South Africa, more than in the rest of Africa combined. The most widely read Sunday newspaper is *The Sunday Times*, with more than half a million readers. In Durban, it is the *Sunday Tribune*. The Afrikaans Sunday equivalent is *Rapport*. The top daily newspapers in South Africa are:

Johannesburg: The Sowetan (black readership), The Star, Business Day, Beeld
    (Afrikaans), and The Citizen;
Cape Town: The Cape Times, Die Burger (Afrikaans) and the Cape Argus;
Durban: The Daily News and The Natal Mercury;
East London: Daily Dispatch;
Pietermaritzburg: Natal Witness;
Port Elizabeth: The Eastern Province Herald, Evening Post and Oosterlig
    (Afrikaans);

Pretoria: the Pretoria News.

A sign of the times is *Woza*, an online Internet newspaper that was launched at the end of 1996 targeting the business market and is updated five days a week. *Woza* highlights local and international sites that offer good value, for things like free software, trading opportunities, and initiatives under way by government, non-governmental and commercial organisations. Visit *Woza* free at http:/ /www.woza.co.za

Magazines. During the apartheid years South Africans did not have a great deal to laugh about and there was correspondingly a lack of an alternative press, with no magazines similar to Britain's *Private Eye* or America's *Mad* magazine to poke fun at politics, politicians and the pompous wherever they might be found. The Publications Control Board kept a firm lid on anything remotely satirical or thought to be prejudicial to the order of the day. Like much else, all that has changed. The Board itself has gone — although it has been replaced by a film and publications watchdog — and the first stirrings of what hopefully is a burgeoning alternative press have become more noticeable. If you prefer satire and comedy to the pontificating of the establishment press get hold of a copy of *Noseweek* magazine or, while you are in Cape Town, take a stroll around Greenmarket Square. This is the stamping ground of a dreadlocked, outrageous character from the Cape Flats who calls himself Zebulon Dread and sells a self-produced zany newspaper called *Hei Voetsak!*, which in polite terms means 'Go away.' Dread writes every article himself, including the letters page. This can truly be called the gutter press, not because the language is crude, but because that is where Dread sets up his pitch.

There has been a huge growth in the number of sports magazines over the past few years. Not too long ago there were only six titles checked by the Audit Bureau of Circulations. Now there are around a dozen. The bulk of the readership of most of these magazines is young and black, who make up the majority of sports fanatics in the country. Most magazines cater for niche interests. The bottom has fallen out of the male magazine market following the dumping of the old strict censorship laws, and the women's magazine arena is over-catered. There has been no significant growth in newspaper readership, which could be the result of a depressing never-ending diet of politics and crime. This tends to be borne out of the fact that the country's largest circulating magazine (more than a million) is M-Net pay television's monthly TV guide. Happily, there are some excellent publications catering for the booming outdoor and travel scene. For the really serious outdoor man or woman there is *Go*, and for the fraternity who like to tackle the outdoor pursuits in lycra and designer gear there are *Getaway* and *Out There*. In all there are some 300 consumer magazines and more than 500 trade, technical and professional publications. Those catering to black readerships are showing continuing growth. This target market should expand even more as education becomes more widespread and is also extended to the older generation. Currently, there are more than 15 million functionally illiterate people in a population estimated at 44 million.

Accommodation

Accommodation in South Africa caters for everyone, from those who revel in five-star hotels, to those who feel more at home in informal flats and cottages, inns, game lodges and reserves, guest-houses and holiday farms, youth and backpacker hostels, and B&Bs. With the plummeting of the South African rand the price of hotel accommodation is extremely reasonable by European or American standards. Cheaper still are guest-houses, YMCAs, YWCAs, municipal bungalows, rest camps in national parks, youth hostels, and the caravan and camping sites dotted around the country. There are about 8500 establishments offering tourist accommodation, with about 166,000 rooms/units and nearly 610,000 beds. Camping and caravan sites are in the majority, accounting for 28% of the total, followed by hotels (25%), holiday flats (11%), resorts (11%), guest houses and farms (9%) and game lodges (6%). National and provincial game parks account for a mere 2% of visitor accommodation (4% including camping sites). B&Bs, hunting lodges, timeshare units, serviced apartments, youth hostels and backpacker lodges are also part of the mix. Most hotels, inns, country houses and some guest houses are licensed to sell alcohol. Although the range of licences may vary, most serve liquor to guests without restriction, including Sundays and religious holidays. Many also offer bedrooms and restaurant facilities for non-smokers. Although health authorities restrict pets in hotels and restaurants, some places welcome them. Enquire about this if you are travelling with a pet. Most establishments accept major credit cards affiliated to organisations such as Visa and MasterCard. Diners Club and American Express are not always accepted and you should check this when booking or on arrival.

MAJOR HOTEL CHAINS

The following are South Africa's major hotel groups and chains:

Sun International is one of the most prestigious hotel and casino groups on the African continent. In the days when South Africa's racial policies created various independent homelands the group built hotels and casinos in some of them to side-step South Africa's anti-gambling laws. The best known is Sun City in the former Bophuthatswana, now reincorporated in the country as part of the North-West Province (see page 267).

> *Sun International:* PO Box 784487, Sandton 2146, tel (011) 780-7444, fax (011) 780-7701;
> *Central reservations:* tel (011) 780-7800, fax (011) 780-7457.

Southern Sun is the largest hotel operator in Africa and has 60 hotels, game lodges and resorts in South Africa, with some 13,000 rooms. The five-star Southern Sun Inter-Continental hotels are situated in Johannesburg, Cape Town and Durban. Central reservations toll-free 0800 12 13 77. The group's *Holiday Inns* offer medium-price accommodation. The four *Holiday Inn Crowne Plaza* hotels cater for the four-star deluxe market and are located in the three major centres. The *Holiday Inn Garden Court* chain of 26 three-star hotels is sited throughout the country and provides good value. *Holiday Inn Express* is an economy hotel chain offering limited service in the two-star market (only R179 for a room with two complimentary breakfasts; £23.85/$39.40). The 16-strong *Formule 1* chain is operated by Southern Sun in partnership with the French-based Accor Group and claims to offer the world's most affordable hotels (R114 per room for up to three guests).

The Southern Sun group also has a number of *Sun Game Lodges* offering a high-quality wildlife experience.

> *Southern Sun Group:* PO Box 782553, Sandton 2146, Gauteng, tel (011) 780-0200, fax (011) 780-0262;
> *Central reservations:* tel (011) 482-3500, fax (011) 726-3019;
> *Holiday Inn Express reservations:* tel (011) 482-3500;
> *Formule 1:* PO Box 480, Bramley 2018, Gauteng, tel (011) 440-1001, fax (011) 440-2800.

Protea Hotels has 67 hotels and resorts in South Africa, ranging from two-star country hotels, seaside and lake resorts, mountain retreats and city centre hotels to four-star *Premier Protea Hotels*, such as *The Capetonian* and *Victoria Junction* in Cape Town, the *Balalaika* and *Parktonian* in Johannesburg, the *Marine* in Port Elizabeth, the *King David* in East London and the *San Lameer* and *Tropicana* hotels in KwaZulu-Natal. Prices range from R120 (£16/$26.40) per person per night sharing at a two-star hotel, R375 each at a four-star establishment, to R980 for a loft at the Victoria Junction Hotel. If you are 60 or over you can get a 50% discount on accommodation; you need to show your passport to qualify.

> *Head Office:* PO Box 6482, Roggebaai 8012, Cape Town, tel (021) 419-5320, fax (021) 25-2956;
> *Central reservations:* toll-free 0800 11 9000, tel (021) 419-8800, fax (021) 419-8200;
> *International central reservations:* United Kingdom: tel (01233) 21-1811, fax (01233) 21-1309; North America: toll-free 800 323-3210, tel (516) 661 6779, fax (516) 661 6914;
> *Web site:* http://www.protea-hotels.co.za
> *e-mail:* uwelcome@protea-hotels.co.za

City Lodge Hotel Group is an inexpensive no-frills hotel group, with accommodation ranging from its *Courtyard* suite hotels at the top end, through business-class *City Lodges*, good value *Town Lodges* and budget-priced *Road Lodges*. Contact PO Box 782630, Sandton 2146, Gauteng, tel (011) 884-5327, fax (011) 883-3640, e-mail info@citylodge.co.za

Gooderson Hotels, PO Box 10305, Marine Parade 4056, Durban; central reservations, tel (031) 37-42222, fax (031) 37-2621, e-mail glczulu@iafrica.com, web site http://www.glczulu.co.za

Karos Hotels has 15 hotels throughout the country in the R255–550 a night bracket; contact PO Box 87534, Houghton 2198, Johannesburg; central reservations tel (011) 484-1641, fax (011) 643-4343.

Stocks Hotels and Resorts has some premier hotels and lodges in its portfolio, from its flagship five-star *The Michelangelo* in Sandton, Johannesburg, and the *Portswood Hotel* on the V&A Waterfront in Cape Town, to the three game lodges of *Bakubung*, *Tshukudu*, and *Kwa Maritane* in the Pilansberg National Park, 10 minutes' drive from Sun City. Contact PO Box 3410, Rivonia 2128, Gauteng, tel (011) 806-4192/3 or 806-4145, fax (011) 806-4105, central reservations tel (011) 445-8383.

Park Hyatt Johannesburg, PO Box 1536, Saxonwold 2132, Gauteng, tel (011) 280-1234, fax (011) 280-1238.

Best Western has two hotels, one in Johannesburg (PO Box 75825, Garden View 2047), which has apartments only from R345, and the other in Pretoria (PO Box 40663, Arcadia 0007), which has bed and breakfast from R286 (£38/$63) per person. Central reservations for both is on 0800 12 0886 (toll-free).

The *Relais et Châteaux* chain has seven establishments in South Africa. These are the *Cellars-Hohenort*, Cape Town; *Cybele Forest Lodge*, White River, Mpumalanga; *Ellerman House*, Bantry Bay, Cape Town; *Grande Roche*, Paarl; *Londolozi Private Game Reserve*, Mpumalanga; *The Plettenberg*, Plettenberg Bay, Western Cape; and *Singita Private Game Reserve*, Mpumalanga. Contact Relais Hotels of the Cape, PO Box 23864, Claremont 7735, tel (021) 794-6676, fax (021) 794-7186.

Grading System. In October 1993, the South African Tourism Board (Satour) changed the grading of the country's accommodation industry to make it more user-friendly. Hotels are graded from one to five stars and some establishments have also been awarded bronze or silver classifications, denoting exceptional standards of service and hospitality. A voluntary system has also been introduced to star-grade guest and country houses, bed and breakfast places and self-catering establishments. Included in this system are timeshare apartments, game parks and holiday resorts.

Accredited guest houses and bed and breakfast establishments are those that meet or exceed guest expectations for service and hospitality. One-star means standard comfort, two very good, three excellent, four outstanding, and five-star means the lap of luxury (during the Rugby World Cup in 1995, 85% of all visitors stayed in three-star hotels). All display distinctive plaques that enable you to check their grading. A rectangular burgundy plaque shows the star rating; those which are accredited have an oval plaque with the word 'Approved'. When you see these plaques, you know what to expect before you check in. Since Satour started this system more than 700 hotels, inns, guest and country houses, and bed and breakfast places have applied for grading, and a further 250 guest houses and bed and breakfasts are on the approved list. Tariffs range from as little as R85 (£11.35/$18.70) to as high as R1500 per person per day according to the type, grade, location and style of the establishment.

The *National Accommodation Guide* lists establishments that have been graded and approved by Satour. This is available from leading book stores and tourism associations, or contact the South African Tourism Board, Private Bag X164, Pretoria 0001, tel (012) 347-0600, fax (012) 45-4889. Other useful guides are *AA Hotels, Lodges and Guest Houses* (R24.95); and Portfolio's *Town and Country Retreats*, *Bed and Breakfast*, and *Country Places*, available from PO Box 132, Newlands 7725, Cape Town, tel (021) 686-5400, fax (021) 686-5310.

Reservations. In certain parts of the country accommodation is in great demand in peak seasons. Reserve your accommodation well in advance if you are planning your holiday during the high season, school vacations, or public holiday/long weekend periods. The summer months from 1 October to 30 April are considered high season. Winter months (May to September) are low season. In addition, some establishments charge extra for Christmas, New Year, Easter weekend and public holiday long weekends. If you expect to arrive after 6pm at the place you have booked into you should let them know, as many hotels and country inns have a policy of letting rooms at this time and unless you have made arrangements you might find yourself without a bed. This does not apply where you have a guaranteed booking and have paid a deposit.

Computicket's Accommodation Bank offers central reservations to hundreds of hotel rooms, bed and breakfasts, self-catering resorts and lodges throughout South Africa. Call central reservations, tel (011) 445-8300. Reservations at hotels and self-catering establishments throughout southern Africa can be made through any AA branch, or by contacting the *AA Travel Information Centre* in Johannesburg, tel (011) 466-6641. The *Johannesburg Publicity Association* can book nationwide hotel accommodation for you through any of its three offices:

Johannesburg International Airport, tel (011) 970-1220, fax (011) 394-1508;
City centre, tel (011) 336-4961, fax (011) 336-4965;
Sandton, tel (011) 784-1354, fax (011) 883-4035.

Other useful contacts include:

Portfolio of Places central reservation office, PO Box 52350, Saxonwold 2132, Gauteng, tel (011) 880-3414 and (011) 788-0287, fax (011) 788-4802;
Caraville Central Reservations, PO Box 139, Sarnia 3615, KwaZulu-Natal, tel (031) 701-4156, fax (031) 701-4159.

For hotels, country houses and game lodges in the R300–700 plus per person bracket (bed and breakfast) contact The Hotelogue, PO Box 160, Green Point 8051, Cape Town, tel (021) 434-1954, fax (021) 434-0489; Johannesburg tel (011) 453-5635, fax (011) 453-5968; Durban (031) 84-0295, fax (031) 83-5106, web site AT URL.http://aztec.co.za/wwmarket

GUEST HOUSES AND FARMS

Farmers in South Africa are helping to develop eco-tourism by offering holidays and hiking trails on their farms. Accommodation ranges from luxury guest houses to rooms, chalets, homesteads and even caves. Contact:

> South African Farm Holiday Association (Safha), PO Box 1140, Oakdale 7534, Western Cape, tel (021) 689-8400, fax (021) 689-1974;
> Safha (Natal), PO Box 10592, Scottsville 3209, tel (0331) 94-8364, fax (0331) 94-8368.

Safha publishes the *SA Farm and Country Holiday Guide* (R25) and has a booking service.

Between them, *Bundubeds*, *Jacana Country Homes and Trails* and *Underberg Hideaways* have a wide range of self-catering cottages, country homes, game farms, bush camps, and bed and breakfast accommodation for tourists and budget travellers:

> *Bundubeds*, PO Box 810, White River 1240, Mpumalanga, tel (013) 751-3950, fax (013) 751-1575;
> *Jacana Country Homes and Trails*, PO Box 95212, Waterkloof 0145, Gauteng, tel (012) 346-3550/1/2, fax (012) 346-2499;
> *Underberg Hideaways*, PO Box 1218, Hilton 3245, KwaZulu-Natal, tel/fax (0331) 43-1217; UK contact Alison Whitfield, tel (0181) 875 1404, fax (0181) 874 8394;
> *Guest House Association of Southern Africa (Ghasa)*, tel (021) 461-0635 or (0234) 42351, fax (0234) 42418.

Internet users can visit the web site of African Alternatives: http://www.a-frica.com:80/-venture/country/index/htm, e-mail PC@alpha.futurenet.co.za

BED AND BREAKFAST, SELF-CATERING AND HOMESHARE

The bed and breakfast way of travel is becoming popular in South Africa and offers an alternative, and cheaper, way to see the country. *Homeshare Holidays* is a company specialising in exactly what its name says, homesharing holidays. It has a computerised network listing more than 1000 private homes in South Africa that offer you reasonably priced bed and breakfast accommodation. All the establishments on the list have been graded in terms of comfort, friendliness and expertise. In addition to a home-cooked breakfast, your hosts can give you helpful information and advice about local attractions. Homeshare has a central booking service, which means you can make one phone call and book your accommodation throughout the country. If you are touring around in a car, this is particularly useful. Contact Homeshare in Johannesburg at tel (011) 907-8206, fax (011) 907-4031, and in Durban contact Len and Alma Boucher, tel (031) 94-1016, Cell 082 449-9501.

Other useful contacts:

> *Home Accommodation Hotline*, a central reservation service for bed and breakfast or self-catering accommodation in private homes, tel (021) 75-7130, fax (021) 72-3340;
> *Bed and Breakfast*, PO Box 2739, Clareinch 7740, Cape Town, tel (021) 683-3505, fax (021) 683-5159;
> *Bed 'n Breakfast*, PO Box 91309, Auckland Park, 2006, Johannesburg, tel (011) 482-2206, fax (011) 726-6915;
> *International Home Exchange*, affiliated to HomeLink International in the UK, can arrange home swaps; contact PO Box 23188, Claremont 7735, Western Cape, tel/fax (021) 794-3433.

The Automobile Association of South Africa publishes a guide called *Self-Catering Getaways*, available from book stores and AA branches countrywide at R24.95.

TIMESHARE

Disparaging attitudes towards timeshare in South Africa have changed with international timeshare brokering through the Internet and the post-apartheid opening up of the country. South Africa is now the fourth largest timeshare market in the world and timeshare swaps are bringing in visitors from as far away as Russia. Resort Condominiums International (RCI) is the best-known name in the local timeshare field. RCI has a wide selection of accommodation at resorts in all the popular holiday areas, such as the North and the South Coasts of KwaZulu-Natal, the Garden Route in the Western Cape, and Mpumalanga — all areas known for their scenic beauty and wildlife. As well as holiday resorts, timeshare is available in hotels, which use timeshare space for normal occupancy out of season. Contact RCI Southern Africa, PO Box 783940, Sandton 2146, Gauteng, tel (011) 780-4444, fax (011) 780-4440. The local industry is regulated by the Timeshare Institute of South Africa (Tisa), PO Box 87660, Houghton 2041, Gauteng, tel (011) 483-3587, fax (011) 483-3595.

HEALTH SPAS

South Africa has an abundance of hot springs, and while there is nothing to rival Yosemite, Iceland or the geysers of New Zealand there are enough to support a fair number of health spas. There are about 90 hot springs scattered throughout South Africa, with temperatures of 25°C/77°F or higher. The main ones developed as resorts are at Aliwal North, near the Eastern Cape border with the Free State; Badplaas, in Mpumalanga; and Warmbaths and Tshipise in the Northern Province. Many of these springs are believed to have curative properties, but no analysis of their water has so far supported the belief that they are medicinal.

The hot springs at the old Cape frontier town of Aliwal North, named after a British victory in 1846 at Aliwal in India, have attracted sufferers of lumbago, arthritis, rheumatism and similar ailments since the early 19th century. The springs have been channelled into the *Aliwal Spa*, where they fill an indoor Olympic-size swimming pool (27.7°C/82°F) and an outdoor pool directly over the eye of a spring, where the water temperature is 31.1°C/88°F. There is another enclosed pool, where gassy water gushes out at 34.4°C/94°F and where you can enjoy the effect of what has been described as bathing in warm champagne. The spa resort also has pools for children, chalets, caravan and camping sites and lots of other amenities. Aliwal Spa Holiday Resort, tel (0551) 2951; Aliwal and Whittal's Chalets, tel (0551) 3142/3202.

The *Badplaas* health resort is near Buffelspruit, 48km/30 miles east of Carolina, on the road to Barberton. Its Northern Sotho name is *Emanzana*, which means 'Healing waters', referring to the supposed medical properties of the hot sulphur springs. The Aventura Badplaas resort has 200 caravan sites and features mineral water pools, hiking trails, super tubes, horse riding and sports. Sites cost R50 a day with power in peak season. Contact PO Box 15, Badplaas 1190, Mpumalanga, tel (01784) 41020, fax (01784) 41391.

The Hydro Spa at *Warmbaths* is also part of the Aventura chain of resorts, which used to be state-run. The spa is 100km/62 miles north of Johannesburg. It is on a 1040-hectare nature reserve, but it is the spa complex that draws up to 400,000 visitors a year, with its 40°C/104°F mineral water pool rich in salts, vast outdoor hot or cold swimming pools, water slides, and continuous cable water-skiing on the lake. There is even an artificial beach. Modestly priced modern, comfortable, self-contained cottages in convenient locations throughout the grounds offer family accommodation. There is also an extensive caravan park. As well as a licensed steak-house with reasonably priced meals, there is a flea-market selling handicrafts, art work, clothing and other souvenirs. Buyskop, 6km/4 miles to the north, was a mail coach staging post between Pretoria and Pietersburg in the days of the old Transvaal Republic, but this sandstone hill also has another claim to fame: from its slopes came the rock used to build the Union Buildings in Pretoria. Contact Aventura Warmbad, PO Box 75, Warmbaths 0480, Northern Province, tel (014) 736-2200, fax (014) 736-4716; central reservations, PO Box 720, Groenkloof 0027, tel (012) 346-2277, fax (012) 346-2293.

Aventura *Tshipise* Mineral Baths Resort is 66km/41 miles south-east of Messina and 84km/52 miles north-east of Louis Trichardt in the northern bushveld. The name is derived from the Venda words *chia fisu*, meaning to burn or be hot, referring to the mineral springs, which are a constant 65°C/149°F. There are three pools as well as private pools for you to relax in and soothe away any aches and pains. On a nearby farm is an immense baobab that is believed to be about 4500 years old. Contact PO Box 4, Tshipise 0901, Northern Province, tel (015539) 624, fax (015539) 724.

Sagole Spa in the Northern Province is situated at a hot spring adjoining a Venda village. You can take tours and walks from here to historical ruins, rock paintings and other places of interest. Six-bed fully equipped self-contained cottages, each with an exclusive plunge pool fed from the nearby hot spring, cost R180 (£24/$39.60) per cottage per night, and three-bed rondavels are R45 a night or R60 a night with showers and toilets. You can pitch a tent for R10 (£1.35/$2.20) a night or park a caravan for R12. Contact Venda Tourism, Private Bag 5045, Thohoyandou 0950, Northern Province, tel (0159) 41577, fax (0159) 41048.

Probably the best known health hydro in the country is *High Rustenberg*, outside Stellenbosch, in the Western Cape. It is also equally well known as an expensive 'fat farm'. Its woodland setting is magnificent; the hydro itself is a mix between a hospital, a holiday camp and an ordinary hotel. It is a haven for people who want to shed weight, as well as those intent on giving up alcohol or tobacco. Rates range from R1490 (£199/$328) for single accommodation in a cottage with a shared bathroom for three nights to R6840 for top-quality single accommodation for 10 nights, or you can try a one-day health vitality programme for R235 (this includes a salad and baked potato). If you feel like an expensive detox contact PO Box 2052, Stellenbosch 7600, Western Cape, tel (021) 883-8600, fax (021) 886-5163, reservations (021) 883-8680.

The mountain range stretching roughly east to west, between Potgietersrus and Thabazimbi, is called the Waterberge, or 'Water Mountains', because of the extensive hot and cold mineral springs found in the area. You will also find other smaller, hot springs and health resorts around the country in places such as Goudini, Caledon, Calitzdorp, and Barrydale in the Western Cape.

Resorts. The biggest and best-known chain of holiday resorts (*oorde* in Afrikaans) in the country is the Aventura consortium's 14 self-catering establishments. As they used to belong to the State they are naturally well equipped and located in some of the best spots. They offer everything from four-star chalets and rondavels, to caravan and camp sites, with all mod cons and usually a swimming pool, shops and eateries. You can book up to 11 months in advance and you pay in full on arrival. If you are over 60 you get substantial discounts outside of peak and high seasons, which roughly cover September to April, depending on the resort. If you want a cheap holiday and do not mind crowds the Aventura resorts are a good bet. Rates range from R25 a day per person to around R450 for a four-bed luxury unit. Contact central reservations, PO Box 720, Groenkloof 0027, Gauteng, tel (012) 346-2277, fax (012) 346-2293, e-mail aventura@iafrica.com, web site http://www.aventura.co.za

CARAVANNING

Caravanning in South Africa is extremely popular. More than 700 caravan parks and resorts offer clean, secure, well kept sites with facilities ranging from excellent to adequate. Most parks offer hot and cold showers, laundry and ironing facilities, ablution blocks and braai (barbecue) areas. Others, which also have hutted accommodation, offer restaurants, shops and swimming pools. Many parks, especially on the coast, are fully booked in December and January, so try to book in advance. You can rent a caravan and a car to tow it.

The Caravan Club of Southern Africa (CCSA) has promoted caravanning and the interests of caravanners since 1947 and grown to be the biggest and most respected caravan club in Africa. You can join the club either as a regular or temporary member. It costs R25 entrance fee, and R84 annual subscription, valid from 1 July to 30 June. You do not have to own a caravan to join. The club organises social activities, rallies and tours and offers a wide range of benefits to members. While a lot of these are of interest only to locals, you can save money by taking advantage of others, among them Budget Car Rental giving a 20% discount on both hire and kilometre rates, and Avis Car Rental offering a 20% discount on its standard daily rates. KwaZulu-Natal coastal caravan parks offer a 10% out-of-season discount for extended stays and weekends if you show a CCSA membership card. You may be asked to produce your passport before you can get the discount. Some parks offer up to 15% discount out of season. Supa Quick outlets offer special discounts on tyres, exhaust systems, shock absorbers and batteries on production of your CCSA card. Members needing their customer care helpline to sort out problems can contact (011) 315-1123.

Other club benefits are discounted subscriptions to a variety of outdoor-oriented publications, such as *Caravan and Outdoor Life*, *Getaway* and *Fish Eagle* magazines, as well as 25% discount on hundreds of books, maps and guides from the publishing group Struik. You can also get buying privileges at a number of shops, stores and services. Among them are two of the country's largest cash and carry chains, Makro and Trade Centre. You can get more details from the CCSA National Council Offices, PO Box 50580, Randburg 2125, Gauteng, tel/fax (011) 789-3202.

Detailed listings of caravan parks and resorts recommended by the CCSA are included in the provincial chapters. For other caravan parks around the country contact Satour, publicity associations or local municipalities.

Incidentally, it is an offence to tow your caravan or trailer with a chain, rope or rigid tow bar longer than 3.5m/11.5ft. Unless you are using a tow-bar you should not travel at more than 30km/h (19mph).

CAMPING

There is no closed season for camping as it is more or less warm all year round, except on high ground. Unless you have permission to put up your tent on private land, such as someone's farm or estate, you will have to camp at a recognised site, usually a caravan and motor-home park. This is not only convenient for showers and other amenities, it is also safer. What the French call wild or savage camping — i.e., wherever you drop your pack — is definitely not recommended. The only exception is in designated Wilderness Areas, where you can camp freely. The South African Camping Club (SACC) is the only organisation catering for and protecting the rights of campers, or tenters as they are known. Established in 1964 in response to the banning of tent campers from parks and resorts nationally, the club set standards for campers that led to the dropping of the ban. The club has branches in KwaZulu-Natal, the Eastern Cape, the Western Cape, and the former Transvaal region. Its membership also includes caravanners and SACC is a member of the Federation of Caravan and Camping Clubs. The organisation is a friendly, unregimented body asking only that you enjoy the outdoor life and follow the International Camper's Code of Behaviour. They welcome contact with visiting campers and will do what they can to help with information and advice about local conditions. This can be invaluable as there is no national guide listing all camp sites.

Contacts:

SACC: Jean Lewin, National Chairperson, Private Bag X2, Paardekraal 1752, Gauteng, tel (011) 954-0229, Cell 083 274-5914;

KwaZulu-Natal: Doug Wheeland, Chairperson, 18 Methven Road, Westville 3630, tel (031) 82-2034;

Eastern Cape: Ken Simpson, Chairperson, 7 Versailles Road, Kraggakamma Park, Port Elizabeth 6070, tel (041) 73-1833;

Western Cape: Cliff Shears, Chairperson, 120 Clovelly Road, Clovelly 7975, tel (021) 782-5222;

Gauteng: Johan van Vuuren, Chairperson, 4 Tay Drive, Three Rivers, Vereeniging 1929, tel (016) 54-9821; Ray Dummer, Secretary, PO Box 1884, Cresta 2118, tel (011) 792-1732;

Federation of Caravan and Camping Clubs: Piet Louw, Secretary, PO Box 15127, Sinoville 0129, Gauteng, tel (012) 543-1010.

The best place for hiking and camping guides is outdoor shop Camp and Climb, which has major branches in Johannesburg, tel (011) 403-1354; Cape Town Central, tel (021) 23-2175, fax (021) 23-2177; and Claremont, Cape Town, tel (021) 61-8839, fax (021) 61-5329.

YOUTH HOSTELS

Hostelling, whether at the YHA or the growing network of backpackers' lodges and hostels, offers great value for money and some of the best locations in the country. Most hostels have communal kitchens, lounges and recreation rooms, which means not only can you save money on meals, you also get to meet like-minded adventurous travellers. Most hostels are also sources of useful information and can arrange budget-cost tours. If you stay at hostels and lodges belonging to the Hostelling International South Africa (HISA) chain, for instance, not only do they organise tours, they have also negotiated special discount fares with long-distance bus operators. Hostelling International is the worldwide name of the International Youth Hostel Federation (IYHF). HISA is the local, non-profit-making operation that provides an umbrella body for 36 hostels throughout the country ranging from an old-style mine house on the outskirts of Johannesburg, through African-style huts, to a hostel in an old hunting lodge on the slopes of Table Mountain. Other hostels in South Africa are a mixture of traditional youth hostels and backpacker-type lodges geared towards the budget travel market. HISA also covers approved, privately owned hostels and backpacker lodges, all of which are R28–35 (£3.75–4.65/$6.15–7.70) per person per night for a dorm and R75–105 for a double or twin room. There are no niggling restrictions, such as your age or mode of transport; you can arrive in a limousine if you wish, but some are not keen on taking very young children as most hostels have bars and pool tables.

As affiliates of HISA these private hostels offer standards of customer service that all visitors expect in the five key areas of welcome, comfort, cleanliness, security and privacy. All affiliated hostels conform to the standards laid down by the IYHF. All have a common room and TV lounge, cooking facilities and outdoor barbecue area. Each hostel offers an information and travel service, often including a free shuttle. If you have an international hostel membership card you can book accommodation at any HISA hostel by getting HISA accommodation vouchers from leading travel agents in your own country or from the HISA national office. HISA brochures detailing the hostels, facilities and tariffs can be found at regional international hostelling offices in 75 countries throughout the world. Location details are given in the provincial chapters later in this book. HISA hostels are linked to the International Booking Network (IBN), which can be accessed through the YHA or its foreign equivalents. This enables you to book your budget accommodation in South Africa from anywhere in the world up to six months in advance and pay for it in your own currency. There are currently 14 hostels in South Africa linked to the IBN, located in Johannesburg, Durban, Cape Town, George and Kimberley. Hostels not linked to the IBN can be booked through the HISA office in Cape Town. Contact Fiona Jones, HISA, PO Box 4402, Cape Town, 8000, Western Cape, tel (021) 419-1853, fax (021) 21-6937.

YMCA and YWCA. There cannot be many organisations better known worldwide by their initials. Hostels run by them in South Africa maintain the same high standards as in other countries and provide the same unpretentious but clean and inexpensive accommodation. The Young Men's Christian Association (YMCA) hostels that have accommodation for students and overseas visitors are listed in the provincial chapters. The national YMCA office can be contacted at PO Box 31045, Braamfontein 2017, Gauteng, tel (011) 339-1385/8, fax (011) 339-7184.

The Young Women's Christian Association (YWCA) of Southern Africa has short-term and holiday accommodation available at its residences in Johannesburg, Pretoria, Cape Town and East London. Tariffs vary from hostel to hostel and can be obtained when making a booking. The National Council can be contacted at PO Box 31746, Braamfontein 2017, Gauteng, tel/fax (011) 403-2423.

Maps and Guides. The best maps of South Africa are topographical maps on a scale of 1:50,000, which means that 2cm represent 1km on any given map. The entire map will cover an area of 25sq km/10sq miles. Maps of 1:250,000 are also available, but the smaller the scale the more use it is to you if, for instance, you are hiking. For drivers, Automobile Association of South Africa road maps are the best you can find. These range from general reference route and provincial maps to touring and drive-about maps. They are free to AA members or members of affiliated motoring organisations, otherwise they cost a few rands. You can get 1:50,000 topographical maps from the Government Printer, Private Bag X85, Pretoria 0001, Gauteng, tel (012) 323-9731, fax (012) 323-0009, and 1:10,000 orthophoto maps, which combine the advantages of photographs and topographical feature maps, from the Surveyor General, Private Bag X10, Mowbray 7705, Cape Town, tel (021) 685-4050. In all the main centres you will find CNA stores, which stock a wide selection of maps. If you need something special try the following:

> *In Johannesburg:* Map Office, Standard House, 40 De Korte Street, Braamfontein, tel (011) 339-4941, fax (011) 339-4951; Map Studio, 32 Thora Crescent, Wynberg, tel (011) 444-9473, fax (011) 444-9472;
> *In Durban:* Map Centre, 42 Fisher Street, tel (031) 37-8531, fax (031) 32-4814;
> *In Cape Town:* Map Studio, 80 McKenzie Street, tel (021) 462-4360, fax (021) 461-9378.

BY AIR

Airlines. *South African Airways (SAA)* and its partner airlines provide an extensive network of 599 air services a week between all major centres in South Africa. There are also 20 licensed scheduled domestic carriers flying a variety of aircraft over 200

feeder routes to connect more than 80 of South Africa's sma██
larger towns and cities served by SAA, SA Airlink, SA Express█
There are more than 20 flights a day between Cape Town and Jo██
Scheduled flight times from Johannesburg International Airport t█
are:

Bloemfontein — 1h 25min	Nelspruit — 1h
Cape Town — 2h 5min	Pietermaritzburg — 1h 10min
Durban — 1h	Pietersburg — 1h
East London — 1h 20min	Port Elizabeth — 1h 40min
Kimberley — 1h 15min	Upington — 1h 15min

An air fare price war has become the most notable feature of the local travel market. Ticket prices are fluctuating wildly in both the international and domestic markets, so any prices given now would be overtaken before the ink dried. Shop around. Given the price war and the depreciating rand, air travel within the country is becoming cheaper by the day. Normal price for a ticket on the Johannesburg–Cape Town route is R1573 (£210/$346), and on the Johannesburg–Durban route R889 (£119/$196). SAA and SA Express have discounted these by more than 50% in their price war with other local airlines. Check all the airlines listed here before you buy a ticket. SAA, for instance, has some bargains on domestic routes through its Costcutters packages; contact SAA Costcutters, tel (011) 356-1144.

You should arrive at the airport at least an hour before departure time (two hours for international flights). If you can, pay for your ticket by credit card. This makes it easy to check back, as well as possibly giving you free insurance. Let airlines know in advance if you are travelling with young children, and if you need any special meals. SAA has a speedy reservation and check-in system for passengers flying between Johannesburg and Cape Town. Phone (011) 356-1111 to make a credit card booking and ask for electronic ticketing. Without collecting the ticket, you then go straight to the electronic check-in counters at the airport. Quote your flight number, provide identification, and you will get a boarding card.

The main SAA domestic offices are:

Johannesburg: 12th Floor, SAA Towers, corner Rissik and Wolmarans Streets, Braamfontein, tel (011) 356-2036, fax (011) 356-2019; *SAA Domestic Customer Care*, PO Box 7778, Johannesburg 2000, tel (011) 773-9900, fax (011) 773-9533; *Johannesburg International Airport*, Domestic Departures, Terminal 4, Room 119, tel (011) 978-3525, fax (011) 978-4377;

Pretoria: De Bruyn Park Building, corner Vermeulen and Andries Streets, tel (012) 315-2929, fax (012) 326-8545;

Bloemfontein: Liberty Life Building, corner Church and St Andrews Streets, tel (051) 408-2922, fax (051) 408-3331;

Cape Town: Cape Town International Airport, tel (021) 936-2662, fax (021) 936-2664;

Durban: Shell House, corner Smith and Aliwal Streets, tel (031) 305-6491, fax (031) 304-8530;

East London: 6th Floor, Caxton House, Terminus Street, tel (0431) 44-5299, fax (0431) 43-7798;

George: Elsa le Roux Building, Van der Stel Square, tel (0441) 76-9003, fax (0441) 76-9009;

Pietermaritzburg: Shop 6, Southern Plaza, Church Street, tel (0331) 45-7313, fax (0331) 45-7311;

Port Elizabeth: The Bridge, Langenhoven Drive, Greenacres, tel (041) 34-4444, fax (041) 33-7165.

Comair is the country's largest privately owned airline and offers some of the lowest economy air fares. A Comair Business Class air fare is the same as the

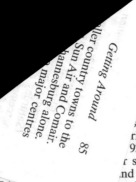
...ly Comair flights connect Johannesburg, Cape
...ichards Bay, Manzini, Skukuza, Hoedspruit and
...ates two return flights a week (Tuesday and
...and Victoria Falls, and two return flights a week
...Cape Town and Windhoek. Following a franchise
...the airline is now officially known as BA-Comair.
...seamless connections between domestic and BA
...passengers also qualify for BA's Frequent Flyer
...fully inclusive fly-in safari packages to the Kruger
...rivate game reserves. Contact PO Box 7015, Bonaero
...921-0111, fax (011) 973 3913/1659.

...r scheduled flights linking Johannesburg, Cape Town,
Por... ...nd also offers charter flights. It has interline agreements
with SAA, ...ess, TAP Air Portugal and Sabena. Contact PO Box 943,
Cramerview 206u, ...g; Johannesburg International Airport, tel (011) 390
1660/1/2/3/4, fax (011) 9/0 1556; Cape Town International Airport, tel (021) 936
2050/1/2, fax (021) 936 2053.

SA Airlink is the official tertiary domestic carrier for southern Africa and links the
country's towns and regions to the main commercial and industrial hubs. Daily flights
connect with other airlines to service the following routes: Johannesburg to Nelspruit,
Sun City, Mmabatho, Pietersburg, Phalaborwa, Pietermaritizburg, Margate, Plettenberg Bay and Umtata; Durban to Port Elizabeth, Plettenberg Bay, Nelspruit, Ulundi
and Bloemfontein; Port Elizabeth to Bloemfontein, Umtata, Plettenberg Bay and
Durban. SA Airlink runs a service between Durban, Pietermaritzburg and Ulundi for
the KwaZulu-Natal provincial government to ferry civil servants between the
province's three main cities, but empty seats are sometimes available to the public.

Discounts of 15% are offered on tourist fares, 30% on Super Savers, and 50% on
Apex fares, depending on when you book and seat availability. Any SAA office can
issue you with an SA Airlink ticket. SA Airlink offers fly-in safaris to the Northern
Province and Mpumalanga to such famous lodges as Ngala, Londolozi, Motswari and
others. Golfing packages to Sun City, the Wild Coast Sun and Phalaborwa are also
available, as well as packages into KwaZulu-Natal, highlighting the battlefields, and
Umfolozi and Hluhluwe game reserves. Contact SA Airlink, PO Box 7529, Bonaero
Park 1622, Gauteng; central reservations and information, tel (011) 394 2430, fax
(011) 394 2649, toll-free 0800 11 47 99.

SA Express Airways is one of Africa's major regional airlines, serving 11
destinations, with 53 city-pair options. It is part-owned by, but operationally
independent of, SAA. Schedules are co-ordinated with SAA to provide connections
for onward travellers, regionally and internationally. Current destinations include
Bloemfontein, Cape Town, Durban, East London, George, Johannesburg, Kimberley,
Port Elizabeth, Richards Bay, Upington and Walvis Bay. It shares a number of routes,
such as Johannesburg to Bloemfontein and Johannesburg to George, with SAA.
Contact SA Express Airways, PO Box 101, Johannesburg International Airport 1627,
Gauteng, tel (011) 978 5569/77, fax (011) 978 5578, web site http:/
/www.saexpress.co.za

State-owned *Sun Air* was voted the country's best domestic airline by local travel
agents in 1996. It operates on the Johannesburg to Cape Town to Durban routes. It
has no special packages or concessions, although it does offer Sun Saver and Super
Sun Saver seats. These vary from a 25% to 40% discount of the full economy adult
fare. Only a limited amount of discounted seats are available on each flight. Children
under the age of 12 pay 50% of the full adult economy class fare. Sun Air has a
partnership agreement with Virgin Atlantic that enables Virgin passengers arriving on
international flights to connect with Sun Air domestic flights to Cape Town and
Durban from Johannesburg. Sun Air is up for privatisation and it is likely Virgin will

become a major shareholder. Contact Private Bag 145, Johannesburg International Airport 1627; Johannesburg passenger services, tel (011) 394-7842, fax (011) 394-9117; Durban, tel (031) 469-3444, fax (031) 469-3443; Cape Town, tel (021) 934-0918, fax (021) 934-9014.

Atlantic Air is a scheduled Garden Route airline that flies three services a week from Cape Town to Mossel Bay and Oudsthoorn, Plettenberg Bay to Oudsthoorn, and Mossel Bay to Cape Town. There are discounts for children under 12, pensioners, and passengers paying seven and 30 days in advance. Enquiries, tel (04457) 30518; reservations, tel (021) 934-6619, fax (021) 934-3751.

Charter Flights. South Africa is a great country for private flying. Flying weather is superb most of the time and many of the most attractive safari spots are best reached by light aircraft. Air charter rates are among the lowest in the world and comparable to the cost of some up-market car rentals. Even for a group of only four passengers it can be more cost-effective to charter an aircraft and fly directly to your destination. No matter how small or remote a place may be in southern Africa you can be sure there will be a landing strip nearby. The following are some leading air charter companies offering hassle-free services if you are in a hurry or planning to visit a spot off the beaten track.

The *Dragonfly Group* specialises in air charter, as well as coach and car hire. It has its own fleet of vehicles for transfers, sight-seeing trips and safaris, both in Johannesburg and in game country. Dragonfly owns the up-market Cybele Forest Lodge, close to the Kruger National Park. This is considered one of South Africa's top country hotels and is a member of Relais et Châteaux. Cybele Forest Lodge, PO Box 346, White River 1240, Mpumalanga, tel (013) 764-1823, fax (013) 764-1810, e-mail cybele@iafrica.com

A helicopter flight is one of the most spectacular ways of experiencing scenic highlights. Dragonfly can copter four to seven people on some of the most popular trips, including scenic flights over Johannesburg and Soweto, with lunch at a country restaurant; a day at Sun City to enjoy gambling, golf and watersports; and a half-day air safari to see the best of the 'Big Five' in a private game lodge. In Cape Town you can fly along the Atlantic coast all the way to Cape Point and return over False Bay and Table Mountain, or spend a day in the winelands and have lunch at a private wine estate. Contact the Dragonfly Group, PO Box 987, Northlands 2116, Gauteng, tel (011) 884 9911, fax (011) 884 9915/6, e-mail dfgroup@iafrica.com

For visiting pilots who want to fly themselves, *Cross Country Air Safaris* offers its service and experience on a consultancy basis. The company can provide information about suitable venues from a pilot's as well as a non-flying guest's point of view; detailed aviation-related information; airfields, frequencies, procedures, refuelling, immigration, temporary aircraft importation, route planning, suitable checkpoints and reporting points; help with administration, validation procedures, useful addresses, telephone numbers, procurement of maps; and other assistance. Depending on reservations made, this help can be free of charge, or provided at reasonable rates. Cross Country Air Safaris is a good bet if you can make up the numbers – four is ideal for economy and comfort – and want to decide your own itinerary. They are not tied to any particular chain of hotels or lodges and its pilots are all experienced bush flyers and between them can muster fluent English, Afrikaans, German, Italian and Ovahimba, as well as a working knowledge of French. If you have your own private, light aircraft licence bring it along. Cross Country Air Safaris, PO Box 95282, Waterkloof 0145, Gauteng, tel (012) 46-3740, fax (012) 346-3473, Cell 082 453 5865.

Rossair Charter is based at Lanseria airport, near Johannesburg, but also operates from Grand Central, Rand and Wonderboom airports, which are situated near the main business centres of Johannesburg and Pretoria. The company can also arrange flights to and from most of the major centres in the country. Rossair, PO Box 52690, Saxonwold 2132, Gauteng, tel (011) 880-9175, fax (011) 447-3211.

African Ramble fly-in tours do air transfers from Johannesburg to any lodge in the Sabie Sand, Timbavati and Manyaleti game reserves bordering the Kruger National Park; tel (012) 46-7983/4, fax (012) 46-1794.

Federal Air operates out of Durban's Virginia Airport and flies charter services all over southern Africa. Contact PO Box 20400, Durban North 4016, KwaZulu-Natal, tel (031) 84-1357/8 and (031) 83-8020/1, fax (031) 84-5416.

Other operators of charter services include:

> *Chopper Flying Services*, PO Box 201132, Durban North 4016, KwaZulu-Natal, tel (031) 84-8085, fax (031) 83-3226; fly out of Virginia Airport;
>
> *Streamline Air Charter*, PO Box 18152, Rand Airport, Germiston 1419, Gauteng, tel (011) 824-1650, fax (011) 824-1757;
>
> *Lowveld Helicopter Service*, PO Box 2801, Nelspruit 1200, Mpumalanga, tel (013) 758-1103, fax (013) 758-1440;
>
> *Court Helicopters*, PO Box 2546, Cape Town 8000, tel (021) 934-0560, fax (021) 934-0568 (Cape Town International Airport); scenic flights, tel (021) 25-2966, fax (021) 21-5920;
>
> *Kwena Air*, PO Box 4565, Rivonia 2128, Gauteng, tel (011) 803-4821, fax (011) 803-4566.

Airports. South Africa has three international airports. They are Johannesburg International Airport, the country's principal gateway, 30km/19 miles from Johannesburg and 60km/38 miles from Pretoria; Durban International Airport, 15km/10 miles south of the city; and Cape Town International Airport, 25km/16 miles east of the city. Johannesburg handles more than 7 million passengers a year and Cape Town handles more than 3 million. More than 70 flights for major foreign cities take off from Cape Town every week, some flying direct.

Scheduled bus services are available at all three international airports. There is coach transport to Johannesburg's main rail terminal every half hour between 6.15am and 11pm, and a reciprocal service from town from 5.30am to 10pm. The bus leaves the city from the Rotunda, in Leyds Street, tel (011) 974-6561. There is also a coach service to Pretoria. The airport bus stops *en route* at the suburbs of Randburg, Sandton and Rosebank. The Magic Bus also picks up and drops arriving and departing passengers at Johannesburg International Airport. The bus runs scheduled hourly shuttles from Sandton. The cost is R40 (£5.35/$8.80) one way and R70 for a return trip, which is at least half the price of a regular one-way taxi fare. The Magic Bus also runs a door-to-door service, but booking is essential for this. MasterCard and Visa are accepted. There is a Magic Bus booth at the airport, or tel (011) 884-3957.

Cape Town has a 24-hour bus shuttle service run by Intercape at regular intervals between the airport and the central terminal in Adderley Street, close to the railway station, on the city's Foreshore. This costs R30 (£4/$6.60) from the airport to the station or R60 door-to-door. Contact tel (021) 934-0802, fax (021) 934-0702. There is also the Airport Shuttle Service, which operates a pre-booked service from the airport, tel (021) 934-5455, fax (021) 934-5448, toll-free booking, tel 0800 22 22 20. There is a regular coach service between Durban International Airport and the terminal at the corner of Smith and Aliwal streets in the city centre run by Airport Bus Services, tel (031) 465-5573 and (031) 21-1133. The ride to or from the city centre costs R15 (£2/$3.30), and R20 to the beachfront. Super Shuttle 24-hour door-to-door transfer service, tel (031) 469-0309 and (031) 203-5407.

There are taxi ranks at most airports, and the larger car rental companies have offices there. Some of the larger hotels transport guests to and from airports.

There are also six national airports, at Bloemfontein, Port Elizabeth, East London,

Kimberley, Upington and George. All are state-owned and have been operated individually as business units by the Airports Company since 1993. There are also about 300 airport/airfields in use, ranging from landing strips in the veld to hi-tech operations such as Lanseria, Wonderboom and Grand Central, Virginia Airport at Durban North, and Rand Airport near Germiston, which is the busiest civil airport in the country. Some 150 operators fly non-scheduled services from about 90 of these airfields, but there is air traffic control at only 20 airports, and only 140 have permanent surfaced runways.

Contact details for the international airports:

Johannesburg: Private Bag X1, Johannesburg International Airport 1627, Gauteng, tel (011) 921-6911, fax (011) 390-1736, flight information tel (011) 975-9963;

Cape Town: Private Bag X9002, Cape Town International Airport 7625, Western Cape, tel (021) 934-0444, fax (021) 934-0932, flight information tel (021) 934-0407;

Durban: Private Bag, Durban International Airport 4029, KwaZulu-Natal, tel (031) 42-6156, fax (031) 42-4398, flight information tel (031) 42-6111.

For information on national airports contact the Regional Office, PO Box 5787, Walmer, Port Elizabeth 6054, Eastern Cape, tel (041) 507-7337/9, fax (041) 507-7340.

BY SEA

Coastal Passages and Cruises. The South African Marine Corporation (Safmarine) is the country's largest shipping line. Their ships link South African ports with the major harbours of the world and their container vessels take limited numbers of passengers. Another South African option is Unicorn Lines, whose 9600-ton *MV Gamtoos* can take six passengers on the coastal voyages it makes carrying containers and cargo between Durban, Cape Town and Walvis Bay in Namibia. The vessel has three cabins of two berths each, with a sleeper couch that can accommodate one extra person. The cost is R1140 (£152/$251) per person for a single passage between Durban and Cape Town (R2280 for the round trip), R2151 for the Durban to Walvis Bay leg, and R1011 for the Cape Town to Walvis Bay trip (the round trip on either leg is double the single fare).

Safmarine, PO Box 2171, Cape Town 8001, tel (021) 408-6911, fax (021) 408-6370;

Unicorn Lines, PO Box 1345, Cape Town 8000, tel (021) 21-1820, fax (021) 25-2262.

Coastal Cruises. If you have plenty of time to spare the *RMS St Helena* has regular round cruises from Cape Town to the Atlantic islands of St Helena, Ascension and Tristan da Cunha at various times of the year. There are also two round mini-cruises from Cape Town to Tristan da Cunha only. Cruises taking in two of the islands — usually St Helena and Ascension — take from 18 days to more than three weeks. The mini-cruises take 12 days. Round-trip fares for the longer cruises range form R16,100 per person for the sole use of an outer double cabin to R9660 if you share an outer two-berth. Fares for the mini voyages to Tristan da Cunha range from R15,260 for sole use of an outer double cabin to R5460 for budget accommodation sharing a four-berth. Children under 2 pay 10% of the fare and those between 2 and 12 years pay 50%. Contact the St Helena Line, PO Box 484, Cape Town 8000, tel (021) 25-1165, fax (021) 21-7485, telex 521192 STHL SA, telegraphic address Helenaship, Cape Town. In the UK, contact Curnow Shipping Ltd, The Shipyard, Porthleven, Helston, Cornwall, tel (01326) 563434, fax (01326) 564347.

Starlight Cruises is a popular cruising company. They usually have more than 30 cruises each season, which is between November and May every year. Cruises in the

16,495-ton *Symphony* include three and four night coastal party cruises between Cape Town and Durban and to the Mozambique islands of Bazaruto and Inhaca; longer cruises to the Indian Ocean islands of Madagascar, Mauritius and Seychelles; and spice island cruises to the East African ports of Mombasa and Zanzibar. They will even sail you to Europe and back on a three-week cruise for R5610 to R11,220 (£748–1496/$1234–2468) each for two adults sharing a cabin.

Contact Starlight Cruises, PO Box 786331, Sandton 2146, Gauteng. tel (011) 807-5111, fax (011) 807-5085; Pretoria, tel (012) 342-4499, fax (012) 342-1942; Durban, tel (031) 301-3614, fax (031) 301-2392; Cape Town, tel (021) 23-6263, fax (021) 23-7166.

BY RAIL

With the vast distances to travel you need to be assured of clean toilets, somewhere to wash or shower and a decent bed so that you arrive at your destination fit for action. First and second-class travel are good value and well worth it. The following are first-class single fares from Johannesburg, with the distance in brackets to show you how reasonable the fares really are:

Beit Bridge — R186	Durban — R164
(655km/406 miles)	(722km/449 miles)
Bloemfontein — R95	East London — R215
(407km/308 miles)	(1023km/636 miles)
Cape Town — R326	Port Elizabeth — R240
(1530km/951 miles)	(1112km/691 miles)

A single first-class fare on the Trans-Orange Express from Cape Town to Durban costs R425 (2010km/1249 miles) and to Kimberley R224 (1035km/643 miles; £29.85/$49.30). All return tickets cost double the single fare.

International travellers can also purchase Rail Passes before departure to South Africa. Four variations of passes are available depending on how many days you wish to use the train: these are available from R990 (£132/$218) for first-class travel.

There can be few better ways to see the breathtaking expanse of South Africa's countryside than by train. There is an extensive rail network — 33,800km/21,002 miles — linking all major cities and towns in South Africa as well as neighbouring Mozambique and Zimbabwe. Distances between centres are vast but travelling by train is comfortable and cheap. Spoornet has Main Line Passenger Services to all the main centres in southern Africa. The main 'name' semi-luxury express trains are:

Algoa — Johannesburg to Port Elizabeth (via Bloemfontein);
Amatola — Johannesburg to East London (via Bloemfontein);
Bosvelder — Johannesburg to Messina (via Louis Trichardt);
Diamond Express — Pretoria to Bloemfontein (via Kimberley);
Southern Cross — Cape Town to Oudtshoorn;
Trans-Karoo — Pretoria to Cape Town (via Johannesburg and Kimberley);
Trans-Natal — Johannesburg to Durban (via Pietermaritzburg);
Trans-Oranje (Orange Express) — Durban to Cape Town (via Bloemfontein and Kimberley).

You have a choice of three classes. First class (four and two bunks), second class (six and three bunks), and third class (six bunks or open coach seating). Compartments and coupés — half the size of compartments — are comfortable and compact. A washbasin and foldaway table form part of the fittings in first and second class. All first-class coaches have toilets and showers. All second-class coaches have toilets, while showers are fitted to newer coaches. Dining or catering cars on main line trains offer meals and are stocked with a variety of South African wines and other beverages. Lunch and dinner are à la carte. You can get tickets for bedding and breakfast on the train or from ticket offices when booking.

Reservations. First and second-class accommodation must be pre-booked. This can be done up to three months in advance at a railway station, reservation office or travel agent. Travel in third-class accommodation is economical and no advance reservations are necessary. Requests for non-smoking accommodation, lower bunks, wheelchairs and so on should be made when booking.

Discounts. Children under the age of seven, accompanied by an adult, travel free of charge. Those between seven and 12 years pay half the adult fare. If you are 60 or over you are eligible for a 40% discount on the normal full fare in first and second class only. Proof of age and identity is required.

Rent-A-Comp. This is ideal for a family or a group travelling first or second class and guarantees that no one else will be booked in with you. There is also a saving on the fare, depending on numbers, but it could be 25% of the whole fare. Rent-a-Comp is available on all main line trains except the Blue Train. First-class compartments have four bunks and second class compartments have six bunks.

Rent-A-Coupé. This also ensures that no one else will share your accommodation. It is available on all main line trains, with the exception of the Blue Train. First-class coupés have two bunks and second-class coupés have three bunks. If your family or group takes a full coupé the overall saving on fares is 25%.

Commuter Services. Many South Africans use commuter trains between the network's 374 stations in or close to the major metropolitan areas. All these services are provided by the South African Rail Commuter Corporation (SARCC) operating as Metro Rail Services. The SARCC moves 2.1 million people to and fro daily on 2574 train services over a rail network in the country's six main urban centres. Fares are subsidised. In peak periods the urban commuter trains can often be crowded, dirty and unpleasant to use. Steps are being taken to improve their image and standards. Avoid them if possible. Metro has launched a campaign to make its trains safer and more popular by distributing pamphlets in English, Xhosa, Zulu and Northern Sotho, with cartoons illustrating entertaining storylines. Contact Metro passenger services, Private Bag X47, Johannesburg 2000, Gauteng, tel (011) 773-5878, fax (011) 773-7475.

All rail travel falls under the control of state-owned Spoornet, which provides services for passengers travelling long distances, as well as for goods and containers. Contact Spoornet, Main Line Passenger Services, PO Box 6135, Johannesburg 2000, tel (011) 773-8920/774-2082. Reservation offices:

Cape Town: tel (021) 405-3871/3581;
Durban: tel (031) 361-7621;
Bloemfontein: tel (051) 408-2941;
Pretoria: tel (012) 315-2401;
Port Elizabeth: tel (041) 507-2400/2222;
East London: tel (0431) 44-2719/2819;
Kimberley: tel (0531) 88-2631/2731.

In the UK, contact LEISURAIL, PO Box 113, Peterborough PE3 8HY, tel 01733-335599, fax 01733-505451, brochures 01733-335556.

LUXURY AND SCENIC RAIL TRIPS

The Blue Train. Train-travel lovers the world over know about South Africa's Blue Train, which for more than 50 years has taken passengers in pampered luxury between Pretoria and Cape Town. In August 1997, South Africa launched a magnificent new Blue Train, which is probably the most luxurious train in the world. It costs R4500 per person sharing a luxury-class compartment for a one-way trip between Pretoria and Cape Town, and R4200 deluxe, but for this the Blue Train offers the ultimate in luxury accommodation, and elegant wining and dining. The train has 18 carriages, accommodates 84 passengers — with a staff of 27 to look after them — and travels at a maximum speed of 110km/h/68mph. It travels three times a week between Pretoria and Cape Town (1600km/994 miles), with one night on the train; and Pretoria and Victoria Falls (1596km/992 miles) six times a year, with two nights aboard.

The Blue Train's reputation for comfort, excellent service and food, punctuality, Irish linen, crystal and silverware in the heart of some of the world's most exquisite scenery has spread around the world and if you are travelling between Johannesburg and Cape Town you can also take your car on the Trans-Karoo Express at an additional cost of R684.

Contact Blue Train Reservations, PO Box 2671, Joubert Park 2044, Gauteng, tel (011) 773-7631, fax (011) 773-7643; Pretoria, tel (012) 315-2436; Cape Town, tel (021) 405-2672; Durban, tel (031) 361-7550; toll-free 0800 11 77 15.

In the UK, contact LEISURAIL, PO Box 113, Peterborough PE3 8HY, tel 01733-335599, fax 01733-505451, brochures 01733-335556.

Rovos Rail. For lovers of steam locomotives a trip with Rovos Rail is a must. Rovos has revived the golden age of steam trains and luxury travel in the heart of the African bush with beautifully restored vintage locomotives and coaches that carry you on steam safaris through some of the most spectacular scenery in Africa. Rovos operates two fully restored and refurbished trains — the *Classic Pride of Africa* (1940s style) and the *Edwardian Pride of Africa* (maximum 46 passengers). The *Classic* carries a maximum of 68 passengers and is dedicated to fortnightly departures on the route between Victoria Falls, Pretoria, Cape Town and George/Knysna. Trips include a 50-hour 1600km/994 mile journey between Pretoria and Cape Town, with off-train excursions to the 'Big Hole' and Mine Museum in Kimberley, breakfast at the Lord Milner Hotel in Matjiesfontein, a quaint Victorian oasis village in the veld, and a 24-hour, 620km/385 mile journey along the spectacular Garden Route between Cape Town and George/Knysna, with a side excursion into the winelands. Rovos also runs steam train safaris between Pretoria and the Kruger National Park and a four-day tour through the wilds of Mpumalanga.

Epic journeys into the heart of Africa are also undertaken by South Africa's own Orient Express. Rovos takes up to 68 passengers on a 12-day (6100km/3790 miles) Edwardian safari from Cape Town to Dar-es-Salaam, via Kimberley, Pretoria, Mpumalanga, Beit Bridge, Bulawayo, Victoria Falls, Lusaka and through Tanzania to Dar-es-Salaam ('Haven of Peace') on a trip that is expected to become one of the world's most famous train journeys. The Cape Town–Dar es Salaam leg costs US$6500 per person sharing a deluxe suite, and the return trip costs US$7800 per person sharing a Royal Suite.

The use of steam locomotives is increasingly difficult as more and more water and coaling facilities are scrapped, so while Rovos trains may be drawn by any of four vintage steam locomotives, diesel or electric locomotives are used where facilities no longer exist. Arrivals and departures in Pretoria, Cape Town, Victoria Falls and Knysna are, however, steam-hauled. Prices vary per person sharing from R3995 (£533/$879) for either the Cape Town–Pretoria or Pretoria–Victoria Falls trip, R2295 for the Cape Town–George legs, to only R195 for the George–Knysna stretch. Rovos Rail also runs the Victoria Hotel in Pretoria, conveniently across the road from the railway station, which makes an ideal stopover during north or southbound journeys.

Contact Rovos Rail, PO Box 2837, Pretoria 0001, Gauteng, tel (012) 323-6052/3/4, fax (012) 323-0843; Cape Town, tel (021) 21-4020, fax (021) 21-4022. International representatives are:

UK: Three Cities Hotels, tel (0171) 225 0164, fax (0171) 823 7701;
USA: Kartagener and Associates, tel (212) 465 0619, fax (212) 268 8299;
Australia: Rovos Rail Australia, tel (02) 6688 5170/6685 6180, fax (02) 6685 5728/6685 5608.

Scenic Rail Trips. Another gracious living and wildlife experience is offered by Spoornet, which has linked its *African Safari Train* to the Shamwari Game Reserve in the Eastern Cape. The African Safari coaches are connected to the scheduled Algoa rail service (Johannesburg/Port Elizabeth/Johannesburg) and you travel in style and air-conditioned comfort. Alternatively, you can visit Shamwari first and return to Johannesburg on the safari train. Shamwari ('friend') is a game reserve on the Bushman's River, close to the Addo Elephant National Park, and is a haven for lion, rhino, elephant, hippo, hyena, kudu, gemsbok, zebra and other game, as well as a wide variety of bird, reptile and plant life. Union Limited in Cape Town also organises scenic rail tours.

Shamwari, tel (042) 851-1196, fax (042) 851-1224;
Spoornet, Main Line Trains, PO Box 2671, Joubert Park 2044, Gauteng, tel (011) 773-6978/87, fax (011) 773-7643;
Union Limited, tel (021) 405-4391, fax (021) 405-4395.

The *Banana Express*, which chuffs along the Kwazulu-Natal South Coast from Port Shepstone, is one of only two narrow-gauge steam trains left in South Africa (the other is the Apple Express in Port Elizabeth). The original Banana Express ran from 1911 until the old SA Railways closed down its route in 1986 because it was unprofitable. A few years later the service was brought back to life and privatised by local businessmen as the Port Shepstone and Alfred County Railway. Today the Banana Express is once more a successful freight carrier, as well as a major tourist attraction. Alfred County Railway operates four Garratt-type NGG16 locomotives, painted in a black or bright red livery, which haul you in coaches dating back to 1907 on the 90-minute to two-hour round trips through banana and sugar cane plantations and countryside dotted with traditional thatched huts. The turnaround points are at Izotsha and at Imbube, where there is a Zulu tribal village selling curios and artefacts. First class fares are R36 (£4.80/$7.90), children (3–12) R18, and tourist tickets are R24, children R12. There is also a 6½-hour day trip to Paddock, whose little station 39km/24 miles from Port Shepstone is a national monument. Here, you can have a barbecue lunch, visit the old stationmaster's house, now a museum, or watch the loco being watered and the trucks loaded with timber, sugar cane and bananas for the return trip. You can also take the Baboon View Trail from Plains station, where a ranger meets the train and leads a ramble through the Natal Parks Board's beautiful Oribi Gorge Nature Reserve. There is also a combined steam train and bus trip to the spectacular Oribi Gorge view sites. Fares for the Paddock trip are R80, children R40, with the Baboon View Trail an extra R6 for the Natal Parks Board entrance fee. The Oribi Gorge trip costs R100 (£13.35/$22), children R50. There are also occasional longer trips to Harding, 120km/75 miles by rail from Port Shepstone. These take eight hours in each direction, including photographic stops *en route*, and cost R300 return or R200 one-way. Contact PO Box 572, Port Shepstone 4240, tel (039) 682-4821, fax (039) 682-5003. Tickets are also available at Hibiscus Coast and Country Publicity, tel (03931) 22322.

The famous narrow-gauge steam train the *Apple Express* operates regularly on the 53km/33 mile track from Port Elizabeth to Thornhill Village, departing from the Humewood Road station. One of the stops is the famed Van Stadens River Bridge, where you can disembark and stroll across this spectacular span and admire the view before photographing the oncoming train as it slowly steams across. The trip to Thornhill takes two hours and you can lunch, picnic, or simply slake your thirst under the shady trees at the Thornhill Hotel, which is near the halt. The Apple Express returns to Port Elizabeth two hours later. Excursion tickets cost R40 for adults and R20 for children (under 12). Contact the Apple Express Society, PO Box 21847, Port Elizabeth 6000, or the Spoornet Information Centre, The Bridge, Greenacres, Port Elizabeth 6045, Eastern Cape, tel (041) 507-2333, fax (041) 507-3233.

BY ROAD

Coach and Bus. Luxury buses and coaches link all major South African cities and operating companies also offer numerous scenic sight-seeing tours from major centres providing comfortable, reasonably priced access to a wide variety of attractions in the country's hinterland. Long-distance intercity coaches run daily, and transport having the high profile it does in the tourism industry, all involved — operators, suppliers and manufacturers — have introduced a coach grading system to ensure these meet international standards.

Greyhound Coach Lines pioneered luxury intercity coach services in South Africa and has an extensive intercity network covering all of South Africa and some neighbouring countries. Greyhound runs a daily Rapide Service from Johannesburg to Durban and back. The six-hour journey costs R160 (£21/$35) single, one way. A single fare for Johannesburg to Cape Town is R340 (£45/$75), to Port Elizabeth R275 and Express to Kimberley is R88. The standard discount for children aged 3 to 11 is 50% of the adult fare; children under 3 go free, if not using a seat. There are also bargain travel days when senior citizens are eligible for a 20% discount on tickets booked in advance, and a go-as-you-please Houndabout pass allowing you unlimited travel and stopovers. You can stop over as often as you want where you wish, so long as you complete your travel within the specified 7, 15 or 30-day time limit. Bookings can be made through the Central Reservations Office in Johannesburg, provincial reservations offices, Computicket outlets or any travel agent.

Greyhound offices are:

> *Johannesburg*, tel (011) 830-1400, fax (011) 830-1527, reservations, tel (011) 830-1301, fax (011) 830-1528;
> *Pretoria*, tel (012) 323-1154, fax (012) 323-1294;
> *Durban*, tel (031) 309-7830, fax (031) 309-7746;
> *Cape Town*, tel (021) 418-4310, fax (021) 418-4315;
> *Port Elizabeth*, tel (041) 56-4879, fax (041) 56-4872;
> *Credit card hotline reservations*, tel (011) 830-1301.

Springbok Atlas is one of the heavyweights in tour travel and has offices in Cape Town, Johannesburg, Durban, George, Port Elizabeth and Windhoek. Services include scheduled luxury coach and minibus tours, group tours, special interest tours and tailored itineraries for travellers. Tours in and around Johannesburg include Johannesburg day tours, Soweto, Gold Reef City, De Wildt Cheetah Research Centre and Pretoria, Diamond Digging tour, Pretoria city and traditional African cultures, Loopspruit Wine Estate and Ndebele Village, a Johannesburg early night tour and an African cultural experience. Other tours are around Cape Town and its environs, Port Elizabeth and Durban, with long-distance tours of the Garden Route from R219, the Kruger National Park from R307 (£41/$68), and Sabi Sabi at R1636. Contact Springbok Atlas, 1st Floor, Port Elizabeth Airport Building, Eastern Cape, tel (041) 51-2555, fax (041) 51-2550, e-mail elizem@springbokatlas.co.za

Good news for backpackers often faced with a weary slog to out-of-the way hostels and campsites is the *Baz Bus*. Modelled on the Slow Coach in Britain, this is a hop-on, hop-off bus that offers an inexpensive way of getting around. There are two Baz buses continuously circling the country. A complete circuit is about 4100km/2548 miles, stopping at 17 cities and towns *en route*. You can buy a four-month ticket for the complete circuit or take a cheaper, shorter stage. You can board anywhere on the route, and likewise jump off anywhere. Baz will drop you off at the door of a hostel or backpacking place, although you are not obliged to stay there. The bus leaves Cape Town for Johannesburg every Monday and Thursday, stopping *en route* at Hermanus, Swellendam, Mossel Bay, George, Oudtshoorn, Sedgefield, Knysna, Plettenberg Bay, Nature's Valley, Jeffreys Bay, Port Elizabeth, Port Alfred, Hamburg, East London, Cintsa, Umtata (for Coffee Bay), Port St Johns, Port Shepstone, Durban, Pietermaritzburg, Drakensberg, Johannesburg/Pretoria. The bus leaves Johannesburg/Pretoria every Tuesday, Friday and Sunday and does this route in reverse. Cape Town to Johannesburg tickets cost R535 one way (R850 return), and for Cape Town to Durban one way it is R435 (R700 return). You can buy tickets at youth hostels, Hostelling International, or at one of the following:

> *Student Travel*, Johannesburg, tel (011) 447-5551, fax (011) 447-5775;
> *SA Adventure Centre*, Cape Town, tel (021) 418-6570, fax (021) 418-4689, or tel (021) 439-2323, fax (021) 439-2343.

A similar service is offered by the *Garden Route Hopper Bus*, a hop-on, hop-off minibus that operates daily in both directions along the Garden Route between Mossel Bay and Port Elizabeth. The Hopper takes you through some of the country's most beautiful mountain passes, along a breathtaking coastline and through mysterious indigenous forests. There are 11 stopover points and you can start your journey from any of them. Tickets are valid for four months, cost R18 (£2.40/$3.95) for a single leg, and there is plenty of space for surfboards, bikes and other gear. Contact Rockey Street Backpackers in Johannesburg, tel (011) 648-8786/96.

Other intercity coach and tour services for Johannesburg are:

> *Biz Bus*, tel (011) 908-1253, fax (011) 908-3026;
> *Impala*, tel (011) 974-6561, fax (011) 974-1346;
> *Translux*, tel (011) 774-3333, fax (011) 774-3871;
> *Mini-Zim Travel*, tel (012) 543-1236 and (012) 567-4264;
> *Panthera Azul* (Johannesburg to Maputo), tel (011) 337-7409;
> *Rand Coach*, tel (011) 339-1658.

Intercity coach services for Cape Town:

> *Chilwan's Bus Service*, tel (021) 934-4786;
> *Springbok Atlas*, tel (021) 448-6545;
> *Intercape*, tel (021) 934-0802 and (021) 419-8888;
> *Munnik's Intercity*, tel (021) 637-1850;
> *Translux*, tel (021) 405-3333.

Intercity coach services between Durban and Johannesburg (Durban station and Johannesburg Rotunda):

> *Golden Wheels*, tel (031) 29-9229 and (031) 307-3363; Johannesburg, tel (011) 773-4552 and (031) 28-5032.

Journey times from Cape Town are: Johannesburg 17 hours, Pretoria 18 hours, Durban 19 hours, and Port Elizabeth 11 hours.

Hitch-hiking. It is still fairly easy to hitch-hike between major centres. The best way to start is to take a train or bus to one of the quieter nearby towns where vehicles are likely to refuel before hitting the highway. South Africans are not keen on picking up fellow South Africans and are much more likely to stop for you if they can see you are a visitor, so stick your country's flag on a sign saying where you want to go. Hitch-hike only on main city and national roads. The South African police constantly warn against hitch-hiking and picking up hitch-hikers. If you have to hitch-hike, do not do it alone. The rule for drivers is, if you are driving alone, do not pick up hitch-hikers. Dial-A-Lift is a link between motorists and hitch-hikers that might help, tel (011) 648-8136/8602.

CITY TRANSPORT

Municipal Bus Service. Public and urban transport is generally a mess and incomprehensible to all but locals, and mostly not even then. One of the problems is that most bus services operate on the basis that all their passengers are heading into the city centre every day to work. The opposite is true. Few people work in the Central Business District if they can avoid it and businesses have been moving out of the cities to the suburbs for years to avoid rising crime. In urban areas bus services are run by local municipal authorities and private bus companies. They operate scheduled bus services between peripheral areas and city centres, and during the week daytime bus services in most cities are fairly regular and punctual — but do not rely on this at night or at the weekend.

Minibus Taxis have largely taken over the role of mass transport and they have achieved phenomenal growth during the last few years. They are the preferred mode of travel by most of the country's poorer commuters and these 12 to 18-seater minibus taxis carry up to 50% of them daily. There are more than 90,000 of these taxis, a quarter of them in Gauteng, and half of them operating illegally. They are owned mostly by black businessmen with small-scale operations in specific local areas. The struggle for turf between the legals and the thousands of pirate operators has led to the widespread violence and gangster-type killings that plague the industry. The taxis are commonly known as Zola Budds because of their tendency to crash (the South African athlete of that name was involved in a famous track collision with Mary Decker during the 3000m race at the 1984 Los Angeles Olympics). Every visitor should take a ride in one — once. They have a poor safety record and even if the tyres do not burst you might find yourself dodging bullets from a rival member of one of the country's 480 taxi associations.

To hail a minibus taxi you first of all have to learn the signals. Point your index finger down and you tell the oncoming driver you are going a short distance; finger up, long distance. Fares vary, but R15 (£2/$3.30) for the Johannesburg to Pretoria trip and R5 for Sandton to the city centre are ballpark figures. When boarding a taxi remember that what the taxi driver says, goes. You are not allowed to eat or smoke in the taxi (although the driver can smoke). Women are not allowed to sit next to the door, they must sit in the middle, or next to the driver. No fat people are allowed to sit in front. Some taxis have stickers saying: 'Fatty boom-booms at the back'. People with strong body odour may be asked by the driver to get out. Women who have been to the hair-dressing salon for a perm are greeted by a sticker saying: 'I like your perm, but not on my windows'. Travelling by minibus taxi is definitely an experience. Long-distance minibus taxis are the same as the city runarounds, except they are more tolerant about luggage — they even take chickens.

Taxis. Unlike their counterparts in New York, London and other cities, taxicabs in South Africa do not cruise the streets looking for fares. They wait at ranks until called. You will find them listed under 'Taxi' in the telephone book Yellow Pages, or ask your hotel reception to call one for you. If the taxi you are using has a meter always ensure that it starts from zero, otherwise first agree the fare for your journey.

Walking and Cycling. These modes of locomotion might be popular in Europe and the USA but they are generally a no-no in South Africa, unless you are going for a hike or a weekend spin with a cycling club. If you see someone walking in a suburb of a city or large town it usually means their car has broken down. Bikes are not allowed on the freeways and, so far, no municipality has taken the step of providing dedicated cycling lanes for pedal-pushers. If you do walk or cycle on your own you take your life in your hands.

Rickshaws. Among Durban's main tourist attractions are the Zulu rickshaws that line up waiting for customers along the beach front. You cannot miss this unusual form of city transport. The two-wheeled rickshaws are brightly painted and ornately decorated, but it is the man-power that attracts attention. The rickshaws are drawn by strapping Zulus who appear even more gigantic in their colourful, top-heavy head-dresses fashioned from beads, feathers, animal horns, and any other bits and pieces that amuse the wearer.

DRIVING

LICENCES

On 4 January 1897 President Paul Kruger declined to take a ride in the first horseless carriage to arrive in South Africa, an 1896 model Benz Velo imported from Germany by a Pretoria businessman. Since then millions have taken to the roads in South Africa, and there are currently more than 7 million drivers — 10% of them without licences. Your driving licence will be accepted in South Africa if it carries your photograph and signature and is printed in English (or accompanied by a letter of authentication, written in English by an embassy or other authority). Alternatively, you can take out an international driving licence before you leave and this is the easiest option. An international driving permit is accepted if the holder is a visitor. If there is a chance your international licence could expire during your visit, you should get a new one in advance. It is compulsory for drivers to carry their licences with them at all times and there are heavy fines if you do not comply.

RULES AND REGULATIONS

Throughout the country, you drive on the left-hand side of the road and overtake on the right. Give way to vehicles already in intersections or circles. You can get a copy of the *Road Code of South Africa* from any CNA store or bookshop.

Speed Limits. The maximum legal speed limit is 120km/h (75mph) on national roads and specified freeways in urban areas. On other rural roads the limit is 100km/h (62mph), unless a sign indicates a lower limit. The general speed limit within urban areas is 60km/h (37mph), except where signs indicate otherwise.

Speed Traps. These are operated by traffic police who use electronic timers, stopwatches, cameras and pace-cars fitted with calibrated speed-measuring devices. Speed traps may operate at any time of the day or night, and along any section of road. The sensor-type trap — including the gatsometer — operates by means of two pressure-sensitive cables laid close together on the road. Watch out for them. It is an offence to try to warn other motorists of a speed trap, by flashing your lights, for example. If you are caught in a speed trap you will be given a summons to appear in court, but there is usually the option of a fine. If you are caught driving at more than 150km/h (93mph) you could be arrested.

Seat Belts. The wearing of seat belts is compulsory, so always belt up. This will not only protect you in an accident, it will also prevent your being jerked out of the car by an attacker.

Drink. Driving under the influence of liquor or drugs is a serious offence, and drink-driving laws are among the toughest in the world. The law says that if you are stopped and checked the concentration of alcohol in your blood should not exceed 0.05g/100ml. If it does, there is a maximum fine of R120,000 and/or a six-year jail sentence. As in other countries you can be guilty of an offence even if your vehicle is not moving; you merely have to be in the driver's seat with the engine running. The law applies to anything travelling principally on wheels, so you should be careful even if you are riding a bike or a horse and cart. It is also as well for European drivers to remember that, generally, alcoholic drinks in South Africa have a higher alcoholic content by volume than those they might be used to. For instance, beer is 5%, wine 10–13%, fortified wine — such as sherry, port, marsala and muscadel — can be up to 20%, and spirits are a hefty 40–50%.

Cell Phones. There is no legislation forbidding the use of hand-held cell phones while driving, although it is in the offing. However, it would be difficult to convince a magistrate that you had exercised the necessary care and diligence if you were chatting on your cell phone when involved in a collision. A conviction for reckless or negligent driving would be the likely outcome.

Insurance. Third-party insurance is compulsory and separate from comprehensive motor insurance. In South Africa, the premium is built into the price of fuel and no additional charge is payable. The display of a third-party token on the windscreen is no longer required. Third-party insurance claims go to the Multilateral Motor Vehicles Accidents Fund (MMF), PO Box 2743, Pretoria 0001, Gauteng, tel (012) 323-9203, fax (012) 323-7345.

ROADS AND FREEWAYS

To anyone used to the congested roads of Europe driving in South Africa can be a pleasure. Roadside facilities are usually of a high standard and the road network is excellent, the most highly developed in Africa. There are more than 200,000km/ 124,274 miles of roads, with a relatively low car density that makes travel quick and easy. Most of the roads are well signposted in English and Afrikaans, are serviced by filling stations and have rest areas where you can picnic in the shade of a tree and stretch your legs. However while most of the roads are in good condition, in some remote areas they may become impassable after heavy rain.

South Africa has a well established network of primary and secondary roads and most routes are numbered. The 7000km/4350 miles of national roads carry the prefix 'N' — for example, 'N3' — and provincial routes carry the prefix 'R', followed by a three-digit number — for example, R531. Metropolitan routes in urban areas and all major cities carry the prefix 'M' — for example, 'M1'. These routes are generally the most direct way of reaching your destination by road. When planning your trip use all sources of information, such as updated maps and publicity brochures, available from information centres throughout the country.

Toll Roads. There are about 20 toll plazas in South Africa, servicing more than 750km/466 miles of high-standard roads. Large signs by the roadside indicate that you are about to enter a toll road and also say how much the toll will be for your class of vehicle. These signs appear before you reach the turn-off to a free, alternative road. If you take the toll road have the correct change ready, and enter the lane that has a green overhead indicator arrow. Some credit cards are accepted, such as Visa and MasterCard. Bright yellow SOS radio telephones are available at regular intervals along most toll roads, for use in case of breakdowns or accidents. A patrol car drives along most toll roads with emergency items such as fuel, water, jumper leads and tools to perform minor repairs. They also give travel information and help to lost or stranded motorists and notify the appropriate authorities, such as police, ambulance

Distances in kilometres

Distances in kilometres	Beaufort West	Bloemfontein	Cape Town	Colesberg	Durban	East London	George	Grahamstown	Johannesburg	Kimberley	Ladysmith	Maseru	Mbabane	Nelspruit	Pietersburg	Port Elizabeth	Pretoria	Umtata
Bethlehem	822	240	1288	495	400	740	1040	729	256	364	162	175	463	574	846	312	681	681
Bloemfontein	558	–	1024	231	640	568	779	557	426	175	402	141	703	750	760	649	482	509
Cape Town	466	1024	–	793	1654	1038	433	870	1450	965	1450	1143	1751	1798	1739	753	1461	1230
Colesberg	327	231	793	–	857	464	548	393	657	276	657	350	958	1005	991	418	713	462
Durban	1161	640	1654	857	–	655	1221	784	608	764	238	575	524	683	883	901	664	424
East London	582	568	1038	464	655	–	605	168	994	740	755	595	1085	1244	1328	285	1050	231
George	237	779	433	548	1221	605	–	437	1205	736	1202	895	1503	1550	1539	320	1261	797
Grahamstown	452	557	870	393	784	168	437	–	983	669	884	584	1214	1373	1317	117	1039	360
Johannesburg	984	426	1450	657	608	994	1205	983	–	447	370	431	356	364	334	1075	56	894
Kimberley	499	175	965	276	764	740	736	669	447	–	526	316	801	862	818	694	540	684
Ladysmith	984	402	1450	657	238	755	1202	884	370	526	–	337	349	444	645	1001	426	524
Maseru	677	141	1143	350	575	595	895	584	431	316	337	–	349	685	765	701	536	536
Mbabane	1285	703	1751	958	524	1085	1503	1214	356	801	349	349	–	159	487	1331	335	854
Nelspruit	1332	750	1798	1005	683	1244	1550	1373	364	862	444	685	159	–	573	1490	331	1013
Pietersburg	1318	760	1739	991	883	1328	1539	1317	334	818	645	765	487	573	–	842	278	1169
Port Elizabeth	408	649	753	418	901	285	320	117	1075	694	1001	701	1331	1490	842	–	1126	477
Pretoria	1040	482	1461	713	664	1050	1261	1039	56	540	426	536	335	331	278	1126	–	950
Queenstown	511	364	977	260	650	204	623	193	790	536	750	391	854	1013	591	310	841	226
Umtata	737	509	1230	462	424	231	797	360	894	684	524	536	854	1013	1169	477	950	–
Upington	549	577	776	575	1166	984	786	898	789	402	928	718	1118	1153	1089	884	811	1261

The distances given are in kilometres over the shortest practicable routes; these are not necessarily the best or the fastest.

Source: The Automobile Association of South Africa.

services, breakdown units or traffic officers, when needed. Service areas along the road provide refuelling points, repair facilities, restaurants and take-aways, emergency breakdown help, washing facilities and overnight parking; rest areas provide only the last two. For information on toll roads contact the Department of Transport in Pretoria, tel (012) 290-9111, fax (012) 325-8004.

Road Signs. The national and provincial freeways are well signposted. South Africa uses the metric system and all distance signs are in kilometres and speed limits in kilometres per hour. A revised road traffic sign system is being phased in. Many of these new signs use symbols rather than words to make them easy to understand and reduce observation time. The main ones are the signs developed to help tourists. Apart from the usual regulatory, warning, guidance and information signs, tourist attractions, facilities and services are identified by distinctive brown and white signs. When you see such a sign you know that the facility meets national and regional tourism standards. Tourism signs are usually posted well in advance of the turn-off and where necessary a further sign is located at the final turn.

FUEL

Since the first filling station was established at Sea Point, Cape Town, in 1922 the country's network of service stations has grown to more than 4000, supplied in the main by the Caltex, Shell, Engen, BP and Total oil companies — others are Zenex and Trek — and except in out of the way hamlets you will usually find cheerful 24-hour, seven-days-a-week service. There are no restrictions on fuel-selling hours; these are determined by the garage owner. The concept of the self-service garage has not caught on and with high unemployment rates and government pressure for labour-intensive enterprises it is not likely to do so. The result is that once you pull into a filling station for fuel you will be surrounded by helpful petrol pump attendants who will not only fill your tank, but check the oil and battery water levels, tyre pressures, and wash the windscreen. It is all part of the service. A tip of R2 (25p/45 cents) is usually given, but seldom expected, for this attention. Payment for fuel is made to the attendant, but note that credit cards are not usually accepted. A word of caution: when filling up, drive to a pump where you can easily see the cash and litre indicators and make sure both are on zero before the attendant starts filling your tank.

Two grades of petrol are available at South African garages and filling stations, a low octane and a high octane, low for the Highveld areas and high for the coastal plain. These grades are available leaded and unleaded. If you drive from one area to the other there is no need to change the octane grade you were using; the refineries have already taken the change in altitude into account and doctored the petrol accordingly. A slight drop in the pulling power of your engine might be noticed when changing altitude. Taking normal sea level power as 100%, your engine will lose 1% for every 100m/328ft climbed. Nothing is gained by using a higher octane than the octane rating of the engine. Petrol gets cheaper the closer to the coast — and the refineries — you get.

Compared to Europe and the USA petrol is expensive. An Automobile Association of South Africa study shows that an hour's earnings will buy 9.7 litres of petrol in South Africa, 13.2 litres in Britain and 31.8 litres in the USA. In February 1997 petrol at inland pumps was R2.23 (30p/50 cents) a litre for leaded 93 octane, while at the coast, leaded 97 octane was R2.13 a litre. Lead-free petrol was introduced in February 1996 and to encourage motorists to use it the pump price is a few cents a litre less than for leaded petrol. Unleaded petrol (ULP) inland is 91 octane, and at the coast it is 95 octane. If you borrow or hire a car and are not sure what fuel to use you can contact vehicle manufacturers on toll-free numbers for advice. Some of these are:

Delta — 0800 42 27 77   Toyota — 0800 13 91 11
Nissan SA — 0800 11 24 48   Volkswagen — 0800 43 47 37

You can also check with the National Association of Automobile Manufacturers of South Africa (NAAMSA) on (012) 323-2980.

Fuel prices will keep rising if the value of the local currency continues to nose dive. The only good thing about these increases from your point of view is that the higher the local fuel price goes the more rands you must be getting for your pounds, dollars or whatever.

Tyre Pressures. Pressures are metricated from pounds per square inch into bars and kilopascals (kPa). One bar equals 100kPa or 14.5 pounds per sq inch. It is usual to give your pressure in bars when you ask pump jockeys to inflate your tyres.

VEHICLE RENTAL

You are spoilt for choice when it comes to vehicle hire. There are 33 car hire companies with a total fleet of some 25,000 vehicles. Hertz Rent-a-Car returned to South Africa at the end of 1996 to offer another option to the three main players in the market: Imperial, Avis and Budget. Hertz is operating through a franchise agreement with Alisa Car Rental, which has a fleet of 1100 vehicles. Imperial has a fleet of 8000, Avis 7800 and Budget 4500. To hire a car in South Africa, you must have a valid international driver's licence and a minimum of five years' driving experience. Generally, you must be aged 23 or over. Cars can be hired at any of the nine major airports, through travel agents, tourist and publicity associations, or by checking the telephone book Yellow Pages under Car and Camper Hire.

There are various restrictions and requirements if you plan a cross-border trip in a rented vehicle, so first check with the hiring company. Generally rental rates for vehicles are in line throughout the country. A 1300cc run-around should be R60–75 (£8–10/$13.20–16.50) a day, plus 68 cents per km, and a 2.6 VW Microbus R235 a day, plus R2.10 per km; check first, though, as at the time of writing these rates were set to rise. Rates naturally drop the longer the rental period. Insurance is extra and compulsory. Car rental companies usually have branches in all major cities and airports, as well as in some game reserves, and often offer package deals with airlines and hotels. They can rent you anything from a campervan, fully equipped with kitchen, stove, fridge, cooking utensils and linen, to a four-wheel-drive vehicle. A variety of sedans (mainly Japanese and German) are available. Details of rental companies can be obtained from the SA Vehicle Rental Association (Savra), PO Box 2940, Randburg 2125, Gauteng, tel (011) 789-2542/3, fax (011) 789-4525.

Local rental companies might be cheaper than the international ones, but the big companies, which are usually franchises, are worth the extra as you can make reservations in advance. You can get prepaid vouchers from travel agents or major rental companies in most countries. Pay by voucher or credit card; if you pay cash you might have to leave a large deposit. Always check that the vehicle you rent has a fully inflated spare tyre and a reliable jack and lug wrench before you drive off, and make sure the door and boot (trunk) locks work.

Budget Rent A Car, one of the top three franchised car rental organisations in the world, has nearly 60 branches throughout southern Africa. Charges fluctuate, but expect to pay about R75 (£10/$16.50) a day plus 81 cents a kilometre for a small 1300cc four-seater to R394 a day and R3.09 a kilometre for an air-conditioned Mercedes-Benz E220 or similar. An air-conditioned 2.3 VW Microbus costs about R625 a day if you take it for a minimum of five days. You get 200km/124 miles a day free with this deal. It is cheaper if you hire for the weekend or by the week. Then, not only is the daily rate lower, you also get 125km/78 miles to 200km/124 miles a day free. Paraplegic hand controls and child safety seats are available for certain models at no extra cost in Johannesburg, Durban and Cape Town. Budget has branches at all the main airports or you can make a reservation on toll-free numbers 0800 016622 (domestic) and 0800 117722 (international). The company's head office is in Johannesburg, tel (011) 392-3907, fax (011) 392-3015.

Avis Car Rental has branches in all major centres and airports in South Africa. Daily rental rates range from R73 (£9.75/$16.05) for a five-door economy car to R344 for a four-door luxury vehicle, such as an Audi 500 V6.

Central Reservations, tel (011) 392-3240, fax (011) 974-1030, toll-free 0800 02 11 11, international toll-free reservations 0800 03 44 44;
Head Office, Johannesburg, tel (011) 392-2023, fax (011) 974-1884.

Other rental companies include:

Hertz (Alisa Car Rental), tel (021) 386-1560, toll-free 0800 02 15 15; Cape Town tel (021) 22-1700; Sea Point tel (021) 439-1144; Johannesburg tel (011) 394-4610; Pretoria tel (012) 324-4782; Durban tel (031) 368-1013; and Port Elizabeth tel (041) 51-6550;

Imperial Car Rental, tel (011) 337-2300, fax (011) 336-8695, toll-free 0800 21 02 27, domestic reservations tel 0800 13 10 00, international reservations tel 0800 11 03 44; emergency (after hours) tel 0800 11 88 98; has offices in all cities and most towns;

Europcar Interrent, toll-free 0800 011 344; Johannesburg International Airport, tel (011) 394-8832, fax (011) 394-8833; Cape Town International Airport, tel (021) 934-2263, fax (021) 934-6620; Cape Town reservations, tel (021) 439-9696, fax (021) 439-8603; Durban International Airport, tel (031) 469-0667/8, fax (031) 469-0041; focuses on incoming and outbound international travellers;

Tempest Car Hire, Johannesburg International Airport, tel (011) 394-8626/7309, fax (011) 394-0316, Cell 083 228-1896; Cape Town International Airport, tel (021) 934-3845, fax (021) 934-3853; Durban International Airport, tel (031) 469-0660, fax (031) 42-4416; focuses on the local leisure markets with vehicles from a 1.4 runaround at R66 a day and 74 cents per km to a 10-seater 2.6 Microbus at R250 and R2.60 per km;

Venture Autorent, PO Box 700, Randburg 2125, Gauteng, tel (011) 792-8240, fax (011) 793-3426, Cell 082 600 5032; has 1300cc cars from R70 per day and 60 cents a km to a 2.5 Microbus at R240 per day and R1.90 a km;

Panther Rent-A-Car, Cape Town International Airport, tel (021) 386-5051/2/3/4, fax (021) 386-5058/9; city, tel (021) 418-6688, fax (021) 418-6689;

Cabs Car Hire, tel (021) 934-3306/3336, fax (021) 934-3310; offers new vehicles from R43 per day, plus insurance and a kilometre rate, and will even meet you at Cape Town International Airport.

Motorhomes. Most hire companies do not like their motorhomes and campervans to leave South Africa. If you want to drive across the border they levy a substantial surcharge and you must have the hiring company's written permission to take the vehicle out of the country. There is usually a minimum rental period of a week, deposits of at least R1000 (£133.35/$220) are usual when booking and full payment is expected in advance on major contract periods. All reputable hire companies are listed in the telephone book's classified Yellow Pages under Car and Camper Hire. The following should give you an idea of what to expect:

Buffalo Campers hires out fully equipped holiday motorhomes and 4x4 vehicles. The cheapest two-berth motorhome costs R2905 (£387/$639) a week, with 1750km/ 1087 miles a week free. A five-berth is R4480 a week with unlimited km and a four-berth 4x4 is R4830 a week, with unlimited km. Contact PO Box 536, Northriding 2162, Gauteng, tel (011) 704-1300, fax (011) 462-5266, Cell 082 412 3099, e-mail buffcamp@global.co.za

Britz:Africa Camper Van Rentals hires out customised touring motorhomes and campers from compact Cubs for two to three people from R600 a day to spacious Explorer five-berths at R740 a day and 4x4 campers from R700 a day, all with unlimited km. Contact PO Box 4300, Kempton Park 1620, Gauteng, tel (011) 396-1860, fax (011) 396-1937; Cape Town, tel (021) 981-8947; Durban, tel (031) 72-9326.

A Landcruiser 4x4 Safari Camper with camping equipment for four people from *Camp Car Hire* costs R540 to R480, with unlimited km, depending on hire period. VW Microbus Campers can be hired for R2450 per week with 1750km/1987 miles a week free. After that you pay R1.30 a km. Contact PO Box 700, Randburg 2125, Gauteng, tel (011) 792-8240, fax (011) 793-3426.

Holiday Camper Hire is the oldest mobile home company in South Africa and the only company owning its own luxury camper ranch, just 20 minutes' drive from Johannesburg, at Inchanga Ranch, Inchanga Road, Witkoppen, Johannesburg, Gauteng. If you hire one of their campervans you can use the ranch free of charge. There is also a budget-priced hostel (R35 a day) at the ranch, where you can stay in a tented camp or in an old farmhouse. You can also hire motorbikes and bicycles. Contact Private Bag X3, Bryanston 2201, Gauteng, tel (011) 708-2176, fax (011) 708-1464, e-mail ivi@pixie.co.za

Motorhome Abroad has motorhomes and 4x4 campers, as well as holiday apartments in Cape Town. Vehicles range from two to five-berth and can be picked up from Johannesburg, Cape Town or Durban. Prices vary from about R405 to R610 a day depending on the hire period. Motorhome Abroad represents a number of reputable motorhome and campervan hire companies. Contact PO Box 221, Constantia 7848, Cape Town, tel (021) 794-7702, fax (021) 794-7703, e-mail campavan@aztec.co.za, web site http://www/aztec.co.za/biz/campavan/

Other motorhome hire companies include:

Campers Corner Rentals, PO Box 48191, Roosevelt Park 2129, Gauteng, tel (011) 787-9105 and (011) 789-2327, fax (011) 787-6900 and (011) 886-3187; Cape Town, tel (021) 905-1503, fax (021) 905-4493, e-mail campers@iafrica.com, web site http://www.campers.co.za

Bobo Campers, PO Box 803, Westville 3630, KwaZulu-Natal, tel (031) 44-8633, fax (031) 44-8614;

Knysna Camper Hire, PO Box 1286, Knysna 6570, Western Cape, tel (0445) 22444, fax (0445) 82-5887;

Leisure Mobiles, PO Box 48928, Roosevelt Park 2129, Gauteng, tel (011) 477-2374, fax (011) 477-2321; campers and camping equipment for independent safaris.

EMERGENCY SERVICES

The Automobile Association (AA) is a household name in South Africa. This is largely due to the Emergency Rescue Service, or Road Patrol Service, whose yellow patrol vehicles are cause for sighs of relief when they appear at a breakdown. The AA belongs to the International Touring Alliance (AIT), a worldwide organisation of touring clubs and automobile associations. AIT clubs provide a wide range of services to each other's members when they are travelling abroad. The AA provides services to tourists belonging to other AIT clubs, and these are available to you if you present your club membership card. The Head Office of the Automobile Association of South Africa (AASA) is at Dennis Paxton House, Kyalami Grand Prix Circuit, Allandale Road, Kyalami, Midrand 1685, Gauteng, tel (011) 799-1000, fax (011) 799-1010.

You can get free roadside repairs and towing services from AA Road Patrols and AA tow-trucks in all major centres through the national toll-free Supernumber 0800 01 01 01. In rural areas where these do not operate you can get the services of an AA-appointed contractor through the same Supernumber. Touring services and information are available free from all AA Auto Shops or from the AA Travel Information Centre in Johannesburg, tel (011) 466-6641. Road information in English is available by telefax, teletex or mail. Free technical advice is available from the AA Technical

Division, tel 0800 033 163 or 0800 033 164. Free advice is given by the AA's Legal Division, tel (011) 466-6604 or (011) 466-6620.

Breakdowns. Most motorists these days find that the best first-aid for their car in the event of a breakdown is an Automobile Association membership card and a cell phone. If you can get to one, there are well equipped garages throughout the country that provide breakdown and repair services. Even so, they can be far apart so carry a spare tyre (inflated), a wheel spanner, a jack and a puncture repair aerosol, a tow rope and, on long journeys, a torch, a good knife, a spare battery, jumper cables, a spare fanbelt, a variety of fuses, insulation tape, a selection of tools, and at least two litres/3.5 pints of oil and the same of water. Quickset Epoxy putty is good for fixing a leaking radiator or a metal pipe. Emergency kits worthy of the name should also include a six-pack of beer and some biltong (dried beef).

Accidents. There are 445,000 collisions on South Africa's roads every year and the fatality rate is one of the highest in the world — 10,000 road deaths a year, or 130 deaths for every 100 million kilometres travelled by car. There is a road accident every 73 seconds and someone dies every 56 minutes as a result of a crash. We presume we now have your attention if you are a driver.

If you are the first person at the scene of an accident (if you have a cell phone call 10177 with the details), do not move anyone unless there is a danger of further injury, such as the vehicle bursting into flames. Switch off the ignition and disconnect the battery if you can. Put up warning signals for following and oncoming traffic. Only do what first-aid you can to the limit of your training and knowledge. If you know nothing about first-aid at least try to calm the injured by talking to them until qualified help arrives. Once the emergency services have arrived, move out of the way. If you are involved in a collision resulting in death, injury or damage you should stop and find out the nature and extent of any injuries, give first-aid if you can, check the damage to the vehicles and exchange your name and address, the name and address of the vehicle's owner and the registration number of the vehicle with the other driver or passengers. You must not move any vehicle that has been in an accident in which a person has been killed or injured, unless it blocks the road, in which case mark its position on the road before moving it. Report the accident to a police station or traffic office within 24 hours and to the insurance company within 14 days.

HAZARDS

Human and Animal. Potential hijacking, armed robbery and theft can be added to the normal human and animal hazards you face on the roads and the AA recommends the following survival skills.

Make sure all the doors of your vehicle are locked, especially when driving in city traffic. Always lock the car door when you get out, even if it is only to open a gate. Make sure all the windows are closed or at least three-quarters closed to prevent someone sticking their arm into your car at a stop street, traffic light or in slow-moving traffic. Do not leave valuables in view while you are driving; keep them in the boot or locked in the glove compartment; and never leave money, valuables or documents in your vehicle, even if you leave it for a short time. Never leave the key in the ignition when the vehicle is unattended; and never leave children alone in the vehicle. Beware of anyone who approaches you when you are parked or stopped in traffic asking for information or help. He might have a partner on the other side of the vehicle ready to grab whatever is lying around while your attention is diverted; and be wary of anyone banging on the side of your vehicle. He may be trying to distract you so that his partner can jerk open your door or steal something through an open window. Do not pick up hitch-hikers; hitch-hikers used to be perfectly normal people on their way from one place to another, but nowadays it is safer to assume that the person flagging a lift could be a potential hijacker or robber, even though this makes it tough on genuine hitch-hikers. Stay alert and beware of anyone lingering around four-way stops and traffic lights. If you are being followed, drive to the nearest police station or service station, or to any house and ask for help. If you lose your way, look for a public place where you can look at a map and ask for directions. If you stop behind a car in traffic, leave a big enough gap so that you can pull away in an emergency. Criminals often bump into cars from behind at traffic lights; they wait for you to get out to inspect the damage, then drive off in your car. If you do get out, lock your door. If anyone acts suspiciously around your car blow the hooter continuously. Have the key ready in your hand when you return to your car. Do not get to your car and then start searching in your pockets or handbag for keys, especially in unguarded, isolated or dimly lit parking areas. If alone, do not stop where there is a body or a seemingly injured person lying on the road. Rather drive on and report it to the police. This may seem callous, but these 'bodies' often spring to life waving a gun at Good Samaritans. Do not spend the night in your vehicle in a parking lot or alongside the road; and request identification before opening your window if you are stopped by police or traffic officers at an unusual roadblock. Another good idea is to make photocopies of all your documents (passport, ID document, driver's licence) and have them certified before leaving home; this will help you to get new ones if the originals are stolen. Keep the copies apart from the originals.

These are sensible precautions to take, but they are not meant to paralyse you with fear. Do not panic even when the situation seems threatening. Keep calm. Vehicles and possessions can be replaced: a human life cannot.

Animals are a big hazard in some parts of the country, particularly in the rural areas where you are more likely to find wild animals using the road to cross from one patch of veld to another than you are dogs, cats, cattle and donkeys. Watch out for triangular warning signs showing a leaping buck. In the Knysna Forest area there are even road signs warning of elephants crossing. Remember that animals caught in your headlights at night usually freeze rather than run. If you hit and kill a wild animal on the road you must inform the police or the Department of Environmental Affairs within 24 hours.

HINTS

To ensure a safe and enjoyable trip plan your journey well before departure. Remember to carry your driver's licence — it is a legal requirement in South Africa.

Driving on the Beach. We do not recommend driving on the beach, but sometimes it is necessary to reach a fishing spot or a secluded nook. A 4x4 vehicle is the safest to drive. Make sure your vehicle is in good running order and has plenty of fuel. Drive between the high and low-water marks on the wet sand part of the beach. The best time to travel on the beach is from two hours before to two hours after low water. Never travel on the beach at high tide. Reduce tyre pressure to less than 1.4 bar before driving on to the beach. Try to keep to existing tyre tracks and keep a good lookout for rocks. Avoid hard braking and do not stop facing uphill. Do not allow anyone to ride on the outside of your vehicle. If you are trapped by the tide your vehicle may be extensively damaged, so enquire about local conditions before you hit the beach.

Publications dealing with all major towns, resorts, places of interest and tourist attractions, as well as excellent maps, are available free of charge from AA Auto Shops on production of a valid membership card from your home motoring organisation. There are AA branches with Auto Shops in all the main centres:

Johannesburg, Braamfontein, tel (011) 407-1373, fax (011) 407-1295;
Pretoria, tel (012) 322-9033, fax (012) 322-5660;
Bloemfontein, tel (051) 477-6191, fax (051) 447-6797;
Kimberley, tel (0531) 82-5207, fax (0531) 3-2882;
East London, tel (0431) 21271, fax (0431) 43-5781;
Port Elizabeth, tel (041) 34-1313, fax (041) 33-1413;
Cape Town, Claremont, tel (021) 683-1410, fax (021) 61-9222;
Durban (Workshop), tel (031) 301-0340, fax (031) 301-7673;
Pietermaritzburg, tel (0331) 42-0571, fax (0331) 94-2475.

We recommend as the most interesting and comprehensive book for visitors to the region TV Bulpin's *Discovering Southern Africa*. Other useful books are the *Southern African Book of the Road*, *Off the Beaten Track* and *Illustrated Guide to the Southern African Coast* (all AA publications), *Touring in Southern Africa* and *Pictorial Motoring Atlas of Southern Africa*, both by Maxwell Leigh, and Andrew White's *Four-wheel Drive in Southern Africa* and *Southern Africa 4x4 Trails*. These are all good for motoring trips, but are generally too bulky for other travel.

If you are driving from Johannesburg to Cape Town allow 15 hours for the trip, to Durban six hours, and to Port Elizabeth 11 hours.

Conversions:

Kilometres into miles: multiply by 0.62;
Miles into kilometres: multiply by 1.61;
UK gallons into litres: multiply by 4.54;
US gallons into litres: multiply by 3.78;
Litres into UK gallons: multiply by 0.22;
Litres into US gallons: multiply by 0.26.

TOP ATTRACTIONS

Without doubt, the country's premier and best known attractions are the massive Kruger National Park and the flat-topped Table Mountain whose distinctive outline has beckoned travellers for centuries. The Victoria and Alfred Waterfront complex in Cape Town's dockland area has climbed in popularity since it was developed in 1988 and now pulls in an incredible 60,000 visitors a day in the holiday season. In fact, Cape Town and the Peninsula can claim to have the lion's share of top tourist attractions, with the famed Kirstenbosch National Botanical Garden, Cape Point and its nature reserve, the nearby winelands, and since the beginning of 1997, Robben Island, the museum and national monument islet where President Nelson Mandela spent so many years as a political prisoner.

The North-West Province draws punters and revellers to try their luck on the tables and one-armed bandits at Sun City and the Lost City entertainment resort, a sort of Las Vegas in the African bush. Gauteng has the MuseumAfrica, Gold Reef City, the palaeontological treasure caves around Krugersdorp, and South Africa's best known black city, Soweto. The 200km/124 miles-long Garden Route along the Cape coast is a natural wonder world of forests, mountains and beaches, and the Drakensberg and game parks of KwaZulu-Natal offer an unforgettable experience. Then there is the renowned Blue Train, the quaint gold prospectors' village of Pilgrim's Rest, and the even quainter hamlet of Matjiesfontein in the Karoo, the Cango Caves, the Augrabies Falls, the Tsitsikamma forest, the Kalahari Gemsbok National Park... that is 21, and the list of attractions goes on and on.

WINE ROUTES

Detailed descriptions of the many and varied wine routes in the Cape — which conveniently link vineyards, estates and wineries into organised tourist trails — are included in the Western Cape chapter (see page 431).

BATTLEFIELD ROUTES

From the earliest days clans, tribes and nations have fought for possession of portions or all of the land that is now South Africa and conflict is tightly woven into the country's history. The wars that undoubtedly made the most enduring mark were those fought over the past turbulent century and a half between Boer and Zulu, British and Zulu, and British and Boer. Both the Zulus and the Boer in turn surprised the seemingly invincible forces of the British by inflicting on them a series of resounding defeats. In the end, however, superior numbers, fire-power and the technological might of Europe's foremost industrialised nation carried the day and reversed these defeats, but to this day British military historians seem to have more than a sneaking admiration for these two doughty foes of the African veld. These battles more than anything else shaped the modern history of South Africa and changed the course of what was believed to be an empire on which the sun would never set. For more than half a century KwaZulu-Natal was the focus of many of these conflicts and today, as the area with the largest concentration of battlefields in the country, it draws visitors from all around the world.

For details of battlefield routes in particular provinces see page 341 (KwaZulu-Natal), page 302 (the Free State) and page 279 (the Northern Cape).

DIAMONDS, GOLD AND SEMI-PRECIOUS STONES

Diamonds and gold go together with South Africa like peaches and cream. These are the two glittering minerals that laid the foundations for a modern nation. The diamond fields of Kimberley started the country on the march and the gold reefs of the Witwatersrand completed the process. No one should visit South Africa without seeing something of these twin wonders, from their extraction to their wrought finishing as faceted gemstones and intricate jewellery.

De Beers, which grew out of the Kimberley diggings, is the world's largest producer of gem diamonds and controls most of the world sales through its Central Selling Organisation's marketing agreement. In effect, this keeps the price of diamonds artificially high by restricting their release on to the open market. De Beers Consolidated Mining Company still has its head office in Kimberley, where you can see a selection of diamonds worth £1 million (see page 276).

Diamonds are found in kimberlite pipes, known to diggers as blue ground. In South Africa there are only about a dozen areas economically exploitable, including the Kimberley group — Kimberley, De Beers, Dutoitspan, Bultfontein and Wesselton — Jagersfontein in the Free State, the Finsch mine near Postmasburg and the famous Premier mine east of Pretoria.

The first South African diamond was picked up at Hopetown in 1866, on the Orange River, and weighed nearly 22 carats. An even bigger stone weighing 82.5 carats and called the Star of South Africa was found two years later. This started the diamond rush as alluvial or river stones were slowly traced from Hopetown as far as

Vereeniging and down the Orange River to Prieska, and eventually to the rich area near Kimberley. Apart from these major mines, alluvial deposits are still worked along the Orange River below Aliwal North, the Vaal River, stretching down to its confluence with the Orange and along the coast of Namaqualand, including Alexander Bay, at the Orange River mouth. The kimberlite pipes in Dutoitspan, Bultfontein and Jagersfontein were discovered in 1870 and others followed. The largest pipe, the Premier, was found in 1902 and the celebrated Cullinan diamond weighing 3030 carats — about one and one-third pounds — was recovered here in 1905. This is the largest diamond ever found.

In 1907, General Louis Botha presented this stone to Queen Alexandra of England to commemorate the granting of self-government to the Transvaal Republic. The stone was sent to the Netherlands where it was cut into two large diamonds, which now decorate the British Sceptre and the Crown. Other famous diamonds from South Africa include the Jonker, whose 726 carats were cut into nine stones in 1904, and the 69.68 carat Excelsior I, one of 21 polished gems cut from the white, pear-shaped 971-carat monster Excelsior diamond discovered in 1893 by a worker at Jagersfontein (his reward was £500, a horse, a saddle and a bridle). Until the Cullinan diamond was found the original Excelsior was the largest stone ever discovered. Diamonds are still big business in South Africa and can still set pulses racing among the most hard-bitten buyers.

Gold

Ceremonial objects, jewellery and other artefacts recovered from archaeological digs in the north of the country show that gold was mined and worked by black craftsmen in South Africa many centuries before white prospectors announced the discovery of gold in the Cape and the Transvaal. Such prospectors probably first discovered gold as alluvial nuggets in southern Cape rivers and it was found in this form in the Gamka River in 1851. At Millwood, near Knysna, there was a minor gold rush towards the end of the century and some 2500 ounces of gold were recovered. A small deposit near Pietersburg was worked from 1868 and other discoveries followed. Deposits at Pilgrim's Rest have been worked consistently since 1872. The Barberton area gave up alluvial gold in 1877 and reefs were discovered and worked from 1886.

Gold was discovered on the Witwatersrand in the same year on the farm Langlaagte by George Walker and George Harrison. The site of the discovery is now the George Harrison Memorial Park. The main reef of the ridge stretches for 65 miles and is one of the richest in the world. More than 80% of all gold mined in South Africa comes from a geological feature known as the Wits Basin, a gold deposit stretching from Johannesburg in Gauteng to Virginia in the Free State, in a wide arc that includes the goldfields around Orkney in the North-West Province. About 100,000 miners descend daily some 2500m into the bowels of the Earth to extract it. No other country has produced as much gold as South Africa, where about five tons of ore have to be blasted from surrounding rock to produce a single ounce. Almost all of the gold mined — about 500 tons a year — goes to the Rand Refinery at Germiston where silver and other impurities are removed and 400oz gold bars are poured. The South African Reserve Bank buys the entire gold output and arranges for its global marketing.

South Africa has the deepest gold mine in the world at Western Deep Levels, where the main shaft goes down more than 3588m/11,772ft. Workers in deep mines labour in temperatures of 46°C/115°F. Visits to working gold mines are strictly controlled and organised under the auspices of the six major mining houses through the offices of the Chamber of Mines of South Africa. Gold mine tours leave the office of the Chamber every Wednesday morning and cost R200 (£26.65/$44) per person, payable in cash in rands. Credit cards are not accepted, and early booking is essential. You must be in good health and no one under the age of 12 is permitted underground.

Before you go underground you are given a presentation on mining operations and local geology, and the whole extraction, melting and pouring process is explained. You are underground for up to two hours, with a visit to the actual working areas at the rock face, before watching a gold pour in the Smelt House. The tour winds up with drinks and lunch with senior mine management before returning to the Chamber of Mines building in Hollard Street, in central Johannesburg. For information and bookings contact Betty Elliott, Chamber of Mines, tel (011) 498-7204, fax (011) 838-4251.

You can also visit a gold mine of your choice with *FIT Tours and Safari* if you book well in advance. Tours last a day and start and finish in Johannesburg. A one-day tour costs R710 per person, although a party of four pays R250 per person. Bed and breakfast and a second day adds R376 per person to the cost. Contact them at PO Box 1037, Stilfontein 2550, North-West Province, tel (018) 484-2984, fax (018) 484-2700.

Semi-Precious Stones

South Africa and its neighbours produce staggering quantities of semi-precious stones. Most consist of some variety of quartz with a great range of colour, transparency and texture. Colourless clear quartz is called rock crystal; amethyst is the best known coloured variety of quartz; rose quartz is pink; there is also smoky quartz and a yellow variety, citrine. Chalcedony is a fine-grained variety of quartz, the yellow-brown variety is carnelian. Chalcedony is perhaps best known in the form of agate. Jasper is also a variety of chalcedony. Tiger's eye, one of the best known banded semi-precious stones is another stone that is essentially quartz. Garnet has lots of varieties and different colours. Two types are of special interest to collectors; one is known as South African jade, which is not jade at all, but a grossularite garnet. Serpentine is an ornamental stone and the green variety from the Barberton area called verdite is well known, as is topaz.

If you are interested in gemstones you will probably know that the term precious stone is generally used for diamonds, corundum and beryl; all other gems are regarded as semi-precious. The precious varieties of corundum are ruby and sapphire. Different names are used according to the colour of beryl, aquamarine being the commonest, with a bluish green or sea-green colour. Emerald is the most valuable variety of beryl. Other varieties of beryl are yellow heliodor and pink morganite, but these are quite rare.

ARTS AND CRAFTS

For details of arts and crafts routes in particular provinces, designed to introduce visitors to a wide variety of craftsmanship and artistic expression, see page 343 (KwaZulu-Natal), page 200 (Gauteng) and page 453 (Western Cape).

COAST OF WHALES

South Africa's Coast of Whales stretches from Gansbaai in the south to St Helena Bay on the West Coast, with Hermanus as the main base for visiting whale watchers. Although other bays along the coastline attract these migrating mammoths, most of them call in on Hermanus and adjacent Walker Bay, which is one of the best spots on the coast for whale-watching between June and November every year when the whales come to court, mate, calve and nurse. The species most commonly seen is the southern right whale, but humpback and Bryde's whales have also been spotted in the area (see page 428).

Some 29 species of whale visit South African waters, from the monarch of them all, the blue whale, which can weigh as much as 25 African bull elephants, to the humpback and southern right whale, which can reach 16m/53ft in length. Southern right whales come to calve and raise their young, while humpback whales are migrating between breeding areas to the north, or feeding grounds to the south. Bryde's whales live year-round on the continental shelf. Modern whaling with cannon-fired harpoons started in South Africa in 1908 and brought southern right whales perilously close to extinction. Right whales were hunted for their oil and baleen (whale bone) and got their name because they were the 'right' whales to kill, being very fat, easy to spot, and they floated when dead. South Africa closed its last whaling station in 1975 and today probably has the strictest whale conservation legislation in the world.

As a result of this the population of southern right whales has been increasing along the south coast for the last decade at a rate of about 7% a year. Though it has taken half a century, numbers have now reached the stage where the whales come close inshore during their winter breeding travels. Humpback numbers are also increasing and Cape Vidal, on the northern coast of KwaZulu-Natal, is a particularly good place to see them. It is estimated that nearly 1000 humpbacks pass Cape Vidal between mid-June and late August, with peak viewing in the second half of July. Southern right whales can be seen cavorting just metres from the shore in False Bay, off the Cape Peninsula. They start arriving at the end of May and stay in the region up until November. Peak viewing is in October. Blue-grey Bryde's whales, black on grey humpbacks and black and white killer whales also visit the bay. You might also see bottlenose dolphins on the east side of the bay and dusky dolphins on the west.

West False Bay. The Muizenberg–Simon's Town coastal road, Boyes Drive above St James and Kalk Bay, and the coastal road from Simon's Town to Cape Point frequently provide outstanding whale watching. In particular, the coastal walkway from Muizenberg to St James, Kalk Bay's harbour wall, and the walkways at Fish Hoek, can give excellent views. Kalk Bay, Fish Hoek and Muizenberg were once all open-boat whaling stations.

East False Bay. The coastal road from Gordon's Bay to Cape Hangklip, the easternmost point of False Bay, provides outstanding views of southern right whales. South of Hangklip is Stony Point, once the site of a whaling station and now home to a breeding colony of Jackass penguins.

Atlantic Coast. The coastline from Yzerfontein to Cape Point provides numerous opportunities to watch whales. The coastal road between Sea Point and Scarborough takes you through Hout Bay and along Chapman's Peak Drive, which has some of the finest sea views in the Western Cape and has plenty of sites for whale spotting. Whales perform a variety of antics and on a good day you might see them putting on a show with many of the following:

> *Breaching:* This is probably their most impressive performance. They leap clear out of the water like a trout or salmon with an arching back flip and fall back into the sea with a thunderous splash. Whales often breach four or five times in a row.
>
> *Lobtailing:* Slapping their flukes on the surface, creating a sound that carries for a considerable distance.
>
> *Spyhopping:* Standing vertically with head and body, as far as the flippers, above the surface. This gives them a whale's-eye view of their surroundings.
>
> *Blowing:* Exhaling and then inhaling through the blowholes when surfacing.
>
> *Grunting:* Emitting a roaring sound that can be heard 1–2km away, especially at night.
>
> *Mating:* Groups of whales may often be seen interacting in the mating season, when several males may attempt to mate with a single female.

A pamphlet sponsored by Safmarine detailing whale-watching spots is available from the Captour Information Bureau in Adderley Street, Cape Town, tel (021) 418-5214.

GREAT WHITE SHARK WATCHING

It is estimated that there are more sharks in the seas and oceans of the world than there are people on Earth — but the chances of a fatal, or even dangerous, encounter with one are pretty remote; more people die each year from bee stings. There are about 350 species roaming the world's oceans, but only about 27 of these have been implicated in attacks on man — and only half a dozen of these species have been recorded in South Africa.

The most feared of them is *Carcharodon carcharias*, which used to be known in South Africa as the Blue Pointer, but since US moviemaker Peter Gimble terrified audiences around the world with his film *Blue Water White Death* it is known as the Great White, or White Death. It is unlikely that swimming, snorkelling or scuba diving you will ever have the privilege of seeing one of these beauties, unless you join a shark-watching expedition and glimpse one from the safety of an underwater cage. Thrill-seekers are doing just this in a variety of spots along the South African coastline known to be the regular haunts of these efficient killing machines. In 1991, South Africa became the first country in the world to declare the Great White a protected species, but there is no doubt that they had long before fallen prey to efforts by fishermen, divers and others to exterminate them, or at least reduce their numbers.

The South African record for the Blue Pointer brought to the gaff by a shore-based angler after a six-hour battle was the 753kg/1660lb specimen caught off Durban back in 1953, a baby compared to the 11.8m/39ft monster caught in the 1930s off Hawaii.

In 1962, the biggest Great White ever recorded from South African waters was harpooned while it was feeding on a dead whale 210km/130 miles off Durban. This was only 4.8m/16ft-long, but it weighed in at a whopping 3175kg/7000lb. The world angling record for a Great White is 1208kg/2664lb.

Dyer Island and neighbouring Geyser Island, near Gansbaai in the south-western Cape, are home to colonies of penguins and Cape fur seals. The seals of these islands are a natural attraction for Great Whites and the predators are particularly prolific in the vicinity of the islands. Seals and other large mammals such as dolphins form an important part of the Great White's diet; but contrary to popular belief, human beings do not. Great White attacks on humans are rare and only one has ever been recorded in the vicinity of Dyer Island.

Maybe it is the Great White's unwarranted reputation as a man-eater that encourages tourists to pay up to R800 a time for the thrill of diving with these supreme predators. The channel between Dyer and Geyser islands is shallow and usually calm and an ideal place to watch patrolling sharks from the safety of a small wire cage. Cages are level with the surface of the water, making it possible for non-divers to observe the sharks with only a mask and snorkel. The cage, which can hold two divers, is roped to the boat and large sacks containing bait are dumped within three metres of the vessel.

The sharks are attracted by what is known as chumming. This entails pouring buckets of mashed pilchards, blood and offal into the sea. This usually brings curious sharks circling. It is not uncommon to see up to eight Great Whites in a single day when cage diving. The sharks come within a metre of the circular cage and — if they take the bait — put on a thrilling show, thrashing the water with their giant tails and displaying their fearsome jaws. If you have had the privilege of seeing these monsters in their natural habitat you can buy a tee-shirt announcing *I dived with a Great White Shark in South Africa* — which must be the ultimate in one-upmanship.

Further east along the southern coast, Mossel Bay also has a growing cage-diving fraternity. About 1.5km/0.9 miles from the beach is a small rocky island that is home to some 5000 seals. This is a favoured place for lowering shark-watchers into the icy waters for their eyeball-to-eyeball thrills, and divers see great Whites on virtually every outing. Up to 11 of the monsters have been spotted here on a good day. Only eight shark attacks have been reported in the area since 1927. In the three years since cage-diving started in Mossel Bay there has been only one definite attack, and this was on a surfer who swam ashore after a Great White bit a chunk out of his board. Shark-watching dives in South Africa are much cheaper than in California or Australia, which also have big Great White populations.

TRIBAL VILLAGES

Traditional tribal lifestyles and dwellings are rapidly becoming a thing of the past, but it is still possible to visit — and stay in — re-creations of the vanishing villages in various parts of the country. For details of tribal villages in particular provinces see page 332 (KwaZulu-Natal), page 298 (the Free State), page 202 (Gauteng) and page 226 (Mpumalanga).

THE CRADLE OF MANKIND

Many people believe that South Africa can justly claim to be the cradle of mankind; others, that the hominids who were our remote ancestors sprang from the plains of East Africa. Whatever the merits of either claim, one thing seems certain: Man's earliest roots were in Africa. World famous palaeo-anthropologist Professor Phillip Tobias, of the University of the Witwatersrand, says, 'It is not a question of South Africa versus East Africa; the emergence of human beings is a pan-African phenomenon. This was the continent which was the cradle of humanity, perhaps four to five million years ago.'

The discovery in the past few years of new sites puts South Africa on centre stage in world evolutionary studies and these are expected to draw scientists and visitors in what Professor Tobias has dubbed the new field of palaeo-tourism. American Dr Lee Berger is working at Gladysvale, which lies within a privately-owned game reserve, and South African Dr Andre Keyser is digging at Drimolen, two sites within a dozen kilometres of Sterkfontein (see page 203), and the latest to yield early human teeth and bones. There must be a hundred other known sites waiting to be explored.

Professor Tobias and Dr Berger are prime movers behind the development of palaeo-tourism. They and their eminent colleagues — among them Dr Ron Clarke, Dr Kathy Kuman and Dr Francis Thackeray — will conduct tours to famous and historic caves near Johannesburg and to more distant sites, including Makapansgat, Cave of Hearths, Buffalo Cave, Ficus Cave and Peppercorn Cave, all of which lie amid beautiful bushveld surroundings near the Kruger National Park. Parties of up to 25 people are usual at US$1000 a day, which includes a visit to Wits Medical School to see prehistoric 'Crown Jewels' such as the Taung skull, *Australopithecus* remains from Makapansgat and Sterkfontein, and fossils of the first known modern humans from Border Cave, on the KwaZulu-Swaziland border, and dated at 100,000 years. Money raised in this way is used to further research.

Contact Professor Phillip Tobias, Dr Lee Berger, or Dr Ron Clarke at the Palaeo-Anthropology Research Group, University of the Witwatersrand, Medical School, 7 York Road, Parktown 2193, Johannesburg, Gauteng, tel (011) 647-2516 and (011) 647-2017, fax (011) 643-4318, e-mail 055pvts@chiron.wits.ac.za

Archaeological Sites. Although there are many Stone Age sites around the country the National Monuments Council stipulates that only a few open archaeological excavations can be visited by the public. Sterkfontein is one and the neighbouring site of Swartkrans can be seen by appointment. Others are the Doornlagte Stone Age site of the McGregor Museum in Kimberley; the Wonderwerk Cave, near Kuruman, in the Northern Cape; and the Matjies River rock shelter, a few kilometres east of the Robberg Peninsula, in the Western Cape. All of these sites have been declared national monuments. You can visit a number of other sites by prior arrangement — Kromdraai, Makapansgat, Florisbad and Mapungubwe — and there is no problem if you want to visit caves and rock shelters where excavations have been abandoned.

MUSEUMS AND ART GALLERIES

South Africa is endowed with a variety of major museums and art galleries, all reflecting the country's collective memory and culture. These include the South African Art Gallery in Cape Town, the Transvaal Museum in Pretoria, the National English Literature Museum in Grahamstown, the Afrikaanse Taalmuseum (language museum) at Paarl, and MuseumAfrica in Johannesburg. All of these museums and many more are described in the provincial chapters. On International Museum Day on 18 May museums throughout the country present special programmes and exhibitions.

Art Galleries. South African art is an eclectic range of styles, from classical and contemporary Western to distinctly African. As with South African painting, sculpture finds its inspiration both in Western international trends and in African traditional art. Painters and sculptors are now in a transitional period, which is seeing a struggle to fuse the two influences into one distinctively indigenous art form.

A roll call of the country's better known modern painters, sculptors and ceramic artists of all population groups would total about 200 names. Many of these have studied abroad and introduced modern styles and themes. Trevor Makhoba is a leading painter in the new South Africa. Winner of the 1991 Natal Biennale and the 1996 Standard Bank Young Artist award, Makhoba has exhibited in New York and Cairo, and is regarded by the critics as one of the country's most incisive commentators on social and political change. Other rising stars are Jackson Hlungwane and Simon Morobe.

There are numerous art galleries of various types in all major centres. Important collections of Africana include the Strange Collection in Johannesburg and the William Fehr Collection in Cape Town, as well as collections in the MuseumAfrica in Johannesburg, Koopmans De Wet House in Cape Town, and the Museum of Culture in Pretoria. The two best-known galleries are undoubtedly the South African National Gallery in Cape Town, and the Johannesburg Art Gallery, set in a garden enclave not far from the city centre.

The best of the books on South African art is Grania Ogilvie's *Dictionary of South African Painters & Sculptors*. If you are interested in early South African painting, get Alfred Gordon-Brown's *Pictorial Africana*. Africana prints are well covered up to 1870 by RF Kennedy's *Catalogue of Prints in the Africana Museum* available from MuseumAfrica at R125 (£16.65/$27.50).

BUSHMAN (SAN) ROCK ART

South Africa's earliest and greatest art treasure is its wealth of rock art, which compares favourably with the more famous cave art at Lascaux, in the Dordogne, France, and in the caves of Altamira — the 'Sistine Chapel of prehistoric art' — in northern Spain.

The rock art of the Bushmen (San) has been described as probably the most striking and exquisitely detailed hunter-gatherer art in the world. Their paintings and engravings are found in thousands of natural rock galleries all over South Africa and fascinate and awe viewers from all over the world with their uncanny rendition of animals and people. Striking characteristics of Bushman art are boldness and simplicity. With a limited palette of natural pigments — their reds and yellows came from iron oxides, white from fine clay or ground sea shells, and black from manganese oxide and bone charcoal — these vanished artists deftly brought to life scenes around them, not only by the use of vibrant colours, but often by incorporating a swelling or bulge in the rock to suggest vigorous movement and life. There are two types of rock art: petroglyphs (engravings) comprising pecked or incised images of animals, human figures and geometric symbols engraved into dolomite rocks; and paintings of human figures and animals on the walls of open shelters under boulders and over-hangs. There is much academic debate about why these stylised paintings and engravings were originally done, often in perilous and inaccessible places.

Most experts, however, agree that they were not meant to be simply pretty pictures, done to amuse or be admired; their significance is thought to be occult, or shamanistic, representing the Bushman's deeply felt identification with the animals he hunted and the rituals he used to achieve power over them. They played an important role in the Bushman's rich spiritual life and the little hunters believed their favourite, the huge eland, chief among all animals and their link to the creator of all things. Some of the finest of their paintings are dominated by this, the largest of the African antelopes, which is the most frequently painted animal in the Drakensberg galleries. Apart from hunting scenes, another common theme in rock art is the trance dance of clan shamans, or medicine men, who danced until they were transformed and entered a terrifying supernatural world. Rock paintings often depict half-man, half-animal figures representing the medicine man in a trance hallucination where he is merging with his animal power.

South Africa has one of the largest and richest rock art traditions in the world with more than 15,000 recognised sites with rock paintings and rock engravings ranging in age from 20,000 years to paintings done as recently as 100 years ago. The oldest definitively dated rock art in Africa is in neighbouring Namibia and is 27,000 years old. Dating accurately is a difficult business, as the rock art fragments have to be found buried alongside other, carbon-dateable remains and this is a rare occurrence. The oldest are thought to be those that depict animals in profile, usually done in a single colour. The most spectacular are usually from the final stage of the Bushman art tradition. These are the shaded polychrome paintings from the Eastern Cape mountains and the Drakensberg and are the paintings most people associate with rock art.

The biggest concentrations of this vivid and often startling art are found in the eastern and southern Free State, the Drakensberg, the Eastern Cape — particularly the north-east region — and the Koue Bokkeveld of the Western Cape. The sites are invariably sited inland, in the areas where the little hunters dug for nut-grass and ran down the fat buck. Sandstone caves and shelters with fine-grained, smooth walls were favoured galleries.

Good examples of Bushman rock art can be seen in the eastern Free State, which not only has a wide range of rock shelters but, equally importantly, they are reasonably accessible without strenuous feats of mountaineering. Many prime works of rock art in the Drakensberg, for example, are at remote sites in terrain forbidding to all but the fittest and most ardent enthusiast. There is no established guiding industry in this field, although some tour companies include one or two sites on their itineraries. The Natal Parks Board has several rock sites under its management and can arrange viewing trips under the supervision of knowledgeable NPB wardens.

A rich area for rock paintings is in the upper valley of the Bushmans River. Within 4km/2.5 miles of the guest huts in the Giant's Castle Game Reserve are some 20 painted rock shelters. Get directions from local residents, game rangers or forest officers. Proprietors and managers of hostels and hotels usually know rock art sites in their area. Other sites in the Drakensberg include The Cavern, the Stream shelter in the Cathedral Peak area, Sunday's Falls Christmas Cave in the Game Pass Valley, near the south end of the Giant's Castle Game Reserve. Battle Cave is in the Injasuti Valley (one of the remotest sites, but it has some of the best preserved paintings). For those who do not want to scramble to sites the Royal Natal Park Museum has a display of rock paintings removed from the Ebusingata shelter.

Near Elliot, in the Eastern Cape, is a 32m/105ft-long gallery of beautifully detailed rock paintings, which can be viewed on the farm Denorbin, between Barkly East and Elliot.

There are numerous caves in the Hex River Valley, and many in the sandstone cliffs of the Piketberg Range on such farms as Bushman's Hollow, Langeberg, Bangkop and Staweklip. In the Olifants Valley are paintings depicting Europeans in the costumes of 250 years ago.

In the area around Beaufort West in the Karoo are a number of interesting rock shelters and there are paintings of horses, ostriches and game at Grootplaat, on the town commonage.

At Driekops Island in the Riet River, east of Douglas, are hundreds of stylised rock engravings. The site is reached via a turn-off on the main Douglas–Kimberley road marked Plooysburg.

In the Outeniqua Mountains are some unusual paintings, which apparently depict women with fish-tails; the paintings in the Queenstown are among some of the finest known; Barkly East also has some superb galleries. Among the last paintings to be done by Bushmen to the south of Ugie are some depicting ox-wagons and redcoat soldiers. There are others in the Echo Caves, not far from the Blyde River Holiday Resort and faded paintings in the Kruger National Park. In the Wonderwerk Cave, near Kuruman, in the Northern Cape, engraved stone fragments have been positively dated as being 10,000 years old; there are excellent paintings 5km/3 miles from Schweizer-Reneke.

One of the most puzzling aspects of rock art distribution in the south-western Cape — where there is a wealth of it between the coastal plain and the Karoo — is the virtual absence of paintings on or around the Cape Peninsula. The nearest of any note are situated well to the north-east in the mountains of the Cape Fold Belt, although there are plenty of Later Stone Age occupation sites on the Peninsula and no lack of sandstone shelters and recesses on Table Mountain. The lack of rock art on the Peninsula, apart from rudimentary examples at Peer's Cave on Skildergatkop, near Fish Hoek, is an enigma. These at Peers Cave are the only examples within 100km/62 miles of the Peninsula.

On a rock overhang in Garcia Pass, 14km/9 miles north of Riversdale on the road to Ladismith, is the Cave of Hands, so called because of its Bushman handprints.

In Die Hel (The Abyss) is a large cave adorned with scenes of hunters and elephants. This was an important Bushman centre as it was a source of pigments used in their art.

A comprehensive collection of rock art photographs is housed in the Woodhouse Gallery of the Anderson Museum in Dordrecht, Eastern Cape, between Aliwal North and East London. These photographs represent 40 years of exploration and recording by noted rock art author and photographer Bert Woodhouse and are representative of sites throughout the whole of South Africa. The exhibits provide the perfect overview and should enable you to decide which site you want to visit. As the majority of rock art sites are on private property, farms and reserves, local help to find them and get the requisite permission is a necessity. The secretary at the Anderson Museum, Lorna Bradfield, is a mine of information and more than willing to help. Write to her at PO Box 215, Dordrecht 5435, Eastern Cape, tel (045) 943-1746, or the Curator, Anderson Museum, c/o Municipality, Grey Street, Dordrecht 5435.

Bert Woodhouse is president of the Institute for the Study of Man in Africa (Isma), which can be contacted at Room 2B10, University of the Witwatersrand Medical School, York Road, Parktown, Johannesburg 2193, Gauteng, tel (011) 647-2203.

There is also a Rock Art Research Unit (RARU) at the University of the Witwatersrand. Neil Lee, well known for his work in photographing and recording rock paintings all over southern Africa over the past 35 years, donated his collection of more than 15,000 colour slides to the Unit. These have been incorporated into material already held, and augment what is arguably the largest and most important archive of Bushman painting records in the world. Contact the RARU at Private Bag 3, Wits 2050, Gauteng, tel (011) 716-1111, fax (011) 716-8030. Neil Lee leads tours to rock art sites and can be contacted at Unit 129, PO Box 4215, Randburg 2125, Gauteng, tel (011) 792-6992.

As all sites fall under the National Monuments Council, Dr Janette Deacon, who has special responsibility for rock art at the Council, can also be approached for information. Contact her at PO Box 4637, Cape Town 8000, tel (021) 462-4502, fax (021) 462-4509.

An association that welcomes visitors to its meetings and field trips is the Friends of Rock Art (Rocustos), in Pretoria, run by National Cultural History Museum archaeologist Ansie Steyn, who specialises in indigenous art and history. Ansie, as an accredited Satour eco-tourism guide, also takes individuals and small groups on private tours of rock art sites. Contact her at 356 Hill Street, Arcadia 0083, Gauteng, tel (012) 43-3417 and (012) 341-1320, fax (012) 341-6146.

Satour-registered guides Tessa Redman and Australian Trevor Earl, operating out of Cape Town, include visits to Bushman sites in their wilderness adventure tours. The Cedarberg mountain range, about 50km/31 miles inland from the Atlantic coastline, and the Koue Bokkeveld Mountains, south of Citrusdal, contain excellent examples of rock paintings and are on their tour itineraries. Some of the sites cannot be reached by road, and their actual locations are kept secret, but a number are accessible, with nearby accommodation ranging from campsites and self-catering chalets, to five-star lodges. Both areas have lots of walking and hiking trails; mountain biking is also available, and the area is famous for its weird sandstone formations, magnificent fynbos and wildflowers. Set aside at least three days to enjoy this wilderness where the Bushmen roamed 6000 years ago. You can visit sites in the Bushmanskloof Private Game Reserve, and at Kagga Kamma, where a Bushmen clan still lives.

Contact Tours and Trails, PO Box 50239, Waterfront 8002, Western Cape, tel (021) 47-6755, fax (021) 47-3561, Cell 082 894-0039.

Bert Woodhouse is a name to look for if you want to read about rock art. He has written seven books on the subject, including the acclaimed *The Rain and its Creatures*, and his *Rock Art of the Golden Gate and Clarens Districts* is a good introduction to the sites of the eastern Free State.

STEAM TRAINS

South Africa is one of the last strongholds of the steam locomotive and steam buffs pour in from all over the world to view, and ride on, these beauties of what is a bygone age of travel in most other countries. If you are one of these enthusiasts your first port of call should be the Transnet Museum in the old railway station in Johannesburg (see page 194). Apart from its fascinating collection of rail relics and mementoes, what the staff there do not know about steam trains in South Africa is not worth knowing, and they can point you in the right direction for a wide variety of nostalgic trips.

Transnet Heritage Foundation in the museum is the preservation arm of Spoornet, the national railway network, and has bases in Cape Town, Johannesburg and George. From Cape Town the foundation runs Union Limited's steam-hauled trains on long distance 14-day safaris, as well as the six-day *Golden Thread* trains along the Garden Route. Tours depart from Cape Town and travel through Worcester and George to Knysna, and then climb the spectacular Montagu pass over the Outeniqua Mountains between George and Oudtshoorn. Accommodation on all Union Limited

Steam Railtours trips is in first-class four-berth compartments (maximum of two persons for space and comfort) and two-berth coupes (with one person). Contact Union Limited Steam Railtours, PO Box 4325, Cape Town 8000, tel (021) 405-4391. From George the *Outeniqua Choo-Tjoe* runs along the preserved scenic George to Knysna branch line. Daily departures are from Monday to Saturday from both towns, crossing each other at the little coastal town of Sedgefield. Motive power on this line is limited to the lighter classes of locomotive. The Outeniqua Choo-Tjoe is one of the more popular of the remaining steam trains in the country. Steam enthusiasts are in their element on this line and everyone enjoys the splendid views of lakes, forests, beaches and cliffs on the train's coastal route between George and Knysna. The one-way trip takes just over three hours. Tickets can be bought at George and Knysna railway stations. George, tel (0441) 73-8288; Knysna, tel (0445) 21361.

Other popular outings are on the *Banana Express* and the *Apple Express* (see page 93).

The following are some of the main groups and companies operating steam train excursions:

Alfred County Railway: Privatised narrow gauge railway from Port Shepstone to Harding. Regular steam trips from Port Shepstone to Izotsha, as well as to Paddock. Contact PO Box 572, Port Shepstone 4240, KwaZulu-Natal, tel (03931) 76443.

The *Champagne Express* steam train runs 30km between Paarl and Franschhoek, Western Cape, tel (02212) 3000 or Paarl Publicity Association, tel (02211) 24842/23829.

Friends of the Rail: Steam enthusiasts group at Capital Park loco depot, Pretoria, run regular steam trips from Pretoria to Cullinan, Oberon and Warmbaths. Contact Courtenay Champion, tel (012) 46-5988.

Hartebeespoort Steam Train, tel (012) 315-2432.

Magalies Valley Steamer, tel (011) 773-9238.

Magaliesburg Express, tel (011) 888-1145. From Johannesburg there are regular steam specials to Magaliesburg. PO Box 3753, Johannesburg 2000, Gauteng, tel (011) 774-2649.

Natal Railway Museum, Hilton Station, Pietermaritzburg, KwaZulu-Natal: Monthly steam trips from Hilton to a variety of destinations every second Sunday of the month (except May to October). Details from Allen Duff, PO Balgowan 3275, KwaZulu-Natal, tel (033234) 4110.

Oosterlyn Express: Steam trips every Sunday from Waterval Boven to Waterval Onder and return. Depart Waterval Boven at 11am, arrive Waterval Onder 11.30am. Depart Waterval Onder at midday, arrive Waterval Boven 12.30pm. Contact (01362) and ask for 14 or tel (013262) and ask for 176.

Reef Steamers: Steam enthusiast group at Germiston locomotive depot run monthly steam trips from Johannesburg to Potchefstroom Dam. Contact Richard Hamilton, PO Box 14564, Farramere 1518, Gauteng, tel (011) 315-2620.

Rovos Rail: Luxury rail travel Cape Town–Pretoria–Victoria Falls, as well as Pretoria–Mpumalanga, and Cape Town–Knysna. Regular steam on trains out of Pretoria. One of the world's great trains. See page 92 for details.

South African National Railway and Steam Museum (SANRASM): Volunteer group has open days on the first Sunday of each month, with 15km/9 mile round trip steam rides, also day trips to Magaliesburg. Contact PO Box 1419, Roosevelt Park 2129, Gauteng, tel (011) 888-1154.

Steamnet 2000: Occasional steam trains on the Kimberley to De Aar line. Contact J Schrenk, PO Box 2534, Kimberley 8300, Northern Cape, tel (0531) 23044.

Trains Galore: Charter train operator often uses steam locomotives. Contact Cathy or Geoff Pethick, PO Box 3136, Witbeeck 1729, Gauteng, tel (011) 762-2351.

Trans Karoo (Johannesburg to Cape Town): Steam haulage on Fridays Johannesburg to Klerksdorp. Depart Johannesburg 12.30pm, arrive Krugersdorp 3.56pm. Return

Saturday, depart Klerksdorp 6.56am arriving Johannesburg 10.15am. Possibly the last regularly steam-hauled express train in the world. Contact Spoornet, Marketing Manager, Main Line Trains, PO Box 2671, Joubert Park 2044, Gauteng, tel (011) 773-2944.

Umgeni Steam Railway: Pinetown, Durban, KwaZulu-Natal. Monthly steam trips operate on the last Sunday of each month between Kloof and Botha's Hill. Contact Jeremy Hathorn, PO Box 33202, Montclair 4061, KwaZulu-Natal, tel (031) 309-1817 (a/h).

As well as these Union Limited runs other regular day tours, such as Heidelberg Express, Port Elizabeth's Green Apple Express, the Jacaranda Express (Johannesburg–Cullinan), and the Strelitzia Steam train (Durban–Kelso).

BOTANICAL WONDERS

South Africa has six distinct biomes, or fairly uniform land communities, formed by climatic influence:

Forest. This is the smallest biome in South Africa, containing less than 1% of the country, and is covered by indigenous trees. Most of this forest is in the Knysna area of the southern Cape and further east.

Fynbos. This is a word (fine bush) used for heath-like vegetation and is usually confined to mountainous areas. Most people associate *fynbos* with the Cape.

Grassland. Veld dominated by grasses. Although grasslands are found in the eastern parts of South Africa they are particularly characteristic of the central plateau area of the country.

Nama Karoo. This covers the grass shrubveld of Namaland in Namibia and the Karoo region of South Africa, where it provides grazing for sheep and goats.

Savanna. Most of this biome is in the summer rainfall areas, and its grasses, scrub and trees are the favoured habitat of most game animals.

Succulent Karoo. This is the winter rainfall area of the Karoo. The number of succulent plant species in this biome is among the highest in the world. The landscape is flat to undulating and lies mainly west of the western escarpment.

Without too much effort you can see the attractions of many of these biomes in the space of an hour or two by visiting Kirstenbosch National Botanical Garden on the eastern slopes of Table Mountain, 12km/7.5 miles from Cape Town, in the suburb of Newlands. This magnificent 560-hectare garden grows plants from all over South Africa — in addition to the Cape flora, about a third of South Africa's 24,000 indigenous species — and is one of the finest in the world, being known as the Kew of the southern hemisphere (see page 402).

Kirstenbosch is the headquarters of a nationwide network of eight regional National Botanic Gardens, which in 1992 amalgamated with the National Botanical Research Institute to form the new National Botanical Institute. The Institute has valuable, living plant collections, as well as the largest and best documented collections of preserved plant specimens, and the most complete botanical libraries and data banks in Africa. A highlight of their research is the tissue culture of rare and endangered plants, which makes it possible to propagate thousands of identical plants from the growth tissue of a single specimen.

As well as Kirstenbosch, there are seven other national gardens: the Karoo National Botanic Garden is at Worcester (100km/62 miles from Cape Town) and is devoted to semi-desert and succulent flora; the Harold Porter National Botanic Garden, at Betty's Bay, Western Cape, which has one of the densest concentrations of *fynbos* in the area; the 57-hectare Free State National Botanic Garden; the Natal National Botanic Garden in Pietermaritzburg, which started in 1870; the 154-hectare Lowveld National Botanic Garden at the confluence of the Nel and Crocodile rivers in Mpumalanga, which was established in 1969 and has one of the largest collections of indigenous trees in the country; the Witwatersrand National Botanic Garden, within easy reach of Johannesburg, which has a dramatic 70m/230ft waterfall as a scenic backdrop to its trees and aloes; and the Pretoria National Botanic Garden, 8km/5 miles outside the city, which covers 76 hectares on Silverton Ridge. Between them, these regional gardens represent the many variations of South Africa's soil, climate and vegetation.

Other gardens developed and maintained by local and provincial governments include the Wilds Botanic Garden in Johannesburg, the Johannesburg Botanic Garden in Emmarentia, the Melville Koppies Nature Reserve, Johannesburg, and the Municipal Botanic Garden in Durban. All are well worth visiting.

Viewing tips. Apart from the season — not all regions flower at the same time — flowering is dependent on the weather. Wind and cold prevent flowers from opening, even if it is sunny. Travel with the sun at your back as the flowers always face the sun, which makes the best viewing time between 11am and 3pm. Flowers vary from region to region, with expanses of daisies typical of the Namaqualand region, and *fynbos* more common in the south-west.

Namaqualand: South African Wildflower Guide by Annelise le Roux and Ted Schelpe (published by the Botanical Society of South Africa in association with the National Botanical Institute), and *Wild Flowers of South Africa*, by JP Rourke, of the National Botanical Institute, Kirstenbosch (Struik, Cape Town 1996) are two good introductory books.

Cape Floral Kingdom. Botanists recognise six major plant kingdoms on Earth, the largest of which is the Boreal Kingdom of the northern hemisphere containing about 10,500 plant species and occupying 40% of the Earth's surface, but in this instance small is beautiful. The tiny Cape Floral Kingdom, or Cape *fynbos*, covers a mere 90,000sq km/34,740sq miles and is the only kingdom to be found entirely within the borders of one country. This botanical wonder contains an incredible 8600 plant species, more than the famed Amazon Basin, and at least a thousand of them are described as rare. Probably the most famous family found in the *fynbos* is the Proteaceae. As similar plants are found elsewhere in the southern hemisphere palaeo-botanists and geologists believe this could be proof that the continents of the southern hemisphere did at one time form the immense land mass known as Gondwanaland. The *Protea* is South Africa's national emblem. In 1605 it became the first South African plant to be described and illustrated by a European botanist.

Many of the unique plants in the Cape Floral Kingdom are bizarre-looking; almost without exception they have magnificent flowers. Since many of these plants are small and not easily seen from the windows of a speeding vehicle, and since many interesting plants grow off the beaten track, you usually need the guidance and interpretive skills of a specialist to enjoy these wonders to the full. Few are more qualified than botanist Penny Mustart, who acts as an eco-tour consultant and guide to the floral kingdom of the Western Cape and is a registered Specialist Environment Guide. She plans nature-based eco-tours that are tailor-made around your special interests. As well as a guided tour of the area's spectacular plant biodiversity, you can see *Protea* farming, birdlife and Bushman rock art, and sample local wines. Specialists in these fields are co-opted from local universities and conservation organisations to guide you. Group size is kept to a minimum (6–16) and travel is in comfortable, air-conditioned mini-buses or coaches. Alternatively, Penny will accompany you in your own vehicle to act as your own private guide.

Some of the stunning areas that Penny has intimate knowledge of are the Cedarberg and the Agulhas Plain. The Cedarberg is a scenic, mountainous wilderness area about 200km/124 miles north of Cape Town. It is renowned for its rock formations, and is an area rich in plants and rock art. Trips to this area also include visits to the Wuppertal, a remote and charming mission station village well known to

South Africans for the stout *velskoen* (hide shoes) made there, as well as to Clanwilliam, the home of *rooibos* (red bush) tea and the only area in the world where it is grown. For those who are interested, a special trip to see the dwarf, succulent plants of the *Knervlakte* (Plain of the Gnashing of Teeth) can be organised. Other trips in this area include a visit to Lambert's Bay on the West Coast for seal and bird watching. There are gannet colonies and, in season, Greater and Lesser Flamingoes. The Agulhas Plain, about 200km/124 miles east of Cape Town, is the undiscovered jewel of the Western Cape.

The Agulhas Plain is situated at the southernmost tip of Africa, between Hermanus and Arniston. Some 2000 indigenous plant species grow here, and more than 100 of them are found nowhere else on Earth. The trip includes a visit to the attractive mission village of Elim, home of a unique type of dwarf *fynbos* — and a community that still bakes bread and makes food in the old way — and a diverse coastal limestone flora. There is also the attraction of game and wetlands bird life, and in season there is whale-watching. Contact Cape Specialist Ecotours, PO Box 326, Rondebosch 7701, Western Cape, tel/fax (021) 689-2978.

See page 408 for details of flower shows and gardens throughout the Western Cape.

Cycads. These fern-like plants with a fruit that looks like a pineapple are South Africa's rarest plants. Their ancestors were growing as long ago as 300 million years. In 1915, between 400 and 500 of these prehistoric relics were collected from all over the country and planted out at Kirstenbosch, where you can see them today. It is estimated that there are fewer than 10,000 individual plants left in the wild of the 30 surviving South African species, and these are threatened by illegal collecting and sales. A cycad conservation project was launched in 1992 by the National Botanical Institute to protect and conserve the plants by propagating and cultivating them in the National Botanical Gardens as threatened species. The tallest and most famous cycads grow in a forest near Duiwelskloof, in the Northern Province, where some are 13m/43ft tall. These cycads have had royal protection from successive tribal queens (all named Modjadji) of the Lobedu people.

Palms. A favourite destination for lovers of palm trees is the swamp forest at Mtunzini, about 150km/93 miles north of Durban, on KwaZulu-Natal's sub-tropical coast. The palm colony was started in 1916 by a local magistrate in the mistaken belief that the species was the raffia palm, whose fibre could be used to make brooms and brushes. Although the plants flourished, the fibre was too short to use and commercial interest petered out. The original handful of palms has grown into a prolific grove as a result of the helpful activities of palmnut vultures and the vervet monkeys, which scatter the seeds after eating the fruit. The magnificent palms at Mtunzini have been declared a national monument.

BLACK TOWNSHIPS

It is now possible to visit Soweto, the Johannesburg township that came to epitomise the oppression and injustice of the apartheid era. See page 193 for details.

WILDLIFE

One of South Africa's main attractions is its abundant wildlife in scenery stunning in its beauty and diversity. Nine out of ten people come to experience just this and while other attractions never pall it is the lure of the 'Big Five' — elephant, white rhino,

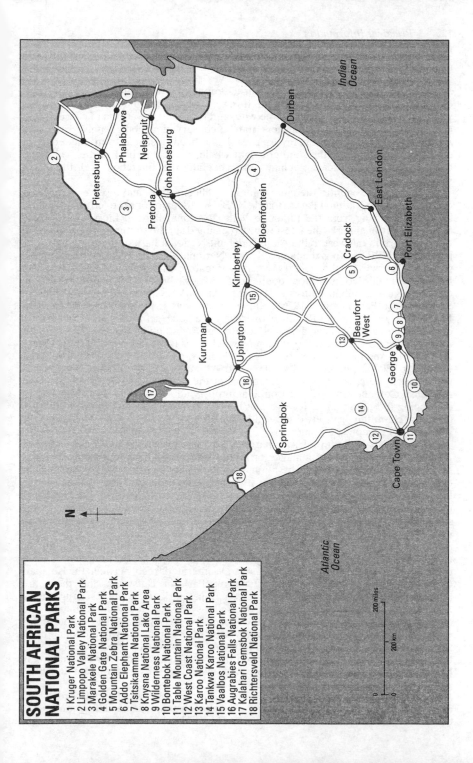

SOUTH AFRICAN NATIONAL PARKS

1 Kruger National Park
2 Limpopo Valley National Park
3 Marakele National Park
4 Golden Gate National Park
5 Mountain Zebra National Park
6 Addo Elephant National Park
7 Tsitsikamma National Park
8 Knysna National Lake Area
9 Wilderness National Park
10 Bontebok National Park
11 Table Mountain National Park
12 West Coast National Park
13 Karoo National Park
14 Tankwa Karoo National Park
15 Vaalbos National Park
16 Augrabies Falls National Park
17 Kalahari Gemsbok National Park
18 Richtersveld National Park

N

Indian Ocean

Atlantic Ocean

Durban

East London

Port Elizabeth

Cradock

Bloemfontein

Kimberley

Beaufort West

George

Cape Town

Springbok

Upington

Kuruman

Pretoria

Johannesburg

Nelspruit

Phalaborwa

Pietersburg

200 miles

200 km

lion, buffalo and leopard — and the countless other species of game, bird, reptile and plant that entrances and captivates. South Africa's wildlife can be seen in its natural habitat in the national parks and nature reserves, some of which are privately owned. South Africa has an enviable and well earned reputation as a country in the forefront of wildlife conservation and protection. It is, for example, the only country left where you can be sure of seeing rhinos in the wild, and thanks to the efforts of conservation authorities, zoos, private landowners, nature conservation bodies, universities and various other institutions, many species have been rescued from the edge of extinction, among them the southern right whale, the leatherback turtle, white and black rhinos, the African elephant, the cheetah, the bontebok and the black wildebeest.

Throughout the country there are some magnificent parks and reserves set up and controlled by the National Parks Board (NPB) — 18 major ones covering 3.6 million hectares stretching from the Limpopo Valley National Park in the north to Table Mountain National Park (the latest to be proclaimed) in the south; from Richtersveld National Park in the west to the Addo Elephant National Park in the south-east. The jewel in the NPB crown is the famed Kruger National Park tucked up in the topmost north-east corner of the country where Zimbabwe and Mozambique abut. The Kruger National Park is without doubt South Africa's best known tourist attraction, drawing nearly a million visitors every year. The park was founded by an Act of the South African Parliament in 1926, although as early as 1898, when Paul Kruger was President of the Transvaal Republic, districts were being set aside for the protection of game. The park covers an area of 19,685sq km/7690sq miles, which makes it about the size of Wales, or slightly larger than New Jersey. It is the largest wildlife sanctuary in the world, and it contains more than a million large game animals, including about 1500 lions, 7800 elephants and 15,000 buffalo. Although it bears his name, the park is not so much the creation of Paul Kruger as of the distinguished British soldier and naturalist Colonel James Stevenson Hamilton, who devoted most of his life to developing the then remote reserve that is now a comfortable four-hour drive from Gauteng. Hamilton privately dismissed Kruger as having 'never in his life thought of wild animals except as biltong.'

The emphasis in South Africa's national parks is placed on the preservation of natural assets and the maintenance of natural processes. Included in the accepted definition, however, is that conservation is a human activity performed for the benefit of mankind. Within the framework of its conservation mandate the National Parks Board makes national parks as accessible as possible to all people. The variety of topography and habitats in the parks is deliberate; the purpose of the national parks system is the conservation of representative areas and ecosystems in as pristine a state as possible. There are plans to extend existing parks and, if possible, acquire and proclaim new ones. The possibilities include trans-frontier parks such as a 'mirror image' of the Kruger National Park across the Mozambique border and the extension of Richtersveld into Namibia. Game has always migrated freely between the Kalahari Gemsbok Park and the adjacent Gemsbok Park in Botswana and there are negotiations to formalise this link. A mega-national park extending the Kruger Park conservation area into the Lowveld as well as Mozambique and Zimbabwe is envisaged, and a new national park is proposed for the Agulhas Plain at the south-western tip of Africa to preserve the biodiversity of the area. The wildlife found in all the country's parks and reserves covers the entire biodiversity spectrum. Nearly all the parks offer a range of accommodation from rudimentary to luxurious and many have trails where you can cover large areas of unspoilt nature areas on foot under the guidance of a trail ranger.

The other major conservation body in the country is the Natal Parks Board, which controls 76 formally protected parks and sanctuaries running in an almost continuous chain of forest and game reserves from the Royal Natal National Park in the north to beyond the Loteni Nature Reserve in the south, and preserving in its great natural beauty an area of some 644 sq km/251 sq miles in KwaZulu-Natal. The oldest established game reserves in Africa — Umfolozi, St Lucia and Hluhluwe — are found in the province. They celebrated their centenaries in 1995. More luxurious and offering more intimate game-viewing are the privately owned game reserves, some bordering on the Kruger National Park, and including Timbavati, Sabi Sand, Klaserie, Manyeleti, Londolozi, Mala Mala and, just outside the main reserve area, Thornybush game reserve. All except Klaserie have lodge accommodation, often luxurious in the extreme. Each of the nine provinces manages the nature reserves, mountain catchment and wilderness areas within its borders. At present, there are more than 300 provincial nature reserves. Accommodation is available at most of them.

There are another 300 wildlife and nature reserves in the country, most of them proclaimed within the past 25 years and most of them privately owned. Nearly three-quarters of these cover less than 5000 hectares, but with the country's other parks and reserves they are host to more than 900 bird species, some 338 terrestrial and aquatic mammal species, a great variety of reptiles and more than 24,000 types of plant. All the reserves together total less than 6% of South Africa's surface area, which is far from the ideal 10% advocated by the International Union for the Conservation of Nature (IUCN). You will often hear the terms 'vulnerable', 'threatened', 'endangered' and 'rare' used to describe various imperilled species and may wonder where the lines are drawn to distinguish one from another. This, in fact, has been an ongoing problem since the inception of the IUCN's Red Data Book programme in the 1960s, which collects scientific data on endangered species. The main problem lies in designing a classification system that is objective rather than subjective. A new system was placed before the IUCN's Species Survival Commission in May 1994 in which there are nine main categories, ranging from 'extinct' to 'low risk'. Although these terms are precisely defined according to scientific criteria, they are often bandied about quite carelessly.

As well as being a founder member of the IUCN, South Africa is also a signatory to the Ramsar Convention, aimed at the conservation of wetlands of international importance, and the Convention on International Trade in Endangered Species of Wild Fauna and Flora (CITES). South Africa's commitment to the preservation of biodiversity is reflected in its stable elephant and white rhinoceros populations, survival successes with the cheetah, mountain zebra and leatherback turtle, and marked increases in the numbers of southern right and humpback whales in its territorial waters. South Africa was one of the first countries to publish its own Red Data Books on threatened and endangered species, a joint venture by the CSIR, the Endangered Wildlife Trust and the Department of Environmental Affairs and Tourism (DEAT).

To enjoy fully the country and its wildlife you should:

- Find out what you can about South Africa before you leave home. What are the social and environmental problems facing the country and its communities?
- Show respect for the country's cultural history, beliefs and social conventions. Find out more about them.
- Check out your tour operator. Does your tour operator promote awareness of the need for the sustainable use of natural resources, and how is this demonstrated?
- Be aware of your impact and what effect it could have on local eco-systems.
- Know where your money goes. Find out how much of the money you spend will benefit the places you visit. What does your tour operator, lodge or resort do to support local environmental and community-based projects?
- Help to employ. Do the places you will be staying in employ local people, and are

any of them managers or business partners, or do they merely fill menial roles with little opportunity for advancement?
- Be prepared to lobby politicians, the media, environmental and conservation groups to draw attention to issues you believe to be of importance.
- Help indigenous communities by buying local products and services. Do not buy curios and mementoes without checking the source of the materials used and whether they have been legally obtained.
- Help in the wise use and management of the environment by joining or supporting a caring conservation organisation.
- Question your lifestyle. Does your lifestyle at home have any negative affect on the area you are visiting? If so, what can you do to change it?

Parks and accommodation are open throughout the year, but it is advisable to book well in advance. Contact the National Parks Board:

Reservations, PO Box 787, Pretoria 0001, Gauteng, tel (012) 343-1991, fax (012) 343-0905;
Foreign Desk and Group Bookings, tel (012) 343-2007, fax (012) 343-2006;
Cape Town Office, PO Box 7400, Roggebaai 8012, tel (021) 22-2810, fax (021) 24-6211.

BIRD-WATCHING

Bird-watching is the fastest growing natural history hobby in the world, and South Africa is a bird-watcher's paradise. More than 920 species occur, with 600 of them breeding within its borders. By comparison, Australia, which is six times the size of South Africa, and the continental USA, which is seven times the size, each has only about 650 bird species. South Africa covers a mere 0.8% of the world's land surface but is home to nearly 10% of the world's birds. You can spend an enjoyable hour or two watching passing bird life from your hotel window or campsite, it is that prolific, but for real bird-watching you have a choice of every imaginable habitat, from wetlands and seashore, to mountains, forests and bushveld, where you will see an unparalleled variety of species.

Before you set off, arm yourself with at least one of these local bird-watcher's bibles:

Roberts' Birds of Southern Africa, edited by Gordon Maclean. This is definitely the choice guide to southern Africa's avifauna and at the price (R84) the best value for money.
Newman's Birds of Southern Africa (R100). Next to Roberts this is regarded as the standard field guide and the colour coding and speedy index make it a time-saver.
Sasol Birds of Southern Africa, by Ian Sinclair, Phil Hockey and Warwick Tarboton (R91).
Ian Sinclair's *Field Guide to the Birds of Southern Africa* (R100) is illustrated with photographs instead of the more usual drawings and paintings.

If you have not brought them with you, you will also need a good pair of field glasses. Suitable glasses are 7x50, 8x30, 8x40, 9x35 and maybe 10x50. Of these, 7x50 and 8x30 are regarded as the best for African conditions (the first figure is linear magnification, while the second is the diameter of the frontline in millimetres). You will also need a notebook to jot down the bird-watcher's six main identification characteristics: size, legs (colour and shape), habitat, plumage, colour or markings, and beak size and shape, and perhaps a tape recorder and camera. Once equipped, you can head for the Kruger National Park, which has more than half of the country's bird species within its borders, the Drakensberg, which provides a stunning backdrop to a rich birdlife, and Maputaland, South Africa's own Everglades with its 472 recorded species — including the rare Palmnut Vulture, Rudd's Apalis and the Green Coucal — in the fabulous transitional area from tropical to sub-tropical. There is also the Western Cape, with its impressive sunbirds and loeries, its wetland flamingoes and waders of the sandpiper and other northern families, and its Jackass penguins, the only species of penguin resident on the African continent. You might even spot one or more of the threatened or endangered species of wattled, blue and crowned cranes, and the endangered Egyptian vulture, roseate tern and blackrumped button-quail, and the blue swallow, of which there are only 60 breeding pairs in South Africa.

If you want to get in touch with local 'twitchers' — which is what South African birders call each other — the national organisation is BirdLife South Africa, PO Box 84394, Greenside 2034, Gauteng, tel (011) 888-4147, fax (011) 782-7013. This is affiliated to BirdLife International and associated with the Royal Society for the Protection of Birds in the UK.

MARINE RESERVES

Only in recent years has the attention given to the country's wildlife sanctuaries since the turn of the century been extended to the wonders off the 3000km/1864 mile shoreline. When the Tsitsikamma National Park in the Eastern Cape was proclaimed in 1964 it became the first marine reserve on the African continent. Nearly 50 reserves and protected areas have since been proclaimed to conserve the teeming life that thrives in one or the other of the two great ocean currents, the Mozambique-Agulhas and the Benguela, which keep one side of the sub-continent warm and the other chilly.

Off KwaZulu-Natal the warm waters shelter the continent's southernmost coral reefs, while on the West Coast the smaller reserves and sanctuaries provide a haven for such heavily exploited species as *perlemoen* (abalone) and rock lobster. Zululand's coral reefs attract scuba divers all year round and powerboats arrive by the score in summer for some of the best marlin fishing in the world, along with barracuda and kingfish. There are three major marine reserves along the KwaZulu-Natal coastline: Trafalgar, St Lucia and Maputaland. The St Lucia and Maputaland marine reserves also contain sanctuary areas within their boundaries.

The reserves were proclaimed to protect marine resources and provide a pantry from which stocks can disperse to other areas along the coast. The sanctuaries serve as pristine environments and reference points for marine biologists measuring the effect of man's disturbance on marine life outside of the sanctuary. Sanctuaries are closed to any form of utilisation. The Trafalgar Marine Reserve contains fossil beds which are 90–100 million years old and these are visible during spring low tides. The St Lucia Marine Reserve was established specifically to protect South Africa's only coral reefs, and the Maputaland Marine Reserve, which runs up to the Mozambique border, was primarily proclaimed to protect the large numbers of marine turtles which come ashore to breed in the area. All eight species of marine turtles are endangered or threatened.

The main marine reserves and sanctuaries on the West Coast are at St Helena Bay, Saldanha Bay, and False Bay, and between the Cape Peninsula and Port Elizabeth at Betty's Bay, Hermanus, Cape Agulhas, Robberg, Tsitsikamma and Sardinia Bay. Without these and other protected areas there would be no way of controlling exploitation of marine resources, and the result would be over-utilisation and degradation, making them valueless for present and future generations. Policing of all these protected areas by officers of the Directorate of Sea Fisheries and the Natal Parks Board is strict and heavy fines can be the result of any negligence on your part. Enjoy these pristine areas, but make sure you know what rules and regulations apply to each one.

HUNTING SAFARIS

Hunting animals and birds for sport probably raises blood pressure worldwide more than any other conservation and environmental issue. It is one of those love it or hate it topics with no real resolution. What is important is a better understanding of hunting's niche in the tourism and ecological sectors of South Africa, where every year visiting trophy hunters inject some R350 million into the economy (most of them from the USA). They do not shoot everything in sight; permits are expensive and strictly controlled and the professional hunters who take visiting sportsmen and women on hunting safaris can be relied upon to see to it that clients follow the letter of the law and operate within a strict code of ethics.

In effect, the responsible hunter has become an important part of the overall nature conservation picture, and the game ranches that cater for them have an excellent reputation for the conservation of numerous otherwise declining animal species, such as the bontebok, Sable antelope and Cape mountain zebra.

The Kruger National Park's two million hectares, for instance, are insufficient to allow animals — especially elephant and buffalo — free run and the National Parks Board has at times to embark on controversial culling programmes. The bald fact is that human settlement has come to mean fences, and fences mean the restriction of animal populations, which in turn requires man's artificial intervention to maintain the animals' viability and their home territory's sustainable resources. Much of the disapproval that falls on hunters and hunting seems to stem from the widespread belief that the huge herds of game that roamed the country for centuries were completely wiped out by thoughtless, bloodthirsty hunters who left the vast plains empty of wildlife. While there is no gainsaying that immense numbers of plains animals did fall to the farmer's gun during the years of settlement, scientific conservation measures have today ensured there is once again an abundance of game and, in many places, an ecologically embarrassing surplus. One of the country's leading conservation bodies, the Wildlife Society of Southern Africa, was actually started by hunters in 1926 (as the Wildlife Protection and Conservation Society of Southern Africa).

The development of the safari business since 1980 under the aegis of the Professional Hunters Association of South Africa (Phasa) has resulted in hunting that goes hand in hand with conservation. Today, South Africa offers some of the finest, and cheapest, trophy hunting in the world. More than 60 species and sub-species can legally be hunted, including the Big Five. Specially protected game such as the klipspringer, giraffe and black rhino may not be hunted. Most hunting is on private game farms, which range in size from 2500ha (more than 6000 acres) to more than 40,000ha (nearly 100,000 acres) and there are about 11,000 of these throughout South Africa, although only a third of them are open to hunting. Some of the best hunting is in KwaZulu-Natal and the Northern Province, although the Free State also offers excellent hunting, with wing shooting in particular being outstanding. The province boasts 35% of the country's enormous spurwing goose, 50% of the Egyptian goose, and 30% of the yellow-billed duck populations. The Barkly East area of the Eastern Cape is held to provide some of the world's best grey-wing partridge shooting.

Hunting popularity is usually determined by the rarity of the species and the perceived danger involved in a successful hunt, with lion heading the list, followed by elephant, leopard, rhino and crocodile. Other popular trophy animals are buffalo, eland, sable antelope, kudu and gemsbok. Bird hunting is the favoured pursuit of Spanish and Italian hunters. On average, only 5% of a specific game population is of trophy quality, and shooting the trophy member of a herd invariably has no detrimental affect on the rest of the animals. In the case of antelope it is the size of the horns that place it in the trophy category, and as these usually belong to the dominant or herd ram — the biggest and oldest animal — his removal simply means that a younger, more virile, male takes his place. The record kudu horns, incidentally, are 1.82m/6ft. Trophy hunters target the biggest and best of the species and it is for this reason that the sport is strictly monitored and carefully controlled. Permits have to be obtained for certain species and hunters are limited in terms of the number of animals they shoot and the way in which it is done.

Hunting is a natural process for both the human and animal world and it provides an important check against over-population. Money generated from hunting is reinvested in conservation and the economy — it pays for lodges, vehicles, staff and, most importantly, the protection of certain species and their unique habitats. For the wildebeest, for example, a trophy hunter must pay an average of R2000 (£267/$440). The meat hunter is charged R1500 while the sale of a live wildebeest brings an average of R1000. Game farms cause less damage to the environment than cattle or sheep farming, as different species have different grazing habits. A farm will carry more game, as a cow weighs around 400kg/882lb, while the average impala weighs 80kg/176lb. Game farming is thus a more productive and natural way of generating income and if more farmers did it they would be able to dedicate more and more land to conservation, giving the environment a chance to return to its natural state. Strictly controlled and supervised hunting is not as heartless, ruthless a sport as many believe it to be. Hunting is done on foot (which requires more skill and adds a measure of fair play) and only during certain periods of the year, allowing the animals to recover and increase their numbers. Where predators are absent in man-made reserves, man can himself assume the task of keeping the population in check by becoming the predator. National parks and game reserves conserve a small part (only about 6%) of South Africa. Wildlife in most areas within the region faces its major threats, not from hunting, but from the destruction of its natural habitats for agriculture, forestry and human settlement.

South African hunting associations:

Confederation of Hunting Associations of South Africa (Chasa), PO Box 1807, Kimberley 8300, Northern Cape, tel (0531) 31098, fax (0531) 31001;

Professional Hunters Association of South Africa (Phasa), PO Box 10264, Hennopsmeer 0046, Gauteng, tel (012) 663-2417, fax (012) 663-7212;

Border Hunting Club, PO Box 3047, Cambridge 5247, Eastern Cape, tel (0431) 43-5838, fax (0431) 54813;

Bushveld Hunters and Game Conservation Association, PO Box 1771, Pietersburg 0700, Northern Province, tel/fax (0152) 293-8224;

Highveld Hunters and Game Conservation Association, PO Box 12054, Leraatsfontein 1038, tel (0135) 72223;

Cape Hunters and Game Conservation Association, 9 Ackerman Street, Krigeville 7600, Western Cape, tel (021) 887-6418, fax (021) 887-9697;

Kalahari Hunters Association, PO Box 1356, Kuruman 8460, Northern Cape, tel/fax (05373) 22711;

KwaZulu-Natal Hunt and Conservation Association, PO Box 352, Westville 3630, KwaZulu-Natal, tel (031) 86-7003, fax (031) 86-2345;

Lowveld Hunters and Game Conservation Association, PO Box 1134, Nelspruit 1200, Mpumalanga, tel (01311) 23575;

Northern Cape Hunters Association, PO Box 1807, Kimberley 8300, Northern Cape, tel (0531) 81-1266, fax (0531) 21832;

North-West Hunters and Game Conservation Association, PO Box 4888, Vaal Reefs 2621, tel (018) 478-4127, fax (018) 478-4435;

Free State Hunters and Game Conservation Association, PO Box 1314, Bloemfontein 9300, Free State, Cell 082 558-7189;

SA Hunters and Game Conservation Association, PO Box 18108, Pretoria North 0116, Gauteng, tel (012) 565-4856, fax (012) 565-4910;

Southern Cape Hunters and Game Conservation Association, PO Box 2040, George 6530, Western Cape, tel (0441) 71-1713, fax (0441) 71-1171.

Rules and Regulations. You can hunt legally only during the official hunting season, which is traditionally in the winter months of May, June and July, but can be from April to August. The season is announced every year in the Hunting Proclamation. As a visiting hunter you must have an appropriate permit allowing you to hunt wild animals that are on the protected, but not the endangered list. You must also have written permission from the person on whose land you hunt. Generally speaking, animals and birds that can be hunted fall into three groups: ordinary game, protected game and unprotected wildlife for which no licence is necessary. There is also a special list of game animals that enjoy specially protected status and that may not be hunted under any circumstances. Usually, the hunting season coincides with winter, when surplus animals would otherwise face death by starvation. No shooting of game is allowed from a vehicle. The smallest calibre rifle usually used for smaller buck is .243. Hunting with an automatic firearm (one that fires more than two shots without having to be reloaded by hand) is not permitted. Calibres of less than 5.6mm (such as a .22) are allowed for any bird for which the hunting season is open or any other wild animal that is not an endangered or protected wild animal. A wide variety of hunting rifles in the small (.22), medium (.243 to .375), and heavy (.458 to .560) calibre range are obtainable in South Africa, although it is usual for hunters to bring their own weapons. Most local hunters regard the .375 as the best all-round rifle, and if they were asked to choose three rifles to cover all conditions and possibilities they would probably plump for a 12-gauge shotgun, a .375 and a .458, as these weapons can cope with anything from guinea-fowl to elephant. High-quality ammunition is widely available locally. All rifles must be sighted in before you go into the veld and if you miss three shots in a row at game you must return to the camp and ensure your rifle is correctly sighted. No-one may take a shot at moving or partially hidden game. If you wound an animal during a hunt you will not be allowed to shoot at any other game until it has been tracked down and killed.

Permitted Species. South Africa has 29 antelope species in all, more than any other country in Africa, and of these 26 can be hunted. Roan, Sharpes' grysbok and Lichtenstein's hartebeest are scarce and no permits are issued for them. Among the species you can hunt are Vaal rhebok, bontebok, blesbok, Cape grysbok, southern mountain reedbok, black wildebeest (white-tailed gnu), and Cape mountain zebra. These cannot be hunted anywhere else in Africa. Of the larger carnivores, cheetah, leopard, lion and spotted hyaena as well as a variety of smaller carnivores, are open to hunters, as well as elephant, white rhino, Burchell's zebra, Cape buffalo, giraffe, bushpig, warthog, and hippopotamus, which means South Africa is the only country where you can hunt all the Big Five. A limited number of permits for these are issued every year.

There is also what local hunters regard as the mini-five. This bag is made up of small antelope species, among them grey, red, and blue duiker, Livingstone's suni, oribi, steenbok, klipspringer, and Cape grysbok. Hunting these can be as challenging as hunting the Big Five and as the habitats of these small antelope differ markedly, such a hunt would take you from the open plains of the Free State and the sub-tropical vegetation of KwaZulu-Natal, to the bushveld of Mpumalanga and the Northern Province, and the mountains and plains of the Cape.

South Africa has a wide variety of game birds, some 14 huntable species of duck, two of geese, 10 partridge (francolin), two pheasant-size birds (guinea fowl), pigeons, doves and quail. Some hunting outfitters offer bird-only safaris — shooting over dogs, shooting driven birds, and shooting over decoys.

Endangered wild animals include the scaly ant-eater (pangolin), cheetah, black rhinoceros, square-lipped (white) rhinoceros, Cape mountain zebra, oribi and riverine rabbit. Endangered birds are the bearded vulture and the bald ibis. Virtually all indigenous birds are protected, including game birds, waterfowl, waders and raptors, but some may be hunted with a licence. Most of the animals on the protected list are not rare or endangered but their hunting is controlled and they can be hunted only with a licence. If all this sounds complicated, it is — but it is the job of the professional hunter or safari outfitter to sort it all out for you long before you line up anything in your sights.

Safari Operators. A hunting outfitter is the person or company arranging the hunt for you; the professional hunter is the person who accompanies you and supervises the hunt, although he can be an outfitter as well. The outfitter is otherwise the link between the client and the professional hunter, and is legally responsible for all your hunting requirements once you are in South Africa, taking care of all the red tape — contracts, licences, permits and the like — and organising the facilities, such as camp accommodation, equipment, vehicles, cooks, skinners, trackers, preparation and despatch of trophies and all the other odds and sods that make a hunting safari a memorable experience rather than a gruelling ordeal. Outfitters organise hunts tailored to the client's trophy needs and pocket. Many provide hunts with only 5–10 species or less, and cater for the hunter who is satisfied with a trophy that is a good representative of the species, as opposed to a world record trophy. Bow, handgun and black powder gun hunts are also available on a limited scale.

The Big Five. The area covered by the former Transvaal, which is now made up of Gauteng, Mpumalanga, the North-West and Northern provinces, is regarded as one of the best hunting-grounds in the world and is one of the few areas where the Big Five (elephant, rhino, buffalo, lion, leopard) can be hunted legally. Weight for weight, leopards are the strongest of the big cats and a male can weigh more than 91kg/200lb. The region contains nearly half of all the country's game hunting ranches and traditional bushveld hunting centres are Alldays, Thabazimbi, Ellisras and Pietersburg. Rhinos are the most endangered of the Big Five but thanks to the work of the Natal Parks Board, they have been brought back from the edge of extinction. Continuing exploitation of these lumbering giants by Eastern cultures is forcing them, especially the black rhino, back to the edge again and there are fewer than 3000 left.

Trophy Taxidermy. Trophies are skinned for a flat skin, tanned for use as, say, a floor covering, when the client does not want a shoulder mount, a full mount or a rug mount. A rug mount is the common mount for the skins of carnivores such as lion and leopard. This includes the mounting of the head with jaws open, with the rest of the skin tanned and mounted on a felt lining. The skinning and preparation of a mask or cape (head skin) for a shoulder mount demands more skill than any other form of taxidermy, as head skins are usually irreplaceable. This is the trophy mount most usually seen on the walls of old homes and hotels in Africa. Unless the hunter is extremely wealthy and has a special trophy room a full mount is usually reserved for small animals; not many people have enough space in their home for a four-metre/13ft tall jumbo or a five-metre/16ft long crocodile. These can take at least six weeks to recreate and six months to deliver. The cheapest way to take your trophy home — if it is a buck — is in the form of either skull and attached horns or simply the horns mounted on a shield. South Africa is a signatory to the Convention on the International Trade in Endangered Species (CITES), so it is important if you intend to ship home a trophy from South Africa that your own customs authority will allow its importation. Safari operators and professional hunters are aware of restrictions and changes in regulations and will advise you of any potential problem areas.

Some taxidermist contacts for hunting and fishing trophies:

Nico van Rooyen Taxidermy, PO Box 911-217, A1 De Waal Street, Rosslyn 0200, Gauteng, tel (012) 541-2053/4, fax (012) 541-2220;
Nel Hayman Taxidermist, 60 Ivan Smuts Avenue, Silverfields Park, Krugersdorp 1739, Gauteng, tel (011) 955-1097;

Robinson Derek Taxidermist, PO Box 1470, Roodepoort 1725, Gauteng, tel (011)
763-5792, fax (011) 763-8159;
Trans African Taxidermist, Riverside Farm, Nooitgedacht, PO Box 740, Muldersdrift
1747, Gauteng, tel (011) 659-0660/0496.

PHOTOGRAPHIC SAFARIS

If you are planning a photographic safari you will probably be going with a
professional who will advise you on what camera equipment to take. If you are
travelling solo, make sure that as well as your camera you pack standard, wide-angle,
telephoto, and zoom lenses, a tripod or monopod, close-up attachments, lens brush
and tissues, flash equipment, all-purpose plastic bags, spare batteries, and plenty of
film. All major brands of film and cameras are available in South Africa but it is
cheaper to bring your own. You can buy the usual photographic film, positive and
negative, and there is no problem getting it processed locally, either by same-day or
one-hour service if it is colour print. When buying film ask whether processing is
included in the price of the film. Keep all your film in an insulated cool box or bag,
especially if you are out in the bundu where temperatures can climb to around
35°C/95°F, and make sure it is kept separately from the beer and soft drinks. The
natural beauty of the country and its amazing diversity are enough to inspire even the
most amateurish photographer but remember that like other sensitive places in the
world certain buildings and installations — especially those connected with defence
and internal security — should not be photographed.

Most people know how to use a simple camera and if yours is not a simple point
and click job you presumably know more about photography than most happy-
snappers. What you might need are some tips on how to make sure you take home
decent pictures of wildlife. First of all, it is important to remember that animals in the
wild are likely to be most active from a photographic point of view early in the
morning and late in the day. This happily is when the light is best for photography. The
telephoto lenses most used for game photography are 180mm and 300mm, mounted
on a good tripod. For photographing birds a lens with at least a focal length of 400mm
is necessary, or you will be staring at pictures with birds the size of pin-heads when
you get home. Fast film is also a must — at least ASA 200 is needed to shoot with
telephoto lenses at high speed and to avoid blurred images.

HIKING AND BACKPACKING

The best way to explore South Africa, from its rolling savanna and snowy mountain
peaks to its arid desert and wild coastal areas, is undoubtedly on foot, as more and
more people are discovering each year. Hiking and backpacking in South Africa
along trails defined and maintained by a variety of private and parastatal bodies has
become an extremely popular way of getting close to nature, so much so that many
of the more popular trails are booked up many months in advance. The coastal Otter
Trail, for instance, is usually fully booked for at least a year. The Department of
Forestry initiated the National Hiking Way System in 1972 and the National Hiking
Way Board was established in 1973.

The idea for a National Hiking Way goes back to 1968 when the 41km/26 mile
Otter Trail (now extended to 80km/50 miles) was established between Storms River
and Nature's Valley. After a study of the Appalachian Trail and other US systems the
SA Department of Forestry opened the country's first National Hiking Way Trail, the
Fanie Botha, near Sabie, in 1973, during Green Heritage Year. A National Hiking
Way Board was set up and it was envisaged that an integrated system of trails would
eventually make it possible to trail-walk 3000km from the Soutpansberg in the
Northern Province to the Cedarberg in the Western Cape. The trail concept has
grown ever since. Trails are well marked, usually by easily spotted metal route

indicators, or white or yellow footprints painted at intervals on rocks, trees, and fence posts. In 1993, the Government decided that the trails and their control should be privatised and they were offered to private owners — provincial administrations and others — and in the case of those on forestry land to the South African Forestry Company Ltd (Safcol), which came into being in April 1993. Safcol now administers trails on forestry land throughout the country. The National Hiking Way Board is now involved with hiking trails in an advisory capacity only and allocates funds to organisations who want to develop more.

There are at least 800 hiking trails in South Africa (nobody really knows the total number), of which nine are controlled and administered by Safcol; the rest fall under municipal and provincial authorities, the National Parks Board, the Natal Parks Board, and sundry private land owners. They range from the almost effortless to the very strenuous, and can last from an hour or so to a week or more. Some are self-guided; others conducted. Some have basic overnight huts, caves or tents *en route*; others nothing at all. A few provide comfortable to luxurious accommodation. Some have been designed for physically disabled people. Most are privately owned, but open to the public on payment of a moderate fee. New trails are opening all the time and the choice is wide, depending on your fitness, preference of scenery and the time you have available. Each trail has its own special features — panoramic views, wildlife, birdlife and botanical wonders, as well as areas of fascinating geographical and historical significance. If you have two or three months to spare, and you are fit enough, you can even backpack the entire 3000km/1864 mile coastline from Alexander Bay in the Western Cape to Kosi Bay in northern Zululand.

Safcol's thousands of hiking kilometres include a combination of five well established trails, which now form part of Safcol's Big 5 trail network. These trails are all five days and longer and take you through some of the most spectacular scenery in South Africa. The trails are Magoebaskloof ('The Mystical Trail'), 60km/37 miles; Prospectors ('The Fortune-Seekers Trail'), 58km/26 miles; Fanie Botha ('The Sustainable Forestry Trail'), 73km/45 miles; Kaapschehoop ('The Conservation Trail'), 69km/43 miles; and Tsitsikamma ('The Scenic Trail'), 72km/45 miles. If you have the energy to complete all five trails, totalling 332km/206 miles, Safcol will award you honorary status within the hiking fraternity.

Some important points to consider when choosing a trail:

Travel distance: Try to avoid long, costly and tedious travelling time by choosing a trail relatively close to your base.

Degree of difficulty: It is recommended that beginners first attempt an easier route. Many day routes are available and these are a good introduction for families.

Facilities: These range from none on wilderness trails to huts with electricity and hot and cold running water on others.

Seasons: Take into account rain, wind, cold and heat, as this will determine your choice of clothing. For security reasons, do not hike alone, make sure you have a good map and let someone know where you are going and when you will be returning.

The Hiking Federation of Southern Africa (HFSA) produces a booklet with all hiking trail booking details. This is available from HFSA for R10 (£1.35/$2.20), or you can simply telephone the Federation, whose staff are always happy to answer hiking queries. When booking a trail, you will be advised of rates, directions and any restrictions in force. Reservations are confirmed by post. Deposits are required and trail permits are posted on receipt of the deposit. The Federation is one of the main organisations promoting hiking throughout the region. It comprises individuals, clubs, trail owners/managers and companies involved in hiking, trail-walking and back-packing. HFSA's main activities include the promotion of hiking as an activity for the young, and among previously disadvantaged communities; and planning, building and maintaining trails and disseminating information on hiking clubs, trails and hiking in general. The National Hiking Way Board in Pretoria still has a limited stock of its excellent detailed 1:50,000 trail maps for sale, but generally the bodies administering the trails provide maps when you have made a booking. Safcol produces a guide to its nine hiking trails. Contact:

> *HFSA*, PO Box 1420, Randburg 2125, Gauteng, tel (011) 886-6524, fax (011) 886-6013;
> *National Hiking Way Board*, Pretoria, tel (012) 299-3382, fax (012) 326-1760;
> *Safcol Ecotourism*, PO Box 1771, Silverton 0127, Gauteng, tel (012) 481-3615, fax (012) 481-3622.

Trail Linx Africa offers a wide range of information on hiking and other outdoor activities on the Internet. TLA's cyber service gives a comprehensive list with basic details of all trails in southern Africa; an on-line booking service through e-mail or fax; a search facility that allows you to find an available trail in any area during a specified period; a list of trail places that become available at short notice because of cancellations; and an e-mail notification service personalised to notify you of any cancellations by way of e-mail. Trail Linx Africa is part of Rural Linx Africa, which gives information on publicity associations in South Africa, and can be found under the Travel and Tourism category on Worldnet Africa at http://africa.cis.co.za/tourism/linx/trails.html

Useful books, available from newsagents and bookshops, include Jaynee Levy's *Complete Guide to Walks and Trails in Southern Africa*; Willie and Sandra Olivier's *Guide to Hiking Trails of Southern Africa* and *Guide to Backpacking and Wilderness Trails*; and David Bristow's *Drakensberg Walks* and his *Best Hikes in South Africa*.

WILDERNESS TRAILS

Wilderness trails are not for the unfit or fainthearted. These trails through the unspoilt wilds of South Africa are few but jealously guarded, cared for by conservationists, and the zenith of the hiking and backpacking experience. A wilderness area is an area of land that has been set aside and managed in such a way that its pristine character is not altered in any way; it is the highest form of conservation. To ensure that the character of a wilderness area remains unaltered and undamaged a number of principles are applied in their control. The number of visitors is limited to ensure a quality experience; management input is kept to a minimum so that natural processes continue without undue interference; and no man-made structures are allowed in the area. For the visitor to a wilderness area this means there is an emphasis on solitude and self-reliance; you may only walk or ride horses on the trails (lone hikers are discouraged); you must relieve yourself away from any cave and must not bury your faeces, as this encourages erosion; you may leave your footprints but nothing else so that others have a real wilderness experience; and what you take in, you must take out, including litter.

Some of the finest wilderness trails are in the proclaimed KwaZulu-Natal Drakensberg Wilderness, controlled by the Natal Parks Board. Within the Natal Drakensberg Park you can criss-cross forests and mountains, camping or sleeping in caves at more than 60 memorable spots, from the Royal Natal Park at the northern end of the mountains, along the whole sweep of the range to Bushman's Nek in the south. As this area was once the home of large numbers of Bushmen there are numerous caves on the trails where you can spend the night, and this is one of the major attractions of the area. As many of these caves were used as rock art galleries by the little hunters extra care must be taken by hikers not to damage their fragile paintings. This means no fires or candles can be lit inside the shelters. The Parks Board restriction on numbers ensures that impact on the eco-system is minimal. While you are tramping through the wilderness only 50 to 200 other people are doing the same thing within an area of 644sq km/400sq miles. The maximum number of people allowed in one party is up to a dozen, and all caves are booked by one group at a time. Even if you are using caves on the trail you are advised still to carry camping equipment.

As well as these do-it-yourself wilderness trails there are also guided wilderness trails. These are available in some of the major national parks and reserves. The Kruger National Park, for instance, has seven guided wilderness trails conducted through spectacular areas of the park that most tourists never see. They are one of the Kruger's success stories. The idea is to get people close to nature, not necessarily to view big game on foot. With your guide you examine trees, spoor, termite nests, the habitat created by a fallen tree and, for instance, the difference between elephant and rhino dung.

Trails do not follow fixed game paths; rangers take you to different areas depending on vegetation, season, time of day or your special interests. It costs about R935 to go on one of these trails, which lasts for two days and three nights, and you must be between 12 and 60. Guided trails in KwaZulu-Natal's game parks include the Umfolozi Game Reserve, where the first wilderness trail was conducted back in 1959, Mkuzi Game Reserve and the St Lucia Wetlands Park, all in the game-rich bushveld area of northern Zululand. Most travel agents and tour operators can organise wilderness trails for you or you can arrange your own through the National Parks Board or the Natal Parks Board.

THE RAINBOW CUISINE

Cookery in South Africa has come a long way since Jan van Riebeeck started growing vegetables in the Cape to ward off scurvy among the crews of passing ships. Bushmen (San) and *strandlopers* (beachcombers) shared their knowledge of edible wild plants with the settlers, a hundred years later Malay slaves arrived, followed in turn by Huguenots, Indians, Chinese, and men and women from virtually every nation. For several centuries all the wild and domestic produce of the land was grist to the cook's mill, although when you go looking for traditional South African food nowadays you will no longer be offered tortoise or turtle soup, egg dishes made variously with penguin, gull and molly mauk eggs, seaweed jelly, breast of flamingo, heron liver, seal and whale steaks, porcupine crackling, or crisply fried locusts — which South African epicure C Louis Leipoldt declared taste 'not unlike whitebait that, somehow, have been stuffed with buttered toast.'

All these dishes were once regarded as tasty treats on Cape tables; now, strict conservation methods and a more squeamish modern diner have resulted in their disappearance from the menu. What you can expect to sample, however, are *boontjiesop* (bean soup), the slow-simmered meat and vegetable *bredies* (ragout), the *boboties* (spiced mince), green mielies (corn on the cob), and a wide variety of game, fish and seafood dishes, including the delicious Cape snoek, the now prohibitively expensive perlemoen (abalone) and the incomparable rock lobster (known to all South Africans as crayfish). The influence of the stolid Dutch has made heavy, creamy puddings a staple of the dessert menu although *melktert* (milk tart) is a very more-ish way to go on to coffee.

Out of this melting pot has come a truly rainbow cuisine. South Africans are most at home with ample servings of meat, preferably steaks and lamb chops, backed up by potatoes, rice, mealie meal, and fresh vegetables, and if the meat has been *braaied* to perfection over a fire in the open so much the better. The *braaivleis,* or barbecue, is a national institution; virtually anything can be braaied, not only meat and the popular *boerewors* (spicy sausage) and *sosaties* (kebabs), but a haunch of game, maize on the cob, sweet potatoes, and pumpkin, and the coast specialities of snoek, rock lobster, mussels, and almost anything else that comes dripping from the sea. Sooner or later, as a visitor, you will be asked to a *braai.* Nowadays you will probably have to take your own packet of chops or sausage and a bottle of wine, unless you are travelling in the countryside and are lucky enough to be invited to a farm braai. There you will see the braais as they were done in the old days, mountains of chops and boerewors charring over the open coals while the mealie meal cooks in a three-legged iron pot that looks rather like a witches' cauldron.

Once in the city it is back to inexpensive steakhouses and fast junkfood, or a choice of international fare ranging from Thai, Chinese, Indonesian and Japanese, to Mexican, Cajun, German, French and Italian. There are also a growing number of vegetarian restaurants and some whose food is kosher or halaal for Jewish or Muslim customers. Most restaurants are licensed to sell wine and beer, and some also the hard stuff. If you are keeping a watch on the purse strings look for the ones that advertise BYO (bring your own); this alone can cut your bill in half. All newspapers and most magazines carry food and drink sections and every publicity and tourist bureau keeps restaurant guides for visitors.

Alternatively pop into the nearest Internet Café and check out *Style* magazine's restaurant guide on http://www/webfeat.co.za/style. This sophisticated guide not only lists restaurants in the Cape, the Highveld and Natal, it also lets you surf menus to find exactly what you feel like eating before you go out. It tells you about things like ambience, price range, wheelchair access, options for music and dancing, whether a restaurant is halaal or vegetarian, opening times and days closed, and lists a wide variety of cuisines. It breaks down prices into very low (R20–35; £2.65–4.65/$4.40–7.70); low (R35–55); medium (R55–70); and high (R70 and over). Most restaurants in the Cape fall into the medium-price bracket; on the Highveld there is a mix of medium and high-priced restaurants; and in Natal those listed are overwhelmingly medium-priced. Budget travellers should stick to cafés and take-aways, or visit the supermarket or deli and buy stuff for a homemade dinner or picnic lunch. This is not only cheaper, it can often be just as tasty.

Seafood. The two major currents washing South Africa's 3000km/1864 mile coastline bring to its tables some of the finest seafood imaginable, particularly from the Western Cape coast, where the icy Atlantic serves up what is arguably the finest seafood in the world. Unless you catch it yourself, a plate of the Cape's finest will make quite a dent in your budget. Holiday resorts, towns and villages along the south-west Cape coast used to hold annual perlemoen festivals, during which restaurants would vie with each other to produce seafood dishes featuring the tasty mollusc. Not any more. With a retail price of R165 a kg perlemoen, known to Americans as abalone, to the Aussies as mutton fish and to Kiwis as paua, is definitely off the menu at most eateries and exports find a ready market in the Far East at up to a staggering R1200 a kg. Little wonder that perlemoen is taking over from crayfish as the prize delicacy of the sea, although crayfish (rock lobster) is still, with oysters, the crowning glory of any seafood supper. Until well after World War Two, South Africans despised crayfish, and regarded it as fit only for fish bait. Now it will set you back the best part of R100 for a crayfish platter. Squid, known as *chokka,* was also once regarded with the same disdain and used as bait. Now it has new social status. The perlemoen seems to be going through the same culinary metamorphosis. We hope the same thing does not happen to the humble black mussel, which can give all other shellfish a run for its money. There is nothing to beat freshly gathered mussels bubbling on the beach in a pot of white wine, garlic and herbs — unless it is a newly caught crayfish, that most sought after of all South African crustaceans, simmering in a tarragon, wine and brandy bath. If that has not whetted your appetite you are not a lover of seafood; if you are, then treats are in store for you at many a Cape restaurant. The most rewarding are those specialising in open-air feasts along the Cape's west coast. These are no-frills places where you eat literally on the beach with tables and benches of driftwood, around open fires cooking a mouth-watering array of fresh line fish and seafood. You might get mussel shells for cutlery — and you can have a dip in the sea between courses. If the sharks don't eat you, you can always trot back to the restaurant and eat them, as shark brochettes.

Boerekos. This literally means farmers' food, and it is hearty stuff that sticks to your ribs, not really the sort of food you want to eat in hot weather, although it is the perfect meal in winter — or if you are famished. A typical plate would be heaped with slices from a couple of roasts — game, beef, mutton, perhaps pork — barricaded by a mountain of yellow rice, sweet potatoes, *stampkoring* (boiled crushed wheat kernels), and various in-season vegetables, but definitely spiced *pampoen* (pumpkin). Before this main course would have come a filling *boontjiesop* (dried bean soup), and afterwards a variety of sweetmeats, including a custardy sweet *melktert* (milk tart) washed down by strong coffee and some syrupy koeksisters (there is no real translation of the name for this sweetmeat; it is supposedly the noise made by the plaited dough when it is plunged into hot oil). Definitely not for the faint-hearted, or anyone practising girth-control.

Before the Boers developed this trenchman cuisine, based firmly on the Dutch country cooking of the 17th century, their chief food was meat and pot-baked bread. Honey was often used in place of scarce sugar. The main vegetables were mealies (maize), pumpkin and potatoes. Everybody drank coffee and ate *boerebeskuit* (biscuits or rusks), *vetkoek* (little deep-fried cakes made of flour and fat) and *souskluitjies* (dumplings). Ant-heaps were hollowed out for use as ovens in the veld, and three-legged iron pots were used for cooking most of the food, which came to be known as *potjiekos,* or pot food. A *rooster* (a grill or gridiron) was used for a *braaivleis,* when meat was grilled over the open fire. A lot of this fairly primitive food has enjoyed something of a revival and is found on menus in most restaurants featuring traditional South African dishes.

Biltong. You cannot spend much time in South Africa before someone offers you what at first glance looks like a gnarled piece of dried wood. This is biltong (jerky), strips of sun-dried game, beef, or even ostrich, and without it in their saddlebags and covered wagons the Boers would never have been able to trek or fight their commando campaigns. Lots of South African men still keep razor-sharp knives specially to cut their biltong. The best biltong comes from the round eye muscle (this is also used fresh as scotch fillet) that runs from the thick rib to the leg along either side of the backbone, and it can be made from almost any animal (fish biltong, called *bokkoms,* is made from the little grey mullet and in the country districts around Malmesbury, snoek is lightly pickled before being wind-dried and turned into snoek biltong). The distinctive flavour of biltong comes from coriander and crushed pepper mixed with the other ingredients used to preserve it. Salting, drying and pickling meat were the traditional means of preserving before the advent of refrigerators and freezers.

Curry and Spice. Cape cookery owes many debts to Dutch, German, Flemish, English, Portuguese, French and Indian culinary traditions, but undoubtedly the people who married all the strands into a savoury whole and put a 'Made in SA' stamp on it were the Malays, who first arrived as slaves shipped from the East by the Dutch East India Company not long after the Cape was settled. From the earliest days, Malays were prized as cooks and acknowledged artists of the kitchen. They were magicians with all the spices of the East: ginger, cinnamon, cassia, nutmeg, mace, cloves, allspice, saffron, turmeric, garlic, chillies, caraway, coriander, cumin, cardamon, tamarind and various herbs, nuts and fruits. They still are, even though over three centuries or so their lifestyle has become a blend of East and West, and they still prepare the spicy, colourful foods of their ancestors that are as enticing to the visitor as they were to the slave-owning Dutch. Their dishes, now part and parcel of the country's traditional cuisine, use spices and seasonings with rare subtlety. Among their better known dishes are bredies, bobotie, sosaties, breyani (or buryani), smoorsnoek, and accompaniments such as sambals, blatjang and atjar, or achaar. Bredies are usually made with mutton and can be made with anything from beans, cabbage, carrots, pumpkin, tomato and, in our opinion, the best of all, *Waterblommetjies,* the buds of the beautiful white water hawthorn that covers the shallow dams and vleis of the southern Cape like snowflakes in the spring. Stewed gently with mutton, onions, garlic, potatoes, white wine, ginger, a sliver of chilli, a blade of mace, and a handful of the *suuring* (wild sorrel) this is food for the gods — and something you can eat nowhere else in the world. In true Eastern tradition, the Malays like to eat rice with their meat dishes. This is invariably yellow rice mixed with raisins. This was traditionally served to mourners after a funeral and is still often referred to as *begrafnisrys,* or funeral rice.

Smoorsnoek (literally smothered, or braised, fish) is another Cape Malay speciality, made with the barracuda-like fish that throngs the waters off the Western Cape between April and June every year. Fresh snoek has its place — usually with chips — but for real flavour the Malays prefer salted and dried snoek. Another Malay treat is *ingelegde vis,* commonly translated as curried fish, although it is closer to a pickled fish curry. This is always eaten cold. With the march of progress you are more likely to find it in inexpensive tins in the supermarket than on any restaurant menu. Bobotie is another truly traditional dish bequeathed by the Malays. It is made from lightly spiced minced mutton blanketed by an egg custard and is to South Africa what lasagne is to Italy and moussaka is to Greece. Sosaties are better known in other countries as kebabs, shish kebabs, or brochettes; breyani has relatives all over the world under names such as rice pilau, pilaff, polo, and paella; it is the Malay magic that makes them different.

The Malays generally have a very sweet tooth and their confections and puddings are lovely to look at, but unless you share their love of sugar and have a figure like a twig you should give them a miss. What you should try if you can find it is a type of blancmange called *gooma,* which is made from the dried pinkish seaweed collected from the stalks of the giant kelp, which abounds in the sea off the Western Cape. Until recent times the hollow dried stems of this sea bamboo were used by wandering Malay fish vendors as horns to announce the approach of their carts. Budget travellers especially should get into the deliciously savoury Malay takeaways, roti and bunnychow, which are cheap and filling, although even if they were expensive they would be worth every cent or penny. Roti is basically an unleavened griddle-fried pancake. This is filled with wonderful spiced mince (and a potato for bulk), also known to the Malays as a *salomi.* Bunnychow is even more basic: it is a loaf cut in half with the dough pulled out and the hollow shell filled with spiced mince or — even cheaper — curried beans.

Bunnychow is also a popular takeaway in the Durban area where curries and climate alike are hotter. Durban is the heartland of South Africa's Indian cuisine, developed with a local flavour by the descendants of the Indian labourers who were brought to Natal in 1860 to work in the sugar-cane fields. From there curries of every stripe spread to the rest of the country. An oddity was the Free State, where old laws did not allow Asians to settle in the province. Now, it is a poorly served town that does not have at least one tandoor or curry palace and curry lovers no longer need to give the prairie province a miss.

Black Soulfood. Until recently, African traditional fare never got far beyond the black townships and back-street cafés of the industrial areas where workers needed to snatch a bite of something sustaining and cheap. Dedicated to changing this low-rent image of his people's food, President Mandela's son-in-law Zweli Hlongwane has opened the first of what will be a chain of countrywide restaurants specialising in authentic African cuisine. Zweli's first restaurant is called *Kofifi*, and it is in Commissioner Street, in downtown Johannesburg. He has the support of the Spur restaurant group, whose steakhouses are familiar throughout South Africa. Kofifi has a township ambience and plays the hottest jazz around. Its menu features South Africa's traditional braaied meat and poultry, but with the African accompaniments of *pap* (maize porridge), *ting* (sour porridge), *samp* (maize hominy grits), rice and dumplings. You can also order bowls of various salads, as well as a hot and spicy African version called *chakalaka,* which is a salad made from spiced pickles, chillies and sliced raw tomatoes. In place of the usual chipped or mashed potatoes you will be served *ubhatata,* which is the local sweet potato. If you are feeling really adventurous you can ask for *omiley.* You will be served up an African delicacy — sheep's head — and if you are really lucky you might be sharing it with President Mandela.

In the black townships fast food outlets, popularly known as Fish and Chips, are fast losing business to the butchers who have introduced a buy and braai policy, which means the customer who buys meat there can either take it home or barbecue it on the spot. The butcher provides a braai stove, spices, forks and plates, and a pap or maize porridge. This buy and cook idea is doing well because *pap en vleis* (mealie-meal porridge and meat) is black South Africa's favourite dish. Buy and braai originates from a well known Chinese fish and chip shop in Johannesburg. Popularly known in the townships as *Magogo Zulu* ('Granny Zulu'), the shop has for many years sold meat you can braai on the premises.

Fast Food. Junk food freaks finally knew South Africa was out of the political doldrums when McDonald's opened up 20 or so of their restaurant takeaways throughout the country. Their Big Mac is now almost as well known as the Coke that usually washes it down. Food franchising first came to South Africa in a big way in the 1960s and today you will see the signage of chains such as Milky Lane, Spur, Steers, Squires, Burger Ranch, Kentucky Fried Chicken, Wimpy, Mike's Kitchen, Porter-house, and a variety of pizza outlets. The Mighty Pie chain caters for the emerging lower sector of the fast food market, Steers outlets are aimed at the middle, and Longhorn's target the upper sector. Good value-for-money family restaurants are those in the MacRib chain (open 365 days a year) and Mike's Kitchen restaurants, which are especially good for veggie-loading. A McGinty's Irish Pub and Grill, a Southern Sun franchise chain, is a good place to eat and drink if you want to feel you are in an old pub in the Emerald Isle.

Cheese. South Africa is not historically a cheese-loving country, although this is fast changing as people travel more to places that used to refuse them entry and two-way trade opens up with these countries. Cheddar in its various guises is the top seller, followed by Gouda, better known as sweet-milk cheese. Apart from these there are at least 40 other kinds of cheese available sold under more than 250 different brand names. If you are a cheese lover that should be enough. You can buy most of the better known cheeses at delicatessens and even at increasingly enterprising supermarkets, but the nicest way to buy and eat cheese is at the farm or place where it is made. In Johannesburg you should head for Cremona and Sons' cheese factory shop in the veld, on a dirt road off Main Reef Road, in Roodepoort. Go mid-week if possible or you will be crushed by the weekend crowds. Cremona makes the largest range of Italian cheese in South Africa. They are of unsurpassed quality, so if your fancy runs to Caciocavallo, Robiola, Mascarpone, Kasseri, Pecorino or Mozzarella, beat a path to Cremona's door. Tel (011) 765-1533. You will also find good cheese selections on sale at the weekend at the Michael Mount Organic Market in Bryanston, Johannesburg, tel (011) 706-3671, at the Hillfox Market in Weltevreden Park, Johannesburg, and the Rooftop Market in Rosebank, Johannesburg, both at tel (011) 442-4488.

In the KwaZulu-Natal Midlands, not far from one of the country's most prestigious private schools, Michaelhouse, is Swissland Cheese, where you can sit in the garden and eat cheeses made from the milk of their Saanen goats. Well worth a visit, tel (033) 234-4042. In the Western Cape, you could take a jaunt out to Bloublommetjieskloof ('Ravine of the Little Blue Flowers'), a biodynamic farm on the hills overlooking the town of Wellington. Nothing that is not natural is fed to the Jersey cows, so the milk they produce makes very special cheeses; tel (021) 873-3696. If you do not make it out to the farm, you may find some in Cape Town health shops, or at the weekly market held outside the Rondebosch Public Library every Saturday morning. Another biodynamic farm worth a visit for the cheeses made there is the Camphill Farm Community at Hemel-en-Aarde, just outside Hermanus, tel (0283) 21120, fax (0283) 23555. An advantage here is that in the same valley are a couple of wine farms whose products are the perfect partners for Camphill cheese — or any other cheese for that matter. Further east along the coast, on a farm outside the resort of Plettenberg Bay, you can do more than simply taste the cheese — you can learn how to make it. During a 2½-day course you will be taught how to make Feta, Gouda, cream cheese, and yoghurt. The course costs R250 and includes lunches (with plenty of cheese), wine and a final tea with cheesecake. Accommodation and transport can be arranged if necessary. Contact Finest Kind, PO Box 1, Plettenberg Bay 6600, Western Cape, tel/fax (04457) 31623. If you want to know more about the subject, read *The Complete Book of South African Cheeses*, by Leslie Richfield.

DRINKING

Wines. In South Africa climatic blessings ensure that every year is a vintage year and you have to search hard to find a truly bad wine. You do not have to be an expert to enjoy what are some of the best-value quality wines in the world. Most of the praiseworthy come from the Cape's wine estates, most of them — though not all — in the Stellenbosch and Paarl areas; the good to drinkable come from the numerous co-operatives scattered throughout the wine-growing regions. Decent wine comes in 750ml corked bottles, and cheaper, but often amazingly palatable, reds and whites come in anything from capped 750ml bottles to 5 litre/1 gallon bag-in-a-box wines — known to tipplers as suitcases or briefcases — and a variety of returnable jars.

Most of the natural white and red table wines come from the coastal belt of the Western Cape whose reliable winter rainfall and its Mediterranean climate cooled by ocean breezes make it an ideal area for quality vineyards. The main producing areas are Paarl, Stellenbosch, Franschhoek, Groot Drakenstein, Tulbagh, and Constantia in the Cape Peninsula. The sweet and fortified wines come from Worcester, Robertson, Montagu and Bonnievale on the plateau beyond the first range of mountains, where the climate is hotter and drier. The best place to buy wine is naturally at the estate or winery where it is made, but it is easier to browse the shelves at the supermarket for cheaper wines, or the bottle store for something more up-market.

Most grapes are harvested in February and March and while the Cape is the premier wine-growing area, passable wines also come from the lower reaches of the Orange River in the Northern Cape, in the vicinity of Upington and Kakamas. More than 330 million vines are grown on about 103,500 hectares in South Africa, producing a million tons of grapes. About 90% of the grapes are used to make wine and spirits, 6% are table grapes and the remainder are dried as raisins and currants. Wine production in 1996 was a record 1 billion litres. South Africa's 78 estates, 105 wineries and 71 co-operatives produce some 2000 different wines to choose from.

The country's largest wine producer is Stellenbosch Farmers' Winery, whose range includes Nederburg and Plaisir de Merle wines, two names to look for on the wine list, especially the reds. Nederburg's flagship red is Edelrood, a masterly blend of Cabernet Sauvignon and Merlot. Nederburg Paarl Cabernet Sauvignon is one of South Africa's best-selling red wines. Both Plaisir de Merle's Cabernet Sauvignon and Merlot are outstanding. Their 1994 Cabernet Sauvignon is a steal at just over R30 (£4/$6.60) a bottle. The Nederburg estate in the Klein Drakenstein district of the Paarl valley is the scene of the prestigious Nederburg Wine Auction of fine and rare wines every year, usually in March or April. This is not open to the public — although it attracts plenty of gatecrashers — and two or three months later wines bearing the distinctive 'Sold at the Nederburg Auction' appear on shelves around the country and are well worth trying if you can afford the premium prices.

The wines of Thelema Mountain Vineyards, on the crest of Helshoogte, near Stellenbosch, have propelled the estate into deserved prominence and they have won numerous awards. Their 1994 Chardonnay was the highest-scoring white wine tasted by an international panel for the 1995 South African Airways wine list and the Thelema 1992 vintage Merlot achieved the same distinction in SAA's 1996 list. Winemaker Gyles Webb was Diners Club Winemaker of the Year in 1994 and again in 1996.

The historic estate of Vergelegen, in Somerset West, has released its first varietal red wine, a 1994 Merlot, which is regarded as one of the best reds around. The 1995 vintage is arguably even better, and winemaker Martin Meinert has also produced a Chardonnay Reserve 1995, which should appeal to those who prefer a fuller wine with greater wood contact. Sauvignon Blanc is the world's most popular dry white wine, and in the Cape this grape makes the best of the white wines, with the pick of the bunch coming from Buitenverwachting and Klein Constantia estates, and the Stellenbosch estates of Thelema and Mulderbosch Vineyards. No list is complete without a mention of South Africa's very own unique red, Pinotage.

In 1925, viticulturist Professor Perold crossed the cultivars Pinot Noir and Hermitage (Cinsaut). The result was a brand new cultivar, which he naturally called Pinotage. It is the only known instance in the world where a single crossing resulted in a new varietal. The Pinotage grape adapted extremely well and today wine made from it is popular both locally and overseas. The world's best, with the trophies to prove it, is made by Beyers Truter at Kanonkop Estate, near Stellenbosch.

Good wine can cost as little as R10 (£1.35/$2.20) a bottle. Some of the best budget buys include: Alphen Cellars Sauvignon Blanc, Boland Chenin Blanc, Bon Courage Riesling, Drostdy Hof Claret, Delheim Light, Goue Vallei Weisser Riesling, La Cotte Blanc de Blanc, La Cotte Sauvignon Blanc, Robertson Red, Spier Chardonnay, Swartland Pinotage, Van Loveren Blanc de Blanc, and Van Loveren Cape Riesling. They are not going to bring tears of joy to your eyes, but neither are they going to remove the varnish if you spill your glass on the table.

Out of curiosity you might like to try !Um Hap Red. If you can pronounce the click represented by the exclamation mark on this label you must be a !Kung Bushman (it is pronounced 'cum cap'). This 1995 wine blended mainly from Cabernet Sauvignon and Merlot comes from the Boland Wine Cellar in Paarl and has a ripe fruity character with an appealing combination of berry and pepper flavours. Drink up, as profits from its sale go to a nature reserve at Kagga Kamma between Ceres and Calvinia, which is home to a clan of Bushman families. The wine, with its interesting rock-art label, was served to Queen Elizabeth on her visit to South Africa in 1995. The cellar has also released !Um Hap Sauvignon Blanc/Chenin Blanc 1996, a wine combining the freshness and fruit of Sauvignon Blanc with the extra dimensions of Chenin Blanc. It has an asparagus flavour.

A wide range of excellent sherries is made in South Africa and one important factor in the general high quality is the similarity of climate and soil between Paarl, the heart of the sherry producing area, and Jerez, in Spain. Ports are fortified by the addition of brandy to fermenting grapes. The 1993 vintage of Vergenoegd is a good buy at around R25 (£3.35/$5.50) a bottle.

If you like your wine fortified try to find one that is at least a year old. Look for muscadels, which can be either red or white, are made with muscadel grapes (black or white), and are officially known as muscat de frontignan. Fortified sweet hanepoot is made from muscat d'Alexandrie. Jerepigos can be made from any grape variety — the name simply indicates a fortified wine. Swartland hanepoot is consistently fine, sweet as barley-sugar and Thelema Muscadel is to treasure, but it is rare outside the Cape. KWV Hanepoot Jerepigo (1953) — if you can find any — is a golden honeyed wine of great intensity and richness.

Spirits, Buchu and White Lightning. Only seven years after stepping ashore Dutch settlers produced the first Cape wine. It must have been adequate because it took a further 13 years to distil the first brandy. Once the production of the stuff popularly known as **Kaapse Smaak** (Cape taste, or flavour) was established it was the start of a long South African love affair with **brandewyn,** or brandy. So much so that apart from the esteemed Constantia wine, most vineyards grew grapes for crummy white wines for distillation into brandy and it was not until the early 1960s that the country really produced decent table wines. During the intervening couple of centuries brandy has matured from the rotgut of earlier days when, its name corrupted by English-speakers to 'Cape Smoke', it fuelled the Irish navvies who helped to build the first railways in the Cape. It is said that people on the Highveld developed their taste for spirits in the days of the Voortrekkers, who needed a drink that travelled well. KWV is the name to conjure with (try saying *Ko-operatiewe Wijnbouwers Vereniging van Zuid-Afrika Beperkt*) if you are a brandy — or wine — drinker, or want to take a truly South African present home for your favourite uncle. Since 1918, when it was established, KWV has become the guru organisation for South Africa's export wines, liqueurs and fine brandies. KWV put an end to private brandy distillation in 1924 and set up the standards that ensured today's quality product. Brandy still has a special place in the life of South Africans, who usually drink it *dop en dam* (tot and water), or with cola.

For the finest liqueur brandy that can stand beside cognac look for the KWV label that states that the brandy is an aged liqueur brandy. A bottle of 10-year-old KWV costs just over R50. If you want to know more about its history and production a trip to the KWV wine and brandy cellars complex, in Kohler Street, Paarl, is recommended. This is the largest complex of its kind in the world. Cellar tours are conducted in English, Afrikaans, German and French. There are slide shows and tastings, and child care facilities for touring parents. Open weekdays from 8.30am to 5pm, Saturdays and public holidays from 8.30am to midday, tel (021) 807-3008, fax (021) 863-1942.

The SA Brandy Foundation, at 39 Herte Street, Stellenbosch, tel (021) 887-3157, fax (021) 886-6381, is also a good port of call, as is the Van Ryn Brandy Cellar, just outside Stellenbosch, on the Vlottenburg road, which has tours at 10.30am and 3pm Monday to Thursday, and on Friday at 10.30am. Tours of the cellar start with a brandy cocktail and an audio-visual presentation that introduces you to the art of brandy making. Next stop is the distillery where the wine is distilled in copper potstills. At the cooperage you can see the craftsmen shaping the staves, curving the wood over the fire, and then fixing the iron bands around them to make a barrel tight enough to mature the brandy. When the barrel is finished, the cooper tests it by playing a rhythmic tune on it. In the maturation cellar you will smell the 'angels' share' in the air — the brandy evaporating from the maturing casks. The tour ends with tastings. Contact tel (021) 881-3875, fax (021) 881-3127. Paarl Rock Brandy Cellars in Drommedaris Street, Daljosafat, Paarl, also has cellar tours explaining its complete brandy production flowline, with an audio-visual presentation, tasting and sales on weekdays at 11am and 1pm, tel (021) 862-6159, fax (021) 862-6024.

Buchu brandy is made from a shrub belonging to the citrus family. The two species used medically grow on the slopes of the Cedarberg in the south-western Cape and can be taken to relieve colds, flu and an unsettled stomach. For stomach ache mix buchu brandy with port. Buchu vinegar is applied to sprains and bruises and buchu tea is drunk to cure disorders of the bladder and kidneys. In the USA it used to be prized as a cure for hangovers, and it is strange that it does not have this reputation in its country of origin. In the old days, Khoikhoi women seldom washed in water, but smeared their bodies with animal fat mixed with sweet-smelling powdered buchu leaves.

Moonshine is part of most modern nations' folklore and South Africa is no different, except here the product of the forbidden still was known as *witblits* (**white lightning**) and **mampoer**. Witblits is virtually as old as South African viticulture. When the Voortrekkers packed their covered wagons to leave the Cape and British rule, they took their witblits with them. Mampoer on the other hand was born in the old Voortrekker Republic of the Transvaal and takes its name from Mampuru, a local tribal chief from the Marico district who developed a definite predilection for this spirit, which has a kick like an ostrich. Both witblits and mampoer were very much home industry stuff and frowned on until some commercial distillers gave it respectability by producing it for the local market. Today, they use a variety of fruits, including peaches, apricot, cherries, apples, oranges and figs to produce this legendary liquor. A pleasant but instant amnesia version is made in KwaZulu-Natal from pineapples. Both witblits and mampoer are 44% alcohol by volume.

Distilling witblits and mampoer is time-consuming and it takes a lot of fruit to produce a few bottles of the stuff, so it is fairly expensive (R38.65 — £5.15/$8.50 — for a 750ml bottle of mampoer and R35.95 for witblits). After fermentation in stainless steel tanks it goes into red copper stills for three distillations. Only part of the second distillation — called the *middelloop* (middle run) — is deemed pure enough for drinking. Most things taste best on their home territory and these two fiery drinks are no exception. The bushveld is where they are traditionally produced and that is the place to savour them. Less than an hour's drive from Pretoria is Loopspruit, the only registered South African wine estate north of the Orange River. It is situated on the banks of the Loopspruit River, about 35km/22 miles from Bronkhorstspruit. Loopspruit produces witblits from grapes and mampoer from peaches and apricots, as well as an interesting range of wines. The estate offers a R50 package that includes wine tasting and a cellar tour, as well as lunch in the estate restaurant, which is decorated with Ndebele beadwork and ethnic motifs — but do not forget to sharpen your appetite first with a tot of witblits or mampoer. Loopspruit Estate is open Tuesday to Sunday from 8am to 4pm, tel (01212) 24303, fax (01212) 33138 for information and directions. Bookings for the restaurant tel/fax (01212) 24352.

There are witblits and mampoer festivals every year in various places, but no-one can seem to remember where or when they are held. There are some in the Groot Marico area and if you are there around September check with the Groot Marico Information Centre, tel (014252) and ask for extension 85. The pleasant little town of Philippolis, in the southern Free State, has a witblits festival every year in April, when local farmers and visitors get together to generate mammoth hangovers. Luckily it only goes on for two days. More information from Louw Vorster, tel (051772) and ask for 6.

Beer. Early records indicate that beer brewing was under way even before wine was made at the Cape. The first private licence to brew beer was granted on February 28 1664, and the first major brewery at the Cape was established in 1696 near the farm Nuweland, where South African Breweries' (SAB) Newlands Brewery still operates as Ohlsson's Cape Breweries, using barley and hops grown in the Cape and the spring water from nearby Table Mountain that was the reason for the brewery's original location there more than three centuries ago. Beer from Newlands went with prospectors to the diamond diggings of Kimberley, washed the grit out of the throats of miners on the Witwatersrand goldfields and was a welcome pick-me-up for British soldiers during the Anglo-Boer War. Since then it has become as South African as braaivleis, boerewors and biltong. Today most of the beer in South Africa is brewed by SAB, which, in 1996, won two highly rated international beer awards, competing against hundreds of beers from more than 50 countries. The first was for its Carling Black Label, which won, for the second time, the gold medal for best beer in its class at the Brewing Industry International Awards at Burton-upon-Trent, England. At the Australian International Beer Awards, SAB's Castle Lager, Lion Lager and Carling Black Label scooped five gold medals and four silvers. Carling Black Label was awarded the overall grand champion trophy.

Like Australian brews, South African beers are brewed to be served cold, ideally around 4°C/39°F. Most SAB beers are 4.5–5% alcohol by volume; the exceptions are Castle Lite (4%), Carling Black Label (5.5%) and Castle Milk Stout (6%). Castle and Lion are the most popular local lagers. Others are Hansa Pilsener, Amstel Lager, Ohlsson's Lager, and SAB imports Heineken, Guinness draught in kegs and cans, and Kilkenny Draught, a traditional Red Irish Ale. A recent addition to the local market is Redd's, an alcoholic apple-flavoured malt beverage. SAB is the fourth largest brewer in the world — after Anheuser-Busch Inc (US), Heineken NV (the Netherlands), and Miller Brewing Co (US) — supplying 99% of the R7.5 billion local market, which guzzles 2.35 billion litres a year.

Parts of the Newlands Brewery in Cape Town dating back to 1859 have been declared national monuments and now house a visitor's centre (open daily). It provides a lively record of SAB's first 100 years. In Johannesburg, you can explore the history of beer in South Africa in an entertaining and hospitable way at SAB's Centenary Centre, in the downtown Newtown Cultural Precinct. The *Ukhamba* display reveals the secrets of African sorghum beer brewing, and the Heritage Hall shows how beer was brewed in the good old days. You can even take a trip back in time and experience a real Soweto shebeen, circa 1965, and wind up your visit by sampling a glass or two. The centre is open Tuesday to Saturday, 11am–6pm, at 15 President Street, Newtown, Johannesburg 2000, tel (011) 836-4900. Admission is R10.

Worldwide interest in real ales and beers found its first echo in South Africa in 1983 when an innovative brewer called Lex Mitchell started a brewery in the small resort town of Knysna, on the scenic Garden Route. At first, a single beer was produced, called Forester's draught, a light, medium-strength beer tending to pilsner. Two years later the brewery produced its first ale, Bosun's Bitter, modelled after the Yorkshire ale Mitchell. Winter saw the introduction of a full-bodied milk stout called Raven Stout. Next came a lighter ale called Stork Ale and then Millwood Mild — Millwood being the name of the old local gold-mining area — a dark, flavourful mild ale. In 1989 came Mitchell's Old 90/- Ale, a heavy winter ale spiced with cinnamon. On special occasions a barley wine, Mitchell's Special Brew, is brewed; this powerful concoction is known locally as Old Wobbly. Since 1989, Mitchell's Waterfront Brewery, next to the Ferryman's Tavern in the Cape Town harbour, has been producing Mitchell's ales under licence. In conjunction with British brewing giant Scottish and Newcastle International, which now has a major shareholding in the Cape Town and Johannesburg breweries, a highly popular Mitchell's Scottish Ale House has been developed in the Waterfront brewery, which is a must for all visiting beer lovers. Mitchell's Gauteng Brewery supplies beer only to Johannesburg and Durban. The three breweries together produce about 1.6 million litres of beer a year, a drop in the ocean compared to the volumes of market giant SAB, but the concept of micro-breweries seems to be greater than the sum of its parts, as anyone interested in CAMRA and similar real ale bodies will know.

Both the Knysna and Cape Town breweries offer tours and tastings and have many brewery related products for sale in their shops (you can even buy beer). Tours of the Johannesburg plant can also be arranged. At Mitchell's Knysna Brewery, contact Dave McRae, tel (0445) 24685, or Lex Mitchell, tel (041) 51-4560. At Mitchell's Waterfront Brewery, contact Andre Swart, tel (021) 419-5074, and contact Mitchell's Gauteng Brewery, tel (011) 493-8640.

In Johannesburg, independent brewer Bavaria Bräu has since 1992 produced a fine drop, brewed according to the German *Reinheitsgebot* (purity law) of 1516. As this stipulates no artificial preservatives, the beers — Edel lager and Kaltenburg Royal lager — do not keep too long or travel far, luckily for the beer drinkers of Gauteng. The brewery also produces an interesting alcoholic soda called Sirocco, and was the first local producer of the Australian alcoholic lemonade Two Dogs. Windhoek and Hansa beers from neighbouring Namibia Breweries are also brewed from imported German malt and hops according to the old purity rules, and are popular tipples. If you do not like the local beers once you have tried them — South Africa is, after all, lager country — you will undoubtedly find your home country's six-packs lining the shelves of any large bottle store (the local name for an off-licence or liquor store).

Liqueurs. There are only two uniquely South African liqueurs for those who like a sticky ending to their meals. The oldest and most famous is Van der Hum, which means the equivalent of 'what's his name'. Van der Hum was invented early on when Dutch settlers tried to produce a local version of Curacao. They used *naartjies* (tangerines) instead of the usual oranges and the result was a spiced and aromatic fruit liqueur that is still a best-seller at about R28 (£3.75/$6.15) a bottle. The other liqueur, which did not appear on the scene for another couple of centuries, is Amarula Cream (R28), which is a delight for anyone with a sweet tooth. It is made from the fruit of the wild marula tree, which grows in the northern low-lying parts of the country, and is packed with Vitamin C (four times more than orange juice). The marula tree bears in abundance between February and April — anything from 17,000 to more than 90,000 fruits during the season. The tree is also known as the Elephant Tree, because its delicious fruit is a favourite with jumbos, who are prone to gobble the over-ripe fruit after it has been lying on the ground fermenting and get the monumental staggers. For Amarula Cream it is fermented in copper pot stills and thereafter matured for two years in oak casks like wine. The liquor is then enriched with a pure marula extract and blended with fresh cream. It is delicious on its own, over fruit or with your coffee. The marula fruit also makes a potent mampoer spirit, a sort of farm poteen.

Soft Drinks. About 275 million cases of soft drinks are sold each year in South Africa, with more than half being downed in the Gauteng area. The market is dominated by colas, which account for more than 60% of the volume, but fruit-flavoured carbonated soft drinks are becoming increasingly popular. Coca Cola has more than 50% of the $860 million-a-year carbonated soft drinks market. South Africans drink 90% of all soft drinks sold in Africa and this makes it the eighth largest market in the world.

Spring Waters. There are about 30 different bottled mineral and spring waters to choose from. In line with the trend towards healthier living worldwide, there has been a rapid increase in the popularity and consumption of bottled water locally. The South African Natural Bottled Water Association (Sanbwa), comprising most of the larger bottled natural water producers, states that all water called mineral, spring, or natural is bottled at source, not kept in tanks for more than 48 hours before bottling, and comes from an underground source free from harmful bacteria. The water can be filtered, but nothing added except carbon dioxide to make it fizz. Ordinary cold springs are found all over the country and particularly large supplies come from limestone formations. Some sparkling and still spring waters you might like to try are Caledon, Valvita, Schweppes, Schoonspruit, Valpré, Maluti and Sparkling Breeze. You can buy most of the well known European bottled waters in delicatessens and speciality stores, but they are prohibitively expensive. A new name in the market is Karoo bottled water. Springbok rugby great Mannetjies Roux and his family are making a big splash with this in the Great Karoo. They are bottling the water from a desert spring on their farm, Nobelsfontein. Behind the old farmhouse on the remote farm, outside Victoria West, is a spring with an estimated 320 million litres waiting to be bottled.

Fruit Juices. Port Elizabeth-based company Valor produces some of the best budget fruit juices in South Africa. Its one-litre packs carry a nutritional fact sheet on the back giving carbohydrate, vitamin, mineral and kilojoule content. This is good for dieters who often drink fruit juice thinking they are kilojoule-free and healthy, only to find out later that they are filled with cane sugar. Valor fruit juices sell at R3.89 (50p/85 cents) in leading supermarkets. Other packs likely to catch your eye in the café or supermarket are Liqui-Fruit and Ceres. Both are excellent. Just Juice in bottles or cans is easier to carry on hikes or trips to the beach.

Tea and Rooibos. At least 10,000 million cups of tea are drunk every year in South Africa, which makes it the country's most popular beverage. Tea was first planted locally in 1880 in Natal and more than 50% of local demand is met by tea grown in South Africa; the rest is imported from Sri Lanka, Malawi and Mauritius. In KwaZulu-Natal's Nkandia district is the Ntingwe tea estate. In the October to April season Ntingwe produces only 100 tons of tea, but when it exports its leaf to London, it commands top prices and is compared by buyers with Darjeeling and other premium teas from the Far East. Unblended Ntingwe tea used to be sold in the UK under a plain brown wrapper on which was handwritten 'Zulu Tea'. Now, however, it is sold worldwide with the name of the estate prominent on the smart tin caddie. Apart from KwaZulu-Natal you will find fine tea plantations in the Northern Province around Magoebaskloof, where verdant blankets of tea plants all but cover the slopes of the escarpment, part of the Sapekoe Group's tea estates. Tea-growing began here in 1967 when a planter from Kenya settled in the area and started producing Sapekoe, or South African Tea ('Pekoe' is a Chinese word for tea). The picking season is from September to May, and if you like the smell of tea a visit to the Sapekoe estates is an interesting experience.

Rooibos (red bush) tea is one of the few plants that has made the transition from a local wild resource to a cultivated, economic crop and it is widely used as an alternative to ordinary tea by people who enjoy it either hot or cold and regard it as a healthy drink. It is also gaining popularity as a beverage in other countries, notably Japan, Germany and the USA, following reports of its healthful properties. It is often prescribed for nervous tension, allergies and various stomach and digestive problems.

Rooibos tea is the processed form of a plant that in its natural state is found only in the mountains of the Western Cape. It grows nowhere else in the world except on the slopes of the Cedarberg and Olifants River mountain ranges, where it is produced on an intensive scale, particularly in the districts of Piketberg, Clanwilliam, Van Rhynsdorp and Calvinia, as it grows best 450m above sea-level. Swedish botanist Carl Thunberg reported in 1772 that the Khoikhoi used the plant to make a hot drink. Once white settlers discovered the pleasant flavour and medicinal qualities of this wild bush tea, rooibos became popular. It used to be difficult to propagate because each plant bears only a single seed, which shoots out as soon as it is ripe. Then it was discovered that ants collected and stored them. Today, more modern collecting methods are used.

Rooibos tea is packaged locally under a variety of brand names. Some of the best known are Eleven O'Clock, Freshpak, Laager, and Vital. In Japan, rooibos tea is marketed as Dr Rooitea and regarded there as an excellent source of anti-oxidants, which counteract free radicals in the human body, increasing the body's immunity and reportedly delaying ageing. Rooibos is a good pick-me-up in the morning, a refreshing drink after a meal, a thirst-quencher after exercise, and a flavouring agent for desserts, bakes, soups and stews, and even a marinade for meat and chicken. It is also a natural meat tenderiser. Rooibos is prepared like ordinary tea and served with or without milk and sugar. It is also good with lemon or apple cider vinegar. It contains nine essential minerals, is caffeine-free, and contains far less tannin than normal tea. The more research reveals about this humble bush the more it seems that rooibos should be called Wonder Tea. Guided tours of the rooibos tea factory at 64 Rooibos Avenue, Clanwilliam, take place daily at 2pm and 4pm. Contact Rooibos Ltd at tel (027) 482-2155.

Honey Tea. *Heuningtee* (Honey tea) is a bushy shrub whose foliage and young flowers have long been used as a bush tea, especially as a soothing drink for coughs and colds. It has a pleasant odour of honey and is free from stimulating alkaloids. It grows mainly in the south-western Cape districts down to Riversdale. Like rooibos, it is packaged and sold in supermarkets.

In general the performing arts and entertainment are alive and reasonably well in South Africa, although interests such as classical music, opera, ballet, modern dance, theatre and other diversions perceived as Eurocentric are feeling a chill wind following the government's decision to stop subsidising the four former provincial performing arts bodies that previously provided an umbrella for their activities. They have been told they must become privately funded as their subsidies have been transferred to a new single National Arts Council, which will use a R10 million budget — to be doubled in 1998 — to fund artists and promote art. The biggest blow in all this is seen by white communities to be the muffling of the nation's four premier symphony orchestras, which for years have been a source of pride and joy to lovers of classical music and the source of most serious concerts. The Department of Arts, Culture, Science and Technology (an odd enough combination) says the issue is not about subsidies but about equity and redress, and redirecting spending to make the arts accessible to all South Africans. Deputy minister Brigitte Mabandla says only when South Africans embrace ballet alongside gumboot dancing as equally valid art forms will a truly multicultural society start to take shape.

The annual festival, or *fees,* is a big event in South Africa and the performing arts feature prominently on local festival calendars. Most towns and even the smallest villages stage a festival or two every year. Every year around July the Eastern Cape university town of Grahamstown hosts the Standard Bank National Arts Festival, which showcases South Africa's top creative talents and is probably the country's most important cultural event. A substantial indigenous fringe component complements the main programme, and for many this is the most entertaining part of the festival. Every two years musicians and dancers from all over the world flock to Roodepoort, in Gauteng, to take part in the biennial International Eisteddfod of South Africa. Those who know about these things rate the Durban Tattoo among the world's best and in the same league as the Edinburgh Military Tattoo and the Royal Tournament in London, and it is regarded as an annual event not to be missed.

MUSIC

South Africa's repertoire includes European and traditional African sounds, jazz, folk, rock, pop, and the special *mbaquanga* sound many visitors associate with South Africa. A new sound emerging is a synthesis of African and European music, and this can be heard at festivals and at clubs found all over the country in the big cities. Although there is still recognisable European and African-based ethnic music the borders are blurring and the fusion of the two is gaining in popularity and giving South Africa a new export. Durban is regarded as the cradle of South African pop, Johannesburg is the recording capital of the music industry, but Soweto is the workshop for new trends. The new music has been popularised by groups such as the Soweto String Quartet and Ladysmith Black Mambazo. Whatever your taste, from classics to township jazz, you are sure to find something to your liking. Newspapers publish details of clubs, concerts, festivals and so on, usually in the Friday and weekend editions. Albums, tapes and CDs of the country's talented musicians and their works are now being played around the world, and many composers, soloists and groups have taken the high road to fame and fortune in Europe and the USA.

South African music used to be characterised by lilting Afrikaner farmer's music played on the squeeze-box and the guitar on the one hand, and the cheery sound of the penny whistle playing the *kwela* music of the black townships on the other. These clichés are almost gone, although you can still hear the odd *boereorkes* playing *vastrap* and *tiekiedraai* music at traditional Afrikaner gatherings. Folk music as it was played in the 1960s and 1970s is a dying melody of the sandals and print-dress era and does not command much of a following any more; country and western has a few devoted fans; jazz remains hugely popular, especially in the uniquely black South African blending of traditional rhythms with American mainstream; but it is pop in all its forms — rock and techno to *kwaito* — that dominates the airwaves and packs them into festivals, warehouses and clubs. Travelling around the country you will notice that the same names keep popping up at gigs and on the club scene. Groups to watch out for are Qcumba Zoo, who have made it big in the USA, Springbok Nude Girls, The Pressure Cookies, Famous Curtain Trick, Urban Creep, Peppa Lizards, Squeal, Mean Mr Mustard, Lithium, Arapaho, the Blues Broers, Live Jimi Presley, Karoo, Landscape Prayers, Gutted Remains, Groinchurn, and the Truly Fully Hey Shoo Wow Band. These are some of the groups likely to feature at such major pop and rock festivals as Splashy Fen, in the southern Drakensberg of KwaZulu-Natal, and Rustler's Valley, near Ficksburg, in the Free State.

After years of exile black music legends such as singer Miriam Makeba (Mama Afrika) and trumpeter Hugh Masekela returned to South Africa to find themselves replaced by new icons such as saxman Sipho 'Hotstix' Mabuse, Sipho Gumede, Lucky Dube, Jabu Khanyile, Jonas Gwangwa, Sibongile Khumalo, West Nkosi, Ringo Madlingozi, and Ray Phiri whose work on the Paul Simon album *Graceland* made him an international star, and his old group Stimela a household name in South Africa. Another internationally celebrated musician is Caiphus Semenya, who is home after a stint in the USA where he composed the music for the TV series *Roots*. Lebo M progressed from backing the popular musical *Sarafina* on Broadway to winning a Grammy for his work on the soundtrack of the Disney hit *The Lion King*.

A word you will hear a lot of is *kwaito,* which is old township ghetto slang for a gangster, but now refers to a type of township pop that is all the rage among black teenagers, even though it is slated by black music critics. The 'King of Kwaito' is Arthur Mafokate whose lyrics — often punctuated by abusive language — are delivered in *iscqamtho,* a lingo mixing Zulu, Sotho, English and Afrikaans, which he believes should be South Africa's 12th official language. Jazzy interpretations of *kwaito* are done by Sipho 'Hotstix' Mabuse. An interesting newcomer now recording is Nothembi Mkhwebane, a former domestic worker who swapped the scrubbing brush for the guitar and now plays popular Ndebele numbers.

JAZZ

Stalwarts of old-style jazz are the African Jazz Pioneers, who have ben belting it out locally since no one remembers when. Hugh Masekela, Denzil Weale, Mike Makhalemele, Abigail Kubeka, McCoy Mrubata, Azval Ismail, Philip Tabane, Johnny Fourie, Surendran Reddy, Vusi Mahlasela, Darius Brubeck and Bheki Mseleku are some of the musicians and singers you will come across if you are a music fan, and while most of these names might mean little to you now, they will mean more once you have heard them. One person who does recognise the talent of South African jazzmen is King Bhumibol of Thailand, who blows a mean sax himself. At the end of 1996, he invited Darius Brubeck and Bheki Mseleku to appear with an international array of top jazz musicians flown into Bangkok to celebrate his 50 years on the throne.

DANCE

Dance has always been an integral part of African life, as the overture to a hunt, waging war, courting, marriage, initiation and work. European and Asian dance traditions have also blossomed. The development of dance over the past two decades has been part and parcel of performance and protest theatre, with its mixture of song, movement and dance. The protest musical has established certain styles of dancing and stage techniques, such as the *toyi-toyi* (struggle dance of the people), the *mapantsula* (township jive), the *isicatamiya* (a choir tradition from the mines) and Zulu dances.

The most memorable Zulu dancing is the foot-stamping warrior dances performed for tourists in kraals and villages in various parts of Zululand. These are the forté of the men dressed in animal-skin kilts, ostrich plumes, cow-tails and seed-pod rattles, rhythmically pounding the earth as they did before they wiped out the British redcoats at Isandhlwana in 1879. The women's dances are more sedate shuffles, typified by the annual Reed Dance in September/October when bare-breasted, beaded maidens perform a dance for the Zulu king. A national Zulu dance competition is held near Estcourt in KwaZulu-Natal every November and there are various other cultural happenings where you can see the finest dancers, including Zululand's dancing dynamos, the Othukela Ngoma Zulu Dance Group, acclaimed as the best in the country. These dancers have performed before Queen Elizabeth, and at many international dance festivals. In Durban, you can even learn the awesome Zulu kicks, stamps and jumps from award-winning choreographer and traditional Zulu dancer Vusabantu Ngema.

Gumboot dancing has always intrigued visitors to South Africa. The nearest thing to it in Europe is the Bavarian and Austrian folk dance that includes slaps on heels and thighs. This, strangely enough, is the origin of the African gumboot dance, which came to full flower in the mine compound dances that used to be held on the Reef at the weekends. The dance is called the *isiCathulo* (boot dance), and a missionary is said to have forbidden lewd and pagan dances and taught the Bhaca tribe to do this genteel European folk dance instead. As some of the men were working in the docks at Durban and were issued with rubber boots, or gumboots, these became incorporated in the dance. You can see exponents of this amusing dance mainly on the Reef, where dance troupes include it in their exhibitions of tribal dancing at festivals, outdoor markets, school fêtes and the like. Look out for Soweto's Rishile Dancers, who jive in gumboots and ankle rattles.

AFTER DARK

Cities and the bigger towns throughout the country offer the usual nightlife attractions — action bars, theme pubs, clubs, night clubs and discos — and details are carried in the local newspapers.

Probably the only kind of relaxation in this area you won't find at home is the shebeen, which was black South Africa's answer in the old days to the strict apartheid laws, which not only forbade their entrance to 'white' bars and hotels, but restricted sales of alcohol to them. Shebeens are now established or traditional township gathering places where you meet your friends and neighbours over a few drinks and where you can buy a plate of food to keep you going. Some of these were known by poetic names such as Back of the Moon and Falling Leaves, and were even immortalised in black musicals such as *King Kong*. Nowadays, most are more up-market taverns with ghetto blasters, a wide range of drinks and an à la carte menu. Many have even made it into the tourist brochures but their names — Freda's, Freddy's, Lily's, and Tickey's — do not have the old ring. An oddity is that the word shebeen is so deeply entrenched in the South African vernacular that its origins are never questioned. Shebeen is an Anglo-Irish word for an illicit liquor shop, but no-one knows how it came to be adopted by the black community.

CINEMAS

Once better known as bioscopes in South Africa but now known as the movie theatre or the movies, cinemas are reviving their popularity, although they have reduced in size from the old opulent palaces where the women patrons wore furs and jewellery and everyone stood for the anthem to mini jobs with a few dozen seats, with up to a dozen or more venues crammed into one massive complex. There also used to be bio-cafés, or cine-cafés — now mercifully gone — which remained in total darkness for days on end while patrons drank tea (or something wrapped in a brown paper bag) and watched flickering old movies. It was often rumoured that patrons believed to have passed out had, in fact, passed on and were left unnoticed for days on end.

The South African film industry itself has never risen to the heights currently occupied by, say, Australia. Movies were of the *skop, skiet en donder* (kick, shoot and beat-up) variety and even the ones produced nowadays with American know-how and actors are B-grade offerings. The government has plans to change this and has established a South African Film and Television Trust and a Television Foundation to help budding TV and film producers. Two major distributors run the country's main movie theatres. They are Ster-Kinekor and Nu Metro, and if you check the daily newspapers for movies you will find them in every town and city listed under these names. These will probably be joined by Virgin cinemas. There are a few independent art cinemas, whose menu of serious and usually sub-titled films attracts a loyal following of film buffs.

THEATRE

Theatre flourishes in South Africa, virtually against all odds, and in Johannesburg alone there are nearly 20 theatres catering for all tastes. There are two established theatrical traditions in the country, the black African tradition, which developed over centuries, and the imported European tradition. This has resulted in part in a hybrid theatre, which like its fusion counterpart in music has created a vibrant form. South Africa has produced some fine actors and actresses and some notable playwrights, the best known and internationally acclaimed being Athol Fugard.

Computicket, which has more than 300 branches countrywide, sells tickets for virtually all entertainment and leisure events in South Africa. As well as movies, theatre, pop and orchestral concerts, you can book for sporting events, festivals, and other tourist attractions, tel (011) 445-8445. Ticketline (011) 445-8200 takes advance bookings for credit card holders only. Open seven days a week, 9am–8pm.

RAVES

There used to be tribal gatherings — now there is the rave scene. Nobody is quite sure what it is all about, least of all the ravers, but it is the latest place to tune in and drop out for a few hours or a few days. A recent magazine survey showed that only one in ten local ravers knows what music is being played. This is not all that surprising considering that it could be any one of a myriad number of categories. Trance is the most popular rave music in South Africa, followed by Jungle, House, Dream and Hardware. It is all a digital bubblebath of head-banging sound, but it draws at least 10,000 under 25s in Gauteng alone for regular weekend raves (anyone over this age is regarded as geriatric). The raves that pull them in are the ones with imported DJs, usually from the UK, who are role models and folk heroes rolled into one. Raves are so far a predominantly white phenomenon. There is a string of rave clubs throughout the country — you can even get tickets through nationwide Computicket at R40 to R50 — but raves are like mushrooms, they pop up when its dark, and the best ones are advertised by word of mouth. They start on Thursday or Friday evening and can go on until Sunday evening. Apart from the pumping music, the lasers and the strobes, they all offer Chill Rooms for dancers to chill out — or E out — from the hyper-activity. No alcohol is sold, nor is it popular with ravers, who prefer to keep going with imported Smart Drinks laced with vitamins and amino acids for stamina, now commonplace on the shelves of most supermarkets. Most users of the drug Ecstasy are ravers and this has led to rising concern and the formation in Johannesburg of a rave association that runs a national campaign called Rave Safe. This is an information service telling ravers how to be intelligent about drug use, with the message: 'If you do drugs, don't let drugs do you.'

Rave festivals have also sprung up, the biggest in the middle of the vast Karoo. Called Desert Storm, this was first held towards the end of 1996 at Verneukpan ('Deception Pan') in the Northern Cape, a bleak spot that was, until the ravers arrived, best known as the flats on which Sir Malcolm Campbell failed to break the world landspeed record in 1928 in his car Bluebird. The Karoo rave was based on similar festivals at Black Rock in the Nevada desert and in the Australian Outback. It will be held every September until interest fades.

Although South Africa relies on Europe for most of its rave music there is a minor local upsurge. A couple of ex-Urban Creep musicians have come up with what they call Trance Sky and they have the bizarre achievement of taking ANC veteran Walter Sisulu's first speech after his release from jail and making a techno dance mix of it.

GAMBLING

Apart from a harmless flutter on the horses, gambling was not only frowned on under the old National Party government but legally restricted by the 1965 Gambling Act, which prohibited all gaming operations in the country. The apartheid policy that established so-called independent black homeland states within the Republic had the unforeseen effect of creating gambling havens, which major hotel interests such as Sun International were not slow to exploit. This saw the rise of opulent US-style hotel-casino complexes in places such as the Transkei, the Ciskei, Venda and Bophuthatswana — the latter home to the most famous of them all, Sun City, later joined by an architectural extravaganza called The Lost City. The homelands are gone — reincorporated in the new South Africa — but the casinos remain as major attractions. Their dominance in an industry that is now estimated to be worth about R4 billion a year will be whittled away now the government has legalised gambling and casinos, by which act it hopes to create an extra 100,000 jobs and generate R1.5 billion a year for Reconstruction and Development Programme projects.

Under the new gambling dispensation the country will get a total 40 casinos, whose licensing is in the hands of the nine provincial governments. Sun International has been given until 1999 to rationalise its 17 licences to eight. It will have to reduce its seven casinos in the North-West Province and its seven in the Eastern Cape to three in each region. The group has already reconstituted some of its casino operations as Sun International South Africa, and others as Africa Sun International, which includes black business and labour organisations among its partners. When all the new casinos are up and spinning there will be six in Gauteng, five each in the Western Cape, KwaZulu-Natal, the North-West and the Eastern Cape, four each in the Free State and Mpumalanga, and three each in the Northern Cape and the Northern Province. This breakdown has been decided by the relative wealth of each province, and therefore the likelihood of its residents contributing in ratio to casino incomes. Gauteng, for instance, should account for 47% of the R4 billion expected to cross the tables every year.

Some fierce battles are being waged over the licences up for grabs. As in other areas, preference is being given to consortiums with visible signs of black empowerment. British corporation Bass Leisure is involved in gambling — slot machines and Bingo — and among its local partners are Southern Sun and black labour umbrellas Fabcos (Foundation for African Business and Consumer Services) and Nafcoc (National African Federated Chamber of Commerce).

Lotteries. These are viewed worldwide as a way to raise funds for charity and estimates suggest a national lottery could net about R4 billion and contribute at least R1.5 billion to reconstruction and development as well as various charities. Lotteries should be in evidence by early 1998 and while control of a national lottery will rest with the state, it will be operated on its behalf by a private organisation.

Horse-Racing. The Sport of Kings got off to an early start in South Africa. Shortly after the British took the Cape from the Dutch, officers were racing their mounts against each other while soldiers and locals placed wagers on the outcome. Fortune-hunting *uitlander* took their love of horse-racing and gambling with them to the Highveld when they left the Cape and headed upcountry to the new goldfields of the Transvaal (present day Gauteng). Johannesburg was not six months old when, in December 1886, the first horse race was held and President Paul Kruger, who believed all forms of gambling to be expressly forbidden by the Almighty, gave it a wink, if not a nod, when he opined that men had a duty to exercise both themselves and their horses. By 1889, the Johannesburg Turf Club has been established and has remained at the forefront of the lucrative sport, with racing assets worth R400 million in a province whose punters place stakes worth R1.3 billion a year. Club assets include three of the country's best known racecourses — Turffontein, Gosforth Park and Newmarket — as well as the Totalisator (Tote) Board. In KwaZulu-Natal, the main tracks are Greyville and Clairwood Park in Durban, and Scottsville, the home of the Pietermaritzburg Turf Club. In the Western Cape, the Western Province Management Board holds race meetings at Milnerton, Durbanville and Kenilworth, all tracks within easy commuting distance from Cape Town. In the Eastern Cape, there are racecourses in Port Elizabeth at Arlington and Fairview, in the Northern Cape at Griqualand West, and in the Free State at Bloemfontein and Vaal.

The red letter days on the racing calendar are the Durban July Handicap at Greyville, which is regarded as the South African Ascot, the J and B Met in Cape Town at Kenilworth in February, and the R750,000 Gold Bowl, run in November over 3200m at Turffontein. As with Ascot, the premier races are as much a fashion show as a race meet and some weird and wonderful sights are to be seen at the tracks. Apart from the fact that the sun is usually beating down — and the sprinkling of traditional African costume among the chiffon, silk and lace — the races could be anywhere, with the bookmakers tick-tacking furiously and despondent punters shredding their last betting slips.

For those unable to get to the races bets can be placed at Tote offices around the country, or by placing a Tab Telebet through Computicket. The racing pages of all newspapers are avidly read and the Johannesburg morning paper *The Citizen* is particularly esteemed by punters for its tips and advice. Paul Kruger would be scandalised but there is now horse-racing on Sunday, as well as at night on floodlit racecourses, which has doubled the number of punters since it was first introduced by Greyville and Newmarket. The regulatory body for all horse-racing in the country is the Jockey Club of Southern Africa, PO Box 74439, Turffontein 2140, Gauteng, tel (011) 683-9283, fax (011) 683-5548.

SPORT AND RECREATION

South Africans are mad about sport — everything from traditional jukskei and morabaraba to golf, football, cricket and, crowning glory, rugby. More than 100 sports are officially recognised by the controlling body, the National Sports Council. Outdoor sport naturally predominates in a country blessed with the perfect climate for these events and the ones with the most spectator appeal are soccer, rugby and cricket. Even the years of sporting isolation as a result of apartheid have not stifled the country's competitive skills and spirit, as it has shown by winning the 1995 Rugby World Cup and the soccer African Cup of Nations. There have also been impressive successes in cricket and boxing, and at the Atlanta Olympics in 1996, South Africa won three golds, a silver and a bronze, outperforming many established Olympic nations, such as the UK. At these games marathon-runner Josia Thugwane became the first black South African ever to win an Olympic gold. Furthermore after an absence of 36 years, South Africa was welcomed back to the Commonwealth Games in Canada in 1994; the last time a South African team had participated in these Games had been at Cardiff in 1958. The 2004 Olympic Games may well be held in South Africa if Cape Town succeeds in its bid to host them.

One of the major challenges facing sport is not in the field, but in redressing historical imbalances, which have — with the notable exception of soccer and athletics — hamstrung black competitors in their efforts to improve their standards — or even take part in some sports. This is changing rapidly as government, sports bodies and business leaders combine to develop all major sports at grass roots level for all communities. Since 1994 sport has done more to promote national unity and racial reconciliation than any amount of tub-thumping by politicians. This was epitomised by President Mandela when he donned the green and gold jersey of a rugby Springbok captain to congratulate his country's team after they quelled the All Blacks in 1995 to win the Rugby World Cup. Mandela is patron-in-chief of the Sports Trust, a joint venture between the government, sports bodies and the private sector, set up not only to redress sporting imbalances, but to encourage more women to take part in sport and to support the development of sport among those with physical or mental disabilities. The Trust is spending millions on a series of sports development projects.

Many believe that the sports boycott of South Africa did as much to crack apartheid as economic and other boycotts. Sport, and in particular rugby, plays a major role in the life of the Afrikaner and the years of isolation when no sporting nation would play against the country's national team, the Springboks, had the effect of sapping morale. Since the boycotts ended, South Africa has bounced back with remarkable vigour.

Rugby is the first love of most sports fans and the country's premier national game, virtually a religion. The winning of the World Cup in 1995 was the Springbok side's crowning glory after more than a decade out in the cold, excluded from all international competition. Following this revitalising win the Springboks remained unbeaten in 14 successive Tests.

In 1995, the National Sports Council objected to the continued use of the Springbok emblem — which first appeared in 1906 — seeing it as a symbol of the apartheid era. They suggested the protea instead, but with pressure from several people, including President Mandela and Minister of Sport Steve Tshwete, the Springbok has remained the national rugby team's emblem, while the protea is the emblem for other sports. The Springboks are affectionately known now by the whole nation as the *Amabokoboko,* a name they were given by the black newspaper *The Sowetan.* South African rugby administrators have tried for some years to increase interest in rugby and now have a comprehensive and far reaching development programme to achieve this.

The main event of the rugby year is the Currie Cup, which is competed for by the provinces throughout the season, culminating in the final in August. For more information contact the South African Rugby Football Union, PO Box 99, Newlands 7725, Cape Town, tel (021) 685-3038.

Cricket. If rugby is king in South Africa then cricket is the crown prince. They don't like cricket in South Africa — they love it, and it is one of the few things that can knock everything else off prime viewing time on TV.

Since South Africa staged its re-entry into world competition with a short series against India at the end of 1991, and followed it with participation in the 1992 and 1996 World Cup matches, the team has been making an impact in world cricket. Today, the South African eleven are a feared Test-playing team and regarded as the best fielding side in the world. South Africa's leading Test run scorers are Hansie Cronje, Andrew Hudson and Brian McMillan. Star bowler is Allan Donald, who has proved himself one of the greatest match-winning bowlers in South African Test cricket history. Batsman Gary Kirsten took his total of runs in limited overs internationals in 1996 to a world record 1352, three more than the 1993 score of that other great left-hander, Brian Lara of the West Indies. Paul 'Gogga' Adams' bowling is an unorthodox frog-in-a-blender action but it has brought him the acclaim of his peers and the admiration of the crowds and remains potentially one of South Africa's best match-winners. This left-handed leg-spinner rose from a junior development player to become, at 18, the youngest player to be selected for South Africa; President Mandela rates his as one of the most important individual efforts towards reconciliation and nation-building in the country. In an assessment of 1996 Test cricket results, South Africa and Australia were the world's joint Test champions. Both had a 60% win-rate, winning three of the five Tests they played.

Like most other sports, cricket is in transition and under the supervision of its controlling body, the United Cricket Board, the sound of leather on willow is increasingly being heard in the townships. In Alexandra, for instance, on the outskirts of Johannesburg, the cricket nets are up among a sea of shanties in the townships' notorious 'Beirut' area. The Alex Cricket Oval's well tended grass and white-clad players contrast sharply with the surrounding poverty. Limited overs cricket is extremely popular and played at all the famous venues: Wanderers in Johannesburg, Newlands in Cape Town, Kingsmead in Durban, St George's Park in Port Elizabeth, and Springbok Park in Bloemfontein. Contact the United Cricket Board, PO Box 55009, Northlands 2116, Gauteng, tel (011) 880-2810.

Soccer. While all communities support rugby and cricket, soccer's most fanatical following comes from black supporters who are loyal to teams with such colourful names as Kaizer Chiefs, Moroko Swallows, Mamelodi Sundowns, Orlando Pirates, Qwa Qwa Stars, Warriors, Witbank Aces, Jomo Cosmos, AmaZulu, and Hellenic (there is even a team called Dangerous Darkies). Soccer is the largest participatory sport in the country, with around 12,000 clubs and more than a million regular players; the showpiece stadium is Soccer City, an ultra-modern facility on the outskirts of Johannesburg. There are stadiums in every large township and the soccer is played virtually all year round.

South Africa's soccer equivalent of the Springboks is the Bafana Bafana, who won the African Nations Cup in February 1996, unquestionably the greatest moment in local soccer history. While soccer was hailed after this victory as yet another sport to unite the nation, security at matches is not all it could be and there have been scenes disturbingly reminiscent of European soccer hooliganism. Contact the South African Football Association (Safa), tel (011) 494-3522.

Golf. Golf escaped the bleak years of isolation that put rugby and cricket into suspended animation and names like Gary Player, David Frost, Harold Henning, John Bland and Simon Hobday were well known and welcomed on the fairways of the international golf scene. A friendly climate makes golf a year-round pursuit and there are more than 400 registered courses to choose from — many of them among the best in the world. Gary Player's legacy lives on in golf's top-earning golden boy Ernie Els, who with Wayne Westner won the World Cup at Erinvale, near Somerset West, Western Cape, at the end of 1996 — a feat that put them in the record books for notching up the largest victory margin (18 strokes) in the history of the event.

The Sun City Million Dollar golf tournament is the most prominent event on the golf calendar, overshadowing even the SA Open. The Million Dollar had its beginnings in what was then the self-governing 'state' of Bophuthatswana and was a (successful) attempt to evade the sports boycott. Its popularity — and its prize money — has enabled it to survive its dubious birth and today it is a massive drawcard and has increased its field to 12 players. The 1996 event drew an international television audience of 400 million to watch the fun in the sun at the former bastion of apartheid. Seven other tournaments constitute the FNB Golf Tour, which boasts prize money of R11,925,000. Contact the Professional Golfers Association of South Africa, PO Box 79432, Senderwood 2145, Gauteng, tel (011) 880-1459.

There are 99,058 male amateur golfers affiliated to 46 clubs, 10,000 amateur women golfers, and 2000 junior golfers. The South African Golf Federation and its various provincial members control amateur golf in South Africa. Contact PO Box 391994, Bramley 2018, Gauteng, tel (011) 442-3723.

Boxing. South Africa can boast seven current world champions. IBF lightweight champion Phillip Holiday and IBF junior featherweight champion Vuyani Bungu are among South Africa's highest paid boxers. As with disadvantaged Afro-Americans, boxing is regarded by black South Africans as a quick way out of poverty and the gyms of the townships are full of aspiring champions.

South Africa's latest blood sport is bar-room brawling as public entertainment. These fights without rules combine boxing, wrestling, martial arts and kickboxing and usually attract as contestants bouncers from the seedier night clubs who make the fights like the gladiatorial battles of ancient Rome. Matches rarely last more than five minutes, but they continue without pause until one of the participants falls unconscious or submits. The South African Boxing Commission condemns the brawls and wants to stamp them out, saying that people who believe they are free to assault each other are confusing democracy with anarchy. Contact the South African

National Boxing Control Board, PO Box 2276, Southdale 2135, Gauteng, tel (011) 494-3538.

Running. South Africa has produced some of the world's top long-distance runners, marathoners and ultra-marathoners of the stature of Bruce Fordyce, nine times winner of the country's premier road event, the 86.7km/53.9 mile gruelling slog between Durban and Pietermaritzburg known as the Comrades Marathon. If you are an early riser you will see men and women of all ages on the streets and roads of the country in their shorts and trainers jogging or running, either for fun, for health reasons, or in preparation for one of the many races held throughout the country every weekend. Long slow distance (LSD) is very popular and continues to grow in numbers while the running boom of the 1970s and 1980s peters out in other countries. It is every runner's ambition to at least complete the Comrades Marathon, which has been going since 1921, 'up' in odd-numbered years from Durban to Pietermaritzburg and 'down' between the two cities in even-dated years. It is run on Youth Day, 16 June, every year and its prize money of R278,000 makes it the richest ultra in the world, with the first man and woman home receiving R65,000 each. The first 10 runners home get gold medals, silver goes to all finishing in seven hours or under, and bronze for all finishers within 11 hours. If you want to take part in the marathon you will need proof of a qualifying time of 4hr 30min for at least a standard marathon.

Long distance is the main arena for the country's black runners who excel at distance and regularly carry off all the medals at top events, although the Comrades' crown has only once been won by a black South African, Jetman Msutu in 1992. Other top distance races are the Two Oceans Marathon, held in Cape Town every Easter over 56km/35 miles, and the Washee 100-miler, run between Port Alfred and East London, in the Eastern Cape.

Contact Athletics South Africa (ASA), PO Box 15616, Doornfontein 2028, Gauteng, tel (011) 402-4973; Comrades Marathon Association, PO Box 100621, Scottsville 3209, KwaZulu-Natal, tel (0331) 94-3510.

Cycling. Since cycling became popular, the sport has seen some interesting developments, among them mountain biking and bikepacking, the two-wheel version of backpacking. Although bikepacking is still in its infancy, there are already tour guides organising ventures, and Satour has registered specialist bikepacking guides. Rowan Bouttell is one of these; contact him on Cell 082 652-7090, or e-mail rowan@ilink.nis.za

Mountain biking has taken off in a big way and there are lots of people and bodies organising trips and tours into the bush and the mountains. Contact Mountainbike Information Line, PO Box 1227, Pinetown 3600, KwaZulu-Natal, tel (031) 78-4839.

Sport and tour cycling is also doing well and the country's big annual events draw big fields, and many entrants from top cycling nations such as Italy, France and Belgium. The 1996 week-long Boland Bank Tour over 850km/528 miles drew 10 teams from overseas, as well as 13 from South Africa, including the national team's Douglas Ryder, Blayne Wikner, Rudolph Wentzel, David George and Alan Wolhuter — all Gauteng-based except Wolhuter from the Western Province. The Argus Pick 'n Pay cycle tour through the Cape winelands is another big annual event. Contact the South African Cycling Federation, PO Box 271, Table View 7349, Cape Town, tel (021) 557-1212.

Tennis. South Africa's top tennis players are usually prophets without honour in their own land and most find fame and fortune on the international circuit. The country has no ATP tournament for men, no WTA tournaments for women and no South African Open of any stature or consequence, although the sport has received a boost from K-Swiss, the sporting apparel manufacturers who pulled out of the country during the apartheid era, and have sponsored a nationwide junior Grand Prix tournament. The ITF-sponsored Tennis Centre adjoining Ellis Park in Johannesburg is in great demand among up and coming tennis-playing countries throughout Africa, but it remains neglected by those on its doorstep. The complex has been told by the South African Tennis Association (Sata) that until its development programme is in full swing the association will not be using the facility. Contact the South African Tennis Association, PO Box 15978, Doornfontein 2028, Gauteng, Cell 083 300-7770.

Squash. Squash South Africa is an umbrella body to which 27 provinces are affiliated. There are 367 registered clubs sprinkled throughout South Africa, with about 24,000 regular players, although some put the number as high as 500,000, making it one of the country's five most popular participant sports. Most of the Health and Racquet clubs and gymnasiums in the country have squash courts.

League forms an important facet of the squash arena and is played in all provinces for at least six months of the year. Development programmes at grass-roots level have been successfully initiated since 1987, mainly in Cape Town, Port Elizabeth, Durban and Johannesburg. The only squash court to be erected in a black township was built in 1992 in Chiawelo, Soweto. Contact Squash SA, PO Box 613, Northlands 2116, Gauteng, tel (011) 442-8056.

Bowls. There are 720 bowling clubs throughout South Africa with a combined membership of 50,000. South African men and women are the current Commonwealth Games champions — the SA Women's Team recently won the World Championships in England. The World Bowls tournament will be staged in South Africa with 24 participating countries in the year 2000. Contact Bowls South Africa, PO Box 47177, Parklands 2121, tel (011) 880-7959.

Equestrian Events. Love of horses and equestrian events goes back a long way in South Africa. The Boers were born to the saddle and the British brought with them their traditions of racing, polo, carriage-driving and show-jumping. The main body is the South African National Equestrian Federation (SANEF), whose disciplines include dressage, driving, equitation, eventing, showing, and showjumping.

The Dunhill Derby is considered the most prestigious equestrian event in the country. It is the only event that brings together top competitors in showjumping, dressage, showing, compleat horse — which combines performance in the previous three — and the increasingly popular sport of carriage driving. The course at Inanda, Johannesburg, is the only true derby course in South Africa, longer and more difficult than any other and it is only used once a year in October, and is now in its 33rd year.

SANEF is pursuing the search for talent in the disadvantaged communities to change the perception that equestrian sport is an elitist activity in South Africa, and supports a riding school in Soweto, near Johannesburg.

Contact the South African National Equestrian Federation, PO Box 374, Lanseria 1748, Gauteng, tel (011) 701-3062 for information on equestrian events. The South African Pony Club has about 1000 members and 50 branches countrywide. Contact the secretary, PO Box 32418, Braamfontein 2017, Gauteng, tel (011) 339-6484.

Polo has a small but dedicated following in 300 playing members and is organised nationally by the South African Polo Association (SAPA). Major annual tournaments during the polo season (March to September) are those in the BMW International Series, in which a touring team plays against the national side in two Test matches. The dates vary from year to year, but are usually in May. The SA Polo Championships, to which every club in the country sends representative sides, is usually played late in July. The tournament is held at Karkloof, in the KwaZulu-Natal Midlands, and the Inter-Provincial Tournament, in June, is held at Shongweni, near Durban. Contact SAPA at 197 Innes Road, Durban 4001, KwaZulu-Natal, tel (031) 303-3903.

Swimming. Impressive successes at the 1996 Atlanta Olympics put swimming back in the spotlight as a sport, with 6000 registered swimmers participating in disciplines including diving, water polo, synchronised swimming, short-course and aquatic at swimming clubs throughout the country. Pools used for events are the main pools used in South Africa. Contact Swimming South Africa, PO Box 1608, Saxonwold 2132, tel (011) 880-4328/9.

Scuba Diving. South Africa and its offshore islands offer scuba — and snorkelling — divers a wide variety of dive sites, some of them acclaimed internationally as among the world's finest, from the bone-chilling waters of the Atlantic to the warmer ambience of the Indian Ocean. Diving is a popular sport in South Africa, as are all water activities, and the underwater world off its 3000km shoreline proffers a wide choice of conditions and dive sites, from the granite caves and rock lobster haunts at Oudekraal, near Cape Town, to Port Elizabeth's beckoning Thunderbolt Reef and Umkomaas's famed Aliwal Shoal, where you can dive in safety among fearsome ragged-tooth sharks.

Further north along the KwaZulu-Natal coast, up near the Mozambique border, Sodwana Bay's array of accessible coral reefs (the only coral formations which have crept this far south) are a mecca for sport divers. If you prefer more serene waters there are numerous fresh water cave systems in the country. More than 120,000 people have been trained to scuba dive here and many others have discovered the delights of shallow reefs and tidal pools by snorkelling. Contact the South African Underwater Union (SAUU), PO Box 557, Parow 7500, Cape Town, tel (021) 930-6549. NAUI (National Association of Underwater Instructors) and PADI (Professional Association of Diving Instructors) offer qualifications that are recognised internationally and which will open up the oceans of the world when you plan your next holiday.

Sailing. From KwaZulu-Natal to the Orange River, the coastal waters offer everything the keen yachtsman or anyone who simply loves messing about in boats, from dinghies to racing keel boats, would enjoy. Main centres are Cape Town and Durban, although there are smaller yachting fraternities and clubs at virtually every little nook and cranny along the coast. Contact Royal Cape Yacht Club, PO Box 772, Cape Town 8000, tel (021) 21-1354/5; Point Yacht Club, 3 Maritime Place, Durban 4000, KwaZulu-Natal, tel (031) 301-4787.

Surfing. South Africa is one of the world's top surfing nations and its southern coast has been a mecca for board riders ever since little St Francis Bay was immortalised back in the 1960s in the US cult movie *Endless Summer*. St Francis Bay and Jeffrey's Bay, an hour's easy drive from Port Elizabeth, are two of the world's legendary surfing spots, known for the flawless waves that sweep their beaches. Jeffrey's Bay is known internationally for its Supertubes, but it was St Francis Bay, 20km/12 miles further along the coast, that has gained renown as the birthplace of the world's most perfect wave. Classic surf events are held annually along the beaches of KwaZulu-Natal and the Eastern Cape. Contact the United Surfing Council, PO Box 799, East London 5200, Eastern Cape, tel (0431) 35-3069.

A variety of other watersports have followings, not only on the coast but also on inland dams, rivers and wherever else it is wet enough. **Boardsailing**, **water-skiing** and **boating** are popular in all these spots and you can join South Africans of all ages in their watery pursuits, whether they are paddling or deep-sea diving.

Water-skiing. There are 23 water-skiing clubs with about 1200 members and 160 competitors. There is a ski school at Ski World, Benoni, Johannesburg, tel (011) 421-3715. The South African waterski championships are held at Buffelspoort, North-West Province, in May, barefoot waterski in April and cable ski at Warmbaths, Northern Province, also in May. Contact the South African Waterski Federation, PO Box 7896, Centurion 0046, Gauteng, tel (011) 634-0430.

Ice-skating. There are ice-skating rinks in various towns and cities but they are not very popular and many have been closed down. However In-line Skating pages, described as 'the most aggressive, up-to-date and hardcore' Internet site of its type in South Africa, includes places to skate and other details. You can find it at http://www/rapid.co.za/sean/skate.htm

River Rafting and Canoeing. South Africa has a wide variety of rafting and canoeing rivers, from KwaZulu-Natal's turbulent Tugela to the Northern Cape's mighty Orange, which offer wild rodeo rides. In the south-western Cape, the Doring River provides good rafting in the rainy winter months, but this is more suitable for novices preferring a more sedate ride. There is also regular rafting and canoeing on the Umkomaas, Berg, Breede and Vaal rivers. River routes are graded from 1 (easy water) to 6 (white-knuckle stuff where mistakes can be fatal). Inner-tubing for novices is done only on Grade 1 stretches, otherwise you can become what is known in river-raftese as 'hole bait.' There are more than two dozen river rafting and canoeing tour companies to choose from. Contact the South Africa Rivers Association (Sara), PO Box 472, Magaliesburg 2805, Gauteng, tel (0142) 77-1888; on the Internet try the White Water Rafting Guide at http://whirl.speech.cs.cmu.edu/WhiteWaterRafting.html

Marathon canoeing events are competed on all types of water conditions and are 20km/12 miles or longer. It is the backbone of canoeing in South Africa and most enthusiasts take up the sport with the intention of competing in one of the classic races around the country, such as the Dusi in KwaZulu-Natal, the Fish in the Eastern Cape, the Berg in Western Cape, or the Vaal in Gauteng. Internationally South Africa is among the top nations in canoe marathons and will host the World Championships in 1998. Contact the South African Canoe Federation, PO Box 212005, Oribi 3205, KwaZulu-Natal, tel (0331) 94-0509.

Aerobics. The fitness industry in South Africa is booming and there are about 73 major health clubs, operating in most of the main centres. Overseas visitors can take out temporary membership and should be impressed with facilities and equipment that compare with the best offered anywhere. As well as recreational aerobics, sport aerobics has been going strong in South Africa since 1992. For information on health clubs, contact Ross Faragher Thomas, PO Box 3882, Rivonia 2128, Gauteng, tel (011) 807-2344; for sport aerobics, contact Danielle Clack, PO Box 380, Gallo Manor 2052, Gauteng, tel (011) 802-2378.

Aerial Sports. South Africans take to the air in a variety of ways, so whether you are into flying, sky-diving, parachuting, hang-gliding, paragliding, gliding, microlighting, hot-air ballooning or even whistling through the air at the end of a bungi-jumping tether, you will find something to watch or take part in. All these forms of aerial derring-do are ardently pursued throughout the country and have their clubs and organising national bodies, which welcome visitors, participants and interested onlookers. For details contact the Aero Club of South Africa, PO Box 1993, Halfway House 1685, Gauteng, tel (011) 805-0366/8/9.

All 22 **gliding** clubs in the country offer instruction and, even if you don't want to take up the sport, an introduction to flight costing from R100 to R150, depending on the method of launching (land winch or air tow). Overseas **hang-gliding** pilots who have toured and competed in South Africa say the country has some of the best sites in the world — among them the Drakensberg, Table Mountain, Mpumalanga, and the Wilderness.

There are 15 **microlight** schools in southern Africa and about 1200 microflights flying in South Africa. Of the two types of microlight available the Trike is the most popular — the one that looks like a hang-glider mounted on a tricycle. To fly this or the other conventional three-axis microlight you need a microlight pilot's licence. If you have not got one you can still fly with a qualified pilot and enjoy the African skies in a two-seater. Contact the Professional Microlight Association of Southern Africa, PO Box 898, Kempton Park 1620, tel (011) 394-4974.

Ballooning is an elegant way of taking to the skies and getting a bird's-eye view of wandering wildlife herds. It is not a widespread pastime, as it depends for its existence on just the right mix of topographical features and thermals. The Highveld has such a mix, and you can sail over the Magaliesberg or the Pilansberg, near Sun City, Mpumalanga's towering escarpment, and even see the winelands of the Western Cape from above. As a result of the need for the right ambient atmosphere, ballooning flights and safaris usually start before dawn, so it is not recommended after a late night. The benefits are spectacular sunrises, prodigious champagne breakfasts, and unforgettable sights of Africa from an unusual angle.

Bungi-Jumping. Bungi-jumping is rapidly catching on wherever there is a high enough anchor point in South Africa — and where there isn't you can jump off a high crane. The ultimate jump (so far) is organised by a group of Australians, Kiwis and locals, who get paid to throw people off the Victoria Falls bridge, 111m up and 100m from the world-famous Falls. Bungi-jumping has been going in South Africa since 1990 and in 30,000 jumps there have been no fatalities.

Scrambling and Climbing. Scrambling, hiking and backpacking tend to merge into one in the bush and mountain regions of South Africa; climbing is definitely different. There are three types of climbing: adventure, sport and competition. Adventure or traditional climbing consists of climbing large cliffs, 50–500m in height. Sport climbing happens on steep or overhanging crags typically 20–30m in length, and demands incredible power and strength, as routes are seldom more than one pitch. Climbs in South Africa are graded A to H, according to steepness, difficulty and the commitment needed to lead a route.

The focus of Highveld climbers has shifted from the gorges of the Magaliesberg, an hour's drive from Johannesburg, to the village of Waterval-Boven in the Mpumalanga province, which has arguably South Africa's toughest route, although two other places that contend for this title are at Montagu, in the Western Cape, where the Cape Fold mountains have produced a series of vertical rock formations, and in the Drakensberg, KwaZulu-Natal. Cape Town has an incredible range of suburban climbing, from an ampitheatre above the Silvermine naval base of Simon's Town to the pale, hard sandstone of Table Mountain itself.

Competition climbing is one of the world's fastest-growing sports. It has a well established South Africa Competition Circuit, with major events in Cape Town, Johannesburg and Durban. The major indoor climbing centre at Johannesburg, for instance, has 66 routes on 500sq m of wall studded with more than 2000 holds. Contact the Mountain Club of South Africa (MCSA), 97 Hatfield Street, Cape Town 8001, tel (021) 45-3412; Durban, tel (031) 72-7844; and Johannesburg, tel (011) 786-8367.

Freshwater Angling. Both freshwater and saltwater angling are among South Africa's most popular recreational activities. Many game and nature reserves have dams or rivers — or even a stretch of coastline — where fishing is allowed. There are about 250 species of freshwater fish in Southern Africa, and some 1500 sea-water species. Trout fishing with fly in South Africa is probably the least expensive in the world. Major trout fishing areas occur in the southern mountain ranges of the Western Cape and throughout the foothills of the Drakensberg Mountains in KwaZulu-Natal. In Mpumalanga and Northern Province, Dullstroom, Lydenburg, Belfast and Tzaneen are among the best areas. The Eastern Cape has exceptional fly fishing in its mountain streams and along the rugged coastline. Flyfishing is also done for bass, barbel, yellowfish and every saltwater species, but the sport is moving to the catching and releasing of indigenous species — and even of trout, which is not really indigenous to South Africa. Apart from rainbow and brown trout, freshwater anglers inland pursue the carp, which is both prolific and large, and can exceed 20kg/44lb. Bass fishermen head for waters such as Theewaterskloof and Clanwilliam in the Western Cape, Albert Falls and Midmar Dam, in KwaZulu-Natal, the Vaal River and the Heyeshope Dam in Mpumalanga. Those looking for the heavyweights should travel to Hartebeespoort Dam, not far from Johannesburg, or the Vaal and Orange rivers, which are the haunts of the largest indigenous fish, the mighty catfish, which can top 30kg/66lb. For lighter but interesting fishing the warmer waters of the Northern Province hold the blue kurper, which is considered tremendous sport on light tackle, even though it seldom exceeds 3kg/6.6lb. It is also excellent eating. Contact the SA Freshwater Angling Association, PO Box 377, Welkom 9460, Free State, tel (0171) 352-2755 and (0171) 5143; the Federation of South African Fly Fishermen, PO Box 2142, Pietermaritzburg 3200, KwaZulu-Natal, tel (0331) 45-3700 or (0331) 94-7137.

Sea Angling and Big Game Fishing. There are as many as 500,000 anglers who fish in the sea for recreation and saltwater angling is the second most important drawcard for coastal holiday resorts (most people are attracted by the sea itself and the beaches for fun and relaxation). Most sea anglers fit into the rock and surf category and more than 300,000 people take part in this type of fishing, and their numbers are growing by about 6% a year. The rest are ski-boat anglers, who launch small but powerful boats through the surf to reach offshore fishing grounds. There are about 7000 of these ski-boats in the country and most are affiliated to clubs and associations. South Africa's estuaries are fairly modest, but places like Langebaan, St Lucia, Durban Bay and Knysna are immensely popular with sea anglers. Salt water fly-fishing is the new challenge. One good venue is Kosi Bay in Zululand, where the estuary offers excellent sport with kingfish, barracuda and skipjack in the summer months. Productive flies are said to be deceivers, sprat and squid pattern, and poppers. The choice of fishing is in tropical or temperate waters, and even a choice of two oceans, the Atlantic and the Indian. More than 50 species of fish are commonly caught along the coast, divided into reef fish and other bottom-feeders, gamefish, sharks and flatfish. The greatest variety occurs along the east coast, especially in KwaZulu-Natal. The cold waters of the Cape's West Coast offer only a handful of species to the angler, but what they lack in diversity they more than make up for in numbers, and with the exception of gamefish, species from cold water usually make better eating.

Contact the SA Federation of Sea Angling and SA Federation of Deep Sea Angling, PO Box 35936, Menlo Park, Pretoria 0001, Gauteng, tel (012) 46-1912; SA Marlin and Tuna Club, Jubilee Square, Simon's Town 7975, Western Cape, tel (021) 786-2762/2124.

Shop till you drop could well be your motto in the cities of South Africa, where shopping seems to be the favourite weekend pastime of the majority of people, certainly the better half. The most popular bumper sticker (apart from 'My other car is a Porsche') is 'Born to Shop.' The international mall culture has arrived and most stores and shops are now situated out of the town and city Central Business Districts (CBDs) in suburban one-stop malls that offer not only the basics of life but are complete lifestyle complexes and often *the* place to meet and socialise. Their parking and security are also better.

A good example in Johannesburg is Sandton Square (which drew on San Marco Square in Venice for its architectural inspiration), next to Sandton City; in Cape Town the whole city centre seems to be a shopping mall, radiating around the Golden Acre complex at the bottom of Adderley Street; and in Durban they have turned a vast old Victorian railway workshop into, yes, The Workshop, a showpiece for speciality shops (in Pretoria a tramshed has been converted into The Tram Shed), and there is also The Wheel, an ultra-modern, multi-themed shopping and entertainment complex with the world's largest Ferris wheel inside a building. Other cities have their local versions of these shopping wonderlands, malls with anything up to 300 shops, as well as hotels, restaurants, bars, office suites, banks, cinemas, beauty salons, supermarkets and children's amusement areas. Many malls have special facilities for disabled shoppers, who can phone ahead and arrange for staff to meet them at designated disabled parking areas with a wheelchair. Some also provide push-chairs for mothers with toddlers. There seems to be nothing you cannot buy, and if it is not in the shops, you will probably find it among the thriving informal kerbside traders who have become a feature of every town and city, selling everything from Chinese junk and stolen car parts to intricately woven baskets, beadwork and coverings, as well as badly made carvings and gross soapstone sculptures (this is not to say you may not find a curio or carving worth buying).

Shopping Hours. Normal shopping hours are 8.30am or 9am to 5pm Monday to Friday and 8.30am to 1pm on Saturday. Many of the larger supermarkets close later on weekdays and are open on Saturday afternoons, Sundays and public holidays. Shops in malls generally open until 6pm weekdays and Saturdays until 5pm, and on Sunday from 10am to 2pm. Corner cafés and suburban mini-markets open early and close late every day of the week throughout the year and are used as convenience stores for bread, newspapers, cigarettes and other casual purchases. You naturally pay more for this convenience.

Liquor Stores. Antiquated laws prevent liquor stores selling alcoholic drinks after 1pm or 2pm on Saturday until they open again on Monday. This has resulted in a traditional Saturday lunchtime rush to stock up for the weekend, which is when most people do their social drinking, something akin to the old 6 o'clock swill in Australia before they civilised their opening and closing times. The current legislation prohibiting the sale of liquor by retailers on Sundays is set to change as the law currently ignores the fact that many South Africans do not celebrate their holy day on Sunday. Supermarkets are allowed to sell wine, but not beer or spirits, from Monday to Saturday. All these restrictions have led to the growth of shebeens and bush pubs in private houses and properties.

Value Added Tax (VAT) is levied on almost every shopping and service transaction — though some basic foodstuffs are excluded — and this is expected to increase from 14% to 15%. By law the price you see is the price you pay, with VAT inclusive. As a visitor you can claim a refund on some of the VAT you pay and collect it at your departure point, provided the value of all the items you bought and are taking with you exceeds R250. You cannot claim refunds on services, such as hotels, cars and restaurants. You should obtain proof of payment for all items you buy during your stay. To qualify for a refund, you must have a valid passport, the necessary forms, and purchase slips. It can be an unprofitable hassle, although the maximum refund is R3000 (£400/$660), which is not to be sneezed at. For more information contact the VAT Refund Administrators, PO Box 9478, Johannesburg 2000, Gauteng, tel (011) 484-7530, fax (011) 484-2952.

Chainstores. Prices are comparable with — and often lower than — those in most Western countries, although some items such as electrical appliances and books are more expensive. Some of the bigger South African retail chains you are likely to notice are Woolworths (a variety of departments, including first-rate food halls); the

OK Bazaars, which stock a wide range of basic goods and foodstuffs; Shoprite Checkers and Pick 'n Pay supermarkets; Clicks (general purpose, mainly household goods); and Edgars, Truworths and Foschini for clothing. Pick 'n Pay's Hypermarkets and OK's Hyperamas are vast, no-frills, suburban shopping complexes whose bulk buying and price-paring make them good places to stock up if you are doing any self-catering. CNA (Central News Agency) stores are the popular outlets for paperbacks, stationery, cards, magazines and music tapes and CDs and watch out for Virgin Megastores, which will probably follow Virgin Airlines into South Africa. Shoprite Checkers is widely regarded as the cheapest supermarket in South Africa, and so it is — if only fractionally. An independent survey shows a basket of goods costing R1461.22 at Shoprite Checkers was nearly R8 more at Pick 'n Pay and R28 more at OK stores. At Spar supermarkets you would have to fork out an extra R75 for the same basket. When buying anything in local stores give preference to goods bearing the mark of the South African Bureau of Standards (SABS), which is a guarantee of quality. If you are into healthy foodstuffs look out for the Heart Mark, which is a logo depicting a red circle, a white heart and a knife and fork. This tells you that stringent Heart Foundation standards have been followed and independently tested by the SABS and the Council for Scientific and Industrial Research (CSIR). The Heart Mark indicates a low-fat, low-cholesterol, low-salt, high-fibre product.

Markets. Markets of every description have sprung up around the country over the past few years along the lines of those familiar in other countries — organic markets, flea markets, roof-top markets, farmers' markets — even car-boot markets. There is nothing of the size of the Paris *Marché aux Puces de St-Ouen* or the variety of London's Petticoat Lane and New Caledonian Market, but give it time. We have listed the more interesting markets under the relevant provincial shopping sections, but two deserve a quick mention here.

One is the oldest and most famous market of them all, the Grand Parade in Cape Town, where for years locals and visitors alike have browsed and bargained informally in the shadow of the old pentagonal castle's walls. The market at the Grand Parade is open on Wednesday and Saturday mornings and as well as colourful displays of fresh fruit and veg to tempt you, you can rummage through old books and the bric-á-brac of centuries in open-air stalls manned by some of the city's more colourful characters. You can also snatch a bite while you listen to the rantings of various religious and political fanatics who use the Grand Parade as a local Speaker's Corner to let off steam.

The other market you should visit if your travels take you to KwaZulu-Natal — and they should — is the famous Indian market in Queen and Victoria streets, in central Durban. This is officially the Victoria Street Market, but no one calls it that. The Indian market has all the mysterious scents of the east, coming from more than 180 stalls, where you can buy everything from African and eastern curiosities to curry powders and exotic spices from one of the biggest ranges to be found outside of India. If you like your curry hot try Hotazell, Mother-in-Law Killer or Volcano.

Cigarettes and Cigars. You will have no difficulty finding your favourite brand of cigarettes if you smoke — although you might find it a little more difficult to find someone to light up your coffin nail. There is an increasingly vociferous and powerful anti-smoking lobby in the country, which has already brought local airlines, restaurants and other public places into line with trends in other countries. Cigars are usually only smoked when the other person is paying for your meal, but there is one curiosity in this aromatic field. The Gauteng Cigar Factory is a small family business operating out of a garage on the West Rand. Its founder and master tobacco blender is Tom van der Marck, who hand-rolls coronas, half-coronas and senoritas like a Cuban maestro, using tobacco mainly from Indonesia, fax (011) 768-5754. For details of cigar nights and cigar clubs contact Colin Wesley in Johannesburg, tel (011) 788-7413, or Theo Rudman in Cape Town, tel (021) 905-3600.

Clothing. If you are looking for a present for someone who likes beer you will find the ideal gift in Pretoria at Cheers to Beers, Shop 13 in The Tram Shed, at the corner of Van der Walt and Schoeman streets, in the city centre. This is the only shop that sells clothing and other gifts with South African beer-branded labels, and it also stocks Springbok rugby, soccer, and cricket jerseys, caps and jackets, as well as T-shirts, sweatshirts, bar accessories, ties and other goodies guaranteed to cheer up any beer lover. Tel (012) 320-4033.

Books and Periodicals. Along with other things, the weakness of the South African rand has meant rocketing prices for imported books, newspapers and magazines. The local book market is worth R350 million a year and there is little you cannot buy, if you are prepared to pay the inflated prices. For a fairly run-of-the-mill selection of books, but an excellent range of periodicals, the stores of the CNA stationery chain are the ones to try. They are particularly good for reasonably priced tourist-oriented books on South Africa and for their range of street and road maps.

For the more serious bookworm the names to look for are Facts and Fiction, and Exclusive Books. Facts and Fiction has seven outlets in Gauteng, one in the university town of Stellenbosch in the Western Cape and two mega-stores in Cape Town. Their outlet in The Firs, Rosebank, Johannesburg, claims to be Africa's largest multimedia bookshop and a quick browse will convince you they are not hyping. This superstore occupies more than 1000sq m and stocks more than 40,000 titles, a comprehensive range of multimedia titles, and it has two floors dedicated to classical, jazz and popular music. There is also a specialist Judaica section, South Africa's largest selection of science fiction, and arguably the biggest range of paperback fiction in the country. You can browse and relax in their subsidised coffee shops and surf the Internet free of charge. They stay open until 10.30pm on weekdays and midnight on Fridays and Saturdays. Exclusive Books have branches in the major centres and sell periodicals and music as well as an impressive range of books.

Wines and Spirits. You can buy South African wines, spirits and liqueurs at the duty-free shops at the international airports, if you have not already stocked up while visiting the winelands, or you can use a very reliable service provided by KWV, which runs a year-round, duty-free delivery of gift packs of selected South African wines, spirits, liqueurs, and food and wine hampers to countries in Europe, the Americas, Australia and the Far East. Contact International Wine Distributors, PO Box 239, Bergvliet 7864, Western Cape, tel (021) 72-0212, fax (021) 72-0268. If you prefer to choose your liquid gifts in a bottle store the outlets of Solly Kramers Discount Liquors are virtually everywhere, and Benny Goldberg's in Johannesburg claims to be the largest liquor supermarket in South Africa. It is on Louis Botha Avenue, Kew, tel (011) 786-3670.

Craftwork and Curios. You will find examples of indigenous crafts and a variety of curios on sale everywhere you go, from the pavement vendors to very chi-chi galleries where the price tags are like telephone numbers. Most of the local wood carvings come from KwaZulu-Natal and Mpumalanga and some 60 tons a year of these curios are turned out in these and other areas. Most popular woods with indigenous carvers are tambotie, mopane and African olive. Carvings in teak, mahogany, ebony and other exotic hardwoods are usually brought in by itinerant traders from countries to the north, particularly East and West Africa. Pop art carvings of animals, masks, bowls and utensils can be found in profusion at street corners and pavement displays are common in all the major tourist centres. Be prepared to haggle, it is expected and part of the fun. If you are looking for genuine traditional African artefacts give the street markets a miss and head for the recognised galleries dealing in the authentic and, therefore, expensive items. Good buys at street level are carved salad bowls and servers, animal figures and human figurines, beadwork, baskets, clay pots, and crochet work. The latter articles are well worth seeking out. They are usually beautifully made, relatively inexpensive, and easy to pack and post or carry home.

Do not let anybody talk you into buying ivory in any form; it is illegal to trade in ivory and you could wind up in trouble if you are found with any in your possession. The same goes for seashore curios, such as coral and shells. Make sure they have been legally collected and that they are not threatened species.

The mopane worm is well known as an ingredient in African cuisine, usually as a crunchy sun-dried delicacy munched like peanuts or added to stews. Another use is possibly far more appealing. Mopane silk, spun into golden strands, can be knitted into shimmering jerkins or woven into cloth. When they have turned into moths — the Emperor moth, in this case — the insects leave cocoons behind. These are treated at the Council for Scientific and Industrial Research's textile department in Port Elizabeth, where they undergo a process that turns them into silk that looks like fine, golden cotton wool. At Lindele, her studio near Lanseria airport, Johannesburg, spinner and artist Hazel Hele uses the silk to knit and crochet superb one-of-a-kind garments. Sometimes, she dyes the silk, usually in colours close to the original, such as rusts and subtle browns.

Although mopane silk is quite rare, it is not astronomically expensive, costing about R400 (£53/$88) a kg in its unspun state, compared to R150 to R200 for wool, and angora at around R550. Hazel sells her wearable works at from R300 upwards, depending on how much silk she has used and how much labour was involved in spinning it. She also sells some of the silk lengths that come from farms in the Northern Province, which harvest mopane worm pods and weave the silk into cloth.

Gold, Diamonds and Semi-Precious Stones. The best place to buy gold, diamonds and semi-precious stones is the hub of the South African mining world, Johannesburg. Within 10 minutes of Johannesburg International Airport is the Erikson Diamond Centre, an international wholesaler and retailer of gold and diamonds. The centre has almost as many facets as the diamonds it cuts. Start with the diamond cutting and jewellery manufacturing tour. You can browse through the diamond museum while absorbing the knowledge you need before buying a diamond. You can view the process through which a diamond passes from its rough to fully faceted state, watch craftsmen hand-make and cast designer jewellery and precious gems into the pieces, and watch a video summarising all you have seen. The tour is free of charge, but bookings should be made at least two days in advance.

There is more to the centre than silk and diamonds. You can visit the Madiba Freedom Museum, which is a tribute to the liberation struggle and a curio shop with a wide selection of unusual and typically South African artefacts. At the heart of the centre is Baguette Jewellers, the place to stop if you are looking for something special. The Baguette stocks loose and set laboratory-certified diamonds as well as gold jewellery. They will also make any item to your own design. You can find the Erikson Diamond Centre at 20 Monument Road, Kempton Park, or contact PO Box 2774, Kempton Park 1620, Gauteng, tel (011) 970-1355/69 or (011) 394-2477/8. You can combine a trip to the splendid re-creation of old Johannesburg at Gold Reef City with a visit to a diamond-cutting factory and watch the experts at work. You can buy gems from a large selection of fully certified diamonds set in designer jewellery, duty and tax-free for tourists. The cutting works are open every Sunday and public holiday and they are at Upper Terrace, Gold Reef City, tel (011) 496-1106.

At the SA Diamond Centre in central Johannesburg is a concentration of jewellery manufacturers, diamond cutters and associated industries. An hour-long tour at the centre includes a presentation on the history of the diamond industry, and the cutting and polishing of diamonds. You can learn how to evaluate a cut diamond. The four Cs — carat, cut, colour and clarity — that determine the ultimate value are explained, after which you will know what you are doing when you buy quality export diamonds and items made of gold. Contact 240 Commissioner Street, Johannesburg 2001, tel (011) 334-8897.

Pay a visit to the South African Mint Coin World, where you can see the full range of coins, medallions and jewellery produced by the South African Mint. For the first time, these are available direct to the public. Coins make unusual gifts, to collect, for an investment or to wear. Coin World is open Monday to Sunday from 9am to 4pm, admission free, tel (012) 677-2342; the Mint, tel (012) 677-2911.

South Africa's best known semi-precious stones are agate, amethyst, aquamarine, garnet, jasper, tiger's eye, turquoise, zircon, chalcedony, carnelian, malachite, Amazonite and topaz. Any of the above gemstone dealers will be able to tell you where you can buy these.

Traditional Delights. If you want to get South Africans really going — apart from a discussion on rugby — ask them where the best biltong and boerewors comes from. If they are from the north, they will undoubtedly say Pretoria; if they are descended from the Afrikaners who did not leave the Cape with the Great Trek, then they will probably say Malmesbury. Butchers in both places do in fact produce excellent examples of the old art and both have their vocal adherents. In reality, discussing the relative merits of what are scrumptious to eat but fairly off-putting to look at is as unrewarding as comparing different wines — you pay your money and you take your choice. Biltong, as explained elsewhere, is basically salted, dried beef or game, like American jerky and Mexican *carne secca,* and is similar to Swiss *Bündnerfleisch.* It is also made in small quantities from ostrich meat. It is like peanuts — once you start eating it you find it difficult to stop. Boerewors, without which no South African braaivleis would be complete, is literally farmer's sausage. This is usually heavily spiced and seasoned and can be an acquired taste. If you know next to nothing about either delicacy take our tip and, if you are in Cape Town, go to a little butcher's shop in quaint old Long Street — 265 to be exact — and chat to Morris the Butcher, whose windows and walls are plastered with clippings extolling his boerewors. Morris has been making his delectable spicy farm sausage for more years than he cares to remember. His customers are unanimous that Morris makes the best boerewors — known to aficionados as boeries or wors — in the land. Contact him at tel (021) 23-1766.

If you want to compare Morris's product with another, you can drive to the little town of Malmesbury, about 60km/37 miles from Cape Town, where at 30 Voortrekker Street you will find Roers. The biltong and boerewors of this butchery are so famous that they have been obliged to open shops all over the Western Cape so that their fans do not have far to travel to get their fix. Expect to pay about R65 to R75 a kg for biltong, R16 a kg for the boerewors and R55 a kg for dried wors. Contact tel (0224) 71007. If you are in Gauteng you will have to get a pointer from someone at a braaivleis, as sources of the right stuff on the Highveld are closely guarded secrets. You can, of course, get ready-chopped biltong in little plastic packets in supermarkets and cafés and while this is all right, the true biltong lover likes to buy it in hefty dried sticks, to be lovingly pared and savoured (it is delicious grated over scrambled eggs). Boerewors does not travel well (except when it is preserved by drying and known as *droëwors*), so it is not advisable to take any back with you in your luggage. Biltong is another matter. Take some home as a curiosity. The customs officer will probably think that dried-out stick you fish out to declare is an African carving.

Snoek is the favourite fish of the Cape fishermen, both to catch and to eat. It is a long — up to a metre — silvery, streamlined predator with fearsome teeth and its name, meaning pike, was given to it by the early Dutch settlers. It is not related to the pike, but to the barracuda. When the snoek are running after the first north-westerlies bring rain in the autumn there is excitement in the fishing communities all the way along the Cape's west coast. The teeming, glistening shoals are the lifeblood of these communities and in a good season, between April and July, up to 2 million snoek have been hauled in on the hand lines. Spend a day snoek fishing and it is an experience you will never forget. Once the snoek start biting they will take virtually anything, even the bare barbless hooks the fishermen use. They will also take your finger if you are not careful, and a bite from a snoek is difficult to staunch, as its mouth releases a powerful anti-coagulant. Like the famous *bacalhau* of the Portuguese the snoek changes in taste and texture once it is salted and dried, the traditional way of preserving it, but the true delicacy is smoked snoek. This firm, golden flesh is sold locally in small packets, or you will find whole snoek in long, flat cardboard boxes for sale at Cape Town International Airport, along with the proteas and wine.

Another speciality of the Cape is **glacé fruit**. You will find this in stores and at airports, or you can also buy it in Malmesbury, where the farm Protea, in the Paardeberg mountains, has been preserving fruit in this manner for the past 50 years. Their range of glacé pineapple, ginger, apricot, pears, figs, watermelons, oranges and cherries goes all over the world under the label Sugar Bird. Contact Sugar Bird at 21 Prospect Street, Malmesbury, Western Cape, tel (0224) 21144.

Traditional South African preserves, jams and marmalades, many using uniquely indigenous fruit, make good gifts. You will find them in any supermarket or deli but two places that even have the ambience of bygone days are Oom Samie se Winkel, 84 Dorp Street, Stellenbosch, tel (021) 887-0797, and (021) 887-2612; and Tan' Malie se Winkel at Hartebeespoort Dam, in the North-West Province, a pleasant hour's drive from Johannesburg, tel (01211) 53-0778.

Wildlife Videos. If you want to do some game-watching from the comfort of your arm-chair when you get home, the most popular wildlife videos available locally are: *Last Feast of the Crocodiles* and *Etosha: Place of Dry Water* (National Geographic), both by Dave and Carol Hughes; *Journey to the Forgotten River* (Wildlife Films Botswana), *Reflections of Elephants* and *Eternal Enemies: Lions and Hyenas* (National Geographic), all by Dereck and Beverly Joubert; *Meerkats United, The Sisterhood* (Mala Mala Video) and *Beauty and the Beast* (Mala Mala/National Geographic), all by Richard Goss; *Survivors of the Skeleton Coast* (National Geographic), by Des and Jen Bartlett; and *Super Hunts, Super Hunters* (Londolozi), by John Varty. The National Geographic Special *Last Feast of the Crocodiles* captures the drama of animal life around one of the last water-holes in the riverbed of the Luvuvhu River in the far north of the Kruger National Park, and is a must-see video if you can bear to watch nature red in tooth and claw.

Complaints and Advice. South Africa is not a grousing nation and you will rarely hear a voice raised in complaint in a shop or restaurant, more's the pity. The government has set the tone by appointing a Public Protector, along with a couple of other Ombudsmen. If you think you have been ripped off you can contact the National Public Protector, Private Bag X677, Pretoria 0001, Gauteng, tel (012) 322-2916. All provinces are formulating new consumer laws and setting up consumer courts and the Auditor General's Office and the Human Rights Commission will both hear complaints.

VIOLENT TIMES

A joke doing the rounds says that the new South African anthem is the sound of a car alarm going off — but it is no joke. A vehicle is stolen nearly every five minutes, which adds up to 288 a day, or 105,120 a year. About 40% of stolen vehicles are never recovered. This has sent car insurance premiums soaring to the point where they are now among the highest in the world, but then the rate of serious crime is similarly high, having increased by more than 30% over the past five years.

Johannesburg is the hijack capital of South Africa and cheeky hijackers even contact radio phone-in chat shows to discuss their gangs and operations in what is wryly regarded as the country's fastest-growing employment sector. One intriguing development has been the spin-off business for black witch-doctors. Increasing numbers of white motorists are turning to them for protection against hijackers. Solomon Mahlaba, who runs the Traditional Medical Practitioners and African National Healers Association in central Johannesburg, does a roaring trade in beads that he swears will protect your vehicle for a year. If you plan to hire a car for your holiday and are worried about hi-jackers you can contact him at tel (011) 333-6430.

Almost every fifth person in South Africa packs a firearm and the Gauteng government has turned its buildings into gun-free zones as a first step towards a gunless society. Government departments have begun placing gun-free-zone notices on their buildings, and installing metal detectors and gun safes at entrance foyers. Guns are as common in the minibus taxi industry as good music systems and bald tyres, and taxi violence is a national problem.

South Africa has a murder rate per capita nine times the international average and a national crime survey shows that nearly half of all South Africans regard crime as the country's most serious problem. Of every 1000 crimes committed, only 450 are reported and of these, only 230 are solved. In addition, only 100 of the criminals involved are ever prosecuted, and only 77 of these are convicted; a mere 36 go to jail, but only eight get two years or more inside.

The government's response has taken several forms. In its National Crime Prevention Strategy (NCPS) the government blames apartheid and its legacy of violence for the crime wave, and points to high unemployment, marginalised youth, endemic poverty, and the absence of adequate social security as some of the reasons for it. The NCPS identifies a number of key categories as posing the greatest threat. These are crimes involving firearms; organised crime, including smuggling illegal immigrants and narcotics, and gangsterism; white-collar crimes against children; violence associated with inter-group conflict, such as taxi violence and land disputes; vehicle theft and hijacking; and corruption in the criminal justice system. Nobody is sacrosanct, and even diplomats have been victims. An attack on the Lebanese ambassador at his home in Johannesburg sent him hurrying home, saying it was safer in Lebanon, and late in 1996 death threats forced the Minister of Justice, Dullah Omar, to move out of his Cape Town home. The average South African detective supposedly handles more murder cases in a year than his UK counterpart sees in his entire career. Hand in hand with government moves Business Against Crime has been launched by the private sector, which has channelled more than R40 million into various anti-crime projects, including fund-raising for the police, and it has even pledged to start building jails to stop the current early releases of hardened criminals because there is no room for them in overcrowded jails. Stricter gun control laws are in the pipeline, along with tougher laws on crime generally, sophisticated hi-tech drug detection equipment for airports, and the formation of a special unit to root out corrupt members of the police.

To help visitors to South Africa, the South African Police Service (SAPS) has established Tourism Protection Units in all major tourist centres to provide more visible policing. This anti-crime support is provided in places such as airports, hotels, banks, bus stations and theatres. Part of police strategy is to ensure that specially trained officers are on hand at the international arrivals area of airports to help and advise tourists regarding their safety and security while they are in the country. The units also co-ordinate preventative safety measures with private security organisations employed by hotels. During peak seasons these units draft in extra officers and equipment for highly visible policing, which is seen as one of the most effective deterrents to crime. This means increased foot, vehicle and air patrols, as well as regular patrols by the SAPS Water Wing at a number of the country's most popular beaches. Mobile police caravans are placed at popular venues to give help and provide information to visitors. Closed circuit TV monitoring systems are used to deter and prevent crime in the Central Business Districts of a number of cities and towns, and on Durban's beachfront.

In addition to these policing activities a Tourism Safety Task Group (TSTG) comprising representatives of the Department of Environmental Affairs and Tourism, Business Against Crime, the Tourism Business Council, the South African Tourism Board and the SAPS has been established to co-ordinate and guide initiatives to create a secure environment for tourists. You can contact SAPS Protection Units at:

Gauteng: Johannesburg, tel (011) 333-1169/1150/1154; Pretoria, tel (012) 324-3616, Cell 082 653-3039;
KwaZulu-Natal: Durban, tel (031) 368-4453/2207;
Western Cape: Cape Town, tel (021) 418-2852/3;
Eastern Cape: Port Elizabeth and Umtata, tel (0471) 2654.

In an emergency, you can call the SAPS Flying Squad throughout the country on toll-free tel 10111, any time of the day or night, and the Police Crime Stop number is toll-free 0800 11 12 13. If you have problems with the emergency number call 1022 (free).

Avoiding Theft and Mugging. The following simple precautions are recommended by the police:

– Use only the main entrance of your hotel and plan your journey before you go out;
– Tell hotel staff at the reception desk where you are going;
– If you intend travelling off the beaten track, ask hotel staff to check your intended route with local community liaison officers;
– Do not draw attention to yourself by displaying large amounts of cash, expensive jewellery or cameras;
– Leave all your valuables in the hotel's safe;
– Ensure that your hotel room door is locked when you are in the room and whenever you leave it;
– If someone knocks at your door, do not open it until you have identified the person;
– Leave your room keys with the reception desk whenever you leave your room;
– Never leave your luggage unattended in front of the hotel or in the lobby;
– Report any incident, no matter how small, to the SAPS Flying Squad or Police Crime Stop number given above.

If you need an **ambulance**, tel 10177. Info Africa operates a 24-hour helpline if you need any assistance, tel (011) 390-1444.

Street Crime. Be observant when walking in the street and guard against snatchers; do not walk around on your own, and do your sightseeing with a group, if possible, especially in city centres; choose a well lit and/or busy street if walking at night, and avoid isolated areas. Keep car doors locked when driving; and do not leave valuables in your vehicle. Carry your valuables in a pouch inside your clothing or in a money belt. Do not become involved in pavement games or gambling; they are usually operated by gangs ready to relieve you of your valuables while you are distracted. Be aware that diamonds, gold and other seemingly expensive items offered to you in the street are likely to be fakes. The National Institute for Crime Prevention and Rehabilitation of Offenders (Nicro) recommends you carry a whistle and blow the emergency signal of two long shrills in an emergency; police have agreed to regard two long blows on the whistle as a signal for help. About 500,000 whistles are available countrywide at Nicro offices and Shoprite Checkers stores for R3 each. Victimline, Nicro, tel (012) 324-2800.

There is a Business Against Crime (BAC) Internet site at http://www.web.co.za/bac providing information, tips and news on crime and the campaign waged against it by the BAC initiative. Among the user-friendly features of the site are tips on how to avoid crime, and what to do and who to contact if you become a victim.

POLICE AND SECURITY SERVICES

The forerunner of the South African Police Service was the South African Constabulary established in 1900 during the Anglo-Boer War by British General Baden-Powell. For decades the SA Police was identified by the black masses as a repressive arm of successive apartheid governments. Within days of the election in April 1994 the new government began to restructure the police into one national and nine provincial forces with new responsibilities and chains of command. In essence, the restructuring is an effort to reach out to black communities and change their old negative perceptions. There are roughly 2.8 police officers for every 1000 people in South Africa. The ratio of policemen to civilians is higher in Gauteng, where 23% of all police are concentrated, which averages out at one policeman to every 250 civilians. Throughout South Africa more than 27,000 police reservists back up the regular force. They help not only by patrolling neighbourhoods, but also by doing administrative work in police stations. The security industry employs an estimated 200,000 people, making it big business. Vehicle security is a prime objective. The South African Police Service is helpful and can be contacted 24 hours a day if you want to report anything. The police are listed under SA Police Service in the Government Departments section at the back of the telephone directory.

DRINK, DRUGS AND THE LAW

Drunkenness. South Africans swig at least 4.9 billion litres of alcohol a year and consumption is growing faster than the size of the population. Between 1978 and 1994, per capita consumption of alcohol increased by 150%. Some of this was due to the shift from traditional sorghum to malt beer, but most was simply due to people drinking more, probably because of increased national stress levels. During the same period the population grew about 50%. The government estimates that alcohol abuse results in more than R5-billion a year being lost to the country's economy through work accidents, lost productivity, damage to health, crime and family breakdown and disintegration. It also estimates that as many as 60% of the people who die on South Africa's roads lose their lives in alcohol-related crashes. New drink-driving legislation has slashed the permissible legal blood alcohol limit, making the law among the most Draconian in the world. While all this suggests a nation of drunkards, public drunkenness is a rare sight. South Africans do most of their drinking at home, at parties or, in the black community, at sociable shebeens, which are usually in somebody's home anyway. The British habit of regularly visiting a local pub for a few pints is virtually unknown, although immigrants from the UK have generated a few pub-type places where they can discuss British football scores.

Drugs and the Law. Special police units focusing almost exclusively on the known 140 drug syndicates have been set up in an attempt to curb the avalanche of narcotics pouring into South Africa. Only 10–15% of all drugs being smuggled in is actually seized. Drug abuse is a growing social problem. Trading in and possession of illegal drugs, including marijuana, known as *dagga* in South Africa, are criminal offences and carry severe penalties. Marijuana is the most common drug as it flourishes literally like a weed all over the country, and is an easy cash crop for the impoverished to grow and sell, especially in KwaZulu-Natal, where the most sought after variety is called Durban Poison. When mixed with crushed Mandrax (methaqualone) tablets and smoked it is known as a 'white pipe,' a combination that seems to be known only to South Africans. The country has the world's highest incidence of Mandrax abuse — an estimated 70% of the world's supply is used by South Africans. Heroin and cocaine are latecomers but are a growing part of the local drug scene. Some appetite suppressants that are obtainable only on prescription elsewhere can be bought over the counter in South Africa from pharmacies, as can a wide range of painkillers and cough mixtures containing drugs. Of the hard drugs, cocaine is the main cause for concern and its derivative, crack, is fast overtaking Mandrax in popularity, especially in Durban, Cape Town and Johannesburg.

When the walls of apartheid came tumbling down a host of hitherto unavailable commodities flooded in. One of these was 3,4-methylenedioxymetamphetamine (MDMA), better known as Ecstasy, a popular designer drug being smuggled in from Europe, particularly Germany and the UK. Known as the 'hug drug' it is often taken with LSD and other drugs smuggled in from Europe. Many users regard it as penicillin for the soul and one of the biggest dangers is the widespread ignorance about the drug and the confusion among those claiming knowledge. There are about 64 different 'Doves' on the international market (this is just one name for the variety of Ecstasy tablets available; others in South Africa are Capital Es, ITs and Hearts). Users are playing Russian roulette everytime they fork out between R80 and R160 for a tablet, as tablets have been found to contain many adulterating substances, such as ketamine, an animal tranquilliser. According to the White Paper for Social Welfare, substance abuse is recognised as one of South Africa's major social problems and drug takers and dealers are getting younger by the day.

Publications such as the MIMS directory of *Permitted and Banned Drugs in Sports* list drugs containing prohibited substances by their trade names, along with the names of the taboo substances. The latest edition lists a massive 536 banned drugs available in South Africa, including certain cough mixtures, suppositories, eye drops, cold and flu capsules and numerous sinusitis treatments. Some 700 pharmacists have been trained under the auspices of the SA Association of Community Pharmacists to provide Drug Wise campaign advice to drug users and their families. For more information on Drug Wise, tel (011) 788-8725/1355 and (011) 728-6668. Other contacts are: Anti-Drug Outreach, tel (012) 329-2670, and the SA National Council for Alcoholism and Drug Abuse, tel (012) 542-1121/2/3/4.

TOURIST INFORMATION CENTRES

The South African Tourism Board (Satour) promotes tourism locally and overseas and has offices in many cities. Tourist information is obtainable abroad from any of the branch offices of Satour and any of its regional offices. For other tourist information offices contact the nearest publicity association or visitor's information bureau (there are more than 50 such associations in South Africa) through the local telephone directory. Most of these offices display the internationally recognised symbol for information, a green and white 'i'.

For information contact: Satour, South African Head Office, 442 Rigel Avenue South Erasmusrand, Pretoria; Private Bag X164, Pretoria 0001, Gauteng; tel (012) 347-0600; fax (012) 45-4889; e-mail gcoetzee@is.co.za. Satour has a brochure request line in the UK on (0541) 550044.

Regional offices are as follows:

Bloemfontein, tel (051) 47-1362, fax (051) 47-0862.
Cape Town, tel (021) 21-6274, fax (021) 419-4875.
Durban, tel (031) 304-7144, fax (031) 305-6693.
Jan Smuts Airport, tel (011) 970-1669, fax (011) 394-1508.
Johannesburg, tel (011) 331-5241, fax (011) 331-5420.
Kimberley, tel (0531) 3-1434/2-2657, fax (0531) 81-2937.
Nelspruit, tel (01311) 44405/6, fax (01311) 44509.
Pietersburg, tel (01521) 95-3025, fax (01521) 91-2654.
Port Elizabeth, tel (041) 55-7761, fax (041) 55-4975.
Potchefstroom, tel (0148) 93-1611/2/3, fax (0148) 22082.

The Southern Africa Tourism Association represents the private sector of the local tourism industry; contact PO Box 65924, Benmore 2010, Gauteng, tel (011) 883-9103, fax (011) 883-9002, e-mail satsa@pixie.co.za.

If you are surfing the internet you will find more information on tourism in South Africa at the TravelInfo Southern Africa web site: http://rapidttp.com

Tourist guides. Satour registers four categories of guides: local tourist guides, who are registered for a specific area in a region and who take tours not lasting longer than a day; regional tourist guides, who operate in a specific province; national tourist guides, who operate in all regions; and specialist tourist guides with expert knowledge of one particular area or subject. All guides wear an identifying badge. You can get more information on guides providing these helpful services from the Registrar of Tourist Guides, Satour, Private Bag X164, Pretoria 0001, Gauteng, tel (012) 347-0600, fax (012) 45-4768.

SA TOURIST OFFICES AND REPRESENTATIVES ABROAD

The South African Tourism Board has offices in the following countries (the tel/fax digits in brackets are the area codes used when dialling from within South Africa):

Australia and New Zealand: Level 6, 285 Clarence Street, Sydney 2000, NSW
Australia, tel (2) 9261 3424, fax (2) 9261 3414, e-mail satbsyd@ozemail.com.au
Canada: Suite 2, 4117 Lawrence Avenue East, Scarborough, Ontario M1E 2S2, tel
(416) 283-0563, fax (416) 283-5465, e-mail Satour@baxternet
Germany: Alemannia Haus, An der Hauptwache 11, 60313 Frankfurt am Main 1;
Postfach 101940, Frankfurt am Main 60019, tel (69) 92 91 290, fax (69) 28 0950,
e-mail 100705,744@compuserve.com
The Netherlands: Jozef Israëlskade 48, 1072 SB Amsterdam; Postbus 75360, 1070 AJ
Amsterdam, tel (20) 664 6201, fax (20) 662 9761, e-mail satour@pi.net
United Kingdom and Scandinavia: 5–6 Alt Grove, Wimbledon SW19 4DZ, UK, tel
(181) 944 8080, fax (181) 944 6705, e-mail satour@satbuk.demon.co.uk
USA: Suite 1524, 9841 Airport Boulevard, Los Angeles, CA 90045, California, USA,
tel (310) 641-8444, fax (310) 641-5812, e-mail satourla@ad.com

Addresses of South African representatives abroad are:

Australia and New Zealand: South African High Commission, Rhodes Place, State
Circle, Yarralumia ACT 2600, tel (2) 6273 2424/7, fax (2) 6273 3543;

Canada: South African High Commission, 15 Sussex Drive, Ottawa, Ontario K1M
1M8, tel (613) 744-0330, fax (613) 741-1639;

Germany: South African Embassy, Auf der Hostert 3, Bonn, tel (228) 82 010, fax
(228) 820 1148;

Ireland: South African Embassy, Alexandra House, Earlsfort Centre, Earlsfort
Terrace, Dublin, tel (1) 661 5553, fax (1) 661 5590;

The Netherlands: South African Embassy, Wassenaarseweg 40, The Hague, tel (70)
392 4501-4, fax (70) 346 0669;

United Kingdom: South African High Commission, South Africa House, Trafalgar
Square, London WC2N 5DP, tel (171) 930 4488, fax (171) 451 7284;

USA: South African Embassy, 3051 Massachusetts Avenue, NW, Washington DC
20008, tel (202) 232-4400, fax (202) 265-1607/232-3402; Consulate-General, 333
East 38th Street, New York NY 10016, tel (212) 213 4880, fax (212) 856 1575;
Consulate-General, Suite 600, 200 South Michigan Avenue, Chicago, Illinois
60604, tel (312) 939 7929/7932/7143, fax (312) 939 2588; Consulate-General, Suite
300, 50 North La Cienega Boulevard, Beverly Hills, CA 90211, tel (310) 657
9200-8, fax (310) 657 9215/3725.

EMBASSIES AND CONSULATES

Most foreign embassies and consulates are situated in Pretoria, Johannesburg,
Durban or Cape Town. Consult local telephone directories, the Yellow Pages,
telephone enquiries on 1023, or contact the Department of Foreign Affairs in
Pretoria, Private Bag X152, Pretoria 0001, Gauteng, tel (012) 351-1000, fax (012)
328-6937, or the Protocol Division, tel (012) 325-1000.

British High Commission, Liberty Life Place, 256 Glyn Street, Hatfield, Pretoria
0083; PO Box 13611 and 13612, Hatfield 0028, Gauteng, tel (012) 342-2200, fax
(012) 342-4955; Consulate-General, Dunkeld Corner, 275 Jan Smuts Avenue,
Dunkeld West 2196, tel (011) 327-0015, fax (011) 327-0152; Southern Life Centre,
8 Riebeeck Street, Cape Town 8001; PO Box 500, Cape Town 8000, tel (021)
25-3670, fax (021) 25-1427; Suite 1901, 19th Floor, The Marine, 22 Gardiner Street,
Durban 4001; PO Box 1404, Durban 4000, tel (031) 305-3041, fax (031)
307-4661;

US Embassy, 877 Pretorius Street, Arcadia, Pretoria 0083; PO Box 9536, Pretoria
0001, tel (012) 342-1048, fax (012) 342-2244/2199; Consulate-General, 11th Floor,
Kine Centre, corner Commissioner and Kruis Streets, Johannesburg 2001, tel
(011) 331-1681/3, fax (011) 331-1327; 4th Floor, Broadway Industries Centre
Foreshore, Cape Town 8001, tel (021) 21-4280/3, fax (021) 25-4151; 29th Floor,
Durban Bay House, 333 Smith Street, Durban 4001, tel (031) 304-4737, fax (031)
301-8206;

Australian High Commission, 292 Orient Street, corner Schoeman Street, Arcadia,
Pretoria, 0083; Private Bag X150, Pretoria 0001, tel (012) 342-3740, fax (012)
342-4201;

Canadian High Commission, 1103 Arcadia Street, corner Hilda Street, Hatfield,
Pretoria 0083, tel (012) 422-3000, fax (012) 422-3052;

German Embassy, 180 Blackwood Street, Arcadia, Pretoria 0083, tel (012)
344-3854/9, fax (012) 343-9401;

Irish Embassy, Delheim Suite, Tulbagh Park, 1234 Church Street, Colbyn, Pretoria
0083; PO Box 4174, Pretoria 0001, tel (012) 342-5062, fax (012) 342-4752;

Israel Embassy, Dashing Centre, 339 Hilda Street, Hatfield, Pretoria 0083; PO Box
3726, Pretoria 0001, tel (012) 342-2693/7, fax (012) 342-1442;

Dutch Embassy, 825 Arcadia Street, Arcadia, Pretoria 0083; PO Box 117, Pretoria
0001, tel (012) 344-3910/5, fax (012) 343-9950;

New Zealand High Commission, Sammbou Building, 424 Hilda Street, Hatfield,

Pretoria 0083; Private Bag X17, Hatfield 0028, tel (012) 342-8656/9, fax (012) 342-8640.

GAY TRAVELLERS

Organisations, publications and establishments catering for the needs and interests of gay travellers have blossomed since Nelson Mandela's government outlawed all discrimination and saw through a clause making sexual orientation a constitutional right. This right was further extended when the new Labour Relations Act came into force in November 1996, stating that employers may not discriminate against anyone on the grounds of sexual orientation or marital status. This alone means that gay couples who are able to prove a stable relationship of at least two years can claim benefits from some medical aid schemes, which until recently had restricted this to partners in heterosexual marriages.

Gay travellers arriving in South Africa can orient themselves in a number of ways. Publications are a good start. *Exit* is a monthly tabloid newspaper for gays and lesbians, tel (011) 614-9866, fax (011) 618-3165, which is sold in CNA outlets. Other publications available are *Magayzine, Outright, Gay SA, Gay Pages* and *Flash*.

The National Coalition for Gay and Lesbian Equality (NCGLE) campaigns on behalf of gays, lesbians, bisexuals and transsexuals, and produces material dealing with various issues, including adoption, marriage, partnership, employment rights, domestic violence, immigration and gay bashing. Contact NCGLE, PO Box 1984, Joubert Park 2044, Gauteng (tel (011) 403-3835; fax (011) 339-7762; e-mail coalgr@aztec.co.za).

Launched in South Africa late in 1996 along the lines of the popular gay phone service in the UK, The Phone Bridge is South Africa's first on-line dating service for gays and lesbians. Only Johannesburg and Cape Town have telephone listings to date. Although the system is accessed by phoning a Cape Town number, you can meet partners in nine other areas. Contact PO Box 56538, Waterfront, Cape Town 8000 (tel (021) 434-7759; fax (021) 434-7782).

Nudists. You won't find nudists or topless beauties on public beaches. The strong Calvinist ethic still dominates social convention and nudism has never really caught on, even though Beau Valley, near Warmbaths, once rated an entry in the *Guinness Book of Records* as the world's largest nudist colony. Owner Beau Brummell has had to close down after his decision to move with the times caused trouble in the Northern Province nudist paradise. He announced that black and gay couples would be allowed to live together in the valley. White heterosexual family shareholders reacted by refusing to pay monthly levies on their weekend cabins. That was the end of Beau Valley. It was liquidated at the end of 1996. The only remaining nudist haunts of note are both in the vicinity of less puritanical Cape Town. One is Sandy Bay, a secluded little cove a short walk from Llandudno, on the way to Hout Bay, and the other is men-only Graaff's Pool on the rocks bang in the middle of high-rise Sea Point. A low concrete wall surrounds the pool to give privacy to sun worshippers and bathers. This was built before the blocks of flats that overlook it. If you like shedding all before you take a dip, make sure there are no other people around. You could be arrested for public indecency.

DISABLED TRAVELLERS

It is estimated that some 14–18% of South Africa's population is physically disabled or suffers from some form of impairment (the world average is about 10%). In spite of this relatively high figure the development of facilities for the disabled is not as advanced as in other countries. No provision is made for special access for the disabled on normal buses, coaches and trains and the only regulations in force govern access to public buildings.

Happily this situation is changing. The government is setting guidelines for new developments that will ensure that adequate provision is made for the disabled and the handicapped, and many attractions, such as Kruger National Park and the adjacent private game reserves, already cater for disabled visitors. In 1995, the government launched a National Accessibility Scheme, which has the aim of making all involved in the tourist industry aware of the needs of the disabled, and setting up a national database of accessible attractions and accommodation. Resort and tour operators, hoteliers and others are being asked to submit details of accessibility to the co-ordinator of the scheme at Satour, so that information can be evaluated and included in the database. In the not too distant future Satour plans to be able to provide reliable information for disabled people on the whole tourist spectrum in South Africa. Contact the National Co-ordinator, National Accessibility Scheme, South African Tourism Board, Private Bag X164, Pretoria 0001, Gauteng, tel (012) 347-6000, fax (012) 45-4289.

We have discovered fewer than half a dozen tourist enterprises catering specifically for disabled visitors, but what they lack in supportive numbers they make up in innovation and ingenuity, and they form a bridge to other operations that incorporate disabled accessibility in their programmes. Rob and Julie Filmer of Johannesburg run Eco-Access, a registered non-profit, fund-raising organisation that promotes accessible environmental education, conservation, eco-tourism and recreational opportunities, based on the premise that people with disabilities are often handicapped by barriers resulting from the attitude of environmentalists and the facilities they develop. Remove these barriers, they say, and the handicaps fall away. They are constantly adding to a register they have compiled of barrier-free facilities to make permanently or temporarily disabled people aware of accessible and semi-accessible opportunities for them to enjoy South Africa's natural heritage. The Filmers also encourage disabled tourists to supply access information to Travelphone in Pretoria — Hennie and Heather Nel, tel (012) 664-6404 — an organisation that provides information on all aspects of tourism in South Africa. Contact Rob and Julie Filmer, Eco-Access, PO Box 1377, Roosevelt Park 2129, Gauteng, tel (011) 673-4533.

The National Environmental Accessibility Programme (NEAP) has as its main aim the setting of standards and evaluation of accessibility to buildings. Plans for new buildings, such as new additions to game lodges, are evaluated. With Satour, NEAP sets the standards. The Satour scheme, whose slogan is 'Tourism Without Barriers', checks features ranging from the gradient of ramps and the width of doors for wheelchair users, to the availability of vibrating alarm clocks for deaf visitors and braille menus for blind guests.

Another organisation working in eco-tourism is the Centre for Eco-tourism at the University of Pretoria. This centre is involved with hiking trails and outdoor adventure. Their approach is sufficiently inventive to suggest that if you cannot see or experience something on foot or by wheels, you can experience it from the air, or even from the back of a donkey cart. The South African Hiking Federation has a physically disabled person on the technical committee to advise on accessibility to hiking trails. One of their projects, completed in conjunction with Cape Nature Conservation, is the 6km/3.7 mile Palmiet Trail in the Western Cape. In addition to being a pleasant hike for everyone, pine logs have been placed along the entire trail so that a blind person, using a cane, can do the trail alone. There are a few clubs around the country that cater for the needs of disabled people who enjoy an outdoor challenge. One such club is Disabled Adventures. Their members, who are mainly physically disabled, get involved in various outdoor activities including scuba diving, camping and hiking. Adventure safaris for paraplegics, other disabled people and their families are available through Wilderness Wheels of Johannesburg. Operator

Phillip Roberts has put lots of thought, effort and money into his bush camps to make everything user-friendly for the disabled. Wheel chairs are loaded on to the 4 by 4 by hydraulic lift, windows open downwards so that everyone has the same viewing opportunity. Once you have arrived at your destination, accommodation is in custom-made tents that are suitable for wheelchairs, beds are wheelchair height for easy access and there are even specially designed shower cubicles. Disabled bush-whackers can enjoy game drives, eco-adventuring, rafting and canoeing, fishing, bungi-jumping, microlight flying and water parasailing, or simply relaxing round a fire in the great outdoors. Examples are a three-day tour to the Kruger National Park for R2144 (£286/$472), and a 14-day round South Africa trip for R18,200. WWA also runs budget tours for backpackers, such as four days camping in the Kruger National Park for R680. Contact Phillip Roberts at Wilderness Wheels Africa, 117 St Georges Road, Observatory 2198, Johannesburg, Gauteng, tel/fax (011) 648-5737.

A similar organisation is Roll-A-Venture, which offers active holidays for groups or individuals. Roll-A-Venture's packages have been put together by people who know all about access. Local wheelchair user Jean de Saint Clair and André Thomas of Austria, together with John Elliott of Felix Unite Tours, have made sure the activities they recommend are accessible. The company offers two main options. Firstly, there is a self-drive tour: Roll-A-Venture meets you at the airport and off you go independently in your hired car to the adventures you have booked, or transport is provided to the various adventure activities. The second option is a two-week guided tour from Johannesburg in a Microbus with a maximum of six people. This takes you to the Kruger National Park, then along the Garden Route in the Western Cape, ending in Cape Town. While in Cape Town you can choose further activities, such as bungi-jumping, rafting down the Breede River, deep-sea fishing, horse riding, microflight flying, Great White Shark and whale watching, photo safaris, canoeing on the Orange River, sailing, seaplane flights, and water parasailing. There are also trips to the Victoria and Alfred Waterfront and the Cape winelands. Contact Roll-A-Venture, PO Box 50565, Waterfront, Cape Town 8001, tel (021) 23-0871, fax (021) 23-2262, Cell 083 625-6021, e-mail saint@iafrica.com.

Other useful contacts for information on accessible environmental facilities are:

> *Disabled Adventures*, c/o Carol Schafer, Sports Science Department, Sports Science Institute of South Africa, PO Box 2593, Clareinch 7740, Western Cape (daytime tel (021) 686-7330 ext 297), organises hiking and outdoor adventure for mobility-restricted people, such as paraplegics, amputees and those with cerebral palsy.
>
> *Independent Living Centre*, PO Box 32099, Braamfontein 2017, Gauteng, tel (011) 720-6546, fax (011) 720-6565.
>
> *Titch Travel*, PO Box 671, Rondebsoch 7701, Western Cape (tel (021) 689-4151), specialises in tours for the disabled and visually impaired.
>
> *The Two Oceans Aquarium* at the Victoria and Alfred Waterfront in Cape Town has a limited number of wheelchairs available free of charge. Ask at the desk. All aquarium exhibits are accessible to the disabled. Visitors with special needs (hearing or visually impaired) can call the Aquarium, tel (021) 418-3823, to facilitate their visit.

All major airlines have a range of aids and facilities for handicapped passengers. Virgin Atlantic provides a good example of the forethought that enables disabled passengers and those with restricted mobility to travel with dignity. The airline is a participating member of 'Access to the Skies', a committee that operates under the auspices of RADAR (the Royal Association for Disability and Rehabilitation) and aims to facilitate air transport for passengers with special needs. Cabin crew and airport staff undergo special training in assisting passengers with restricted mobility and/or impaired sight or hearing, assistance to and from aircraft is available, passengers in wheelchairs are invited to Virgin Upper Class lounges, there are on-board wheelchairs on Boeing 747s and Airbus 340s and these planes have toilets fully accessible to wheelchair passengers. Nebulisers for asthmatics or passengers with breathing problems are carried on all flights, and automatic defibrillators are available on long-haul aircraft. South African Airways (SAA) provides passenger aid units at all major airports and the larger car hire companies provide vehicles with hand controls.

Chaplins restaurant in Mellville, Johannesburg, is sensitive to special needs, such as vegetarians, diabetics, calorie-counters and people with heart conditions, and their menu is also available in Braille. Chaplins is at 85 4th Avenue, Mellville, Gauteng, tel (011) 726-5411.

The Wheelchair Travel Club realises that a hotel's suitability can be determined by features such as 80cm/32 inch entrances to lifts, doors and ramps, and grab-rails alongside baths and toilets. Contact Ron or Christina Coleman in Johannesburg at tel (011) 725-5648/50, fax (011) 725-5639, Cell 082 492-8859.

Durban Rotaract Club has compiled a guidebook called *Wheeling Around Durban* that measures accessibility to Durban's clubs, restaurants, shopping centres, tourist destinations, parks and sports venues. This is free from Disabled People of South Africa (DPSA), tel (031) 709-2750, or you can find it at the Durban International Airport.

> *Association of the Physically Disabled*, Private Bag X1, Parkview 2122, Gauteng, tel (011) 646-8331/2/3/4, fax (011) 646-5248; *Eastern Cape:* PO Box 11149, Southern-wood, East London 5213, tel (0431) 29680, fax (0431) 29355; *Western Cape:* PO Box 1375, Cape Town 8000, tel (021) 685-4153, fax (021) 685-3438
>
> *Cripple Care Association*, 8 Dr Savage Road, Pretoria 0002, Gauteng, tel (012) 328-6447, fax (012) 328-6759
>
> *Disabled People of SA*, PO Box 39008, Booysens 2016, Gauteng, tel (011) 982-1130, fax (011) 982-2181
>
> *Friends of Disabled Riders*, tel (011) 702-1349 and (011) 468-2756
>
> *Quadriplegic Helpline*, Durban, tel (031) 72-2733
>
> *SA National Council for the Blind*, PO Box 11149, Brooklyn 0011, Gauteng, tel (012) 346-1171, fax (012) 346-1177
>
> *SA National Council for the Deaf*, 22 Napier Road, Richmond, Johannesburg 2000, Private Bag X04, Westhoven 2142, Gauteng, tel (011) 482-1610/726-5873, fax (011) 726-5873
>
> *SA Riding for the Disabled Association (SARDA) Centre*, Honeydew, Johannesburg, tel (011) 958-1319/1992 or (011) 708-1974

Most shopping centres do their best to accommodate disabled drivers; some fence off bays and post guards to remove the chains for disabled parkers; others issue a special access card to a separate section. Some clamp the wheels of offending cars. Culprits have to pay a fine for the key to the clamp, which is donated to an organisation for the disabled.

USEFUL INFORMATION

Time Zone. Standard Time in South Africa is two hours ahead of GMT, one hour ahead of Central European Winter Time and seven hours ahead of Eastern Standard Winter Time (USA). Details of world time zones can be found in the international section of the local telephone directory.

Electrical Appliances. Generally, urban power systems are 220/230 volts AC at 50 cycles per second, although there are variations with Pretoria at 250 volts and Port Elizabeth at 220/250 volts. Plugs are 5amp two-pin and 15amp three-pin (round pin). Adaptors for electric razors and hair dryers can be obtained from the reception desk in most hotels or from electrical shops, supermarkets and hardware stores. US-made appliances may need a transformer.

Weights and Measures. South Africa operates on the metric system and all weights and measures are given only in this form. In the rural areas an oddity is that farmers still measure the area of their land in morgen. A morgen is about 12,000 sq m, or two acres, and its name comes from the amount of land that could be ploughed in a morning.

Useful Addresses and Numbers. Information, advice and support are available by contacting the following:

Computicket bookings, tel (011) 445-8000 (open 9am to 8pm, 7 days a week), information, tel (011) 445-8445, hotel central reservations, tel (011) 445-8300.

Crime Stop, toll-free 0800 11 12 13.

Hiking Federation of South Africa, PO Box 1420, Randburg 2125, Gauteng, tel (011) 886-6524, fax (011) 886-6013.

Life Line, 24-hour service, any crisis, tel (012) 343-8888. Counselling by phone is also available on the following numbers: Cape Town, tel (021) 461-1111; Johannesburg, tel (011) 728-1347; East Rand, tel (011) 422-4242; East London, tel (0431) 22000; Pretoria, tel (012) 46-0666; Port Elizabeth, tel (041) 55-5581; Durban, tel (031) 23-2323; Welkom, tel (057) 352-2212; Vaal, tel (016) 33-7333.

Passport office, 77 Harrison Street, Johannesburg, tel (011) 836-3228.

Rape crisis centres: Cape Town, tel (021) 47-9762 or 21-5400; Pietermaritzburg, tel (0331) 45-6279; Johannesburg, tel (011) 642-4345.

For the *time* telephone 1026.

Weather information: Gauteng, Mpumalanga, Northern and North-West Province, tel (012) 21-9621; Cape Peninsula, South-Western Cape interior and the coastal region up to Plettenberg Bay, tel (021) 40881; the coastal region from Plettenberg Bay to Port Edward, as well as the Eastern Cape interior, tel (041) 52-4242; KwaZulu-Natal, tel (031) 307-4121; Maritime, tel (031) 307-4135; Free State, Northern Cape and the Karoo, tel (051) 430-4058.

Womens' Bureau of SA, tel (012) 47-6176.

Public Holidays

Banks and businesses that are closed on Sundays will also be closed on public holidays and public transport will run less frequently. If a public holiday falls on a Sunday, then Monday is a holiday.

January 1	New Year's Day
March 21	Human Rights Day
March 28	Good Friday
March 31	Family Day
April 27	Freedom Day
May 1	Workers Day
June 16	Youth Day
August 9	National Women's Day
September 24	Heritage Day
December 16	Day of Reconciliation
December 25	Christmas Day
December 26	Christmas Day

School Holidays. During these you can expect to find most of the popular holiday spots jam-packed and difficult to get into without long-standing bookings. The dates vary from year to year (and from one province to the next), but usually cover late March to early April, late June to late July, late September to early October, and early December to mid-January.

Calendar of Events

January 1–4	Cape Minstrels Carnival	Cape Town
February	Dias Festival	Mossel Bay
March 28–April 13	Rand Easter Show	Johannesburg
March 29–April 5	Klein Karoo National Arts Festival	Oudsthoorn
April	Game and Wine Festival	Kuruman
April	Mardi Gras Festival	Durban
April	Port Elizabeth Splash Festival	Port Elizabeth
April 25–28	Music in the Mountains Festival	Drakensberg
May	East London Show	East London
May 1–4	Splashy Fen Music Festival	Underberg
May 20–1 June	Grahamstown Eisteddfod	Grahamstown
May/June	Royal Show	Pietermaritzburg
June 10	Regional Traditional Dance	Badplaas
June 16	Comrades Marathon	Pietermaritzburg
July	Hibuscus Festival	Margate
July	Knysna Oyster Festival	Knysna
July 3–13	National Arts Festival	Grahamstown
August	Pretoria International Show	Pretoria
August	Mpumalanga Eisteddfod	Nelspruit
August	Umhlanga (Reed Dance)	Badplaas
September	Graaff-Reinet Karoo Festival	Graaff-Reinet
September	Whale Festival	Hermanus
September	Zululand Show	Eshowe
September 4	Kora All Africa Music Awards	Johannesburg
September 19–27	Stellenbosch Festival	Stellenbosch
September 20–October 5	Magoesbaskloof Spring Festival	Magoesbaskloof
September 26–October 5	International Eisteddfod of SA	Roodepoort
October	Jacaranda Festival	Pretoria
October	Rose Festival	Bloemfontein
October 25	Tulbagh Festival	Tulbagh
November	Bush Festival	Prieska
November	Cherry Festival	Ficksburg
November	National Zulu Dance Competition	Estcourt
November	Philippolis Show	Philippolis
December	Kenton-on-Sea Neptune Festival	Kenton-on-Sea
December	Million Dollar Golf Challenge	Sun City
December 17–31	Rustler's Valley Christmas Festival	Ficksburg
December 27–28	The Drakensberg Auld Lang Syne	Drakensberg Festival

Gauteng

Johannesburg skyline

Gauteng, which is a Northern Sotho word meaning 'Place of Gold', covers 18,810sq km/7263sq miles and encompasses an area that used to be known as the Pretoria-Witwatersrand-Vaal Triangle, or PWV, one of the largest industrial regions in the southern hemisphere. It is the smallest of South Africa's nine provinces but economically speaking the most significant. The province's concentrations of gold, diamonds, platinum, coal, iron, vanadium and other natural resources have made it the country's engine room, accounting for 37% of its gross domestic produce (GDP), 27% of its labour force, 60% of its fiscal revenue and a personal per capita income of R4992 for its 7.4 million people, or just about double the national average. Some of the country's biggest companies, corporations and financial institutions operate out of heartland capital Johannesburg, which is also home to the largest of Africa's 14 stock markets. With Pretoria, South Africa's administrative capital 56km/35 miles to the north, Johannesburg is the country's focal point and barometer of the nation's economic health. Johannesburg's infrastructure is one of the finest in Africa and is the apex of the entire country's communications network and from here, the hub of international arrivals and departures, the country is an open book for travellers. Within Gauteng, with the exceptions of Pretoria and Krugersdorp most towns, such as Randfontein and Roodepoort to the west, Kempton Park and Benoni and to the east, and the industrial regions of Vanderbijlpark and Vereeniging to the south, are relatively modern, unsightly centres which generally owe their existence to the central mining and industrial activities of the Reef. They are not totally bereft of interest, but they are not on the tourist highway. Johannesburg is the magnet for the unemployed, not only of the country, but of neighbouring countries whose own economies are in tatters. It is estimated that Greater Johannesburg's population of 3 million is increasing by 30,000 a month and this is one of the reasons for the city's unenviable crime rate, the highest in the country.

JOHANNESBURG

When visitors flew into Johannesburg during the apartheid years, goes the old joke, the pilot would switch on the intercom and advise passengers, 'We are now descending to land in Johannesburg. Please put your watches back 40 years.' Today there is very little that is out of date in this bustling, modern, high-rise city on the windswept Highveld. Indeed, its residents seem to have a passion for pulling down anything remotely old-fashioned and replacing it with a geometric tower of glass and steel, to the degree that when one British notable visited Johannesburg and was asked what he thought of the city, he replied 'It will be wonderful when it's finished.' Jo'burg, Joeys, the Golden City and iGoli — the Nguni word for gold — the city is known by all these names to South Africans. Johannesburg is South Africa's most populous city and is a financial centre of world importance. The city stands 1760m/5774ft above sea level on the Witwatersrand (the Ridge of White Waters), which is a range of hills covering the ore deposits rich in gold which gave it birth in 1886.

The origin of its name is open to dispute but the nickname Golden City says it all. One thing that has barely changed since the days of the apocryphal pilot is the ring of immense mine dumps which seem to enclose Johannesburg like gigantic molehills, the waste and crushings the mines discarded as they burrowed deeper and deeper into the fabulous golden reef, the richest the world has ever known. These days the dumps which are such a well known feature of the cityscape are, in fact, gradually vanishing. Environmental pressure has led to the greening of many, but the real pressure has been — in true Jo'burg fashion — commercial. The rising value of the metal has led to the dumps being re-worked to recover the gold left behind by earlier, more primitive, mining methods. While this might remove some old landmarks the city dwellers won't miss the ochre dumps that coat the area with powdery mine dust when the wind blows in August to herald spring. Johannesburg is the Big Apple of southern Africa, a modern, cosmopolitan metropolis, the largest city on the continent after Cairo — but still an inexpensive place to visit. A global cost of living index rates Johannesburg as the third cheapest city in the world if you have pounds or dollars in your pocket. Only La Paz in Bolivia and Caracas in Venezuela are cheaper. It is full of vitality and verve, with scores of first-rate hotels, some 2000 restaurants, 22 museums, 30 art galleries, more than 20 markets and countless shopping centres whose bustle contrasts with leafy suburbs such as Parktown, Houghton and Dunkeld, where stylish mansions, many of them designed by famous British architect Sir Herbert Baker, stand bracketed by BMWs and Mercs in exquisitely manicured gardens. Probably the best known area of Johannesburg to visitors is Hillbrow, the most densely populated residential area in the country, which sits atop Hospital Hill, 20 minutes' walk from the CBD. It is a cosmopolitan hotch-potch similar but on a smaller scale to New York's Greenwich Village, Sydney's Kings Cross and London's Soho. Its landmark, poking an ugly 269m/883ft finger into the sky and visible from afar, is the Hillbrow Tower, built in 1971 for telecommunications. The area is vibrant but sleazy, with theatres, cinemas, music, restaurants, bars and boutiques, sex shops, skin shows, prostitutes, and drug-dealing all part of the scene. Interesting, but it can be dangerous, so take in your money belt an extra notch if you visit. Another New Age suburb is Rockey Street, between Yeoville and Bellevue, which is a short walk from Hillbrow. Rockey Street is where it all happens, so far as young revellers are concerned. Mixture as in Hillbrow, and same advice, but more so. Melville, whose main street and 9th Avenue are lined with attractive shops and atmospheric caf'es and restaurants, is a more sedate slice of bohemia, as is Brixton, a homing beacon for the trendies in the shadow of the 235m/771ft high towering landmark, the Brixton Tower which relays TV transmissions.

In the central business district (CBD) skyscrapers rear over haut couture boutiques, aromatic Indian bazaars, and African *muti* (medicine) shops where traditional healers throw the bones and dispense herbal remedies while jets roar overhead and pin-striped brokers hurry to the Stock Exchange, founded in 1887. Johannesburg sprang to life the year before, in 1886, when a semi-literate Australian miner named George Harrison found gold on the farm Langlaagte in what was then a pastoral Boer republic ruled by President Stephanus Johannes Paulus Kruger. Until then, the patriarchal Boer had watched with misgivings the flood of prospectors into his Zuid-Afrikaansche Republiek, and once started a speech in Johannesburg with the words, 'Burghers, friends, murderers, thieves and robbers...' He believed that 'he who finds gold, finds trouble,' but digger pressure and a near-empty treasury obliged him to proclaim public gold diggings on a number of farms on the Main Reef. Four thousand diggers were in the first mad stampede to peg claims. Langlaagte became the cradle of Johannesburg — at first better known as Ferreira's Camp — and a Government Gazette proclamation on 15 September 1886 was the birth certificate of the city founded literally on gold. When the government auctioned the first stands two months later Johannesburg was laid out on a grid along American lines. City blocks were kept short so that there would be more of the corner stands which brought the highest prices. This helped to swell Kruger's coffers but it left modern Johannesburg with the makings of traffic problems the City Fathers are still trying to sort out. Digger George Harrison sold his claim for £10 and became a footnote to history, his only monuments a street in central Johannesburg bearing his name and the George Harrison Park, Langlaagte, the site of his original claim 5km/3 miles west of Johannesburg, which houses a forlorn old ore crusher.

In little more than a decade the original huddle of tents and corrugated iron shanties on the bleak veld became a bustling mining town producing more gold than the entire USA, and enjoying nearly all the amenities of a modern European or American city, and some of the more dubious ones, such as bars, brothels and gambling saloons. Johannesburg gained official city status in 1928. Once the city was firmly on the map its history became in virtually every respect the history of South Africa itself. Johannesburg is the powerhouse that charges South Africa and the sub-continent and is still fuelled by the increasingly elusive precious yellow metal that men now have to wrench from workings up to an incredible 12,000ft below its pavements and other mining towns along the 105km/65 mile-long Main Reef. This Reef is the largest, most concentrated and apparently endless treasure trove ever found and continues to produce most of the world's gold supply. Gold mining activity has largely moved away from Johannesburg itself, although the city remains the home of the Chamber of Mines of South Africa, representing most of the gold mines in the Republic. Over the years the city has been rocked by political chicanery, local and international conflicts, strikes, mining tragedies, gangster activities, and ruinous financial debacles, and today still reflects the frontier brashness and spirit of its early days, although it has achieved a veneer of refinement and culture.

The city stands on a series of east-west ridges, the Witwatersrand, which originally extended from Springs in the east to Randfontein in the west, corresponding to the concentration of gold-mining and other industry. Archaeological digs have revealed evidence of continuous human occupation of these ridges for at least 1.25 million years. Prior to European settlement, they were inhabited by Iron Age people who lived in semi-permanent villages, grew crops, reared domestic livestock and produced iron and earthenware implements. Remains of their homes, implements and furnaces cans still be seen in the Melville Koppies Nature Reserve, a small wilderness area within sight of the skyscrapers. Scenically the ridges are very attractive and many mining magnates built their homes on them after the discovery of gold. From the earliest days, Jo'burgers believed in working in the south but living in the north, whose suburbs still reflect the days of gracious living. While Johannesburg is the undisputed commercial heart of South Africa, much of the area has escaped development and in dozens of country retreats and resorts surrounding the City of Gold, there are ample opportunities for fun and relaxation.

Getting Around

Arrival and Departure. Johannesburg International Airport is about 20km/12 miles east of Johannesburg and 50km/31 miles south of Pretoria. Since it opened in 1952 it has grown to become the gateway to South Africa and now handles more than 7 million passengers a year. There is a regular bus service from the airport to Johannesburg and Pretoria, as well as taxis and hire cars.

Arrival/departure enquiries, tel (011) 975-9963.
Other enquiries, tel (011) 333-6504.
Lost property (international), tel (011) 978-4777.
Lost property (domestic), tel (011) 978-5671.
Grand Central Airport, Midrand, tel (011) 805-3166.
Lanseria Airport, on the road to Broederstroom, tel (011) 659-2750.
Rand Airport, tel (011) 827-8884.
Springs, tel (011) 818-5578.

City Transport. The Greater Johannesburg areas has some 2750km/1709 miles of roads, so you can forget walking, apart from the security risk. The municipal **bus services** are reasonably reliable during daylight hours, but not at night or the weekends. City bus times are available on request from tel (011) 403-4300, 838-2125/6 or 838-2164/5, or you can get timetables from the Van der Bijl and Bree Street information offices in the city centre. A dedicated complaints office has been established, tel (011) 403-4300. Monthly tickets can be bought at the ticket offices in Van der Bijl Square, Bree Street, Johannesburg Hotel (corner Eloff and Kerk Streets), Westgate and selected pharmacies.

For **taxis** try:

City Taxi, tel (011) 336-5213/4/5/6;
Taxi Bureau, tel (011) 487-1716;
Taxi Maxi Cabs, tel (011) 648-1212;

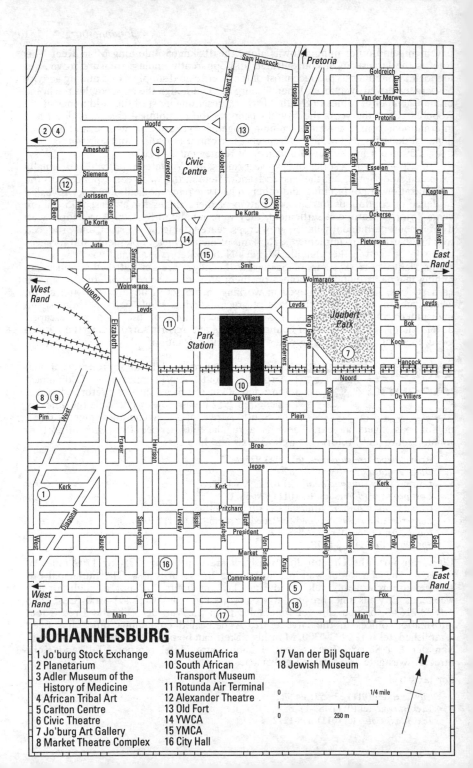

JOHANNESBURG

1 Jo'burg Stock Exchange
2 Planetarium
3 Adler Museum of the
  History of Medicine
4 African Tribal Art
5 Carlton Centre
6 Civic Theatre
7 Jo'burg Art Gallery
8 Market Theatre Complex

9 MuseumAfrica
10 South African
   Transport Museum
11 Rotunda Air Terminal
12 Alexander Theatre
13 Old Fort
14 YWCA
15 YMCA
16 City Hall

17 Van der Bijl Square
18 Jewish Museum

0   1/4 mile

0   250 m

N

Egoli Taxi, tel (011) 648-0614;
Fax-a-Cab, fax your address to (011) 648-8555 and they will send you a taxi;
Nation Taxi Services, tel (011) 339-2289/2379;
Rose Radio Taxis (24-hour service), tel (011) 725-3333/1111;
Mohammed's Taxi Service (Durban to Johannesburg), tel (011) 855-8876/2911;
South African Black Taxi Association (Sabta), tel (011) 832-1911.

Car hire is a better option, especially if you are going to be in Gauteng for any length of time:

Avis, tel (011) 974-2571;
Budget, tel (011) 392-3929, toll-free 0800 01 66 22;
Europcar, tel (011) 885-1122;
Hertz, tel (011) 394-4610.

Hotels. *The Michelangelo*, in the heart of Sandton's exclusive shopping malls, charges from R1000 (£133/$220) per person per night. With a R3500 a night suite you get a butler, your own fax machine and hotel stationery with your name embossed on it. Sandton Square, West Street, Sandown. PO Box 784682, Sandton 2146, tel (011) 282-7000, fax (011) 282-7171.

The *Cullinan Hotel* in Sandton offers first-class service and luxury at 115 Katherine Street, Sandown. Its three-star sister, Cullinan Inn, provides a down-to-earth, value-for-money alternative and can be found at No 1 Cullinan Close, Morningside, tel (011) 884-8544, fax (011) 884-8545.

Best Western's Premier Lodge in the Johannesburg suburb of Bedfordview is an eight-minute drive from Johannesburg International Airport. Rates from R295 per person per night. 33 Bradford Road, Bedfordview 2047. PO Box 75825, Gardenview 2047, tel (011) 622-1556, fax (011) 622-8725.

The Grace in Rosebank, Johannesburg, is a five-star sister hotel. Rates are R460 a night per person sharing a double or twin room and R900 per person for a one-bedroomed suite. Contact PO Box 2536, Parklands 2121, tel (011) 880-1675, fax (011) 880-3282.

Sandton Sun and Towers, five-star accommodation in an exclusive suburb surrounded by chic boutiques and restaurants and two of the classiest shopping malls in South Africa, tel (011) 780-5000, fax (011) 780-5002, toll-free 0800 12 13 77.

The five-star *Carlton Hotel* is an enduring African landmark situated in the heart of Johannesburg's commercial and financial centre. The hotel prides itself on its service and excellent restaurants, including the up-market Three Ships, which ranks among the finest in the country, the lively El Gaucho for carnivores and the all-day Koffiehuis. Facilities include a gymnasium and a rooftop pool. Tel (011) 331-8911, fax (011) 331-3555.

Self-catering accommodation is available at:

The Bostonian, 29 Abel Road, Berea, Johannesburg, tel (011) 643-7211;
The Don Apartments, in Illovo, Melrose, Bruma, Rosebank and Sandton, tel (011) 788-1853;
Don Palazzo, 245 Oxford Road, Illovo, Sandton, tel (011) 880-2503;
Protea Gardens Apartments, O'Reilly Road, Berea, tel (011) 643-6611;
St Tropez, Linbro Park, Sandton, tel (011) 974-8834.

Hostels. Budget travellers usually make Johannesburg the first stop on their peregrinations, and the suburb of Yeoville is the cosmopolitan magnet that attracts them with its clubs, cheap eateries and accommodation. As a known drug centre it is also heavily policed, which makes it safe as well as friendly. *Rockey Street Backpackers* caters exclusively for young, international travellers. Accommodation is provided in dormitories (6–8 beds) and single and double rooms. A fully equipped self-catering kitchen is available and breakfast can be provided for group bookings. Dormitory beds are R35 (£4.65/$7.70) per person per night, single rooms R65 and doubles R85 to R100 per room.

One of Rockey Street's most important services is its travel advice — where to go, what to do and how to get there — and it offers a wide choice of budget tours and car hire at reasonable rates (for example, three-night, four-day trips to Kruger Park from R490 to R690 per person, camping with meals). Tickets are available for the Baz Bus round-the-country hostel-hopper service, the Garden Route Hopper Bus and other services. Contact Rockey Street Backpackers, 34 Regent Street, Yeoville, Johannesburg 2198, Gauteng, tel (011) 648-8786, fax (011) 648-8423.

The *Backpackers Ritz* (BR) of Johannesburg is situated between the up-market suburbs of Rosebank and Hyde Park, which are noted for their cafés, restaurants, cinemas and shopping malls. As well as inexpensive accommodation. BR provides free pick-up once you reach Johannesburg and can also arrange transport when you leave. The hostel acts as an agent for buses, trains, a backpackers bus and car hire companies. They can recommend the companies to contact if, for instance, you want to tour Soweto, Johannesburg city centre, the Kruger National Park, take weekend hikes or longer tours through South Africa. Dorm beds cost R35 (£4.65/$7.70) per person, per night, single rooms R60, and double rooms R80 to R100 per room, per night. The Backpackers Ritz is at 1A North Road, Dunkeld West, Johannesburg 2196, Gauteng, tel Mark Baines at (011) 325-7125/327-0229, fax (011) 327-0233.

Other budget lodges and hostels in Johannesburg, all charging R28–35 (£3.75–4.65/$6.15–7.70) a night in a dorm, up to R45 per person for a double, are:

> *Backpackers Lodge ITH*, 119 Ascot Avenue, Bez Valley, tel (011) 614-2555.
> *Egoli Backpackers Goldmine*, 109 Third Avenue, Bez Valley, tel (011) 614-7014, fax (011) 648-9701.
> *Explorers Club*, 9 Innes Street, Observatory, tel (011) 648-7138, fax (011) 648-4673.
> *Fairview Youth Hostel*, 4 College Street (off Commissioner), Fairview 2094, tel (011) 618-2048, fax (011) 614-2823.
> *Inchanga Ranch*, Inchanga Road, Witkoppen 2068, tel (011) 708-1304, fax (011) 708-1464.
> *Johannesburg Central Youth Hostel*, 4 Fife Avenue, Berea 2001, tel (011) 643-1213, fax (011) 643-1412.
> *Kew Youth Hostel*, 5 Johannesburg Road, Kew 2090, tel (011) 887-9072, fax (011) 643-1412.
> *Travellers and Backpackers Retreat*, 55 First Avenue, Bez Valley, tel (011) 614-4640, fax (011) 614-2497.
> *The Pink House*, 73 Becker Street, Yeoville 2198, tel (011) 487-1991, fax (011) 487-1991.
> *Zoo Lodge Backpackers Retreat*, 2 Ashwood Road, corner Jan Smuts Avenue, Saxonwold 2091, tel (011) 486-0011, fax (011) 838-7322.

The *Orlando YMCA* can be contacted at PO Box 5, Orlando, tel/fax (011) 935-1022, and the *Johannesburg YWCA* on 128 De Korte Street, Braamfontein, tel (011) 403-3830.

Caravan parks and resorts include *Murray Park Recreation Resort*, tel (011) 816-1104, and *Riebeeck Lake Caravan Park*, tel (011) 411-0184.

Further Afield. An hour's easy drive from Johannesburg is the four-star *Mount Grace Country House Hotel*, set in magnificent gardens in the Rietpoort valley, not far from the little village of Magaliesburg. Accommodation is in thatched cottages. There are marked walking trails, and bird lists in each room. People fly in just for their Sunday lunch buffet. Something extra is a chamber music theatre where classical concerts are held. B&B rates range from R233 (£31/$51) a night per person sharing to R408, tel (0142) 77-1350, fax (0142) 77-1202. Central reservations, PO Box 2536, Parklands 2121, Gauteng, tel (011) 880-1675, fax (011) 880-3282.

Igoli Guest House is within one hours' drive from Johannesburg and two minutes from the Vaal River. 4 Beethoven Street, Vanderbijlpark 1911, tel (016) 32-4242.

West Winds, three-star country house in the old Cape Dutch style, in Magaliesburg, tel (0142) 75-0560.

Utopia, self-catering chalets and campsite set in the Magaliesberg mountain bushveld, tel (0142) 75-0352.

Eating and Drinking

There are more than 2000 restaurants in the Greater Johannesburg area, and this keeps prices keen, unless money is no object and your taste runs to haute cuisine and imported wine. There is a thriving café society during the day; night is for restaurants and music, and preferably restaurants with music. Always the best bet for hungry budget travellers are carveries and buffet places where you can eat your fill. A good alternative is anything run by Portuguese, trenchermen who can be relied on to produce tasty, nourishing dishes at reasonable prices. You can find Portuguese restaurants in virtually every suburb, but the most authentic tend to be in the low-rent, working-class southern suburbs. A good start would be the *Parreirinha Restaurant and Beerhall*, in 6th Street, La Rochelle, tel (011) 435-3809; another is the *Radium Beerhall*, at 282 Louis Botha Avenue, Orange Grove, tel (011) 728-3866. There is another Radium in Rivonia, but it lacks the down-at-heel charm of the original. Another Portuguese restaurant is the *Vilamoura* — there are three of them — which has been voted the best in town by local radio listeners, who rated *Linger Longer* in Sandton the ritziest, and the *Baron and Quail* the best for pub grub.

You will often eat better fish and seafood in Gauteng than on the coast, as the pick of the catch is flown up to the Highveld daily, where it brings better prices. Fish lovers should follow the queues outside *The Fishmonger*, in the Grosvenor Shopping Centre, off Main Road and William Nicol Drive, in Bryanston. Queues for this restaurant are not unusual as you cannot make reservations. There is a wide variety of fish dishes, as well as a meze bar and Japanese menu offering first-class sushi, sashimi and rolls. The fish is superb and the children's favourite, a generous portion of battered hake and chips, costs R14 (£1.85/$3.10). An assorted sushi platter which easily satisfies four adults as a starter is R40, and a prawn, calamari and sole platter is R45. Tel (011) 463-7826.

Other top finny places are:

> *The Codfather*, 3 Corlett Drive, Illovo, for line fish to sushi, tel (011) 447-4317;
> *Horatio's*, at the corner 3rd Avenue and 7th Street, Melville, tel (011) 726-2890;
> *The Fish House*, Shop 30, Milpark Galleries, opposite Milpark Holiday Inn, tel (011) 726-5803;
> *Pescador Restaurant*, in Sandown's Grayston Centre, tel (011) 884-4429.

For some of the best Japanese fish dishes in Johannesburg try:

> *Fuji* in Sandown, tel (011) 884-0114;
> *Tokyo* in Sandton Square, tel (011) 784-3156;
> *Yamato* in Illovo, tel (011) 880-9781;
> *Daruma* in Melrose North, tel (011) 447-2260;
> *Osho* in Rosebank, tel (011) 442-9109.

For traditional South African and ethnic food try:

Anton van Wouw, 111 Sivewright Avenue, Doornfontein, next to the Alhambra Theatre, tel (011) 402-7916;

Iyavaya African Restaurant, 42 Hunter Street, Yeoville, tel (011) 648-3500;

Jahnito's African jazz bar and restaurant, 43 Rockey Street, Bellevue East, tel (011) 648-9288;

Leipoldt's, 94 Juta Street, Braamfontein, good for buffet, tel (011) 339-2765;

Gramadoelas, at the Market Theatre, corner of Wolhuter and Bree streets, Newtown, spicy dishes of Africa (try the fried mopane worms), tel (011) 838-6960;

Africa Upstairs Downstairs, 185 Oxford Road, Rosebank. There is even an Ndebele hut in the middle of the restaurant, tel (011) 442-2836;

Die Koper Ketel, 236 DF Malan Drive, Blackheath, tel (011) 678-6011.

President Mandela's son-in-law Zweli Hlongwane has opened a downtown restaurant called *Kofifi*, in Commissioner Street, specialising in authentic African cuisine. It has a township ambience and jazz is played.

If you take a tour of Soweto, ask to make a detour to the *Blue Fountain* for a R15 bar lunch, 1437 Moroka Street, Mapetla, tel (011) 986-1142.

For the really hungry meat-eater *The Train* is reputed to have the biggest buffet in the world (more than 140 dishes). You eat in immaculately restored Blue Train dining coaches. Renowned for its game dishes, buffalo, elephant, warthog, crocodile, giraffe, kudu, ostrich — to mention a few. There is, in addition, a massive selection of starters, fish, stews, curries, salads, pies and puddings. Eat as much as you like at no extra cost. The Train has an exceptional wine list and a remarkable selection of imported beers. Old Pretoria Road, Halfway House, tel (011) 805-1949/3639/2906.

You can mix food, drink and entertainment at the following:

Gold Reef City Hotel (at the Gold Reef City Theme Park), with trad South African grub on call breakfast, lunch and dinner, seven days a week, tel (011) 496-1626;

Consolidated Saloon has live entertainment on Friday, Saturday and Sunday evenings and a good selection of local and imported beers and draught on tap. Open Tuesday to Sunday for pub lunches, tel (011) 496-1626;

Rosie O'Grady's Good Time Emporium is next to *Digger Joe's Grill*, where theatre suppers are laid on before and after shows, as well as family fare lunches, tel (011) 496-1600;

Barney's Tavern is another popular attraction. Set in Gold Rush surroundings there is entertainment, draught beer, sports videos and a rollicking atmosphere. Pub lunches are available daily, tel (011) 496-1600;

Crown Restaurant specialises in wild game, served in authentic Victorian surroundings, tel (011) 835-1181.

Kapitan's Café at 11a Kort Street, between Market and President streets, in central Johannesburg, is something of a shrine for politically correct foodies. The café specialises in curries. These are greasy, mediocre assaults on Indian cuisine but you can at least say you have eaten at the place that was a favourite hang-out of Nelson Mandela in the days when he was plotting the downfall of white South Africa. Open Monday to Saturday from midday to 3pm, tel (011) 834-8048.

One of Gauteng's best-kept secrets has got to be the *Hotel School*, Smit Street, Braamfontein, offering the most reasonable meals in towns from Tuesdays to Fridays. Lunch is just R28.50 for a four-course meal, including coffee, and dinner a measly R38 (£5.05/$8.35) and you get the silver service treatment, tel (011) 406-2956.

You can get a value-for-money dinner at *Milner's* restaurant at the Holiday Inn Crowne Plaza in Parktown, a historical landmark which, during the Anglo-Boer War, was the official residence and headquarters of British High Commissioner Lord Milner. Opt for the buffet as either a starter at R18 or as your main course for R35. On the à la carte menu are things like smoked ostrich with tropical avocado salad

(R22), Cape Malay bobotie (R35), and mutton bredie (R35). The restaurant is open seven days a week, tel (011) 643-7226.

Rodizio Brazilian restaurant. Eat as much as you like for R39. Shop 28, The Terrace, Rustenburg Road, Victory Park, tel (011) 888-7633.

The *Judge 'n Brewery*, corner of Bordeaux and Ryder roads, Randburg, has pub lunches from R9.95, with live entertainment on Wednesday and Friday evening, tel (011) 781-1387.

The *Münchner House* restaurant at 44 Tungsten Street, Strijdom Park, Ferndale, has a Friday and Sunday lunch beef carvery at R16 per person. There is a live German Oompah band on Friday and Saturday evening, tel (011) 792-8156.

A good place to spend sheepless nights is the *Outback Bar & Grill*, 135 Rivonia Road (opposite Village Walk), Sandton. Open 10am till late Monday to Saturday, with jazz on a Sunday from noon. Homesick Aussies can drink Two Dogs Lemonade, in the can and the draught version, imported frosties such as Fosters, Emu, Toohey's, Castlemaine XXXX and Jacob's Creek wines. These can wash down Kookaburra Winga (barbecue chicken wings with hot sauce), Haha (New Zealand mussels wrapped in bacon and served with a sweet and sour sauce), Mad Max's lamb shank, Kylie's kingklip, Thunder from Down Under (peri-peri chicken) and Priscilla, prawn of the desert. There is a giant TV screen for watching international sport, even if the pub has to open at dawn because of time differences. Tel (011) 883-9303/4.

Chuckleberrys is the place for char-broiled burgers. Size starts at the 150g Regular (R10–15), or twice the basic universal fast-food burger. It then doubles to Super (R15–24), trebles to Great (R22–26), and on demand quadruples to the Big Four. There is a choice of three dozen toppings. You can also get vegetarian (big black mushroom) burgers. Bring your own (BYO) wine and beer. Rivonia Square, Rivonia Boulevard, tel (011) 803-5024.

Rock 'n' rollers from 20 to 60 head for the *Rattlesnake Roadside Diner*, Mutual Village, Rivonia Boulevard, Rivonia, for Tex-Mex food and music. Platters of fajitas, ribs, corn, fritters, chimichangas, beef scalopini, wings, nachos with guacamole, .the works. Their Angel Food Cake and Key Lime Pie are the Real McCoy. Tel (011) 803-9406.

Hard Rock Café, good for modestly priced food, good for partying. Live music. It's trendy and terrific. Open seven days a week till very late. Happy hours 5–7pm. Thrupps Centre, 204 Oxford Road, Illovo, tel (011) 447-5059/2583.

Surf into the *Cyber Café*, 7th Street, Melville, the suburb's gateway to the world of Internet. The coffee is good and the patrons are trendy and arty, or cruise at the *FullStop Café*, 7th Avenue, Mellville, tel (011) 726-3801. Melville's only 24-hour restaurant is *Catz Pyjamas*, at 7 Main Road, where you can order extraordinary hamburgers and check the glazed ravers, tel (011) 726-8596.

Green Pastures specialises in breakfasts from around the world — English, American, German, Swiss and New South African — eggs, boerewors, steak or chop — you name it, as well as vegetarian dishes. Pub lunches from R11 (£1.45/$2.40). Shop 1, Total House, Corner Smit and Rissik Streets, Braamfontein, tel (011) 339-1246/8.

Vegetarians used to be regarded as unhealthy health-nut freaks in meat-eating South Africa. Not so now. There is a wide array of **vegetarian restaurants** and even places like the Carnivore do not flinch if you request a vegetarian platter. *Mary-Ann's* wholefood emporium and restaurant chain has vegetarian breakfasts and an all-day Eco-Buffet that serves up a smorgasbord of additive-free and delicious dishes from fresh and unusual garden salads to quiches, hotpots and home-made bread, fresh fruit and veggie juices, plus a selection of teas and caffeine-free coffees. Find them at:

The Colony, 345 Jan Smuts Avenue, Craighall, tel (011) 442-3836;
Heathway Centre, DF Malan Drive, Northcliff, tel (011) 478-1563;
Rivonia Junction, Rivonia Road, 7th Avenue, Rivonia, tel (011) 807-5515.

Pomegranate is a vegetarian cult temple at 79 Third Avenue, Mellville, serving creative light vegetarian meals and legendary Tomato Tart. Tel (011) 482-2366. They say if Zen Buddhists wrote a menu it would probably be the same as Pravina's, 83 Fourth Avenue, Melville, where there is an outstanding selection of vegetarian Gujerati dishes and you can have a bowl of food for as little as R5. Be sure to try the drink called matho, tel (011) 482-6670.

Vegetarian breakfasts at R17–24 are dished up at Anderson's Nursery & Coffee Shoppe, 10 Grant Avenue, Norwood, as well as lunch and all-day snacks. A sandwich costs R7–13, lunches R18–32. There is also the classic English full-house breakfast, bolstered by chicken sausages and mushrooms. Ask about the Romanian breakfasts and the meal-size pancakes brimful with savouries (creamy mushroom and parmesan) or sweets (banana, maple syrup and ice-cream), enveloped in soft thick dough, tel (011) 728-6802.

Speaking of breakfasts, *Scandies*, in the Upper Mall at Hyde Park Corner, Jan Smuts Avenue, does a brisk Saturday morning trade in eggs Benedict, Florentine, or better still, a soufflé Omelettes Supreme of smoked salmon, shrimps, duck and oysters for only R17.50, tel (011) 325-6049.

Further Afield. *The Carnivore* at Muldersdrift Estate is for carnivores par excellence. The massive central charcoal fire is the focus of the restaurant, from which a procession of carvers carry roast-laden spits, and slice a selection of 12 different types of meat, ranging from the usual chicken, lamb, beef, pork to the unusual, which may be crocodile, springbok, zebra, and a variety of other game. You can eat until you are fit to burst. The carving stops when you surrender by waving the white flag on your table. If you still have room there is now a choice of six desserts, with coffee or tea to follow. The restaurant is wheelchair-friendly, tel (011) 957-2099, fax (011) 957-3132, e-mail 100100.3245@compuserve.com

Jenny de Luca owns one of the most successful country restaurants in Gauteng, the *Casalinga*, on Rocky Ridge Driving Range, Muldersdrift Road, Honeydew. People do not go there because she is the daughter of legendary international golfer Gary Player, they go for the fabulous Italian food of her husband, Peter, concocted with fruit, veg and herbs plucked fresh from the 32ha/79 acre farm on which the thatched restaurant — built from sections of old houses from Randfontein Gold Mining Estates — is situated, tel (011) 957-2612.

Ramkietjie country restaurant, on the Wilge River, serves ostrich, springbok potjie, pot roast, venison and lamb bredie, to name a few traditional dishes. Vegetarian meals and pub lunches are also available. 35 Peter Road, Honeydew, tel (011) 958-1050.

Set amid mine dumps some 50km/31 miles from Johannesburg, Krugersdorp is most famous for a Boer act of defiance against the annexation of their Republic by the British in 1877. If this doesn't grab you as a reason to visit, the *Simply Chapat* restaurant could be. Operating in a charming old Victorian-style house in the middle of town, the cuisine is haute and the creations of chef Daniel Chapat and his wife Colleen are likely to give you decision neurosis. Dress is semi-formal. 046 Luipaard Street, corner of Paardekraal Drive, Krugersdorp, tel (011) 953-4093. Also in Krugersdorp is *Greensleeves Medieval Kingdom*, good, bawdy fun every Friday and Saturday night, with foaming tankards and groaning banquet, friendly wenches and rollicking music, tel (011) 956-6300.

No foodie should leave Gauteng without making the pilgrimage to *Mount Grace Hotel* to tuck into their legendary Sunday buffet lunch. It is an hour's drive from central Johannesburg, but there is also a helipad on the property and Court Helicopters will deliver parties of between four and six, tel (011) 827-8907. Regular classical concerts are an added attraction, tel (0142) 77-1350, fax (0142) 77-1202.

Gay Restaurants:

Café della Salute, Sandton Square.

Café Frankfurt, Lower Level Sanlam Centre, Pretoria Road, Randburg, tel (011) 878-6802.
Elaine's, 9a Rockey Street, Yeoville, tel (011) 648-0801.
Gershwin's, 6 Rockey Street, Yeoville, tel (011) 648-9761.
Jojo's, Civic Theatre, Main Entrance, Braamfontein, tel (011) 403-7373/2321.
Jose's, 21 4th Ave, Parkhurst, tel (011) 788-4308 or (011) 880-7450.
L'Incontro, basement of The Firs, Rosebank, tel (011) 447-6769.
Pravina's Gujerati Cuisine, 83 4th Avenue, Melville, tel (011) 482-6670.
Quasimodo, 430 Commissioner Street, Fairview, tel (011) 614-5585.
Scooza Mi, corner 4th Avenue and 13th St, Parkhurst, tel (011) 442-7778.
The Jazz-A-Fair, Lower Level Sanlam Centre, Pretoria Road, Randburg, tel (011) 789-4703.
The Squirrel, 111 Main Road, Newlands, tel (011) 673-1111.
The Tearoom, Constantia Centre (below Krypton), Rosebank, tel (011) 442-4706.

There is plenty to do in the Greater Johannesburg area (508sq km/196sq miles); there is a large selection of natural and man-made attractions, such as walking trails, lakes, botanical gardens, the fascinating MuseumAfrica, a variety of theatres, a wide range of ethnic restaurants which have bubbled up from the flow of immigrants from all over the world, a large tribal kraal with accommodation and Zulu dancing displays, an authentic mine village, underground mine visits and gold pouring, and any number of wildlife attractions. In Gauteng, you also have a choice of top-class hotels, self-catering accommodation, game lodges, bushveld hideaways and budget youth hostels. Sitting as it does at the centre of the country's communications system there is easy access from Johannesburg and Gauteng to many of the country's major tourist destinations, such as the Kruger National Park, its adjacent private game reserves, the Sun City and Lost City resort complex, superb zoological and botanical gardens and the Vaal Dam, which has a circumference of 700km/435 miles and is a magnet for anyone attracted by water.

Johannesburg has one of the top four medical history museums in the world, the **Adler Museum of Medicine**, which attracts hundreds of international visitors every year. The museum is housed in a 1913 Herbert Baker national monument and displays 19th and 20th century medical instruments, from a foot-operated dental drill to 100-year-old wooden stethoscopes. The outside display areas have a reconstruction of a herbalist's shop, a traditional healer's consulting room, a turn-of-the-century pharmacy, doctor's and dental surgeries, an optician's room and a hospital display room. The Adler Museum of Medicine is at the South African Institute for Medical Research, at the corner of De Korte and Hospital streets, Hillbrow, Johannesburg, tel (011) 489-9000.

African Herbalist Shop. At 14 Diagonal Street, near the Stock Exchange. One of Johannesburg's more interesting *muti* (traditional African medicine) shops, where advice and medicines obtained from herbs, bark, roots, bulbs, and other ingredients are dispensed. Open Monday to Saturday from 7.30am to 5pm. Guided tours are available, tel (011) 838-7352.

African Tribal Art. The Gertrude Posel Gallery in Senate House at the University of the Witwatersrand, Braamfontein, focuses on a variety of African art forms. Tel (011) 716-3632 for an appointment to view.

Bensusan Museum of Photography, at the MuseumAfrica, 121 Bree Street, Newtown, has a display of early photographs and equipment recording the history of the photographic art, from magic lanterns to CD-ROM, tel (011) 833-5624.

Bernard Price Institute. This world-famous institute for palaeontological research is where rock-lined shelves hold a priceless treasure — the history of how the creatures of the modern world evolved and how the continents came into being. In the institute are the fossils of some 10,000 mammal-like reptiles, most of them collected from the Karoo. The institute is open to the public Monday to Friday, 8.30am–5pm, tel (011) 716-2727.

Bird's-Eye Views of Johannesburg: Court Helicopters has a service out of Rand Airport, with tours over the city and Soweto as well as lunch and game tours daily. Choppers can take up to four passengers, tel (011) 827-8907. Hot Air Balloon Adventures offers a romantic (and quiet) way of viewing the city and its environs, gliding over river estates and small game lodges, tel (011) 705-3201/397-1445. Pleasure Plane Trips have flights for a minimum of three and a maximum of five people, tel Lanseria Airport, (011) 659-1111, Rand Airport (011) 827-3675, Soweto (011) 659-2649, Johannesburg (011) 659-2930 or Magaliesburg (011) 701-3161. Gold Reef City Helicopters has seven-minute hops over Johannesburg and flights over Soweto, Saturday and Sunday from 11.30am, tel (011) 496-1600, fax (011) 496-1135.

Carfax Experience. An artistic onslaught on the senses in an abandoned factory on Pim Street in Newtown, which has been painted light blue and renovated as a cavernous atelier for painters, poets, sculptors and musicians. Developed by a German artist and named after the original Carfax, which was a lunatic asylum in Germany at the turn of the century.

Carlton Centre. From the observation deck on the 50th floor of the Carlton (Top of Africa) in the middle of the city, you get a 360-degree view that is unsurpassable. On a clear day, you can see as far as the Magaliesberg mountains. Telescopes are provided. Open daily from 9am to 11.30pm. The centre has a restaurant, a cocktail bar and a wide range of shops, including a souvenir shop and specialist boutiques, tel (011) 331-6608.

Civic Theatre. Guided tours of the backstage world highlights historical features of the buildings, and demonstrates technical aspects of stage, sets, sound and lighting. Tours take place on Tuesdays and Thursdays at 11am and 2pm, tel (011) 403-3408 ext 264.

First National Bank Museum. See the fascinating history of money come alive. An audio-visual presentation of bank history is screened on request. Admission is free. Open on weekdays from 9am to 4pm, Saturday by arrangement. 90 Market Street (between Harrison and Loveday streets, tel (011) 836-5887.

Gold Reef City. A gigantic theme park 8km/5 miles south of the city, which is a reconstruction of Johannesburg as it was during its early gold rush days, built around No 14 shaft of Crown Mines, in its day the deepest (3000m) mine on the central Reef. Diversions include a Victorian fun-fair, miners' houses, a brewery, pubs, a hotel, restaurants, and a stock exchange. You can watch molten gold being poured, take a trip down a mine shaft, and ride an old Puffing Billy. Can-can, gumboot and tribal dancing adds to the fun. Multilingual conducted tours are available, tel (011) 496-1600.

Historic Johannesburg. The Parktown and Westcliff Heritage Trust organise educational bus and walking tours of suburbs such as Parktown, Westcliff, Kensington, Yeoville, Florida and Roodepoort. These are far more than dry history lectures. The past is brought to life by volunteer tour guides in Edwardian costume. Tel (011) 482-3349 (mornings only).

The **Johannesburg Art Gallery** in King George's Street, Joubert Park, was designed by British architect Sir Edward Lutyens, who unfortunately made it face south as if it were in the northern hemisphere. Until the birth of the new South Africa, the gallery tended to be Eurocentric, marginalising indigenous art. Mining giant Anglo American has enabled the gallery to change its past emphasis by financing the repatriation of major collections of southern African art. Large-scale works by South African sculptors are in the gallery grounds and in adjacent Joubert Park. Admission is free. One-hour guided tours. Ramps and lifts are available in most areas for disabled visitors. The gallery is open Tuesday to Sunday, 10am–5pm, tel (011) 725-3130/3180.

Johannesburg Botanical Gardens. The 125ha/309 acre gardens encompassing the Emmarentia Dam are the setting for bonsai trees, herbs, succulents, cycads, and a 10-hectare rose garden, believed to be the largest in the world, which is a must-see when the roses are in bloom between October and April, open 7am–4pm. For guided tours, tel (011) 782-0517.

Johannesburg Public Library. The library on Market Square opened in June 1890, only four years after the discovery of gold on the Witwatersrand. You can read a wide range of South African and foreign newspapers in the basement, there is a music library. a lending library and reference section and the Michaelis Art Library has a wonderful collection of books on architecture, painting, sculpture, ceramics, drawing and other decorative arts. Visitors can enjoy the library's large collection of books, magazines and pamphlets and many books are available on loan. Open Monday to Friday 9am–5pm, Saturday 9am–1pm, tel (011) 836-6165, fax (011) 836-6607.

Johannesburg Stock Exchange. This is at 11 Diagonal Street in the city centre, where you can watch from a public gallery as fortunes are made and lost, although all the old excitement has gone now that the traditional open-cry trading has been abandoned and all dealing is done by computer. Book for tours conducted from Monday to Friday at 11am, tel (011) 833-6580 and (011) 377-2200.

Johannesburg Zoo. The Zoo on Jan Smuts Avenue, Parkview, contains in its 5.5-hectare gardens more than 300 species of mammals, birds and reptiles, including rare, exotic species, mainly from other parts of Africa. Ask at the entrance about animal feeding times. Tours are available, including night tours to see nocturnal animals and birds, followed by hot chocolate and toasted marshmallows around a bonfire. The Museum of South African Rock Art is at the Zoo and has a collection of engravings from all over South Africa. Open daily, 8.30am–5.30pm, tel (011) 646-2000.

For years No 19 Albemarle Street, in Troyeville, has been a shrine, regarded as the house where **Mahatma Gandhi** lived from late in 1904 to April or May 1906. It has been declared a national monument. A US historian, Dr James Hunt of Shaw University in North Carolina, says this is the wrong house: The right one is No 11. South Africa was the crucible from which Mohandas Karamchand Gandhi rose to become a *mahatma* ('great soul'). The 21 years spent in South Africa from 1893 had a profound impact on his life and he told followers, 'I was born in India but made in South Africa.'

Market Theatre Complex. The old Johannesburg produce market has been restored and converted into three theatres, an art gallery, restaurants and pubs. Tel (011) 832-1641.

Melrose Wild Bird Sanctuary. A 10-minute drive from the centre of Johannesburg. More than 120 wild bird species nest in the reedbeds and indigenous trees around a lake. The best time to visit is in the early morning and late evening, tel (011) 782-7064.

Johannesburg's Africana Museum spent 59 years in temporary premises in the public library before moving in 1994 to the Newtown Cultural Precinct in downtown Johannesburg and being renamed **MuseumAfrica**. It is next door to the Market

Theatre and near a host of other cultural and entertainment venues. The museum has a number of different sections. One is devoted to the African National Congress and its history, another has squatter shacks, where you can walk into the dwellings. Permanent exhibitions include *Tried for Treason*, a display on the 1956 to 1961 treason trial at which Nelson Mandela was sentenced to life imprisonment; *Johannesburg Transformations* — tracing Johannesburg's early roots and history; the **Geological Museum**; the **Museum of South African Rock Art**; and the **Bensusan Museum of Photography**, displaying the history and technology of photography, from early equipment to video, digital imaging, photo CD, CD-ROM and multimedia.

The museum complex is open Tuesday to Sunday, 9am–5pm. Closed Mondays, Good Friday, Christmas Day and the Day of Goodwill (26 December). Admission is R2 (25p/45 cents) for adults, half-price for children. MuseumAfrica is at 121 Bree Street, Newtown, Johannesburg. Contact PO Box 517, Newtown 2113, Gauteng, tel (011) 833-5624.

MuseumAfrica has a number of branch museums. There is the **Bernberg Fashion Museum** near the zoo on Jan Smuts Avenue, Johannesburg, which is open Monday to Saturday from 9am to 4.30pm, and the **James Hall Museum of Transport**, on Rosettenville Road, La Rochelle, with its vast collection of carts, cars, tractors, buses and fire engines, tel (011) 435-9718. The **George Harrison Memorial Park** is on the outskirts of Johannesburg on the site where the main gold reef was first discovered.

The **Mine Museum** and entertainment complex at Gold Reef City, Johannesburg, is a reconstruction of Johannesburg as it was during its mining camp days. It is built around a shaft of Crown Mines gold mine. You can watch molten gold being poured and take a trip down the old mine shaft. The museum is open daily, 9am–4pm.

Musical Fountains. Multicoloured fountains at Wemmer Pan synchronised to popular tunes are popular with children, tel (011) 407-6833.

Newtown. This is an area at the western end of the CBD that is being developed as a cultural precinct to do for Johannesburg what Waterfront has done for Cape Town. It is already home to SA Breweries' museum and visitors' centre, MuseumAfrica, the Afrika Cultural Centre, Mega Music Warehouse, the Dance Factory, Workers' Library and Museum, and a host of related activities, tel (011) 834-2102.

The **Pharmacy Museum** is housed at Pharmacy House, 80 Jorissen Street, Braamfontein, Johannesburg, and has an interesting collection of medicinal plants and antiquated laboratory equipment.

Planetarium. Located in the grounds of the University of the Witwatersrand. Educational and entertaining programmes on different aspects of astronomy are held every Friday, Saturday and Sunday. Children under 12 must be accompanied by an adult, tel (011) 716-3199 for programme details and times.

Randburg Waterfront. This is an extraordinary development in Randburg, where former dumping ground and hang-out for down-and-outs has been transformed into an attractive complex of pubs, restaurants, shops, cinemas, a flea market with 360 stalls, all around a man-made lake, tel (011) 886-0208.

Santarama Miniland. A miniature version of a city built to a scale of 1:25, complete with airport, railway, docks, soccer stadium, game reserve, and race-course. Miniland depicts many of South Africa's most impressive buildings, including old Cape Dutch houses. Kimberley's 'Big Hole' and Van Riebeeck's ship *Dromedaris*, which brought him to the Cape in April 1652, are also featured. You can explore on foot or take a mini-train trip. Open daily from 10am to 4.30pm, tel (011) 435-0543.

SABC Tours. Guided tours of the South African Broadcasting Corporation can be arranged from Monday to Friday at 9am and 10.30am only. No children under 12, tel (011) 714-3744.

More people visit the **South African National Museum of Military History** in Hermann Eckstein Park, Saxonwold, than any other in Johannesburg. No aspect of military life and endeavour is ignored in this comprehensive indoor and outdoor collection, from aircraft, tanks and weapons, to uniforms, medals, maps and propaganda material. Tucked away in the museum are two watercolours by that famous British Quaker of the Anglo-Boer War, Emily Hobhouse. The museum is open daily, 9am–4pm, and costs R5 (65p/$1.10) for adults, R3 for pensioners and R2 for schoolchildren. Tel (011) 646-5513.

Soweto. The name of Soweto rang around the world on 16 June 1976 when black pupils protesting against the imposition of Afrikaans as a medium of instruction in their schools staged a protest march in their township, part of the 33 South West Townships (So-we-to). The response of the authorities was quick and brutal, and (officially) 95 blacks died as a result of police gunfire.

Today, Soweto is a city of four million and remains a symbol to the black liberation movement, a symbol of young resistance at a time when their elders had been cowed into virtual submission by a series of harsh repressive laws during more than two decades of apartheid. The Soweto complex of townships on the outskirts of Johannesburg was largely developed after 1956, when the post-war years turned South Africa into a highly industrialised society, with Johannesburg as its dynamic hub. While the city of gold threw up massive high-rise blocks within its surrounding mine dumps, Soweto grew into a sprawling, festering peri-urban sore, with rudimentary water and electricity supplies, and inadequate sanitation and roads. In spite of all this, it developed its own vibrant ethos and lifestyle and it is the blossoming of this, as well as its apartheid struggle memorials, that make it the embodiment of all South Africa's townships and squatter camps, and the reason why it has become such a popular draw for tourists. Commercial activity is expanding fast and Dobsonville Shopping Complex, the newest and the best, is worth a visit.

Delegates at the United Nations Conference on Trade and Development (Unctad), held in Johannesburg in May 1996, were taken on a tour of Soweto, and expressed surprise on discovering that the huge township was 'not as bad as we thought it would be.' See for yourself. Tour operators offer a variety of options, from half-day to all-day tours, from a special jazz tour, to an overnight visit. There is even a three-day tour if you really want to soak up the township atmosphere.

All the operators will show you Soweto's now famous landmarks and highlights – the Regina Mundi cathedral, the school where the 1976 uprising started, and the Hector Pietersen monument commemorating this catalytic event, President Nelson Mandela's humble old house, and the more palatial residence of his ex-wife Winnie Nomzamo Madikizela-Mandela, and the fortress-like house of Bishop Desmond Tutu, Freedom Square, and Kliptown, the oldest squatter camp in the area. All these are must-sees, but the real spirit of Soweto is in the spirit, hospitality and friendliness of the people who live there. This you will experience when your guide takes you into a shebeen, usually a room in someone's house, that is the focal point of the street's social life. Here you will eat the *pap en vleis* (maize porridge and meat) that is the staple fare, drink beer, vodka, whisky or Pepsi (the preferred drinks) and listen to some of the best music around on a ghetto-blaster. For the real live stuff, take the tour of the township's jazz clubs. Places like these gave rise to musos of the stature of singer Miriam Makeba, trumpeter Hugh Masekela and sax-man Kippie Moeketse.

Some shebeens have risen to sophisticated levels and can compare with any hotel bar in their range and services. DJ's Inn, for instance, is a flashy tavern that is also a pool room and restaurant; not far away is Vincent Mpho's shebeen in a ramshackle house; Sipho Motsamai's watering hole is where you will find customers who can talk to you in Spanish, German and French, as well as English, Afrikaans and even Russian. Lancelot Ntsepileng Sello, who runs Abantu Tours, speaks seven African languages as well as fluent English and Afrikaans, which is useful not only for the tribal groupings in the townships, but for the tour groups he takes out on off-beat trips into the countryside. Transport for all tours is usually by ubiquitous mini-bus.

Tours. *Abantu Tours* will take you on a half-day tour for R90 (£12/$20) per person, a full-day for R170, Soweto by night for R90, overnight R150 or the three-day tour for R690. The two nights in Soweto are spent with a township family. Abantu will also show you the sights of Johannesburg for R95 per person, and take you on a six-hour tour of Soweto's jazz clubs for R90, where you will hear jazz played like nowhere else. Contact Abantu Tours, PO Box 93737, Yeoville 2143, Gauteng, tel (011) 648-7066.

Half-day tours of Soweto seem to be the most popular of all these options and *Africa Excursions* specialise in these. Morning and afternoon tours are guaranteed, seven days a week. Contact PO Box 2051, Gallo Manor 2052, Gauteng, tel (011) 726-8088. If you prefer a personal guide rather than a tour group leader contact *Visit Soweto*, tel (011) 326-0073.

Jimmy's Face to Face Tours promise to show you the good, the bad, and the ugly in Soweto. For close encounters in this black city of surprise and contrast Jimmy Ntintili runs morning and afternoon tours from most hotels. Among other outings with a black perspective on offer are tours of Johannesburg (day and night), Pretoria, Gold Reef City, Sun City and Lost City, as well as mini day safaris and a two-day special to the Kruger National Park. Jimmy's Face to Face Tours, 2nd Floor, Budget House, 130 Main Street, Johannesburg, Gauteng, tel (011) 331-6109/6209. A similar range of tours is offered by *Sam Selomah's Molepe Tours and Safaris*, PO Box 192, Dube 1800, tel (011) 452-0610/0611.

Ubuntu ('humanity') is a word you will hear and read a lot about in the new South Africa. *Imbizo Tours* will take you on a Soweto Ubuntu Experience, where you can eat traditional meals in a five-star shebeen, walk around the 'California' of Soweto, visit schools, clinics, orphanages, hospitals, cemeteries, and see witchdoctor Credo Mutwa's collection of sculptures, or share a drink in a shanty house and meet (strange but true) people who drink *imbambha*, home-made beer pepped up with battery acid. Day tours cost R85 (£11.35/$18.70), plus R20 pick-up charge, and a four-hour night tour of shebeens costs R180. Contact Mandy Mankazana at PO Box 25031, Ferreirasdorp 2048, Gauteng, tel and fax (011) 838-2667, Cell 083 700 90 98. If you are interested, Soweto tour operators will take you to a black gay bar, usually the popular one run by Scotch Dube and his sister at 940B Malunga Street, where black homosexuals continue to celebrate the freedom from discrimination conferred by the new Constitution.

Steam Train Trips. For information about these contact:

> *Hartbeespoort Steam Train*, tel (012) 315-2432;
> *Historical Transport Association*, tel (011) 640-4739;
> *Magalies Valley Steamer*, tel (011) 773-9238;
> *Magaliesburg Express*, tel (011) 888-1145.

The **Transnet Museum** is in the concourse of the old Johannesburg South Station Building in the city centre, and fits in naturally with the architecture of its surroundings, which date from the 1920s. The museum houses a large collection of items depicting the origin, growth and development of South Africa's largest transport enterprise. Open Monday to Friday, 7.30am–3.45pm, tel (011) 773-9118.

Workers' Museum. This is a restored Electrical Department workers' compound in the Newtown Cultural Precinct, in downtown Johannesburg, where performances of traditional dance and music are staged, tel (011) 834-2181.

Zoo Lake. A large, well established park surrounds Zoo Lake which is frequented by breeding bird colonies. Other attractions include rowing boats for hire, a swimming pool, tennis courts, a bowling club, a tea garden and a restaurant. Artists Under the Sun, a popular open-air artists' market, is held on the shores of the lake on the first weekend of every month, 8am–5pm.

Durban and Cape Town have the sea. The tide never comes in on the Highveld, so the people of land-locked Gauteng have to make do with each other. Johannesburg in particular is a people place, where the citizens make up for the lack of sea, sand, rivers, and mountains by living an intensely social existence. Unlike Cape Town, where you might be asked where you come from, Jo'burgers will ask you what you do for a living and from this try to figure out how much you make. Life revolves around dinner parties, parties, cinema, theatre, restaurants and clubs.

As there are only two major movie distributors you can see the latest on the circuit no matter what town or city you are in. You can find details of Nu Metro and Ster-Kinekor cinemas in the newspapers. Movie-going is not what it was, although the city's 20 or so theatres still draw the faithful. Johannesburg's large Jewish community has always supported the theatre and contributed some fine actors and actresses to the profession – and this has tided theatre over through the periodic depressions brought on by previous political and economic upheavals and now by crime.

The plum theatre in terms of size and opulence is undoubtedly Pretoria's *State Theatre*; Johannesburg's answer to this is a rather more muted *Civic Theatre* complex, in Loveday Street, Braamfontein. The complex houses four theatres, the main auditorium (1065 seats), the Tesson (215), the Thabong (176) and the Pieter Roos (95). Tel (011) 403-3408. The politically correct theatre in Johannesburg is the *Market Theatre*, which was a centre of theatrical dissent during the apartheid years and the place where you are most likely to see ethnic and avant-garde productions. The Market Theatre Complex, in Newtown, houses three theatres, the Main Auditorium, the Barney Simon Theatre and the Laager Theatre. Tel (011) 832-1641. The complex also has a Workshop Theatre Laboratory, which runs courses for theatre hopefuls. Tel (011) 836-0516. The nearby Dance Factory centre also runs courses, tel (011) 833-1347. Other off-the-wall productions can be seen at places such as the *Windybrow Theatre* in Nugget Street, Hillbrow, tel (011) 720-7009, and the *Victory Theatre*, in Louis Botha Avenue, Orange Grove, tel (011) 483-2793. For relaxing drawing room comedy, farce and whodunits the middle-aged and over patronise the *Alhambra Theatre*, in the Ellis Park precinct, Doornfontein, tel (011) 402-7726, and the *Alexander Theatre*, in Stiemens Street, Braamfontein, tel (011) 402-7726. If you are travelling with youngsters take them to the *People's Theatre*, in Rissik Street, Braamfontein, which specialises in family musicals, tel (011) 403-1563. The *Roodepoort City Theatre*, part of the Civic Centre complex in Florida Park, is a venue for ballet, drama and the visual arts, serving the Greater Johannesburg area. It seats 320 people and has a resident orchestra, Pro Musica, which has received acclaim as both an opera and a concert orchestra. Tel (011) 674-1356.

Theatre and film bookings can be made through Computicket, tel (011) 331-9991. See the Entertainment section of South African newspapers for details on shows.

Nightlife. The days of stylish night-club evenings where patrons dressed to the nines and drank cocktails probably lasted longer inside the apartheid fortress than anywhere else, but they have now given way to the New Age; even discos are passé. The in thing is the rave club, or at least bars and restaurants with live music, and if it is ethnic so much the better. In the vanguard are the *Mega Music Warehouse* in the Newtown precinct and nearby *Carfax*, a club so hot it is reportedly nearing auto-combustion and advertises nightlife for the next century. Starts at 10pm. 39 Pim Street, Newtown, tel (011) 834-9187.

Ravers dance off substance abuse at a wide variety of clubs which, like many other music venues, tend to be shared by Yeoville's Rockey Street area and the more up-market suburb of Rosebank, although for the bold there are clubs in risky central and downtown Johannesburg. On the upper level of Thrupps Centre, in Oxford Road, Illovo, is *Insomnia* for the older (25 and over) raver, tel (011) 447-3344; *Club Krypton* is on Jan Smuts Avenue, in Rosebank's Constantia Centre, tel (011) 788-4708 and (011) 442-8306, Cell 082 659-3015. Other clubs have names like *Roxy Rhythm Bar, Adrenochrome, Sub-Zero, Nexus, The Workshop, ESP, OMO's,* and *Wonderland.* Clubs come and go, change names, change addresses, but you can get the latest details from the press, or from Computicket, which also sell tickets. For something really alternative there is *Pandora's Piano Lounge* in Rosebank where the beat meet the elite, cruising territory *Camp Elsies* in Rockey Street, Yeoville, and if you are into black leather, tattoos, bikes and heavy metal there is *Club Whiplash,* corner of Goud and Marshall streets, central city. Not for the faint-hearted, tel (011) 781-1390.

Since the scrapping of old laws preventing black South Africans from living and owning property in white residential and business areas the result has been good news for music and musicians. Returned exile Hugh Masekela runs a jazz venue in Yeoville called *J&B Junction,* styled after Ronnie Scott's famous London club; also in Yeoville is *The Shebeen* at the *Tandoor,* in Rockey Street, where they play black township *kwaito* street music, reggae and jungle fusion, tel (011) 648-9451; *Jahnito's* also in Rockey Street is two venues under one roof, the *Jahnito Jah Centre* for jazz and *Jahnito Live House* which showcases African poetry and *kwasa-kwasa* music, tel (011) 648-9288; *Kartouche,* in Raymond Street, Yeoville, is a favourite with bumpies (black upwardly mobile people), tel (011) 648-5553 and Cell 083 253-4844; *La Frontiere* in the Squash Court Centre, Pretoria Street, Hillbrow, features local, Zairean and West African music. Thursday nights free entrance to students with cards, tel (011) 642-8593. At the *Guest House* restaurant, on the corner of Thulane and Kutlwanong streets, in the black township of Kagiso, near Krugersdorp, you can hear the real grass-roots stuff and get a dish of mealie-meal porridge and steak or ribs for only R10, tel (011) 410-0539.

Jazz. Top jazzmen can regularly be heard jamming at the *Bassline Jazz Club,* at 7, 7th Street, Melville, tel (011) 482-6915, and at *Club 206,* on Louis Botha Avenue, Orange Grove, tel (011) 728-5333, which also has next door at *208* a rave and chill scene; down the road in Orange Grove the *Radium Beer Hall* has jazz at lunchtime on Sunday. At Mutual Square, in Rosebank, you can usually hear jazz at the weekend while you are shopping or grabbing a coffee. Good jazz is played on a wider scale throughout the black townships, such as the *707i* in Soweto, but it is not advisable to go looking for it on your own. Go in a group or, better still, join a night tour or one that specialises in the township shebeen and jazz scene, such as Abantu Tours in Yeoville, which has a jazz club tour for R90 a person, tel (011) 648-7066.

Folk. Gauteng has its headquarters in Braamfontein at *Wings Beat Bar,* 8 Ameshoff Street, in the shape of Buskers Acoustic Music Club, tel (011) 803-1137 and (011) 339-4492.

Gay Bars and Clubs

Blues Bar, Corner 8th Street and Long, Greymont.
Bob's Bar, 76 Op De Bergen Street, Fairview, tel (011) 624-1894.
Champions, corner Wolmarans and Loveday Streets, Braamfontein, tel (011) 720-6605 or 725-2697.
Club Camp Elsies, 70 Rockey Street, Bellevue East, tel (011) 487-2465.
Club Zoo, Hopkins Street, Yeoville.
Connections, 1 Pretoria Street, Hillbrow, tel (011) 642-8511.
Gotham City, 58 Pretoria Street, Hillbrow.
Illusions Bar at the Kine Centre, Ster Kinekor Section, Carlton Centre.

Krypton, 17 Constantia Centre, Tyrwhitt Avenue, Rosebank, tel (011) 442-7372.
Pandora's Piano Lounge, 77 Cargo Corner, Tyrwhitt Avenue, Rosebank, tel (011) 447-3066. Anything goes here, in a club that looks like Liberace's bedroom.
Punchline Pub, Civic Theatre, Braamfontein, tel (011) 403-3408.
Skyline Bar, Harrison Reef Hotel, Pretoria Street, Hillbrow.
Stonewall, behind Yeoville Books, Rockey Street, Yeoville.
Steamwork Health and Leisure Club, Fortuna House, 727 4th Street, Wynberg, Sandton, tel (011) 887-2266.
Talking Heads, 163 Meyer Street, Germiston, tel (011) 873-0211.
The Barn, 73 6th Road, Clovedene, Benoni, tel (011) 968-2719.

Gautengers love to shop and they love bargains, which is why you will find malls, markets and kerbside traders in every town, city and village doing roaring business, particularly at the weekend and on public holidays. There are several large shopping centres in and around Johannesburg, among them Sandton City, Eastgate and the Rosebank Shopping complex, which retail a variety of goods, from curios to up-market clothing. The Oriental Plaza in Fordsburg covers 16 city blocks and specialises in merchandise with an eastern flavour. This is the place to go if you are into spices and exotic vegetables. There are 300 shops to browse through. The main flea markets are held regularly at Bruma Lake and Randburg Waterfront, Newtown Africa Market, Rosebank Mall, Hillfox Flea Market, Roodepoort, and Michael Mount Waldorf School, Bryanston.

Flea Market World, Bruma, has more than 600 bargain stalls and a variety of wholesome food stalls and entertainment. For tired parents there is free entertainment for the kids every Thursday and Saturday all day long, from pony rides and battery cars to jumping castles and face painters. Professional child finders look after your kids while you enjoy buskers and Zulu dancers. Corner of Ernest Oppenheimer and Marcia streets, Bruma, Johannesburg, tel (011) 622-9648/9.

The *Randburg Waterfront* on Republic Road, Randburg, has a full range of boutiques, shoe stores, jewellers, salons and cosmetic shops. Speciality boutiques include gift shops, antiques and *objets d'art* outlets, book shops and CD dealers, as well as outdoor adventure specialists, and a watersports shop. The Harbour Market, whose 360 stalls are open every day, offers a flea-market atmosphere with works of art, ethnic jewellery and clothing just a few of the items on offer. Open every day from 10am to 8pm, tel (011) 886-0208 and (011) 789-5052.

Newtown Africa Market is Johannesburg's original flea market. Open Saturdays from 9am to 4pm, it has 350 stalls selling arts and crafts, antiques, bric-a-brac, clothing, curios from all over Africa, traditional African clothing and collectables. Mary Fitzgerald Square, corner of Bree and Wolhuter streets, opposite the Market Theatre, tel (011) 832-1641.

Rosebank Mall *Rooftop Market*, open every Sunday, is the largest and most colourful flea market in the area, with more than 500 stalls offering everything from spices and electronic equipment to clothing and African crafts. Good local entertainment, including jazz and gumboot dancing, and a good variety of home-made foods. Open from 9.30am to 5pm on Sundays and public holidays only, tel (011) 788-7931.

Michael Mount Organic Market, on Culross Road, Bryanston, is probably the most exclusive of all the markets hawking arts, crafts, food and clothing. People queue to buy cheese and health foods here, and the breadth of its wares is unsurpassed. Open Thursday and Saturday only from 9am to 1pm, tel (011) 706-3671.

Hillfox Flea Market, Hillfox Tower Centre, corner of Hendrik Potgieter and Rhinoceros roads, Roodepoort. Features 300 stalls, all under cover, with a variety of goods, arts and crafts, prepared and wholesale food. Open from 9.30am to 5pm on Saturday, Sunday and public holidays, tel (011) 442-4488.

The *Crafter's Marketplace* showcases the work of more than 100 craftsmen and artisans. It is open daily at the Top Crop Centre, DF Malan Drive, Johannesburg, tel (011) 476-8114.

Horwoods Plaza Flea Market, Homestead Road, Edenvale. 140 trading stalls display only hand-made items on a farm with a lake, ampitheatre, picnic sites, kids playworld, and restaurant. Open every weekend from 9.30am to 3pm, tel (011) 648-1310.

Bedford Centre Flea Market. This up-market flea market in Bedfordview has more than 200 stalls. Open every Sunday and public holiday from 10am to 4pm, tel (011) 622-1840.

Rockey Street Free People's Market in Yeoville features 150 stalls of diverse goods, crafts and food halls. Open Saturday, Sunday and public holidays from 9.30am to 4.30pm, tel (011) 648-1310.

Pavement Art at Village Walk is a weekly arts and crafts market exhibiting multicultural displays of fine, applied and functional arts and hand-made crafts. It takes place in the forecourt at the fountain steps at Village Walk in Maude Street, Sandton, from 9am every Saturday, tel (011) 883-1501.

Mutual Square Arts & Crafts Market on Cradock Avenue, Rosebank, features 120 stalls with work by artists from all over Gauteng. Open on Saturday and public holidays from 10am to 3.30pm, tel (011) 442-4488.

Farmers Markets. In the middle of the south plaza of the *Oriental Plaza* in downtown Johannesburg Tara Daya's stall, SR Fruiterers, is crammed with an astonishing array of fruit and unusual vegetables — binda (okra), ginger, amadumbi, dhanya, ambraaraadi for Thai cooking, green mangoes, and the green bananas used as a vegetable in many African dishes. Much of this exotica comes from KwaZulu-Natal, and some comes from Kenya. You can buy a wide variety of peas and beans, such as flat pea-like papri, toovar pods with lumpy seeds inside which become dhal when dried, gadra (half-dried sugar beans), tiny goovar beans and the larger dalibla, or double beans. Fresh fronds of the edible elephant ear plant are sold to make the wrapped vegetarian Hindu rolls called patha. Pinch off bit of fresh leaf and chew it and you are in for a surprise.

Boksburg Farmers Market has fresh produce, flea market stalls and flowers on Saturdays, 7am–1pm. It is on the west side of the lake, off Trichardt Street, Boksburg, tel (011) 482-2900.

Horison Farmers Market on the corner of Sonop and Swart streets, Horison, is open on Saturdays, 7am–1pm, tel (011) 662-1306.

Kew Farmers Market has fresh vegetables, meat, eggs, mieliemeal, crafts. Open Monday to Saturday, 8am–5pm, and Sundays, 8am–midday, with 180 stalls under thatch. Ninth Road, Kew, tel (011) 887-3888 or (011) 882-0967/8.

Krugersdorp Farmers Market includes arts and crafts, meat and other fresh produce. Open on Saturdays, 7am–1pm. Corner of Luipaard and Viljoen streets, Krugersdorp (Monument Dam), tel (011) 482-2900.

Petticoat Lane Market for home-made cheeses and farm fresh milk. Open on Saturdays and Sundays, 9am–4.30pm, moonlight market on Friday, 3–9pm. On the Jukskei River, tel (011) 464-1780/1866.

Roodepoort Farmers Market is open on Saturdays, 7am–1pm. Opposite Florida Lake, Fourth Avenue, Roodepoort, tel (011) 672-9501/3 or 674-4211/01.

Traders Village is open on Saturdays from 6am, and on Sundays, 7am–4pm. Corner of South Klipriviersberg and Outspan roads, South Hills, tel (011) 613-4177 or (011) 485-2197.

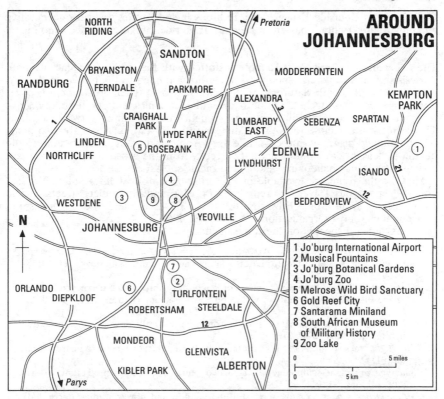

AROUND JOHANNESBURG

1 Jo'burg International Airport
2 Musical Fountains
3 Jo'burg Botanical Gardens
4 Jo'burg Zoo
5 Melrose Wild Bird Sanctuary
6 Gold Reef City
7 Santarama Miniland
8 South African Museum of Military History
9 Zoo Lake

Further Afield

Braamfontein Spruit Hiking Trail. A 25km/16 mile network of self-guided urban trails of varying lengths. Each can be completed in a day. The trail can be joined from various suburbs in Johannesburg. It runs along the Braamfontein Spruit through Johannesburg, Randburg and Sandton as far as the Kleinjukskei River. Bird life (about 225 species), small mammals and waterfalls are among the attractions. For safety, hikers should walk in groups.

Bullfrog Pan. This sanctuary in President Steyn Street, Benoni, is the second largest bullfrog reserve in the southern hemisphere. It hosts a variety of frog species and makes an unusual outing. Since the pan was cleaned of pollutants more than 50 species of birds have returned, including flamingoes and the pollution-sensitive Cape wagtail, tel (011) 849-5466.

Carletonville. The principal town in the gold mining area known as Westonaria. Nearby, the Abe Bailey Nature Reserve covering some 4000 hectares of grassland and a marsh is home to small game and about 180 bird species. Overnight facilities and game rangers are available. Contact The Wildlife Society of South Africa, tel (01491) 93431, fax (01491) 3015.

Coronation Park. A pool and playground are among the attractions of this beautifully laid-out park in Krugersdorp. Some grand old steam locomotives are on display at the open-air South African National Railway and Steam Museum at Randfontein Estates

Gold Mine, just outside Krugersdorp. Exhibits include a diesel electric locomotive and more than 50 vintage passenger coaches. Train rides are offered once a month, tel (011) 888-1154/5/6.

The **Crocodile Arts and Craft Ramble** is dotted with the studios of some of South Africa's top artists and craftspeople. The studios are open to the public on the first weekend of each month, Saturday and Sunday, 9am–5pm. Their arts and crafts cover a wide spectrum and include sculpture, painting, ceramics, pottery, jewellery, glass, designer clothes, custom-built furniture, wrought iron, spinning, knitwear and lace. This scenic route is close to both Johannesburg and Pretoria. There are also many restaurants and places of interest in the area. You can drive from one studio to the next in a pleasant day's outing and buy directly from the artists. *En route* there are restaurants, fishing, ballooning, hiking and picnic spots.

Maps of the route are available in Pretoria at the Tourist Information Bureau, Tourist Rendezvous Travel Centre, corner Prinsloo and Vermeulen Streets, and in Johannesburg from Mike Edwards, tel (011) 659-2917, and the Johannesburg Metropolitan Tourist Organisation, tel (011) 336-4961/2.

Artists and craftspeople on the route include:

John and Tina Dunn's Studio. Art stoneware, matt glazed tiles, hand-made wash basins, vanity slabs, large platters, lamps and wildlife paintings, tel (011) 662-1139;

Chris Patton Pottery. Stoneware and terracota pottery, thrown and decorated by the artist, ethnic and decorative ware, bird feeders and house signs, tel (011) 662-1017;

John Curteis Forged Iron. Fine wrought iron, architectural ironwork, furniture and lighting, tel (011) 957-2821;

The Right Track. Hand-crafted furniture, made from naturally weathered hardwood, tel (011) 957-2830;

Khanya Craft. Hand-sculpted jewellery, artwork and gifts, hand-painted ethnic cloths and cushions, tel (011) 957-2988;

Susan Orpen Gallery. Landscapes, still-life, wildlife and flower studies, decorated ostrich and goose eggs, tel (011) 957-2025;

The Lace Place. Hand-made lace, furniture, bobbin-lace demonstrations and lace-making lessons, tel (011) 958-1463;

Mickey Korzennik. Sculptures in concrete, timber, steel, railway sleepers, lead and bronze, graphics, paintings, drawings and wall-panels, tel (011) 659-0423;

The Woods. Traditional furniture and miscellany crafted from indigenous timbers, such as stinkwood, yellowwood and wild olive, tel (011) 659-0515;

Hulley's Haven. Painting (watercolours and oils), birds, African studies and Japanese brushwork, tel (011) 659-0774;

The Ibis Gallery. Sculptures in wood, metal and stone, drawings, paintings and watercolours, tel (011) 957-0211;

Lindley Sculpture Garden. Landscape and architectural sculptures, portraiture and fountains in bronze, wood and steel, tel (011) 659-2915;

Lindele. Hazel Hele's handspun knitwear in angora, wool, cotton, and mopani silk, hand-dyed, tel (011) 659-2486;

Riverbend Studio. Hand-made rustic furniture and children's furniture, tel (011) 957-3188;

Dietmar Wiening. Bronze sculptures of marine life and birds, as well as paintings, architectural features and intimate interior work, tel (01205) 51193;

Shades of Ngwenya. Hand-formed and mouth-blown recycled glassware, bowls, plates, vases, storm lanterns and paperweights, tel (011) 957-3180.

Lunch is available at the Riverbend Studio (pizza baked in an outdoor oven), La Picnique (French-style picnic hampers), or light bistro meals from Millbank. Tel (011)

659-2486/622-1017. Restaurants on the ramble include *The Moon and Sixpence*, tel (011) 659-0429, *The Post and Rail*, tel (011) 662-1491, and *Petezarea*, tel (011) 957-2580.

Delta Park. An environment centre set in a park with dams and a wide variety of bird life. A twitcher's delight, this serene oasis is in the Johannesburg suburb of Victory Park, tel (011) 888-4831.

Easter Gorge. Stroll up in this gorge in the Magaliesberg for a swim in the mountain pools. Call the Mountain Club of South Africa for entry permits and more information, tel (011) 786-8367.

Germiston. Named after a farm near Glasgow, Scotland, this city some 54km/34 miles south of Pretoria and 16km/10 miles south-east of Johannesburg has the largest railway junction in South Africa and the largest gold refinery in the world.

Hartebeeshoek. Site of a radio space research station between Magaliesburg and the Hartbeespoort Dam. It was established in 1966 in collaboration with NASA.

Heia Safari Ranch. You can watch game roam in natural surroundings, spend an evening in a Zulu kraal or, on Sundays, watch a Mzumba troupe perform tribal dances — all only 45km/28 miles from Johannesburg. Booking is essential, contact PO Box 1387, Honeydew 2040, Gauteng, tel (011) 659-0605.

Heidelberg Transport Museum. 55km/34 miles south-west of Johannesburg. Complete with restored railway station and a steam locomotive built in Britain in 1919 standing at the platform. In the goods sheds you can admire a magnificent collection of vintage motor cars, motor-cycles and bicycles. You can even take a ride on one, or on a replica pennyfarthing. Open Tuesday to Saturday from 10am to 5pm and on Sunday from 11am to 5pm, tel (0151) 6303.

Historic Flights. South African Airways Tante Ju is a large lady, weighing in at nearly 11 tons. She is SAA's historic flight section Junkers Ju52, one of only six restored Junkers in the world still flying, and which takes passengers on 20-minute flips over the city, the suburbs and Johannesburg landmarks. Flights are on the first Saturday of every month from the Transvaal Aviation Club at Rand Airport and the first Sunday of each month from Lanseria Airport for R100 (£13.35/$22) a time. Flights start at 10am and continue every hour. The Ju52 is also available for charter flights and occasional package tours which include game watching from the air. Two vintage Douglas DC-3 Dakotas and two DC-4 Skymasters are also used for charters. For aviation enthusiasts there is a static display at Johannesburg International Airport of a Lockheed Constellation, Lockheed Lodestar, Vickers Viking, and a De Havilland Dove. Tel (011) 978-5625 and (011) 978-5685, or contact any SAA office.

Krugersdorp Game Reserve. An African bush experience within 45 minutes of Johannesburg, with large herds of the blesbok, impala, sable antelope, eland, black wildebeest, springbok, zebra and rhino that once roamed Gauteng's great plains. A pride of lion can be seen feeding at 10am on Sundays. The Ngonyama Lion Lodge serves a popular Sunday buffet lunch. The à la carte restaurant is open for breakfast, lunch and supper, seven days a week, as is the ladies bar, which serves a good pub lunch every day except Sunday. The 1400-hectare reserve is on the R24, Rustenburg Road about 7km/4 miles outside Krugersdorp. You pay R50 (£6.65/$11) a car for up to six people, R5 for each additional person. There are organised game drives with qualified rangers, a camping site, caravan park, guest lodge, four swimming pools, and a supermarket-style store is located within the resort. Bungalows painted in colourful African tradition offer comfortable accommodation at prices ranging from R150 per night for a self-catering two-bed rondavel, to R260 per four-bed lodge per night.

Caravanners pay R60 a site. Directions and enquiries, tel (011) 953-1770, fax (011) 665-1735.

Lesedi Cultural Village. Less than an hour's drive north of Johannesburg, at Broederstroom, Lesedi gives you an opportunity to experience the culture and architecture of rural Africa. You are hosted by Xhosa, Pedi, Zulu or Sotho families in rural African homesteads, and encouraged to join in the rituals and routines of your host family. Guest accommodation combines authentic architecture — woven beehive huts — with all mod cons. At night you gather around a fire in the boma for an evening of singing, dancing and storytelling. It costs R495 per person sharing, dinner, bed and breakfast, or R610 single, tel (01205) 51394/5, fax (01205) 51344.

Lion Park. You can drive on 16km/10 miles of trail and see lion and game animals in their natural habitat on 354 hectares of veld, visit the curio shop, pet's corner, the Ndebele village and enjoy a dip in the swimming pool, tel (011) 460-1814.

Lippizaner Stallions. In Kyalami every Sunday, starting at 11am, a team of white stallions perform in the elegant style of the famous Spanish Riding School in Vienna. Book at Computicket or tel (011) 702-2103.

Magaliesberg. This picturesque mountainous area, with its little village of Magaliesburg 75km/47 miles from Johannesburg, is a favourite with walkers and climbers. The Makalani Bird Park between the mountains and the Hartbeespoort Dam, has the largest selection of loeries in southern Africa, and is a sanctuary for an impressive array of exotic birds. Guided tours, walk-in aviaries and swimming pools are among the attractions. Zanandi Pleasure Resort, on the northern slopes of the Magaliesberg, is noted for a wide selection of indigenous trees. Pleasure resorts and hospitable country inns abound in the area, and quaint craft shops invite a leisurely browse. On Sundays, the Magaliesburg Express steam train leaves Johannesburg Station at 8.45am for Magaliespoort (a trip of just under two hours) arriving back in Johannesburg at 5.45pm. Tel (011) 888-1154. For a different perspective Bill Harrop's Original Balloon Safaris will float you up, up and away over the hills and valleys for an hour or two, ending with a champagne brunch. The balloon goes up every day, weather permitting. Special game-viewing balloon safaris can also be arranged. Contact Bill and Mary Harrop, PO Box 67, Randburg 2125, Gauteng, tel (011) 705-3201/2, fax (011) 805-3203, e-mail travels@aztec.co.za

Melville Koppies. This 80-hectare nature reserve in the western suburbs was once the site of a Stone Age village and iron-smelting works. The flora includes 80 per cent of the species recorded on the Witwatersrand. The trail along the Louw Geldenhuys View Site, through Mellville Koppies Nature Reserve and the Western Section to its extremity covers nearly 5km/3 miles. It fits into a number of existing trails, and connects with the Braamfontein Spruit Trail at the top of the Johannesburg Botanical Garden and offers several paths to the Montgomery Spruit Trail. The reserve is open only between September and April. Guided tours are available, tel (011) 782-7064/888-4831.

Mountain Sanctuary Park. In the Magaliesberg valley, 90km/56 miles from Pretoria and 106km/66 miles from Johannesburg. This 960-hectare reserve is a delight to walkers, climbers, botanists, birders and anyone who appreciates untouched wilderness. It is watered by crystal mountain streams and natural pools and has a caravan and camp site, each with its own barbecue area, as well as self-catering chalets. A variety of small buck, vervet monkeys and inquisitive baboons share the kloofs and cliffs in the reserve. Tel (0142) 75-0114 (only between 8am and 5pm).

Ndabushe Wildlife Sanctuary. Barely 30km/19 miles from Johannesburg, south of the Magaliesberg, this game sanctuary protects many antelope species, from the giant eland to the dainty steenbok. There are hippos in the dam as well as water mongoose and otters, and 150 species of birds. Game drives and walks with a game scout are available, tel (011) 956-6338.

New Vaal Meander. This arts and crafts route provides an opportunity to view and buy a wide variety of works from artists' studios, selected art galleries and tea gardens. Open on the first weekend of every month, Saturday 9am–5pm, Sunday 11.30am–5pm. Contact Vaal Tourism Committee (Vereeniging), tel (016) 50-3009.

Pelindaba. Site of a nuclear research reactor near to the Hartbeespoort Dam, in the Pretoria district. The name means 'the matter is settled,' and refers to the dam which was completed when the water reached its highest level.

Pretorius Park in Krugersdorp is home to a number of bird species. The African Fauna and Bird Park harbours various species of wildlife and birds, demonstrations by feathered 'stars' (birds used in local TV commercials) take place on Sundays at midday and 2pm, tel (011) 660-2623.

Roodepoort owes its prosperity to gold, which is the main theme of the Roodepoort Museum. Walks and trails lead through the Kloofendal Nature Reserve, which is home to more than 120 bird species. Within the reserve, the Kloofendal Ampitheatre, seating 10,000 spectators, is the venue for popular entertainment events, tel (011) 470-3600. Leisure options at Florida Lake include boating and angling, a play park, a swimming pool and rides on a miniature train. Facilities at the Little Falls Pleasure Resort, Wilgespruit, include a swimming pool, barbecue areas and picnic spots, tel (011) 475-1433.

Sparkling Waters. Amble through the mountains in the heart of the Magaliesberg. Abundant birdlife, tennis, squash, bowls, trampoline, jungle-gym, guided walks, trails, horse-riding, pony rides, and tasty country fare. Tel (0142) 75-0151/7.

The Rhino and Lion Nature Reserve, in the Kromdraai Conservancy, is just 30 minutes' drive north-west of Johannesburg. It is a haven for white rhino, lion, buffalo, hippo and more than 20 other species of game. Game drives, day and night, take you close to the wildlife. You can see and photograph the rare Cape vulture, hippo and South Africa's five smallest antelope, the klipspringer, blue duiker, suni, steenbok, and grysbok. There is a rest camp with three fully equipped chalets, with *en-suite* bathrooms, each sleeping four. You can make your visit to the reserve a two-in-one excursion by visiting the Wonder Cave, which is also in the Conservancy, tel (011) 957-0109.

The Wonder Cave. This was formed about 2.2 billion years ago and is regarded as one of the most beautifully naturally decorated caves in South Africa. Difficulty of access has preserved its formations in pristine condition. The cave was opened to the public in 1991, and the installation of an elevator now makes it easy for small groups to enter. The cave has massive formations of stalactites and stalagmites and there are also less common formations, such as rimstone dams, cave pearls and a complete calcified animal skeleton. It is open daily, 8am–5pm, tel (011) 957-0106.

Sterkfontein Caves. These are nearby and are the site of the discovery of 'Mrs Ples' (*Plesianthropus transvaalenis*) by Dr Robert Broom. He described the caves as the anthropological treasure house of the world. They comprise a series of caverns with many stalactites and stalagmites and a huge underground lake.
    You can view the excavations in progress by following the cave exit up to the perimeter fence, after you have seen the caves. The Robert Broom Museum at the caves has a comprehensive fossil display and there is a bronze bust of the great man holding the skull of Mrs Ples at the exit of the caves. There is also a tea room and a well tended picnic area. The caves are in the Isaac Edwin Stegman Nature Reserve, about 10km/6 miles north-west of Krugersdorp, and nearby is the Kromdraai Palaeontological Reserve. The caves are open from Tuesday to Sunday and on public

holidays, 9am–5pm. One-hour guided tours start on the half hour, 9am–4pm, tel (011) 956-6342.

Transvaal Snake Park. At Midrand, midway between Johannesburg and Pretoria, this privately owned park holds South Africa's premier live reptile collection. There are daily demonstrations with pythons and venomous snakes. If you are a bit squeamish about snakes, there are also owls, monkeys and crocodiles. There is a curio shop and a restaurant at the park. Open every day from 9am to 5pm, tel (011) 805-3116.

Trout Fishing. This is a bit like shooting fish in a barrel, but it is fun for the whole family at Rainbow Trout Farm, River Country Estates, and Footloose Trout Farm. Catch your own and barbecue it on the spot. You can hire fishing tackle. Open seven days a week from 7am to 6pm, tel (011) 957-0008, (011) 957-0014, (011) 957-1014, (011) 464-1545.

Vaal Dam. Take away this sheet of water between the province and the Free State and you remove all the money and all the power from Gauteng. The 2572 million cubic metre/90,829 million cubic feet reservoir built in 1935 is nothing less than the heart of the region. It is also a favourite weekend getaway, with its opportunities for fishing, boating, sailing, waterskiing and other water sports.

Witwatersrand National Botanical Garden. The 225-hectare grounds at Malcolm Road, Poortview, Roodepoort, include a large portion of mountainous area and contain more than 600 species of flowering plant, 180 species of bird (including a magnificent pair of black eagles nesting on the cliff face next to a 70m-high waterfall), 30 species of reptile and many small mammals. There are major plantings of cycads, aloes, and frost-hardy shrubs and trees. There is a small visitor's centre and restaurant. Guided tours take place every Sunday at 3pm, starting from the main entrance. Wheelchairs are available by arrangement. The garden is open every day of the year, 8am–5pm. The entrance fee is R4 (55p/90 cents) per adult, R1 per child (no charge for pre-school children), and R1 for senior citizens. Guided walks are conducted on Sundays at 3pm, tel (011) 958-1751.

PRETORIA

Johannesburg grew up virtually in the shadow of Pretoria, which was the capital of the Transvaal when the diggings to the south were still a Wild West mining camp. The city is some 50km/31 miles north of Johannesburg and is renowned for its graceful buildings and colourful gardens, flowers and trees, particularly beautiful in spring when 70,000 jacarandas fill the city avenues from September to November with a mauve haze. The city has a noticeably more laid-back atmosphere than Johannesburg, an echo of the days when it was the capital of a pastoral Boer Republic, and being 382m/1253ft lower it is always a few degrees warmer. The city has an abundance of open spaces, with more than 100 parks, bird sanctuaries, dams and nature reserves. Within easy reach, day walks provide a relaxing introduction to the region's natural habitats, many inhabited by indigenous animals and birds. Pretoria was founded by Mathinus Wessel Pretorius, the first President of the South African Republic in 1850. He named it after his father Andries Pretorius, the Voortrekker hero of the Battle of Blood River. It became the capital of the Transvaal in 1860 and has been the country's administrative capital since the Act of Union amalgamated the provinces of the Cape, the Orange Free State, the Transvaal, and Natal in 1910. To its Sotho-speaking residents it is also known as Tshwane, and to millions of other people as the Jacaranda City.

Church Square is the heart of Pretoria. Looming over it is the bronze statue of Paul Kruger, with its attendant burgher sentries. The work of sculptor Anton van Wouw, the figures were cast in Italy at the turn of the century but it was not until 1954 that they were given their dominant position in the city centre. It is surrounded by such fine buildings as the Old Raadsaal (Council Chamber), the Palace of Justice and the Reserve Bank. The Ou Raadsaal was designed by a Dutch architect and built in 1887 by a Scotsman from the Orkney Isles and is a good example of early Transvaal architecture. Church Square is the hub around which the city has grown and spread. The square was the site of the first church, the first open-air markets and the first shops. Progress has brought to Pretoria hi-tech shopping centres, museums and art galleries and a wide variety of restaurants. The city has four universities and a number of scientific institutes, including the Council for Scientific and Industrial Research (CSIR) and, 12km/7.5 miles north, the Onderstepoort Veterinary Research Institute, both internationally renowned. The commanding ridge above the city is crowned by the impressive red sandstone horseshoe of the Union Buildings, which houses the office of the State President and is now recognisable to millions worldwide since the inauguration of President Mandela was televised globally from that venue. The greater Pretoria metropolitan area covers more than 900sq km/348sq miles and has a population of more than 1.6 million.

Pretoria has some fine museums, historic houses and monuments, ranging from the Voortrekker Monument and Museum, the Miriammen Hindu Temple, Melrose House, the Union Buildings, Paul Kruger's unpretentious house, the State Model Schools from which Winston Churchill made his celebrated escape after being taken prisoner during the Anglo Boer War, and the cenotaph in Atteridgeville, a memorial for the men of the Native Corps who died in World War Two. Between Gerhard Moerdyk Street, Kotze Street and Van Boeschoten Lane are some of the last remnants of old Pretoria, 25 original houses built between 1895 and 1920, which have been meticulously restored and house a variety of excellent restaurants, art galleries, antique shops and exclusive boutiques in a vibrant area known as the Oeverzicht Art Village. Pretoria is a multi-cultural and multi-lingual city representative of all indigenous languages spoken, although English and Afrikaans are the languages most commonly used to bridge cultural and ethnic divides. It is host to a large international colony of diplomats whose presence adds spice to the restaurant and entertainment scene.

Arrival and Departure. Shuttle transport to and from Johannesburg International Airport departs on the hour from the Tourist Rendezvous Centre in Pretoria city centre, 6am–7pm every day of the week. Last shuttle from the airport leaves at 8pm from Terminal 3. Your hotel or hostel can advise on other alternatives, but you should avoid using taxis from Pretoria to Johannesburg International Airport, as charges can be prohibitive.

Bus services. *Elwierda* scheduled bus services between Pretoria and Johannesburg (mornings only). Depart Monday to Friday from State Theatre, Prinsloo Street at 6.25am to Carlton Hotel, Johannesburg. Return at 4.45pm from Carlton Hotel to Pretoria, tel (012) 664-5880, fax (012) 664-5317.

North Link and *Translink Transport*: Pretoria–Pietersburg–Phalaborwa departs from Bosman Street, between Church and Pretorius Streets, at the Merino Building, tel (012) 323-0379, fax (012) 323-5242.

Translux departs from Pretoria Station for Cape Town, Durban, Bloemfontein and Nelspruit, tel (012) 315-2595.

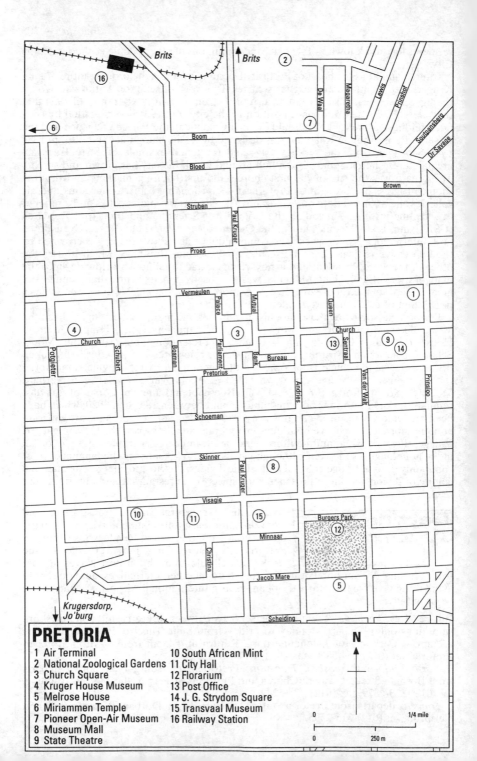

PRETORIA

1 Air Terminal
2 National Zoological Gardens
3 Church Square
4 Kruger House Museum
5 Melrose House
6 Miriammen Temple
7 Pioneer Open-Air Museum
8 Museum Mall
9 State Theatre
10 South African Mint
11 City Hall
12 Florarium
13 Post Office
14 J. G. Strydom Square
15 Transvaal Museum
16 Railway Station

N

0   1/4 mile

0   250 m

Other services:

Putco, tel (012) 372-0061;
Brits/Pretoria, tel (01211) 22354;
Pretoria/Ellisras, tel (014) 763-2511.

Travelling times from Johannesburg/Pretoria to:

Cape Town, by air (1hr 50mins), by car (14hrs), by bus (16–19hrs), by rail (28hrs);
Bloemfontein, by air (50 mins), by car (5hrs), by bus (6–7hrs), by rail (15hrs);
Durban, by air (1hr), by car (6hrs), by bus (8–9hrs), by train (14hrs).

City Transport. Timetables for municipal buses are available in pharmacies, on buses, and at the Information Office on Church Square, Pretoria, tel (012) 313-0839/0840. Metered **taxis** (cabs) pick you up by appointment – you cannot flag them down. You can book taxis through the Tourist Rendezvous Travel Centre:

City Bug, tel (012) 663-6316
City Taxis, tel (012) 21-5742/3/4
Rixi Taxis, tel (012) 325-8072/3/4
Buzz-a-bee, tel (012) 335-6565
Flash Taxis, tel (012) 323-6376

United Long Distance Taxi Association, covering Gauteng routes from Johannesburg and Mpumalanga as far as Lydenburg and Nelspruit, tel (0135) 656-5830.

Car hire:

Avis, tel (012) 325-1490, toll-free 0800 02 11 11
Budget, tel (012) 341-4650, fax (012) 341-1688
Citybug, tel (012) 663-6316
Europcar, tel/fax (012) 326-3716
Rent a Jalopy, tel (012) 333-4374

Rail. Commuter trains, tel (012) 315-2007. Mainline railway services enquiries, tel (012) 315-2757, and reservations, tel (012) 315-2401.

Accommodation

Four-star hotels:

Centurion Lake Hotel, PO Box 7331, Hennopsmeer 0046, tel (012) 663-1825, fax (012) 663-2760.
Holiday Inn Crowne Plaza, Beatrix Street, Arcadia, tel (012) 341-1571, fax (012) 44-7534.
Pretoria Hof Hotel, 291 Pretorius Street, central Pretoria, tel (012) 322-7570, fax (012) 322-9461.
Courtyard Hotel, 950 Park Street, Hatfield, tel (012) 342-4940, fax (012) 342-4941.

Three-star hotels:

Arcadia Hotel, 515 Proes Street, central Pretoria, tel (012) 326-9311, fax (012) 326-1067.
The *Pretoria Hotel* is centrally situated at 230 Hamilton Street, Pretoria, 52km/32 miles from Johannesburg International Airport and 150km/93 miles from Sun City. Tel (012) 341-3473, fax (012) 341-4449.
Karos Manhattan, 247 Scheiding Street, central Pretoria, tel (012) 322-7635, fax (012) 322-0721.

Two-star hotels:

Host International, 573 Church Street, Arcadia, tel/fax (012) 341-7455.
Park Lodge Hotel, 240 Jacob Mare Street, Arcadia, tel/fax (012) 320-8230

Guest Houses/Bed and Breakfast.
The Farm Inn, a privately owned country estate, is situated on 162 hectares of wildlife

sanctuary on the eastern outskirts of Pretoria, at Die Wilgers, tel (012) 809-0266, fax (012) 809-0146.

If you converse best in German, Russian or Slovak, then *Papa Joe's Slovak and International Guest House* at 470 Frederick Street, Pretoria West 0183, could be the right spot for you. Contact Papa Joe or Natalia, PO Box 4187, Pretoria 0001, tel (012) 327-0344, fax (012) 327-0343, Cell 082 453-1662. They also speak English.

Jane-Anne's Junction has B&B in Murrayfield, eastern Pretoria, with twin beds (R100 per person sharing) and single-bedded rooms (R120 a night). 175 Rubida Street, Murrayfield Ext. 1, Pretoria 0184, tel/fax (012) 83-3535, Cell 083 212-1989.

Silverton Guest House, 460 President Street, Silverton, offers a wide variety of short term self-catering and B&B accommodation, with special rates for backpackers. Tel/fax (012) 804-1597.

Boggers Pozzie, 503 Reitz Street, Sunnyside, Pretoria, tel (012) 343-7782, fax (012) 343-7782.

For guest houses and bed and breakfast contact the *Guest House Association of South Africa*. Pretoria branch of GHA, tel (012) 46-2887/2970 and for Pretoria guest and private house reservations, tel (012) 46-5327. Farm and Country Holidays, central reservations, tel/fax (012) 333-8021.

Hostels:

Econo Lodge, 252 Grosvenor Street, Hatfield, Cell 082 454-6580.

Pretoria Backpackers, 34 Bourke Street, Sunnyside, Pretoria, tel (012) 343-9754; has an hourly shuttle service to Johannesburg International Airport.

Word of Mouth Backpackers, 145 Berea Street, Muckleneuk 0002, tel (012) 341-9661.

Kia Ora Embassy Gasthaus offers a 24-hour check-in, private rooms from R100 (£13.35/$22) and dormitory from R25 per person. As well as the usual amenities they have a job-finder service and a pub with live music daily between 5pm and 7pm. 257 Jacob Mare Street, Pretoria 0001, tel (012) 322-4803, fax (012) 322-4816.

The *Pretoria YWCA* is at 557 Vermeulen Street, tel (012) 326-2916.

Among the larger **caravan parks** and **campsites** are:

ATKV Buffelspoort, tel (01427) 23214/7, fax (01427) 23215.

Fountains Valley Caravan Park, tel (012) 44-7131, fax (012) 341-3960.

Oberon Pleasure Resort, tel (01205) 51353.

Roodeplat Dam Resort, tel/fax (012) 808-0361.

Zanandi Caravan Park, tel (01211) 313454.

Eating and Drinking

Pretoria is big on Italian food and meat and there are plenty of places to eat a reasonable, inexpensive steak, pizza or pasta dish. For its size, Pretoria has probably got more coffee shops than any other South African city and you will have no trouble finding a cup of the stuff that kept the Voortrekkers going on their trek north. *Café Riche*, on Church Square, has the extra fillip of being located in one of the most beautiful corner buildings in Pretoria, tel (012) 328-3173.

Ed's Easy Diner looks like something out of the 1950's US comics. It has a rock 'n' roll dance floor, pinball machines, double-malts, and juke boxes. The waiters and waitresses reflect the era and they dance on the tables at midnight. It is open 24 hours, seven days a week at 1066 Burnett Street, Hatfield. For the ravenous there are mighty one-pounder burgers or a Grand Canyon Sandwich, tel (012) 342-2499.

On Sunday morning all the diplomats in town seem to head for *Der Zuckerbacker* bakery and coffee shop for their heart-starter of genuine Continental coffee and croissants or a choice of 60 varieties of bread and a host of irresistible confections with unpronounceable names. The buzz starts around breakfast (popular with the Harley Davidson club) and ends with imported beers from the bar to round the day off. Club Centre, Dely Road, Hazelwood, tel (012) 46-2845.

For traditional South African food in and around Pretoria try:

Die Werf, tel (012) 991-1809;
Gerhard Moerdyk, tel (012) 344-4856;
Oeka Toeka, tel (012) 341-0082;
Wildlife Lapa, tel (012) 342-7243;
The Boma at Silkaatssnek, tel (01211) 50-2680;
Die Stoep, tel (01212) 25101.

Oscar's American Diner, 501 Beatrix Street, Arcadia, tel (012) 341-2812; and *Paradise Alley*, on the corner of Schoeman and Prinsloo streets, tel (012) 322-6041. If you like music with your beer try the *Crossroads Blues Bar*, Upper Level, The Tram Shed, corner of Schoeman and Van der Walt Streets, central Pretoria, tel (012) 322-3263. The *Ringside Diner* in Groenkloof is a novel rendezvous set in the arena round a boxing ring, tel (012) 46-1238.

Shebeens are casual drinking places, like pubs, in black townships. They have emerged as instruments for black economic empowerment, especially for the unemployed, and specialise in a powerful cocktail of music, beer and spirits, and food. In Atteridgeville, try Fana Maseko, tel (012) 373-6402, Sarah Nohabeleng, tel (012) 373-9242, Tickey Maleka, tel (012) 373-0957, and Vesi Bazil Phala, tel (012) 373-4743. In Mamelodi try Mafosha's Tavern, tel (012) 805-9338, Maggie's Jazz Club, tel (012) 805-0323, and Sunny's Shebeen, tel (012) 805-2081. If you need help there is a country pub crawl which costs R65 per person for a trip on a luxury bus and a tour of country shebeens and pubs, snacks and eats at various venues, a lamb on the spit at the final stop and drinks. Cell 083 268-2737.

For more information on eating out in Pretoria see *Be My Guest Restaurant Guide*.

Gay Restaurants:

Fillings, 315 Esselen Street, Sunnyside, tel (012) 343-1683.
Pancake Palazzo, Gerard Moerdyk Street, Oeverzicht Art Village, Sunnyside.

The granite *Voortrekker Monument* commemorating the Great Trek from the Cape Colony dominates the hilly skyline on the approach to Pretoria from Johannesburg. The foundation stone was laid on 16 December 1938, on the centenary of the Voortrekker's victory over the Zulus at the Battle of Blood River in Natal and on this day every year a shaft of sunlight falls on the altar inside. In the car park at the foot of the flight of 260 steps leading up to the monument, designed by Gerhard Moerdyk, is a metal replica of the type of ox-wagon the Afrikaner trekkers used on their epic journey to the Highveld. Nearby is an informative little museum and a restaurant, which unimaginatively serves toasted sandwiches and burgers rather than the coffee, pot bread and koeksisters you might expect at an Afrikaner national shrine. The museum charts the most important migratory patterns in the history of southern Africa, with a focus on the lifestyle of the Voortrekkers, as well as life in the interior after the Great Trek (1835-1852). Entrance to the monument is R5 (half-price for children) and R5 for the museum, children R3. Open Monday to Saturday from 9am to 4.45pm, Sunday from 11am to 4.45pm, tel (012) 326-6770, Museum, tel (012) 323-0682. Restaurant, tel (012) 21-6230.

Air Force Museum depicts the history of the South African Air Force and displays a collection of old aircraft, uniforms, medals and paintings. Open Monday to Friday from 8am to 3pm, Saturday to Sunday from 10am to 3pm. Route R101 Valhalla, Swartkops Airforce Base, tel (012) 351-2153.

Austin Roberts Bird Sanctuary. Named after an authority on South African birds, the park provides sanctuary for more than 100 species, including the blue crane, crowned crane, sacred ibis, heron and a rare black swan. Birds can be viewed from an observation hide. Open weekends and public holidays. Tel. (012) 344-3840.

Burgers Park. Next to Melrose House on Jacob Maré Street in central Pretoria. Established in 1874 this is the oldest park in Pretoria. It has been declared a national monument. Open daily from 8am to 6pm.

Correctional Services Museum is the only one of its kind in South Africa. It portrays the development of the penal system as well as some hobbies of prisoners, and illegally manufactured items. Open Tuesday to Friday from 9am to 3pm. Central Prison, Potgieter Street, Pretoria, tel (012) 314-1766.

Fort Klapperkop ('Rattle Hill'). Now an interesting military museum on a hill south-east of Pretoria, which takes its Afrikaans name from a tree which grows there and whose seeds rattle in the dried fruit. The fort, built in 1897, reflects military preoccupations from Bushman times to World War Two. A curiosity is a nine-seater cycle constructed by the British during the Anglo-Boer War to run on railway lines. The central seat was where the officer sat in style while he was peddled along by eight subordinates. Fort Skanskop, near the Voortrekker Monument, was built at the same time and is also a military museum. Both are open every day, 10am–3.30pm.

Fountains Valley Nature Reserve. This was Africa's first proclaimed reserve (1895). It is the source of the Apies River which runs through Pretoria and is the setting in Groenkloof for indigenous and exotic plants, as well as a prolific bird life. Restaurants, swimming pool, caves, fountains, a miniature railway and an open-air theatre are among the attractions. There is also a caravan park and a tennis court. It is the start of the 18km/11 mile Groenkloof hiking trail. Open daily until midnight, tel (012) 44-7131/8316.

Heroes' Acre Church Street Cemetery at the corner of Church Street and DF Malan Drive, was established in 1867. The central part, known as Heroes' Acre, contains the graves of many historical figures, among them that of 'Breaker' Morant, an Australian executed for the murder of a missionary during the Anglo-Boer War.

Kruger House Museum. This simple house on Church Street West, gives you a feel for the life of this extraordinary man. It contains the possessions of President Paul Kruger and his wife, who lived in the house from 1884 to 1901. Tributes presented to Kruger and the Boers during the Anglo-Boer War are also on display. Open Monday to Saturday, 8.30am–4pm, Sunday and public holidays, 11am–4pm, tel (012) 326-9172.

Melrose House. One of the best preserved examples of Victorian architecture in South Africa and a national monument. The Peace Treaty of Vereeniging, which ended the Anglo-Boer War, was signed here on 31 May 1902. Melrose House contains lovely period furniture. Delicious teas in the garden. Guided tours are conducted at 3pm on the last Sunday of each month. Open Tuesday to Saturday, 10am–5pm, Sunday midday–5pm. 275 Jacob Mare Street, central Pretoria, tel (012) 322-2805, and (012) 322-0420.

Miriammen Temple. On Sixth Street, Asiatic Bazaar, in the city centre, is the oldest Hindu Temple in Pretoria (1905). It is dedicated to the goddess who controls smallpox and other infectious diseases. Remove your shoes before entering the cellar or assembly hall.

Museum of Culture. This new museum in Visagie Street, central Pretoria, is custodian of 2 million years of South African history. It houses magnificent archaeological and anthropological material, as well as Cape silver; historical furniture; the General Louis Botha collection and replicas of General Hertzog's study and General Smuts' bedroom. A fine collection of rock art and an ethnological display dedicated to the African tribes of Gauteng are also on view. In March 1997 a satellite called the African Window was opened to promote living culture, through song, dance, and visual arts. It also displays for the first time artefacts and works of art previously scattered all over the city. Tel (012) 328-4075.

Museum Mall. Located on Visagie Street from Van der Walt to Schubart streets in the city centre this has been designed along the lines of the American Smithsonian Institute in Washington. When complete it will encompass Melrose House, Burgers Park, the Transvaal Museum, the City Hall, a Children's Museum, the Museum of Culture, the Museum for Science and Technology and the State Library. Tel (012) 322-7632.

National Botanical Gardens. The first plantings were made in 1946 and by 1979 the living plant collection was so important it was declared a national monument. The indigenous plants reflect every major type of southern African vegetation. The garden is a 75-hectare urban oasis. Six vegetation types and nearly 1700 species of flowering plant occur in the Pretoria area – this is the same range as the total for the British Isles in an area one-hundredth their size. More than half these species grow in the garden. Half of South Africa's 1000-odd tree species also grow here. A self-guided nature walk follows a meandering landscaped path for several kilometres around the top of the ridge. An annotated map gives you details on 15 viewpoints. The whole walk takes a leisurely hour and offers close encounters with natural *bankenveld*, the name given to the vegetation of Pretoria and its surrounding area. The garden lies 8km east of the city centre, near the junction of the N1 and the N4 highways at Cussonia Avenue, Brummeria. Roads to the garden are sign-posted. For more information about buses, tel (012) 28-3562. The garden is open every day, 8am–6pm. Admission is R3 (40p/65 cents) a head for adults and R1 for pensioners and students. Paved walkways in the developed garden are suitable for the use of people in wheelchairs. Tel (012) 804-3200.

National Zoological Gardens. One of the largest of its kind, it has been voted one of the 10 best in the world, with more than 140 mammals and 320 bird species. There is an aquarium and reptile house, and a cable car to transport you to various lookout points. The zoo exhibits animals as naturally as possible, with the emphasis on conservation, education and research, and does pioneering work in the breeding of endangered species. These breeding programmes are aimed at re-introducing endangered species to their natural habitat. At the De Wildt Breeding Centre cheetahs were bred so successfully that they were removed from the Red Data list. Open daily, 8am–5.30pm, tel (012) 328-3265.

Pierneef Museum. This houses a collection of art from various periods of South African artist Pierneef's work (1904-1954) at 218 Vermeulen Street, city centre, Pretoria. Open Monday to Friday, 8am–4pm. Accessible to the disabled, tel (012) 323-1419 or (012) 323-0731.

Pretoria Art Museum. This showcase for some of South Africa's finest art also houses displays of international graphic art and collections of 17th century Dutch art. Open Tuesday to Saturday, 10am–5pm, Sunday 1–6pm, tel (012) 344-1807.

Puppet Collection. The University of Pretoria's collection of more than 1000 puppets is displayed in the Education and Law Building on the University campus, corner of Faculty and Tindall Avenues, Hillcrest. Visits are by appointment only. Tel (012) 420-3031.

Sammy Marks Museum. A splendid Victorian mansion (1884) on the Old Bronkhorstspruit Road, which was the residence of the magnate Sammy Marks, a friend of President Paul Kruger who made a significant contribution to the industrial, mining and agricultural development of the old Zuid-Afrikaansche Republiek. Open Tuesday to Friday from 9am to 4pm, Saturday to Sunday from 10am to 4pm. African arts and crafts on sale. Victorian garden tours are conducted between October and December by guides in period costume, tel (012) 803-6158.

Science and Technology Museum situated in Skinner Street, central Pretoria, this is a hands-on museum and the only one of its kind in South Africa. Themes include nuclear energy, biology, space, mechanics, water, holograms and a weather satellite-receiving station. Open Monday to Friday from 8am to 4pm, Sunday from 2pm to 5pm, tel (012) 322-6404.

Transvaal Museum. This famous natural history museum on Paul Kruger Street houses a superb collection of mammals, birds, reptiles, amphibians, insects, fossils, prehistoric man and archaeological and geological material, including one of the largest collections of Bushman rock art in the country. The original fossils found by Dr Robert Broom are housed in a strong room not usually open to the public. The Geological Museum has a fascinating display of precious and semi-precious stones. The Austin Roberts Bird Hall contains a comprehensive collection of South African birds. Open Monday to Saturday from 9am to 5pm, Sunday from 11am to 5pm, tel (012) 322-7632.

Union Buildings. Designed by Sir Herbert Baker and completed in 1913 these are considered to be his greatest achievement and South Africa's architectural masterpiece. The administrative headquarters of government stand on Meintjeskop Ridge, overlooking the city. In the grounds are the Deville Wood War Memorial, a tribute to South African troops who died during World War One, and statues of various Prime Ministers, as well as a Police Memorial. The Union buildings are surrounded by beautifully laid-out gardens. This was the setting for President Nelson Mandela's historic inauguration on 10 May 1994. The buildings are closed to the public, but the spacious, terraced gardens offer fine views of the city. Garden tours on Monday to Friday by appointment only, tel (012) 325-2000.

Unisa Art Gallery. This non-commercial, academic gallery in the Theo van Wyk Building, B Block, Preller Road, Muckleneuk, presents a wide range of stimulating exhibitions. Open Monday to Friday from 10am to 3.30pm, Saturday from 2.30pm to 4.30pm. Accessible to the disabled. Guided tours, tel (012) 492-6255.

Wonderboom Nature Reserve. The Wonderboom ('Wonder tree') that gives this reserve 13km/8 miles to the north of the city its name is a giant wild fig tree that is one of South Africa's oldest trees. The main tree is about 1000 years old and 20m/65ft high and has spread over the years to form five concentric rings of tangled growth that can literally shelter a thousand people. You can see the remains of the old Wonderboom Fort in the reserve, which has a hiking trail along the slopes of the Magaliesberg to a view site providing a fine vista of Pretoria, tel (012) 542-9918.

Pretoria is fairly well provided with theatre, clubs and other entertainment venues. Theatre's flagship is the *State Theatre*, on Church Street, in the city. Seven auditoriums in the complex provide venues for opera, theatre, ballet, choirs and symphony concerts. The interior is decorated by the work of South African artists. Guided tours of the complex and areas not usually seen by the public can be booked. Partially accessible to the disabled, tel (012) 322-1665.

The *Aula Theatre, Lier Masker, Musaion* and *Ampitheatre* are all part of a cultural centre at the University of Pretoria, where opera, ballet and concerts are regularly presented, tel (012) 420-2315.

> *Breytenbach Theatre*, Gerhard Moerdyk Street, Sunnyside, Pretoria, tel (012) 44-4834.
> *Little Theatre*, Skinner Street, Pretoria, tel (012) 322-8484.
> *Piet van der Walt Theatre*, Showgrounds, Soutter Street, Pretoria West, tel (012) 327-1487.
> *Café Riche Basement Theatre*, 2 Church Square, central city, tel (012) 328-3173.

A theatre guide is available from the Pretoria Tourist Information Bureau, tel (012) 313-7694 or (012) 308-7980. Bookings can be made through Computicket, tel (012) 328-4040.

Being the capital of Fortress South Africa for so many years kept the lid on the club scene more than in Johannesburg, but now Pretoria claims to have South Africa's biggest gay club, *Steamers*, on the corner of Paul Kruger and Railway streets, Pretoria. Weekly programmes offer drag nights, oldies nights, ladies' night (stripshow for the girls), men's night (stripshow for the boys), rave nights, and weekend parties. Open 7 days a week, from 8pm till late, tel (012) 322-6278/9.

For jazz fans, try the *House of Jazz*, at the Host International Hotel, Church Street East, Arcadia, tel (012) 341-7455; for more serious stuff there is the *Medical Music School*, in Atteridgeville, tel (012) 373-7442. *Moretele Park*, in Mamelodi, is the venue for occasional jazz and other music festivals; and there is live music at *Dreamers*, 139 Esselen Street, Sunnyside, tel (012) 341-0604, and the *Café Galleria*, 20 Esselen Street, tel (012) 341-1710. Often to be heard at the Galleria is a heavy metal group called Wizard. One of its guitarists is a young Pretoria businessman, Chris Paulet, who would probably be recognised in more elevated circles as the Earl of Wiltshire.

Casinos and gambling places in general are in a state of flux but the main ones in the area are *Carousel Entertainment World*, where there is the *Cheyenne Saloon* for musical extravaganzas, and *Gentleman Jim's* music pub. N1 Freeway to Pietersburg, Maubane offramp, tel (01464) 77777; *Morula Sun*, Mabopane Freeway R80, Rosslyn offramp, tel (0146) 23320; and *Sun City/Lost City*, N4 freeway to Rustenburg, tel (014651) 2100.

Gay Bars and Clubs

> *Klub 113*, 113 Diamond Street, Rosslyn, tel (012) 542-4928 or (011) 892-5004.
> *Mieke Exclusive Club*, Meintjies Building 92, Meintjies Street, Sunnyside, tel (012) 341-8917.
> *Steamers*, corner Paul Kruger and Railway Street Extension, tel (012) 322-6278.

There is no shortage of shopping complexes in the Pretoria area. In and around the CBD there are centres with boutiques, speciality shops, and trading stores, among them Sunnypark, Sanlam Centre, Arcadia Centre, Die Meent, deBruynpark, Barclay Square, the Standard Bank Centre, FedLife Forum, Sancardia, The Tram Shed, and Sammy Marks Square, which is home to the oldest commercial buildings in Pretoria. In the south there is the Elardus Park Shopping Centre, as well as open-air Centurion Park, which is built around a man-made lake and offers relaxing space for strollers. Specialist shops abound in and around Pretoria and the Oeverzicht Art Village, in Gerhard Moerdyk Street, housing art and craft shops and restaurants, should be on your shopping list.

Regular flea markets are held throughout Pretoria and its suburbs at Sunnypark (on Sundays), the Fedlife Forum, on the corner of Beatrix and Vermeulen streets, at the Wierda Park Shopping Centre, at Checkers Pretoria North, Centurion Centre, Sanlam Centre Alkantrant, the Quagga Centre, Gezina City, Poyntons, Brooklyn

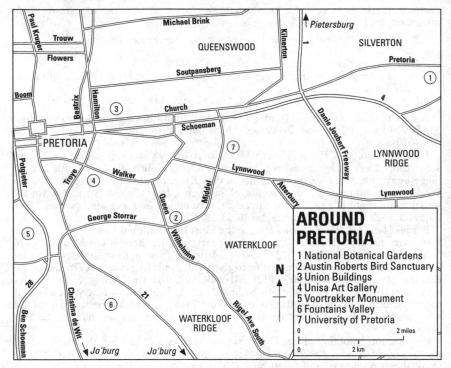

AROUND PRETORIA

1 National Botanical Gardens
2 Austin Roberts Bird Sanctuary
3 Union Buildings
4 Unisa Art Gallery
5 Voortrekker Monument
6 Fountains Valley
7 University of Pretoria

Mall, Crack Roadhouse and at the State Theatre. Under the weeping willows at *Magnolia Dell* a very upper-class flea market is held on the first Saturday of every month from 9am to 3pm, an art-in-the-park exhibition every last Saturday and moonlight markets in the summer, corner of Queen Wilhelmina and Charles streets, New Muckleneuk, tel (012) 98-1557 and (012) 811-0552. Pretoria's *International Flea Market* is in the Park Building, at the corner of Beatrix and Schoeman streets, Sunnyside. Curios from all over African are a speciality and there is live music every weekend, tel (012) 341-1591. One that is worth going out of town for is the *Village Market* at Smuts House Museum, Irene, where there are 220 arts and crafts stalls every second and last Saturday of the month. It is open from 9am to 2pm and has a tea garden with live classical music, tel (012) 667-1659/2266.

Zoo Craft Market. A wide variety of African hand-crafts are sold outside the main entrance of the National Zoological Gardens in Pretoria.

Bronkhorstspruit. 58km/36 miles east on Pretoria on the road to Mpumalanga is a pleasant little farming centre that is chiefly remembered for the massacre of 66 British soldiers, ambushed there by Boers at the start of the First Anglo-Boer War in December 1880. Today peach trees flourish on the spot where they fell and it is believed they grew from the peach-stones of the fruit the soldiers were eating when they died. There is a small resort at Bronkhorstspruit Dam, which has abundant birdlife and opportunities for angling, sailing and watersports, tel (01212) 20061.

Cullinan. The old mining village 40km/25 miles east of Pretoria grew up around the

Premier Diamond Mine, and many turn-of-the-century sandstone houses still stand. The mine, the world's biggest diamond mine, has produced some of the world's most famous diamonds, among them The Cullinan, at 3024 carats the largest ever found. The 530-carat Star of Africa was cut from this and is now in the British Crown Jewels. Surface tours take place at the mine from Monday to Friday, tel (01213) 40081, or contact Betty Elliott at the Chamber of Mines of South Africa, PO Box 61809, Marshalltown 2107, Johannesburg, tel (011) 498-7204, fax (011) 838-4251, Cell 083 263-7776.

Klipgat. You can see people of the Ndebele tribe, in their traditional dress, living in a kraal with its geometrically painted houses at Klipgat village, 48km/30 miles north-west of Pretoria. The village is open every day except Sunday.

Loopspruit Wine Estate. 35km/22 miles north of Bronkhorstspruit, this is the only registered wine estate north of the Orange River. It is open Tuesday to Sunday from 8am to 4pm for cellar tours and wine and spirit tastings (try the witblits and mampoer). There is a restaurant on the estate and an Ndebele village open to visitors is near the entrance, tel/fax (01212) 24352 for restaurant bookings. Estate tel (01212) 24303.

Pioneer Open-Air Museum. A restored thatched Voortrekker cottage complete with dung-smeared floor and reconstructed farmyard dating from about 1848. Daily demonstrations include bread, butter and candle-making, and other pioneer skills. Souvenirs are available. Watermeyer Street, Silverton. Open daily, 8.30am–4pm, tel (012) 803-6086.

Rietvlei Dam is ideal for canoeing, sailing, game-viewing and picnicking. There are also several game farms and lodges in the area. In the reserve you can see rhino, zebra and several species of antelope. Contact tel (012) 345-2274 and 313-7694.

Smuts House Museum 13km/8 miles south-east of Pretoria on Nelmapius Road, in the village of Irene, is the modest iron and wood house of former South African Prime Minister Field Marshal Jan Christiaan Smuts, Doornkloof. The house, a corrugated iron British officer's mess originally used at Lord Kitchener's head-quarters at Middelburg during the Anglo-Boer War, was once described by Smuts as 'an ideal refuge for stoics', as it was hot in summer and bitterly cold in winter. It contains the original austere furnishings of the family. There is a tea garden nearby. Open daily, tel (012) 667-1176.

Tswaing Crater is one of the best preserved meteorite impact craters in the world. The meteorite crashed into the Earth 45km/28 miles north of Pretoria 200,000 years ago. The water-filled crater is now 1.13km/0.7 miles wide and 120m/394ft deep. Stone Age people occupied the area for 120,000 years, drawn by the salt from the lake (the name comes from a Tswana word meaning *the place of salt*).

The **Tswaing Crater Museum** was established in 1992 and is one of the nine satellite museums of the national Museum of Culture in Pretoria. The museum site is 2000 hectares in size and is still being developed. There is a large variety of plant life and a population of about 300 species of birds in the wetland on the north-eastern part of the crater. Visits can be arranged by prior booking. Contact the museum at (01214) 98-7302 (tel and fax) or tel (012) 341-1320.

Voortrekkerhoogte. Military centre 10km/6 miles south-west of Pretoria. Founded in 1900 as headquarters of British Commander-in-Chief Lord Roberts, it was originally named Roberts Heights. In 1938, it was renamed Voortrekkerhoogte to commemorate the centenary of the Great Trek.

Willem Prinsloo Agricultural Museum. This farmstead on the Old Bronkhorstspruit Road dating from 1880 has a blacksmith's shop, dairy, working water mill and a peach brandy still. You can watch traditional farming activities such as bread baking and candle-making and sample a traditional meal at Tant Miertjie se Kombuis or picnic in the barbecue area. Open daily, tel (01213) 44171/2/3.

 **Entertainment**

SPORT AND RECREATION

Greater Johannesburg will be the venue for the 1999 All Africa Games. More than 5000 athletes, 3000 officials and a huge media contingent are expected to converge on the city in September 1999 for these, which will stamp Johannesburg as the sports capital of the continent. For spectator sports the main stadiums in Gauteng are Ellis Park for rugby and athletics and the Standard Bank Arena, which stages everything from tennis and basketball to indoor soccer and pop concerts. Both are in Johannesburg. In Pretoria Loftus Versveld is the home of rugby, and there is a fine sports venue in Germiston at the Herman Immelman Stadium; in Roodepoort the Ruimsig Athletics Stadium is the most modern in the province. It is part of a complex designed to accommodate more than 50 sporting codes. Cricket is played at Centurion Park in Pretoria and at the Wanderers in Johannesburg, which also has a top golf course.

Motor sport has a big following in South Africa, which has produced such top drivers as Jody Scheckter. 25km/15 miles north of Johannesburg Kyalami (Zulu for 'My Home') is the province's main motor racing track, an internationally renowned racing circuit for Formula One, saloon car and motor-cycle events. Tel (011) 702-2305, or AA Motor Sport, tel (011) 466-2440, for information on race dates and track events. Motorsport South Africa controls 42 different branches of motorsport, tel (011) 466-2440, fax (011) 466-2450. e-mail insport@iafrica.com or visit http://rst.nis.za/rst/msa

Drag and stock car racing are favourite weekend attractions and take place not far from Krugersdorp, at Tarlton International Raceway, tel (011) 952-1044, or contact Tarlton Motor Sport Club, tel (011) 762-5431. Motorsport takes place in Pretoria at Zwartkop Raceway, tel (012) 374-1692.

Oval track motor racing features at the new Wembley Raceway, on Turffontein Road, Stafford, in Johannesburg, which closed in 1976 when spectators turned on TV sets for the first time. Now that TV has lost its charm Wembley again provides race fans with sprint, saloon and stockcar events, as well as sidecar and speedway motorbike racing on Friday nights, tel (011) 683-8383.

Four-wheel drive off-road events and expeditions are extremely popular. The bundu provides plenty of opportunities for this activity and there are hundreds of 4x4 trails throughout the country, and even in some of the national parks. A good guide to a range of these is *Southern Africa 4x4 Trails*, by Andrew St Pierre White and Gwynn White (International Motoring Publications, Johannesburg), and White's Continental 4xForum is probably the foremost information Internet web site on the local scene, featuring vehicle manufacturers, off-road equipment manufacturers and resellers, 4x4 clubs, magazines, trails and safari operators. Contact the Continental 4xForum on: http//www.4xforum.co.za or e-mail andreww@aztec.co.za or write to PO Box 347, Randburg 2125, tel (011) 787-6933, fax (011) 886-3760. The Continental Offroad Academy holds courses to help you master the basics of 4x4 vehicles and teaches vehicle dynamics, driving and winching techniques, basic life support, and camping and touring know-how. Courses are held at Gerotek vehicle testing facility near Hartbeespoort Dam, about 30 minutes' drive from Sandton, tel (011) 883-7427/8/9.

The Four-Wheel-Drive Club of Southern Africa is the largest club of its kind in Africa, and is headquartered in Johannesburg. The club runs driver training, rescue, conservation, radio, motorsport, marshalling and driving sections, and organises 4x4 driving venues. The club also holds social, competitive and other event, and arranges day and weekend outings and extended trips to out-of-the-way places. It also has an active scuba diving section. Chairman is George Wolff, tel (011) 975-3293, and PR officer is Peter van Der Walt, tel (011) 704-1329, or contact PO Box 8860, Edenglen 1613, Gauteng, tel (011) 452-3860, fax 452-3860.

Other 4x4 clubs in Gauteng which welcome visitors and offer advice and a variety of services and facilities are the Jeep Club, PO Box 28354, Sunnyside 0132; Land Rover Owners Club of SA, PO Box 23507, Joubert Park 2044; and Honeydew Toyota Four-Wheel-Drive Club, PO Box 466, Honeydew 2040.

British-based Safari Drive can provide 4x4 hire vehicles and organise all bookings, as well as guided safaris. Tel London (0171) 622-3891, fax (0171) 498-0914.

Gauteng is, like the Cape and KwaZulu-Natal, a horsy province, with plenty of opportunities for hacking, jumping, eventing, and trails and safaris. The most prestigious equestrian event in South Africa is the four-day Dunhill Derby, which is held in October at the Inanda Country Club, Johannesburg. It features showjumping, dressage, showing, compleat horse, which combines performance in all three disciplines, and carriage driving. Contact Nina Fiddian-Green, tel (011) 783-0908 or Cell 083 601-2542. To see something of Gauteng from the saddle try Equus Horse Safaris, who will show you Africa's big game from horseback on a 22,000ha/54,363 acre private game reserve north of Johannesburg. Contact Equus Trails, 36 12th Avenue, Parktown North 2193, Gauteng, tel (011) 788-3923, fax (011) 880-8401. Roberts Farm Horse Trails can take you on one to three-hour, half and full-day cross-country rides in the foothills of the Magaliesberg mountains. Moonlight and sunset rides are available from September to May, tel (0142) 77-1498. Other contacts are the Association for Horse Trails and Safaris in Southern Africa, tel (011) 788-3923, and the Gauteng Horse Society, tel (011) 702-1657.

Horse racing takes place regularly at Turffontein in Johannesburg, tel (011) 683-9330; Gosforth Park, in Germiston, tel (011) 873-1000, and at Newmarket, in Alberton, tel (011) 907-9753. All newspapers carry full racing reports and details of meetings.

There are more boats **sailing** on the dams of Gauteng than down at Durban or Port Elizabeth. There is even a National Sea Rescue Institute (NSRI) rescue station on the Vaal Dam, at the Manton Marina across the Free State border in Deneysville. The width of the dam is such that it takes 15 minutes to cross it – and that's in a powerboat at 40kmh (25mph). An annual single-handed Round the Island regatta is held every New Year's Day at the Vaal Dam, starting near the Deneys Yacht Club. The NSRI has published an informative and affordable book (R30; £4/$6.60), *Small Vessel Seamanship, A Guide to Safe Inland Boating*, which is recommended reading if you plan to take to the water on any of Gauteng's rivers or dams. If you prefer angling in the dams and waterways contact any tourist information centre, the Gauteng Flytyers Guild, Dries de Bruyn, tel (012) 325-2100 or (012) 64-5936, or the Requin Angling Club, tel (011) 893-1554.

Even the smallest *dorp* has a **golf** course of sorts and the quality rises from there to the super courses of Gauteng, such as the Wanderers, Houghton Golf Club, and Randpark Club, in Johannesburg, and the Glendower Country Club, in Edenvale. Contact Golfline, tel (011) 907-1632, or SA Golf Federation, tel (011) 442-3723.

Johannesburg and Pretoria are surrounded by excellent **walking and climbing** country, from the Magaliesberg mountains to Suikerbosrand and the Klipriviersberg. The most accessible walk close to Johannesburg is the 32km/20 mile Braamfontein Spruit trail, which provides hours of walking from Melville Koppies, past Emmarentia, through Johannesburg's north-western suburbs and on through Sandton, where it links with the Sand Spruit trail. Another popular walk is Phalandingwe Nature Trail near Broederstroom. In the Suikerbosrand Nature Reserve, near Heidelberg, you can choose between two routes on the Bokmakierie Nature Trail, one of them 10km/6 miles and the other of 17km/11 miles. As well as these better known ones, walks and trails criss-cross virtually every rural area. The Hiking Federation of South Africa has a R10 booklet listing trails, location, distances and contact numbers. HFSA, tel (011) 886-6524, fax (011) 886-6013. Cyrildene Hiking Club has rambles for the fit and the unfit every Sunday and some Saturdays, weekends away, outings and backpacking trails, tel (011) 616-5256. Before you set off climbing you can limber up at Climb Inn, an indoor climbing centre at Kya Sand, on the outskirts of Johannesburg. You can rent gear, but you should at least have your own stretch-pants and a decent pair of rubber-soled trainers. It costs R27 (£3.60/$5.95) per person per day (this includes the equipment) or R20 (if you bring your own). It is R15 for the under 12. If you want instruction Thrillseekers runs rock-climbing courses. All instructors are members of the Mountain Club of South Africa and the courses follow the syllabus devised by the MCSA, with an evening's discussion on the theoretical aspects at the MCSA clubhouse in Waverley, an evening on the indoor climbing wall at Kya-Sands, and a weekend climbing routes from relatively easy 10m/33ft to 20m/66ft on Northcliff Ridge to a day's climbing on more challenging pitches in the Magaliesberg mountains, tel/fax (011) 462-8282, Cell 083 491-6483,

There is good **hunting** within an hour's drive of Johannesburg and Pretoria. Johannesburg-based Sporting into Africa can take you on trophy hunting safaris throughout the country for anything from US$300 a day per person (this includes the services of a licensed professional hunter and the usual staff) to US$950 a day for an 18 to 28-day sable and Big Five safari. They also organise bow-hunting trips. Contact David van der Meulen, PO Box 782067, Sandton 2146, Johannesburg, tel (011) 884-4974, Cell 082 442-1906. Professional Hunters' Association of SA, tel (012) 663-2417.

In September 1996 some 12,000 pigeons took to the skies at the debut of South Africa's biggest and most lucrative pigeon race from Cradock to Gauteng, about 700km/435 miles, with R2 million in prize money being shared by the first 301 pigeons home. **Pigeon racing** is still in its infancy in South Africa, although the country is ideally suited to it with its climate, wide open spaces and relatively low-population density. There are 6000 to 8000 pigeon fanciers in the country and more than 145 clubs in Gauteng alone. Races take place most weeks during the season between June and October.

You can get more detailed information about other sports and other venues from the Greater Johannesburg Tourism Authority, tel (011) 337-6650, or the Publicity Association, tel (011) 336-4961. In Pretoria, contact Mitratour, tel (012) 313-7694/8835.

Crime and Safety

The central business district of Johannesburg is the most crime-ridden area of Gauteng and as in Pretoria and other major centres you should avoid walking in the streets alone after shopping hours or over the weekend; use taxis at night and use only those you book through a reputable taxi company; do not carry cameras or wear expensive jewellery and do not carry large amounts of cash; for shopping and other expenses use travellers' cheques or credit cards; keep your car doors locked at all times; do not stop and talk to strangers; stay away from cars parked along the road with their engines running; do not allow yourself to be distracted when buying something or when opening your purse or wallet; do not wait alone at a bus stop at night; do not carry too many packages at once. Finally, do not resist if confronted; you can always replace stolen articles.

Help and Information

In Johannesburg:

Police Flying Squad, Ambulance and Fire Brigade, tel 10111.
Crisis Centre, tel (011) 787-9555.
Radio 702 Help Line, tel (011) 331-9889.

Life Line, tel (011) 728-1347.
Poison Information Centre, tel (011) 642-2417.
Traffic Department, 24 hours, tel (011) 492-1900.
Automobile Association (AA), toll-free tel (011) 0800 01 01 01.
Citizen's Advice Bureau, tel (011) 836-0817.
St John Ambulance Service, tel (011) 403-4227.
SA Red Cross Society, tel (011) 646-1384.
AIDS Outreach, tel (011) 725-6724.
Community AIDS Info and Support Centre, tel (011) 725-6710.
Friends for Life (HIV+ and AIDS support group), tel (011) 484-6705 or (011) 650-5050.
Gay Library, 38 High Street, Berea. Open Tuesday, 7.30–9.30pm, and Saturday, 2.30–4.30pm, tel (011) 643-2311.
GLOW, PO Box 23297, Joubert Park, tel (011) 336-5081. Open from 3pm to 8pm. 24-hour AIDS Info line, toll-free 0800 01 23 22.
Life Line (AIDS), 24-hours, toll-free 0800 01 23 22.
Oasis (HIV+ and AIDS support centre), 128 8th Avenue, Mayfair, tel (011) 402-8181 or (011) 837-2026.
Organisation for Gay Sport, tel (011) 624-1460 (o) or (011) 487-3058 (h).

In Pretoria:

Police, 24-hour, toll-free, tel 10111.
SA Police Services Tourism Unit, tel (012) 324-3616, Cell 082 653-3039 for emergency calls only.
Central Police, tel (012) 353-4233 and (012) 353-4250/1/2.
Robbery Reaction Unit, tel (012) 353-4229.
Life Line, 24-hour advisory service, tel (012) 343-8888/46-0666.
Ambulance, 10177.
Fire Brigade, tel (012) 323-2781.
AIDS Programme, tel (012) 325-5100.
Gay and Lesbian Organisation of Pretoria, tel (012) 46-9888 or 325-6664. Support group, tel (012) 341-7110.
Gay Help Line, tel (012) 46-2336.

TOURIST INFORMATION

Gauteng Tourism Agency, tel (011) 836-5060, fax (011) 836-8558.
Johannesburg Metropolitan Tourist Association, PO Box 4580, Johannesburg 2000, tel (011) 337-6650, fax (011) 333-7272, e-mail brebnor@iafrica.com, web site http://osz.iafrica.com80/travel/safrica/gauteng/jnbpub.htm
Contact the *Johannesburg Publicity Association* at: Johannesburg International Airport, tel (011) 970-1220, fax (011) 394-1508; and City Centre, tel (011) 336-4961, fax (011) 336-4965.
East Rand Tourism Association, tel (011) 917-1931, fax (011) 917-5117; Western Gauteng, tel (011) 412-2701, fax (011) 412-3663; Southern Gauteng, tel (016) 81-0165/6, fax (016) 33-8801.

Northern Gauteng Tourism, tel (012) 313-7694, fax (012) 313-8460.
Pretoria Tourist Information Bureau, situated in the *Tourist Rendezvous Travel Centre*, at the corner of Prinsloo and Vermeulen streets, in the central area of the city. Tel (012) 323-1222 and (012) 313-7694/7980, fax (012) 313-8460. The Rendezvous is a one-stop to check out and book accommodation, car hire, tours, game reserves, air, sea and land travel, entertainment and everything else you might want to know.

Alberton, tel (011) 907-9710.
Benoni, tel (011) 422-3651, fax (011) 421-6462.

Boksburg, tel (011) 899-4256, fax (011) 917-3671.
Broederstroom, tel (01205) 51003, fax (01205) 51201.
Bronkhorstspruit, tel (01212) 20061, fax (01212) 20641.
Carletonville, tel (01491) 72131, fax (01491) 91105.
Cullinan, tel (012) 313-7694.
Hartbeespoort, tel (01211) 30037.
Heidelberg, tel (0151) 3111.
Krugersdorp, tel (011) 953-3727, fax (011) 660-4865.
Magaliesburg, tel (0142) 77-1432.
Meyerton, tel (016) 62-0060, fax (016) 62-2791.
Midrand, tel (011) 314-2320.
Muldersdrift, tel (011) 957-3254, fax (01205) 51201.
Pretoria, tel (012) 313-8259/7694/7980, fax (012) 313-8460.
Randfontein, tel (011) 412-2701.
Roodepoort, tel (011) 672-9503, fax (011) 672-9501.
Sandton, tel (011) 881-6911.
Vanderbijlpark, tel (016) 33-2222, fax (016) 33-8644.

Mpumalanga

The Big Five

Mpumalanga, Zulu for 'the place where the sun rises', should be on your destination list if you are a lover of wildlife and the great outdoors. The matchless beauty of the lowveld and the soaring escarpment of the Drakensberg offer exceptional opportunities for hiking, climbing, bird-watching, fishing, horse riding and dozens of other leisure pursuits in a region of panoramic passes, valleys and canyons, rivers, waterfalls and forests. Fascinating little towns and villages abound, among them old gold rush towns of the 1880s such as Barberton and Pilgrim's Rest, and the region is full of haunting names from this wild era — Eureka City Pass, Starvation Creek, Devil's Office, Valley of Death and Revolver Creek. This is also big game country, the land of the Big Five and the setting for more than 70 game parks and conservation areas teeming with birds and animals. Foremost among them is the renowned Kruger National Park and its luxurious satellite private game reserves, where it might cost you an arm and a leg (but only when you get the bill). Close to the Park towns such as Hazyview, Sabie and White River provide attractive, comfortable hotels, inns, guest and country houses, camping and caravanning sites and other accommodation.

Mpumalanga is the smallest of South Africa's nine provinces — 81,816sq km/ 31,589 sq — and with 2,900,000 people the least populated. Nelspruit is the capital, a sophisticated town offering high-quality amenities and entertainment and a useful base for exploring the region. Main economic centres are Middelburg and Witbank in the west, White River in the east and Ermelo and the more industrialised Trichardt-Evander-Kinross-Secunda complex in the south. Other important towns are Standerton, Piet Retief, Barberton and Sabie. Occupying much of the former Eastern Transvaal, the province is a mix of the middleveld, a highveld plateau with an altitude of between 1300m to 1700m, the bushveld to the north and at the foot of the escarpment a sub-tropical lowveld. In the south-eastern corner of the province, the Songimvelo Game Reserve straddles the lowveld, escarpment and highveld, with bushveld elements to stir the pot. This makes it a unique reserve of mixed landscapes and an unusual range of weather conditions. From the reaches of Gauteng the middleveld stretches eastwards for hundreds of kilometres. Witbank, the first major town in this region, is the centre of the local coal-mining industry, while the Botshabelo Mission Station near Middelburg is a reminder of the days when the African veld was frontier territory. Peaceful, spacious and invigorating, the region has numerous dams and rivers for boating and angling. The region is the home of the Ndebele people, noted for their strikingly attractive dress, characterised by vivid colours, metal rings and beaded hoops. They are also known for the exceptional quality of their beadwork and the colourful, geometric designs on the walls of their houses.

To the east, the brisk cool highlands around Belfast, Dullstroom, Machadadorp and Lydenburg comprise one of the few remaining natural highveld areas and provide well stocked trout streams as well as spectacular scenery. In the north-east, the grasslands climb towards the mountains, ending in an immense and breathtaking escarpment noted for its wild beauty. The escarpment plunges, with startling abruptness in some places, hundreds of metres to the low-lying lowveld. North-west of Graskop, God's Window provides a seemingly boundless view across miles of forested mountains and fertile lowlands. Further north is one of the wonders of Africa, the magnificent Blyde River Canyon.

The lowveld is rich with memories and relics of its exploring, pioneering and mining history and it is intensely evocative of the old Africa. Barberton, made famous by Sir Percy Fitzpatrick's book *Jock of the Bushveld* and the centre of riotous gold rush days, was the site of the Transvaal's first stock exchange. The highveld south of the main N4 route has rich historical associations and many tourist attractions; it also offers an alternative route to KwaZulu-Natal. There are a number of battlefields in this region and Ermelo, a mining and agricultural centre, has attractions ranging from the corbelled huts of the vanished Leghoya-Tlokoa tribes to well preserved Bushman paintings.

The fortunes of Mpumalanga are due for a change as the Maputo Development Corridor, South Africa's first attempt at genuine regional economic co-operation, takes shape to improve the infrastructure of the area and revitalise old trade links with the Mozambique capital of Maputo. Existing roads will be upgraded, a multi-million rand toll road will link Witbank to Maputo, and South Africa is helping its poverty-stricken neighbour to build a railway from the South African border to Maputo and upgrade its run-down harbour.

NELSPRUIT

Nelspruit, the capital of Mpumalanga, is a neat, prosperous and friendly city in park-like surroundings in the fertile valley of the Crocodile River. It is a thriving commercial and administrative centre of a vast citrus-growing area, from where good roads radiate to many of the most beautiful and interesting parts of the lowveld, among them vast game sanctuaries, craggy mountains and quaint historic towns. It is 330km/205 miles from Gauteng and hotels, caravan parks and camp sites in and around the town make it a convenient stop-over or base. Nelspruit was named after three Nel brothers, Gert, Louis and Andries, who used the land here as winter grazing for their cattle during the 1870s. They camped at Nel's spruit (Nel's stream), from where the town grew up around the railhead during the 1890s and gradually developed into the main service centre of the lowveld.

GETTING AROUND

Nelspruit Airport is 8km/5 miles from town, with daily scheduled flights from Johannesburg and Durban, tel (013) 741-1238. There is no regular bus service to town, but **shuttle services** are operated locally by *City Bug*, tel (013) 755-3792, and *Lowveld Shuttle Service*, tel (013) 755-2205, Cell 082 447-6787. Major **car hire** companies have rental vehicles at the airport, among them *Budget*, tel (013) 741-3871, and *Avis*, tel (013) 741-1087.

Air. *Metavia Airlines* has daily return flights between Johannesburg and Nelspruit, Johannesburg and Maputo, Nelspruit and Maputo. Contact PO Box 1023, Nelspruit 1200, tel (013) 741-3141; *Nelair Charters* will fly you anywhere, tel (013) 741-2012, fax (013) 741-2013, Cell 082 444-7994/5/6; for flights over the scenic lowveld, *Lowveld Helicopter Services*, Nelspruit Airport, tel (013) 741-4651.

Rail. For train services contact Spoornet, tel (013) 288-2203/2257.

Intercity Buses. *Greyhound*, tel (01311) 25134; *Translux*, tel (011) 774-3333; and *Pro Tours*, tel (01311) 52901.

ACCOMMODATION

In the centre of Nelspruit the old town hall has been converted into the *Hotel Promenade* in the Promenade Shopping Centre. Rates on application to PO Box 4355, Nelspruit 1200, tel (013) 753-3000, fax (013) 752-5533.

Crocodile Country Inn, Schagen, is a three-star establishment 26km/16 miles from Nelspruit where it costs R180 (£24/$39.60) a night per person sharing. Contact PO Box 496, Nelspruit 1200, tel (013) 753-3000

There are 18 B&Bs in Nelspruit, among them *Loerie's Call*, 2 du Preez Street, tel (013) 752-4844; Shandon Lodge, 1 Saturn Street, tel (013) 744-9934; and Pension Hans Schmidt, 21 Von Braun Street, tel (013) 744-9984. All cost about R120 a night per person sharing.

The local *Youth Hostel* is *Laeveld Verblyfsentrum*, on Old Pretoria Road, tel (013) 753-3380.

Local **caravan and camping parks** include:

Polka Dot, N4 Johannesburg Road, tel (013) 755-6173;
Nelspruit Holiday Resort, Graniet Street, tel (013) 741-3253;
Rippling Waters, tel (01311) 27847.

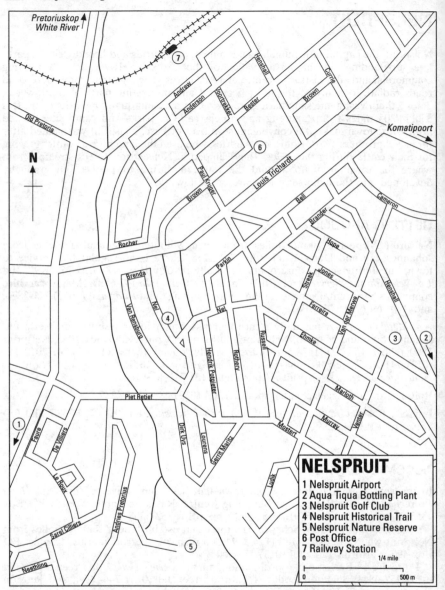

NELSPRUIT

1 Nelspruit Airport
2 Aqua Tiqua Bottling Plant
3 Nelspruit Golf Club
4 Nelspruit Historical Trail
5 Nelspruit Nature Reserve
6 Post Office
7 Railway Station

EATING AND DRINKING

Nelspruit has the usual selection eating places and pubs. There are 20 restaurants in the town where steaks are the staple, with trout from the many rivers, lakes and streams a close second. The *Wild Horse Restaurant* in Kaapsehoop, along a lovely hilly road from Nelspruit, is worth the drive. You will also probably see the wild horses for which the area is known, tel (0134) 734-4161.

EXPLORING

Aqua Tiqua Bottling Plant. About 30 different brands of water are bottled and sold in South Africa, but the locals swear that the crystal-clear spring water bottled at source among the granite rocks of the farm Vierhoek here is the best of them all, tel (01311) 49986.

Lowveld Botanical Gardens. These are set in stunning scenery on the banks of the Crocodile River, 3km/2 miles outside the town. The gardens house one of the most comprehensive cycad collections in the world and you can also see a fine herbarium and one of the country's best fern and tree fern collections, as well as a Rain Forest, 500 indigenous tree species and rare lowveld plants. A feature of the gardens is a waterfall and cascades. Many pleasant trails meander through the garden and you can get a trail map at the entrance. Open daily, 8am–5pm, tel (013) 752-5531.

Nelspruit Historical Trail. Stretching from the Promenade Centre to the Civic Centre, the one-hour historical route brings interesting facets of Nelspruit's past to life. A restored ox-wagon in the library gardens will give you an idea of how the founding fathers got around. The plant sundial in Louis Trichardt Street and the Art Gallery are also worth a visit.

Nelspruit Nature Reserve. Among several walks through the 50-hectare reserve, lasting from one to six hours, the Green Heritage Hiking Trail offers a pleasant, relaxing way to enjoy the indigenous vegetation, a wide diversity of birds and small antelope.

MIDDLEVELD

The middleveld lies in south-east Mpumalanga between the cold highveld and the hot lowveld and has a more temperate climate. Summer rainfall averages 800–1000mm (32–39 inches), while winter frost is common in the west on high ground. The region has a wealth of plants, birds and animals and is ideal for hikes and rambles. Waterfalls are plentiful, filling cool pools along the many trails and there are also relaxing and invigorating hot mineral springs in the area.

ACCOMMODATION

Avontuur Rest Camp, self-catered rondavels and camp sites, with prolific birdlife on hiking trails along Buffel River. 2km/1 mile from Badplaas on the R38 to Carolina. Contact PO Box 8, Badplaas 1190, tel (017) 844-1411.

Aventura Badplaas, self-catering family hotel and 250 caravan/camp sites. Hot mineral spring baths are the resort's main feature, as well as cool pools, hydro spa, playground, walks and sports. Satour self-catering establishment of the year 1996. From R180 (£24/$39.60) a night for a one-bed unit to R320 for two beds. Contact PO Box 15, Badplaas 1190, tel (017) 844-1020.

Critchley Hackle Lodge is a three-star country hotel where trout fishing is usually the passion of its guests. R350 a night per person sharing. Contact PO Box 141, Dullstroom 1110, tel (01325) 40415, fax (01325) 40246.

Valley of the Rainbow is a 1200ha/2965 acre private wilderness reserve in the Steenkamps mountains between Dullstroom and Roossenekal offering hiking, fly-fishing, abseiling, horse-riding and clay pigeon shooting. There is a guesthouse and a luxury tented camp in the mountains. Rates from R350 per person per night sharing. Contact tel (011) 782-5358, e-mail rainbow@cis.co.za

Boven Trout Lodge, self-catering, 10 rooms, communal kitchen. Trout fishing, rod hire and tuition. Contact PO Box 50, Waterval Boven 1195, tel (013262) ask for 26 or 253, Cell 083 227-3755.

Redwing Trout Farm, between Machadodorp and Waterval Boven, lies on top of the escarpment and offers angling in a choice of a dozen well-stocked dams. There is also game viewing, hiking and rock-climbing in the spectacular mountain gorges. Spring water is so pure it does not even have to be chemically tested before being bottled and distributed. Contact George and Greta Havermahl, tel (013252) ask for 5513, or for fax direct dial tel (01325) 31118.

Walkerson's, near Dullstroom, was the runner-up in the 1996 Satour Hotel of the Year awards. It has a well stocked cellar, daily game-viewing and bird-watching drives through the mountain reserve, and forest and river walks. If you fish, there are stocked lakes and long stretches of private river. Equipment — and even tuition — is provided (the chef will prepare the ones that did not get away). Tel (01325) 40246, fax (01325) 40260.

Dullstroom Caravan Park offers fishing at the dam, fishing tackle available in the village. Contact PO Box Dullstroom 1110, tel (01325) 40151.

EATING AND DRINKING

Whistle and Trout restaurant/pub/museum, in Waterval Boven opposite the railway station. Quaint 1896 stone house restaurant. Open Tuesday to Sunday from 8am. Trout dishes and speciality pies, tel (013262) ask for 699.

Ye Wayside Tearoom, opposite Krugerhof Museum in Waterval Onder. Specialises in trout dishes. They also have a large variety of curios. Open seven days a week, tel (013262) ask for 1712.

EXPLORING

Badplaas. The mineral spa at Badplaas between Carolina and Barberton is set in picturesque surroundings. Accommodation and sports facilities, including a swimming pool, are available. An attractive 1000-hectare nature reserve supports species such as red hartebeest, black wildebeest, blesbok, eland and springbok. There are trails for walking and horse-riding.

Botshabelo Mission Station. This colourful restored village provides glimpses of the traditional lifestyle of the South Ndebele people and the daily routine of a 19th century mission station. The name Botshabelo means 'place of refuge'. Ndebele women do beadwork and other handicrafts and paint the attractive murals that are a prominent feature of their culture. You can explore on your own or enquire at the open-air museum about guided tours, tel (0132) 23897.

Ndebele arts and crafts are also available at Papatso, an Ndebele village between Pretoria and Warmbaths and at the strikingly decorated Ndebele village near KwaMhlanga, north-east of Pretoria. This village is 35km/22 miles from Bronkhorstspruit near the entrance to Loopspruit, the only registered wine estate north of the Orange River. Tel (01212) 24303, fax (01212) 24350.

Dullstroom. Superb trout fishing is usually what brings people to this peaceful village 35km/22 miles from Lydenburg. Bird-watching and walking trails are also popular. The Steenkampsberg Nature Reserve, outside town, provides sanctuary for the rare wattled crane. Dullstroom is one of the coldest towns in South Africa and has the highest station (2076m/6811ft). It is the only place in the country where beech and elm trees grow.

Jericho Dam Nature Reserve is 76km/47 miles from Ermelo, not far from the Swaziland border. The dam is popular for competitive anglers. The reserve, which conserves an area of high altitude grassland, also features some excellent bird-watching spots. The reserve has no facilities for campers, but day visitors are welcome.

Loskop Dam Nature Reserve. One of the largest (15,000 hectares) and most beautiful of the province's reserves, the dam stretches for 23km/14 miles in the foothills of the Waterberg, between Groblersdal and Middelburg. Good angling for yellowfish, barbel, kurper and carp. Crocodiles and bilharzia are present in the water, so do not swim. A resort on the north-eastern shore has a swimming pool and water slides, and offers boating, fishing, a restaurant and accommodation. You have a good chance of seeing white rhino, giraffe, kudu, sable and smaller antelope species, as well as some 250 species of birds. It is open 24 hours a day.

Mabusa Nature Reserve. A reserve of 15,800 hectares situated on the edge of the highveld plateau 60km/37 miles north of Bronkhorstspruit and within easy reach of Johannesburg and Pretoria. The southern section of the reserve features open grassland which breaks into a network of kloofs and valleys further north. A number of antelope species have been introduced into the reserve. There is no accommodation at the reserve.

Machadodorp. This town 26km/16 miles east of Belfast is a popular health resort with hot mineral springs.

Mdala Game Reserve. An hour's drive from Pretoria, this reserve has a large walk-in aviary and a snake park. Camp sites at Mkolwane, Zwelabo and Manala offer accommodation for up to eight people; the latter two are self-catering. The Mkholwane Lodge is situated within the reserve and has six well appointed thatched cottages, a dining complex, and swimming pool, tel (013) 753-3931.

Mkhombo Nature Reserve. This is on the border of the Mdala Reserve and features a large dam with good fishing. There is a self-catering tented camp.

Nooitgedacht Dam Nature Reserve. A highveld grassland reserve 10km/6 miles from Carolina on the Komati River. Main leisure activities are yachting, fishing and camping.

SS Skosana Nature Reserve. This is a small but unusual nature reserve with guided bush walks. The three-day Tjhetjhisa Hiking Trail is in the reserve and takes two parties of eight people at any one time. The CN Mahlangu Lodge is the main base camp. The lodge has accommodation in 16 twin-bed cabins and self-catering facilities.

Verloren Valei Nature Reserve. On 5900 hectares of grassland on the Steenkamps-berg plateau north-east of Dullstroom, the area offers exceptional birdwatching. The rare Wattled Crane breeds in the area. Visitors must make arrangements to visit by contacting the Mpumalanga Parks Board. There is no accommodation.

Waterval Boven. Horse-riding and trout-fishing are popular pastimes in this region. Among a number of hiking trails, the Elandskrans Trail includes a 30-minute train ride between Waterval Boven (the name means 'above the waterfall') and Waterval Onder ('below the waterfall'). Krugerhof, at Waterval Onder, was the last residence of President Paul Kruger before he left the country for Europe.

LOWVELD

ACCOMMODATION

Blue Mountain Lodge, near Sabie in Mpumalanga, was the runner-up guest house in the 1996 Satour awards, tel/fax (013) 737-8446.

Komati River Lodge is not far from Barberton and 150km/93 miles from Nelspruit on the banks of the Komati River in Songimvelo Game Reserve, where there is birdlife in abundance and a wide variety of antelope, as well as giraffe, zebra, elephant and white rhino. Accommodation is in a tented camp. Contact PO Box 1990, Nelspruit 1200, tel (01311) 53931 ext 2202.

Jock of the Bushveld Huts, are on a litchi and mango farm where you can sleep in fully equipped, self-catering Zulu huts on the plains where old-time diggers once panned for gold. Contact PO Box 54, Barberton 1300, tel (013) 712-4002, fax (013) 712-5915, Cell 083 376-1199.

Elmwood B&B is on the Mpumalanga escarpment, with major scenic attractions all within 60km/37 mile radius. Rates R105 (£14/$23.10) per person sharing. Contact PO Box 363, Graskop 1270, tel (013) 767-1553.

Safcol runs *Hlalanathi*, a forest lodge where you can unwind in the subtropical Sabie-Hazyview Valley. This secluded retreat is situated on Safcol's Frankfort plantation and avocado farm, an hour's drive from the Kruger National Park and the Blyde River Canyon. There is ample opportunity for bird-watching, hiking and mountain biking, while fishermen can lure the trout in the Sabie River. Accommodation consists of serviced three self-contained two-bedroom rustic flats and a spacious three-bedroom house. All you need to take is charcoal and hiking boots or comfortable shoes. You can rent mountain bikes. Hlalanathi is 17km/11 miles from Sabie and 380km/236 miles from Johannesburg. Contact Private Bag X503, Sabie 1260, tel (013) 764-1058/1392, fax (013) 764-2071.

Famba Farms, set in 5000 hectares of mountainous riverine bushveld along the Crocodile River, offers self-catering accommodation in either luxury three-bed-roomed cottages, cottages sleeping four each, or hikers and mountain biker's chalets that sleep 12–16. There are also camp sites. Contact PO Box 436, Lydenburg 1120, tel (013) 51839.

Trout Hideaway. You do not have to be a fisherman to enjoy this spot between the Drakensberg and Kliprots ranges. Five dams fed by a crystal river for anglers and superb walks with a wide range of flora, birdlife, especially sunbirds. You can get fly-fishing instruction and hire tackle. Self-catering log chalets for 2 people cost from R1060 (£141/$233) for 2 nights and R3440 for 8 people. PO Box 880, Lydenburg 1120, tel/fax (013) 768-1347.

The *Royal Hotel*, is a national monument and the focal point of Pilgrim's Rest. It has been restored and furnished in its original Victorian style. It nestles in a valley alongside the meandering river where gold was discovered more than a century ago. Contact PO Box 59, Pilgrim's Rest 1290, tel (013) 768-1100, fax (013) 768-1188. Also in Pilgrim's Rest are self-catering miner's cottages. Contact Private Bag X516, Pilgrim's Rest 1290, tel (01315) 81211, fax (01315) 81113.

Mount Sheba Hotel. 600m above Pilgrim's rest is this 4-star hotel in a private nature reserve offering luxury accommodation on a dinner, B&B basis for R395 per person sharing. Nature trails and towering rain forests. Contact PO Box 100, Pilgrim's Rest 1290, tel/fax (01315) 81241. For reservations tel (011) 788-1258/9, fax (011) 788-0739, toll-free 0801 11 44 48.

Fern Tree Park. Three-star Satour-graded cottages with a turn of the century mining settlement theme. Fully equipped, self-contained accommodation. Close to Sabie waterfalls and the Kruger National Park. Also near the Loerie, Fanie Botha and Prospectors' hiking trails. Rates from R174 (£23/$38) for two people to R278 for six.

Pensioners get 10 per cent discount out of season. Contact PO Box 145, Sabie 1260, tel/fax (01315) 42215.

Shunter's Express. 16 old railway coaches provide the accommodation and dining-rooms. Dam abundantly stocked with bream and large-mouth bass. Hiking and horse trails. Bed and brunch R150 per person; Dinner, bed and brunch R175. Self-catering boathouse R200 for up to 4 people. PO Box 2696, White River 1240, tel/fax (013) 764-1777.

Cybele Forest Lodge. Once described by the British *Tatler* as 'the smartest hideaway in South Africa' and one of the 50 best hotels in the world, this is an old hunting lodge on 121 hectares of timber and coffee plantations. The luxury accommodation is limited to 28 people and costs from R635 per person for a cottage, inclusive of dinner, B&B, to R1550 per person for a suite with its own private pool. Contact PO Box 346, White River 1240, tel (013) 750-0511, fax (013) 751-2839.

Bushveld Breakaways offers a variety of bushveld destinations, from up-market and low tariff game lodges, to rustic bush camps and self-catering retreats. Contact PO Box 2703, White River 1240, tel (013) 750-1998, fax (013) 750-0383.

Mpumalanga Guest and Private House Reservations has a wide choice of guest and private homes. They are all Satour-accredited and range from budget to ultra-luxurious. Accommodation on game farms, hunting safaris and plane charter can also be arranged. Rates from R100 to R400 per person sharing. There is no charge for making reservations. Contact them at (0135) 71032, Cell 083 228-9011, or (012) 46-5327 and (012) 87-1931.

Crystal Springs Mountain Lodge was runner-up in the 1996 Satour hotel awards, and is set in a game reserve above Pilgrim's Rest, tel/fax (013) 768-1153.

Backpackers include *Jock of the Bushveld*, Main Road (behind Wimpy Bar), Sabie 1260, tel (013) 42178, and *Kruger Park Backpackers*, Main Road, Hazyview 1242, PO Box 214, Hazyview 1242, tel/fax (0137) 67224.

Caravan parks:

Siesta Caravan Park and Holiday Resort, Lydenburg, tel (01323) 2886;
Uitspan Caravan Park and Rondavels, Lydenburg, tel (01323) 2914;
Pilgrim's Rest Caravan Park, tel (01315) 81367;
Aventura Blydepoort, Blyde River Canyon, tel (01323) 80155;
Municipal Tourist Park, Graskop, tel (01315) 71091;
Castle Rock, Sabie, tel (01315) 41241/6;
Merry Pebbles, Sabie, tel (01315) 42266, fax (01315) 41629;
Barberton Caravan and Chalet Park, tel (01314) 23323;
Aventura Loskopdam, tel (01202) 3075;
Aventura Swadini, tel (01528) 35141.

Private Reserves

Exeter, a small private exclusive game lodge in 65,000ha of Sabie Sands Game Reserve, comprises 10 thatched chalets. After a game drive you can enjoy breakfast on Leopard Lookout and dinner in the boma with a crackling fire and traditional African dancing. Leadwood Lodge is self-catering and has five double suites, while Hunters Lodge, also self-catering, offers five luxury bedrooms. Central reservations, PO Box 373, Morningside 2057, Gauteng, tel (011) 884-6438, fax (011) 783-1631.

Londolozi. This private game reserve adjacent to the Kruger National Park — its name is Zulu for 'Protector of living things' — ensures an intimate and ultra-luxurious African bush experience. Game drives (including night safaris) are led by experienced game rangers in open Land Rovers, and you're likely to end up a stone's throw (not advisable) from the Big Five. Contact PO Box 1211, Sunninghill Park 2157, Gauteng, tel (011) 803-8421, fax (011) 803-1810.

Sabi Sabi private game reserve lies in the Sabie Sand where you can still observe the natural relationship between predator and prey. Sabi Sabi has three lodges.

Central reservations, PO Box 52665, Saxonwold 2132, Gauteng, tel (011) 483-3939, fax (011) 483-3799.

Savanna Tented Safari Lodge is in the Sabie Sands reserve. This is sleeping under canvas with a difference; the top of the accommodation is tented, the bottom brick. There are four *en suite* tents which, at the most, can accommodate only 8. Contact tel (013) 751-2205, fax (013) 751-2204.

Inyati Game Lodge is set in 65,000 hectares of bushveld, in the Sabi Sand Game Reserve. Inyati means buffalo in Shangaan and the reserve is home to this bellicose member of the Big Five. A night at Inyati will cost you R850 (£113/$187) per person sharing a double; from October 1997 this increases to R1350 each. Contact Inyati Game Lodge, PO Box 38838, Booysens 2016, Gauteng, tel (011) 880-5907/5950, fax (011) 788-2406.

Mala Mala is one of South Africa's most exclusive and best known game reserves, and borders the Kruger National Park. It is in 45,000 acres of pristine bush, and the Big Five can often be seen at close quarters on guided drives. Accommodation is in spacious, air-conditioned, thatched chalets. Dinners are served in a reed-enclosed *boma* around a log fire. It is about as up-market as you can get at R2700 per person per day sharing in the main camp, although this drops to R975 for Harry's bush camp. Contact PO Box 2575, Randburg 2125, Gauteng, tel (011) 789-2677, fax (011) 886-4382, e-mail jhb@malamala.co.za

EATING AND DRINKING

The Diggers Den pub and restaurant and historic bar at the Royal Hotel, Pilgrim's Rest, is something you should not miss, tel (01315) 81100. Other good places for foodies are the Chandelier Restaurant at Mount Sheba, Pilgrim's Rest, tel (01315) 81214; the Inn on Robber's Pass, Lydenburg, tel (01315) 81491; and the restaurant at the Sabie Country Club, on Main Street, Sabie, tel (01315) 42282.

EXPLORING

Barberton. The town, 350km/218 miles east of Pretoria, developed 10 years after the first traces of gold were discovered in the area in 1874. By 1888, the boom was over, and a mass exodus took place. There are still many reminders of the early gold rush days. Belhaven, one of Barberton's most elegant old buildings, is now a museum furnished in the style of a wealthy Edwardian family home. Two other museums depicting the early days are Fernlea House and Stopforth House. The only known verdite deposits in the world are found in the rocks of the Barberton district. Powdered verdite has been used for centuries by *sangomas* (traditional healers) to increase fertility. Barberton is the departure point for hikers following the Gold Nugget, Pioneer and Umvoti trails, the same paths that were used by early miners.

Blyde River Canyon Nature Reserve. The Blyde River Canyon stretching for 26km/16 miles and its 29,000 hectares reserve take in some of the most dramatic scenery in the country, set along the Greater Drakensberg Escarpment. The weird geological features at Bourke's Luck Potholes, the Three Rondavels and the breathtaking view from God's Window are all easily accessible from Graskop. There are a number of hiking trails in the reserve catering for all ages and levels of fitness, including the 65km/40 mile Blyderivierspoort Hiking Trail, which starts at God's Window and takes five days to complete, tel (01315) 81216.

Crocodile River. This is one of many rivers with this name, testifying to a time when this mighty reptile was found wherever it was damp enough. This one still has lots of them. Mpumalanga is a major tributary of the Komati River which runs thorugh Mozambique to the Indian Ocean. It rises north of Dullstroom and flows 306km/190 miles, mainly eastwards, to the confluence at Komatipoort.

Graskop is perched at 1430m on the very edge of the Drakensberg escarpment. From here a 100km/62 miles round trip will ensure that you see some spectacular natural features. If you are pressed for time a whistle-stop tour of the following places can be done in a weekend. Mpumalanga's Panorama Route is punctuated by The Pinnacle, God's Window, Wonder View, Lisbon Falls, Bourke's Luck Potholes, and the two viewpoints into the Blyde River Canyon, Lowveld Viewpoint and three Rondavels Viewpoint. Westward is the historical gold mining town of Pilgrim's Rest, the only town in the country to be declared a national monument, and just over Robber's Pass is Mount Sheba Nature Reserve and the Orighstad Dam Nature Reserve. 30km/19 miles to the south lies Sabie with its multitude of waterfalls — Sabie Falls, Bridal Veil Falls, Horseshoe Falls, Lone Creek Falls — and its Forestry Museum. On the way to Sabie is the Natural Bridge, Maria Shires Falls, Forest Falls, the Jock of the Bushveld monument, Mac Mac Falls and Mac Mac Pools. Beyond Sabie, on the way to Lydenburg, is the Long Tom Pass with its magnificent views. The 1000m/3281ft drop to the Kruger National Park in the east takes you through the only avalanche bridge in the country on the scenic Kowyn's Pass.

Hazyview. The town is in the Sabie River Valley. It is close to the Kruger and has several lodges, hotels and holiday resorts catering for Kruger visitors.

Kaapsehoop. This quaint historical village high in the hills between Nelspruit and Barberton has a fine panoramic view of the lowveld. Wild horses frequent the district and blue swallows are regular visitors from September to April.

Komatipoort. This agricultural centre is the gateway to Mozambique. Komatipoort offers an ideal entrance to the Kruger via the Crocodile River Gate. Situated as the confluence of the Crocodile and Komati rivers, the area has some of the best tiger fishing in the country.

Lebombo Mountains. Zulu for 'Big Nose', this range extends some 800km/497 miles from beyond the Mkuzi River in the south, along the Kruger National Park to the Limpopo River. It generally follows the borders between South Africa and Mozambique and between Swaziland and Mozambique.

Lydenburg. 320km/199 miles north-east of Johannesburg the town gets its name from the Dutch 'town of suffering' because of the disease and hardship suffered by the early settlers. Set against a backdrop of hills and forests, Lydenburg's major features are its well preserved old buildings. The Gustav Klingbiel Reserve, east of town, has antelope and more than 100 bird species. It is the site of archaeological Late Iron Age ruins and the Lydenburg Museum is at the entrance to the reserve. The Long Tom Pass, the highest road in South Africa, traverses the escarpment near Mount Anderson (2284m/7493ft) and links Lydenburg with Sabie. The highest point on the pass is 2149m and the views are spectacular. The Lydenburg museum portrays local history from the arrival of the Pedi tribe, the Voortrekkers, the story of six wars and ends with the Lydenburg of today, tel (01361) 2031.

Mac Mac Pools and Falls. Idyllic crystal-clear pools for swimming. About a mile further north, two waterfalls plunge into a densely wooded chasm. The 69km/43 mile Prospector's Trail from the Mac Mac Forest Station to Bourke's Luck Potholes takes five days to complete. Open daily from 7am to 5pm, admission R3 (40p/65 cents) per person, tel (01315) 41058.

Mount Sheba Nature Reserve. Best known for its indigenous forest, one of the few left in the region. More than 100 tree species have been identified, including yellowwood, white stinkwood, Cape chestnut and mountain cedar. Forest mammals such as red duiker, bushbuck and samango monkey are occasionally seen in the 400-hectare reserve.

Mthethomusha Game Reserve. In mountainous country north of the Crocodile River on the south-western corner of the Kruger National Park, this 7200-hectare reserve is owned by the Mpakeni community. It is home to the Big Five, along with numerous other bushveld mammals and birds. Several Iron Age settlement sites and some excellent examples of Bushman rock paintings can be visited. Accommodation is limited to Southern Sun's Bongani Lodge, which can arrange guided walks and game drives.

Ohrigstad Dam Nature Reserve. This dam offers exceptional fishing for yellowtail, catfish, tilapia, and carp. Camping sites are available with rustic facilities. There is no running water. Take your own food and supplies.

Echo Caves. These caves with their interesting dripstone formations are a national monument. There is an open-air museum and an art gallery on the way to the caves. The caves are open daily from 8am to 5pm and guides are available.

Pilgrim's Rest. Picturesque town 15km/9 miles north-west of Graskop and 45km/28 miles north of Sabie. So named because here, after so many false trails, gold prospectors found gold in 1873 and a place of rest. The village is a living museum frozen in time. Many restored miners' houses serve as shops. The Alanglade House Museum offers guided tours of the former mine manager's house, exquisitely furnished in Victorian, Edwardian and Art Deco styles. The Diggings Museum, just over half a mile south of town on the Graskop road, has conducted tours of gold-panning activities. A popular tourist destination and definitely worth visiting.

Sabie. The town began life in the 1880s as a gold-mining camp but today is the centre of the largest man-made forest in South Africa. The Cultural Historical Forestry Museum houses exhibits depicting various aspects of South Africa's forestry industry. It is open weekdays, 9am–4pm, Saturdays, 9am–1pm. Some 12km/8 miles of the Sabie River have been reserved for trout fishing, which is stocked with rainbow trout. Brown trout are found in the upper reaches. For information about licences tel (01311) 32686.

Songimvelo Game Reserve. This conserves 49,000 hectares of bushveld, middleveld and grassland on the Barberton mountain slopes against the Swaziland border. 45 species of animals and more than 300 species of birds along with numerous reptile and tree species make this one of the very special destinations in Mpumalanga. Locals call it one of South Africa's best kept secrets.

Sterkspruit Nature Reserve. This mountain escarpment reserve, 10km/6 miles south-east of Lydenburg towards the Long Tom Pass, is the starting point for the Rooikat Hiking Trail which takes you 32km/20 miles across some spectacular mountain scenery via three well-equippped rest camps.

Sudwala Caves. A series of caverns in the Houtbosloop Valley 33km/21 miles from Nelspruit. In the 19th century, the caves were used as a fortress by a Swazi king and take their name from one of his captains, Sudwala. The temperature stays at a constant 18°C throughout the year and even at some distance from the entrance, cool air from an unknown source permeates the passages. The caves are illuminated and spotlights throw into relief the strange formations created by water and erosion over the centuries. Watch out for the Screaming Monster, a huge calcium carbonate formation believed once to have been worshipped by primitive cave dwellers. Guided tours are offered seven days a week from 8.30am to 4.30pm. The six-hour Crystal Cave Tour takes place on the last Saturday of the month. At the adjacent PR Owen Dinosaur Park, full-scale replicas of long-extinct giant reptiles are on display, tel (013) 733-4152.

White River. The streets of White River are lined with date palms, bougainvillaea and jacaranda trees. About 3km from the town, Rottcher Wineries, in Nutcracker Valley, offers cellar tours which will introduce you to their unusual orange wines and liqueurs, tel (013) 751-3884.

KRUGER NATIONAL PARK

Mpumalanga shares this famous game sanctuary, the largest in the world, equally with neighbouring Northern Province, with the Olifants River running east to west through the park to form a natural boundary. Each province has access through four of the park's eight main gates. This is Africa in the raw — apart from the tarred and neatly gravelled roads that enable you to comfortably tour the park and get eyeball to eyeball with the Big Five (elephant, lion, leopard, rhino and buffalo) and other wild inhabitants. The Kruger lies in the north-east corner of the country between the Crocodile and Sabie rivers, and the Lebombo and Drakensberg mountains. It is 350km/217 miles long from north to south and has a maximum width of 90km/56 miles. It covers 20,000sq km/7722sq miles, roughly the size of Wales or Massachusetts. The Kruger is the ultimate in do-it-yourself game-viewing. The park has five major rivers flowing through it and has such a vast land area that there are distinct ecosystems to which different species of wildlife are naturally attracted. From south to north the four main gates into the park from Mpumalanga are the Crocodile Bridge Gate to Lower Sabie Camp, the Malelane Gate to Berg-en-Dal Camp, the Numbi Gate to Pretorius Camp, and the Paul Kruger Gate to the main rest camp at Skukuza. All these gates are easily reached from Nelspruit and there are daily Comair flights from Johannesburg to the main camp at Skukuza.

South of the Olifants River and extending east towards the Lebombo Mountains are large tracts of knobthorn and marula savanna, which provide excellent grazing for zebra, wildebeest, impala and buffalo, and their attendant predators, the hyena, cheetah, leopard, lion and wild dog. West of this area lies the wettest and most mountainous region of the park, where the bushwillow woodlands around Pretoriuskop and Malelane are the habitat of browsers such as giraffe, duiker, kudu and impala, as well as a significant population of white, or square-lipped, rhino. The wooded south-western regions are favoured by rhino and buffalo, while the grassy cover interspersed with acacia in the south east attracts herds of impala, zebra, wildebeest, giraffe, and black rhino. These antelope also attract the big cats. Another area is made up of river systems throughout the park where the greatest variety of vegetation is found and favoured by grazers, browsers and predators, especially the wary leopard. Within the entire park you will find an unparalleled diversity of wildlife, with an impressive 114 reptile, 147 mammal, and more than 500 bird species — the feathered Big Five are the saddlebilled stork, lappetfaced vulture, martial eagle, kori bustard and ground hornbill — as well as more than 300 different types of trees and shrubs and some 227 different kinds of butterfly. The park has an embarrassment of around 7800 elephant and authorities have been upsetting people by periodically culling them, although rangers are experimenting with jumbo-size contraceptive vaccinations to avoid shooting them. Game viewing is easiest in winter, although many people prefer the lusher vegetation of summer. The park falls within a summer rainfall area. Summer temperatures sometimes exceed 40°C/104°F, but winters are generally mild and frost-free.

Wilderness Trails. Six of the seven guided trails throughout the park are in the Mpumalanga section — Bushman, Wolhuter, Napi, Metsimetsi, Sweni, and Olifants. The Nyalala Trail is near Punda Maria in the north. Up to eight people are allowed on each trail. You must be between 12 and 60 and reasonably fit. The trails last three nights and two days and start either on Sunday or Wednesday. There has not been a single fatality among hikers since the trails started in the late 1970s — although 16 animals, mainly elephant and rhino, have been shot to protect trailists. Rangers

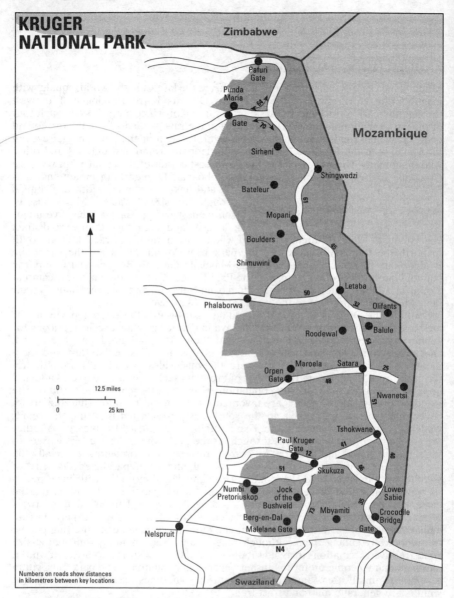

accompany you, bearing .458 Winchesters, just in case. Trails cost R935 a person, which includes all meals. Demand for trails is excessive and preference is given to written applications received up to 13 months in advance. There are no trails in December, it is too hot. Best months to go are during winter from July to September when the highest the mercury will rise will be about 30°C/86°F and the nights are cold. Good reference books are essential for the Kruger. Recommended are Ken Newman's *Birds of the Kruger National Park;* Piet van Wyk's *Field Guide to the Trees of the Kruger National Park;* Chris and Tilde Stuart's *Field Guide to the Mammals of Southern Africa; Kruger National Park Questions & Answers,* by PF Fourie; and *Kruger National Park: A Visitor's Guide,* by Leo Braack.

Camps and modern amenities take up only 3 per cent of the park, but they provide comfortable accommodation from tents and rustic rondavels to 6-bed family cottages. The following are in the Mpumalanga section of the Kruger:

Rest Camps. All accommodation is provided with bedding, towels and soap. Services at most of the rest camps include electricity, a first-aid centre, fuel supply, restaurant, swimming pool, laundry, shops, barbecue facilities and public telephones. All the camps are fenced.

Balule is a small camp 11km/7 miles from Olifants Camp. Consists of six three-bed huts with public ablution facilities and camping and caravan facilities.

Berg-en-Dal, on the banks of the Matjulu Spruit. A wide range of accommodation, from houses to six-bed and three-bed huts. All have en-suite facilities, air-conditioning and kitchens. Some are equipped for the handicapped. Camping and caravanning sites and a swimming pool are available. There is a rhino walking trail in the camp and night drives are available.

Crocodile Bridge lies on the Crocodile River, not far from the Mozambique border. It consists of three-bed huts with an equipped kitchen, air-conditioning and en-suite facilities. Some are equipped for the handicapped. Caravan and camp sites available.

Lower Sabie is on the banks of a dam on the Sabie River. There is a house and two cottages, as well as other various-sized cottages. Some are equipped for the handicapped. Caravanning and camping available. Night drives.

Orpen is a peaceful little camp at the Orpen Gate of six-bed cottages to smaller two-bed cottages, which share ablution facilities. A communal freezer is available. There is no restaurant, but a small shop sells basic foodstuffs.

Maroela, 4km/2.5 miles from Orpen Camp, is the only camping area where there is no other accommodation. There is a communal kitchen and an ablution block.

Pretoriuskop is the oldest rest camp in the park and has a milder climate than the rest of the park. It comprises houses which accommodate up to nine people and smaller cottages and huts. All are air-conditioned. There is a swimming pool. Night drives. Sabie walking trail in the camp. Caravanning and camping.

Satara lies in the knobthorn veld which attracts the largest concentrations of game. The camp consists of houses accommodating up to nine people and smaller cottages and huts. All are air-conditioned and some are suitable for the handicapped. Night drives. Caravan and camp sites available.

Skukuza. This is the Kruger Park's headquarters and the usual first port of call for visitors. It takes its name from the sobriquet of the Kruger's first warden, Col J Stevenson-Hamilton, who was called Skukuza ('to scrape clean') because he cleared the region of poachers. The camp is situated on the banks of the Sabie River and is said to have the largest thatched building in the world. There are 200 huts and cottages. Furnished tents with 2 to 4 beds at R100 (£13.35/$22) a night and camp and caravan sites are available. Night drives. The camp has a bank, a post office, and a well stocked minimarket-cum-curio shop. The Stevenson-Hamilton Memorial Library and museum are well worth visiting.

Bushveld Camps

Biyamiti is on the bank of the Biyamiti River, about 41km/26 miles from the Malelane Gate and 26km/16 miles from Crocodile Bridge Gate, in the south. It consists of 15 family cottages with barbecue facilities at each hut, a gas stove and fridge.

Talamati is on the bank of the Nwaswitsontso Spruit, about 31km/19 miles from Orpen Gate and has similar facilities to those at Biyamiti.

Jakkalsbessie is on the banks of the Sabie River, about 7km/4 miles from Skukuza and near the airfield. It comprises eight family cottages, one of which is suitable for the handicapped.

Private Camps

Malelane is 3km/2 miles from the Malelane Gate on the Berg-en-Dal road and accommodates 18 visitors in two three-bed huts and three four-bed huts. There is a communal dining-room and kitchen.

Jock of the Bushveld is 40km/25 miles from Berg-en-Dal rest camp on the Skukuza road. It can accommodate up to 12. It consists of three two-bedroom family huts, with *en suite* facilities and a dining-room. A communal kitchen is provided.

Nwanetsi is 27km/17 miles from Satara on the Nwanetsi road. it can house up to 16 people in four three-bed huts and two two-bedhuts, each with *en suite* facilities. There is a communal dining-room and kitchen.

Roodewal is 40km/25 miles from the Olifants rest camp on the gravel road to Timbavati. It can accommodate 19 people and consists of one family cottage with two bedrooms, each with its own bathroom, and three huts, each with five single beds and *en-suite* facilities. A separate dining-room and kitchen are available. All these camps have barbecue facilities.

Costs. A camp site for up to 6 people costs R40 a night; a two-bed chalet or rondavel at Skukuza (this is the most expensive) costs R300 (£40/$66) a night; a two-bed cottage in a bushveld camp costs R570 a night. All these camps are linked by a network of 2600km/1616 miles of good roads. A motor vehicle is essential; microbuses are ideal because they are spacious and their extra height makes game viewing easier. Getting information out of the National Parks Board — especially about the Kruger Park — is like drawing teeth. Staff freely admit that the Kruger is so popular there is no need for them to promote it or sing its praises. It is usually fully booked and if you want to stay there you are advised that preference is given to written applications for accommodation received 13 months in advance. Reservations are only made and confirmed between 11 and 12 months in advance. After these applications have been processed other applications are then considered. Some visitors are, however, allowed to enter the park without reservations to take whatever accommodation is available through cancellations.

Private Reserves. Fences between the Kruger National Park and the private game reserves on its western border are all coming down to enable animals to move more freely and this is helping to restore natural migration patterns. Private reserves will, however, stay private and exclusive. Justly world famous for the splendour of their setting, their wealth of game and birdlife, and their accommodation and services, are the Sabie Sand Game Reserve, Mala Mala, Londolozi, and Sabi Sabi which share the Kruger's western border.

SPORT AND RECREATION

Nelspruit Golf Club is a pleasant 18-hole course set in hilly, well grassed surroundings. The fairways and greens are lined with trees, bush and shrubs, and the terrain makes for a challenging round, tel (01311) 22187.

The Off-Road Experience at Nelspruit offers an all-inclusive two-day weekend on a game ranch which is suitable for 4x4 beginners and experienced drivers. Accommodation is in a tented camp, tel (013) 753-2551, fax (013) 753-3578.

Hiking. Most of the 60 and more trails and hikes in Mpumalanga are on the escarpment, among cascading falls, majestic ridges and rolling forests. They vary in length from short walks such as the Fortuna Mine Nature Trail in the hills above Barberton and the Rose's Creek Trail (both about a mile), to Sabie's Fanie Botha Hiking Trail, a five-day 79km/49 mile circular route, although there are shorter variations that require different levels of fitness. In the lowveld, almost all the private game reserves — and the Kruger National Park itself — are cross-hatched by hiking trails. Seven National Parks Board Wilderness Trails traverse normally unseen corners of the Kruger Park and concentrate on historical features and game-viewing. These must be booked in advance. For the average walker the best way to experience the beauties of the region is to concentrate on some of the shorter walks. For example, more than 245 species of birds and a wide swatch of indigenous vegetation can be seen during the seven-hour McManus Nature Walk in Nelspruit (open only between November and June). Barberton in the De Kaap Valley was the centre of gold prospecting in the 1880s and the Fortuna Mine Nature Trail (just over a mile) first passes through a park of indigenous trees before entering a tunnel blasted by miners through 4200 million-year-old rock to transport ore to the crushing mill. To the north, Pilgrim's Rest has within its nature reserve the Rambler's trails, a complex of walks and horseback trails. Above the village Mount Sheba has 10 nature trails, all of them shorter than 6km/4 miles in length. Waterfalls, fascinating rock formations, birdlife, flora, and scenic views are all part of the Blyde River Canyon walks north of Pilgrim's Rest, where both the Kadishi Valley trail system and the Swadini nature trails offer from 30-minute rambles to hikes of up to three hours. For the serious hiker the following are a few of the more popular two to five-day trails.

Geelhout ('Yellowwood') Hiking Trail, Blyde River Canyon, is a 24km/15 mile two-day trail. The trail crosses the Blyde River above Bourke's Luck Potholes. The first 3km/2 miles winds along the edge of the escarpment, with breathtaking views into the depths. These grassy uplands are dotted with proteas which attract nectar-feeding sunbirds. The trail descends steeply into the Belvedere Valley. The vegetation becomes denser here with the lavender tree and wild pear among the interesting trees. The final stretch of the day sees the trail wind through rugged terrain and through evergreen forest before leading back to the Belvedere Stream and the rustic Salma Hut. The second day you follow a different route back up the valley. Troops of noisy baboons will be watching your progress as you come to a crossroad where you link up to the path of the previous day and head back to Bourke's Luck. All food, utensils, sleeping bags and toiletries must be carried with you. Book well in advance through the Mpumalanga Parks Board, PO Box 1990, Nelspruit 1200, tel/fax (013) 768-1216 or (013) 758-1035.

The 38km/24 mile Protea Hiking Trail, also in the Blyde River Canyon, is a three or four night trail, starting from Bourke's Luck Potholes, along the upper slopes of Belvedere Valley and into the Muilhuis Valley where there is an overnight hut after the 12.5km/8 mile leg. The second day you climb out of the valley into an indigenous forest, past the dramatic rock formations of The Divide, to the Op-de-Berg overnight hut, 6.5km/4 miles from Muilhuis. On three you hike through more forest along the contours of Scotland Hill, and then down the canyon to the Eerste Liefde hut after 8.5km/5 miles. The last day you climb the incline known as the Last Slog before crossing Belvedere Creek and winding along to the edge of the buttress. The final 11km/6.8 mile leg brings you back to Bourke's Luck Potholes. Each of the trail huts has 10 steel-frame bunks with mattresses. Muilhuis and Bourke's Luck have cold water with open-air showers, flush toilets and barbecue facilities. No fires are allowed so take a small stove.

Day walks in the Sabie-Graskop area: Maritzbos, the first overnight stop on the Fanie Botha Trail can be done by reasonably fit hikers. The route starts and ends at the Ceylon Forest station. The Loerie Trail also starts at Ceylon Forest Station and is a full day's walk past the impressive Bridal Veil Falls, passing the Elna Falls on the way back to Sabie. The trail goes through exotic plantations as well as through beautiful indigenous forest.

Fanie Botha Trail. This trail winds through pine plantations, indigenous forest and mountain grassland, with exceptional views of the lowveld. It is a five-day, 73km/46 mile trail. *Prospector's Hiking Trail* is situated near Pilgrim's Rest and provides many trail options, ranging from two days to five days, winding through indigenous forests, exotic plantations and places of interest dating back to the gold rush era. Peach Tree Creek two-day trail 21km/13 miles; Blackhill two-day trail 27km/17 miles; Morgenzon three-day trail 43km/27 miles; Peach Tree Creek/Blackhill combination four-day trail 48km/30 miles; Prospector's five-day trail 58km/36 miles. Toilets, cooking utensils and barbecue facilities are available at overnight huts. Safcol provides a beautifully produced booklet of each trail featuring maps, a detailed route description, geology, historical and archaeological sites, flora and fauna, and other interesting titbits.

Kaapschehoop Geological Route. 33km/20 miles from Nelspruit in the Berlin plantation. The trail can be started at either Barretts Coaches or Kaapschehoop and provides the hiker with tremendous variation. Starvation Creek two-day trail 23km/14 miles; Battery Creek two-day trail; Blue Swallow two-day trail 24km; Starvation/Battery Creek three-day trail 36km/22 miles; Battery Creek/Blue Swallow three-day trail 39km/24 miles; Starvation/Battery Creek/Blue Swallow four-day trail 54km/34 miles; Battery Creek/Blue Swallow four-day trail 51km/32 miles; Kaapschehoop five-day trail 60km/37 miles.

Uitsoek Hiking Trail. 80km/50 miles from Nelspruit, in the Uitsoek plantation. The trail starts at the Uitsoek forest station and is a 52km walk over two days. From Uitsoek to the Lisabon hut 15km/9 miles; from Lisabon hut to Uitsoek 15km; from Uitsoek to Beestekraalspruit and Bakkrans 11km/7 miles.

Abseiling. Thrillseekers operates day and weekend abseil trips at sites near Waterval-Boven, two and a half hours' drive from Johannesburg, but you must arrange your own transport. Although this is a potentially dangerous mountaineering technique Thrillseekers has a 100% accident-free record. All equipment is provided. T-shirts and photographs of yourself doing a Rambo are available. Rap-jumping — a new technique of going over forwards — is also offered for those with high adrenalin thresholds. Participants start on easy rock faces and through the course of the trip, graduate to the finale — a huge 50m/164ft drop next to a pumping waterfall. On an average day, each participant can do about eight to ten abseil jumps at a variety of sites. The cost of the day trip is R200 (£26.65/$44) per person, R495 for the weekend trip. Thrillseekers say they have thrown hundreds of people off cliffs all over the country and they've always come back for more. No previous experience is required. Instructors explain the technique, slip you into a harness and over you go. Experienced Mountain Club of South Africa instructors will also give you an introductory rock climbing course for R850 (R750 for students), tel (011) 455-1670, Cell 082 491-6483.

Down at Secunda the Leslie Gold Mine has dammed a natural pan, Leeupan, to create a 2600-hectare body of water where small carp go up to 1.5kg and bigger carp weigh in at about 5kg. There are also a few bass. There is a lawned site, complete with power points, electric lights and excellent ablutions, for which R25 a vehicle a night is charged. There are only about 20 stands and no pre-booking.

Mpumalanga is the second biggest citrus producer in South Africa and the orange groves are a delight when they are in blossom. Many other kinds of tropical fruit grow in profusion and there are wayside stalls selling a Technicolour range all over the province. The citrus industry has given birth to an unusual orange wine and a potent mampoer, or high-proof spirit liquor made from peaches and other fruits. At

White River, a winery, nuttery and art gallery offer some of these beverages, among them Avalencia orange and ginger liqueurs, packaged nuts, and local craftwork. Other delicacies of the region include Lydenburg's well known peaches and kiwi fruit — both grown extensively in this area.

Flea markets are held in Nelspruit at Prorom Square (Friday) and Promenade Centre (Saturday), tel (01311) 552164, and at Hall's Gateway (Saturday and Sunday). Mingerhout Verdite sells semi-precious stone carvings by local craftsmen, tel (013) 744-7169, and 20km/12 miles from Nelspruit is Umbala Glass Studio, in the Crocodile River valley at the foot of Mt Carmel on the N4 to Johannesburg, where you can choose from artwork on glass, paintings, lampshades, panels and screens, tel/fax (013) 733-3709.

Milly's Country Trout Stall, 3.5km/2 miles before Machadodorp on the N4, produces and sells top quality trout products, tel (01325) 31118; in Waterval Boven Ye Olde Post Office Shoppe near the railway station has handcrafts in wood, glass and cloth, tel (013262) ask for 406; the boerewors, dry wors and biltong at the Ponderosa Butchery, Main Road, Badplaas, are claimed by the locals to be the best in Mpumalanga, tel (017) 844-1118.

Tsakani, South Africa's only silk farm, is situated in the Amashangaan tribal land about an hour's drive from Graskop on the R533. Shangaan women will show you the intricate methods of commercial silk farming and the hand-processing of silk duvets, tel (01311) 55-3214. Ponieskrantz Weavery sells locally made hand-woven rugs, wall hangings and has a variety of other hand-crafted items, tel (01315) 81150; Daisy Craft in Barberton offers African art by locals, such as animal figurines made of recyclable material and non-toxic paint, tel (013) 712-6266. Halls roadside farm stalls offer local fruit and fresh farm produce. Look for them throughout the lowveld — a vegetarian and fruitarian delight.

In Nelspruit:

Police, tel (013) 10111.
Ambulance, tel (013) 10177.
Fire Brigade, tel (013) 753-3331.

TOURIST INFORMATION

The *Nelspruit Publicity Association* is in the Promenade Centre, Louis Trichardt Street, Nelspruit. PO Box 5018, Nelspruit 1200, tel (01311) 55-1988/9. You can use their air-conditioned office to make calls from a pay telephone and to get information on Nelspruit and the lowveld region, as well as on the rest of the country.

The Mpumalanga Parks Board administers and manages many of the game and nature reserves throughout the province. The Kruger National Park is a National Park and under independent management and control.

Mpumalanga Parks Board, PO Box 1990, Nelspruit 1200, tel/fax (013) 758-1035 or (013) 755-3931.
Mpumalanga Tourism Authority, PO Box 679, Nelspruit 1200, tel (013) 752-7001, fax (013) 752-7013.
Mpumalanga Tourism Board, tel (01311) 55-4004, fax (01311) 55-4006.

Middleveld

Dullstroom, tel (013) 254-0175.
Groblersdal, tel (01202) 3056, fax (01202) 2547.
Middleveld Tourism Association, tel/fax (017) 844-1233/843-2088.
Waterval Boven, tel (013) 262-1803.

Lowveld

Barberton, tel/fax (013) 712-2121.
Graskop, tel (013) 767-1316, fax (013) 761-1798.
Hazyview, tel (013) 737-7414.
Komatipoort Tourism Association, tel/fax (013) 790-8070.
Kruger National Park, tel (012) 343-1991, fax (012) 343-0905
Lowveld and Escarpment Tourism Association, tel (013) 755-1988, fax (013) 755-1350.
Lydenburg, tel (013) 235-2121, fax (013) 235-1108.
Nelspruit, tel (013) 755-1988 fax (013) 755-1350.
Pilgrim's Rest, tel (013) 768-1211.
Sabie, tel (013) 764-3492.
White River, tel/fax (013) 115-1599.

Northern Province

Baobab Trees

South Africa's most northerly province is where you can still find untamed Africa. It is the land of the mysterious Rain Queen, Modjadji, of ruins and relics of Stone Age and Iron Age sites, ancient baobabs, the upside-down tree, hot mineral springs sparkling trout waters and waterfalls and of a rich variety of game and birdlife. Much of this 123,280 sq km/47,599 sq mile region has remained unchanged for centuries. In prosaic terms this is the country's poorest province, its 5.7 million people existing on an annual per capita income of only R725. Capital of the province, which merges the old Northern Transvaal and the former homelands of Venda, Lebowa and Gazankulu, is Pietersburg, which is also the cultural and infrastructural hub of the region. Halfway between Pretoria and the Limpopo River, near the Tropic of Capricorn, this attractive town makes a pleasant port of call *en route* to the hunting area of the western bushveld, the scenic Magoesbaskloof area near Tzaneen, or the top half of the Kruger National Park, which falls within the Northern Province. Other important provincial centres are Warmbaths, Nylstroom, Potgietersrus, Ellisras, Messina, Louis Trichardt, Phalaborwa, Thabazimbi, Tzaneen and Thoyoyandou. The province shares borders in the west with Botswana, in the north with Zimbabwe, and in the east, bounding the Kruger National Park, Mozambique. For travelling convenience the region is broken up into the bushveld, the Soutpansberg, and the lowveld.

The Great North Road erratically linking Cape Town to Cairo slices the province neatly in half, running almost due north from Pretoria to the Zimbabwe border at Beit Bridge. For most of its length in the province it passes through typical bushveld and provides easy access to most other areas. The Soutpansberg range lies at right angles to the Drakensberg, not far from the Zimbabwe border. It stretches for more than 150km/93 miles from east to west and climbs from 300m/984ft above sea level to the 1747m/5732ft summit of Letjuma and is one of the loveliest regions in the province. It is best explored in a leisurely way along one of the many mountain and forest trails. Beyond the mountains, mopane trees and giant baobabs dominate the plains sweeping northward to the Limpopo Valley, giving it a 'Lost World' feeling. The Venda, who live in the Soutpansberg believe they are descended from tribes who migrated south from central Africa three centuries ago. They are intensely superstitious and still perform many old rites and rituals. In the Python Dance, bare-breasted teenage girls perform a slow, rhythmic *domba* (fertility dance) to the tribal drums central to their religious ceremonies.

The Great Escarpment sweeps north to south from the Soutpansberg, north of Louis Trichardt, to the massive buttresses of the Drakensberg near Sabie and Kaapsehoop in Mpumalanga, and from the Wolkberg south of Magoesbaskloof the Drakensberg effectively divides the lowveld to the east from the highlands of the interior. Magoesbaskloof lies in an area poetically known as the Land of the Silver Mist and is a scenic pass winding down the escarpment between Haenertsburg and Tzaneen. It is encircled by dense forests and dominated by the cloud-capped Wolkberg and its 2128m/6982ft Iron Crown peak. Some of South Africa's finest private game reserves are situated in the lowveld on the western boundary of the Kruger National Park. All of them offer comfortable — in many cases luxurious — air-conditioned accommodation, gourmet cuisine and conducted 4x4 game drives. South of Phalaborwa are the world-famous game and nature reserves of Klaserie, Timbavati, and Manyeleti which run into each other to become part of the Greater Kruger National Park. There are also numerous game reserves in the mountainous area of the Waterberg offering rewarding wilderness experiences. The northern section of the Kruger is renowned for its herds of elephant and buffalo, increasing herds of tsessebe and sable and its enchanting bird life. In the Pafuri area of the park, where the Soutpansberg melts down, raptors such as the black eagle and the long crested eagle are a common sight. This is also a prime area to see the rare Pell's fishing owl. Not far away is the point where Zimbabwe, Mozambique and South Africa meet, an area once notorious as 'Crook's Corner' because of the shady characters who used to conduct their nefarious business here. To the east, the Limpopo Valley National Park — the 'Peace Park' — is being developed at the confluence of the river Rudyard Kipling called the 'great, grey-green, greasy Limpopo,' and the Shashe River. This will be a transfrontier park encompassing territory in South Africa, Zimbabwe and Botswana and will point the way for similar expansions projected for other parts of the country.

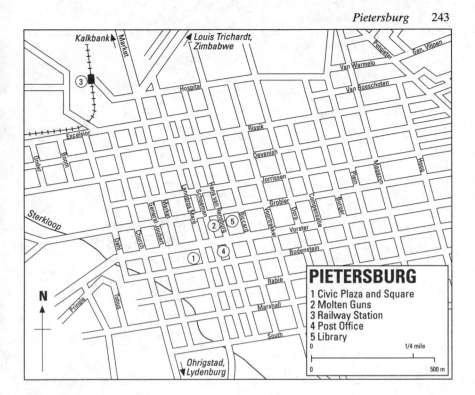

PIETERSBURG
1 Civic Plaza and Square
2 Molten Guns
3 Railway Station
4 Post Office
5 Library

PIETERSBURG

GETTING AROUND

SA Airlink operates daily flights between Johannesburg, Pietersburg and Phalaborwa. **Pietersburg Airport** is 5km/3 miles from town. There is no bus service to town, but major **car hire** companies have rental vehicles at the airport; *Avis*, tel (0152) 291-1877, fax (0152) 291-1834, Cell 082 446-8341. **Taxis** are also available. A daily luxury **coach** service links Pietersburg, Pretoria, Johannesburg, Ellisras and other towns in the province, but there is no local bus service.

ACCOMMODATION

The Ranch Hotel, 22km/14 miles south of Pietersburg, is a 3-star hotel set in 15 hectares of lush gardens and lawns, with opportunities for walking and bird-watching and facilities for the more energetic such as squash, tennis and volley ball courts. PO Box 77, Pietersburg 0700, tel (0152) 293-7180, fax (0152) 293-7188.

There is a 3-star *Holiday Inn* in town close to the centre, R200 (£26.65/$44) a night for a two-bedded room. PO Box 784, Pietersburg 0700, tel (0152) 291-2030, fax (0152) 291-3150.

EXPLORING

Bakone Malapa Open-air Museum. For an insight into an ancient lifestyle this North

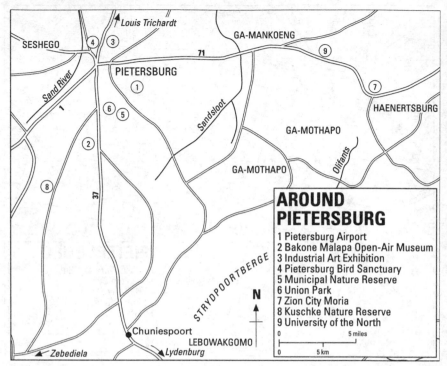

Sotho kraal, 9km/6 miles south of Pietersburg, is a place where you can watch men and women practising traditional handicrafts and making baskets, clay pots, furniture and utensils, preparing hides and brewing beer. Conducted tours are offered and an information centre provides historical background, tel (0152) 295-011.

Civic Plaza and Square. Lovely landscaped gardens with walkways, streams and ponds provide an attractive setting for Pietersburg's Civic Plaza. The Art Museum in the Library Gardens houses an impressive art collection. A wealth of exotic plants in the Conservatory should delight the botanically minded. The Hugh Exton Photographic Museum is housed in the restored Dutch Reformed Church and displays the Exton Collection of 22,000 glass negatives and many other photographs of great historical value. Exton worked as a photographer during the Anglo-Boer War and his pictures graphically record the casualties and destruction of this conflict.

Industrial Art Exhibition. At the northern entrance to Pietersburg the verges of the road have been converted into a permanent 'gallery' of dramatic industrial sculpture made of steel pipes, old railway sleepers and scrap metal.

Molten Guns. At the entrance to the library there is an unusual sculpture made from the molten remains of rifles which were burnt and melted down after being confiscated from Chief Makgoba's tribe following their defeat by Boer commandos of the old Transvaal Republic in 1895.

Pietersburg Bird Sanctuary. Close to town on the R521 route. Entry is on foot only, except for the aged and the disabled, who can drive around. Some 280 bird species have been identified in the acacia bush. Scenic hiking trails link various bird-watching hides and look-out points. Open daily, 7am–6pm, tel (0152) 295-2011.

Pietersburg Municipal Nature Reserve is one of the largest municipal game reserves in the country. About 5km/3 miles south of town, next to Union Park, the 3200-hectare reserve supports rhino, zebra, giraffe and gemsbok. Open grass-covered plains make for easy game-viewing. A 20km/12 mile Rhino Hiking Trail with overnight facilities traverses the more scenic parts of the reserve, which is open daily, 7am–8pm.

Union Park. Some 5km/3 miles south of town, the park offers shady trees, barbecue facilities, a children's playground and a dam where the fishing is good. Camping sites, six-bed luxury rondavels and chalets are available at the adjacent municipal caravan park.

Zion City Moria. Not far from Pietersburg, this is the headquarters of the Zion Christian Church and draws more than a million pilgrims every Easter — which is not a good time to be driving in this area. This is the largest of some 2000 African indigenous churches in South Africa, which generally mix Christian doctrine with elements of traditional African belief.

LOWVELD

ACCOMMODATION

Coach House at Agatha, 15km/9 miles south of Tzaneen, is on top of a plateau with views of the Drakensberg. The food here is famous. Accommodation R230 per person sharing. Contact PO Box 544, Tzaneen 0850, tel (0152) 307-3641, fax (0152) 307-1466, toll-free 0800 11 53 00.

Glenshiel Country Lodge in Magoebaskloof borders on the Ebenezer Dam. There is tennis, swimming, trout fishing, bird-watching, cycling, trail walking or exploring the nearby historic village of Haenertsburg. Contact PO Box 1, Haenertsburg 0730, tel (0152) 276-4335, central reservations, tel (011) 788-1258, toll-free 0801 11 44 48.

Kings Camp in the Timbavati Game Reserve has day and night game drives and bush walks with game rangers and trackers. It has a traversing area of 5750 hectares where leopard, lion, elephant, buffalo, rhino, inyala, and birds such as bee-eaters, steppes eagles, lilac-breasted rollers and hornbills can be spotted. It is a five-hour drive from Johannesburg, or you can fly in to Phalaborwa. Contact PO Box 1255, Hoedspruit 1380, tel/fax (01528) 31123. Johannesburg office reservations, tel (011) 465-9387.

Motswari is a private game reserve which lies in the 15,000-hectare Timbavati Game Reserve, famed as the home of a pride of white lions, adjoining the Kruger National Park. Scheduled daily flights to Phalaborwa with a Motswari air transfer to the lodge. By road it is 521km/324 miles from Johannesburg. Motswari rates are R1450 per person per night sharing *en suite* bungalows, M'Bali bush camp R1550 per person. Central reservations, PO Box 67865, Bryanston 2021, Gauteng, tel (011) 463-1990, fax (011) 463-1992.

Nyati Pools. 45km/28 miles from Kruger National Park's Orpen Gate. Tented self-catering camps with all the kitchen equipment you are likely to need. Full catering is also available. Night game drives. Contact PO Box 664, Hoedspruit 1380, tel (01528) 31676,

Tanda Tula ('to love the silence') bush camp has 8 luxury tents with *en suite* bathrooms and hot and cold running water. Each tent has its own patio overlooking the bush and water-hole. With the removal of the fences between the Timbavati Private Nature Reserve and the Kruger National Park, a 2.8 million-hectare wilderness has been created, where wildlife roams freely. Professional rangers and trackers will take you game tracking on foot or in open safari vehicles, in the territory of the famous white lions and the Big Five. Rates and information from PO Box 32, Constantia 7848, Cape Town, tel (021) 794-6500, fax (021) 794-7605.

Tshukudu Game Lodge on 5000 hectares of game reserve near the Blyde River Canyon has accommodation in thatched bungalows with private facilities. Cost is R590 (£79/$130) per person sharing. A self-catering alternative in a rustic bushcamp offers accommodation in thatched cottages on stilts at R135 per person. Contact PO Box 289, Hoedspruit 1380, tel (01528) 32476, fax (01528) 32078, Cell 083 626-4916.

Some **caravan and camping sites** in the lowveld are:

> *Duiwelskloof Holiday Resort*, tel (0152) 309-9246;
> *Fairview Caravan Park and Chalets*, tel (0152) 307-4809;
> *Knott's Trail Camp*, tel (015253) 4460.

EXPLORING

Duiwelskloof. A picturesque village in a heavily wooded area north of Tzaneen. 19km/12 miles to the north-east is the kraal of the legendary Rain Queen, Modjadji of the Lebedu, who is revered by tribal people throughout southern Africa. The North Sotho people believe she is immortal and that the present Modjadji is the one who settled in the area early in the 16th century. Rider Haggard used her as the central character of his novel *She*. Near the kraal is the Modjadji Nature Reserve, which protects the world's largest concentration of the cycad species *Encephalartos transvenosus*, also known as Modjadji's Palm. On the Leeudraai Road, Platland, is Sunland Farm, where refreshments are served in an unusual setting — inside the hollow trunk of the largest baobab south of the Tropic of Capricorn, tel (0152) 309-9039.

Haenertsburg. The 'capital' of the Land of the Silver Mist area around Magoesbaskloof. In spring the area is a mass of colour from azaleas and ornamental fruit trees and the town hosts events in the area's Cherry Blossom Festival, which is held from the end of September to early October every year.

Hans Merensky Nature Reserve. On the southern banks of the Great Letaba River, 64km/40 miles east-north-east of Tzaneen, the reserve supports a large variety of game and more than 200 bird species, among them the fish, martial, and snake eagles. At the Tsonga Kraal Open-air Museum, arts, crafts and traditional huts reflect Tsonga lifestyle of a century ago. Guided tours are held from Monday to Friday, tel (015) 386-8727.

Hoedspruit. The town started as a small rail-stop and is now an agricultural centre. Citrus fruit and mangoes are the main agricultural crops. The SA Air Force established a base at the town in 1977. Hoedspruit is situated in vegetation known as bush savanna. This type of bush is the favoured habitat of the Big Five — elephant, lion, rhino, buffalo and leopard.

Hoedspruit Cheetah Breeding and Research Centre. The centre provides sanctuary not only for the cheetah, the fastest animal on earth, but also the white rhino, the Cape Hunting dog and a variety of vultures. Open Monday to Saturday, 8.30am–4pm, and on Sundays, school holidays and long weekends. Accessible to the disabled. Admission R20 (£2.65/$4.40) per person, R10 per child (6–12) for a 90-minute tour, tel (01528) 31633/31620.

Kruger National Park (Northern Section). A wilderness experience that ranks with the finest in Africa — see page 233 for main description. Mopane trees dominate the northern part of the Park, which is famous for its elephants and large herds of buffalo.

Private Camps

These are for the use of groups and you must book the entire camp to stay in one. Only residents are allowed inside the camps, which offer complete privacy. There is no caravanning or camping.

Boulders is situated about 50km north of Letaba rest camp...

African elephant in the Kr... holes attract lots of game.

Mopani is 45km/28 miles north of Letaba on the eastern bank of the Pioneer... and consists of houses and cottages for up to eight people to four-bedded huts, one of which is equipped for the handicapped. There is a swimming pool and night drives are available.

Olifants Camp overlooks the Olifants River and the surrounding Lebombo Mountains, which run along the Mozambique border. Fever trees, wild figs and tree euphorbias fringe the river. There are houses, smaller cottages and huts, one of which is equipped for the handicapped. All huts have air-conditioning. Night drives. There are no camping or caravanning facilities.

Shingwedzi has various types of accommodation. Some huts are equipped for the handicapped. There are delightful drives along the Kanniedood Dam road and there is a swimming pool. Night drives. Caravanning and camping sites are available.

Punda Maria is a cosy little camp lying at the foot of Dimbo Mountain with a view over the valley. It comprises modern cottages and huts made from clay and slates. The latter date from the 1930s, but the interiors are modern. The camp is in the Sand Veld, often described as the botanical garden of the Kruger. Plant species occur in the vicinity which are not found anywhere else. The Luvuvhu River is 50km/31 miles away, with its fever tree forest and picnic site. The Paradise Flycatcher Nature Trail Meanders through the camp. Caravanning and camping sites are available. Expect to pay from R100 (£13.35/$22) a night for a two-bed hut to R680 for a six-bed cottage in any of these camps.

Bushveld Camps

If you prefer smaller, more remote camps, these are ideal. There are no shops, restaurants or filling stations. No camping or caravanning. The most you will pay for a three-bedroomed cottage sleeping six will be R640 a night, while the cheapest is R295 a night for a one-bedroomed cottage with four beds.

Shimuwini is on the upper reaches of the Shimuwini Dam on the Letaba River, about 50km/31 miles from the Phalaborwa Gate on the Mooiplaas Road. It has a total of 15 family cottages, which can accommodate 71 people.

Bateleur is on the bank of the Mashokwe Spruit, about 40km/25 miles south-west of the Shingwedzi rest camp. It consists of seven family cottages, which can accommodate 34 people.

Sirheni is on the bank of the Shirheni Dam, about 54km/34 miles from Punda Maria rest camp on the Shingwedzi road. It consists of 15 family cottages, accommodating 80 people.

All camps have similar facilities — barbecue areas, fridges, and solar panels generating electricity for lights and fans only.

...and can sleep 12. It consists of a main sleeping unit, with two rooms and *en-suites*, four separate rooms with two single beds and a bathroom. There is a communal dining-room and kitchen, as well as barbecue facilities. The cost is R2070 (£276/$455) a night for up to 12 people.

Contact The National Parks Board, PO Box 787, Pretoria 0001, tel (012) 343-1991, fax (012) 343-0905, or at Private Bag X402, Skukuza 1350, tel (01311) 65159, fax (01311) 65154.

Letaba. This tributary of the Olifants River rises near Haenertsburg at the northern extremity of the Drakensberg and flows eastwards for almost 100km/62 miles to its confluence with the main stream near the border of Mozambique. The name comes from Northern Sotho *le hlaba*, 'sandy river.' The district of Letaba, with Tzaneen as its principal town, takes its name from the river.

Magoebaskloof. 35km/22 miles south of Tzaneen and 61km/38 miles east of Pietersburg, the Magoesbaskloof Pass leads through beautiful mountain scenery where picknicking, fishing, swimming and hiking are popular. The Dokolewa and Grootbosch hiking trails traverse forests and valleys, providing an excellent introduction to the region. In a tangle of indigenous trees, 3km/2 miles from the main road, the Debegeni Falls plunge into a clear pool suitable for swimming, before cascading 800m/2625ft down the cliff. A hazy cloak of mist can envelop Magoesbaskloof for days on end in winter and summer. In geographic terms, Magoebaskloof refers to more than just the kloof, it includes the areas below and above the edges of the escarpment where the road — along one of the most scenic drives in the country — drops 600m/1969ft in 6km/4 miles. The valleys are gardens of fruit, flowers and trees and the area's lush vegetation is without equal in the province. From early September Magoesbaskloof is ablaze with colour when the azaleas bloom, and a few weeks later when the cherry trees blossom. The spectacle is celebrated every year with a Cherry Blossom Festival. Nature lovers, gardeners, botanists, photographers and artists by the score come to admire and record this event. Along the forested Cheerio Road is the organic Wegraakbosch dairy farm, source of piquant Mutschli cheese. There are guided tours of the farm and the cheese-making process and there is a rustic rondavel on the property for overnighting and several beautiful picnic sites, tel (0152) 276-1811. Also well worth doing is the scenic George's Valley drive between Tzaneen and Haenertsburg. The valley was named after road builder George Deneys, who combined his work with a love for the area by creating a road full of detours and wayside halts to give travellers a chance to admire the magnificent scenery in a more leisurely manner.

Moholoholo Wildlife Rehabilitation Centre. This is part of a game farm near Hoedspruit, which enables rehabilitated injured animals and birds to be returned to the wild on site, the only such centre doing this in South Africa. A forest camp on the farm offers overnight accommodation, tel (01528) 31676.

Phalaborwa. Town in the Letaba district, 104km/65 miles east of Tzaneen. The name means 'it is better here than in the south,' and refers to the peaceful existence tribal refugees enjoyed here after fleeing from bloodthirsty Swazis and Zulus. Major attractions, including the Blyde River Canyon and historic Pilgrim's Rest in neighbouring Mpumalanga, are within easy reach of the town, which has the biggest open-cast copper mine in Africa. Tours of the mine are conducted every Friday, tel

(01524) 4848. Golfers should make a point of playing a round or two at the Hans Merensky Golf Course, which is one of the finest in the country (hippos, crocodiles and the occasional elephant sometimes wander across the course). The town is only 3km/2 miles from the Kruger National Park's Phalaborwa gate. Inside the park, the Masorini Open-air Museum, 12km/7.5 miles from town, is a reconstruction of an Iron Age village.

Tzaneen. Situated in an area of exceptional beauty along the eastern escarpment of the Drakensberg the town, 104km/64 miles east of Pietersburg, lies in a district growing tea, coffee, fruit, vegetables and nuts. North of the town, whose name is Sotho for 'Place where people gathered,' the Tzaneen Dam Nature Reserve is popular with anglers and bird-watchers. Hiking trails, mountain views, a warm climate and numerous waterfalls, trout streams and forests make the surroundings a walker's and nature lover's paradise.

SOUTPANSBERG

ACCOMMODATION

Cloud's End Hotel. Swiss-owned hotel with rooms at R150 (£20/$33) per person sharing. Private Bag X2409, Louis Trichardt 0920, tel (015) 517-7021, fax (015) 517-7187.

Lalani Lodge is a small self-catering resort on an avocado and macadamia nut farm on the Luvhungwe River in the lush Levuba Valley, east of Louis Trichardt. The lodge offers superb views of the Soutpansberg, as well as river walks and mountain hikes. It was recognised as one of the best 'newcomers' in the 1996 Satour Tourism Awards, tel (015) 583-0218, fax (015) 583-0405.

Lapalala Lodge accommodates 16 people in four separate thatched rondavels with *en-suite* bathrooms at R400 per person a night sharing. Rhino Camp accommodates eight people in four safari-style luxury tents set on platforms, with *en suite* facilities, in the bush of the Kgokong River, and costs R295 per person a night sharing. Six self-catering fully equipped bush camps accommodating two to eight people are situated on the banks of a river. The emphasis is on seclusion, walking, birding and relaxation. Contact PO Box 645, Bedfordview 2008, Gauteng, tel (011) 453-7645/6/7, fax (011) 453-7645.

Marakele National Park. A tented camp of six furnished units is sited on the banks of the perennial Matlabas River. Each tent has two single beds and two stretchers with mattresses, a private bathroom (shower, wash basin and toilet), a fully equipped kitchen with a refrigerator/freezer, two-plate stove and electricity. Each tent has a verandah with table and chairs and barbecue facilities. Contact the National Parks Board, PO Box 787, Pretoria 0001, Gauteng, tel (012) 343-1991, fax (012) 343-0905.

Nwanedi Resort and *Nwanedi National Park* in Venda have four-bed fully equipped rondavels with *en-suite* kitchens, bathrooms, ceiling fans and barbecue facilities for R120 a night, as well as more luxurious accommodation and camping and caravan sites. Tents are R16 a night and caravans R30 (£4/$6.60) a night. Mphephu Resort is family oriented with swimming, children's playgrounds, games and dancing. Self-contained fully serviced chalets with 2–4 beds, *en-suite* shower/toilet and kitchen cost R120 a night. Contact Venda Tourism, Private Bag 5045, Thohoyandou 0950, tel (0159) 41577, fax (0159) 41048.

Thornybush Game Lodge has 32 beds and accommodation in four other camps — Serondella, n'Kaya, Chapungu and the Jackelberry Lodge. You can fly SA Airlink from Johannesburg to Phalaborwa with transfers to the Lodge. Private air charters are also available. If you are driving, take the N12 and then the N4 from Johannesburg to Belfast. From Belfast take the R540 to Lydenburg and continue via the Abel Erasmus Pass to Hoedspruit and follow the signs to Thornybush. It is a five-hour drive. Contact tel (011) 883-7918/9, fax (011) 883-8201.

Venda Sun in Thohoyandou, capital of the former Venda homeland, is one of Sun International's chain of hotel-casino complexes with all the usual facilities. Rates on enquiry to PO Box 766, Sibasa 0970, tel (0159) 21011, fax (0159) 21367.

Caravan parks include *Messina Caravan Park*, tel (01553) 2210, and *Ben Alberts Nature Reserve*, tel (01537) 21509.

EXPLORING

Alldays. Behind the Soutpansberg range and stretching all the way to the Limpopo River, which marks South Africa's border with Zimbabwe, is a bushveld region of thorn, acacias and giant baobabs which is the Africa that most people visualise when they think of the Dark Continent. Tucked away in this vast landscape lies the little village of Alldays, which has been here since the days of the early explorers and hunters. Although this is traditionally a hunting area, there is now an increasing emphasis on eco-tourism. Hunting safaris are still operating, but offered as an integral part of conservation, while ranches which specialise in the breeding and selling of game offer superb game-viewing experiences with some of the most spectacular specimens of rare game species to be found in the country. The bushveld has an abundance of indigenous trees and grasses as well as more than 300 bird species. The countryside varies from thornveld and mopane trees to riverine forest, with occasional outcrops of basalt and fascinating weathered sandstone formations. Some well-preserved Bushman paintings, ancient stone fortresses and fossil foot-prints add the unusual to the area's attractions. For more information on the area and its facilities contact Alldays Tourism, PO Box 65, Alldays 0909, tel (01554) 270 or 258, fax (01554) 286.

Ben Lavin Nature Reserve. 15km/9 miles south-east of Louis Trichardt and 450km/280 miles from Johannesburg, this 2500-hectare reserve is well stocked with game, including more than 50 large mammal species and some 238 bird species. Facilities include 40km/25 miles of roads for game-viewing, 18km/11 miles of walking trails and hides at water-holes. There are also mountain bike trails and bikes can be hired at the main camp shop. There is accommodation in tents and in thatched huts and lodges, tel (015) 516-4534, Cell 083 226-7345.

Louis Trichardt. This picturesque town 111km/69 miles north-east of Pietersburg lies in the southern foothills of the Soutpansberg. Named after a Voortrekker leader, the town is the centre of the farming community. Hunting and photographic safaris are available on private ranches in the area. With its many hotels, game lodges, resorts and a private nature reserve, the district is a tourist magnet and a birder's dream.

Mapungubwe. Iron Age sites dating from about 200AD onwards are scattered throughout South Africa and reflect the spread of the black farmers who began moving into the country around that time from the north through the eastern coastal regions. Two that have stirred lots of interest are those at Mapungubwe ('Place of the Jackals'), 72km/45 miles west of Messina on the southern bank of the Limpopo River, and the walled village of **Thulamela** in the northern area of the Kruger National Park. Mapungubwe was a fortified settlement on a flat-topped hillock and was occupied by the vanished Leya tribe from 1220 to 1270AD. These digs have uncovered a dazzling collection of gold beads, chains and other ornaments, as well as a small gold-plated rhinoceros burial offering, all of which seem to link these gold workers with the famous stone-walled fortifications at Great Zimbabwe, across the border.

Thulamela is a fairly recent discovery. Archaeologists have been excavating in this area of the park since 1993 but only in May 1996 were their efforts rewarded when an African queen's magnificent gold bracelets and beads saw the light of day for the first time in four centuries. The skeleton of the queen was uncovered and the nearby grave of the king was located, along with nearly 300 gold beads, and other ornaments and artefacts that link the settlement not only with Mapungubwe and Great Zimbabwe but also, through evidence of trade, with India, China and Europe. The walls and structures at Thulamela have been reconstructed and the site developed as a cultural and ecological museum. Replicas of the ornaments and ceremonial objects found there, and at another pre-colonial site at **Makahane**, 15km/9 miles away (near Pafuri), are on display at the museum.

Messina. This is the northernmost town in the country, 16km/10 miles south of Beit Bridge, on the Limpopo. It is best known for the copper mining which has been carried out in the area since prehistoric times. The Impala Lily Park in the centre of the town is particularly spectacular in spring. About 6km/4 miles south of the town, is the Messina Nature Reserve, with its forest of baobab trees. One gigantic specimen is 25m/82ft high, with a circumference of 16m/53ft. The reserve is a sanctuary for many antelope species, as well as giraffe, leopard, cheetah, and more than 200 bird species, among them martial and black eagles, and crested guineafowl.

Soutpansberg Mountains. The slopes of these imposing mountains ('Salt Pan Mountains') are cloaked with bluegum, pine, rare cycads and yellowwood trees. Since prehistoric times tribes have collected salt from the brine spring at the western end of the mountains. Birdlife is prolific. Forest walks include the Soutpansberg Hiking Trail, the two-day Hanglip section and the three-to-four-day Entabeni section.

Thohoyandou ('Head of the Elephant'). The casino here, housed in a hotel complex, draws thousands of locals. In the mountains behind the town there are tea estates, forests and decorated villages. Lake Fundudzi, surrounded by mountains, is venerated by the Venda people, as the area was originally settled by powerful tribal medicine men and the Venda believe their spirits still inhabit the region. They also believe that the lake is the home of the python god of fertility. No one washes or swims in it and permission is required to visit. On the approach to the lake you can travel through the Venda Holy Forest only by car. According to Venda belief, hikers disturb the ancestral spirits.

Tshipise. Holiday resort 66km/41 miles south-east of Messina and 84km/52 miles north-east of Louis Trichardt. Derives its name from *chia fisu*, meaning burn or be hot, and referring to the 65°C/149°F mineral springs. For centuries sacred to the Venda people, the hot springs of Tshipise lie at the centre of the mineral spa and holiday resort, which has accommodation and other facilities, tel (015539) 624 or 661. Adjacent to the resort, the Honnet Nature Reserve is a sanctuary for a variety of game.

Venda is a small area in the north-east corner of the Soutpansberg whose people trace their roots back to the Great Lakes of central Africa and the culture of Zimbabwe. Traditional arts and crafts, singing and dancing, legends and superstitions dominate the simple lifestyle of the Venda people. To avoid causing offence when visiting their sacred places you should use tour guides and not venture off the beaten track without permission. Signposted places of interest may be visited without a guide. Venda Tourism offers mini-bus and 4x4 tours to scenic, cultural and historic sites, and guided trails and walks, to places such as Lake Fundudzi, the Sacred Forest, and the Phiphidi waterfalls.

BUSHVELD

ACCOMMODATION

Aventura Warmbaths is one of a leading chain of health and holiday resorts with modern facilities, swimming and mineral pools, sauna, tennis, snooker, bar, restaurant, fishing, camping from R30 (£4/$6.60) a person and other accommodation up to a luxury four-bed unit for R550 a day in peak season. Central reservations, tel (012) 346-2277.

Jabulani Guest Farm is in the Waterberg Mountains with 2000 hectares for swimming, rock-climbing, hikes, mountain bike trails and canoeing. There are three fully equipped self-catering houses on the farm, costing R55 per person a night (children under 12 pay R30). Contact Jabulani Guest Farm, PO Box 85460, Emmarentia 2029, Gauteng, tel/fax (011) 486-1794.

Opikopi Game Ranch is a year-round bird watcher's paradise. Accommodation is in air-conditioned fully equipped thatched chalets and evenings can be spent in the lapa around an open log fire. Contact PO Box 590, Ellisras 0555, tel/fax (014) 763-3115.

Podica River Lodge is in the heart of the Waterberg Mountains, with fully equipped self-catering rondavels from R200 a day for two beds. There is also a lodge in a nearby private game reserve with 3-bed and 9-bed rondavels from R100 (£13.35/$22) per person a day. Masses of game and birdlife, including the rare African Finfoot. Contact PO Box 397, Vaalwater 0530, tel (0147552) ask for 2905.

EXPLORING

Ellisras. A town on the banks of the Mogol River, Ellisras is the hub of a region that is world famous among hunters. It is also known for its excellent fishing in the nearby Mokolo Dam.

Kates Hope Nature Reserve. Some 35km/22 miles from Messina, this reserve falls in the baobab belt, weird trees which have fascinated travellers since the earliest times. Some African tribes call them the upside down trees, and that is exactly what they appear to be, with their writhing limbs looking more like the roots than the branches of a tree. They are also known as cream-of-tartar trees for the pleasantly astringent fruit they bear in their large pods. Weight for weight the pulp has four times more vitamin C than oranges. The tart-flavoured pulp is used in several ways, but generally made into a porridge, mixed with milk or honey or some type of cereal. It is also stirred into water to make a refreshing drink, not unlike sherbet. The shiny dark seeds can be ground into meal to make porridge or used as a coffee substitute. The young leaves are like wild spinach. Baobabs can live for centuries and grow to an immense size. If you feel the urge to visit and hug a baobab, contact Peter Skellern at PO Box 2720, Cresta 2118, Gauteng, tel (011) 476-6217.

Lapalala Wilderness is a privately owned reserve of 26,000 hectares in the Waterberg Mountains and one of the wildest regions in the country. The climate is temperate and malaria-free. Lapalala is about 300km/186 miles by road from Johannesburg in an area with a spectacular diversity of plants and trees, unbroken vistas, krantzes and the Lephalala and Kgokong rivers. Within the sanctuary are the first black rhino ever introduced into a private reserve in South Africa. A wide variety of animals roam the reserve, among them white rhino, buffalo, hippo, roan and sable antelope, leopard, giraffe, zebra, and many others. More than 280 bird species have been recorded. There are also Iron Age sites and Bushman rock paintings.

Makapansgat. These caves, near Potgietersrus, have a long and bloody history dating back hundreds of thousands of years. Fossils found there led to one of palaeontology's more embarrassing interpretations – and made at that by the redoubtable Professor Raymond Dart of the University of the Witwatersrand.

Examining the remains of early hominids found with a conglomeration of what seemed to be bone and horn tools, Dart came to the conclusion that early man must have been a ferocious weapon-wielding killer. The discovery at Makapansgat, and other sites, of *Australopithecus* skulls and jaws that appeared to have been crushed by clubs led Dart to believe that the pre-human cave dwellers had also hunted and eaten each other and their close hominid relatives. Skulls with two neat puncture holes in them seemed to support his theory that they had been struck with some sort of spiked bone club. Unhappily for Dart's thesis, later painstaking studies by Bob Brain of the Transvaal Museum showed that hyaenas were largely responsible for creating these 'tools' when they crushed up bones with their powerful jaws. The holes found in the hominid skulls had been made by leopards, Brain showing how their fangs fitted perfectly into the puncture holes. Apparently battered skulls had simply been crushed by the sheer weight of accumulated sediments. In other words, the ape-men were the hunted, not the hunters.

In modern times, Makapansgat saw man-on-man bloodletting. In 1854, after local tribesmen murdered a party of Voortrekkers at Moorddrif, 2000 of them under their chief Makapane sought refuge in the great cavern. A Boer commando tracked them down and stormed the cave after a month-long siege. Some 1500 people lay lifeless inside, victims of thirst and starvation. You can still walk among the ashes of their fires in the cave, an eerie experience. Permission to visit Makapansgat can be obtained from the Bernard Price Institute of Palaeontology at the University of Witwatersrand in Johannesburg, tel (011) 716-2430 and (011) 716-2591, which has been overseeing excavations there and in the nearby lime quarry for nearly 50 years.

Manyeleti Game Reserve. In local Shangaan this means 'Place of the Stars'. The reserve is adjacent to Kruger National Park and its Pungwe Safari Camp houses 10 people in tented units each covered by a thatch A-frame roof. Game viewing and bird watching from open vehicles and guided walks. Central reservations, tel (011) 768-1318, e-mail safari@cis.co.za

Marakele National Park is in the heart of the Waterberg Mountains, 200km/124 miles from the major urban centres of Gauteng. It can be toured only by 4x4 vehicle. The park is characterised by wild mountain landscapes, grassy hills and deep valleys. As the 44,000-hectare park is situated in a particularly interesting transitional zone between the dry and wetter regions of South Africa, arid area gemsbok and savanna impala roam together in the same park. This also contributes to the rich diversity of plants in the area; no fewer than 13 species of ground orchids and 30 fern species have been identified. Other rare plants include the Waterberg cycad, which can grow to 5m in height, yellowwood and mountain cypress. Wildlife species include white and black rhino, elephant, roan and sable antelope, buffalo, giraffe, eland, tsessebe, red hartebeest, gemsbok, kudu, impala, zebra, blue wildebeest, bushbuck, nyala, brown hyena, leopard, caracal, duiker, klipspringer, steenbok, reedbuck and a few smaller mammals. Resident snakes are generally harmless, with the exception of Africa's deadliest, the black mamba. Of the estimated 400 bird species in the area, 280 have been sighted in the park. The world's largest breeding colony of endangered Cape vultures – more than 800 breeding pairs – is also resident in the park.

Nylstroom. Principal town of the Waterberg district, 125km/78 miles north of Pretoria. Afrikaans for 'Nile stream', and called this because the Jerusalemgangers mistook the Mogalakwena River for the upper reaches of the Nile and nearby Kranskop hill for a pyramid.

Nylsvlei Nature Reserve. The 3100-hectare reserve has one of the greatest concentrations of waterfowl and bushveld birds in South Africa. The sprawling 16,000-hectare flood plain of the Nyl River in the vicinity of Naboomspruit attracts more than 400 species of birds to the area. When the river overflows its banks in summer, up to 100,000 wetland birds, including herons, ducks and cranes, flock to the vlei. Spring and summer are the best times for bird-watching here, tel (01474) 31074.

Potgietersrus. The town lies on the main roads north and north-west in an area noted for game and hunting farms. It is also the centre of a considerable tobacco growing industry. The Potgietersrus Nature Reserve supports indigenous and exotic game, and is maintained by the National Zoological Gardens as a game-breeding centre. The Arend Dieperink Museum, said to be one of the finest small museums in the country, has a fine cultural-historical collection. In the museum's aloe garden is a collection of more than 4000 plants of 212 different species, tel (0154) 2244.

Thabazimbi. The town was established after the discovery of vast deposits of iron ore in the area. The name means 'Mountain of Iron.' The district has a large concentration of private game reserves and with the opening of Marakele it is easy to see why this is one of the eco-tourism growth points in the country.

Warmbaths. The southern gateway to the Northern Province is 100km/62 miles north of Pretoria and is renowned for its hot springs, which attract more than a million visitors a year. A strong mineral spring delivers 20,000 litres of water an hour at a temperature of 50°C/122°F. In summer the temperature averages 30°C/86°F and a minimum of 17°C/63°F. All the game farms in this region are home to extensive collections of game. Mabula Game Lodge, a luxurious bush retreat, Sondela Nature Reserve, Kranskop, Mabalingwe, Thaba Monate and Diepdrift all have many species of game in their natural habitats. For more information about the area, tel (014) 736-3694/2111.

Waterberg Range. A malaria-free mountainous area rich in indigenous trees, streams, springs, wetlands and a prolific birdlife. The vertical cliffs and impressive rock formations of the southern slopes of the Waterberg offer some challenging climbing. Facilities in the Waterberg region range from luxury lodges and tented camps to basic self-catering accommodation. Outdoor recreation options are virtually unlimited, encompassing horse safaris, walking trails and hunting safaris. A number of reputable safari outfitters operate in the area. The area is the natural habitat of the rare roan antelope.

Thornybush Game Reserve. Located on a vast tract of wilderness between Hoedspruit and Timbavati, and 64km/40 miles from the Orpen Gate of the Kruger, this is a place where you can bank on seeing the Big Five. The 10,000-hectare reserve lies outside all the other large conservancies along the western border of the Kruger National Park, which is a blessing in disguise as animals cannot leave Thornybush and this means the chances of spotting them are always good. There are open-vehicle game drives, and bush walks ranging from one to four hours. During the peak birding summer season more than 280 species of bird are present in the reserve. The reserve's diverse terrain also sustains more than 50 species of mammal, including bushbuck, nyala, wild dog, cheetah, pangolin, aardwolf and four species of mongoose.

SPORT AND RECREATION

Pietersburg has a modern sports stadium with indoor and outdoor facilities situated to the south of the city, with amenities for squash, netball, golf, bowls, cricket, athletics, rugby, boxing, karate and gymnastics. You can do just about everything in the area – tennis, go-karting, parachuting, badminton, soccer, swimming, kick-boxing, shooting, tennequoit, road-running, cycling, hiking and climbing.

Hiking. One wonderful walking and camping area is the Wolkberg Wilderness area of some 22,000 hectares, about 80km/50 miles east of Pietersburg on the Tzaneen turn-off beyond Haenertsburg. Permits are issued for parties of not more than nine people and you can get one from The Officer in Charge, Wolkberg Wilderness Area, Private Bag 102, Haenertsburg 0730. It is best to phone first as visitor numbers are limited, tel (0152) 276-1303. In the Magoebaskloof area there are two circular hiking trails in the Woodbush and De Hoek forest areas, the Dokolewa and Grootbosch, both three-day stretches. Both start at the De Hoek Forest Station, about 22km/14 miles from Tzaneen, and wind through this and Woodbush State Forest, passing through pine plantations, evergreen indigenous forests, and dense mountain valleys to meander to the top of the escarpment. They also pass through the largest forest in the area, the Grootbosch, and one trail goes along the summit of the northern spur of the Drakensberg, with marvellous views of the lowveld. Tel (01315) 41058.

Some wilderness experiences cannot be fully appreciated from the back of a vehicle, you have to be on foot in the bush with a knowledgeable eco-guide to share his savvy. Wildlife fundi Clive Walker set up trails on which the intricate web of the entire environment could be experienced. Gary Freeman now runs the Klaserie Lowveld Trails Camp and operates the trails established by Walker, with a format and philosophy that remains unchanged. The Klaserie Lowveld Trail is in the Klaserie Private Nature Reserve, which is part of the Greater Kruger Park area. All the fences have been removed between Kruger National Park, Timbavati and Klaserie and there is free animal movement through the whole area, with all the animals (except black rhino) of the Kruger Park also present in Klaserie. The camp is a rustic tented bush camp with open-air shower/toilet facilities and is situated on the banks of the Klaserie River. Tents sleep two people. A maximum of eight people are permitted on the trail. The emphasis is on walking, although there is an open vehicle which is used for night game-viewing drives. The five-day Rhino and Elephant Trail is a dual destination trip with the first two nights spent at Lapalala Wilderness followed by two nights in neighbouring Botswana. Time is spent both on foot and in open 4x4 vehicles looking for black and white rhino, as well as other game species, including the rare and endangered roan and sable antelopes. Klaserie Lowveld Trail costs US$535 per person sharing, the Rhino and Elephant Trail costs US$975 and there is also a three-day Rhino Trail at US$305. Contact Gary Freeman Safaris, PO Box 1885, Nigel 1490, Gauteng, tel/fax (011) 814-2855.

The Stamvrug hiking trail, less than 2 hours' drive from Johannesburg, traverses Jabulani and another farm on the mountain plateau in the Waterberg range. The trail is a two-day circular route starting from either of two base camps, Kloof or Stamvrug. The Kloof camp overlooks a spectacular cliff face and gorge. The Stamvrug camp is set in one of the folds of the koppies, which at 1600m/5249ft offer spectacular views over the upper wetlands and plains. The kloof route is 10.5km/6.5 miles long, but for the less energetic there is an alternative route of 7.5km/5 miles. The Stamvrug route is 6.5km/4 miles long, with an additional 3km/2 mile loop leading to a panoramic view. There are bilharzia-free earth dams on both routes for hikers to cool off. Birdwatchers in particular should enjoy these trails and there is a good chance of spotting the rare Blue Crane. The routes are average to difficult. Some 30 animal species have been sighted on the trails, from otters to Greater Kudu. Contact Jacana Country Homes and Trails for this and other areas at, PO Box 95212, Waterkloof 0145, Pretoria, Gauteng, tel (012) 346-3550/1/2. Other pleasant hikes in the area include the Louis Changuion Trail, Haenertsburg, 11km/7 miles. A circular route taking 3 to 4 hours, it includes some quite steep gradients, but spectacular views. You can get a map from Reflections, Rissik Street, or Aries Associates, Rabe Street, Haenertsburg, tel (0152) 276-4328 or 276-4307. The Rooikat Trail, State Forest, New

Agatha, near Tzaneen, has an 11km/6.8 mile trail, a circular forest route with picnic spots and swimming pools in the river. Some steep gradients, tel (0152) 307-4310. There are one and 3-day trails at Lekgalameetse Nature Reserve, access via Ofcolaco Road, which turns off the R36, at 44km/27 miles from Tzaneen, tel (0152302) and ask for 1514.

Fishing. For the angler, Magoesbaskloof in particular has a wealth of dams. High up in the kloof, near Woodbush forest, is the Dap Naude Dam, while the much larger Ebenezer Dam, 6km/4 miles from Haenertsburg on the George's Valley road, is well stocked with trout, eel, barbel, kurper and black bass. There is also boating, although launching sites are few and far between. Two smaller dams, the Magoesbaskloof and Troutwaters, are close to the main road, one at the bottom, and the other at the top of the kloof, and although no angling is allowed in the Magoesbaskloof Dam, Troutwaters is exactly what its name says. You can get the necessary angling licence from any revenue or magistrate's office.

Hunting. Through the efforts of local hunters and conservationists the Waterberg has been restored to its former glory as a wildlife paradise. The region is one of South Africa's most remote and rugged landscapes and provides a challenging hunting environment. Ellisras and Alldays are the province's north-western bushveld hunting capitals, and there are vast and plentiful game farms offering trophy hunting, as well as game-viewing, hiking trails, and photographic safaris. For information on these areas contact the Ellisras Community Tourism Association at Private Bag X136, Ellisras 0555, tel (014) 763-2193, fax (014) 763-5662 and Alldays Tourism, PO Box 102, Alldays 0909, tel (01554) 270/258, fax (01554) 286.

Golf. The Hans Merensky Golf Club is on the edge of the Kruger National Park at Phalaborwa. The golf course extends over 110 hectares and, with hippo in a water hazard and antelopes on the fairways, your game is enhanced or otherwise by constant interruptions from wandering wildlife. Contact Hans Merensky Country Club, tel (01524) 5931.

For a more unusual form of recreation there is a 25,000-acre cattle ranch in the Waterberg where you can spend your days riding horses and cattle-mustering in real cowboy-style, camping and sleeping out among wild game in the bush. The Triple B Ranch is about 85km/53 miles from Nylstroom and a two-hour drive from Pretoria. If you prefer a roof over your head there is accommodation in a rustic farmhouse, hiking lodges and other self-catering facilities. Contact PO Box 301, Vaalwater 0530, tel (0147552) 2423 or 2141, or tel (012) 998-8157.

 Pietersburg has a wide range of shops and four large malls – Pick 'n Pay complex is to the north, down Market Street; Checkers Complex is in the city centre, in Hans van Rensburg Street; and the Metropolitan Centre is also in Market Street, in the city centre. Others include The Mall, Palm Centre, the Indian Shopping Complex, the Flora Park and Bendor shopping centres. A flea market is held in the Library Gardens on the last Saturday every month. You will find interesting farm stalls, curio shops and craft markets all over the province, but if you are passing by any of the following you are sure to find something good to eat, admire or pack.

In the lowveld, the Pot 'n Plow, near Magoesbaskloof, on the R71 between Haenertsburg and Tzaneen, is a small country store bursting at the seams with locally produced handicrafts. You can browse among the huge selection – preserves, condiments, pottery, carvings, leatherwork, art works and ethnic jewellery – but part of the store's attraction is its freshly baked, feather-light, home-made pies. On the same road is the Wheelbarrow Farm Stall, where if you are planning a hike you can stock up on biltong, dried fruit, nuts, honey and their export quality avocados and litchis. They also have a good range of local art and craft work. For something uniquely local Karosswerkers is a project formed to develop the skills of rural people in the Letsitele area of the Northern Province. Here you can find delicate embroidery done by citrus packers and tractor drivers, and African kaftans from Tsumeri. Products are sold directly to visitors — you won't find them in the local shops — by appointment only, tel (015) 345-1765. Sapekoe has tea estates in the Magoebaskloof area and you can visit and sample their brew before buying their product, tel (0152) 30-5324.

Despite the poverty of the region, statistics show that it is the safest place in South Africa to live — unless you happen to be a witch. Attacks on suspected witches are the most commonly committed crime in the Northern Province. Police say that the rates for rape, assault and robbery are more than five times below the national average, which is obviously good news for visitors.

TOURIST INFORMATION

Northern Province Tourism Board, tel (0152) 295-9300, fax (0152) 295-5819.
Noordtratoer, PO Box 111, Pietersburg 0700, tel (0152) 295-2011, fax (0152) 291-5101.
Satour, tel (0152) 295-3025, fax (0152) 291-2654.

Lowveld

Duiwelskloof and Haenertsburg, tel (0152) 309-9246.
Hoedspruit, tel (01528) 31678, fax (01528) 31912.
Kruger National Park, tel (012) 343-1991, fax (012) 343-0905.
Letaba, tel (015276) 4307, fax (015276) 4386.
Phalaborwa, tel (01524) 85860, fax (01524) 85870.
Tzaneen, tel (0152) 307-1411, fax (0152) 307-1507.

Soutpansberg

Alldays (Soutpansberg/Limpopo Valley), tel (01554) 535/270, fax (01554) 286.
Louis Trichardt, tel/fax (015) 516-0040.
Messina, tel (01553) 40211, fax (01553) 2513.
Thohoyandou, tel (0159) 21885, fax (0159) 21298.
Venda Tourism, PO Box 9, Sibasa 0970, tel (0159) 21-1316/41577, fax (0159) 21298/41048.

Bushveld

Ellisras, tel (014) 763-2193, fax (014) 763-5662.
Naboomspruit, tel (014) 743-1111, fax (014) 743-2434.
Nylstroom, tel/fax (01470) 2211.
Potgietersrus, tel/fax (0154) 2244.
Thabazimbi, tel (014773) 22590, fax (014773) 71069.
Vaalwater, tel (014755) 3605, fax (014755) 3860.
Warmbaths, tel/fax (014) 736-2111 ext 122, fax (014) 736-3288.
Waterberg, tel/fax (014755) 3862.

Gay-friendly tours of the Lowveld and Kruger National Park are arranged by *Southern Star Tourist Services*, PO Box 1238, Hoedspruit 1380, tel (01528) 35219.

North-West Province

The Lost City

The North-West Province is like a gigantic yellow and green striped flag, made up of the fields of sunflowers and maize that cloak the lush plains in a seemingly endless expanse. The region does, in fact, produce a third of the country's staple maize crop, as well as cradling the richest known platinum reef in the world. You do not, however, come to look at something you probably do not eat or at a mineral you cannot see; what you visit North-West for is what draws everyone else: excellent game-viewing within only two hours' drive from Johannesburg and Pretoria and the vast and lavish gaming and entertainment hotel and casino complex of Sun City and The Lost City, which are a cross between Las Vegas and Disneyland.

More than a dozen game parks and nature reserves are scattered throughout the province, which merges into Botswana along its western perimeter, the biggest and most varied being Pilansberg National Park, which is set in and around an extinct volcanic crater. One the park's southern boundary and a few minutes' drive away is the Sun City gambling complex, where you might make enough on the fall of a card to pay for your holiday — or lose your shirt. In the early 19th century all this was the domain of Mzilikazi and his Matabele warriors. In the 1830s white farmers and their Batswana allies drove Mzilikazi and his tribesman northwards across the Limpopo, into Zimbabwe, where they still live.

The capital of the North-West is Mmabatho, a name of Setswana origin meaning 'Mother of the People,' although it seems likely that its suburb, century-old Mafikeng, on the Molopo River, will take over the role of capital from the modern centre which was created largely as a result of the National Party's government's bantustan or homelands policy. In 1857, Molema, the younger brother of the great Barolong chief Montshiwa, settled his Tswana people at the 'Place of Stones' — Mafikeng in Setswana. In 1885, the Bechuanaland High Commissioner gave permission for a white settlement to be established outside the Barolong town and Mafeking became the seat of the Bechaunaland Protectorate Government, the only country with its capital outside its borders. This was moved in 1966 to Gaborone, after Botswana gained its independence. Mafeking reverted to its original spelling, Mafikeng, in 1977. Mafikeng is better known as the town — then Mafeking — which drew the world's admiration when it was besieged and held off Boer forces for more than seven months after the start of the Anglo-Boer War in 1899. The relief of the town gave the English language the new verb maffick, meaning to celebrate or exult riotously. Many places of interest in the area are closely related to this event, which made garrison commander Colonel Robert Baden-Powell world famous and subsequently led him to found the international Boy Scout movement based on the boy cadet corps he formed to run messages in the town. Mmabatho was originally the seat of government of the Tswana homeland of Bophuthatswana ('that which binds the Tswana'), set up in 1977 as an independent but fragmented 'state' of 2 million people. In March 1994, on the eve of South Africa's first democratic elections, the Bophuthatswana government of Lucas Mangope was overthrown and the territory became once more part of South Africa. It now covers a cohesive 117,000sq km/45,174sq miles, with a population of 4 million people, two-thirds of them living traditional lives in the rural areas. Today, the Batswana farm and breed cattle, which, until recently, were considered more valuable than any other possession, representing a family's wealth and used, among other things, to pay *lobola* ('bride price'), to buy favours from the tribal chief and to pay fines. The Batswana believe in the influence of the spirits of their ancestors, to whom they make supplications in ritual ceremonies. Ancient customs such as rain dances are still practised at the start of the ploughing season. The Batswana are naturally creative, with a strong sense of design and colour, and you can buy some exceptionally fine jewellery, curios and works of art in the countryside.

The relatively recent development of Mmabatho has given it some of the most striking and contemporary buildings in Africa and it is noteworthy for its impressive administration buildings designed around the concept of a *kgotla*, the traditional meeting place in a Batswana village. Among the province's important commercial centres are Klerksdorp, Potchefstroom, Vryburg, Lichtenburg, Brits and Rustenburg. The little town of Groot Marico has, for lovers of literature, an attraction disproportionate to its size. The Marico bushveld is the setting of what are arguably South Africa's funniest stories, set down with rare fluency by Herman Charles Bosman, whose immortal fictional character Oom Schalk Lourens captures the essence of the old pre-apartheid Afrikaner. There are still characters in this rural area who could have stepped out of Bosman's pages and the potent *mampoer* moonshine that fuels them is still made in the old way and has its own annual festival and Mampoer Route. If mampoer has no allure, there are Anglo-Boer War battlefields to explore, scenes of the world's greatest diamond rush, the varied attractions of Sun City and the Lost City and, along the southern boundary of the province, its popular playground, the Vaal River, where you can while away the time swimming, fishing, water-skiing, boating and sailing. Further south, near the border with the Northern Cape Province, is Taung ('Place of the Lion') where in 1924 the famous skull known as the Taung Child was found in a local limestone quarry which is now a Heritage Site. Close to Johannesburg is the tranquil watersport resort of Hartbeespoort Dam and village, which is a popular weekend jaunt for Gautengers tired of city stress and bustle.

MMABATHO-MAFIKENG

GETTING AROUND

Mmabatho Airport is 17km from town. There are no buses to town but you can hire a car at the airport. Mmabatho and Mafikeng are small enough to walk around, but you can hire a car or take a taxi if you travel further afield. Check with the tourist office. Unlike the developed countries of the world travel from one place to another usually calls for private transport; unless they are on the main motor freeways, towns and villages are not connected by regular or reliable bus services, nor (with few exceptions) are they linked by train unless they are on the country's main north–south or east–west rail lines. This is where the **long-distance minibus taxi** reigns supreme among those without their own wheels.

EXPLORING

Cannon Koppie is a hill that commands fine views of Barolong Village. The name dates back to a time of conflict between the Tshidi Barolong and the Boers of the Goshen Republic in 1882. The Boers used to fire a three-pounder into the village from here. In 1885, the British sent the Warren Expedition to Mafikeng to halt Boer infiltration and built two forts, Cannon Koppie and Warren's Fort, one on either side of the Molopo River. Warren's Fort on the north side lies within the Imperial Reserve on the Vryburg Road and, except for having its roof raised, is authentic colonial Brit. Warren's Well, a well preserved brick and steel structure, is to the left of the Bokone Road from Mafikeng before it crosses the river. Warren's Weir is on the river below the Methodist Church, and was used by the expedition and during the famous siege to water large herds of horses.

Leopard Park Golf Course is a challenging 18-hole course that attracts golfers from far and wide.

Mafikeng Cemetery holds the siege graves of British soldiers, British South African Police and members of the Town Guard. One row of closely spaced of crosses marks the trench in which the men who died in the attack on Gametree Fort in 1899 are buried. The most distinctive grave is that of Andrew Beauchamp-Proctor, the most highly decorated South African air fighter ace of World War One. **Concentration Camp Cemeteries** contain the graves of Boer women and children who died in the camp.

Imperial Reserve, the unimposing administrative offices of three former governments — Bechuanaland (now Botswana), pre-independence Tswana Territorial Authority

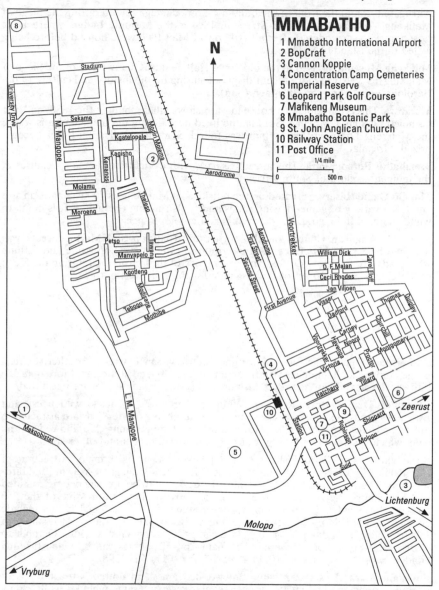

MMABATHO

1 Mmabatho International Airport
2 BopCraft
3 Cannon Koppie
4 Concentration Camp Cemeteries
5 Imperial Reserve
6 Leopard Park Golf Course
7 Mafikeng Museum
8 Mmabatho Botanic Park
9 St. John Anglican Church
10 Railway Station
11 Post Office

and the then Republic of Bophuthatswana — the building today is the local headquarters of the South African Police Service.

Lotlamoreng Dam Cultural Reserve, 'Great Water of the King' is a sanctuary for many species of plants and birds. It is also home to the Cultural Village which is a living museum portraying life in 10 traditional African villages.

Mafikeng Club, built in 1894 at the corner of Robinson and Tillard Street. A piece of corrugated iron in the front of the building shows damage caused during the Siege of Mafikeng. Also built in Tillard Street in 1894 is the **Masonic Lodge**, where Boer prisoners who surrendered after a battle on 12 May 1900 were housed before being exiled to the island of St Helena.

Mafikeng Museum, housed in the old Town Hall, features many relics of the Siege of Mafeking, as well as a more recent display focusing on the history and culture of the Barolong people and the Bushmen (San).

Maratiwa. This is the name of a house in Montshiwa village, built in the 1880s and first occupied by Silas T Molema. Sol Plaatjie lived here during the Siege and it is where the Mafikeng Diary written by him was found. Since its publication it has become prized Africana.

Mmabatho Botanic Park. This attractive park with a Victorian theme specialises in the indigenous flora of South Africa.

Molopo Game Reserve, situated on the outskirts of Mafikeng, is 7000 hectares in size and has a variety of game-viewing roads and trails running through it. It is home to white rhino, buffalo, giraffe and a number of antelope species.

St John's Anglican Church on the corner of Robinson and Martin streets was designed by Sir Herbert Baker. An inscription in the foundation stone laid in June 1907 reads: 'To the glory of God and in memory of those who died during the Siege of Mafeking, and as an act of thanksgiving for the relief of the town.'

FURTHER AFIELD

Barberspan. One of the most important waterfowl sanctuaries in southern Africa. Large numbers of flamingoes visit from time to time to feed at the pan. More than 350 bird species have been recorded. Fishing and certain water sports are permitted.

Bloemhof Dam Nature Reserve. White rhino, blesbok, black wildebeest and Burchell's zebra inhabit the reserve, and large numbers of waterbirds are attracted to the dam. There are picnic sites. Water sports, including fishing, are allowed on the dam, which is stocked with carp, yellowfish, mudfish, barbel and other species.

Borakalalo Game Park. Fishing in the Klipvoor Dam is a major attraction of Borakalalo (14,000 hectares). Leisure options include hiking, game-viewing and bird-watching. There are bird hides at Borakalalo, designed to be used by people confined to wheelchairs. The African fish eagle is perhaps the most impressive of the 350 recorded bushveld and wetlands bird species. Some 35 large mammal species include elephant, white rhino, sable, giraffe and zebra. Borakalalo is within easy distance of Johannesburg for a day trip or there are camps for a longer stay. Open October to March, 6am–8pm; April to September, 6am–7pm. Bookings can be made through Golden Leopard Resorts, tel (011) 465-5437, fax (011) 465-1228.

Botsalano Game Reserve. Magnificent wooded grassland dotted with outcrops of quartzite, ironstone and lava characterises this reserve. Game includes white rhino, giraffe, springbok, impala, other antelope species and a great diversity of birds. There are guided wilderness trails and self-guided walks. Mogobe Camp offers guests exclusive walking trails. Central reservations, tel (011) 465-5423/4, fax (011) 465-1228.

Brits. This area played an important historical role in the history of the old Transvaal. About 5km/3 miles east of the town, on the Brits-Silkaatsnek route, is the *Vredesboom* (Peace Tree). The inscription on the tree reads: 'After the Burgerstryd in the Transvaal and the Crocodile River Battle in this area, on January 5th 1864, the leaders of the Staatsleger and the Volksleger met underneath this tree from the 9th to the 15th January for discussions which led to the restitution of peace and harmony. Paul Kruger in his capacity as Commandant General provided important contributions to the restoration of peace.' Today, Brits is a modern, developing town and is well-known as a citrus fruit and vegetable centre.

Cashan Territory. The Cashan Territory, spanning the area from Renosterspruit in the south, Pretoria in the east, Krugersdorp in the west and Rustenburg in the north, gets its name from chief Kgwashwane of the Kwena Mmatau who settled along the southern slopes of the Magaliesberg mountains in the late 17th century. The area has numerous scenic attractions, quaint shops and villages, arts and craft workshops, galleries and studios, game, cheetah and crocodile farms, and a variety of accommodation, including B&B, cottages, country houses, guest houses and camping sites. Tel (01205) 51003, fax (01205) 51201. Brochures and maps are available from the Johannesburg and Pretoria Publicity Associations.

Christiana. Briefly a boom town after diamonds were discovered in the area in 1870. Diamond digging still takes place. The Vaal River offers opportunities for angling and water sports. Nearby, the Aventura Vaal Spa Holiday Resort has a well-stocked game reserve. Tel (0534) 2245.

Groot Marico. The rich history and Iron Age culture of the Marico district can be traced back to the middle 17th century through Bushmen rock paintings. The remains of Gaditshwene village, headquarters of the Hurutshe tribe, confirm the occupation of the land by the Tswanas from the early 19th century. Names such as Mzilikazi, Robert Moffat, Dr Andrew Murray and Dr David Livingstone dot the history books. To book for mampoer and tobacco tours contact Marico Bushveld Tours, tel (014252) and ask for 85.

Hartbeespoort Dam. About 60km/37 miles and less than an hour's drive from Johannesburg or Pretoria (on the R511 or R512), Hartbeespoort Dam is easily reached on fine roads. The temperature in the area of the dam averages 2°C/36°F warmer than Johannesburg and its vegetation is considerably more subtropical and luxuriant. Under the Magaliesberg Mountains, Kosmos and its surroundings offer some excellent restaurants, picturesque pubs, tea gardens, guest houses, arts and crafts, a well-stocked zoo, a huge aquarium, a cableway, yachting, speed-boating, hang-gliding and a lot more if you look around. Surrounded by the 120km/75 mile range of the Magaliesberg mountains, the dam is popular all year round as a fishing and boating resort and venue for watersports enthusiasts. There is even an Officers Club, where you can play war games or ride go-karts. This beautiful little resort area is a favourite with artists and potters, whose studios are on the Cashan Territory route. The area has an historical heritage ranging from Stone Age to Matabele and Anglo-Boer War sites. The dam wall was completed in 1923, although the first irrigation dam in the Crocodile River was built in 1898, and holds back over 200 million cubic metres of water, which algal growth periodically turns into an unappetising pea soup green. About 12km/7.5 miles from Hartbeespoort Dam is the De Wildt Cheetah Research Centre. Tours of this well known breeding centre for cheetah (including king cheetah), wild dog and brown hyena are available on Tuesdays, Thursdays, Saturdays and Sundays, tel (012) 504-1921.

Klerksdorp. In 1837, a dozen Voortrekker families settled here on the banks of the Schoonspruit. The 11km/7 mile Ou Dorp hiking trail meanders through the old part of the town where they lived. Remains of prehistoric kraals can also be seen. Gold was discovered in 1886 and the rich deposits are still mined near the city. At Goudkoppie ('Gold Hill') you can see old mine shafts dating from the 1880s with inscriptions made by British soldiers who camped there during the Anglo-Boer War.

Gold mine tours can be arranged on request, tel (018) 26220. Fine old buildings include the former jail, now an interesting museum, the Dutch Reformed Church in Anderson Street, and the railway station, opened by President Kruger in 1897. The Schoonspruit, Vaal River and Johan Neser Dam offer water sports and picnics. The Schoonspruit Hiking Trail traverses an area notable for its indigenous vegetation. At the Faan Meintjies Nature Reserve, 13km/8 miles from town, there is a good chance of spotting antelope, giraffe, zebra and white rhino. About 18km/11 miles north of the town on the farm Bosworth you can see excellent examples of Bushmen (San) rock engravings.

Lichtenburg. The National Zoological Gardens, north of the town, administers the Lichtenburg Game-Breeding Centre where rare species of wildlife from all over the world, such as pygmy hippo, derby eland and Pere David's deer, can be seen. Other endangered animals are also bred for the National Zoo in Pretoria. The farm is a haven for thousands of waterbirds. Lichtenburg has an agricultural museum, a cultural-historical museum and an art gallery and 20km/12 miles north is the site of the world's greatest diamond rush, sparked off by the discovery of a magnificent gem on the farm Elandsputte in 1926. Within 12 months there were 100,000 people on the diggings, which spread along the course of an ancient dried-up river. Today, you can follow the route of these prospectors through a number of small villages.

Madikwe Game Reserve, 80km/50 miles north of Zeerust, in the heart of the Marico District, is the North-west Province's Parks Board's newest park. It boasts the 'Big Five' and is malaria-free. The game reserve, the third largest in South Africa, currently covers more than 80,000 hectares and has seen the largest reintroduction of game undertaken by man in any reserve in Africa. The relocation of entire breeding herds of elephant, various antelope species, buffalo, white rhino, zebra, lion, cheetah, spotted hyena and endangered wild dogs have increased the large mammal population of the park to more than 10,000. Some species, such as kudu and leopards, occur naturally in the area. Tel (01466) 55960/1/2/3, fax (01466) 55964.

Montshiwa Nature Reserve. The Lotlamoreng Dam surrounding the reserve offers excellent fishing, especially for barbel, yellowfish and carp. Canoeing is another option. There are barbecue areas and a refreshment kiosk. The reserve is the site of the Lotlamoreng Dam Cultural Village, a functioning representation of life during the African Iron Age. The village provides an opportunity to learn about ancient cultural traditions, including traditional rain ceremonies and story-telling, as well as herbal and spiritual healing.

Pilansberg Game Reserve. At 58,000 hectares, this is one of the largest reserves in South Africa. It is set in the crater of an extinct volcano and supports more than 10,000 head of game, including the Big Five, as well as cheetah, hippo, giraffe, antelope and more than 350 bird species. Among a great many facilities, there are swimming pools, a mini-golf course and a restaurant. A day visitors' area includes a walk-in aviary. You can take part in three-hour safaris in the early morning and late afternoon, the best times for observing game. The best months for game-viewing are between August and May. Guided walks set out at 6am. Park accommodation ranges from safari tents to luxurious chalets and hotels. For the ultimate wilderness experience hikers camp under the stars. Central reservations, tel (011) 465-5423, fax (011) 465-1228. The Sun City/Lost City casino complex and resort is a few minutes' drive away on the park's southern perimeter, but the real 'Lost City' is an archaeological site dating back to 1600 in southern Africa's late Iron Age, and to be found in the Pilansberg National Park only a few kilometres from the resort complex. Four hundred years ago it was a flourishing settlement of Tswana people; now, only the tumbled walls remain to show where they once flourished.

Potchefstroom. The first capital of the old Transvaal Republic, Potchefstroom has evolved into an important agricultural, military and educational centre with many interesting historical buildings. The Dutch Reformed Church — the oldest in the North-West — is an architectural gem, and the Anglican Church has magnificent stained glass windows. The Potchefstroom Museum houses art and cultural history exhibitions. The President Pretorius Museum, built in Cape style in 1868 by the first state President of the South African Republic, and the Goetz/Fleischack Museum, a restored town house of the mid-1850s furnished in Victorian style, are worth touring. The Lakeside Holiday Resort, an extensive recreational complex on the banks of the Potchefstroom Dam, has chalets, swimming pools and water sports facilities. Angling is popular on the dam. There is excellent bird-watching at the Prozesky Bird Sanctuary next to the golf course.

Rustenburg. At the foot of the Magaliesberg range of hills, the town serves a prosperous farming community. Paul Kruger's restored farm Boekenhoutfontein, 14km/9 miles from town, the museum in the Town Hall, and other historical sites are worth visiting. An art ramble, incorporating visits to artists' studios, takes place during the first weekend of every month. Outside town, two platinum mines are reputed to be the largest in the world. About 4km/2.5 miles to the south-west in the Magaliesberg range, the Rustenburg Nature Reserve has a wide variety of game and more than 140 bird species. There are two hiking trails, one of about three hours and the other lasting two days. Tel (0142) 31050.

Schweizer-Reneke. The town is named after Captain CA Schweizer and field-cornet CM Reneke, who were killed in a tribal skirmish in 1885. There are Bushman paintings 2km north-east of the town which are thought to be more than 20,000 years old, as well as rusting relics from the Anglo-Boer War in the nearby veld.

Taung. A plaque marks the spot where in 1924, the front of the hominid skull of the Taung Child was found in the Buxton limestone quarries. This was the first fossil of the African man-ape *Australopithecus africanus* to be discovered. After passing the Taung skull site, there is an attractive valley with a stream and a number of pools. An old mine tunnel has been opened for visitors to explore and there is an ablution block and barbecue facilities. The Boipelo Game Reserve is managed by the Taung Sun Hotel and offers a choice of four walking trails, varying from 0.5km to 3.2km. Some 150 hectares of natural bushveld forms part of the land granted to the hotel for tourist development and paths suitable for walking and mountain biking have been laid out.

Vryburg. When the Republic of Stellaland was proclaimed in 1882, Vryburg was established as its capital. The Republicans called themselves *vryburgers* (free citizens) hence the name of the town. The area is still known locally as Stellaland and also commonly referred to as the Texas of South Africa. There are lots of hiking and horse-riding trails, good hunting, game-viewing, fishing, water-skiing, canoeing, and agricultural tours in the area. Today it is the industrial and agricultural centre of the western region, and annually is host to a variety of events, including an agricultural show, national gliding championships and off-road racing events. Among local places of interest are the Vryburg Museum, Tiger Kloof Educational Institute, Theiler Museum, and the Leon Taljaard Nature Reserve.

Wolmaransstad. The town was founded in 1891 in the valley of the Makwasi, which takes its name from the wild spearmint that flourishes there, and used to be an important halt on the old postal route between Johannesburg and Kimberley. Today it is the hub of a large maize farming community and is an important international diamond trading centre. Every Friday, Dutch, Belgian, Israeli and local buyers arrive with wads of dollars to haggle for gemstones. Sources in the town estimate that about R5 million changes hands at the weekly auctions, making it one of the biggest diamond markets in Africa. Stones range from finest quality blue-whites at R5400 a carat to yellow stones worth peanuts.

You can see the diamond industry at work on a tour of the alluvial diamond diggings in the vicinity of the town and diggers can still be seen searching for the one that will make them rich. Polished gems can be bought at diggers' prices. For information on the Diggers' Tour contact Elizabeth Labuschagne, tel (01811) 22404.

Zeerust. The town is situated in the Marico bushveld region, about 240km/149 miles from Pretoria and Johannesburg. A trail through breathtaking scenery is a recommended hike as well as a visit to at least one of the game ranches in the area. Kaditsweni, on Orion Game Farm, near Zeerust, is a Batswana cultural development where handicrafts such as leatherwork, woodwork and needlework are made and sold. Tel (01428) 23350. At Marula Kop, 50km/31 miles north of the town, is an Iron Age settlement which has an unusual stone wall construction and evidence of terracing on the steep hill slope and iron smelting at the base.

 **Accommodation**

Unless you are on a business trip you should not go to the North-West Province to stay in Mmabatho, although there are two casino hotels which can offer nightclubs and various entertainments, as well as gambling. These are the four-star *Mmabatho Sun Hotel*, PO Box 600, Mafikeng 8670, Lobatsi Road, tel (014) 89-1111, and the three-star *Molopo Sun Hotel*, PO Box 3355, Mmabatho 8681, tel (0140) 24184, fax (0140) 23472. Lower down the scale is the one-star *Surrey Hotel*, Shippard Street, tel (014) 81-0420, and there is a self-catering option at *Cooke's Lake Caravan Park*, tel (014) 32531. There are also half a dozen B&B places, which the local publicity office will tell you about. Sun International runs all of the most up-market hotel and entertainment complexes in the province. The most famous is Sun City and the Lost City, near the Pilansberg National Park (see below).

The *Tlhabane Sun* is 5km/3 miles outside Rustenburg on the road to Sun City. The land was the home of the Bafokeng tribe, and the name means 'You have supported me and seen me through my troubles.' Apart from the normal hotel amenities and slot machine areas, it is best known for its ultra-modern totaliser room which can take up to 400 punters at a times. Bets are taken not only on horse racing, but on all major sporting events. A video screen above the betting window gives live coverage of featured races and there is also a tote bar. Close to the totaliser room is a children's entertainment complex with lots of video game machines.

From *Taung Sun Hotel and Slots Casino* you can visit the world-famous site where the Taung skull was found, 19km away, and the local marble factory. Game trails and mountain bikes are available through nearby Taung Sun Game Park. The *Toroko* restaurant (meaning Prickly Pear in Setswana) offers local and international fare. PO Box 201, Taung Station 8580, tel (01405) 41820, fax (01405) 41788.

The *Carousel Casino and Entertainment World* is at Babalegi, 56km/35 miles north of Pretoria, off the N1 to Warmbaths. The architectural theme and decor is Victorian, and a real carousel is one of the attractions. The split-level casino covers 5200 square metres and is the biggest and most colourful in the southern hemisphere. Two terraces containing 1530 slot machines circle the main gaming area and ramps from here lead down to the casino pit to tables for American roulette and blackjack. There are various eateries, from fast-food outlets to restaurants, live entertainment, a children's theatre, cinemas, a video games arcade, and glittering shopping malls. There is a creche for children aged from 2 to 7, and another supervised room for children ranging from 7 to 14. Contact the Carousel, PO Box 777, Temba 0404, North-West Province, tel (01464) 77777 or (011) 780-7444, fax (01464) 77111.

The *Morula Sun* is near Mabopane, 33km/21 miles from Pretoria on the south-eastern shore of the Nooitgedacht Dam. With its conical roofs it looks like a traditional Tswana village. The 70-roomed hotel has an open-air beer garden, a cinema, slot machine areas and a casino. Sports facilities include two floodlit tennis courts, a children's venture park and a mini-golf course. There is a nature reserve and bird park at the water's edge. Contact tel (01461) 23320. For all these hotel casino complexes contact Central Reservations, PO Box 784487, Sandton 2146, tel (011) 780-7800, fax (011) 780-7726.

At Pilansberg National Park, a few kilometres from Sun City, you have a choice of accommodation – luxury four-star chalets at *Kwa Maritane* ('Place of the Rock') *Game Lodge*, furnished cabins and thatched chalets at *Tshukudu* ('Place of the Rhino') *Camp* and *Bakubung Hotel and Timeshare Lodge*, all tel (01465) 21861/2, fax (01465) 21621/18, a tented camp on the Mankwe Dam, and safari tents at Kololo and Manyane. Tel (011) 465-5423, fax (011) 465-1228.

Tau Game Lodge is a Sun establishment in the Madikwe Game Reserve, located about 300km/186 miles from Johannesburg and 28km/17 miles from Gaborone airport in Botswana and an hour's drive from Sun City. Luxury air-conditioned thatched chalets and suites are spread out on either side of a large natural water hole which attracts prolific game. Tau — it means lion in Setswana — has chefs who prepare dishes with local ingredients such as maroelas, marog and madumbies. Contact Sun Game Lodges, tel (011) 780-0356, fax (011) 780-0033. In the same reserve is *Madikwe River Lodge*. It has 16 split-level chalets under thatch on the banks of the perennial Marico River, each with a private deck overlooking riverine bush. It costs R850 per person sharing, tel (014778) 891/2, fax (014778) 893. Also at Madikwe is the *Wonderboom Guest House*, an authentic colonial farmhouse that has been luxuriously modernised, and *Mosetlha Bushcamp*, owned and run by Honey-guide Trails, which is a rustic camp consisting of two raised wooden bunkhouses which offers up to eight people a true wilderness experience, tel/fax (011) 393-4286.

In the Hartbeespoort area there is Satour five-star graded *Mount Amanzi Lodge*, in the Crocodile River valley of the Magaliesberg mountains, with thatched self-catering chalets and all mod cons. PO Box 169, Hartbeespoort 0126, tel (01211) 53-0541, fax (01211) 53-0510. Between the dam and the mountains is family oriented *Makalani*, with luxury self-catering accommodation around a swimming pool, trampolines, volleyball and games area. There is also a keep-fit gym and an art showroom to take care of your gifts and souvenirs, tel (01211) 53-0436. *Cashan Lodge* is a B&B and **youth hostel** on the road to Sun City, tel/fax (01211) 56-0422. Two places overlooking the dam are *Sally's* guest house, tel/fax (01211) 56-0422, and *Willings Lodge* B&B, in the charming artists' village of Kosmos, tel (01211) 53-0032, Cell 082 454-2073. **Caravanners and campers** should head for Oberon on the shores of the dam, where there is a neat little resort with shady sites with power, clean ablution blocks and sparkling swimming pools, tel (01205) 51353. Hartbeespoort Dam Central Reservations, tel (01211) 5300541 and (01205) 51210, fax (01211) 53-0510, Cell 083 266-5184, can put you in touch with others.

Caravanning facilities are also available at *Rustenberg Kloof Holiday Resort*, tel (0142) 97-1351.

SUN CITY AND THE LOST CITY

Sun City is probably the most successful and famous resort on the African continent and since the addition of The Lost City African fantasy theme resort in 1991, it has become one of the top three tourist destinations in southern Africa. It is South Africa's answer to Las Vegas, and with its palm trees and a man-made sea complete with waves and beaches, the resort is a lush oasis in an arid landscape. It offers up-market accommodation in the *Sun Hotel*, the *Cascades*, the *Cabanas*, and the *Palace of the Lost City*, with dozens of leisure options, including sports facilities of every description, championship boxing tournaments, cinemas, excellent restaurants and an entertainment centre with star-studded extravaganzas. As well as all this there is a Superbowl that can seat 6000 people, a casino that is the largest in the world outside the USA, a golf course of international repute, tennis and squash courts, a bowling green and a health spa. A sky train makes it easy to reach various places in the vast complex.

The Lost City covers 25 hectares at Sun City and was designed to look like the lost city of an ancient civilisation, the sort of place where you might bump into the Sultan of Brunei or Indiana Jones. At the heart of the complex is the Palace of the Lost City, a luxurious 340-roomed hotel. The entertainment centre is situated in a rock cavern linked to the Valley of the Ancients, a fantasy jungle garden. A golf course — with live crocodiles in the water hazard at the 13th hole — was designed by famous South African champion golfer Gary Player. Residents have entry to all other resort and sporting facilities at the complex. For children aged three to 12 there is Kamp Kwena, a daily children's programme packed with fun activities, and the Children's Activity Park. There are good-value dining facilities, from buffet breakfasts in the lush green gardens and sparkling blue pools, to Mexican enchiladas, fish dishes, sizzling steaks and carveries, or top-flight international cuisine. In between times you can snack on pancakes and waffles or schwarmas at the pool. This jewel in Sun International's resort chain is a 90-minute drive from Johannesburg. As well as a regular bus service between the two, there are daily flights between the airport at Sun City and major centres throughout southern Africa.

Eating and Drinking

The North-West is by no means a gourmet's paradise. The hotels dish up filling but standard fare with an international sameness and the fast food outlets offer the hamburgers and other staples that taste the same from Cape to Cairo. Some delicious alternatives can be found at Groot Marico, in the dry bushveld between Rustenburg and Mafikeng where home-cooked traditional fare using recipes passed down from generation to generation is the order of the day. Try Flori-Anne Esterhuizen's delicious cooking at *Ouma's Kitchen*, a small restaurant in the *Bobbejaanskrans Guest House*. You get generous portions of traditional bobotie, mutton fried in the oven or chicken pie. A favourite from the Voortrekker days is *doek poeding*, a steamed pudding covered in a cloth and served with brandy, herb or wine sauces. The ginger beer is made in the old style and you can also buy homemade jams or other farm fare. Rina du Preez at *Vergenoeg Guest House* prepares tasty *skaap-afval* (tripe) and at *Doornkraal* rondavel on the banks of the Marico River, Bets Swart specialises in game sausage. Breakfast at the *Groot Marico Bosveld Hotel* or at one of the area's guest houses is usually a grand affair. A typical farm-style breakfast includes mielie-pap (maize porridge), sausages, home-baked bread, bacon, eggs and tomato. Prices are similar wherever you stay. R125 (£16.65/$27.50) for two people sharing at the quaint *Groot Marico Bosveld Hotel;* guest houses charge about R50 per person sharing, including bed and breakfast. Contact Groot Marico Information Centre, PO Box 28, Groot Marico 2825, tel (014252) and ask for 85.

In the Hartbeespoort Dam area, in the north-east corner of the province, you can get hearty, no-nonsense meals and snacks at the *Lapa Pub and Restaurant*, tel (01211) 53-0534, the *Makalani* family restaurant, tel (01211) 53-0436, the *Thatchaven Tea Garden and Pub* — overlooking the dam it claims to be a registered stress-free environment — tel (01211) 31798, and the *Cock and Bull* pub at the Cashan Lodge, tel (01211) 56-0422. More up-market are the restaurants at the *Magaliespark Country Club*, tel (01207) 71315.

SPORT AND RECREATION

Sun City is the mecca for anyone who likes to swing a club. You can follow in the footsteps of the world's finest golfers by playing on the world-renowned Gary Player Golf Course, which is home to the Million Dollar Golf Challenge in December every year. The course is a spectacular spread of fairways and greens carved out of the rugged Pilansberg bushveld. The Pro Shop caters for a golfer's every need and you can hire golf clubs and carts. The terrace bar serves light snacks and drinks. The new 18-hole desert-style Lost City Golf Course, also designed by Gary Player, has a driving range, a halfway house and four of the most spectacular par-3 holes in the world. There are waste bunkers for the first time in southern Africa – and live crocodiles in the water at the 13th hole. You can take lessons at the Lost City Driving Range from the resident professional. Visitors can play all year round, when no tournaments are taking place. The cost for hotel resort residents is R100 (£13.35/$22) green fees, and R50 caddy fees; non-residents pay R125 green fees and R50 caddy fees. Contact the Gary Player Country Club in advance to book your time, tel (01465) 21000.

A memorable way of viewing the Pilansberg National Park and its game is by hot-air balloon. Flights are generally early in the morning to take advantage of the cool air and you should allow about four hours for the full itinerary, which includes early morning collection from your hotel, launch of the balloon from the centre of the park, an hour drifting serenely above the park, a hearty bush breakfast with champagne, and the return drive through the park by game vehicle. Contact Airtrack Adventures, tel (011) 957-2322. Bookings can be made through Pilansberg Safaris, tel (01465) 21561.

The Mega City Shopping Centre in Mmabatho is an industrial-modern shopping centre and the biggest in the province. It houses department stores, restaurants, speciality boutiques, cinemas and theatres. Batswana curios and works of art are on sale here and traditional wood carvings in marula, mopane and ebony, and exquisite unglazed ceramic pieces all make unusual souvenirs and gifts. For carvings in leadwood, visit BopCraft, 861 Modiri Molema Road, which is also a good place for Setswana handcrafted products. Products made of leather, ceramics, sculptures, and finely woven carpets are on sale, tel (0141) 21997.

The area surrounding picturesque Hartbeespoort Dam, 28km/17 miles from Pretoria and 80km/50 miles from Johannesburg International Airport, is known as Cashan Territory, after a powerful tribal chief who ruled in the area in the 19th century. There are arts and crafts and craft studios and shops to browse through, where you will find everything from pots of preserves, to curios, carvings and delicate glass-blown wildlife figurines. Try the Makalani Curio Shop and Art Showrooms, tel (01211) 53-0436, or watch glassblowers creating wildlife figures and other objects at Shades of Ngwenya Glass Studio, tel (011) 957-3180. Tan' Malie se Winkel, not far from the Hartbeespoort Dam wall, is a traditional South African shop in the style of a typical old country trading post where you can enjoy a barbecue with meat, home-made bread, farm butter and cooking facilities provided. Light meals, coffee, melktert, home-made preserves, bokkems, dried fruit, and breakfast are specialities, tel (01211) 30188/9. There is a large range of African carvings and sculptures round the corner at Art d'Afrique, which claims to have the most exclusive and biggest collection of African sculptures, carvings and curios in South Africa. They deliver worldwide. Open seven days a week, 10am–4pm, tel (01211) 503155, Cell 082 566-7920. Art of Africa, which specialises in leadwood carvings, is 10km/6 miles south of Rustenburg on the R24 from Johannesburg. Look out for the white rhino sign.

Open weekends and normally on weekdays but tel (0142) 92521 to confirm. For cheese lovers it is also worth a trip to nearby Skeepoort cheese farm, where you can watch cheesemaking and choose samples from a wide variety, tel (01207) 71289. You can get an illustrated map of the territory from any local publicity office.

TOURIST INFORMATION

North-West Tourism Council, PO Box 7727, Johannesburg 2000, tel (011) 331-9330/6/8/9, fax (011) 331-9351; Mmabatho, tel (0140) 84-3040/1, fax (0140) 84-2524; Potchefstroom, tel (0148) 293-1611/2/3, fax (0148) 297-2082.

Brits, tel (01211) 58-9111.
Christiana, tel (0534) 3261.
Groot Marico, tel (014252) 85.
Klerksdorp, tel (018) 462-3919.
Lichtenburg, tel (01441) 25051.
Mafikeng, tel/fax (0140) 81-0023.
Potchefstroom, tel (0148) 299-5130/1/2, fax (0148) 294-8203.
Rustenburg, tel (0142) 97-3111 ext 3194, fax (0142) 20181.
Stellaland (Vryburg), tel (05391) 2222, fax (05391) 2401
Vryburg, tel (05391) 78-2200, fax (05391) 3482.
Zeerust, tel (01428) 21081.

Northern Cape

San Gunta

If you really want to get away from it all and you are a lover of silence, solitude and wide open spaces the Northern Cape has it all, plus some unparalleled wilderness scenery, wildlife in abundance and accommodation ranging from the inexpensive to the unusual. The Northern Cape is South Africa's largest province (slightly bigger than Germany), but its most sparsely populated. Only 800,000 people live in this vast territory, which means you will share a square mile with about five others. Although the land is rich in a wide variety of minerals — diamonds, silver, zinc and iron-ore among them — poverty is widespread and the provincial government in the capital, Kimberley, is pinning its hopes on tourism to improve the standard of living for its electorate. The number of tourists visiting the Northern Cape showed a 40 per cent growth in 1996. What they came to see principally was the game and birdlife, and the scenic wonders along the Orange River, South Africa's mightiest and longest waterway. This river dominates the province like the Nile dominates Egypt. On its palm-lined banks and in the fields irrigated by its waters the landscape is emerald green with fertility, where other parts are parched and bare of all but hardy succulents and the umbrella-like aloe trees from which Bushmen once made their arrow quivers. On its way to the Atlantic the Orange River crashes down one of the sixth largest waterfalls in the world to carve an awe-inspiring gorge through the ancient granite at Augrabies, just below Kakamas, an area that wondering Khoi herders called the 'place of great noise.' Without this life-giving artery the Northern Cape would be even bleaker and more sparsely populated than it is, but without diamonds its capital Kimberley would never have risen from the veld and South Africa's history would have been an entirely different story. If you are fascinated by the twinkling stones immortalised in the song as being a girl's best friend you must visit the old-world town with its now water-filled Big Hole from which 50,000 diggers from all over the world scooped diamonds literally by the ton. Around it the area has been restored to the way it looked when Cecil John Rhodes halted his horse outside Halfway House Inn — then the Halfway Hotel — on his way home to order a drink brought to him in the saddle. Kimberley brought fame and wealth to Rhodes and other mining magnates, who all went on to increase their fortunes on the goldfields of the Witwatersrand. This rough and tumble town of tents and tin shanties grew into the diamond capital of the world and even had the first electric street lights south of the equator, and the second in the world, after New York.

Kimberley's last three mines — Wesselton, Bultfontein and Dutoitspan — are today nearing the end of their productive life, but there are still old prospectors sifting for diamonds along the banks of the Vaal River near Barkly West. Alluvial diamonds are also being recovered by dredger and divers off the Namaqualand coast, whose real treasure, however, remains the annual display of spring wild flowers. Even if you have little interest in botany or gardens this seasonal multicoloured carpeting of normally bare veld and mountains is little short of miraculous and merits a special excursion into the region. The province's other natural treasures are its premier national parks — Augrabies Falls, the Kalahari Gemsbok, the Richtersveld, and Vaalbos — which each preserve untamed wilderness and contain game animals, predators, and birds in numbers that astonish.

The province is nominally broken into the Diamond Fields, Kalahari, Lower Orange, Namaqualand and Karoo regions, but overall it presents a common picture of untrammelled vastness where settled areas are few and far between and the main centres outside the capital — Upington, Springbok, Kuruman, De Aar, and Colesberg — blend harmoniously into the landscape. Despite the general poverty crime is far less of a problem here than in other provinces. Explains a policeman, 'Here, people steal diamonds, not tourists' wallets.' Summer temperatures that are often searing should encourage you to visit this province in spring or autumn; even the camel safaris close down in the summer months.

KIMBERLEY

Kimberley does not rate too highly in most guide books. After all, it would not exist if diamond diggers had not chanced in 1871 upon a hillock called Colesberg Koppie standing in the middle of the veld. Diamonds galore were found there and within no time at all the koppie had disappeared to become what is now world-famous as the Big Hole of Kimberley, and the town's prime tourist attraction. In spite of shabby treatment by other guidebooks we believe Kimberley merits a definite detour, especially if you are a history buff or if you would otherwise have gone home thinking that the arid centre of South Africa was given over largely to sheep and goats and poverty-stricken families driving around on rickety donkey carts piled not-so-high with their worldly possessions.

Apart from anything else there are guided tours of sights where ghosts can apparently be seen. There is talk of a riderless horse at Carter's Ridge, a sad-looking uniformed British soldier walking up and down at the local golf club, and a lone piper playing a bagpipe lament on the Anglo-Boer battlefield at Magersfontein — and if you listen hard enough you might even hear echoes of the delirious laughter of diggers celebrating a lucky find. Kimberley, named after the Earl of Kimberley, is world-famous for its diamonds. More diamonds have come from this town than from any other city in the world. You should not miss seeing the Big Hole, the Open Mine Museum and the uncut diamonds displayed by De Beers. Cultural treasures can be seen at the Duggan-Cronin Gallery, which contains a collection of unique photographs of tribal life and African art; the McGregor Memorial Museum; and the Humphreys Art Gallery. The city's museums are generally outstanding.

Getting Around

Kimberley Airport is 8km/5 miles from town. There is no bus service between town and the airport, but taxis are available and major **car hire** companies have rental kiosks at the airport:
Avis, tel (0531) 851-1082, fax (0531) 851-1062;

Budget, tel (0531) 851-1182/3, fax (0531) 851-1375;
Imperial, tel (0531) 851-1131/2, fax (0531) 851-1108.

The province has good air connections and road links to all the country's major towns and cities and driving on uncongested highways is a pleasure, although you should keep your eyes peeled for signs saying *pas op vir koedoes* ('beware of kudu').

Upington also has an airport, the runway of which is 3 miles long, the longest tarred runway in the southern hemisphere. There is also a tarred airstrip of almost a mile in length at Calvinia, in the south-west.

Car hire in Upington:
Avis, tel (054) 25746;
Imperial, tel (054) 23382;
Venture 4x4 Rental, tel (054) 31-1125;
Budget and Upington 4x4 Rental, tel (054) 25441;
Baurent and 4x4 Rental, tel (054) 22251.

Intercape runs intercity routes between Upington, Cape Town, Johannesburg and other centres, tel (054) 27091. 24-hour information from (021) 934-4400.

If you are driving between Johannesburg and Cape Town an interesting alternative to the usual main N1 highway is to travel through the Namaqualand region by way of Springbok. This, the Namakwari Route, is virtually the same distance as the more travelled north–south route, except that on the road through Namaqualand you will never be in nose-to-tail traffic. Various bus and car hire services link Cape Town, Johannesburg and Springbok and some of the smaller towns in the region. There is also an air service to Springbok. For more information on air services, the Namaqualand Bus Service, Intercape coaches and car hire companies contact the Regional Tourism Information Office at tel (0251) 22011, fax (0251) 21421.

Rail. Kimberley's railway station is centrally situated in Florence Street. The luxury

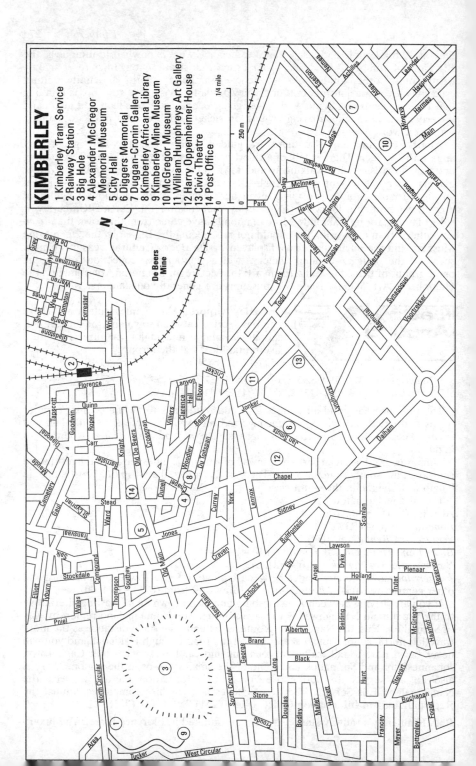

KIMBERLEY

1 Kimberley Tram Service
2 Railway Station
3 Big Hole
4 Alexander McGregor
  Memorial Museum
5 City Hall
6 Diggers Memorial
7 Duggan-Cronin Gallery
8 Kimberley Africana Library
9 Kimberley Mine Museum
10 McGregor Museum
11 William Humphreys Art Gallery
12 Harry Oppenheimer House
13 Civic Theatre
14 Post Office

N

De Beers Mine

0   250 m
0   1/4 mile

Blue Train and Rovos Rail travel from Pretoria to Cape Town via Johannesburg and Kimberley.

Tram. An unusual alternative to walking or driving around Kimberley is a **tram** ride. A restored 1914 electric tram in its bright yellow and black livery clangs along a track between the City Hall and the Big Hole. Tens of thousands of diggers used trams like this in the pioneer days. The route also takes in a number of historically interesting buildings. Buy your ticket on the tram, R5 per person return fare. It runs every hour from 9am to 4pm, tel (0531) 82-7298, fax (0531) 82-7211.

There is a variety of **pleasure resorts** close to Kimberley. Some 30km/19 miles from the city, on the banks of the Vaal River, is the *Riverton Pleasure Resort*, tel (0531) 21703. You can choose between luxury chalets (sleeping eight people), villas (four), double rondavels (three) and single rondavels (two), or make use of one of the country's finest caravan parks. The river is an angler's, water-skier's and windsurfer's dream. Boats and paddleboats can be hired. Next to Riverton is Langley which has well equipped bungalows and a caravan park and camp sites. Popular among birdwatchers, Langleg also offers boating and angling. Rekaofella, 5km/3 miles from Barkly West, has fully equipped chalets and a good overnight stop for day visitors to the Vaalbos National Park.

There is a wide range of accommodation in **guest houses and bed-and-breakfast** establishments in Kimberley, starting at R50 per person per night sharing:

Diamond Guesthouse, 4 Pearl Street, Gemdene, Kimberley 8301, tel (0531) 712064.

Edwardian-style accommodation at *Pembury Lodge*, 11 Curry Street, Kimberley 8301, tel/fax (0531) 81-6965.

Holiday Inn Garden Court, four-star hotel. From R245 (£33/$54) room only. Du Toitspan Road, Kimberley 8301, tel (0531) 31751, fax (0531) 82-1814.

Hotel Kimberlite, three-star, R200 a double room, 162 George Street, Kimberley 8301, tel (0531) 81-1968/9, fax (0531) 81-1967.

Horseshoe Motel, two-star, from R90 per person. Memorial Road, Kimberley 8301, tel/fax (0531) 82-5267/8.

Diamond Protea Lodge, two-star, from R207 for room only, tel (0531) 81-1281.

Big Hole Caravan Park, West Circular Road, Kimberley 8301, tel (0531) 80-6322.

Kimberley Caravan Park, Hull Street, Kimberley 8301, tel (0531) 33582.

Show Grounds Caravan Park, tel (0531) 33581/2.

Backpacker accommodation is available at *Gum Tree Lodge*, Bloemfontein Road, Kimberley 8301, PO Box 777, Kimberley 8300, tel (0531) 82-8577, fax (0531) 81-5409.

Caravan parks include *Kimberley Caravan Park*, tel (0531) 33581, and *Open Mine Caravan Park*, tel (0531) 80-6322.

The **Alexander McGregor Memorial Museum** depicts southern Africa's prehistory, natural history and geology, and has an exceptional collection of Bushman (San) relics, weapons and implements. This building, the original home of the McGregor Museum, was built in 1907 in memory of a former mayor of the city, Alexander McGregor. Open Monday to Friday, 9am–5pm, Saturday, 9am–1pm, Sunday, 2–5pm, tel (0531) 32645/6.

Big Hole. This is the largest hole in the world dug entirely by manual labour. An observation platform offers a good view of this impressive excavation, which has a circumference of about 1.6km/1 mile and a depth of 215m/705ft. Up to 12,000 men worked in this hole at one time, and some 22.5 million tons of diamond-bearing blue ground were dug out between 1871 and 1914, yielding nearly three tons of diamonds, or 14.5 million carats.

You can experience the thrill of searching for diamonds at Engelsman's Prospect, next to the Big Hole. 'Claims' can be bought that entitle you to sift through gravel for diamond tokens, and prizes range from small souvenirs to real diamonds. Tel (0531) 31557 or (011) 638-5126.

Bultfontein Mine. 5km/3 miles from town on Molyneux Road, this mine is still operational and surface tours are offered twice a day — 9am and 11am — from Monday to Friday. These include an audio-visual presentation on the history of Kimberley, modern diamond mining and recovery methods, and a tour of the surface workings. Underground tours on Tuesday at 9.30am and other weekdays at 8am, by appointment, tel (0531) 82-9651, or (0531) 32259 (a/h). Tours are also available at Du Toitspan mine.

City Hall. An imposing sandstone edifice on Market Square, built in ornate classic Roman Corinthian style at the turn of the century. Nearby, in the Public Library, Chapel Street, is the Tourist Information Centre, tel (0531) 82-7298.

Diggers Memorial. This fountain and statue in the form of a diamond sieve held aloft by five life-sized diggers is in the Oppenheimer Memorial Gardens.

Duggan-Cronin Gallery. A truly superb collection of some 8000 photographs of southern Africa's indigenous peoples taken between 1919 and 1939 by Irish mine manager Alfred Duggan-Cronin. Most are of labourers recruited to work on the mines and who kept their traditional clothing, hairstyles and facial markings. In the grounds are tribal huts built with traditional materials. Egerton Road, open Monday to Friday, 9am–5pm, Saturday, 9am–1pm and 2–5pm, Sunday, 2–5pm, tel (0531) 32645/6.

Dunluce and Rudd House. Two of Kimberley's historic homes, which now house museums furnished in period style. Guided tours by arrangement with the McGregor Museum. Lodge and Loch roads, tel (0531) 32645.

Galeshwe. This is Kimberley's satellite black township, named after an old chief of the Batlahapeng tribe. It offers an historical tour that is in startling contrast to the city next door. For an African experience, take a minibus taxi from the City Hall to Galeshwe and see the homes of ANC founder member Sol Plaatje and PAC founder Robert Sobukwe; Plaatje's grave; the Helen Joseph self-help scheme; the park honouring assassinated SA Communist Party leader Chris Hani; and the home of the premier of the Northern Cape. Round off your visit with refreshment at a traditional township shebeen.

Kimberley Africana Library. Contains a superb collection and houses missionary Robert Moffat's printing press and original translation of the Bible into Tswana, the first to be translated into an African language. Du Toitspan Road, open Monday to Friday from 9am to 8pm, Saturday from 9am to 1pm.

Kimberley Mine Museum. Next to the Big Hole, this open-air museum depicts Kimberley in its Victorian heyday during the diamond rush, with shops and houses, a church, diggers' tavern, Barney Barnato's Boxing Academy and the De Beers directors' private railway coach. The Transport Hall contains late 19th century vehicles, and De Beers Hall displays uncut diamonds stones of different colours and various items of jewellery. Also on display are the '616' (616 carats) — the largest uncut diamond in the world — and the 'Eureka', the first diamond officially discovered in South Africa (1866). Open daily from 8am to 6pm, tel (0531) 31557.

Kimberley Station Museum. This is situated on Platform 1 of the Kimberley Station in Florence Street. It portrays the history of railway transport in the Northern Cape from the arrival of the first train in Kimberley on 28 November 1886. Open weekdays from 10am to 4pm, tel (0531) 88-2400.

Market Square. This was originally the centre of the tent town that sprang up in 1871 with the discovery of diamonds on the farm Dutoitspan and modern Kimberley grew up around it. The memorial of balancing rocks from the Matopos commemorates the departure from the square in 1890 of Rhodes' Pioneer Column, which opened the way for the white settlement of Rhodesia (now Zimbabwe). The square was declared a national monument in 1977.

McGregor Museum. Built in 1897 by Cecil John Rhodes to serve as a sanatorium, this magnificent building on Egerton Road was used as a luxury hotel (Hotel Belgrave) and later as a convent school before being taken over by the McGregor Museum. Rhodes lived on the ground floor during the Kimberley Siege. The museum has a notable collection of natural history specimens and Bushman (San) relics, as well as other exhibits reflecting the early history of the city and comparative religions. An interesting circular historical walking tour begins and ends at the museum, providing a glimpse of the affluent lifestyles of those who made their fortunes in early Kimberley. Open Monday to Friday from 9am to 5pm, Saturday from 9am to 1pm, Sunday from 2pm to 5pm, tel (0531) 32645.

Pioneers of Aviation Museum on General van der Spuy Drive, 3.5km/2 miles from the airport, is situated on the site where in 1913 the first flying school had its base. This is where aviation in South Africa began and where the South African Air Force was born. This interesting little museum features a reconstruction of the original hangar, a replica of the Compton-Paterson biplane used in flight training, and early aviation photographs. Open Monday to Saturday from 9am to 5pm and on Sunday from 2pm to 5pm, tel (0531) 32645/6.

Tours. Diamond Tours Unlimited can show you every facet of the industry, with day tours from 7am to 8pm or overnight extended visits. As well as taking you 800m/2625ft underground, DTU can arrange microlight flights over the diggings. They will also organise diamonds at wholesale prices. Contact Big Hole Info Office, PO Box 2775, Kimberley 8300, Northern Cape, tel (0531) 82-9834 or (0531) 81-4006, fax (0531) 34347.

William Humphreys Art Gallery. This exceptionally fine gallery, in the Civic Centre, off Jan Smuts Boulevard, houses a representative collection of South African works of art, as well as works of European artists and 16th and 17th century Dutch and Flemish Old Masters. A statue of Queen Victoria in front of the gallery recalls earlier links with England and the Kottler nudes, which once raised temperatures in Pretoria and were banished in a storm of indignation, are in the gallery's walled garden. Open Monday to Saturday from 10am to 1pm and 2pm to 5pm, Sunday from 2pm to 5pm, tel (0531) 81-1724/5.

Kimberley has the usual range of shops with, unsurprisingly, an emphasis on the diamonds that have made the city famous. You can buy certified diamonds — and curios — at the Big Hole Curio Shop in the Kimberley Mine Museum. Opposite the entrance to the museum is the Jewel Box selling diamonds direct from the factory. While you are debating how many carats you can afford you can watch a goldsmith and diamond cutter at work. As a visitor, all your purchases are duty-free. Remember that the finest stones are either blue-white or colourless, though some coloured diamonds have become famous because of their beauty and size. For the bookworm

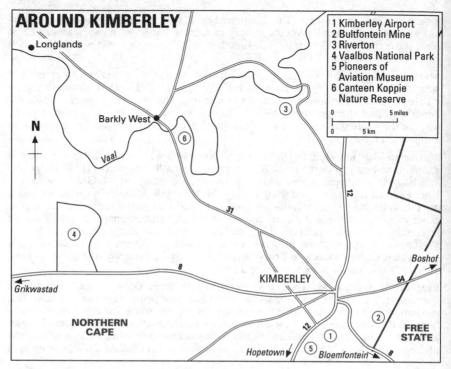

AROUND KIMBERLEY

1 Kimberley Airport
2 Bultfontein Mine
3 Riverton
4 Vaalbos National Park
5 Pioneers of
  Aviation Museum
6 Canteen Koppie
  Nature Reserve

Longlands

Barkly West

N

Vaal

Grikwastad

NORTHERN
CAPE

KIMBERLEY

Boshof

FREE
STATE

Hopetown   Bloemfontein

the McGregor Museum Shop in the Sanatorium has an interesting selection of books on specialist topics that you won't find anywhere else in the country. A flea market is held at Jan Smuts Boulevard, opposite Oppenheimer Gardens, on the first and last Saturday of every month.

Further Afield

DIAMOND FIELDS

Barkly West. Situated on a great bend of the Vaal River, once a convenient crossing place and known as Klipdrift, this was the scene in 1869 of one of the first diamond rushes in the area. At Canteen Koppie, focus of the first alluvial diamond diggings, there is an open-air archaeological museum and nature reserve. The Mining Commissioner's Museum has a variety of interesting exhibits.

Driekopseiland (Three Hills Island). You can see more than 3000 Stone Age engravings on the smooth lava bed of the Riet River, near its confluence with the Modder River, some 40km/25 miles south-west of Kimberley. Tel (0531) 32645 to arrange a visit.

Griquatown. Griquas, people of mixed Khoikhoi and Dutch origin, settled north of the Orange River at the end of the 18th century. The London Missionary Society established a station here in 1801 which was later headed by Robert Moffat. In 1913 it became Griquatown, reputedly the first town founded north of the Orange River. Mary Moffat, wife of David Livingstone, was born in the Old Mission House in 1821. It is now the Mary Moffat Museum, housing a collection devoted to the history of missionary work in the area. The district is noted for its tiger's eye and other semi-precious stones and you can see these at the local polishing factory.

Vaalbos National Park. The 23,000-hectare park gets its name from the Afrikaans word for the abundant camphor bush growing here. The park is split into two parts, 30km/19 miles apart. The largest chunk (16,000 hectares) is about 27km/17 miles from Barkly West, with the smallest section in the Graspan-Holpan area. The park is a sanctuary for white and black rhino and other mammals such as giraffe, buffalo, kudu, springbok, wildebeest and red hartebeest. The 86 recorded bird species include lappetfaced and whiteheaded vultures, kori bustards, bateleurs, martial and fish eagles. There are cabins to rent, tel (05352) ext 9012.

BATTLEFIELDS

The 'Kimberley Battlefields Route' runs from Hopetown (see below) to Paardeberg, 38km/24 miles into the Free State, and covers major battles fought during the Anglo-Boer War.

The first battlefield is that of **Belmont**, which took place on 23 November 1899. The battle was considered a true 'soldiers battle' and was won by the British. Next is **Graspan**, 16km/10 miles closer to Kimberley. A memorial marks the western extent of the battlefield near the main road. It was here that the Naval Brigade suffered heavily, and in horrific heat. The date was 25 November 1899. The battlefield of **Modder River**, which took place on 28 November 1899, still boasts the Crown and Royal Hotel, used by both British and Boers as a first-aid dressing station. It was the British HQ for the Battle of **Magersfontein**, which took place on 11 December 1899 and saw the virtual annihilation of the famed Highland Brigade by entrenched Boers. *Langeberg Guest Lodge* is on the battlefield. The siege and relief of Kimberley are well documented at Kimberley's McGregor Museum, while Boer emplacements can still be seen around the city. A small museum gives a vivid picture of the uniforms, weaponry and equipment used by both armies, while nine memorials commemorate the dead. Several British sites may still be seen, as can the two battlesites of **Carters Ridge** and **Dronfield**. The latter is on private ground.

The battlefield of **Paardeberg** is on the Bloemfontein via Petrusberg Road, about 38km/24 miles from Kimberley. This historic battle was the longest-lasting — 10 days — and suffered the most casualties. The Modder River winds through the centre of the battlefield, where there is an interesting museum. Paardeberg is where the names of Christian de Wet, Gideon Scheepers and Danie Theron came to the fore. The battle of **Sunnyside**, near Douglas, is remembered as the first battle by colonial troops, the first Australian dying on the battlefield on 1 January 1900. **Fabers Put** battlefield, 20km/12 miles past Douglas, is where General Charles Warren fought a pitched battle with the Boer rebels of Griqualand West.

Closer to Kimberley is the battlefield of **Koedoesberg Drift**. This battle, which took place in February 1900, is famous for the death of the champion British golfer Freddie Tait. Situated on the banks of the Riet river, Koedoesberg was the Highland Brigade's first engagement after Magersfontein. **Jacobsdal**, in the Free State, but close to Modder River, was the first Free State town captured in the war. Two battles, including one where the CIV had their baptism of fire, are commemorated by memorials. The church in this beautiful town was used as a Boer hospital. The French Colonel, Comte de Villebois-Mareuil, was killed in a battle with Lord Methuen's forces in April 1900, just outside the town. There is a memorial on the battlefield.

UPPER KAROO

Colesberg. This little Karoo town 800km/497 miles from Cape Town and 630km/392 miles from Johannesburg is in the centre of a thriving sheep and horse stud district. Of particular interest are the Kemper Museum, which includes a display on the Anglo-Boer War, and the Karoo Nomad photographic exhibition compiled by the University of South Africa (Unisa). Other attractions are battle sites and camps, a military cemetery, the Karoo Ostrich Ranch, the Toverberg Game Farm, walks through the Doornkloof Reserve, and the picturesque Cape Karoo cottages in Bell Street. One of the oldest horse-drawn mills in South Africa has been renovated and turned into an English-style pub in Bell Street.

De Aar. This is best known as an important railway junction, with 110km/68 miles of track and trains passing through at the rate of 92 a day. Olive Schreiner, one of South Africa's best-known authors, once lived here in a house on the corner of Van Zyl and Gringling streets, which now contains a museum and a restaurant. Steam trains are still used on the De Aar-Kraankuil and Kimberley routes. Bushman graves and rock engravings can be viewed on the farms Nooitgedacht, south-east of town, and Brandfontein, to the west of town, tel (0571) 3888 and (0571) 3816 respectively. The PK Le Roux, 110km/68 miles from De Aar, offers boating, fishing and water sports.

Hopetown. This town 134km/83 miles south-west of Kimberley is famed as the site of the first discovery of diamonds in South Africa in 1886–7. In 1866 the first diamond (Eureka) was found on the farm De Kalk, and in 1868 an 83.5 carat diamond known as the Star of South Africa was found. Gazella Game Reserve, on the banks of the Orange River, is a sanctuary for gemsbok, eland, kudu and springbok. Outdoor activities in the vicinity include white-water rafting, game-viewing, bird-watching and hiking.

Orania. Established as an Afrikaner preserve in 1991 to protect the Afrikaans language and culture. An oddity in the new South Africa, a sign at the entrance to the village proclaims in Afrikaans: *Welkom in Orania*, but the welcome is a restricted one. English-speakers are tolerated so long as they can speak Afrikaans and live according to Calvinistic tenets. The town has a Museum of Guns, with weapons dating back to the 1700s. If you get stuck, you can overnight at the *Afsaal Kafee* (Off-Saddle Café), tel (053202) 899.

Prieska. Renowned for its semi-precious stones. During the Anglo-Boer War the British even built a fort mostly from tiger's eye on the summit of Prieska Koppie. If you are a rock-hound you can see a collection of semi-precious stones at the municipal offices. Prieska Koppie Nature Reserve and the Ria Huisamen Aloe Garden enclose impressive collections of succulents, and the weird *halfmens* (half-human) and *Kokerboom* (quiver tree) flourish here.

KALAHARI/LOWER ORANGE REGION

Augrabies Falls National Park. This 13,699-hectare park lies 129km/80 miles west of Upington and is set in a region of dramatic contrasts, where the Orange River winds across a rocky lunar landscape before plunging into a deep granite gorge. According to legend, a fortune in diamonds washed down by the river lies at the bottom of the 130m/427ft deep pool. The Augrabies Falls is one of the finest cataract-type falls in the world. The main fall is a spectacular 56m/184ft but together with the cataracts above, the total drop is about 91m/299ft. The average depth of the gorge over a distance of 18km/11 miles is about 250m/820ft, and it abounds with boiling rapids. The falls — the sixth biggest in the world — get their name from a Nama word meaning 'place of great noise.' On game-viewing drives in the park you can expect to see prolific birdlife, and game such as kudu, springbok, klipspringer, baboons, vervet monkeys, and Africa's scarcest species of black rhino. This is the main focus of Black Rhino Adventure, a National Parks Board day excursion which includes a boat trip down a magnificent section of the Orange River. The three-day, 40km/25 mile Klipspringer Hiking Trail, which can be followed between April and October, leads though the southern section of the reserve and there are three one-hour walking trails catering for the less energetic. Air-conditioned chalets and cottages are available and there are caravan and camp sites with shady trees, lawns, and ablution blocks. A maximum of six people are allowed per site, which all have power points. A 2-bed chalet costs R235 (£31/$52) a night, and a camp site for 2 is R33 a night (R9 for each additional person). Night game-viewing drives are available; mountain bikes and canoes can be hired. To reserve accommodation or camp sites within three days of the date of your visit, you should apply direct to the Warden, Augrabies Falls National Park, Private Bag X1, Augrabies 8874, Northern Cape, tel (054) 451-0050/51/52, fax (054) 451-0053. For any period longer than three days in advance contact the National Parks Board in Pretoria or Cape Town, tel (012) 343-1991 or (021) 22-2810.

Kakamas. Egyptian-style working waterwheels and ancient hand-built runnels irrigate vineyards, lucerne and cottonfields and are reminiscent of scenes from the banks of the Nile. Kakamas is a convenient stopover on the way to the Augrabies Falls and the Richtersveld National Park. Wonderful yellow clingstone peaches grow in the area.

Kalahari Gemsbok National Park. The second largest (959,103 hectares) after Kruger, this is truly one of the great reserves of Africa, not least because it shares an unfenced boundary with Botswana's equally wild and remote huge sanctuary, the Gemsbok National Park, which allows the seasonal migration of vast numbers of animals. The combined area of this superpark totals more than 36,200sq km/13,977sq miles, 50 per cent larger than Kruger and slightly bigger than Belgium or Maryland, and this makes it one of the largest unspoilt ecosystems in the world. The park is a sanctuary for a great variety of migratory animal species and these occur in vast numbers. The sight of thousands of antelope on the move across the red Kalahari sands is an experience you will never forget. Roads skirt the dry beds of the Nossob and Auob rivers and the relatively barren terrain makes for great wildlife photography. The park has 215 recorded species of birds and is one of the best places to see large raptors such as martial, tawny and bateleur eagles and pale chanting goshawks. In the heat of the day, when the black-maned Kalahari lions lie under shady bushes and leopards take refuge in the branches of camelthorn trees, you can cool off in the pool or enjoy a drink.

There are three rest camps in the park, an up-market one at Twee Rivieren, with a restaurant, curio shop, and swimming pool, another at Mata-Mata, and one 157km/ 98 miles from Twee Rivieren at Nossob. Twee Rivieren has air-conditioned chalets for 124 people; Mata-Mata has accommodation for 39 people (there is no gate at Mata-Mata); and Nossob has accommodation for 32 people. Each camp has camp sites with ablution blocks, facilities for washing-up and open fireplaces, as well as petrol and diesel pumps. A maximum of six persons per site are allowed. There are no power points. A four-bed cottage costs R270 (£36/$59) a night, a hut sleeping three costs R85 a night, and a camp site is R33. There is a 20% discount on accommodation and camping from 1 November to the end of February. The park is open all year round, but March to October are the most popular months. In summer it is extremely hot, but winter nights can be quite cold, so you should take warm clothes if you visit later than May. There are landing strips for light aircraft. Precautions against malaria are recommended. This park is ultra-wild and a favourite with hardy off-the-beaten-trackers, so written applications must be made 13 months before your intended visit, tel (054) 561-0021.

Tswalu Private Desert Reserve. Tswalu means 'new beginning,' and that is what this 75,000-hectare reserve on the southern edge of the Kalahari represents. This is largest privately owned game reserve in South Africa, and it is all the work of an Englishman, Stephen Boler, who spent £9 million to create it. More than 3000 head of game were relocated here to supplement more than 5000 plains game — springbok, brown and blue wildebeest, giraffe, zebra, nyala, brown and spotted hyena and five major species of antelope — sable, roan, eland, kudu and gemsbok, as well as cheetah and lion. Rare black desert rhino have been brought in from Namibia and white rhino from Hluhluwe, in KwaZulu-Natal. It also has disease-free Cape buffalo and the first-ever translocated desert elephants. It is geared mainly to the well-heeled tourist, with a tariff in excess of R1650 per person a day sharing. You can hire a 4x4 for R1500 a day. The reserve is 560km/348 miles from Kimberley. It has its own landing strip and daily transfers are provided from Kimberley and Upington airports. It is a harsh climate with sub-zero temperatures in winter and 40-plus degrees (over 104°F) in summer. Tswalu encompasses the Korannaberg mountains, a raptor route for tawny, black and martial eagles, as well as bateleurs, Cape, lappetfaced and white-backed vultures. Conservation Corporation Africa (CCA) has a 22-bed lodge here with traversing rights over the reserve. Contact tel (011) 803-8421, fax (011) 803-1810.

Kanoneiland. This is the largest inhabited inland island in South Africa. Virtually every inch is under irrigation as a drive through the vineyards and lucerne fields will show. To book a guided tour of the island, tel (054) 491-1147. This includes a barbecue of spit-roasted sheep, along with home-baked bread, traditional desserts and local wines. You can also visit a catfish farm.

Kenhardt. The oldest town in the lower Orange River region began as a camp under a giant camelthorn tree in 1868. The 600-year-old tree is still growing and is a national monument. 8km/5 miles south of town is a forest of 5000 quiver trees. The 4km/2.5 mile Kokerboom hiking trail goes through the forest. Huge nests of sociable weaver birds are common. Verneukpan 64km/40 miles from town is the vast salt flat on which Sir Donald Campbell unsuccessfully attempted to shatter the world land-speed record in 1929 in his car *Bluebird.*

Keimos. This village 40km/25 miles south-west of Upington takes its name from the Koranna river people's word for 'mouse nest.' The Tierberg Nature Reserve 4km/2.5 miles from town is notable for its prodigious numbers of aloes, its springbok, and a panoramic view of the Orange River Valley. Wine tasting and tours are offered at the Orange River Wine Cellars Co-operative.

Kuruman. This famous mission station established by Robert Moffat is known as the Fountain of Christianity in Africa because it provided Moffat, and later Livingstone, with a base to explore deep into Africa. Nearby is the spring known as the 'Eye' of Kuruman, which rises in dolomite and gushes into a crystal-clear pool at the rate of 18 to 20 million litres — up to 4.4 million gallons — a day. The original buildings, including the church and Moffatt's house, have been meticulously restored and services are still held here. The church is where Moffatt's daughter, Mary, married David Livingstone. Visitors are welcome at the Kuruman Country Club where you can play golf, tennis, bowls and squash, tel (05373) 21242. Halfway between Kuruman and Danielskuil is the **Wonderwerk Cave**, an important archaeological site originally used by Bushmen. Prehistoric rock etchings here can be viewed by appointment, tel (0598) 30680.

Pella. Temperatures here have been known to exceed 50°C/122°F in summer, which is why the Roman Catholic mission station has been able to grow one of the only three date plantations in the southern hemisphere. The station is named after the village in Macedonia which provided refuge for Christians in biblical times. The cathedral here was built by two missionaries with local help and took seven years to complete. They used an encyclopedia as a building guide.

Roaring Sands. A natural phenomenon and strange freak of nature occurring at Witsand, about 20km/12 miles south-west of Postmasburg. Any disturbance of the dunes in hot, dry weather makes the sand produce an eerie moaning sound. You can make the sand roar, or at least murmur, simply by drawing your fingers through it.

Upington. Within easy reach of the Augrabies Falls and the Kalahari Gemsbok National Park, the town developed from a Dutch Reformed mission station founded in the 1870s. The Orange River Wine Cellars here are the largest wine co-operative in South Africa. For bookings and free wine tasting, tel (054) 25651. The South African Dried Fruit Co-operative covers an area of more than 2 hectares and every year processes all South Africa's dried sultanas (some 250 tons). Guided tours daily at 9.45am and 2pm, except Friday afternoons and weekends. At the Kalahari-Oranje Museum is a bronze monument to the donkey, remembering its contribution to the development of the region. There is a similar monument to the camel and rider outside the police station. Other attractions are the Spitskop Nature Reserve, with its herd of camels, 13km/8 miles north of town; the 1041m-long Date Palm Avenue at the entrance to the Eiland Holiday Resort, the longest palm avenue in the world; and the grave of South Africa's own Robin Hood, outlaw Scotty Smith, who died in the 1918 flu epidemic.

WESTERN KAROO

Some 250 million years ago this region was an inland sea fringed by cycads and home to prehistoric mammal-like amphibian reptiles. Floods and erosion have created a moonscape of semi-arid plains, flat-topped koppies like anvils, and rugged mountains.

Calvinia. This is the hub of one of South Africa's largest wool-producing districts. The Calvinia Museum, in an old Art Deco synagogue in Church Street, tells the story of farming, transport and the lifestyle of the early inhabitants. The Tourism Office in the museum arranges guided walking tours to places of interest, tel (0273) 41-1011. Two trails through the Akkerendam Nature Reserve give you an opportunity to admire flowers found only in these parts. During August and September the town and golf course, as well as farms within a 40km/25 miles radius of the town, are covered in blossom.

Fraserburg. A village of typical Karoo houses, many with wrought-iron Victorian *stoep* (veranda) railings, it is best known for the *Peperbus*, ('pepper-box'), on Market Square. This six-sided stone building, 9m/28ft high, with a six-sided tower on the dome of the main structure, was built in 1861. The museum in the Ou Pastorie is furnished in the style of a century ago. Open Monday to Friday from 8am to 1pm. At Gansfontein, 5km/3 miles away, is an ancient Karoo water-hole bearing the fossilised footprints of giant reptiles, the best examples in southern Africa. These, which are complemented by an exhibition in the local museum, can be visited by appointment, tel (02072) 12. There are numerous walks in the area, which in winter offers prime plains-game hunting.

Sutherland. The South African Astronomical Observatory, about 14km/7 miles outside town, is one of the finest observatories in the southern hemisphere. Sutherland also claims to produce the finest mutton in South Africa, which makes it a wonderful place for an outdoor barbecue. It also has, at nearly 1500m above sea level, the more doubtful distinction of being the coldest town in the country.

Tankwa Karoo National Park. A 28,000-hectare reserve bordering on the Western Cape, which is still in its development stage. It has been fenced off to allow the veld to recover from years of overgrazing and bad farming. At this stage there are no roads or facilities in the park, although there are a couple of picnic spots and day visitors are permitted.

NAMAQUALAND

This is desolate semi-desert country, ranging from thorn-bush and scrub inland to windswept dunes along the cold Atlantic, covering an area of 48,000sq km/18,750sq miles from the Orange River to Groenriviersmond in the south. In spring the harshness is softened by extravagant displays of wild flowers, which are unusually fine around Kamieskroon and Springbok on the main road between Cape Town and Namibia. Other picturesque little towns in the region include Garies and Port Nolloth. The region is rich in minerals such as copper, diamonds, gemstones, gypsum and sillimanite, which is a fibrous aluminium silicate.

ACCOMMODATION

Namaqualand offers a real Nama cultural experience at *Matjieshuis Village*, where you sleep in a traditional *matjieshuis* (reed mat hut) and enjoy boerekos from as little as R37.50 (£5/$8.25) per person per night, tel (0251) 22435, fax (0251) 21926. *Namastad* also has accommodation in Nama dome-shaped reed huts, tel (0251) 22435.

Accommodation in Springbok includes:

> *Springbok Hotel*, tel (0251) 21-1161;
> *Kokerboom Motel and Caravan Park*, tel (0251) 22685;
> *Springbok Lodge* (rooms over a café, which has an incredible selection of semi-precious stones for sale), tel (0251) 21321;
> *Ratekraal Farm House*, tel (0251) 5687.

At Port Nolloth:

> *Scotia Inn Hotel*, tel (0255) 8353;
> *McDougalls Bay*, caravan park and chalets, tel (0255) 8657;
> *Bedrock*, tel (0255) 8865.

EXPLORING

Alexander Bay. Alluvial diamonds are mined in this high security area, with entry limited to permit-holders. A large area of the coast is off-limits. There are tours of the diamond mine on Thursdays, starting at 8am. Booking is essential and must be arranged 24 hours in advance, tel (0256) 831-1330.

Garies. On the outskirts of town you can see some huge boulders known as Letterklip, on which the names of early travellers are carved, as well as a coat of arms chiselled into the rock by the British soldiers who built a fort here in 1901.

Hondeklipbaai ('Dogstone Bay'). On the coast 98km/61 miles from Kamieskroon is this neglected inlet, which prompted a trader ordered there in 1855 to consider suicide instead. It takes its name from a large rock next to the police station, which many thought resembled a dog. If it did, it doesn't any longer — a bolt of lightning has decapitated the likeness. This is a good area for crayfish diving. Camp sites are available and there is limited accommodation at two local restaurants.

Kamieskroon. The village is renowned for its spring floral displays (see below). There are excellent hikes in the area, and three strenuous mountain bike trails lead into the Kamiesberg.

Nababeep. Copper mining gave birth to the town in 1860. It is 16km/10 miles north-west of Springbok and gets its curious name from the Nama for 'the place where the giraffe drinks.' At the Mining Museum the history of Namaqualand's mining era is well recorded by photographs and relics. Open Tuesdays, Thursdays and Saturdays.

Okiep. Village 8km/5 miles north of Springbok, established after copper was found there in 1862. The copper mine here was once the richest in the world, until demand for the metal slumped. A Cornish beam pump and smoke-stack in the centre of town were erected in 1882 to pump water from the mine. Both are now national monuments.

Pofadder. Often called the region's treasure-chest because of the geological deposits found here, this portion of Bushmanland is a mass of flowers after good rains. Visits to top dorper sheep studs can be arranged, tel (0020) 532 ask for 43.

Port Nolloth. The port was established in the mid-1880s on the Atlantic Ocean 80km/50 miles south of the Orange River mouth to ship out Namaqualand's copper. Ore went through Port Nolloth for shipment overseas until well into the 20th century, now it is the centre of a marine diamond recovery project and the only holiday resort on the prohibited Diamond Coast. You can watch diamond dredgers and fishing boats leave harbour at sunrise. There is good fishing and crayfish diving.

Richtersveld National Park. The rugged terrain of the Richtersveld in the north-western corner of the province offers a breathtaking experience if you are energetic, adventurous and do not mind roughing it. This 162,445-hectare reserve between the Orange River in the north and east and the Atlantic Ocean in the west offers saw-toothed peaks, wind-sculpted rocks and a wild beauty that make it dream territory for photographers and lovers of the great outdoors. Hidden away in this remote corner, with few of the normal tourist amenities, the park draws few visitors, which is one of the reasons why it has remained pristine. Large areas are poorly known and accessible only to 4x4 vehicles, but you can canoe here down the Orange River, passing through an exceptional wilderness area. The only other ways to explore are on foot or by helicopter.

The Park is noted among botanists the world over for its wide range of rare, endemic plant species. Distinctive desert flowers, many of them succulents, make a blaze of colour in spring. Accommodation is limited to 22 beds. A unit for two people costs R125 (£16.65/$27.50) a night and campers pay R10 each a night. Permits to enter the Park (R25 per person) are available from the Park Warden, Sendelingsdrift, tel (0256) 831-1506.

Springbok. 560km/348 miles north of Cape Town, this is the administrative capital of Namaqualand. Springbok was founded during the copper era and retains echoes of its early mining lifestyle. The synagogue (1929) is now a museum. A small hill in the centre of town is the site of Anglo-Boer War monuments. The beautiful stone Anglican Church, built in 1864, houses the Regional Information Centre. 5km/3 miles to the east of town is the spot where Simon van der Stel, governor of the Cape of Good Hope, sank three shafts while prospecting for copper in 1685. The largest shaft on which he carved his initials is a national monument. Roads around lead through a region unparalleled for its spring flowers. 15km/9 miles south-east is the Hester Malan Wild Flower Garden, which is crossed by hiking, horse, mountain-bike and 4x4 trails. It is open daily from 8am to 4pm, tel (0251) 21880. Just beyond the airport is the 7000-hectare Goegap Nature Reserve. 50km/31 miles west of Springbok is the settlement of Komaggas, on the Kleinzee road, where you can watch high-class spinning and weaving. You can even design your own carpet.

Spring Flowers. In spring the area from Cape Town's doorstep to the Orange River on the border with Namibia is transformed into a blaze of colour as plants blossom in riotous profusion, especially in August and September. Namaqualand is the centre of this transformation; barren land for most of the year, it comes to life in early spring and is unique in being the only desert in the world to stage such an extravagant display of flowers. Locals know they are in for a good flower season when good rains fall in autumn (April and May) and are followed by the regular winter rains. As soon as rain has fallen the Department of Botany at the University of Pretoria can accurately predict when the flowers will blossom.

One of the best places to enjoy the flowers is in the Skilpad Wildflower Reserve, near Kamieskroon in central Namaqualand (true Namaqualand, according to the local inhabitants). The 1000-hectare reserve lies on the edge of the escarpment in a region where there is always enough rain to guarantee a floral display in spring. The reserve was bought by the South African Nature Foundation (now the World Wide Fund for Nature-South Africa), in 1988. It catches much of the rain that blows in off the sea, so that even in years when the surrounding areas have poor displays, Skilpad's is usually magnificent. Tel (0257) 614.

Accommodation In the Upper Karoo, Colesberg has comfortable hotels and motels, affordable overnight chalets, self-catering cottages, guest rooms, and a spacious caravan park. There are also several guest farms, holiday farms and hunting lodges in the district. While the town has more than 1000 beds for overnight visitors, unless you book in advance it is difficult to find accommodation during peak periods.

Central Hotel, Church Street, Colesberg, one-star. Double room without bathroom R100 (£13.35/$22) per room and rooms with bathroom R120 per room. Luxury rooms with bathroom, TV, telephone and air-conditioning R240. Dinner costs R20–40, breakfast R25 and lunch R15–35, tel (051) 753-0734/5, fax (051) 753-0667.

Seekoeirivier offers farm holidays with accommodation in fully equipped cottages or in the farm house. Birdwatching, game-viewing, horse riding, and hiking and mountain bike trails. From R50 per person, tel/fax (051) 753-1378.

Merino Inn, three-star, next to the N1 in Colesberg. From R185 per person, tel (051) 753-0782, fax (051) 753-0615.

Colesberg Caravan Park, municipal caravan park, tel (051) 753-0040.

For something completely different you can sleep at the jail in Colesberg where Correctional Services will let you have a room with either two or four beds for only R30.24 a night. No prison food is available, tel (051) 753-0564.

Britstown Caravan Park, tel (0536712) 3.

Upington has a variety of hotels, home accommodation, B&B, and the Eiland Holiday Resort and Caravan Park, which has 199 beds and 90 caravan sites.

The three-star *Upington Protea Hotel* is on the banks of the Orange River at 24 Schroder Street, Upington 8800, tel/fax (054) 25414.

The *Gariep Lodge* is also on the river. Accommodation in a tented camp, chalets and rondavels, A-framed units and caravan sites. Fishing, horse riding, canoeing, and hiking, tel (054902) ask for 919812.

Eiland Holiday Resort on the outskirts of town has chalets, cottages and caravan sites on the banks of the river, tel (054) 26911.

Yebo Budget & Breakfast, tel (054) 24226.

Farm accommodation varies from a pioneering experience in a corbelled hut to luxury homesteads furnished to reflect the history of the family. Corbelled huts are a distinctive feature of the area and were built as early as 1815 by the first trekboers in the districts of Sutherland, Fraserburg, Williston and Carnarvon.

On the farm *Walkraal* in Williston remains of the Anglo-Boer War are still visible, tel (02052) 2331. *Toekoms Guest House*, Calvinia, also has relics of this war on the farm, tel (0273) 41-2201. *Kliprivier Guest Houses*, form a complex 5km/3 miles from Nieuwoudtville, close to the Klippe River. Accommodation is in *Die Suikerbekkie*, a comfortable room at the main complex for two people; *Kraaifontein*, a thatched cottage for 6 people; or *Uncle Tony's Cabin*, a thatched cottage 3km/2 miles from Niewoudtville, for 4 people. The farm is rich in birdlife and has a home industry selling home-spun wool and warm goose-feather duvets, all made by women on the farm. If you wish, you can join the family around the dining-room table and enjoy tasty farm food with home-produced mutton as the main course, tel (02726) 81204.

Eating and Drinking

Nature is not always kind to the people of the Northern Cape so they make the best of whatever is available, which means, generally, a choice of meat, game, and more meat, although French fries have crept on to the local menu, along with other fast foods and tourist-prompted culinary experiments. If you are in the southern part of the province during the last weekend in August the Hantam Meat Festival at the Calvinia showgrounds is a gastronomical display of typical traditional meat (mainly lamb) dishes. The festival should also appeal if you are interested in folklore and dancing. Contact PO Box 111, Calvinia 8190, tel (0273) 41-1794 (mornings only). Arid territory like this builds pioneer-size thirsts and if you feel like wetting your whistle the way the diggers did in Victorian times Kimberley can still oblige. The town once earned a doubtful reputation because of its plethora of bars. A couple of these watering holes still operate. *Halfway House Inn* is a rarity — a drive-in pub where you can get a drink without leaving your car. This popular pub can thank Cecil John Rhodes for this distinction. Rhodes apparently disliked dismounting from his horse in order to enjoy his pint, so he started the fashion for ride-in drinking. The feature has been retained to this day, making the inn one of the most popular drinking spots in the city. The *Kimberlite Hotel*, in George Street, within walking distance of the Big Hole, also boasts a drive-in bar. Another surviving hostelry from the early days is the *Star of the West*, which still opens for business near the Kimberley Mine Museum. It was built in 1870 from wood and iron and granted the first liquor licence in 1873. The Kimberley Tram will stop for you on request outside the pub if you want to take a closer look. The Northern Cape can even offer you wine tasting. Sherry, pinotage and white wines produced in the province are available from the cellars at Hartswater and Douglas. In Upington, you can sample the natural and fortified products of the Oranjerivier Co-operative Wine Cellars, a five-cellar co-operative that is the second largest in the world. Wine tastings and tours are conducted daily, except Saturday. Cellar tours by arrangement, tel (054) 25651. In October you can also experience, if not enjoy, Upington's Raisin Festival, which keeps the town buzzing for the whole month. There is a market with stalls offering everything from the merely delectable to the divine. You can work it all off afterwards in the SAD-Triathlon.

Entertainment

SPORT AND RECREATION

The sun-baked Northern Cape is not the place to go to watch football or cricket — although all sports are played throughout the province — but it is the region to get away from it all and enjoy challenging sports and recreation such as trail-walking white-water rafting and canoeing, 4x4 off-road safaris and hunting. There are also less demanding activities such as game and bird-watching, photography and botanising in a region renowned for its rare plants and flowers. People are naturally drawn to any expanse of water in a land where rainfall is minimal so you will find watersports of all kinds on the Orange River and on any dam large enough to take a boat or a sailboard. If not, fish. Northern Cape Tourism will provide you with information on these and other leisure activities but the following should give you an idea of the sort of adventures open to you. Lots of sports and social clubs offer temporary membership to visitors.

Hiking. To experience the splendours of what has been called South Africa's last true wilderness area the *Klipspringer Hiking Trail* is a 40km/25 mile three-day trail which ends its way through the Augrabies Falls National Park, with spectacular views of the Orange River and its gorges. Along the way you will become acquainted with a unique diversity of birds, game, desert plants, reptiles, and rodents that have adapted to life in this harsh region. Accommodation is in two overnight huts, with bunks, mattresses, toilets, drinking water, firewood and basic cooking utensils. The trail costs R60 per person. Contact the National Parks Board, tel (012) 343-1991 in Pretoria or (021) 22-2810 in Cape Town; or tel Augrabies National Park at (054472) and ask for Augrabies Falls 4. There are a number of trails for the fit in the rugged Richtersveld area of Namaqualand, open from April to September. Contact the Park Warden, tel (0256) 831-1506. Private guides from Richtersveld Challenge, tel (0251) 21905.

Rooiberg Hiking Trail. East of Garies in the Rooiberge, which has the highest mountain in the Northern Cape, this 50km/31 mile trail takes three days to complete. It is fairly strenuous and overnight accommodation includes a cave and a *matjieshuis* (reed mat hut). Good hiking from May to September. Contact Garies Tourist Information, tel (02792), ask for 14.

The 42km/26 mile *Transkaroo Trail* is a three-day hike in the heart of the arid Karoo between Middelburg and Hanover, midway between Cape Town and Johannesburg. Interesting geological features, historic buildings, Bushman rock art, natural swimming pools in the streams, as well as the game and birdlife, makes this a really worthwhile hike. The trail is well planned and clearly marked and first-timers should have no difficulty in completing it. Overnight accommodation houses 12, but you can bring your own tent. Contact Elmarie van der Merwe at (04924) 22112; or write to Transkaroo Hiking Trail, PO Box 105, Noupoort 5950, Northern Cape.

River Rafting and Canoeing. The 'Augrabies Rush' is a raft trip down 8km/5 miles of the Orange River, tackling rapids with names such as Rhino, Rollercoaster, Klipspringer, Blind Faith and the Cascades, while viewing bird and wildlife as the banks whizz by. Registered guides take you on this four-hour dash, which departs from and returns to Augrabies Falls National Park reception. It costs R95 per person and all rafting and safety equipment, transport and refreshments are supplied. Contact the park's reception, tel (054) 451-0177. Felix Unite, tel (021) 762-6935, will take you white-water riding from Noordoewer down the Orange River for R775 per person for a four-day trip, all inclusive. Adventure Runners, tel (011) 403-2512, charges R565 per person for a weekend rafting trip on the river, including food, guides and equipment. Adventure Runners also do an unusual trail below the Augrabies Falls; you can canoe a stretch and then ride a camel along the banks of the river. Camels are used only in the months March to October when temperatures make riding comfortable.

If this area of the mighty Orange seems a bit too wild and woolly Alleyway River Adventures will raft you down the stretch between Hopetown and Douglas. There are some exciting rapids, as well as more leisurely stretches, tel (053202) 1302. Also on the river near Hopetown is Egerton Game and Rafting Ranch, a wildwater adventure operation in summer and a hunting camp in winter, tel (053202) ask for 1922. In Johannesburg tel (011) 403-2512.

Birdwatching. Keen birdwatchers in particular should not miss the opportunity of viewing waterbirds and veldbirds by canoeing on the Vaal River. A wonderful way to spend a summers day, these canoe trips operate from the Riverton Resort and include full day, half-day and sunset options. Refreshments and an open-air barbecue are provided. Accommodation is available at Riverton. Wildlife weekender canoe trails operate from October to March.

Hunting Safaris. There are lots of opportunities to hunt on game farms in various parts of the province. Safari packages, which include the services of professional hunters, trackers and skinners, accommodation in tented camps or luxury lodges and all meals, are usual. Hunting in the province is conducted under the auspices of the Northern Cape Hunters' Association, tel (0531) 81-1266, which believes that the responsible hunter is also a conservationist. Hunting safaris are conducted out of Upington, tel/fax (054) 27064. For hunting in the Kalahari region, tel (05373) 21001, fax (05373) 22502. In the north-west region hunting is offered by many farmers as part of their springbok culling programmes, tel (0273) 41-1080, fax (0273) 41-1852.

4x4 Trails. Largely rugged semi-desert, the Northern Cape is virtually all outback, and ideal terrain for those enthusiasts who like to have their bones shaken on challenging off-road jaunts. Trails for 4x4 vehicles have sprouted all over the place since the Karoo National Park, near Beaufort West, established its 80km/50-mile trail in 1992, the first national park to do so. Here are a few ranging from novice stuff to experienced drivers only to wet your appetite. You can get information on others from any regional tourist office, or get the *Northern Trails* booklet from Tourism Northern Cape in Kimberley.

The *Kalahari 4x4 Trail* is a two-day 200km/124 mile circular trail in the Mier area, the piece of province wedged between Namibia and the Kalahari Gemsbok Park where the average height of the dunes is 35m/115ft. The trail starts and ends at Molopo Lodge on the road to the park, about 60km/37 miles from the Twee Rivieren Camp. Accommodation at the lodge consists of chalets and a camp site with an ablution block and swimming pool. Lots of driving in Kalahari sand, lots of game, especially gemsbok, make this one to remember. Tel (054902), ask for Askham 2. The *Namaqua 4x4 Route* is a 612km/380 mile route through one of South Africa's most isolated areas. It is divided into two routes, one of 328km/204 miles from the picturesque mission station of Pella to Vioolsdrif on the Orange River, and one of 284km/176 miles from Vioolsdrif and the southern part of the Richtersveld to Alexander Bay. Autumn and spring are best times to do these trails. You can get trail permits from the Regional Information Office, Springbok, tel (0251) 22011, fax (0251) 21421.

For the dyed in the wool 4x4 fanatic there is a two-week (minimum) blockbuster through the Richtersveld National Park, the Augrabies Falls National Park and the Kalahari Gemsbok National Park, three of the wildest areas in southern Africa, mainly mountains and desert. The best time is spring. Budget accommodation all along the route, with designated camp sites in the National Parks. Contact tel (0256) 831-1506, fax (0256) 831-1175, or (021) 22-2810.

Mountain Bike Trails. There are places in Namaqualand that few people ever see because there are simply no roads. These undiscovered gems are now open to pedal-pushers, with most of the routes — marked by a yellow bicycle painted on a rock or signboard — in the Kamiesberg area, east of Kamieskroon. This mountainous terrain is good work-out territory and it is also a floral wonderland between August and October. The four main routes are Nourivier, a circular 29km/18 mile-route, rated as fairly easy with difficult spots; Leliefontein, which has a circular family route of 8km/5 miles; Vissersplaat route is an easy stretch of 7.5km/4.5 miles, with spectacular views; and then there is either a circular route of 49km/30 miles or a straight cycle of 30km/19 miles. This is a fairly difficult trail and a high level of fitness is necessary, especially for the circular route. You get a detailed map and route description when buying your permit. This costs R10 (£1.35/$2.20) and allows you to tackle any of the four routes. Contact the Regional Information Office in Springbok, tel (0251) 22011, fax (0251) 21421. You can also get a permit at the Kamieskroon Hotel, tel (0257) 614, fax (0257) 675.

 In Upington, you can stock up on dried fruit that is rated as the best in the world from the SA Dried Fruit Co-operative factory on the Groblershoop road. The factory is open for visits from Monday to Thursday at 9.45am and 2pm, as well as Friday morning at 9.45am. The shop is open during normal business hours. In the Karoo region of the province, around Colesburg, you can buy lamb of unsurpassed succulence and flavour and it is legend that, like wine farmers at a blind tasting, Karoo housewives can tell if a leg of lamb comes from a local animal after savouring a morsel. The wild herbs and plants the sheep graze give their meat its distinctive taste.

TOURIST INFORMATION

Tourism Northern Cape, Flaxley House, Du Toitspan Road, Private Bag X5017, Kimberley 8300, tel (0531) 31434 or (0531) 82-2657, fax (0531) 81-2937.

Tourism Kimberley, Public Library, Chapel Street, PO Box 1976, Kimberley 8300, tel (0531) 82-7298, fax (0531) 82-7211.

Diamond Fields:

Barkly West, tel (053) 531-0671.
Diamond Fields, tel (0531) 861-4911, fax (0531) 861-1538.
Griquatown, tel (05962) 19.

Karoo:

Colesberg, tel (051) 753-0678, fax (051) 753-0574.
De Aar, tel (05363) 60891/60927, fax (05363) 2529.
Hopetown, tel (053) 203-0008.
Kenhardt, tel (05462) 25.
Orania, tel (053202) 806.
Prieska, tel (0594) 61002/3/4.
Upper Karoo, tel (05363) 60891, fax (05363) 2529.
Calvinia, tel (0273) 41-1080.
Western Karoo, tel (0273) 41-1080, fax (0273) 41-1852.

Kalahari (Lower Orange):

Kalahari, tel (05373) 21001, fax (05373) 22502.
Kuruman, tel (05373) 21095, fax (05373) 23581.
Postmasburg, tel (0591) 30343.
Kakamas, tel (054) 431-0838, fax (054) 431-0836.
Keimoes, tel (054) 461-1016.
Lower Orange River, tel (054) 26911, fax (054) 27064.
Upington, tel/fax (054) 27064.

Namaqualand:

Namaqualand Regional Information, tel (0251) 22011, fax (0251) 21421.
Alexander Bay, tel (0256) 831-1330, fax (0256) 831-1364.
Richtersveld National Park, tel (0256) 831-1506.

Free State

CHRISTIAAN RUDOLPH DE WET
1854 - 1922

The Fourth Raadsaal

Not too many people have the Free State in their sights when they head for South Africa. This is a pity as this landlocked central region stretching from the Vaal River in the north to the Orange River in the south (an area of 129,480sq km/49,992sq miles) has more to offer than the seemingly endless flat prairie lands that produce a third of the nation's maize and wheat and a third of its gold. While the prairie has its own charm, with its chequerboard of tranquil farms and occasional flat-topped koppies, or hillocks, it is the eastern part of the province that beckons the holiday maker, the hiker, camper, and climber and all who want to get close to the animals that once roamed in vast herds across these plains. This is an enchanting mountainous area with a Highland Route which will take you along the border with the neighbouring upland Kingdom of Lesotho to Harrismith, the gateway to the Drakensberg and KwaZulu-Natal.

This region runs roughly from Harrismith in the north-east to Zastron in the south on a road that often straddles great rocky outcrops as it curves through countryside dominated by rugged peaks. This is the area where some of the finest examples of the country's Bushman rock art are found. Rocks and crevices formed natural shelters for the ancient artists who depicted on cave walls the game they hunted in this area, and their legacy of paintings and engravings can still be seen, particularly in the districts of Bethlehem, Ficksburg, Ladybrand and Wepener. The area has lots of pleasant inns and hotels, monuments, battlefields and buildings of the beautiful mellow sandstone which forms striking golden bluffs. The Golden Gate National Park, home of the springbok, eland, red hartebeest and the rare black eagle, is the province's only national park. It is set in the foothills of Lesotho's Maluti Mountains and lies at between 1828m/5997ft and 2743m/8999ft and takes its name from its glowing sandstone surrounds.

The Free State lies entirely on the great interior plateau, 1372m/4500ft above sea level, which means sunny and warm days, and cool and crisp nights. Rain falls mainly in summer. Virtually in the centre of the province is the capital, Bloemfontein, which is also the judicial capital of South Africa. The fountain which gives the city its name still surfaces in the middle of the town. At one time a source of water for Bushman hunters, Sotho farmers, Voortrekkers and their oxen, the spring is now part of a site occupied by a caravan park. From that little fountain Bloemfontein has developed into a prosperous commercial and industrial city, with stately old buildings in the shadow of glass and concrete high-rise buildings. The territory was settled by Afrikaner farmers in the late 1830s and remained largely agricultural until the discovery of gold in the northern part of the province in the 1940s. As you approach from Gauteng the mining towns of Welkom, Odendaalsrus, Virginia and Allanridge thrust their dumps and headgear over the horizon, all towns built on gold and all risen from barren veld within a few decades. The northern border is the willow-lined Vaal River, and Loch Vaal and the Vaal Dam along this major waterway are favourites among anglers and water sport enthusiasts. If you enter the Free State from the Northern or Eastern Cape you will be struck by the contrast in the fertility of the area. The further north you go the more fertile the soil and, with good rainfall, near-perfect conditions for agriculture on an heroic scale are created, as well as for cattle and game farming. Many of the farmers open their doors to visitors, providing opportunities for you to enjoy a reception that has made Free State hospitality a byword. The Free State is the oldest province in South Africa, retaining virtually the borders it has had since the 1870s. It is the third largest of the nine provinces, with the second smallest population (2.9 million). Although it has historically been regarded as the conservative heartland of the Afrikaner people, in the short time since democracy was ushered in its inhabitants of all races have demonstrated a notable harmony and tolerance lacking in many other regions. It is also notable for having the first provincial women premier in the country.

BLOEMFONTEIN

Bloemfontein is a city of many names. In 1840 a Voortrekker built himself a house near the only spring he could find on the dry open plains and named it 'Flower Fountain'. The area was already known to the Tswana people as *Mangaung* or 'the place of the cheetahs'. Today this drowsy capital is also known as the City of Roses and seems to have developed the knack of keeping history alive in a natural manner so that its architectural and historical heritage blends unobtrusively with the lines of the modern city. Stately museum buildings stand at the ends of tree-lined main streets in the city centre and almost unnoticeable small monuments and memorials are preserved even in built-up suburbs. This city of 370,000 has many facets, ranging from sophisticated up-market shopping centres, restaurants and theatres to vestiges of its gracious Victorian past. For a city that was formerly the capital of a Boer republic, Bloemfontein still has many British features that are legacies of the Anglo-Boer War when the town was occupied by British forces. The city has a feeling of leisurely space, enhanced by its setting and natural beauty. There is even a game reserve in the centre of town. The climate is temperate. Average temperatures at Bloemfontein 1422m/4665ft above sea level are 24°C/75°F in summer and 8°C/47°F in winter. Summer is the rainy season. To get a feel for the place a good idea is to start with the historical walking tour of the city, which takes in 25 places of interest in a 5km/3 mile walkabout which starts in the central area. You can get brochures on this from the Publicity Association in the New Tourism Centre, 60 Park Road, tel (051) 405-8489.

Bloemfontein Airport is 14km/9 miles east of the city. There are daily flights linking it with Johannesburg, Cape Town, George, Kimberley and Upington. Smaller aircraft can land at the airports in Harrismith and Bethlehem. There is no bus service between Bloemfontein and the airport, but you can hire a car there or take a taxi.

Car rental at the airport:

Avis, tel (051) 33-2331, fax (051) 33-2352;
Budget, tel (051) 33-1178;
Imperial, tel (051) 33-3511.

Taxis:

Bloem Taxis, tel (051) 33-3776;
Bloemfontein Taxi Federation, tel (051) 33-2543;
Express Hiring Taxi and Bus Operators, tel (051) 430-1430;
Rosestad Taxis, tel (051) 451-1022;
Silverleaf Taxis, tel (051) 430-2005.

An excellent transport and communications network connects this centrally situated city to all major centres in the country, while rail connections from north and south also meet here. There is a local bus service, tel (051) 405-8135, and luxury **buses and coaches** offer easy access to the attractions of the Free State and the hinterland:

Translux, tel (051) 408-3242;
Greyhound, tel (051) 430-2361;
InterCape, tel (051) 33-3876;
Vrystaat Toere, tel (051) 448-4951;
Snel bus, tel (051) 33-1229.

Rail. The railway station is centrally situated in Maitland Street, tel (051) 408-2946. The Orange Express main line train operates once a week between Bloemfontein, Kimberley, Durban and Cape Town. Spoornet Passengers Service, tel (051) 408-2941.

Bloemfontein has a variety of accommodation ranging from star-rated hotels to a wide variety of motels, holiday farms, guest houses, resorts, caravan and camping parks. For 4-star luxury there is the *Bloemfontein Hotel* at the Sanlam Plaza in the heart

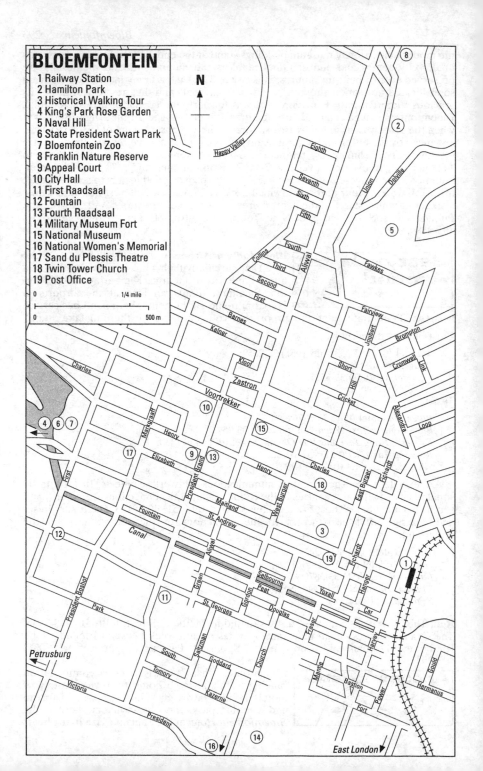

BLOEMFONTEIN

1 Railway Station
2 Hamilton Park
3 Historical Walking Tour
4 King's Park Rose Garden
5 Naval Hill
6 State President Swart Park
7 Bloemfontein Zoo
8 Franklin Nature Reserve
9 Appeal Court
10 City Hall
11 First Raadsaal
12 Fountain
13 Fourth Raadsaal
14 Military Museum Fort
15 National Museum
16 National Women's Memorial
17 Sand du Plessis Theatre
18 Twin Tower Church
19 Post Office

N

0   1/4 mile
0   500 m

Happy Valley

Eighth
Seventh
Sixth
Fifth
Fourth
Collins
Third
Second
First
Barnes
Kellner
Kloof
Zastron
Voortrekker
Charles

Union
Delville
Fawkes
Fairview
Joubert
Brompton
Cromwell
Link
Short
Hill
Cricket
Alexandra
Loop
Aliwal

Markgraaff
Henry
Elizabeth
President Brand
Maitland
St. Andrew
Fountain
Canal
Green
Aliwal
St. Georges
Gordon
Peet
Selbourne
Douglas
Saltzman
Goddard
Church
South
Tomory
Kazerne
Victoria
President
Park
President Boshof

Henry
West Burger
Charles
East Burger
Eichardt
Yoxall
Fraser
Car
Harvey
Mantie
Bastion
Fort
Power
Gould
Hermanus

Petrusburg
East London

of the city, R240 (£32/$53) per person a night sharing, tel (051) 430-1911, fax (051) 447-7102. There are two 3-star *Holiday Inn Garden Courts* in Bloemfontein, one in Brandhof, tel (051) 447-0310, fax (051) 430-5678, and the other at Naval Hill, tel (051) 430-1111. They cost R250 to R275 a night per person sharing.

JR Tolkien, author of *The Hobbit*, was born in Bloemfontein, and a recent Satour guesthouse of the year was the *Hobbit House*, with rooms named after his characters: the Bilbo Baggins Room, and the Room of Galadriel, queen of the elves. What all the rooms have in common is a teddy bear on the bed. Personal touches include the miniature bottles of medium-cream sherry left in your room for nightcaps, along with Belgian chocolates. Tel/Fax (051) 447-0663.

Aventura Maselspoort 23km/14 miles from Bloemfontein, is an oasis on the banks of the Modder ('Mud') River. A two-bed chalet costs R150 (£20/$33) a night. There are self-catering chalets and camping and caravan sites, tel (051) 41-7848. There are also Aventura resorts at the Gariep Dam in the south, tel (052172) and ask for 45, and at the Willem Pretorius Game Reserve, between Ventersburg and Winburg. They cost between R100 (£13.35/$22) and R350 a night for 2-bed units. Central reservations, tel (012) 346-2277. Bloemfontein Publicity Association will provide you with a list of other places to stay. Agents for guest houses are Ansu, tel (051) 436-5154, and Homeshare Holidays, Cell 082 550-1562. There are two *Sun International* casino hotels at Thaba 'Nchu, 75km/47 miles east of Bloemfontein. For reservations, tel (051) 33-1505/9.

Taffy's Backpackers is at 18 Louis Botha Street, Waverley, Bloemfontein 9301, tel (051) 31-4533.

Appeal Court. The Privy Council in England ceased to hear appeals from South Africa in 1950 and the Appeal Court in Bloemfontein became the country's highest judicial authority. The Appellate Division of the Supreme Court is housed in a 1929 building decorated with fine stinkwood panelling, carvings and furniture, tel (051) 47-2631.

City Hall. This well known landmark is regarded as one of the country's finest civic buildings and has a collection of historic paintings and photographs. It is notable for its superb Italian marble and Burmese wood, tel (051) 405-8911.

First Raadsaal (Parliament Building). Built in 1849 as a school, this one-roomed thatched building is Bloemfontein's oldest to survive in its original condition (it still has a dung floor). Open Monday to Friday from 10.15am to 3pm and weekends from 2pm to 5pm, tel (051) 47-9610.

Fountain. A column emblazoned with Bloemfontein's coat of arms marks the site of the spring from which the city gets its name. More unromantically, the old fountain feeds a concrete drainage canal, near the municipal caravan park in Victoria Park.

Fourth Raadsaal. Officially opened in 1893, this dignified sandstone and red brick building is rightly regarded as an architectural masterpiece. Exhibits include the busts of six former Free State presidents. You can visit only by appointment, tel (051) 47-8898.

Hamilton Park. This park at the western foot of Naval Hill has a lovely orchid house, where waterfalls and pools provide a backdrop for magnificent displays of more than 6000 orchids. Nearby is a fragrance garden for the blind. Visiting hours during the week are from 10am to 4pm and at the weekend from 10am to 5pm.

National Museum. Notable for its large collection of fossils, cultural historical exhibits and archaeological displays, including the Florisbad skull discovered in 1932. A highlight of the museum is a reconstructed turn-of-the-century Bloemfontein street scene and there is also a working bee-hive. Open daily from 8am to 5pm, Sunday from midday to 6pm, tel (051) 447-9609.

Naval Hill. There are panoramic views of the city from the flat crest of Naval Hill, which has the vest-pocket 198ha/489 acre Franklin Nature Reserve on its flanks, with animals ranging from giraffes to tiny steenbok. It is the only game reserve in a city centre in the world, tel (051) 405-8124. In the reserve the Lamont-Hussey Observatory once controlled by the University of Michigan is now an intimate theatre and cultural centre. On the south-eastern slopes is the white horse laid out during the Anglo-Boer War by the men of the Wiltshire Remount Depot as a landmark for riders coming in from the plains. Two British naval guns are mounted on the crest of the hill.

Old Presidency. This stately Victorian building dating from 1886 was the official residence of three presidents of the old Republic of the Orange Free State. It houses a museum covering their terms of office, and a cultural centre for art exhibitions, theatrical productions and musical events, tel (051) 48-0949.

Oliewenhuis Art Gallery. This gallery in the elegant residence of former governors-general and state presidents houses a permanent exhibition, as well as temporary exhibitions featuring works by contemporary Free State artists. Open daily, tel (051) 447-9609.

President Swart Park, King's Park Gardens and Zoo. These adjoining parks and gardens form a large green lung in the city and are a blaze of colour almost all year round. There are more than 4000 rose trees in the rose garden at King's Park, which was opened in 1925 by the Prince of Wales. Bloemfontein Zoo is known for its lion-tiger cross ('ligers') and one of the largest collection of primates in the country, as well as its Big Five. Open every day of the year, in summer from 8am to 6pm and in the winter from 8am to 5pm, tel (051) 405-8483.

Queen's Fort Military Museum. Exhibits at this museum relate mainly to the history of Bloemfontein from 1848 — when the British proclaimed the Orange River Sovereignty after a skirmish with dissenting Boers — to the present. There are excellent collections of firearms and uniforms. Open Monday to Friday from 8am to 4pm, tel (051) 447-5478.

Railway Station. Built in 1890, this teak-pillared building draws steam buffs to see the *City of Bloemfontein*, a superb loco built in Germany in 1935 and displayed outside the station, tel (051) 408-2946.

Sand du Plessis Theatre. The superb multipurpose complex houses one of the most technically advanced theatres in the world, which is the venue for opera, ballet, drama and concert performances. It can seat 900. Tours by appointment, tel (051) 447-7771.

Supreme Court. This neo-classical Edwardian building with its magnificent interior was completed in 1909. Visits are by appointment only, tel (051) 447-8837.

Twin Tower Church. Twin spires, modelled on those of the Cathedral of Bamberg in Bavaria, make this one of South Africa's most distinctive churches.

War Museum. Dedicated to the Boer forces that took part in the Anglo-Boer War. Exhibits include weapons and items made by Boer prisoners. You can also get a glimpse of the part played in the 'White Man's War' by coloured and black people. In the grounds is the **National Women's Memorial**, designed by famous sculptor Anton van Wouw, a striking 36.5m/120ft sandstone obelisk which commemorates the 26,000 Boer women and children who died in British concentration camps. The ashes of British Quaker Emily Hobhouse, who alleviated some of the suffering in the camps, lie under the obelisk. Open weekdays from 9am to 4.30pm, Saturday from 9am to 5pm and Sunday from 2pm to 5pm, tel (051) 447-3447.

Bloemfontein has a fair choice of shopping malls and centres containing major chains as well as smaller, more personal boutiques, trendy arts and crafts galleries and outlets for specialist products. Most prestigious is the Middestad Centre in the heart of the city, where you will rub shoulders with some of the 12,000 people who shop there every day in the centre's 76 stores. The centre is on West Burger Street, tel (051) 447-6202. There is a flea market on the first Saturday of every month at Loch Logan in King's Park gardens. Old-fashioned general dealer stores selling everything from snuff to snacks are scattered throughout the towns and villages and many articles on sale there should bring back memories for older travellers.

NORTHERN FREE STATE

Bothaville. The Bothaville district produces maize in immense quantities and the Nampo Harvest Farm and Festival, one of the largest private agricultural show centres in the world, draws more than 20,000 visitors a year. The farm has a permanent exhibition highlighting various aspects of this important South African industry. Witblits made locally can be bought at the town library.

Kroonstad. The holiday resort of Kroon Park is on the banks of the Vals River. A one-day hiking trail just outside town provides good bird-watching and leads past some well preserved Bushman paintings.

Parys. On the south bank of the Vaal River, Parys ('Paris') is a popular highveld holiday venue. The river here is 1.5km/0.9 miles wide and dotted with tree-covered islands. Several of these have been developed into pleasant resorts and one, linked to the town by a suspension bridge, is the setting for a 9-hole golf course. Many have camping sites and chalets. Parys Museum focuses on the cultural, historical and geological features of the region.

Vaal Dam. Gauteng and Free State share this 300sq km/116sq mile dam which is a popular weekend and holiday venue for watersports, with good yellowfish, carp and barbel fishing. Along the dam are resorts and camping and caravan sites galore. Diverse birdlife includes great white egrets, Egyptian geese, and fish eagles. Deneysville village is on the dam and there are four yacht clubs close by. Contact Deneysville Information Centre, tel (01618) 31130.

Welkom. This modern city is one of the only cities in the world planned to completion before a single brick was laid. It lies in the middle of the Free State goldfields and is a good base for a visit to a gold mine. You can also visit the world's deepest wine cellar, 857m/2812ft below ground at the St Helena Mine. All types of sport are catered for, including motor racing. The Goldfields Racetrack is the venue for national car racing championships.

CENTRAL FREE STATE

Erfenis Dam Nature Reserve. The 3200-hectare dam has a 400ha/988 acre reserve on its banks which has a variety of antelope species, including the unusual white springbok and yellow blesbok. The fishing is good and there is a caravan and camping park at the dam, tel (05772) 4211.

Florisbad. Health resort with indoor and outdoor hot springs 45km/28 miles north-west of Bloemfontein. Named after Floris Venter, who first opened up the mineral spring that became famous as the place where the fossiled prehistoric skull of Florisbad Man was found in 1932. It was originally estimated to be 100,000 to 130,000 years old, although other datings make it as recent as 35,000 to 50,000 years old and ancestral to the Bushmen (San). The skull was the first to be found among implements and animal food remains in South Africa, and is now in the National Museum in Bloemfontein.

Free State National Botanical Garden. Some 10km/6 miles north of Bloemfontein, the garden is rich in indigenous plants and wildlife. Divided into formal gardens, natural woodlands and wetlands, it features a man-made lake, herbarium, and an orange tree arbour, tel (051) 31-3530.

Maselspoort Pleasure Resort. About 22km/14 miles east of Bloemfontein on the road to Lesotho this resort on the banks of the Modder River has an enormous swimming pool and facilities for rowing, fishing, tennis and other outdoor activities. There is accommodation in rondavels and a caravan park.

Sandveld Nature Reserve. Gemsbok, blue wildebeest, kudu, rhino, buffalo, giraffe and small mammals thrive in this 37,700ha/93,159 acre reserve, which encompasses the Bloemhof Dam, noted for excellent fishing, and which attracts large numbers of egret, cormorant and ibis. Hunting is permitted in the reserve in winter. Caravan and camping facilities are available, tel (01802) 31701.

Soetdoring Nature Reserve. A 7500-hectare sanctuary near Bloemfontein for Burchell's zebra, wildebeest, blesbok and springbok. A predator park is inhabited by lion and cheetah. Martial eagles and secretarybirds breed in the reserve. The Krugersdrif Dam, when full, attracts large flocks of ducks and geese. There are one-day hikes along the Modder River, tel (051) 33-1011.

Thaba'Nchu ('Black Mountain') was once the stronghold of a 19th century chief. Conducted game-viewing drives and 7-hour to 10-hour hikes are available at Maria Moroka National Park, where you can see up to 150 bird species, including the rare blue korhaan. If you are more of a night owl than a birder, then head for Thaba 'Nchu's cabarets, casinos and discos.

Willem Pretorius Game Reserve. On the Allemanskraal Dam. 160km/100 miles north-east of Bloemfontein, this 12,000-hectare reserve contains a large variety of wild animals, including black wildebeest, eland, buffalo, impala, reedbok, springbok, white rhino, and giraffe. The dam is popular with anglers and draws more than 220 bird species, including martial and fish eagles. In the hills around the dam you can see prehistoric beehive-shaped stone huts. Accommodation at a resort overlooking the dam and a caravan park, tel (05777) 4003/4.

Winburg. Established in 1842 and the first capital of the Republic of the Orange Free State. The Town Hall is built to resemble an ox-wagon and it is decorated with fine murals of South African scenes. Using life-size models, the Free State Voortrekker Museum shows the daily routine of the trekkers, and the Voortrekker Monument, 3km/2 miles outside of town, commemorates five major Trekker groups. There is an Anglo-Boer War concentration camp cemetery west of the town.

EASTERN FREE STATE

Basotho Cultural Village. The Basotho have developed a distinctive culture in the eastern Free State and you can see many facets of this in their 'Cultural Village' in the heart of the Qwaqwa National Park, a stone's throw away from the majestic sandstone cliffs of the Golden Gate area. Here the lifestyle and dwellings of the South Sotho are accurately depicted from the 16th century to the present. The guide will take you into the *khotla*, the gathering place of men, where you will be offered a sip of traditional beer. You can consult the *ngaka*, the captain's advisor, in his professional capacity as traditional healer, and then step into the home of either his first, second or third wife and watch them grinding and sifting maize to make beer.

The huts are built and furnished according to different historical times. Interior and exterior decoration of Sotho huts is traditionally done by women, and is called *litema*. These colourful geometric designs can still be seen throughout the Free State's rural areas. An art gallery displays work of local artists and has a permanent photographic exhibition of village building and *litema* art in the eastern Free State. You can buy a wide variety of Basotho arts and crafts at the local curio shop.

One of the innovations at the Cultural Village is a two-hour trail. A social ecologist and an *ngaka* (healer) will take you on this trail, and they will show you a variety of grasses, roots, herbs, leaves and bark in the veld and explain how these are used in rituals or to cure ailments ranging from toothache to sexually transmitted diseases. *En route* you also visit well preserved Bushman paintings, depicting eland, rhino, a giraffe and lion on a kill. Contact Basotho Cultural Village, Private Bag X826, Witsieshoek 9870, tel (058) 721-0300, e-mail Basotho@dorea.co.za

Bethlehem is roughly equidistant from Johannesburg and Bloemfontein. It was founded in 1864 on the banks of the Jordan river, which form part of the Pretoriuskloof Nature Reserve. The museum in Muller Street depicts the history of this one-time Voortrekkers transit point on the wagon road to Natal. It also houses a steam locomotive. Across the road is the AB Baartman Wagonhouse museum. There is a local tour of 19 beautiful sandstone buildings. Loch Athlone municipal pleasure resort, on the southern outskirts of town, has a range of sports facilities, a swimming pool and hiking trails which take in the nearby Wolhuterskop Nature Reserve. An unusual feature of the resort is a restaurant in the shape of an old Union Castle steamship, the *Athlone Castle*, which contains many fixtures recovered from the ship before it was scrapped.

Caledonspoort. In a shallow sandstone rock shelter overlooking the Caledon River near the Fouriesburg-Butha Buthe road, close to the Lesotho border, are some Bushman paintings of fish, an unusual subject for the little hunter artists. The river marks the Free State-Lesotho border.

Clarens. 10km/6 miles from the Lesotho border the little town of Clarens, named after the town in Switzerland where Paul Kruger died in exile, is a magnet for artists and photographers. The town abounds with studios and 13 of these are open to visitors. Art galleries, a lovely church and a museum are worth a visit. In Naupoort Street is the tiny Cinderella Castle, built with more than 55,000 beer bottles. 12km/8 miles out of town at the farm Schaapplaats is a cave noted for its prehistoric polychrome rock art.

Ficksburg. The cherries and asparagus of this area on the banks of the Caledon River are renowned. To visit growers, tel (05192) 5547/8. The town has a Cherry Festival every November. The Anglican church is known for its stained glass windows and in the centre of town is the General Fick Museum. Hoekfontein Game Ranch, some 10km/6 miles east, has white rhino, hippo, Burchell's zebras, antelope, and abundant waterfowl, grassland birds and raptors. Water sports and angling are popular on the nearby Meulspruit Dam, which is the starting and finishing point for the 23km/14 mile Imparani Hiking Trail. In the area is Rustlers Valley Mountain Lodge, renowned among New Age travellers for its open-air music festival every Easter and its extended Christmas camping party, tel (05192) 92-3939.

Golden Gate Highlands National Park. Just when your eye has grown accustomed to the big sky and an endless, virtually uninterrupted, view the Free State offers you its greatest treasure. This is the eastern highlands where aeons of scouring by the elements have exposed gigantic sandstone outcrops and sculpted their cliffs into wonderful shapes and formations. When the sun strikes them, particularly at dawn and sunset, they take on a rosy golden glow which gives the area and this splendid 11,630-hectare sanctuary its name. The park is on the Highlands Route near Clarens and is as accessible from Johannesburg as it is from Bloemfontein. The climate is invigorating and the scenery is a backdrop to many species of game and birdlife. Outdoor options include tennis, bowls, horse riding, swimming in mountain pools and visits to Bushman rock paintings. You can take leisurely walks along winding nature trails, some of which start at the Glen Reenen camping site, or you can follow the 31km/19 mile (two-day) Rhebok Hiking Trail which leads through stunning surroundings to the summit of Generaalskop (2757m/9045ft), the highest point in the park. You should spot eland, zebra, red hartebeest, black wildebeest, and the endangered oribi, as well as the bearded vulture, bald ibis and the black eagle. The trail and overnight hut costs R33 (£4.40/$7.25) a person. Some 140 bird species have been identified in the park, and a hide at the vulture 'restaurant' enables you to get close to these magnificent raptors. Accommodation at the park is either in hotel rooms or self-catering chalets and rondavels. There are two rest camps: Brandwag is the main building with singles, doubles and even suites. There are four-bed chalets, and the Wilgenhof Youth Hostel, which can take up to 86 people. Glen Reenen rest camp has a house, rondavels, and a caravan and camping site. At these rest camps you will pay from R220 (£29/$48) for a two-bed chalet to R365 for a suite for two people. Camping costs R40 a night for two people, with R9 for each additional person. Tel (012) 343-1991 and (012) 22-2810, fax (012) 343-0905 and (012) 24-6211.

Harrismith. Named after Sir Harry Smith, Governor of the Cape (1847-1852), the town is the starting point of the Highlands Route, and many tourists use the town as a gateway to the Natal Drakensberg and the Golden Gate National Park. The town has seen armies, hordes of adventurers and battles galore, which have all left their mark on this, one of the oldest towns in the Free State. A 27m/89ft petrified tree, 150 million years old, lies on the Town Hall lawn. The Platberg Wild Flower Garden on the outskirts of town harbours 20 per cent of all the flora of the Drakensberg. Open daily from sunrise to sunset.

Highland Route. The beauty of the Free State reaches its zenith in the eastern highlands, where this dazzling scenic route traces the Lesotho border from the north-east to south-east corner of the province. Bushman caves and superb examples of rock art are a feature of the route, which has many outstanding hiking trails.

Ladybrand. 15km/9 miles from the main border post between South Africa and Lesotho. Founded at the foot of the Platberg (Flat Mountain) in 1867. Among the exhibits at the Catharina Brand Museum is an old pharmacy containing *boererate*, farmers' traditional remedies. Leliehoek Pleasure Resort has some pleasant walks, including the two-day Steve Visser Hiking Trail, with views of the Maluti Mountains. There are also riding trails and horses can be hired. There are some important, although disfigured, Bushmen paintings in caves in the area, especially at Rose Cottage (3km/2 miles from the town), Modderpoort (11km/7 miles) and on the farm Tandjiesberg (22km/14 miles). At Modderpoort a cave church dating back to 1869 is a relic of the Anglican Society of St Augustine, a small monastic group who once used the cave as a chapel and living quarters. On the fourth Sunday of each August the Anglican Society of the Sacred Mission holds a service in the cave church.

Qwaqwa. This district has been the home of the Kwena and Tlokwa southern Sotho tribes since 1839, although this name for the dominant flat-topped sandstone mountain was given to it long before by the Bushmen. It means 'whiter than white' and probably refers to its coating of vulture droppings. The main town is Phuthaditjhaba. The Qwaqwa Park, 60km/37 miles from Harrismith and adjacent to the Golden Gate National Park, covers 22,000 hectares of largely mountainous terrain and is home to antelope and rare bird species, including the bearded vulture, bald ibis and wattled crane. Hiking, camping and 4x4 trails are available. The park is largely a hiker's world and the Sentinel Trail traverses magnificent terrain. A chain ladder helps you to reach the Drakensberg plateau and Mont-aux-Sources, tel (05871) 44444, fax (05871) 34342.

Seekoeivlei Nature Reserve. This 4400-hectare reserve 15km/9 miles north of Memel is a bird-watcher's paradise and has a Ramsar listing as wetlands of international importance. Hiking trails through the marshland lead to watchtowers from which endangered birds such as the blue and wattled crane can be seen, tel (0174) 40183.

Sterkfontein Dam Nature Reserve. The grassveld of this 18,000-hectare reserve in the foothills of the Drakensberg provides an ideal habitat for bearded and Cape vultures, black and martial eagles and the long-legged secretarybird. The dam is the largest earthwall dam in South Africa and the second largest in the world. It is an anglers' and windsurfers' paradise, tel (05861) 23520, fax (05861) 21772.

SOUTHERN FREE STATE

Bethulie used to be called Moordenaarspoort ('Murderers defile') because a large number of Griquas and Bushmen were murdered here by Basotho. It lies on the northern bank of the Gariep Dam, not far from the confluence of the Caledon and Orange rivers. Pellissier House Museum depicts the history of the area. Bethulie Dam has attractive picnic spots along its shady banks and is a venue for water sports and angling. There are three hiking trails. Nearby is the Mynhardt Game Reserve.

Fauresmith. Probably of interest only to those besotted by railways is this little town 60km/37 miles north of Philippolis. It is one of the few places in the world where the railway line runs down the centre of the main street. If you are fascinated by things like this you can watch the local loco clatter through at 6am and return at 11am on weekdays. Check in case it has gone into mothballs. If it has, you can admire the retired loco which is a permanent fixture in the middle of the town, or you can visit the Kalkfontein Dam Nature Reserve 30km/19 miles north of town.

Gariep Dam. This huge man-made lake where the Free State is bordered by the Eastern Cape and the Northern Cape is more than 100km/62 miles long and 24km/15 miles wide and is an engineering marvel. Between the dam and Bethulie there is a nature reserve with the country's largest springbok population, other antelope and a breeding herd of Cape mountain zebra. To the west is a holiday resort and great views of this enormous (384sq km/148sq miles) inland sea, islands and distant hills, tel/fax (052172) 26.

Philippolis. Founded as a London Missionary Society station in 1823, this is one of the oldest towns in the province and has many fine old buildings along its main street. The Dutch Reformed Church has a magnificent wild olive pulpit made without a single nail or screw. There is a memorial to Emily Hobhouse (1860–1926), the British Quaker who won the enduring affection of the Afrikaners during the Anglo-Boer War. The Transgariep Museum depicts the history of the area from the time of Adam Kok and the Griquas who settled around the mission. In April every year the museum uses one of its exhibits, a distilling kettle, at the town's annual Witblits Festival. Open Monday to Friday from 10am to midday, tel (051) 7726.

Smithfield. 132km/82 miles south of Bloemfontein, this is a restful, pollution and crime-free Karoo *dorp* which has been revitalised by a colony of artists and craftsmen. Once you have visited the concentration camp cemetery and the Caledon River Museum you can relax and enjoy good local food, exhibitions of South African artists, and some of the estimated 350 days a year of sunshine, tel (055620) ask for 3.

Tussen die Riviere ('Between the rivers') **Nature Reserve.** East of Bethulie, at the confluence of the Caledon and Orange rivers, this reserve reputedly has more game than any other in the Free State, and includes white rhino, Burchell's zebra, wildebeest and a variety of antelopes. Bird life is prolific. It is open from the beginning of September to the end of April. In autumn and winter it is reserved for hunters, tel (051762) 9992 and 2803.

Zastron. A striking landmark above the town is the 'Eye of Zastron' a hole 9m/30ft in diameter in one of the cliffs of the Aasvoëlberg ('Vulture Mountain'). Legend has it that this hole was made by the devil's head when it was blown from his body by the mixture of peach brandy and strong pipe tobacco he shared with a local farmer. From the caravan park in Eeufeeskloof roads lead to vantage points high in mountains notable for Bushman paintings in caves which were their last stronghold in the Free State. The caravan park is also starting point for the two-day 36km/22 miles circular Aasvoëlberg Hiking Trail.

BATTLEFIELDS

The Anglo-Boer War of 1899–1902 was the last major war to be fought on South African soil. It was the first of the modern wars and is regarded as the last of the gentlemen's wars. Remnants of those stormy years are scattered throughout the province in the shape of battlefields, blockhouses and the War Museum in Bloemfontein (see above). As the centenary of the Anglo-Boer war approaches, the Free State is promoting tours of its battle sites, some of which are not so well known, such as Sanaspos and Driefontein, as well as highlighting long-neglected black participation in the war.

Magersfontein (11 December 1899). British troops advancing to relieve Kimberley were blocked here by Boer commandos. There is a museum on the hill and a viewsite with explanatory notes on the battle.

Paardeberg (18–27 February 1900). General JDP French relieved Kimberley on 15 February 1900 after one of the last great cavalry charges in history. The British caught up with the Boers at Paardeberg on 17 February 1900 and prevented them crossing the Modder River. On 18 February, Lord Kitchener, commanding British forces for the day, assaulted the Boer entrenchments, suffering the heaviest losses of any day of the entire war. Following a prolonged bombardment, General Cronje's forces surrendered on 27 February, the anniversary of the British defeat at Majuba in 1881. A museum at the site commemorates the battle, and there is a look-out post on Oskoppies and another at the site of the Boer laager, as well as British graves.

Poplar Grove (7 March 1900). After Paardeberg, Poplar Grove was an anti-climax. General CR de Wet's forces made a stand at Poplar Grove, a drift in the river, in the path of the British forces on their way to Bloemfontein. On 7 March 1900, French's cavalry flanked the Boer positions and to avoid being surrounded they fell back to Bloemfontein, leaving Roberts in command of the position with only a few casualties.

Driefontein (10 March 1900). Driefontein was the last stand the Boer forces made before Bloemfontein fell. General De Wet and General JH de la Rey had 1500 men at their disposal to defend their positions. The Welsh and Essex bore the brunt of the fighting. Under heavy artillery bombardment they advanced and drove the Boers from their positions, forcing them to fall back to Bloemfontein. There are monuments to the fallen of both sides and graves of casualties at the site.

Sannaspos (31 March 1900). Bloemfontein was occupied on 13 March 1900. At the end of March, General de Wet attacked the small British garrison protecting Sannaspos, the main water supply for Bloemfontein. Instead of an expected garrison of 200, De Wet found himself facing Brig Gen R Broadwood's 1800 men, but put them to flight. This violent clash was the beginning of the guerrilla phase of the war. There is a museum open daily from 8am to 5pm.

Mostertshoek (3–4 April 1900). Gen De Wet caught up with a British force of 591 men under Captain McWhinnie, who made a stand in the hills near Mostershoek. De Wet had nearly 2000 men and attacked the British on 3 April 1900. The battle went on until night and although three British officers were killed the British clung to their positions until overwhelmed and defeated. The Boers lost six men, compared to 591 British dead.

Jammerbergdrif (9 April 1900). After Sannaspos and Mosterthoek, the only garrison left in the eastern Free State was that of Lt Col Dalgety of Wepener. De Wet and his 5000 men were unable to penetrate the defences on 9 April 1900, and besieged the garrison until 25 April, when a British relief column arrived. There is a monument commemorating the battle and a cemetery at the site.

Sand River (10 May 1900). On 3 May 1900 Lord Roberts started his march to Pretoria from Bloemfontein with about 25,000 soldiers, 80 guns and 49 machine guns. The Boers had 2000 men ranged against him. After several skirmishes the Boers made a stand at Sand River, but against Gen French's encircling cavalry the Boers fell into disarray and beat a retreat.

Biddulphsberg (29 May 1900). While the battle at Biddulphsberg, near the town of Senekal, was taking place, Boers were also attacking the Imperial Yeomanry at Lindley. When the Yeomanry were besieged, Lt Gen Rundle with his 4000 men at Senekal tried to divert the Boers' attention. When news reached Rundle about Boer positions at Biddulphsberg, he attacked after shelling them. The bombardment set the veld on fire and at first covered the British attack, but a change of wind swept the fire through the British lines and the Boers were left victorious.

Lindley (31 May 1900). Lindley is remembered for the British surrender that never was. After several days of inconclusive fighting between the Boers and the 13th Imperial Yeomanry a heavy Boer bombardment followed by a charge brought a white flag fluttering from the British ranks. This had been raised without the consent of the officer in charge, but was accepted as the Boers were already disarming British troops.

Roodewal (7 June 1900). After occupying Bloemfontein and Pretoria, the British were dependant for provisions on the railway, so the Boers concentrated on disrupting these lines. Gen De Wet attacked Roodewal station on 7 June 1900, overpowering the garrison and making off with war provisions and equipment worth £100,000.

Surrender Hill (30 July 1900). While 4000 Boers camped in the Brandwater basin argued about who should lead them they were encircled by troops under Lt Gen A Hunter and the newly elected Boer leader was forced to surrender. At the place where they surrendered, the Boers burnt their weapons and to this day, it is said, no grass grows on this spot.

Doornkraal (6 November 1900). Early on the morning of 6 November 1900 the Boers at Doornkraal, near Bothaville, were surprised by the British under Lt Col Le Gallais. De Wet and a few followers escaped while the other members of the commando made a futile stand. Le Gallais fell on the battlefield. De Wet lived to fight another day and become an irritating thorn in the British side.

Groenkop (24–25 December 1901). De Wet and his guerrilla commando chose Christmas Day to attack the British at Groenkop, where soldiers were building blockhouses in the eastern Free State. The camp was surprised before sunrise. A third of the British force escaped; the rest were captured or killed.

For more information on the Free State Battlefields Route contact the Bloemfontein War Museum, PO Box 704, Bloemfontein 9300, Free State, tel (051) 447-3447, fax (051) 447-1322.

Time seems to stand still in many little Free State *dorps*, and nowhere more than in Philippolis and Smithfield, in the southern reaches. In Philippolis, 7 Colin Fraser Street, is a very special house. Not only is it one of the few examples of republican architecture to survive the Anglo-Boer War, it was the birthplace in 1906 of the late Sir Laurens van der Post, Afrikaner by birth, British by adoption, writer, friend and mentor of Prince Charles. The house is now a national monument and the *Van der Post Guest House*, neatly positioned between Gauteng and the Cape. Contact Mark Ingle, PO Box 139, Philippolis 9970, tel (051772), ask for 324.

Sleepy Smithfield on the road south to the Eastern Cape is well worth driving the extra hour or so from Bloemfontein to join a group of artists, restaurateurs and craftsmen who have turned this Karoo *dorp* into a cultured, tranquil haven. Julius Bramley and Frans Mulder have transformed a national monument dated 1861 into a guest house called *Adam's Cottage*, which costs R125 (£16.65/$27.50) B&B, with dinner an extra R55. They have also opened a restaurant called the *Colony Room* — rated in the country's Top 10 in 1996 — and the Maggsleigh Art Gallery, which exhibits African tribal art alternating with contemporary art. The gallery is in the oldest Anglican church north of the Orange River. Contact PO Box 73, Smithfield 9966, tel/fax (051) 683-1138.

Maluti Mountain Lodge, near Golden Gate National Park has horse trails, hiking, trout fishing, golf, squash, tennis, bowls, and swimming. There are Bushmen paintings and dinosaur remains nearby, and there is trophy hunting and grey-wing bird shooting in season. From R145 B&B per person sharing. Contact PO Box 21, Clarens 9797, tel (058) 256-1422, fax (058) 256-1306. Another mountain getaway in the Rooiberge, near Golden Gate, is the *De Ark Game Ranch*, which has self-catering chalets from R60 per person. Contact PO Box 25, Clarens 9707, tel (058) 256-1202, fax (058) 256-1181. *Witsieshoek Mountain Resort* in the northern Drakensberg is the highest (2286m/7500ft) resort in South Africa and ideal for hiking, fly-fishing, bird-watching and game viewing. Contact PO Box 17311, Witsieshoek 9870, tel (058) 789-1900, fax (058) 789-1901.

Harrismith is the gateway to the Drakensberg and a good centre for walking and climbing and generally taking the crisp air. 21km/13 miles north of the town is *Mount Everest Game Lodge*, with log cabins and caravan sites or rustic accommodation in a century-old farmhouse. Self-catering costs R105 (£14/$23) per person in chalets, R65 a day for caravans. Contact PO Box 471, Harrismith 9880, tel (05861) 21816, fax (05861) 23493. *Platberg Nature Reserve* on the outskirts of town has basic foresters' huts for hikers and hunters. Take your own bedding and cooking gear. There is no electricity. Self-catering R28.50 per person, tel (05861) 23525. *Harrismith Caravan Park* charges only R27 for four people, and that includes electricity, tel (05861) 23525. The first of its kind in the province is the Township Bed & Breakfast. Contact Harrismith Tourist Information for more details, tel (05861) 23525 or 21583 (a/h).

Near Ficksburg, 300km/186 miles from Johannesburg, *Hoekfontein Game Ranch* can give you a feeling of what it was like on trek in the old days — camping, food and ox-wagon outings. You can sleep in an ox-wagon or tent. Take your own bedding. Contact PO Box 354, Ficksburg 9730, tel (05192) 3915.

Near Bethlehem the *Loch Athlone Resort* on the wooded banks of the Loch Athlone dam has self-catering chalets and 200 caravan and camping sites on the

Jordan river. There is boating and angling and also a heated pool. It costs from R85 per person sharing. Caravan and camping sites are R35. Contact PO Box 60, Bethlehem 9700, tel/fax (058) 303-4981.

Backpacker accommodation includes *Isibongo Lodge*, Olisbiershoek Pass, Harrismith 9880, tel (036) 438-6707, and *Rustlers Valley Backpackers*, Rustlers Valley Farm, Ficksburg 9730, PO Box 373, Ficksburg 9730, tel (05192) 3939/2730, fax (05192) 3939, e-mail wemad@cis.co.za

Caravan parks:

> *Abrahamsrust*, tel (016) 71-2222.
> *Gariep Dam Natuurreservaat*, tel (052172) as for 26.
> *Johan Brits Karavaanpark*, tel (057) 405-8488.
> *Loch Athlone Holiday Resort*, tel (01431) 35732.
> *Mount Everest Wildreservaat*, tel (05861) 23491.
> *Rob Ferreira (Aventura)*, tel (0534) 2245/6.
> *Smilin Thru Nature Reserve and Resort*, tel (0568) 2123.
> *Zastron Karavaan Park*, tel (05542) 397.

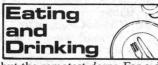

Eating and Drinking

The Free State is no place for the fussy eater. Like the people, the food generally is hearty, down-to-earth stuff — but as the locals say, it is *lekker kos* (nice food). We are in meat territory here, although you can find everything from burgers to pizzas in all but the remotest *dorps*. For a different taste experience ask a local to direct you to a *vetkoek* den. This is the Afrikaner's equivalent of a hamburger joint and serves up massive pockets of deep-fried dough as thick as a hamburger but the size of a pitta. This is stuffed with delicious savoury minced meat. Filling and inexpensive for hungry budget travellers; not for the faint of liver or calorie-watchers.

In Bloemfontein traditional South African restaurants and carveries include *De Oude Kraal*, 40km/25 miles south on the N1, tel (05215) 636; *Die Plaaskombuis* on Jagersfontein Road, tel (051) 441-8535; and *Die Stalle* in President Brand Street, tel (051) 445-2107.

Onze Rust, the Steyn family farm, 40km/25 miles south on the N1, was a remount station for horses during the Anglo-Boer War. You can down a couple in the pub at the rear of the restaurant, where barmen are done up in old-time Boer regalia, before giving the braais, lavish buffets, and *boerekos* your attention. Tel/fax (051) 441-8717. If you only want to go back as far as the 1960s and 1970s try *Harleys Power House*, on the corner of Charles and Henry streets in the city centre. You can get a pub lunch, with live entertainment and strip shows thrown in. There is a massive dance floor and the bar stays open until 4am. You will find *Steer* and *Spur* chain steakhouses throughout the area and, for a friendly tipple, the *Sportsman's*, *O'Hagan's* and *McGinty's* pubs.

In the eastern highlands you'll find a wide choice from traditional treats to local specials — rainbow trout, fresh from the dam, roast venison, vetkoek, boerekos, braaivleis, biltong — and sometimes even crocodile steaks and porcupine pie. If you stay on any of the holiday farms in the area you can be sure of freshly baked bread, home-made cakes and puddings with dollops of fresh farm cream. You can also sample traditional tribal food and beverages at the Basotho Cultural Village in Qwaqwa.

Entertainment

SPORT AND RECREATION

Bloemfontein has some impressive sports facilities, most of them handily cheek by jowl in the central President Swart Park adjoining King's Park Gardens. Here you can watch rugby and soccer at the

Free State Stadium, with neighbouring venues such as Springbok Park stadium for cricket and hockey. This huge park area also has bowling greens, tennis courts, and athletics tracks. The city also sports some excellent golf clubs, gymnasiums and swimming pools, all of international standard. Various dams offer vast areas for all forms of watersports and recreation. Loch Logan is a popular venue, another is Aventura Maselspoort, on the banks of the Modder River, which is a family pleasure resort with first-class fishing, tennis courts, miniature golf, waterslides and a heated pool. Carefully controlled hunting is allowed in the various nature and private reserves at certain times of the year. Would-be off-road enthusiasts might be interested in Continental Off-Road Academy's track 40km/25 miles from Bloemfontein, which is designed to simulate all the off-road obstacles likely to be found in the wild. Contact Carl Barnard, tel (051) 447-0792, or Jannie du Plessis, tel (051) 430-3326. 35km/22 miles from Kroonstad is the *Verblyden 4x4 Playground* with fun for novices and experienced drivers. Contact Breggie, tel (0562) 24036; Jan, Cell 082 558-7878; Jolandi, Cell 083 602-0131; or *Verblyden Guest House*, tel (0562) 24036, fax (0562) 24031. Safari Centre in Johannesburg run 4x4 trails through the eastern highlands and Golden Gate. The route is broken up into sections ranging from a two-hour obstacle course to a full day's mountain drive to Clarens. Allow three days. Contact, tel (011) 465-3813. Near Parys, on the Vaal River, is the river lodge of Sunwa Ventures, tel (0568) 7710, and nearby is the tented camp of Hadeda Creek, tel (0568) 4121. Both organise river trips from Parys on Grade 2 (boisterous) water, as does River Adventures, tel (0568) 77107, using inflatable rafts for safety, comfort and stability. These trips are suitable for all ages. The eastern highlands are the traditional home of the little Basotho ponies, which are renowned for their sure-footedness, endurance and even temperament. Two to three-day pony treks overnighting in farmhouses or caves are available from Golden Gate National Park and from a number of farms in the Clarens area. Connemara Irish ponies are also bred in this area and can be hired. In the eastern Free State Bethlehem has three large dams — Loch Athlone, Loch Lomond and Saulspoort — where you can enjoy watersports and fishing for black bass and yellowfish. Harrismith has a 18-hole golf course at the Harrismith Country Club, where you will also find tennis courts, squash courts and snooker tables. The Harrismith Mountain Race is an annual run which attracts ardent athletes. There is a bowling green and facilities for cycling, mountain biking, and 4x4 routes. In Qwaqwa you can take a scenic drive up to the Sentinel car park (2540m/8333ft). Follow the 4km/2.5 mile contour path and ascend the escarpment by way of the famous chain ladder. Other beautiful hikes are the Metsi Matsho Trail from the Witsieshoek Mountain Inn, and a variety of excellent walks and hikes from Fika Patso Mountain Inn, as well as the 27km/17 mile Spelonken Trail in Qwaqwa Park. The Metsi Matsho and Fika Patso dams are great for trout fishing and on the main road to Qwaqwa is a nine-hole golf course designed by South African golf champion Gary Player.

 There is a number of curio shops in Clarens, but the one in the Cinderella Castle is especially noteworthy. It is the only one in a building made of beer bottles. Golden Gate has a well-stocked curio shop with many unusual African artefacts. Mohair wall hangings, karakul carpets, hand-painted porcelain, baskets, cane furniture, copper, brass and clay pots are made in the Qwaqwa district, the traditional home of the South Sotho people, and sold on the outskirts of Phuthaditjhaba. The Qwa-Hands Centre serves as a retail outlet for many rural crafts and is a delight to visit. North of Theunissen, on the road to Welkom, Goudveld Wine Estate offers cellar tours where visitors can sample and buy these pleasant products of the farm, which also has an interesting cycad nursery.

 **Help and Information**

TOURIST INFORMATION

Free State Tourism Board, Shop 9, Sanlam Parkade, Charles Street, Bloemfontein. PO Box 3515, Bloemfontein 9300, tel (051) 447-1362, fax (051) 447-0862.

Free State Eco-Tourism, Private Bag X826, Witsieshoek 9870, tel (05871) 34444, fax (05871) 34342.

Bethlehem, tel (058) 303-5732, fax (058) 303-5076.

Bethulie, tel/fax (051762) 2.

Bloemfontein Publicity Association, New Tourism Centre, 60 Park Road, PO Box 639, Bloemfontein 9300, tel (051) 405-8489/90.

Central Free State, tel/fax (0562) 22601.

Clarens, tel (058) 256-1406, fax (058) 256-1149.

Ficksburg, tel (05192) 5547/8, fax (05192) 5449.

Harrismith, tel (05861) 23525, fax (05861) 30923.

Kroonstad, tel (0562) 22601, fax (0562) 22601.

Ladybrand, tel (05191) 40654, fax (05191) 40305.

Parys, tel/fax (0568) 2131/3.

Philippolis, tel (051772) 6.

Qwaqwa, tel (058) 713-0576 and (01438) 30903, fax (058) 713-0691.

Transgariep (southern Free State), tel/fax (051732) 158.

Welkom, tel (057) 352-9244, fax (057) 353-2482.

Winburg, tel/fax (05242) 361.

Zastron, tel (05542) 107, fax (05542) 379.

KwaZulu-Natal

Zulu Kraal

If you sport a bumper sticker on your vehicle saying 'Last Outpost of the British Empire', every South African will know you have been to KwaZulu-Natal, a lush province that more than any other treasures the traces of its British colonial past, along with those of the mighty Zulu empire and the hardy Boer Voortrekkers, all of whom had a decisive hand in shaping the history of this beautiful region. The province is a mosaic of 91,481sq km/35,321sq miles, made up of semi-tropical coastal plains on the Indian Ocean, green rolling midlands, the lush hills and valleys of Zululand and its northerly thornveld, home to unnumbered game animals, and the great mountain range aptly called by the Zulus 'the Barrier of Pointed Spears'. This is the Drakensberg, a chain of the highest peaks in southern Africa, which forms the natural frontier between KwaZulu-Natal and the neighbouring upland kingdom of Lesotho. These are the areas that call the fly and saltwater angler, the underwater explorer, the hiker and climber, the game and bird-watcher, the naturalist and photographer, and anyone else who revels in sunshine and some of the most fascinating and diverse scenery and peoples in Africa. Although the climate is subtropical, sea breezes on the coast and the altitude inland temper the summer heat.

KwaZulu-Natal is renowned in particular for its game parks, wildlife sanctuaries and nature reserves. The Natal Parks Board administers more than 60 of these, of which the best known are the joint Hluhluwe-Umfolozi parks in central Zululand, which have won world acclaim for saving the black and white rhino from extinction, and the Greater St Lucia Wetland Park, linking a succession of coastal parks and marine reserves to form a huge conservation area rivalling in size and ecological diversity the world's leading national parks. The sparsely populated northern area of Maputaland has been compared to the American Everglades for its attractions, and its birdlife alone is outstanding.

Some 8.5 million people of African, European and Asian descent live in KwaZulu-Natal, the majority of them Zulus, who say their tribal name means 'the People of the Heavens'. Historically a fierce, warlike nation, the Zulus were probably the only non-European nation to give the British Empire a run for its money, and a succession of bloody and often humiliating military clashes led British Prime Minister Benjamin Disraeli to note in 1879, 'A very remarkable people the Zulu. They defeat our generals, they convert our bishops, they have sealed the fate of a great European dynasty.'

The battlefields where Boer and then British fought the Zulus, and then wound up fighting each other, have been linked together along with some legendary names — Ghandi, Winston Churchill, the Prince Imperial of France, last of the Bonaparte dynasty — in a fascinating historical tourist route, and knowledgeable local guides are available through any of the information offices in the area. Avoid the modern killing grounds where some militant Zulu factions have turned their attention to political enemies in the ruling ANC party and its supporters.

There is still debate about whether the old Zulu capital of Ulundi should dethrone Pietermaritzburg and take over its status as capital of KwaZulu-Natal. The province's largest and best-known city, however, is Durban. As well as being one of the country's most popular holiday resorts, Durban is one of the world's remaining great sea ports, with the finest natural harbour in southern Africa locked between two horns of land called the Point and the Bluff. This harbour has been the focal point of the region since Portuguese navigator Vasco da Gama named it *Terra do Natal* ('Land of the Nativity') after sighting it on Christmas Day in 1497. The British who settled there in 1824 called their trading post Port Natal, renaming it Durban in 1835 in honour of the then Governor of the Cape, Sir Benjamin D'Urban. Between 1860 and 1911 it was the port of entry for Indians who arrived to work in the coastal sugar cane fields, and later for other waves of immigrants, all of whose descendants have helped to give the province its unique multicultural flavour. The Zulus call Durban *eThekwini* — 'the Place where the Earth and the Ocean Meet' — and like most names in this vivid language the name is entirely appropriate. The city has a wealth of parks, gardens and nature reserves spread out within a radius of 30km/19 miles from the city centre where you can watch game and birds or enjoy pleasant walks. Easily accessible are Stainsbank, Beachwood, Bluff, Palmiet, Pigeon Valley, Silverglen and Krantzkloof nature reserves. North and south of Durban the coast is strung with a seemingly endless chain of holiday resorts, which have grouped themselves into areas with names such as the Dolphin Coast, the Hibiscus Coast, and the Golf Coast. Some important commercial centres in the province are Richards Bay, Eshowe, Estcourt, Ladysmith, Newcastle and Kokstad. Scattered among them are towns and villages

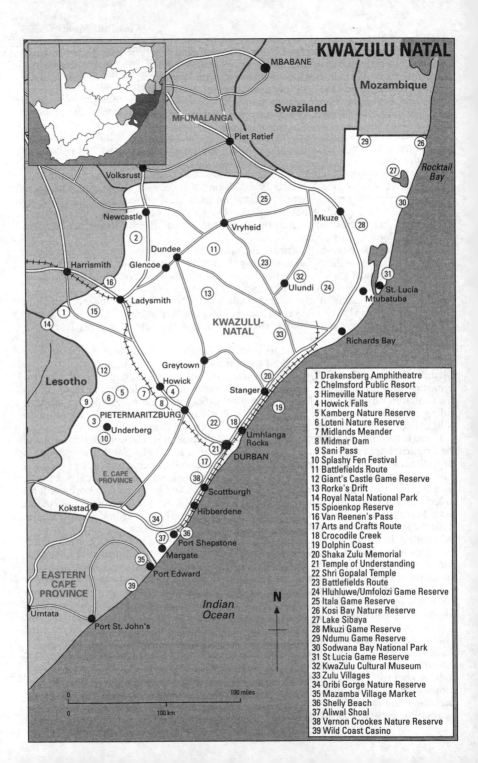

KWAZULU NATAL

1 Drakensberg Amphitheatre
2 Chelmsford Public Resort
3 Himeville Nature Reserve
4 Howick Falls
5 Kamberg Nature Reserve
6 Loteni Nature Reserve
7 Midlands Meander
8 Midmar Dam
9 Sani Pass
10 Splashy Fen Festival
11 Battlefields Route
12 Giant's Castle Game Reserve
13 Rorke's Drift
14 Royal Natal National Park
15 Spioenkop Reserve
16 Van Reenen's Pass
17 Arts and Crafts Route
18 Crocodile Creek
19 Dolphin Coast
20 Shaka Zulu Memorial
21 Temple of Understanding
22 Shri Gopalal Temple
23 Battlefields Route
24 Hluhluwe/Umfolozi Game Reserve
25 Itala Game Reserve
26 Kosi Bay Nature Reserve
27 Lake Sibaya
28 Mkuzi Game Reserve
29 Ndumu Game Reserve
30 Sodwana Bay National Park
31 St Lucia Game Reserve
32 KwaZulu Cultural Museum
33 Zulu Villages
34 Oribi Gorge Nature Reserve
35 Mazamba Village Market
36 Shelly Beach
37 Aliwal Shoal
38 Vernon Crookes Nature Reserve
39 Wild Coast Casino

whose striking Englishness makes it obvious why that 'Last Outpost' bumper sticker is such a popular and apt decal.

DURBAN

Durban — 'Durbs' to generations of South Africans — is the largest city in KwaZulu-Natal and one of South Africa's top holiday attractions. Washed by the Indian Ocean on the east coast, it has a pleasant sub-tropical climate, with sunshine for at least 320 days a year. Temperatures are 16–25°C (61–77°F) during the winter months of June and July, reaching 32°C/90°F during the summer months, when the humidity can be unpleasantly sticky. Sea bathing from beaches within easy reach of the city centre can be enjoyed all year round in water where the temperature seldom falls below 17°C, even during the winter months.

Durban has the largest and busiest port in Africa and the ninth biggest in the world. The harbour, originally a swampy lagoon, is a bare city block from the CBD. Yachting, skiing, powerboating, passenger liner arrivals and departures, container vessels and tankers being loaded and off-loaded and fishing are all part of harbour life. The gateway to the harbour lies between two piers; North Pier is a favourite spot for fishermen, and a ferry service operates to the South Pier. Pleasure trips around the harbour and deep sea cruises are available from the Gardiner Street Jetty, tel (031) 305-4022. The small craft harbour (Yacht Mole) is always a hive of activity with both local and round-the-world yachts coming and going. Both the Point Yacht Club and Royal Natal Yacht Club welcome visiting yacht club members.

Durban's foreshore is known for its famous 'Golden Mile' strung with hotels, restaurants, holiday flats and leisure amenities (ride along the strip in a gaily coloured rickshaw pulled by a beaded Zulu).

Arrival and Departure. Durban International Airport, 15km/9 miles south of the city, caters for international, regional, domestic scheduled and charter flights, tel (031) 42-6145. Virginia Airport, 12km/7 miles north of the city, caters for light aircraft and helicopters, tel (031) 84-4144. Coach services operate regularly between the international airport, the terminal at the corner of Smith and Aliwal streets, in the city centre, and beachfront hotels. Super Shuttle 24-hour transfer service, tel (031) 469-0309 or (031) 203-5407.

Taxis:

> *Zippy Cabs*, tel (031) 202-7067;
> *Bunny Cabs*, tel (031) 32-2914;
> *Eagle*, tel (031) 37-8333;
> *Swift*, tel (031) 32-5569;
> *Mozzie Cabs*, tel (031) 368-1114.

Car hire:

> *Avis*, tel (031) 42-6333;
> *Berea Car and Bakkie Hire*, tel (031) 22-3333;
> *Imperial*, tel (031) 42-4648;
> *Budget*, tel (031) 304-9023;
> *Citi Rent*, tel (031) 368-1013;

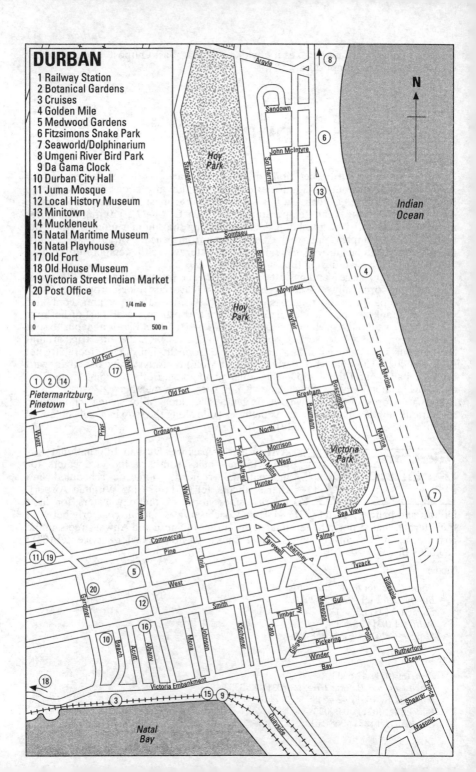

DURBAN

1 Railway Station
2 Botanical Gardens
3 Cruises
4 Golden Mile
5 Medwood Gardens
6 Fitzsimons Snake Park
7 Seaworld/Dolphinarium
8 Umgeni River Bird Park
9 Da Gama Clock
10 Durban City Hall
11 Juma Mosque
12 Local History Museum
13 Minitown
14 Muckleneuk
15 Natal Maritime Museum
16 Natal Playhouse
17 Old Fort
18 Old House Museum
19 Victoria Street Indian Market
20 Post Office

0   1/4 mile

0   500 m

N

Indian
Ocean

Argyle
Sandown
John McIntyre
Hoy Park
Stanger
Sol Harris
Shell
Somtseu
Brickhill
Molyneux
Hoy Park
Playfair
Lower Marine

Old Fort
NMR
Pietermaritzburg,
Pinetown
Wyatt
Prior
Old Fort
Ordnance
Gresham
Boscombe
Baumann
North
Morrison
West
Hunter
Milne
Stanger
Prince Alfred
John Milne
Victoria
Park
Marine
Aliwal
Walnut
Sea View
Commercial
Pine
Palmer
Kearsney
Ume
Farewell
Tyzack
Medwood
West
Smith
Johnson
Kitchener
Cato
Timber
Bay
Mazppa
Gull
Gillespie
Gardiner
Juma
Beach
Acutt
Albany
Mona
Gillespie
Winder
Pickering
Rutherford
Ocean
Point
Prince
Victoria Embankment
Bay
Quayside
Shearer
Masonic

Natal
Bay

Maharani Car Hire, tel (031) 37-0211;
Tempest, tel (031) 307-5211.

Coach services:

Greyhound Citiliner, operates daily between Johannesburg and Durban and calls at Ladysmith and Newcastle, tel (031) 361-7774;

Translux Express, tel (031) 361-8333;

Golden Wheels Intercity, runs a service between Durban and Johannesburg, tel (031) 29-2894;

Skyliner Coach Tours, offers a countrywide service, with daily coaches for Johannesburg, Cape Town, Port Elizabeth and Sun City. Tours can be arranged for the Drakensberg, Hluhluwe, Kruger National Park and the Valley of a Thousand Hills, tel (031) 301-1550/7, fax (031) 301-1566;

Interport has a daily service to Richards Bay and Empangeni, tel (0351) 91791/4.

Rail. Durban railway station is situated between NMR Avenue and Umgeni Road, 2km/1 mile to the north-west of the City Hall. Inter-city and local suburban trains operate from here at regular intervals and it is also the terminus for inter-city coaches. You can book rail tickets at Spoornet Main Line Passenger Services, tel (031) 361-7609, or at the Tourist Junction in Pine Street, Durban, tel (031) 361-8270, fax (031) 361-8280. *Drumbeat Steam Train Travels* offers novelty rides from Durban to Scottburgh. The train leaves from Thirsty's at the Point Waterfront, tel (031) 903-2747.

City Transport. Buses and taxis form the nucleus of public transport, providing an excellent service in and around the city and suburbs. Durban Transport Management Board also offers various daily tours, tel (031) 309-4126. Tuk-Tuks, small motorised tricycles that can carry up to six people, are available for short distances. A convenient service is operated by *Mynah Buses*, which run regularly from North and South Beaches into the city centre and suburbs within a 10km/6-mile radius, tel (031) 307-3503.

For an unusual ride take a **rickshaw** on upper Marine Parade with one of the city's flamboyantly costumed Zulus. Rides last between five and seven minutes and cost roughly R10 (£1.35/$2.20) a person (R5 extra for a photograph). Make sure you agree on the fare before you hop aboard. As always, the best way to explore the city is on foot. Conducted cultural and historical walking tours organised by *Durban Unlimited* are a good introduction to the city sights, tel (031) 304-4934. To see the lights of Durban from the harbour at night take a cruise with *Durban Ferry Services*, tel (031) 361-8727/304-6091, departing from alongside the Maritime Museum at the Victoria Embankment end of Aliwal Street.

Accommodation

Durban's balmy climate attracts visitors all year round and because of this hotels tend to be cheaper than those at resorts depending on seasonal custom. Durban's top five-star hotels are the centrally situated *Royal Hotel* at 267 Smith Street, from R665 a double room, and the well known city landmark the *Karos Edward Hotel* at 149 Marine Parade, which is the only five-star deluxe hotel on Durban's Golden Mile beachfront. It costs from R176 (£23.45/$38.70) per person, although if you have a princely income you might want to stay in the King's or Oppenheimer suites. The Edward's Mandarin and Brasserie restaurants are legendary. Central reservations, tel (011) 484-1641.

Also near the sea are *Blue Waters*, Snell Parade, R141–176 per person a night, tel (031) 32-4272, fax (031) 37-5817; *Lonsdale*, 52 West Street, R56–100 a night, tel (031) 37-3361, fax (031) 37-5962; and the four-star *Marine Parade Holiday Inn*, R180 per person a night, tel/fax (031) 37-3341. There are numerous small hotels charging as little as R50 a night for a room. The *Palm Beach Hotel*, on the beachfront, at 106 Gillespie Street, costs between R55 and R75, tel (031) 37-3451, fax (031) 37-2047.

There is a B&B and self-catering network for the Greater Durban area, Cell 083 626-8470, which will find you accommodation in a private home. No booking fee is charged.

Backpacker accommodation:

> *Backpackers Club International*, 200m/656ft from harbour and 350m/1148ft from nearest beaches, 154 Point Road, Durban 4001, tel (031) 32-0511, fax (031) 32-0541.
> *Banana Backpackers*, 61 Pine Street, Durban 4001, tel (031) 368-4062, fax (031) 304-6340.
> *Durban Beach*, 19 Smith Street, Durban 4001, tel (031) 32-4945, fax (031) 32-4551.
> *Seafarers Backpackers*, 154 Point Road, Durban 4001, tel (031) 32-0511, fax (031) 32-0510.
> *Tekweni Backpackers*, 169 Ninth Avenue, Morningside, Durban 4001, tel (031) 303-1433, fax (031) 309-2854.
> *Travellers Rest*, 743 Currie Road, Morningside, Durban 4001, tel (031) 303-1064, fax (031) 303-1064.

Further out are:

> *Angle Rock Backpackers*, 5 Ellcock Road, Warner Beach 4126, tel (031) 96-2996, fax (031) 96-4947, e-mail rayjan@iafrica.com
> *St Johns Backpackers*, 31 Ridgeside Road, Umgeni Park 4051, tel (031) 83-6570, fax (031) 83-6570.

Durban YMCA is at Anchor House, 82 St Andrew's Street, tel (031) 305-4496, fax (031) 305-4499.

Caravan parks include *ATKV — Natalia*, tel (031) 96-4545; *Karridene Protea Hotel*, tel (031) 96-3332; and *Villa Spa Holiday Resort*, tel (031) 96-4936.

Eating and Drinking Durban's cosmopolitan fare leans heavily on dishes of Indian origin, such as hot and spicy curries made from vegetables, mutton, chicken or beef, the savoury breyani, and *roti*, an unleavened pancake eaten with a variety of curry fillings. Hamburgers apart, one of the most popular and inexpensive takeaways in the Durban area is the bunny chow, a half or quarter loaf of bread scooped out and filled with curried meat or vegetables. *Patels* in Grey Street and *The Sunrise Chip 'n Ranch* at 89 Sparks Road, near Overport City, make these tasty takeaways from R5, tel (031) 29-8417. Scrumptious versions are made at the *Congella Hotel* at 467 Sydney Road, Umbilo, where a chicken bunny costs R6, and a prawn bunny is R10.50. You can also get spare ribs for R8.50 and grilled line-fish for R10 (£1.35/$2.20). This hotel is the original (1895) homestead of Ellis Brown, a tea and coffee magnate, and gives you a choice of seven bars.

The harbour area is a hive of pubs and eateries. *Café Fish* stands on stilts in the waters of Durban Yacht Mole, with indoor and outdoor eating and an upstairs pub area, tel (031) 305-5062. *Charlie Crofts Maydon Wharf Diner* is at 18 Boatman Road, Wilson's Wharf, and is a pub-cum-diner with great seafood, tel (031) 307-2935. There is also a *Charlie Croft's Diner* on Lagoon Drive, Umhlanga, tel (031) 561-1596. *The Famous Fish Company*, at King's Battery at the harbour mouth Point Waterfront, also has a reputation for its seafood. Watch the ships sail past your table, tel (031) 368-1060. *Thirsty's* (the Dockside Tavern) is also at King's Battery and has two bars and an outside deck where you can eat curry and rice and other inexpensive dishes in one of the most scenic pubs in South Africa, tel (031) 37-9212.

If you fancy going into orbit while you are eating try the *Roma Revolving Restaurant* on the 32nd floor of John Ross House, Victoria Embankment, tel (031) 37-6707. You also get breathtaking views over Durban's harbour. Vegetarians will find great lentil moussaka and spring rolls at *SoHo SoHi Café*, 19 Hermitage Street, Durban, tel (031) 305-3127, and authentic Indian vegetarian dishes at *Aangan*, at 86 Queen Street, not far from the Victoria Street Indian market, tel (031) 307-1366.

Real beer drinkers should head for the *Firkin Hop House Brewery* at the Westville Pavilion Mall, a brew pub producing traditional real ale brewed the natural way, on site, with no preservatives or chemicals. While you are quaffing you can watch sporting events on the pub's giant TV screens, tel (031) 265-0155.

Other Durban hotspots are *Joe Kool's*, a popular beachfront bar and restaurant at 137 Lower Marine Parade, North Beach, tel (031) 32-9679; and *Roxies Action Bar*, with a long bar and pub lunches, 174 West Street, central city, tel (031) 32-3293. Rub shoulders with trendy Durbanites at *Billy the BUMS' Bistro and Cocktail Bar* in Windermere Road, tel (031) 303-1988 (BUMS = 'Basic Upmarket Socialite'); and meet homesick Poms at the *London Town Pub* — lunch for R5 and drinks in a red London double-decker bus — at 106 Gillespie Street, off West Street, Beach End, tel (031) 37-3451. Coffee shops abound, but the cyber-inclined should enjoy *Java @ Java*, where travellers can pop in and e-mail home. It is at 13 Marriott Road, Berea, tel (031) 309-1575, javajava@sprintlink.co.za

Gay Restaurants

Two Moon Junction, 45 Windermere Road, Morningside, tel (031) 303-3078;
Late Night Galleon Coffee Bar, Nedbank Centre, corner Point and West Street, tel (031) 32-4689;
SoHo SoHi, late night café and lounge bar (see above).

Beaches. Durban's beaches stretch in a long line north from Addington Beach near the harbour entrance to the Blue Lagoon, all of them protected by shark nets. There are plenty change-rooms, fast-food outlets, and lifesavers. The Bay of Plenty, opposite the Amphitheatre Gardens, is a favourite with surfers. The sunken Amphitheatre Gardens, on Marine Parade, have spacious lawns, fountains, sub-tropical flower gardens, and fish pools, and form a tranquil oasis.

In the **Bergtheil Local History Museum**, housed in an historic 19th century farmhouse at 16 Queens Avenue, Westville, there is an interesting collection of photographs, documents and artefacts relating to 1848 German settlers, tel (031) 86-1131.

The 12ha/30-acre **Botanic Gardens** at the corner of Edith Benson Crescent and Sydenham Road, Greyville, has a celebrated orchid house, as well as flowering trees from many lands, a collection of rare cycads, and a special fragrant garden for the blind. Open daily from 7.30am to 5.30pm, tel (031) 21-1303.

City Hall. This is one of the stateliest buildings in the southern hemisphere, and is an almost exact replica of Belfast City Hall in Northern Ireland. It houses the **Durban Science Museum** and the **Durban Art Gallery**. The museum has a varied wildlife exhibition, as well as displays of game in natural surroundings and a superb bird collection. Guides are provided. Open Monday to Saturday, 8.30am–5pm, and Sunday, 11am–5pm, tel (031) 300-6212.

The gallery displays works by renowned South African and overseas artists, as well as Chinese porcelain and African pottery. Open Monday to Friday, 8.30am–5pm, and Sunday, 11am–5pm, tel (031) 300-6238.

The history of the Indian community is featured at the **Cultural and Documentation Centre**, at the corner of Epsom Road and Derby Street, and shown through exhibits and illustrations covering indentured Indians, Ghandi in South Africa, cultural artefacts, paintings, culinary art, traditional clothing and jewellery, tel (031) 309-7559.

The **Da Gama Clock** on the Victoria Embankment is a fine example of Victorian baroque ironwork. The memorial was presented to the city by the Portuguese Government in 1897 to commemorate the discovery of Port Natal on Christmas Day 1497 by famous Portuguese explorer Vasco da Gama. Further along the Embankment is the **Dick King Statue**, an equestrian bronze of the man who in 1842 rode nearly 1000km/621 miles in 10 days from Durban to Grahamstown to get help for the British garrison besieged by Boer forces at the Old Fort. Also on the Embankment, closer to the sea, is a statue to **John Ross**, who at the age of 15, walked from Durban to Delagoa Bay in Mozambique — present day Maputo — and back in three weeks to obtain medical supplies for the settlers.

The **Fitzsimons Snake Park** on Lower Marine Parade, North Beach, has a wide collection of indigenous and exotic snakes, as well as crocodiles, iguanas, and other reptiles. Venom-milking demonstrations are a popular attraction and you can buy anti-venom serum if you are planning a bush hike. Open daily from 9am to 4.30pm, tel (031) 37-6456.

In the city centre is the **Francis Farewell Square**, named after Lt Francis Farewell, who set up a permanent trading post here in 1824. The square has several statues and plaques commemorating events and people in South Africa's history. The Cenotaph stands behind the Gates of Memory, opened in 1947 by HM King George VI.

The **Golden Mile** is actually 6km/4 miles of beaches, protected by shark nets and flanked by luxury hotels, apartment blocks, and amusement arcades — not to mention pickpockets. Funworld, tel (031) 32-9776, is a favourite with children. A ride in a cable car gives a bird's-eye view of the beachfront and the pools, fountains and lawns of the Ampitheatre Gardens. Waterworld is guaranteed to keep pre-teens amused for hours with a kamikaze slide, speed and body slides, and one of the most exciting river rides in the country. Open 9am to 5pm, tel (031) 37-6336.

The Alayam Hindu Temple on Somtseu Road, is the largest and oldest temple in South Africa and the place of worship for about 75 per cent of Durban's Indians. Open daily from 7am to 6pm, tel (031) 32-2848. Informative tours are conducted round the **Islamic Juma Mosque**, at the corner of Grey and Queen streets, the largest place of worship for Muslims in southern Africa and famous for its massive golden dome and minarets. Contact the Islamic Propagation Centre, tel (031) 306-0026 and (031) 304-4934. Both these religious communities hold annual festivals in Durban. The Hindus have fire-walking rituals at Easter, and in February and May, depending on the full moon, you can watch the spectacle of Hindu penitents piercing themselves with fish hooks, daggers and skewers at the Kavady Festival. A major Muslim celebration is held on the 10th day of the first month of the Muslim calendar.

In Tinsley Road, Durban North, are the **Japanese Gardens**, an enchanting valley of lakes, cascading waterfalls and rustic bridges, with weeping willows and a wealth of birdlife, the ideal spot to relax for a while. There is a licensed restaurant open for lunch and dinner.

The King's Battery was named after British monarch George VI and formed part of the coastal defences during the Second World War. The basement has been turned into the **King's Battery Museum** and reflects Durban's involvement in the war.

The **Local History Museum**, in Aliwal Street, is housed in Durban's original courthouse (1886) and depicts the history of the early settlers. It includes a reconstruction of the city's first white settler dwelling, a sugar mill featuring indentured Indian labourers, a post office, general dealer and an apothecary. There is also a fine collection of period costumes, maps, documents and pictures of Durban and Natal's colonial past. Open Monday to Saturday from 8.30am to 5pm, and Sunday from 11am to 5pm, tel (031) 300-6241.

The **KwaMuhle Museum**, in Ordnance Road, is part of the same museum and depicts the history and the contribution of black South Africans to the development of the city. Open Monday to Saturday from 8.30am to 5pm, Sunday 11am to 5pm, tel (031) 300-6310.

Medwood Gardens in the city centre between Pine and West streets is another of those quiet green oases that dot the city, where you can put your feet up after a shopping expedition and listen to the fountains tinkling and the flowers growing.

Minitown, on Snell Parade, North Beach, is a miniature city built to a scale of 1:24, incorporating many of Durban's best-known buildings, including the harbour and the airport, and enlivened with animated displays, tel (031) 37-7892.

Muckleneuk. This beautiful building houses three important Africana collections. The Killie Campbell Africana Library has rare books, pictures, maps and unpublished manuscripts from all over the world; the Mashu Museum of Ethnology contains artefacts relating to tribal culture; and the William Campbell Furniture Museum displays furniture brought to the province by early English settlers. Guided tours are available, tel (031) 207-3432.

Near the small craft basin at the end of Aliwal Street is the **Port Natal Maritime Museum** where two retired tugs and a minesweeper are the main exhibits. There is also an amusing Pirates' Museum. The Britannia Room has exhibitions on whaling, navigation, Zulu royalty and the sea. Open Monday to Saturday, 8.30am–4.30pm, and Sunday 10.30am–4.30pm, tel (031) 300-6324.

The **Old Fort and Warrior Gate**, on Old Fort Road, is where the British were besieged by attacking Boers in 1842, an event which sent Dick King off on his famous ride. There is now a garden here stocked with a fascinating species of cycads. The former powder magazine has been converted into the Chapel of St Peter in Chains and is a popular venue for weddings. Warrior Gate is a shrine and headquarters of the MOTHS. Open Tuesday, Friday and Sunday from 11am to 3pm, Saturday from 10am to midday, tel (031) 307-3337.

The **Natal Settlers Old House Museum**, on St Andrews Street, is a replica of a settler home in the early 19th century, and highlights settler furniture, domestic ware and oil paintings. The museum is situated at 31 St Andrews Street. Open Monday to Saturday 8.30am–5pm, Sunday 11am–5pm, tel (031) 300-6250/6313.

The **Post Office**, in West Street, city centre, was Durban's Town Hall between 1885 and 1910. A plaque marks the spot where Sir Winston Churchill received a hero's welcome after his escape from the Boers during the Anglo-Boer War.

Sea World and Dolphinarium on the Golden Mile has daily dolphin, seal and penguin shows, and the aquarium displays fascinating tropical fish, sharks, turtles and shells and has one of the world's finest displays of oceanic sharks. You can dive in the aquarium, too — air tanks can be hired, and the dive costs R100 (£13.35/$22) per person for a 30-minute close encounter. Open daily 9am–9pm, tel (031) 37-4079/37-3536.

The Hare Krishna **Temple of Understanding** in Chatsworth is an architectural masterpiece and an opulent landmark. Guided tours of the ornate marble temple and surrounding moat and gardens are conducted daily. There is an audio-visual show, an exotic gift shop and a strictly vegetarian restaurant which is open daily from 11am to 9pm, tel (031) 43-5815/43-3328.

Umgeni River Bird Park, on Riverside Road on the north bank of the Umgeni River, has a collection of more than 1000 indigenous and exotic birds from all over the world, among them Giant Great Hornbills and Rhino Hornbills with brightly coloured beaks almost a foot long. Other species include lorikeets, loeries, flamingoes, cockatoos and macaws. Open daily from 9am to 5pm, tel (031) 579-4600.

Whysall's Camera Museum, 33 Brickhill Road, has one of the world's finest collections of photographica. More than 3 800 exhibits depict the story of photography from 1841 to the present day. Open daily from 8.30am to midday, tel (031) 37-1431.

Durban's **Sugar Terminal** on Maydon Wharf is one of the most advanced in the world. The largest silo has floor space the size of two rugby fields and the entire place can store 520,000 tons of raw sugar. An audio visual tells you all about the process and you can wind up on the terrace with a free cup of tea or soft drink. Free tours Monday to Wednesday at 9am, 11am and 2pm from the SA Sugar Association's reception centre at the corner of Maydon and Leuchars roads, tel (031) 301-0331.

Walkabouts around the city are organised by the tourist association, Durban Unlimited. You can take a R25 (£3.35/$5.50) escorted tour to see various facets of Durban. There are historical and oriental walkabouts Monday to Friday, and an introduction to the ethnic and cultural heart of the city on Tuesday. Book at the Tourist Junction's beachfront or airport offices, tel (031) 32-2595, and (031) 42-0400.

 KwaZulu-Natal is a melting pot where you can experience the theatre, art, dance and music of a variety of cultures and enjoy everything from the Drakensberg Boys' Choir, symphony concerts, Afro-jazz and operatic arias sung in Zulu, to ballet, township jive and Indian classical music and dance.

Durban claims to be the city where the fun never sets and there is a wide spread of entertainment venues, ranging from theatres and night clubs to pubs and discos. *The Playhouse* in Smith Street is a distinctive five-venue theatre which can, and does, stage everything from opera, concerts and live theatre to cabaret, ballet and modern dance. Conducted tours take place once a week, tel (031) 304-3631. Theatre buffs can also find a variety of productions and entertainments in any number of other venues, among them the University of Natal, the University of Durban-Westville, the Durban City Hall, and the BAT Centre, which is a vibrant, alternative cultural centre, best described as South Africa's first arts hypermarket. The centre has a prime waterfront site overlooking the small craft harbour, and embraces visual and performing arts under one multi-coloured roof. Whether you want food, entertainment, arts and crafts, or one of the most unusual shopping treats in town, it is all here. It has a 300-seat theatre, rehearsal rooms, a dance studio, visual arts galleries and shops. There are wood carvers working at benches in the art studios, as well as painters at easels, and potters at the kiln.

Traditional dancer and choreographer Vusabantu Ngema runs a course teaching the awesome kicks, stamps and jumps of Zulu dancing, tel (031) 32-0451. If you want to know what and who is on the programme, tel (031) 32-0468. Durban has a tradition of producing innovative musicians and it is regarded as the cradle of South African music. *Funky's* at the BAT Centre is a good place for live music, tel (031) 368-2029. Jazz lovers should try the *Beachhouse*, 237 Marine Parade, tel (031) 32-3929; the *Centre for Jazz*, University of Natal Durban (UND) campus, tel (031) 260-3385; and the *Club Aladdin*, 33 North Coast Road, tel (031) 579-2774. For folk fans there is the Durban Folk Club, which meets at Le Plaza Hotel in Broad Street. Entry is R6 and the annual membership costs R35 (£4.65/$7.70), tel (031) 23-7161.

The watering hole for all Bob Marley fans in the city is *Cool Runnings*, a bar, restaurant, and 36-bed backpacker's lodge. The place is designed to look like a Jamaican shack — and succeeds. A sign in the bar cautions 'No Drugs', but the barman says that doesn't stop the vice squad staking out the place. There is a franchise in Margate and more are planned for Johannesburg, Pretoria, Cape Town and Jeffreys Bay.

More mature music lovers might prefer Retros, at the Riviera Hotel, 127 Victoria Embankment, for a night out to the sounds of yesteryear, tel (031) 301-3681. The Big Blue at 22 The Workshop plays Seventies and early Eighties music only, tel (031) 306-4748/1585.

Durban is the home of the Natal Philharmonic Orchestra which, apart from its season of concerts, gives Sunset Proms at the Village Green and Music by the Lake concerts at the Botanical Gardens, tel (031) 369-9404 and (031) 21-1303.

There are Indian cinemas in the city and suburbs, Jehan and Shiraz, as well as the Ster Kinekor and Nu Metro circuits. Local newspapers carry details of programmes and locations.

Gay Bars and Clubs

Grumpy's, 124 Point Road, tel (031) 368-1625;
The Makathini Clan, Pietermaritzburg, tel (0331) 44-1135;
The Theatre, night club and coffee shop, Tyzack Street, tel (031) 37-34511.

Durban's shopping centre radiates from two main streets, West and Smith. These are lined by major department stores, but it is the lanes and arcades connecting them and the beachfront that have the interesting bargain nooks. The Durban African Art Centre, in Guildhall Arcade, has some unusual sculptures and beadwork, tel (031) 304-7915. An African craft market is held on top of the Ocean Sports Centre on Marine Parade every Sunday 9am–5pm, tel (031) 23-1416/301-2515. Curiocity at the Tourist Junction in Pine Street, Durban, is a stylish curio shop where you can pay from R6 for a bead necklace to R20,000 for a carving.

Some say The Pavilion, at Westville, is the best shopping centre of them all; it is certainly the biggest. The Workshop, in Pine Street, is housed in a vast Victorian building which was formerly a railway workshop, and some of the old giant girders are still in place. It has been transformed into an upmarket shopping, dining and entertainment complex. It houses more than 120 shops, with the pleasant addition of Victorian-type barrow stalls on the ground floor, and has become a tourist attraction in its own right. The Wheel, between Gillespie Street and Point Road, is a multi-themed shopping and entertainment complex of 140 shops, restaurants, bars and cinemas. It claims to have the world's biggest Ferris wheel inside a building.

If you can't find what you want at the Indian and African markets, next to one another in Victoria Street, among the mosques and the temples, then it probably doesn't exist. The Indian market has finely wrought jewellery, leatherwork, baskets of all shapes, brass, ivory and filigree silverware, as well as volcanic blends of curry powder. You can buy anything from a tiny elephant inside a hollow bean to a massive elephant carved out of ebony — and haggling could bring the price down by as much as 50 per cent. The same applies at the African market, where you can buy assegais, carved masks and walking sticks, cowhide shields, witchcraft potions, and other curios.

The South Plaza Fleamarket is at the Durban Exhibition Centre, Walnut Road entrance, and with more than 750 stalls is one of the biggest fleamarkets in the country. Probably in no other place will you find such a spread of home-crafted leather goods. Jewellery is also a good buy as most items have been impeccably set with attractive gems and stones in unusual metals. Open every Sunday, tel (031) 301-9900. The Bluff Flea Market is held on the first and last Saturday of the month in Tara Road, tel (031) 47-7574 and (031) 47-2579. The Heritage Market in Hillcrest, a 20-minute drive inland, is an elegant Victorian-style shopping complex where each shop is uniquely decorated and the garden setting, with gazebos, walkways, live music, and an attractive garden of 4000 rose bushes, makes for a relaxed and tranquil atmosphere. The Stables market is in Jacko Jackson Drive, off Goble Road (next to King's Park Rugby Stadium). Stalls are in converted horse stables and there is an outdoor tea/beer garden which serves really good cappuccino, as well as German beer and food. Open every Wednesday from 6pm to 10pm and on Sundays from noon to 8pm, tel (031) 29-1242, and Cell 083 786-2110.

Other flea markets in and around Durban include:

The Amphimarket, North Beach, Durban, tel (031) 301-3200/3080;
Farepark Market, between West and Pine streets, Durban, tel (031) 368-2190;
The Bazaar, opposite The Wheel, Durban, tel (031) 368-4361;
Point Waterfront Fleamarket, tel (031) 368-5436;
Church Street Arts & Crafts Market, opposite Durban City Hall, Cell 082 440-9505;
Berea Craft Market, Essenwood Road, Durban, tel (031) 83-6240;
Ridley Park Fleamarket, Malvern, tel (031) 463-1537;
Chatsworth Fleamarket, tel (031) 43-7007;
Southway Fleamarket, Southway Mall, Rossburgh, tel (031) 466-3017;
Pineville Craft Village, corner Stapleton and Old Main roads, Pinetown, tel (031) 72-5149;
Pinetown Japanese Gardens, corner Bartlett and Underwood roads, Pinetown, tel (031) 705-2194;
The Car Boot Market every Sunday at the circus site in Stanger Street, Durban, tel (031) 29-4751.

For a list of factory shops in and around Durban, Di Petersen has completed a booklet, *The Guide to Factory Shops*. She also organises a Factory Shop Tour (R55) for hardened shoppers, tel (031) 903-3198.

PIETERMARITZBURG

The capital city of KwaZulu-Natal is Pietermaritzburg, 77km/48 miles north-east of Durban. It is set in the heart of Zulu country but is essentially British colonial in character, with numerous well preserved Victorian and Edwardian buildings and quaint pedestrian lanes. It has even got a Town Crier.

Outstanding among its red brick buildings is the ornate City Hall (1900), notable for its domes and fine stained-glass windows. According to Ripley's *Believe it or Not* it is the largest load-bearing brick building in the southern hemisphere. It is the ideal place to start a walking tour of the city. Hitching rails here and there are reminders of a more leisurely past: one is outside the Imperial Hotel from where patron Louis Napoleon, Prince Imperial of France, rode to his death in a Zulu ambush in 1879; another is near the entrance to South Africa's oldest newspaper, *The Natal Witness*, founded in 1846 by a Scottish immigrant.

Pietermaritzburg also played an important role in Afrikaner history. A commando led by Andries Pretorius defeated a Zulu army at the Battle of Blood River, near Dundee, on 16 December 1838 and the church they built in 1841 in Pietermaritzburg to commemorate their victory is now a museum. An Eastern flavour has been added to the city by the descendants of the Indian labourers who first arrived to work in the coastal sugar cane fields in 1860. To the colonial skyline they have added mosques and temples, and enlivened the Easter holidays with an annual fire-walking ceremony.

GETTING AROUND

Oribi Airport is about 10km/6 miles to the south-east of the city. Although restricted to smaller aircraft, flights to and from Johannesburg connect with international flights. There are scheduled domestic services to and from several cities and towns, as well as charter flights. There is no bus service between the city and the airport, but **car hire** companies rent out vehicles at the airport:

> *Avis*, tel (0331) 45-4601;
> *Budget*, tel (0331) 42-8433;
> *Imperial*, tel (0331) 94-2728;
> *Airport Limousine Service*, tel (0331) 94-5659.

Taxis:

> *Junior Taxi Service*, tel (0331) 94-5454;
> *Unique Taxis*, tel (0331) 91-1238;
> *Wilken Taxis*, tel (0331) 42-3333.

City Transport. Although there is no bus service within the city, private bus companies run between the central area, surrounding townships and suburbs. City Hopper: Cheetah Coaches, tel (0331) 42-0266. Taxis and minibus taxis are also available.

Buses. Inter-city buses, particularly those operating between Johannesburg and Durban, stop *en route* through the city centre. *Midlands Mini Coach*, airport service from the Midlands, Estcourt–Durban scheduled service, tel (0333) 37110. A bus service operates to and from the Wild Coast Casino.

Rail. Pietermaritzburg is on the main rail link between Durban and other major cities and towns. Commuter trains also serve stations in various areas in the Midlands. The railway station at the top end of Church Street is notable not only for its stone facings and cast-iron lacework, but for being the scene of a historic event: Mahatma Gandhi was ejected from a train here in 1893 in an infamous racial incident that launched him on his political career.

Other Airports. The second largest airport in the province is 4km/2.5 miles from the centre of **Margate**. There are regular flights to and from Johannesburg and Durban, tel (03931) 73267. The airport is the venue for a big airshow in May every year, tel (03931) 20560.

Car hire:

> *Avis*, tel (03931) 20094;
> *Imperial*, tel (03931) 21346;
> *Budget*, tel (03931) 73202.

Margate Mini Coach operates between Margate and Durban, same day return R60, single R40. Check arrival and departure times; they depart and return to Wild Coast Casino, Margate, Port Shepstone, Hibberdene and Scottburgh/Amanzimtoti. Gird Mowat Building, Marine Drive, Margate, tel (03931) 21406, fax (03931) 21600. *Lux Liner* runs a weekly service between Johannesburg and Margate. The coach leaves Margate for Johannesburg at 6pm on Saturday and returns to Margate at 6am on Sunday. Travel time is about 9 hours, tel (03931) 22322.

On the North Coast the **Richards Bay Airport** is not far from the town centre.

PIETERMARITZBURG

1 Railway Station
2 Alexandra Park
3 Botanic Gardens
4 Garden of Remembrance
5 Voortrekker Museum
6 City Hall
7 Post Office
8 Natal Museum

0 ———————————— 1/4 mile
0 ———————————— 250 m

N

There are daily flights to and from Johannesburg. Charter air services from various centres also use the airport.

Car hire:

Avis, Richards Bay, tel (0351) 98-6555, Ulundi, tel (0358) 22261/64;
Budget, Richards Bay, tel (0351) 92-3695;
Ford Rent-A-Car, Richards Bay, tel (0351) 97-3401;
Imperial, Richards Bay, tel (0351) 41414;

Island Rock 4x4 Vehicle Hire, Hluhluwe, tel (035) 562-0251;
Sodwana 4x4 Rental, Mbazwana, tel (035) 517-0092.

ACCOMMODATION

Rob Roy Hotel, three-star, 21km/13 miles from Pietermaritzburg. Scenically situated above the Valley of a Thousand Hills. Accommodation in *en-suite* bedrooms. Contact PO Box 10, Botha's Hill 3660, tel (031) 777-1305, fax (031) 777-1364.

Penny Farthing B&B, 30km/19 miles from Dundee on a stock and game farm in the Biggarsberg mountain range, close to the battlefields of Rorke's Drift, Isandlwana and Blood River. Accommodation is in an old fort, garden cottage or in the main homestead. Contact PO Box 1358, Dundee 3000, tel (03425) 925.

Imperial Hotel, three-star hotel not far from Pietermaritzburg City Hall. Named after the Prince Imperial (Prince Louis Napoleon of France), who was an early patron. Contact PO Box 140, Pietermaritzburg 3200, tel (0331) 42-6551, fax (0331) 42-9796.

Amble Inn, on the main road outside Ixopo, an hour's drive from Pietermaritzburg. R75 per person sharing B&B. Caravans R30 (£4/$6.60) plus R5 per person. Contact PO Box 46, Ixopo 3276, tel (0336) 34-2208.

Sunduzi Backpackers, R25 per night, self-catering. Meals available from R10 (£1.35/$2.20). 140 Berg Street, Pietermaritzburg 3200, tel (0331) 94-0072.

Game Valley, a spacious four-star country lodge, 20 minutes from Pietermaritzburg. The Karkloof Falls are nearby. Rates from R274 per person sharing in lodge rooms to R354 per person in valley-view cottages. Contact PO Box 13010, Cascades 3202, tel (033) 569-0011, fax (033) 569-0012.

Little Switzerland Hotel, Oliviershoek Pass, Bergville. From R185 per person DB&B. Contact Private Bag X1661, Bergville 3350, tel (036) 438-6220.

Sani Pass Hotel, three-star leisure resort, 1500m above sea level. Acclaimed 9-hole country golf course, tennis, bowls, squash, horse-riding. Contact PO Box 44, Himeville 3256, tel (033) 702-1320.

Summer Place Youth Hostel, 85 Pietermaritz Street, Pietermaritzburg 3200, tel (0331) 94-5785.

Pietermaritzburg YMCA is at 1 Durban Road, tel (0331) 42-8106, fax (0331) 45-0313.

Pietermaritzburg Municipal Caravan Park is on Cleland Road, nearly 5km from the railway station, tel (0331) 65342.

EXPLORING

An attractive city landmark and picnic spot is the 65-hectare **Alexandra Park**, which is the setting for a splendid Victorian pavilion and bandstand, as well as a sports stadium, cricket oval, cycle track, swimming pool, and a rock and rose garden.

The **Natal National Botanical Gardens**, founded in 1870, feature both exotic and indigenous trees and plants from all over the world. Other attractions are a plane tree avenue and the bell from the British Admiralty yacht *Lady Enchantress*, which took Sir Winston Churchill to Norway after World War II. Tel (0331) 44-3585. There is a restaurant and tea room, tel (0331) 44-2207.

Chelmsford Public Resort Nature Reserve is a bird-watcher's paradise with its Egyptian and spur-winged geese, spoonbills, yellow-billed ducks and dabchicks. Powerboating and carp and bass fishing are added attractions. Caravan and camp sites and chalets can be booked through the Natal Parks Board, tel (0331) 47-1981, fax (0331) 47-1980.

The **City Hall** in Church Street, the largest all-brick building south of the equator, stands on the site of the old Voortrekker meeting place and on the foundations of the first town hall. It contains one of the largest organs in the southern hemisphere. The clock tower is 47m high and has a 12-bell carillon.

The soaring columns of the elegant **Colonial Buildings** in Church Street are a fine example of Victorian architecture. A central pediment features the Royal coat of arms and minor pediments display the Natal wildebeest emblem and the elephant, symbol of Pietermaritzburg. Opposite the building is the **Ghandi Statue**, which was unveiled in 1993 to mark the centenary of his ejection on racial grounds from a train at Pietermaritzburg Station, an incident which changed the course of history.

Comrades Marathon House is a restored Victorian residence and headquarters of the Comrades Marathon Association. It displays exhibits which include memorabilia, official trophies, photographic and press histories of this famous ultra-marathon, as well as a route model, tel (0331) 94-3510.

Not much attention has been given to the part that the city played in the nation's freedom struggle, so the Pietermaritzburg Publicity Association has established a **Freedom Route** to commemorate this era. The route highlights the struggle for freedom across racial and cultural divides and the grave of Selby Msimang, first secretary-general of the African National Congress in KwaZulu-Natal, can be visited on this trail.

In the **Garden of Remembrance**, commemorating the men who died in the two World Wars, sap oozes from the famous Weeping Cross of Delville Wood on the anniversary of the battle in July 1916 in which 2398 South African soldiers out of a brigade of 3153 died during World War I. The garden is in Leinster Road, alongside the Midlands Club.

On the escarpment north-east of Pietermaritzburg are the **Green Belt Trails**, marked with logos for the benefit of riders and hikers. The Ferncliffe Trail leads through indigenous forest, the Dorpspruit Trail takes in historical aspects of the city, and the World's View Trails follow the route taken by early Voortrekkers. The road to World View's is opposite the **Queen Elizabeth Park Nature Reserve**, which is the headquarters of the Natal Parks Board. The park is 8km/5 miles from the city centre, and is a pleasant spot for picnics and walks on which you can see white rhino, zebra, impala, blesbok and grey duiker.

The **Sri Siva Soobramoniar and Mariammen Temple** in lower Longmarket Street is the main place of worship for the city's Hindus and is the focal point of the annual Firewalking Festival held every year on Good Friday. Devotees end a 10-day fast by walking barefoot across pits of glowing coals in the temple grounds. The temple is open Sundays 8am–6pm and Monday to Saturday 7am–6pm. Visitors are also allowed into the **Islamia Mosque**, in Church Street, the city's largest Muslim place of worship. Take off your shoes before entering.

One of the town's most notable examples of Victorian architecture is **Macrorie House Museum**, at the corner of Pine and Loop streets, which provides glimpses of the elegant lifestyle of early British settlers. Built in 1862, it was the home of William Macrorie, who was Bishop of Maritzburg from 1869 to 1891.

The **Natal Museum** at 237 Loop Street features regional archaeology, African cultural objects, European settler history, and seashells, insects, and other forms of animal life, as well as an important collection of Zulu craft work. The Hall of Natal History is an outstanding display of demolished Victorian houses and shops of the 1850s restored to their original state. Open Monday to Saturday 9am–4.30pm, Sunday 2–5pm, R2 (25p/45 cents) for adults, 50 cents for children, tel (0331) 45-1404.

At the top end of Church Street is the **Old Government House**, home to Governors of Natal from the 1860s until 1910. The mounting block in the portico was used by ladies in the days of the horse and carriage. Also in Church Street is the **Old Presbyterian Church**, the first British church built in town (1852), and **St Peter's Church**, once Bishop Colenso's cathedral following the split in the Church of England in the colony in the 1860s, and now a museum housing church treasures and beautiful stained glass windows.

The **Old Natal Parliament** in Longmarket Street contains many fascinating antiques and relics of colonial days, when it was a parliament of two Houses, including a statue of a stern Queen Victoria in the grounds.

On Commercial Road almost opposite **Publicity House**, is the **Tatham Art Gallery**, in a building built between 1865 and 1871 and used in turn as a post office, a bastion of defence against Zulu attack, and as the Supreme Court. In 1990 it became the home of the gallery, which has an interesting collection of paintings, prints, sculpture and ceramics. Open Tuesday to Sunday from 10am to 6pm, tel (0331) 42-1804.

Vintage steam train excursion trips from Hilton Station to Howick by **Umgeni Steam Railway** take place on the second Sunday of each month, except in August and September. Contact Natal Railway Museum, tel (0331) 43-1857. On the last Sunday of every month Umgeni runs a picnic trip from Kloof to Inchanga, tel (031) 72-6734 and (031) 466-4112.

The city's oldest surviving double-storey **Voortrekker House**, on Boom Street, has been restored and furnished in authentic style. It is part of the **Voortrekker Museum** complex in Church Street which was originally the Church of the Vow, built by Voortrekkers in 1841 to commemorate their victory at the Battle of Blood River in 1838. The museum has a unique collection of trekker relics, including a fine replica of a trek wagon, old flintlock rifles, and a chair carved from ironwood for Zulu King Dingane. In the complex is a modern Memorial Church fronted by statues of trek leaders Piet Retief and Gerrit Maritz — after whom the city is named — and the house of Commandant Andries Pretorius, who led the victorious commando at Blood River. Open Monday to Friday from 9am to 4.30pm, and Sunday from 2pm to 5pm, tel (0331) 94-6834/7.

SHOPPING

Part of Church Sreet is an attractive pedestrian shopping mall. The African Arts and Craft Centre in Fraser Lane specialises in traditional and contemporary work, including sculpture, handwoven rugs and tapestries designed and handwoven by Zulu men and women at the Lutheran Art Centre at Rorke's Drift, hand-printed fabrics and batiks, wooden jewellery and collectors' pieces, tel (0331) 42-1785.

Midlands Meander Arts and Crafts brochures are available at the Publicity Association, which also sells souvenirs. There are some good cheese-makers along the Midlands Meander. Look out for goat's milk cheese from Fran Vermaak at Lidgetton; farmhouse gouda from Dave Kleynhans at Rosetta; feta cheese from Jon Tucker at Curry's Post; natural yoghurts and cheese from Gordon Phipps at Mooi River; and feta and mozarella from Mount West, tel (0332) 30-4308. Cheddar produced by Troutbrook near Underberg in the southern Drakensberg compares with the best the UK has to offer, according to Harrods of London, who have tested it. Open to visitors seven days a week, tel (033) 701-1373.

Craft and fleamarkets are held regularly at the Craft Market in Chancery Lane, tel (0331) 94-8140; the huge Maritzburg Arts & Crafts Market, in Alexandra Park, is held on the first Sunday of every month, tel (0331) 65055; Camps Drift Market, on the Dusi Canal, has bargains galore from a variety of stalls as well as barge rides, tel

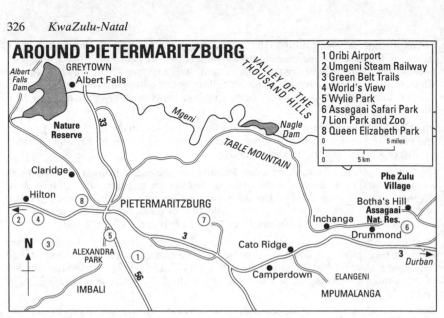

AROUND PIETERMARITZBURG

GREYTOWN
Albert Falls Dam
Albert Falls
VALLEY OF THE THOUSAND HILLS
Nature Reserve
Mgeni
33
Nagle Dam
TABLE MOUNTAIN
Claridge
Hilton
PIETERMARITZBURG
Inchanga
8
2 4
N 3
ALEXANDRA PARK
5
1
3
Cato Ridge
Camperdown
ELANGENI
IMBALI
56
MPUMALANGA
Phe Zulu Village
Botha's Hill
Assagaai Nat. Res.
6
Drummond
3
Durban

1 Oribi Airport
2 Umgeni Steam Railway
3 Green Belt Trails
4 World's View
5 Wylie Park
6 Assegaai Safari Park
7 Lion Park and Zoo
8 Queen Elizabeth Park
0   5 miles
0   5 km

(0331) 45-4797; and the Arts and Crafts Fayre, is at the Pietermaritzburg Botanical Gardens, tel (0331) 44-3035.

Further Afield

DRAKENSBERG

The popular name for the Drakensberg is the Berg, and along this 200km/124-mile barrier between KwaZulu-Natal and Lesotho are some spectacular reserves run by the Natal Parks Board (NPB), mainly on the high land at around 1829m/6000ft. The most popular are The Royal Natal National Park below the weathered black basalt mass of the Amphitheatre, and the Giant's Castle National Park. It is important to note that camp and caravan site reservations must be made directly with the appropriate reserve. For an unusual view of the Berg there is hot-air ballooning, or you can try one of the horseback trails run by the Natal Parks Board during the winter months. A breathtaking but easier way to mount the dragon's back is to take a 4x4 drive up serpentine and hair-raising Sani Pass into Lesotho. At the top you can drink a toast in the highest pub in Africa. Don't forget your passport.

Accommodation

Drakensberg Sun, in the foothills of the mountains, has self-catering chalets against the backdrop of Cathkin Peak, tel (036) 468-1000, fax (036) 468-1224. *Cathedral Peak Hotel* is in surroundings offering some of the finest climbs and walks in the Drakensberg. A helicopter flip above the hotel and along the soaring peaks is something to remember. Budget accommodation R200 (£26.65/$44) per person a day, luxury R280, and executive R300, all DB&B. Contact PO Winterton 3340, tel/fax (036) 488-1888.

   Cayley Lodge, overlooking Cathkin Peak and Champagne Castle. R190 per person per day includes all meals. Contact PO Box 241, Winterton 3340, tel (036) 468-1222.

   Dragon Peaks Park, below Champagne Castle and Cathkin, is a family resort offering self-catering accommodation from R80 per person and caravan and camp sites from R35 per person. Supervised out-rides, hiking trails, bass fishing and bird-watching. Contact PO Winterton 3340, tel (036) 468-1031, fax (036) 468-1104.

Hlalanathi Berg Resort overlooks the Tugela River with magnificent views of the Ampitheatre. Shady, lawned caravan sites and self-contained thatched chalets. Contact Private Bag X1621, Bergville 3350, tel (036) 438-6308.

Royal Natal National Park Hotel, set amidst some of the Drakensberg's finest scenery in the upper Tugela Valley, this hotel hosted the 1947 British Royal Visit. Cost per person from R176. Contact Private Bag 4, Mont-aux-Sources 3353, tel (036) 438-6200, fax (036) 438-6101.

Mambasa Hutted Camp is in the Winterton area in the centre of the Anglo-Boer War battlefields, a short walk from the ruins of early Iron Age settlements, and a few minutes' drive from Spioenkop game and nature reserve. Accommodation is in traditional beehive huts with four beds apiece, a honeymoon suite (a hut with its own cooking and ablution facilities), and a reed hut on stilts overlooking the river. There is no electricity. Cooking is done in iron pots over open fires and hot water for showers is provided by wood-fed stoves. Swimming, canoeing, hiking and bird-watching. Costs are about R25 (£3.35/$5.50) a day per person, but you need to take everything, tel (036) 488-1524/1222.

The *Wild West Sani Youth Hostel*, set in the Drakensberg National Park, is an old trading post, the last stop before the Lesotho border post. Dormitory bunk beds as well as thatched rondavels. Self-catering kitchen. Prices start at R20 for dorms and R25 for rondavels. Contact PO Box 107, Himeville 4585, tel (033) 702-0340.

Backpacker accommodation is available at *Vilamoura*, 5km/3 miles from Winterton, *en route* to Drakensberg Sun, tel (036) 488-1128, and *Sani Lodge*, PO Box 485, Underberg 4590, tel (033) 702-0330.

Exploring

The 243,000-hectare **Natal Drakensberg Park** stretches from Bushman's Nek in the south to Royal National Park in the north and encompasses nearly 20 sanctuaries, reserves and camps of varying sizes.

Bushmans Nek, 49km/30 miles from Underberg, has wildlife typical of that found throughout the Drakensberg park and has excellent trout fishing, day and overnight trails, tel (033) 701-1823.

Cathedral Peak is in the Northern Drakensberg, north-west of Pietermaritzburg. It borders on the upper Thukela area in the north and east, Lesotho in the west and Monk's Cowl in the south and is 32,000-hectares in extent. The mountain peak of the same name is 3004m/9856ft above sea level and located at the eastern end of a spur, branching from the main Drakensberg range some 30km/19 miles south-west of Bergville. Cathedral Peak camp sites are R17 (£2.25/$3.75) a night, and there are 15 caves at R12 a night. There are eight different walks from the camp ranging in length from one to days, tel (036) 488-1880.

Cobham, in the Southern Drakensberg 13km/8 miles from Himeville, is part of the Vergelegen Reserve and together they form 52,000 hectares, with lots of day and overnight walks. The rustic camp site at Cobham is an open area where you can put up a tent or park a caravan for R12 a night. Caves used for overnight hikes cost R12 a night. They are reached by three to five-hour walks, tel (033722) 1831.

Coleford Nature Reserve, 34km/21 miles south of Underberg, is a good base for exploring the Southern Drakensberg. The Ngwangwane and Ndawane rivers provide superb sport during the trout season. Accommodation includes 6-bed chalets at R75 per person a night, 3-bed at R55 a person a night, 5-bed at R55 per person a night, and 3-bed rustic cabins at R45 per person a night. Each has its own barbecue. Bedding, linen, cutlery and crockery are provided. Take your own food and drink.

Alternative accommodation at *Sunnyside Cottage*, near the camp, costs R45 per person a night, tel (033) 701-1982.

Drive through the Drakensberg Gardens Hotel to reach the **Garden Castle**, entry point to the Natal Drakensberg Park. Hiking, trout angling, swimming and bird-watching are some of the attractions. Accommodation is in 30-bed trail huts at R30 (£4/$6.60) per person a night.

Giant's Castle Game Reserve, 56km/35 miles from Estcourt, lies in the central Berg region. The reserve is dominated by a 35km/22-mile stretch of basalt wall which ends in the prominent massif known as Giant's Castle. The scenery is superb and climbs here are both thrilling and difficult. A network of trails in the reserve offers hikes of varying length. Three mountain huts and two caves can be used if you want to hike longer than one day, but prior booking must be made. The 40km/25-mile Giant's Castle Two Huts Hike takes three days to complete. More than 5000 superb cave paintings are among the reserve's attractions and there is a Lammergeyer hide open in winter from which you can watch bearded vultures and other endangered species feeding. The Main Caves Bushman Site Museum is just 2km/1 mile from the rest camp and with its life-size models of Bushmen gives interesting insights into these vanished people, while guided two or three-night wilderness trails, on foot or horseback, overnight in caves or mountain huts. Accommodation in self-contained cottages and bungalows costs R105 (£14/$23.10) a night per person, with communal kitchens. Cooks are provided. *Luxurious Giant's Lodge* costs R170 per person a night, tel (0363) 24718.

Highmoor, to the west of Kamberg, is 2000m/6562ft above sea level. Good walking, trout fishing and bird-watching. Camp sites at R12 per person a night.

32km/20 miles from the main Giant's Castle camp is **Hillside**, the base for all horse trails. Sites for tents and caravans costs R17 per person a night. The 8-bed Hillside rustic hut is R45 per person a night and provides crockery, cutlery, cooking utensils, a refrigerator, and a stove. Take your own sleeping bags and towels, tel (0363) 24435.

In the northern section of the Giant's Castle area is **Injasuti**, cradled between the Injasuti (or 'Little Tugela') and Delmhlwazini rivers. There are fully equipped, self-contained 6-bed cabins at R75 per person a night. There are also 8-bed dormitory cabins at R55 per person a night. You can also stay overnight in Lower Injasuti Cave, Upper Injasuti Cave, and Grindstone Cave for R12 per person. Camp sites are R17 per person a night. There are walks in the adjacent Mdedelelo Wilderness Area and a guided walk to Battle Cave, famous for well preserved Bushman paintings depicting Bushmen engaged in battle, tel (036) 488-1050.

In the foothills of the central Berg, 40km/25 miles from Rosetta, the **Kamberg Nature Reserve** is a haven for trout fishermen and nature lovers. There are a number of walks and self-guided trails through indigenous yellowwoods, tree ferns and proteas. Another trail has been designed for people in wheelchairs. Accommodation is in two-bed huts at R65 per person a night, a five-bedded chalet costs R60 per person a night, and a self-contained six-bedded cottage is R120 (£16/$26.40) per person a night.

Loteni Nature Reserve in the southern Berg is particularly popular with photographers and nature lovers. The Loteni River has good trout fishing. There is a choice of walks and climbs as well as mountain game-viewing and bird-watching. There is an historical settler's museum in the reserve. Accommodation ranges from R75 per person a night in 6-bed chalets to 3-bed at R55. Camp sites cost R17 per person a night, tel (033) 702-1636.

The nearby **Mkhomazi State Forest** charges an entry fee of R6 per person and overnight hiking costs R12 per person a night.

Monk's Cowl is 32km/20 miles, in the Champagne Valley. Most of the Mdedelelo Wilderness area falls within this reserve and its attractions are the mountains, walks and birdlife. Camp sites cost R22 per person a night. Monk's Cowl Country Club has a beautiful golf course in this majestic setting, tel (036) 468-1300.

A twitcher's delight is **Mount Currie Nature Reserve**, near Kokstad in the south of the province, with common sightings of flufftails and bearded vultures. The reserve has a bird list of more than 220 recorded species. Wildlife includes grey and mountain rhebuck, oribi, grey and common duiker, bushbuck and blesbok. Hiking trails follow old cattle tracks and paths. The Crystal Dam is stocked with largemouth bass and bluegill. Camp sites cost R17 per person a night, tel (037) 727-3844.

The **Royal Natal National Park** at the foot of Mont-Aux-Sources (3284m/10,774ft) has some of the most stunning scenery in South Africa. The southern boundary is formed by the magnificent cliff of the Ampitheatre. The park, 48km/30 miles west of Bergville, is probably best explored on horseback. As well as breathtaking scenery, comfortable accommodation, waterfalls and mountain streams stocked with trout, you also have a choice of 25 walks and hikes. The best, leading to panoramic views from the top of Mont-aux-Sources, is strenuous and involves climbing two chain ladders up a sheer rock face. The park is a popular base for climbers. The Tendele Hutted Camp has bungalows ranging from R125–145 per person a night to a luxury lodge with *en-suite* bedrooms at R170 (£22.65/$37.40) per person a night. The Mahai campground caters for up to 400 campers and caravans and sites cost R25 per person a night, tel (036) 438-6303.

Vergelegen Nature Reserve 19km/12 miles from the main Underberg/Nottingham road, lies at an altitude of more than 1500m/4921ft near the headwaters of the Umkomaas River. There is no man-made accommodation but you can overnight in a cave for R12 per person a night, tel (033) 701-1712.

The village of **Himeville** lies in the Southern Drakensberg near Underberg in an area renowned for its wild trout fishing. The nearby Himeville Nature Reserve has two trout-stocked dams which attract a variety of waterfowl, including the rare wattled crane. Camp sites cost R17 per person a night. There are barbecue facilities and rowing boats for hire, tel (033) 702-1036. The **Sani Pass** is one of the most famous passes in southern Africa, and an exciting drive while you are in the Underberg/ Himeville area. It follows an old trade route into Lesotho. There are some scary hairpin bends on the road to the top — especially when there is snow on the ground — and these are best negotiated in a 4x4 vehicle, so bum a lift or pay someone to drive you up. The 41km/26 mile route from Himeville to the top of the pass usually takes about 2.5 hours. At the top you can enjoy a noggin in the highest (2874m/9429ft) licensed hotel in southern Africa, the Sani Top Chalet. The view is superb; a stiff hike away is Ntabana Ntlenyana, at 3482m/11,424ft the highest point in southern Africa. Mike Campbell, who lives in Himeville, drives up regularly to look after his backpacker and tourist lodge at Molumong ('Place of Noise', although the only noise you'll hear is the sound of eagles' wings cutting through the crisp air). Contact Mike at PO Box 44, Underberg 3257, tel (033) 702-1050 and (033) 701-1490, fax (033) 701-1491.

Van Reenen's Pass, sweeping 1680m/5512ft over the Drakensberg into the Free State is one of southern Africa's major road and railway passes and follows the route once used by herds of zebra, hartebeest, blesbok and wildebeest trekking from the Highveld to their winter grazing grounds in the Midlands.

Winterton, in the foothills of the Cathedral Peak area, is the gateway to the central Drakensberg resorts and is best known for the Drakensberg Boys' Choir School close by on the farm 'Dragon Peaks.' When the choirs are not touring visitors can enjoy concerts on Wednesday and Saturday in the school auditorium, tel (036) 468-1012.

Entertainment

The Natal Philharmonic is hitching its wagon to the *Splashy Fen Festival* and now stages an annual classical musical festival in October at this trout farm in the foothills of the Southern Drakensberg, near Underberg. Splashy Fen has been on the South African musical calendar since 1990 as the country's very own Woodstock, although it is modelled more on the pre-Woodstock Festival of the Flower Children at Woburn Abbey, in England. It is arguably the most dramatically located music festival in the country in a natural mountain amphitheatre; a sparkling trout river runs through it. Splashy Fen is 20km/12 miles beyond Underberg village on the Bushman's Nek road. Contact Peter Ferraz at PO Box 186, Underberg 3257, KwaZulu-Natal, tel (033) 701-1932.

MIDLANDS

The Midlands attracts artists and craftspeople and it is the site of the country's original arts and crafts route — the Midlands Meander, where you can browse through galleries and craft shops, visit weavers and potters, leather workers, wood crafters, and sample home-made cheeses and herb teas (see page 344). The rolling pastoral green of the Midlands stretches for 200km/124 miles between the coast and the Drakensberg mountains. The plains and valleys are dotted with towns, villages and country inns, all looking as though they have been transplanted from England. Game parks and sanctuaries throughout the region conserve large numbers and species of wildlife and provide enchanting recreational areas.

The 3090-hectare **Albert Falls Nature Reserve**, 24km/15 miles from Pietermaritzburg, is three-quarters water, and boating, waterskiing, sailing, fishing, bird-watching and game-viewing are its main attractions. Rustic rondavels cost R45 to R55 per person a night, and waterside camp sites cost R22, tel (03393) 202/203.

Set in the scenic Valley of a Thousand Hills, the **Assagay Safari Park** houses a fearsome collection of live crocodiles and other reptiles. There is a Crocodile Museum and a Classy Croc restaurant with jungle gyms to occupy the small fry, who will also enjoy the hands-on experience of an animal touch farm. Open daily from 9am to 4.30pm, tel/fax (031) 777-1208.

Greytown, also known as Umgungundlovana ('Place of the Little Elephant'), lies on the Umvoti River, 64km/40 miles north of Pietermaritzburg. The local museum houses a Hindu and Muslim room, Zulu culture room, Victorian children's room, and a military room. There is a blacksmith's forge in the Coach House. Interesting old steam engines include a Ruston and Hornsby built in England in 1923 and another built by Robey and Company of Lincoln in 1924.

Howick is 115km/71 miles from Durban and 23km/14 miles north-west of Pietermaritzburg, on the Umgeni River in the heart of the Midlands. It is best known for the *Howick Falls*, which plunge 93m/305ft over the edge of a dolerite cliff into a deep gorge. Nearby are the *Karkloof Falls*, with an even higher drop (105m/345ft). The *Midmar Nature Reserve* is on the banks of the Midmar Dam, 26km/16 miles from Pietermaritzburg and 5km/3 miles from Howick. The dam — three times the area of Durban Bay — is popular for yachting, water-skiing, windsurfing, swimming and angling. Launch tours, barge trips and sunset cruises are available. The 1000-hectare game park has red and black hartebeest, blesbok, springbok, reedbuck, oribi and zebra. Accommodation in an 8-bed lodge costs R105 (£14/$23.10) per person a night, chalets are R60 per person, rustic cabins cost R45 per person, and camp sites are R22 per person a night, tel (0332) 30-2067/8. **Midmar Historical Village** is a replica of a Victorian hamlet and includes a number of historical buildings, as well as a steam tug and a Zulu kraal where there is traditional dancing on Sundays. A large attraction is Rob Roy, at two tons the largest Shire horse in Africa, who draws visitors around in a carriage, tel (0332) 30-5351.

Nottingham Road gets its name from a Nottinghamshire regiment garrisoned nearby in the mid-1800s to protect settlers against raiding Bushmen. The village lies at an altitude of 1479m/4852ft in a popular trout-fishing area.

Spioenkop ('Spy Hill') is a hill 25km/16 miles south-west of Ladysmith, the site of a famous Anglo-Boer War battle lasting from 17 to 24 January 1900. It is a dominant feature of *Spioenkop Reserve*, which surrounds Spioenkop Dam. The resort has plenty of outdoor attractions, including fishing, yachting and powerboating. Accommodation in a tented camp costs R60 per person a night and in a rustic camp it is R75. There are also camp and caravan sites at R22 per person a night, tel (036) 488-1578, fax (036) 488-1065.

There is a little bit of Germany in the Midlands, 30km/19 miles from Pietermaritzburg. This is **Wartburg**, a hamlet whose residents take pride in their ancestry and retain the language and customs of their forebears. The local hotel, the Wartburger Hof, is reminiscent of Bavaria and each of its suites is named after a German town. There is also a farm brewery nearby making beer in the German manner, tel (0341) 81735/6.

ZULULAND

Zululand is an area of incredible beauty and diversity. The coastal plains have long unspoilt beaches, while inland there are undulating hills, grassy plains, bushveld, forest sanctuaries and game reserves. Historically, Zululand is the north-eastern region of KwaZulu-Natal, from the north bank of the Tugela River to the borders of Swaziland and Mozambique. The landscape is steeped in the history of past battles, among them Isandlwana, Blood River, Rorke's Drift, Ulundi, Majuba, the Siege of Ladysmith, Spioenkop and Colenso. A round trip from Durban through Gingindlovu, Eshowe, Vryheid and Kranskop, near Greytown, will take you through the heart of the Zulu country. The monument at Shaka's great capital, kwaBulawayo, is 27km/17 miles from Eshowe. The Dundee and Melmoth districts are rich in historical associations and the Nkandla and Dukuduku forests are rare surviving stands of primaeval forest. Zulu villagers still live in lovely beehive huts in many rural areas. In the north are the premier game reserves of KwaZulu-Natal: Hluhluwe-Umfolozi, Mkuzi, Itala, and Ndumo, all controlled by the Natal Parks Board.

Accommodation

Shakaland and *Simunye* give you an opportunity to experience Zulu traditions and lifestyles. A six-bedroom stone lodge called Simunye (Zulu for 'We are One') adds a contemporary dimension to the ethnic Zulu experience at Shakaland. The hotel part of the Shakaland complex, between Eshowe and Melmoth, is on a hill slope below the kraal, with sweeping views of the valley. Overnight in a double room in a huge beehive hut. Meals are normal rural fare of wild spinach, sweet potatoes, fried cabbage, samp (stamped maize kernels), beans and *uphutu* (maize porridge). Fully inclusive rates at Shakaland are R185 (£24.65/$40.70) per person sharing. Simunye charges R285. Contact PO Box 103, Eshowe 3815, tel (03546) 912, fax (03546) 824.

Babanango Valley Lodge is situated on a Natural Heritage Site in the bushveld, with *en suite* rooms in comfortable country style. Tours of Zulu historical sites, the Battlefields of the Anglo-Zulu War of 1879 and to the Umfolozi Game Reserve are conducted by owner John Turner, a Satour specialist tour guide. Dinner, B&B from

R262 per person sharing. Contact PO Box 100, Babanango 3850, tel (0358) 35-0062, fax (0358) 35-0160.

Eagle's View Country House, in Babanango, overlooks the White Umfolozi River, not far from the Umfolozi and Hluhluwe game reserves. Accommodation in *en suite* bedrooms, R225 per person sharing, DB&B. Camp sites and rustic cabins are also available. Contact PO Box 119, Babanango 3850, tel (0358) 35-0054, fax (0358) 35-0010.

Tradewinds Hotel, 132km/82 miles from Durban, two-star. Overlooking the sea and the Umlalazi Nature Reserve. R101 to R140 a night. Contact PO Box 100, Mtunzini 3867, tel (0353) 40-1411, fax (0353) 40-1629.

Some other hotels in Zululand are:

> *Amble Inn*, 116 Main Street, Eshowe, tel (0354) 41300, R100 (£13.35/$22) to R140 a night;
>
> *Ghost Mountain Inn*, PO Box 18, Mkuze 3965, tel (035) 573-1025, R78 to R175 a night;
>
> *Ulundi Holiday Inn*, PO Box 91, Ulundi 3838, tel (0358) 21121, fax (0358) 21721, from R176 a night.

Backpacker accommodation is available at *Amazulu Lodge Backpackers*, PO Box 453, Kwanbonambi 3915, tel (035) 580-1009, e-mail rhino@cdrive.co.za, and *Siyayi Guest House*, PO Box 583, Mtunzini 3867, tel (0353) 40-1165, fax (0353) 40-1166.

Xaxaza Caravan Park, R35 per adult, R18 per child for a site in the peak season. PO Box 101, Mtunzini 3867, tel (0353) 40-1843, fax (0353) 40-1181.

Harbour Lights backpackers and caravan park between Empangeni and Richards Bay has caravan and camp sites for R50 a night with power, or R45 without. Dorms and private rooms are also available. Contact PO Box 7099, Empangeni 3910, tel/fax (0351) 96-6239.

Exploring

Both a mountain and a town north-west of Melmoth are named **Babanango**. The child of a Zulu chief was lost in the mist. He was found by his brother, who called out, 'Baba, nango!' ('Father, there he is!'). The town is a popular jumping off point for the Battlefields Route. This route, from Eshowe to Vryheid via Ulundi, is known as Shaka's Way, and encompasses battlegrounds, memorials, forts and other reminders of various wars between the British, Voortrekkers and Zulus.

Blood River is renowned in Afrikaner history as the site of a famous battle between 12,000 Zulus and 460 Voortrekkers on 16 December 1838. Three Voortrekkers were wounded in the battle and 3000 Zulus were killed. A monument in the form of a circle of 64 bronze wagons stand on the site of the original Boer laager. The battlefield is 48km/30 miles from Dundee.

The historical town of **Colenso** on the banks of the Tugela River, 27km/17 miles south of Ladysmith, was named after Bishop John William Colenso (1814–1883), the first Anglican bishop of Natal and champion of the Zulus. It was the scene of several battles during the Anglo-Boer War. Winston Churchill was captured in this area by the Boers.

North-west of Louwsberg is **Duiwel se Wereld**, a region characterised by rugged, impenetrable ravines. According to legend, at the time of the Creation the Devil was permitted to create a portion of the earth. When he saw that his work was inferior to God's he furiously tore his handiwork to bits. The ruins are still known locally as the 'Devil's World.'

At **DumaZulu Traditional Village**, in the heart of Zululand, you can spend the night in dwellings that from the outside look like the diverse tribal homes of southern

Africa — Zulu, South Sotho, Venda, Xhosa, Tsonga, Ndbele and Tswana peoples — but which are furnished with all mod cons. Two kraals have been built in a circular formation known in Africa as 'boma style' and housing 10 units. The entire complex is connected by wooden walkways in natural bush vegetation. A descriptive board at each of the 20 dwellings explains the culture and heritage of the tribe. Staff are traditionally garbed in keeping with the authenticity of the village and kraal. In the evening you can watch a short Zulu play performed by locals after a sundowner at the shebeen bar. Villagers will demonstrate spear, shield and clay-pot making, basket weaving, beadwork, and a *sangoma* (witchdoctor) will explain the mysteries of bone-throwing. You can even take part in a Zulu dance if you feel energetic.

DumaZulu ('the Thundering Zulu') is surrounded by more than 100,000 hectares of game reserves and can arrange outings or day visits to any of these attractions, as well as big-game viewing, a cruise on Lake St Lucia to watch hippo and crocodile, scuba diving, deep-sea fishing, scenic walks and hikes. A night at DumaZulu costs R210 (£28/$46) per person sharing, children under 12 sharing are free. A half-day trip to nearby Hluhluwe Game Reserve costs R85 and a full day at the reserves of Umfolozi or Mkuze, or the St Lucia Marine Reserve is R160. Contact DumaZulu Kraal at PO Box 79, Hluhluwe 3960, KwaZulu-Natal, tel (035) 562-0144, fax (035) 562-0205, e-mail glczulu@iafrica.com, web site http://www.glczulu.co.za

The cathedral town of **Dundee** nestles in the foothills of the Biggarsberg mountains, at the heart of the Natal battlefields. Much of the town's fascinating history is depicted in the Talana Museum, set in parklike surroundings against Talana Hill and on a portion of the battlefield of Talana, where the first shots of the second Anglo-Boer War were fired, tel (0341) 22654. For guided tours of the Battlefields Route, tel (0341) 22121.

Empangeni, 30km/19 miles from the coast and 160km/99 miles north-east of Durban, is the hub of the sugar industry, a cattle farming district and an important railway centre. The University of Zululand is in the hills on the outskirts. North of Empangeni is *Enseleni Nature Reserve*, which with its coastal grasslands and forest is a botanical paradise. There are two short scenic walks but no accommodation, caravanning or camping in the reserve, tel (0351) 92-3732.

140km/87 miles north-east of Durban is **Eshowe**, named by Zulus after the sound of the wind in the trees and the oldest town in Zululand. The relics of the past include Fort Nongqayi, built in 1883 for the bodyguards of Sir Melmoth Osborn, the British Resident for Zululand. The white mud and brick turreted fort now houses the Zululand Historical Museum which among other exhibits offers a rare look at John Dunn, the only white man to become a Zulu chief and husband to 48 Zulu wives, tel (0354) 41141. The Vukani Arts and Crafts shop is renowned for its Zulu basketry and the Vukani Museum has superlative examples of historical Zulu basketware, tel (0354) 75274. Near the town is a monument depicting the spot where Shaka Zulu is believed to have tortured warriors accused of cowardice. Nearby Shakaland — where the movie *Shaka Zulu* was shot — displays the tribal way of life with daily cultural shows, and has accommodation in a Zulu kraal, tel (03546) 912, fax (03546) 824. North of the town towards Ulundi are the hilltop sites of three great Zulu military kraals, Shaka's kwaBulawayo, Dingane's Umgungundlovu, and Cetshwayo's Ondini.

Estcourt is an industrial centre in the heart of a rich agricultural community on the main route between Durban and Gauteng. Nearby Fort Durnford was built in 1874 to protect the town against Zulu attack. It is now a museum and has a reconstructed Amangwane Zulu kraal at the entrance to the grounds, tel (0363) 23000.

Gingindlovu is a Zulu village 21km/13 miles south-east of Eshowe. The name is Zulu for 'Place of the Elephant' and was originally applied to one of Zulu King

Cetshwayo's nearby military kraals, which was burnt down at the beginning of the Anglo-Zulu War of 1879.

The **Hluhluwe-Umfolozi Game Reserve** is not only highly rated for game-viewing, it is also world-famous for its great conservation successes in saving the white (square-lipped) rhino from extinction. The reserves were proclaimed separately in 1895 but are now joined by a corridor, making the combined complex of 96,000 hectares the oldest officially protected area in Africa. Today 32 per cent of Africa's black rhino live in this sanctuary, which supports more than 2000 white and black rhinos – the largest concentration in the world. The reserve also has impressive numbers of lion, elephant, leopard, buffalo, giraffe and cheetah in its open grasslands and thornveld. Also well established are bushbuck, zebra, blue wildebeest, waterbuck, red and grey duiker, steenbok, klipspringer, impala, kudu, nyala, baboon, warthog, spotted hyena, and black-backed jackal. Accommodation in Hluhluwe is at the Hilltop Camp in 2-bed rondavels at R80 per person a night. There are also a number of chalets at R165 (£22/$36.30) per person a night. The exclusive Mtwazi Lodge and the up-market Muntulu and Munywaneni bush lodges have *en suite* bedrooms at R180 per person a night. Umfolozi has accommodation ranging from rest huts at R80 per person a night and cottages at R140 per person to bush lodges at R180 per person a night. Three-day wilderness trails, led by a ranger and a game guard, are undertaken in this Big Five country between March and November. The average distance covered each day is about 12–15km (8–9 miles). Contact the Natal Parks Board, tel (0331) 47-1981, fax (0331) 41-1980.

Isandlwana is a mountain 16km/10 miles south-east of Rorke's Drift, around which a British force of more than 1500 was surrounded and 1300 killed by Zulus in 1879 in one of the bloodiest clashes ever between British forces and warriors of King Cetshwayo, who lost more than 1000 dead. A few kilometres from Isandlwana is **Fugitive's Drift**, a ford which takes its name from a handful of British soldiers who fled to the Buffels River here after the disastrous battle. Only two survivors of Isandlwana made it to raise the alarm at **Rorke's Drift**, an unfortified Swedish mission used by the British as a hospital and magazine. 4000 Zulu warriors repeatedly attacked the tiny mission station, 139 men defended it. The British lost 17 men before the Zulus withdrew, leaving 600–700 of their impis dead. A record number of 11 VCs were awarded to the defenders, who wound up fighting from behind a fragile barricade of biscuit boxes. At the site today is a fine little museum and an arts and crafts centre.

Itala Game Reserve, overlooking the Pongola River Valley in the rugged, mountainous thornveld of northern Zululand, is a 29,653-hectare sanctuary for white and black rhino, elephant, crocodile, giraffe, buffalo, cheetah, leopard, many antelope species and more than 300 varieties of birds. Accommodation is in bush camps with 2-bed reed and thatch units at R115 per person a night; in a lodge at R150 per person; luxury Ntshondwe Camp's thatched chalets cost R135 per person; and a six-bed luxury lodge with its own swimming pool is R170 per person. There are also camp sites at R12 per person a night, tel (0388) 75105, fax (0388) 75190.

Ladysmith was at the centre of the first and most critical stage of the Anglo-Boer War. The Ladysmith Siege Museum is an exceptional little museum with a display of photographs depicting scenes from the famous 118-day siege and subsequent relief of the town. Two 6.3-inch howitzers used by the British garrison stand in front of the City Hall. The 3m/9ft bronze statue of Mohandas Gandhi was imported from Bombay and erected in the grounds of the Lord Vishnu Temple in memory of his association with Ladysmith (he was a stretcher bearer with the British forces).

Mkuzi Game Reserve, in northern Zululand, has game drives and guided walks through a wide variety of habitats, where you can see rhino, giraffe, zebra, kudu and impala, among other species. More than 380 bird species have also been recorded, including fish eagles, kingfishers and a host of ducks and waders. There is a bird-watching hide that is a highlight of the 40,000-hectare reserve. Rest huts cost R80 (£10.65/$17.60) per person a night, bungalows are R115, and cottages are R140 per person. There is also a reed and thatch bush camp for eight people at R90 per person a night and caravan and camp sites at R20 per person a night, tel (035) 573-0002/3.

Ndumo Game Reserve, just south of the Mozambique border, is considered by many to be the finest birdwatching locality in South Africa and has a checklist of more than 400 species. Many tropical varieties, at the southernmost limit of their range, are also found here. Game in the 10 367-hectare reserve includes hippo, rhino, giraffe, zebra, buffalo and various antelope species. In addition to a lodge, there is a rest camp with communal kitchens and ablution blocks, tel (0331) 94-6696, fax (0331) 42-1948. A night at Ndumo Wilderness Camp, run by Wilderness Safaris, costs R600 per person sharing. This includes all meals, accommodation, game drives and leisure activities. Contact PO Box 78573, Sandton 2146, Gauteng, tel (011) 883-0747, fax (011) 883-0911.

Paulpietersburg is a beautiful rural town 48km/30 miles north of Vryheid. In the area is the Pongola Bush Nature Reserve with its two-day hiking trails. This town has some beautiful colonial buildings from the turn of the century. The nearby German settlement of Lüneburg, has remained culturally true to its forefathers.

Simunye Zulu Lodge is in the Mfule River Valley, 45km/28 miles from Eshowe. You can make the trip in on horseback, on a donkey cart or in an ox-wagon drawn by Nguni oxen. Zulu warriors welcome you with a tribal dance. You can sample traditional food and drink in the neighbouring Zulu village. Contact PO Box 103, Eshowe 3815, tel (035) 45-3111, fax (035) 45-2534.

Ulundi. This possible capital of KwaZulu-Natal is in the heartland of the old Zulu kingdom. Close by is **Ondini**, King Cetshwayo's capital, which was burned to the ground by the British after the Battle of Ulundi in 1879. The royal section of the capital has been excavated by archaeologists and reconstructed to replicate the original and Ondini has been developed as a historical and cultural showpiece by the KwaZulu Monuments Council. There is a museum that shows what life was like in the capital during Cetshwayo's time. You can also see a herd of white Nguni cattle of the type prized by the old Zulu kings. A short drive away is the *eMakhosini* ('Valley of the Kings'), where many of the forebears of the Zulu royal house are buried.

You can sleep at Ulundi in traditional Zulu beehive huts (with modern kitchen and bathroom facilities). There are five beehive huts within a stockade, the largest of which sleeps 16 in double bunks. Contact KwaZulu Monuments Council, PO Box 523, Ulundi 3838, KwaZulu-Natal, tel (0358) 791854/5.

You can stay at other authentic Zulu kraals (villages) and experience traditional Zulu culture first-hand in KwaZulu-Natal at places such as *Kwabhekithunga Kraal*, tel (03546) 644, fax (03546) 867, and *Stewart's Farm*, near Eshowe, tel (03546) 778.

Umlalazi Nature Reserve near the coastal town of Mtunzini, south of Empangeni, covers 1028 hectares of sand dune forest and mangrove swamp. There is good fishing in the lagoon but watch out for crocodiles and sharks. There are three trails through the reserve and an easy walk through one of the best examples of mangrove swamps in South Africa. Another trail leads through pine forest and partly through the mangroves along the edge of the Umlalazi river. The reserve is home to the palmnut vulture, one of the rarest birds of prey in South Africa. Five-bed log cabins cost R100 (£13.35/$22) per person a night and the camp sites are R22 per person a night, tel (0353) 40-1836, fax (0353) 40-1607.

North-west of Durban and east of Pietermaritzburg is the lovely and appropriately named undulating **Valley of a Thousand Hills**, a region covering parts of

Camperdown, New Hanover, Pietermaritzburg, and Pinetown districts. It can best be seen from the Botha's Hill-Drummond road. Just past Botha's Hill is the Phe-Zulu traditional kraal, overlooking the valley where you can watch Zulu dances and visit the art gallery and curio shop. Tours and talks in 7 languages. Open 7 days a week, tel/fax (031) 777-1405.

Boating and fishing are the main activities at **Wagendrift Nature Reserve**, near Estcourt. There is also a 3km/2-mile self-guided trail along the Bushmans River. Birdlife is abundant in the 980-hectare reserve and includes the fish eagle and black eagle. Caravan and camp sites cost R22 per person a night, tel (0363) 33-5520.

Weenen is a small town 35km/22 miles to the north-east of Estcourt, on the banks of the Bushmans River. This town was laid out in 1838 as a memorial to Voortrekkers massacred by Zulus. Nearby is the *Weenen Nature Reserve* covering 5000 hectares of thornveld and supporting a wide variety of game, including rhino, buffalo, giraffe, zebra, and 251 species of birds. A game viewing hide gets you close at one of the many waterholes and there is also a vulture feeding site. There are three short self-guided trails, and guided walks are available to view black rhino and Cape buffalo. A self-contained 5-bed cottage costs R45 per person a night, and caravan and camp sites are R17 per person a night, tel (0363) 41809.

NORTH COAST

The coastal area north of Durban is a green blanket of sugar cane, with beaches, rivers and lagoons fringed by luxuriant forest giving way to mangroves and palm trees the further north you go towards Maputaland and the Mozambique border. Much of the area is protected by parks and reserves administered by the Natal Parks Board. Offshore, you can swim and snorkel among tropical fish, turtles, rays, dolphins, and sharks. The North Coast stretches more than 350km/218 miles from Durban to Kosi Bay and encompasses some of the province's most popular seaside resort towns and villages, among them Umhlanga Rocks, Umdloti, Shaka's Rock, Tongaat Beach, La Mercy, Ballito Bay, Salt Rock, Blythedale Beach, Zinkwazi Beach, Tugela Mouth, Mtunzini, Mapelane, and the vast coastal and estuarine complex of the Greater St Lucia Wetland Park, Cape Vidal, St Lucia, Sodwana Bay and Kosi Bay, which are the two most northerly resorts. Also on the coast, 180km/112 miles from Durban, is Richards Bay, one of the largest coal terminals in the world. 90km/56 miles from Durban is the Tugela River Mouth, historically the beginning of Zululand.

Accommodation

Beverly Hills Sun Inter-Continental, on Lighthouse Road, Umhlanga Rocks, is a five-star hotel, 20 minutes from Durban. The village of Umhlanga is a few minutes' walk away. From R176 (£23.45/$38.70) per person. Contact PO Box 71, Umhlanga Rocks 4320, tel (031) 561-2211, fax (031) 561-3711.
    Oyster Box, at Umhlanga Rocks is one of South Africa's best-known 3-star hotels. The hotel has its own lighthouse and is a shell's throw from the Indian Ocean. Contact PO Box 22, Umhlanga Rocks 4320, tel (031) 561-2233, fax (031) 561-4072.
    Salt Rock Hotel and Beach Resort, two-star, on Basil Hulett Drive, Salt Rock. From R165 B&B per person sharing to R255 DB&B. Choose from hotel rooms, timeshare units and caravan park sites, tel (0322) 5025, fax (0322) 5071.
    Eureka Farm Cottage B&B, 50km/31 miles north of Durban, on a sugar cane and anthurium farm. Golf course nearby, and Salt Rock and Ballito beaches 5 minutes away. Bass fishing on a private dam and scenic walks. R85 per person sharing. French spoken, tel (0322) 71254.
    Dolphin Holiday Resort has caravan sites and self-contained and fully equipped 2-bed cottages sleeping six. Family entertainment, safe sea bathing. Out-of-season

caravanner specials for senior citizens. Contact PO Box 6, Ballito 4420, tel (0322) 62187, fax (0322) 63490.

La Mouette Caravan Park is a highly rated park with paved roads and grassed, level caravan sites, mains power. Swimming pool, entertainment complex, tuckshop and unspoiled, flood-lit and shark-netted beach. Contact PO Box 3090, Stanger 2240, tel (0324) 22547, fax (0324) 91430.

Batama Lodge, 7 Campbell Drive, Umhlanga Rocks 4320, tel (031) 561-3096.

There is a *YMCA* in Richards Bay; PO Box 203, Richards Bay 3900, tel (0351) 53-4086, fax (0351) 32243.

Exploring

Ballito must be the only holiday resort named after an Italian brand of ladies' stocking. No one knows why. There are magnificent rock pools, beaches, safe bathing, and good rock and ski-boat fishing. Nearby **Shaka's Rock** is reputedly where the Zulu monarch ordered warriors suspected of cowardice to jump into the sea. He also threw captured enemies from the high cliff. When Shaka was in holiday mood he visited nearby Thompson's Bay, where he was apparently fascinated by a large rock with a hole in it.

On the banks of the Tongati River, midway between Ballito and Tongaat Beach, is **Crocodile Creek**, a ranch for the breeding and conservation of these reptiles. Conducted tours and lectures are held and you can have your picture taken holding a small croc. Open daily from 10am to 4.30pm, tel (0322) 23485.

The stretch of coastline from Umdloti to the Tugela is known as the **Dolphin Coast**, and schools of bottle-nose dolphins can often be seen gambolling inshore. Larger humpback dolphins are also around but as they are shy they are rarely seen. Many of the first Indian immigrants settled in this coastal area and the markets, mosques and temples reflect their origins.

False Bay Park is to the north-west of Lake St Lucia and part of the Greater St Lucia Wetland Park. There are self-guided trails and you can cool off in the Hippo Pools. Fanies Island and Charters Creek to the south are favoured by anglers, and there are jet-boat trips to neighbouring islands. Accommodation in a 7-bed cottage is R125 (£16.65/$27.50) per person a night, 2-bed rest huts are R70 per person, and camp sites cost R22 per person. Cape Vidal 30km/19 miles north of the estuary, is a haven for powerboat and snorkelling enthusiasts and excellent for surf angling. A bed in a hut costs R46 per person a night, and caravan and camp sites along the shore are R17 per person a night, tel (035) 562-0425.

The **Greater St Lucia Wetland Park** is a wilderness gem and encompasses the *St Lucia Game Reserve* (36,826 hectares), *St Lucia Park* (12,545 hectares), *False Bay Park* (3194 hectares), *Eastern Shores Nature Reserve* (15,151 hectares), the *Cape Vidal State Forest* (10,376 hectares), the *Sodwana Bay National Park* (58,000 hectares), and several other interlinking areas to form one of the largest conservation areas in South Africa. There are also marine reserves and sanctuaries to protect South Africa's only coral reefs, the diverse marine resources of the area, and to provide safe breeding grounds for rare loggerhead and giant leatherback turtles. St Lucia lake is a relatively shallow 60km/37-mile long estuary at the heart of a lake system that is a wetland of international importance and comparable to the Everglades in the USA. High forested sand dunes, at 120m/394ft among the world's highest, run along the length of the lake, supporting a wide variety of tropical plants and animals. Between the dunes and the swamp forest are open grasslands and woody thickets sheltering nyala, bushbuck, waterbuck, buffalo, reedbuck, duiker, suni, steenbuck, and bush pig. The estuary area is one of the few regions left in the province with the grass that Zulus use to make decorative and sleeping mats and every year thousands of them come to harvest it. Wildlife in the St Lucia Game Reserve includes black rhino, suni, pangolin and red duiker, marine turtles, pink-backed pelicans, Caspian terns, flamingoes, and the largest crocodile, hippo and reedbuck populations in South Africa. There is a three-day trail in the reserve and daily guided tours of the estuary on an 80-seater launch. There are three camping and caravanning grounds, with sites at R25–30 (£3.35–4/$5.50–6.60) per person a night, tel (035) 590-1340, fax (035) 590-1343.

The Kosi Bay area has one of the last unspoilt estuarine systems in South Africa. The **Kosi Bay Nature Reserve**, tucked up against the Mozambique border in Maputaland, is part of the Coastal Forest Reserve stretching to Sodwana Bay in the south. The reserve is a network of lakes with mangroves, rare orchids, palms and waterbirds. The Indian Ocean here provides great snorkelling and fishing and there are walking trails around the Kosi estuarine system. There are camp sites on the northern bank of Lake Nhlange, the largest of the Kosi lakes, and self-contained thatched lodges, tel (0331) 94-6696, fax (0331) 42-1948.

Lake Sibaya covers about 77sq km/30sq miles, with an average depth of 13m/43ft. This is South Africa's largest natural freshwater lake and home to many hippos and Nile crocodiles. Excellent birding and coastal forest walks are among its attractions. There is accommodation in a wilderness camp, tel (0331) 94-6696, fax (0331) 42-1948.

Within the Maputaland Coastal Reserve between Sodwana and Kosi bays, **Rocktail Bay** offers a rich environment where snorkelling, scuba diving, surf fishing and nature walks with a naturalist/marine guide can be enjoyed. Birding is excellent and Rocktail has its own unusual Big Five — the rare leatherback turtle, palmnut vulture, snake-eyed skink (lizard), lion fish and Zululand cycad. Turtle spotting is the most popular excursion from November to February when the females return, once in every eight years, to lay their eggs on the beach where they were born. There is accommodation at Rocktail Lodge in wood and thatch A-frame tree built on stilts into the milkwood canopy. It costs R800 per person a night sharing. This includes meals, return 4x4 transfers, excursions to Lake Sibaya and other attractions, and the use of fishing and snorkelling equipment. Contact Wilderness Safaris, PO Box 651171, Benmore 2010, Gauteng, tel (011) 884-1458.

North-west of Lake St Lucia is **Phinda Game Reserve**, a 17,000-hectare reserve of forests, grasslands, rivers, and mountain ranges abundantly stocked with lion, giraffe, white rhino, cheetah, elephant, hippo and antelope, including the rare suni. Game viewing, guided trails and walks, river-boat cruises and canoeing are available in this up-market private reserve, where the inclusive tariff is R1390 per person sharing a twin-bed room in one of the four luxury lodges, tel (011) 803-8421, fax (011) 803-1810.

Not too long ago, crocodiles and hippos had **Richards Bay** harbour to themselves. Today, the port is a hive of shipping and industry and a fast developing town at the mouth of the Mhlatuze River. Wharfs and terminals load bulk coal and various metal ores for export. Tankers discharge oil to a pipeline which serves Gauteng.

Sodwana Bay National Park, 349km/217 miles north of Durban, is a reserve of stunning beauty and a paradise for big-game fishermen and scuba divers. Log cabins cost R105 (£14/$23.10) per person a night and there are camp sites at R25 and R35 per person a night. Take precautions against malaria, tel (035682) 1502.

Stanger, 72km/45 miles north-east of Durban, is incised in Zulu history as the place where Shaka Zulu was assassinated in 1828 while he was relaxing under a fig tree. He was buried upright in a grain pit and the site is commemorated by a monument in Couper Street, the main entrance to the town. Relics of the early days of the sugar cane industry can be seen in the Natal North Coast Museum in Gledhow Mill Street and the Indian market has an aromatic atmosphere all its own.

Between Ndumo Game Reserve and Kosi Bay, on the Mozambique border, is **Tembe Elephant Park.** You can see a number of game species here, but this is elephant territory. The jumbos are fairly nervous and difficult to approach as they made it to the sanctuary of Tembe only by escaping war-torn Mozambique. A 4x4 vehicle is essential to enter the park. The park's tented camp accommodates only eight people. Contact tel (0331) 94-6696.

Tongaat, 45km/28 miles north of Durban, is situated in an area where sugar cane was first planted in 1854. It is predominantly an Indian community, first established here in 1854. Places of interest include the Juggernath Puri Temple, a replica of its namesake in India and thought to be the oldest and tallest Indian temple in the country, and the Vishwaroop Temple.

Umhlanga, 18km/11 miles from Durban, is the most popular resort on the North Coast and has luxury hotels, sophisticated shopping malls and good restaurants. Ski-boating is a year-round activity. The Wildlife Society conducts guided tours of the Hawaan Forest with its rare indigenous trees, tel (031) 561-1101. Regular audio-visual presentations on the life cycle of sharks are held at the Natal Sharks Board, Umhlanga Rocks, with the focus on man-eaters such as Zambezi, Tiger, and Great White sharks. You can also watch shark dissections. The Sharks Board maintains anti-shark nets at 46 beaches along 450km/280 miles of coastline, tel (031) 561-1001.

Verulam, perched on a hill overlooking the Mdloti River, is named after an ancient Roman city and is noteworthy for its Indian character. Worth a visit are the market, the Shri Gopalal Temple, opened by Mohandas (Mahatma) Ghandi in 1913, and the nearby 304ha/751-acre Hazelmere Nature Reserve and dam.

SOUTH COAST

From Durban along nearly 200km/124 miles to the rugged Wild Coast of the Eastern Cape the N2 highway links a virtually unending chain of seaside resorts, so that the entire coastline seems to be one long holiday resort. Heading south from Durban the main holiday resorts and small towns are Amanzimtoti, Umkomaas, Scottburgh, Port Shepstone, Shelly Beach, St Michael's-on-Sea, Margate, Ramsgate, Southbroom and Port Edward. In between, among the paw-paw trees, bananas, mangoes and pineapple plantations that flourish along this coast are lots of other picturesque spots with caravan and camp sites close to the Indian Ocean.

Accommodation

Karridene Protea Hotel, three-star, on the Umzimbazi Lagoon, near Illovo Beach and 20 minutes from Durban. Fishing, boating and other watersports at sea and on the lagoon. From R176 a night. Also has a caravan park. Contact PO Box 20, Illovo Beach 4155, tel (031) 96-3321, fax (031) 96-4093.

St Michaels Sands Hotel, near Margate Airport and St Michaels beach, in a safe protected bay. Bowls, tennis and 9-hole golf course. From R141 to R175. Contact PO Box 45, St Michaels-on-Sea 4265, tel (03931) 51230, fax (03931) 51885.

The Duck Place B&B, 105 Dan Pienaar Drive, Amanzimtoti, 10 minutes from Durban International Airport. R275 (£37/$61) per person sharing, tel/fax (031) 903-7829, Cell 082 440-7160.

Some other South Coast hotels are: *Cutty Sark Protea Hotel*, from R101 to R176, PO Box 3, Scottburgh 4180, tel (0323) 21230, fax (0323) 22197; *Margate Hotel*, R101 to R140 a night, Marine Drive, PO Box 4, Margate 4275, tel/fax (03931) 21410; and *San Lameer Hotel*, R176 upwards a night, Lower South Coast Main Road, Margate, tel (039) 313-0011.

If you prefer a self-catering luxury apartment, Beach Holiday Apartments have more than 500 fully equipped ones to choose from, one to four bedrooms, at Shelly Beach, Uvongo and Margate. Central reservations, tel (03931) 22543.

For backpackers, there is *The Spot*, North Beach, Ambleside Road, Umtentwini, Port Shepstone 4240, tel (0391) 82-4251, fax (0391) 22491.

Caravan parks:

> *Blue Seas Caravan Park*, tel (03931) 51049.
> *Caravan Cove*, tel (0323) 21215.
> *De Wet Caravan Park*, tel (03931) 21022.
> *Margate Caravan Park*, tel (03931) 20852.
> *Marlon Holiday Resort*, tel (0391) 83596.
> *Oasis*, tel (03931) 50778.
> *Paradise Holiday Resort*, tel (03931) 30655.
> *Mac Nicols Bazley Beach Caravan Park*, tel (0323) 98863.
> *Mac Nicols Pennington Park*, tel (0323) 51107.
> *Prairie Park Caravan Resort*, tel (0391) 81-2013.
> *Rocky Bay Caravan Park*, tel (0323) 20546.
> *Scottburgh Caravan Park*, tel (0323) 20291.
> *Umdoni Caravan Park*, tel (0323) 51261.
> *Umtentweni Caravan Resort*, tel (0391) 50531.
> *Voetplaatpark (Edms) Bpk*, tel (0391) 83325.

Exploring

The 7km/4 mile-long beachfront at **Amanzimtoti** (Zulu for 'Place of Sweet Waters') has two safe bathing areas, Inyoni Rocks and Pipeline Beach, where lifeguards are on duty all year round. Places of interest include the Ilanda Wilds Nature Reserve, noted for its birdlife, and the Umbogavango Nature Reserve, which also has an abundance of birds, as well as several trails. Most sports are catered for, and the Shongololo Crawl Arts & Crafts offers a wide range of curios and souvenirs on its route.

Margate incorporates the popular seaside villages of Ramsgate, Uvongo and Shelly Beach and is one of the most popular holiday playgrounds on this stretch of coast, with lots to offer — restaurants, cinemas, good fishing, an amusement park and a skating rink. Discos, cabarets and beach activities are laid on during the holiday season.

There is a little Eden 21km/13 miles inland from Port Shepstone, **Oribi Gorge Nature Reserve**, whose 1837 hectares encompass forests, rivers, rapids and ravines. High sandstone cliffs dominate the 24km/15-mile-long gorge. Leopards, baboons, small antelope and a variety of birds, including five kingfisher species and seven eagle species, are resident. There is a baboon-viewing trail and accommodation is provided in 2 and 4-bed huts at R65 per person a night and in 7-bed self-contained cottages at R125 (£16.65/$27.50) per person. Contact the Natal Parks Board, tel (0331) 47-1981.

Safe swimming and excellent fishing are among the attractions of **Port Edward.** The nearby *Umtamvuna Nature Reserve* is noted for its birdlife and rare plants. Trails in the reserve, especially in spring, rank among the best in KwaZulu-Natal.

The rugged coastline at **Scottburgh** provides excellent fishing throughout the year. The main bathing beach is protected by shark nets and lifesavers. Mini-train rides, a supertube and mini-golf on the beachfront should keep youngsters entertained. Crocworld gives an insight into the private life of the Nile crocodile. Tours every day of the week between 11am and 3pm, tel (0323) 21103.

The Shell Museum in **Shelly Beach** has the largest display of shells in South Africa. You can collect your own on the beach, where there is also safe swimming and good angling. Next door is **St Michael's on Sea**, which has the best surfing waves on the South Coast.

Interesting fossil beds were deposited about 100 million years ago in what is now the **Trafalgar Marine Reserve**, extending from Marina Beach in the north to Palm Beach in the south. The fossils are visible during spring low tides when the inter-tidal zone is exposed. This area is popular with anglers fishing for bronze bream.

The rocky coastline at **Umkomaas** is a magnet for anglers and divers but unsuitable for bathing. Sports facilities include tennis courts and bowling greens. The Umkomaas Golf Course, part of the South Coast Golf Circuit, is the setting for the Natal Amateur Championships. Pottery, woven items, baskets and leather goods are sold at the Umnini Zulu Crafts Centre north of the town. 100 bird species have been identified at the Ezulwini Nature Reserve on the outskirts of town. The coastal forest shelters small antelope, monkeys and mongoose. There are three walking trails and accommodation in 4-bed wooden chalets and a 20-sleeper tree-house. Open seven days a week, tel (0323) 30090, fax (0323) 30600. The Aliwal Shoal off Umkomaas is world-famous for its scuba diving among sharks. For dive operators, tel (0323) 21364.

Set in hilly grasslands just outside Umzinto the **Vernon Crookes Nature Reserve** has abundant bird life and several antelope species, as well as jackal and mongoose. There are 4-bed units and a 20-bed dormitory with kitchen at R45 per person a night. Open seven days a week, tel (0323) 42-2222.

KWAZULU-NATAL BATTLEFIELDS

Midway between Durban and Johannesburg, the Battlefields Route is a fascinating detour and encompasses seven Zulu, eight Voortrekker, nine Anglo-Zulu, five First War of Independence, and 35 Anglo-Boer War sites.

There are 11 main centres on the Battlefields Route, all sharing a common historical theme. Each has its own charm and attractions — arts and crafts, scenic hiking trails, farm resorts, Zulu culture (both traditional and modern) quaint bed and breakfast homes, roadside stalls, and cottage industries. Battlefields in the district are indicated by road signs displaying a cannon.

The route starts at Estcourt in the south and winds north, through Colenso and Ladysmith to Newcastle and Volkrust, and eastwards to Utrecht, Glencoe, Dundee, Nqutu, Paulpietersburg, Vryheid and Ulundi. Each area has specialist guides who will accompany you to the battlefields of your choice and bring their history alive for you. There are also scheduled tours and Walk and Talk tape aids. Contact the Dundee Publicity Association, PO Box 2024, Dundee 3000, KwaZulu-Natal, tel (0341) 22654, fax (0341) 23856, or any of the other information and publicity offices on the Battlefields Route.

Blood River (1838). After their exodus from the Cape to escape British rule, Piet Retief's group of Voortrekkers arrived in Natal in 1838. They negotiated with Zulu King Dingane for land. Retief and some of the trekkers were killed while finalising an agreement with Dingane and subsequently a number of battles took place, particularly in the region of present day Estcourt, where the trekkers where encamped. The Voortrekkers marched on Dingane to exact retribution and at the Battle of Blood River, which the Zulus call *Ncome*, Dingane's impis were defeated and he was forced to flee. Three Voortrekkers were wounded in the battle; 3000 Zulus were killed. The battlefield is now dominated by 64 full-scale bronze ox-wagons, as well as replicas of cannons used during the battle.

Anglo-Zulu War (1879). Mpande succeeded Dingane in 1840 and established friendly relations with the Voortrekkers and the British colonists established south of the Thukela (Tugela) River. Cetshwayo succeeded his father, Mpande, as King in 1872 and set about strengthening the Zulu kingdom, which colonists saw as a threat to their security. An ultimatum was presented to Cetshwayo and on its expiry British troops invaded Zululand.

The first battles of the war were fought on 22 January at 1879 at Isandlwana ('something like a small house'), where the British suffered a disastrous defeat, and on 23 January at Rorke's Drift. At Rorke's Drift Battle Museum you can see an outstanding display and watch an audio visual presentation depicting the battles. Further battles and skirmishes took place at Intombi Drift, Hlobane and Kambula, with a final battle at Ulundi, where the British lost 12 men to the Zulus' 1500 dead. This last clash on 4 July 1879 destroyed the Zulu army and broke the power of the Zulu nation.

First War of Independence (1880–81). The final goal of the Afrikaner Great Trek was accomplished when the Zuid-Afrikaansche Republiek (now part of Gauteng) and the Orange Free State (now the Free State Province) gained their independence from the British in 1852 and 1854 respectively. On 12 April 1877 the ZAR was annexed by the British. After attempts at peaceful protest, the Transvaalers raised the Vierkleur (four-colour flag) at Paardekraal on 13 December 1880, and proclaimed a republic. Three days later the First War of Independence began. To block British reinforcements on the way from Durban to the strategically important town of Newcastle, some 50km/31 miles from the Transvaal border, Boer General Piet Joubert moved 2000 men across the Natal border and advanced to Laing's Nek where he ran into Sir George Colley. On 28 January 1881 Colley attacked Joubert but had to retreat after an hour-long engagement.

During the night of 26 February 1881, Colley and 579 men climbed Majuba (Mountain of Doves) at Laing's Nek to view Boer positions. Next morning 150 Boers climbed the slopes and during their attack Colley was killed. His successor, Sir Evelyn Wood, signed an armistice on 6 March 1881 in the foothills of Majuba. The Pretoria Convention signed in October was never totally accepted by the Boers and eventually led to the Anglo-Boer War in 1899.

Anglo-Boer War (1899–1902). The Transvaal reverted to the Boers to become the Zuid-Afrikaansche Republiek again in 1884. After gold was discovered in the Transvaal in 1886 the Boers, fearing a build up of *uitlanders* (foreigners) restricted their voting rights. The *uitlanders* protested and war between Britain and the ZAR, supported by the Orange Free State, broke out on 11 October 1899. The northern triangle of Natal that bordered on both Boer republics was an especially vulnerable region and the first major battle of the Anglo-Boer War was fought at Talana, just over a mile from Dundee, nine days after war was declared.

The British drove the Boers off Talana Hill but suffered heavy losses and their commanding officer General Penn Symons was mortally wounded. The Boers besieged Ladysmith for 118 days, an action that put the town on the world map. Repeated attempts were made by bumbling Sir Redvers Buller to relieve Ladysmith. At Colenso, Vaalkrans and Spioenkop he failed to break through Boer defences, finally succeeding in a series of engagements now known as the Battle of Tugela Heights. From May 1900 a guerilla war was fought in the northern parts of Natal, the Cape colony and the Boer republics. The second Boer invasion of Natal saw a number of battles in the Vryheid area. The end of the war came in 1902, with 22,000 British dead and 24,000 Boers, of whom only 4000 were actual combatants.

Key towns

Volkrust. This town on the border of KwaZulu-Natal, Mpumalanga and the Free State forms the northern gateway to the Battlefields Route. Majuba Mountain, the final point of conflict between Boer and Brit during the first Anglo-Boer War, is an imposing backdrop.

Utrecht. The museum, housed in the old parsonage, depicts local history and the relationship between the Zulus and the ZAR from the time of the Great Trek.

Newcastle. Midway between Port Natal (Durban) and the ZAR this tiny settlement was a popular halt. The town was also a transport junction for the Transvaal and the Orange Free State with canteens and hotels along the route.

Dundee. The town nestles in the foothills of the Biggarsberg range and was named by one of its founders, Peter Smith, who came from a village near Dundee, Scotland. Today, Dundee is a quiet town with a wealth of historical buildings. Most churches in the town date from the turn of the century and contain commemorative plaques of local battles. The most important battlefields near Dundee are Blood River and Isandlwana. The Talana Museum depicts chapters in Zulu, Boer and British history. In the grounds are graves of British soldiers. Tel (0341) 22677.

Babanango. The town was part of a land grant made to European farmers in 1885 by King Dinizulu and laid out shortly after the Anglo-Boer War. There are guest farms in and around the town.

Paulpietersburg. This picturesque little town lies at the foothills of Dumbe Mountain. On the bank of the Egode river stands the monument where Louis Botha met his troops to sign the peace treaty ending the Anglo-Boer War. Some 30km/19 miles away is Ntombe battlefield and Lüneberg village.

Vryheid. This was once the capital of the Nieuwe Republiek (New Republic), later becoming part of the Zuid-Afrikaansche Republiek (South African Republic) in 1884. In Landdrost Street the Old Raadzaal (Council Chambers), old fort and gaol and the Landdroskantoor (Magistrates offices) form a facade of national monuments.

Ladysmith. Numerous cemeteries and monuments stand to the memory of those who died here. The town was named after the Spanish wife of Sir Harry Smith and made world headlines at the turn of the century when it was besieged for 118 days by Boer forces. Visit the Ladysmith Siege Museum for an insight into the battles of Colenso, Spioenkop, Vaalkrans and Tugela Heights. Guided tours to battlefields can be arranged by staff at the museum, which is open Monday to Friday, 8am–4.30pm, and Saturday, 10am–1pm, tel (0361) 22231.

Colenso. This historic town on the Tugela River lies in the foothills of the Drakensberg. In the vicinity are many memorials erected by the various regiments involved in battles in the area. Several major battles were fought here during the Anglo-Boer War. You can see a diorama showing the battle of the Tugela and military exhibits in the Robert F Stevenson Museum. Get the key from the Colenso Police Station, tel (03622) 2113. Nearby is the Blaauwkrantz monument to Voortrekkers massacred by Zulus in 1838. Lord Roberts' son, Freddy, is buried here and the armoured train cemetery where Winston Churchill was captured while a young war correspondent is nearby.

Estcourt. The town was named after an MP for North Wiltshire and sponsor of British settlers. It lies along the Bushman's River and is close to the central Drakensberg resorts and imposing Giant's Castle.

Glencoe. Named after a valley in Argyleshire by early Scottish pioneers during the late 1800s. General French was stationed here on a number of occasions during the Anglo-Boer War and President Paul Kruger also stayed during the siege of Ladysmith.

Among specialist Battlefield Route guides are Ron Lock and Paul Naish, who run Historical KwaZulu-Natal. Ron is the author of *Blood on a Painted Mountain* a recent book on the Anglo-Zulu War. Tel (031) 75-1244 or (031) 765-7048. Also John

Turner, of Battlefields Guides, tel (0358) 35-0062. David Rattray gives excellent perspectives on the battles of Isandlwana and Rorke's Drift. Rattray is a tour operator and owner of the land on which Fugitives Drift lies, where Lieutenant Teignmouth Melvill and Lieutenant Nevill Coghill died on the banks of the Buffalo River attempting to save the Queen's colours, winning the first posthumous VCs. Caltex produces a useful brochure on the Battlefields Route, which is available from information and publicity offices in the region.

ARTS AND CRAFTS ROUTES

The Midlands Meander

This route in the heart of the province is a network of arts and crafts outlets, country pubs, health hydros, hotels, guest houses and tea gardens. The beautiful Natal Midlands has always attracted artists and craftspeople. In 1985, local artists, potters and weavers got together and created this arts and craft route to encourage visitors to come out into the country and see how various hand-made wares were made. By selling their work from their studios they kept prices down. With the support of hotels, shops and restaurants in the area the route has grown and now attracts many thousands of visitors a year.

The route is only an hour's drive from Durban, less than half an hour from Pietermaritzburg, and 4½ hours from Johannesburg. It wanders between Hilton, a quaint village just north of Pietermaritzburg, and Hidcote, a farming hamlet outside Mooi River. It extends from the lush Dargle Valley and Fort Nottingham in the west, to Rietvlei and Curry's Post in the east. One of the advantages in this area is the good road network linking all the outlets.

Few people lived in this area before Boer settlers arrived in the early 1800s. Previously it was a Zulu royal hunting reserve. A number of trekker families settled in the area and there is evidence of their mark in farm names such as *Geelhout*, *Boschhoek* and *Boschfontein*. In 1889, the latter farm obtained a government grant to import 30,000 trout eggs from Dumfries, Scotland. Many of these hatched successfully and in May 1890 the first 1500 trout were released into the Bushmans, Mngeni and Mooi rivers. Each year more rivers were stocked and this was the start of trout fishing in Natal.

Historical Sites. There are many historical buildings in the Midlands dating back to the 1880s. A number are national monuments, among them well preserved Settler churches, and they include St John's Gowrie; Nottingham Road, built in 1885; St Andrews; The Dargle, built in 1882; St Paul's; Curry's Post, established in 1876 by Sergeant M Curry; St Matthews; Lidgetton; and St Lukes, Howick, first opened in 1869. The Midmar Historical Village forms part of the Midmar Nature Reserve and is a recreation of a Natal country village at the turn of the century. It is open every day. The Natal Railway Museum is in Hilton and is open from Tuesday to Thursday and most weekends. Flying enthusiasts can visit the Goodman Household monument near Curry's Post, erected to commemorate the flight in a home-made glider by Goodman Household in 1871. He crashed, wrecking his glider and his leg, ending what is believed to be man's earliest attempt to fly in South Africa.

There are scores of stops on the Meander but, to make it easy, they have been divided into three one-day outings so that you do not have to travel around at breakneck speed. Route One takes in 17 stops between Hilton, Merrivale, Howick and Curry's Post and includes *Crafts Southern Africa*, tel (0332) 30-5859, and *Nogqaza Crafts*, tel (0332) 30-7533, at the Howick Falls, where you can buy Zulu and other ethnic curios and gifts, and *Kingdom Weavers*, tel (033) 234-4187, where you can watch Zulu women producing beautiful woven rugs and other pieces. Not part of the official Meander but well worth checking out is the viewsite at Howick Falls, where locals sell knick-knacks ingeniously fashioned out of scrap wire.

Route Two includes Lions River, Lidgetton, Balgowan, Nottingham Road and Mount West. This offers 25 halts and includes *Home of the Fisherman*, a tackle, garment and souvenir shop (try the smoked trout) in the grounds of Rawdon's Hotel in Nottingham Road, tel (0333) 36044, famous *Michaelhouse School*, at Balgowan, tel (033) 234-4110, and *Swissland Cheese*, 5km/3 miles from Michaelhouse, where you can watch the Saanen goats being milked between 3.30pm and 4.30pm before sampling and buying their delicious products, tel (033) 234-4042.

Route Three is a nice short one, encompassing Lion's River, Dargle, Fort Nottingham, Nottingham Road, Rosetta and Mooi River. Nine stops on the route include *Dargle Valley Pottery,* for award-winning porcelain, stoneware and terracota, tel (033) 234-4377; *Stokkiesdraai Cottage Weavers* for angora, mohair and wool pieces, tel (033) 234-4243; *The Woodturner* for watercolours painted on wood and bowls crafted from indigenous woods, tel (033) 234-4548; and *Shuttleworth Weaving,* tel (0333) 36818, who can produce mohair and pure wool shawls, jackets and blankets if you are heading for the mountains. There is also a route combination with 19 stops that includes some spots perfect for children, such as *Ballina Farm*, with its rocking horse factory, tel (0333) 37211; the *New Hobbits Hut,* which is full of fantasy and serves great home-made ice-cream, tel (0333) 36715; and *Mother Goose,* tel (0333) 37021, where you can pet miniature horses, dwarf cows and goats, and tiny pigs, sheep, geese, rabbits, ducks and chickens.

There are nine hotels, seven guest houses, eight bed and breakfasts, and six self-catering places on the Midlands Meander, as well as 18 restaurants. For help and reservations contact Selected Mini Stays, tel/fax (0332) 30-3343, Midlands Wanderer, tel (0333) 38714, or Gateway Reservations, tel (0333) 32573. They can also organise tours if you are without transport, or you can hire a mountain bike in Curry's Post for R35 (£4.65/$7.70) a day from Rent a Bike, tel (0332) 30-6092.

A splendid full-colour brochure detailing all the suggested halts is available from any of the publicity offices in the Midlands area or from the Midlands Meander Association, PO Box 874, Howick 3290, KwaZulu-Natal, fax (0332) 30-5510. You can also contact the Howick Publicity Association, tel (0332) 30-5305.

The Shongololo Crawl

This is unlike other craft routes as it has a seaside atmosphere. It meanders around the Amanzimtoti area south of Durban, known as the Strelitzia Coast, and takes place every Sunday during the holiday season and thereafter on the first Sunday of every month.

> *Archies Wrought Iron Crafts.* All types of iron and wire-work on display and made on the premises. Showroom opens at any time, but phone for an appointment during the week. Tel (031) 94-2340.
>
> *Chameleon Arts and Crafts Shop.* Craft workshops and demonstration of paper-making, ceramic painting, and silkscreening. Local artists and crafters exhibit here. Original hand-made gifts. Tel (031) 903-7139.
>
> *Rathbone Jewellers.* Guided tours of jewellery-making. Various jewellery items for sale, specialising in a vast range of charms. Tel (031) 916-6455.
>
> *Wild Boyz Surf School.* Watch surf boards being crafted after 3pm daily. This surf school on Warner Beach also offers surf tuition at R25 (£3.35/$5.50) for 1½ hours. Tel (031) 96-3919.
>
> *Ria van Rooyen Gallery.* Original art exhibited. Painting classes and teas served in the Heart of Art Tea Garden. There is a birdwatchers' park across the road. Tel (031) 96-1742.
>
> *Birdshill Arts and Crafts.* Wildlife paintings, three dimensional paintings, hand-painted fabrics, abstract canvases and intricate cushions. Tel (031) 96-4705.

Art in Wood. Open first and last Sunday of the month from 9am to 4pm. Generally open weekdays during school holiday season. Family crests, hand-carved wooden and African stone curios, as well as numerous items crafted by local artists. Tel (031) 96-2812.

Illovo River Arts and Crafts. Held every Sunday from 9am to 4pm at Illovo River. Numerous arts and crafts, as well as four-wheel motorbike rides, barbecued lamb, and face painting for the children.

For information on accommodation and restaurants on this route contact the Crawl Secretary, PO Box 406, Warner Beach 4140, KwaZulu-Natal, tel (031) 903-2893, fax (031) 916-6456, Cell 083 255-4838. Publicity Association, tel (031) 903-7498.

Rorke's Drift

The fame of Rorke's Drift in KwaZulu-Natal as a battlefield is almost matched by the fame of the Evangelical Lutheran Church Arts and Crafts Centre there. Zulus at the centre specialise in hand-woven tapestries, pottery and silkscreen fabrics. The rugs and tapestries are made from pure karakul wool and each piece is guaranteed unique, as no design is ever repeated. Tel (03425) 627.

Wildabout Arts and Crafts Trail

These are stops you could make if driving from Southport to the Wild Coast on the KwaZulu-Natal South Coast:

Paul Buchel Studio, Southbroom. Watercolours, wildlife, landscape, flora and fauna. Open Monday to Friday 9am to 4pm. Tel (03931) 6178.

Titta and Mary Fasciotti, Leisure Bay. Paintings, homecraft, patchwork and applique. Tel (03930) 92181.

Marita Simpson and Petro Taljaard, Port Edward. Paintings in oils, sculpture, woodcarving, charcoal and pencil sketches. Tel (03930) 32638.

River Bend Art Gallery at the River Bend Crocodile Farm. Tel (03931) 6076.

Jo Arkell Pottery, near Port Edward. Porcelain, stoneware and tableware. Open most of the time. Tel (03930) 31672.

Emithini Clothing, near Port Edward. Hand-dyed and hand-painted clothing, painted pottery and conventional stoneware. Open 9am to 5pm daily. Tel (03930) 32433.

Maureen Holmes, Southbroom. Pottery pieces in stoneware. Tel (03931) 6477.

Edmeé Joubert, Munster. Woven apparel in mohair and karakul. Tel (03930) 92695.

Mzamba Village Market. Watch Transkei craftspeople at work opposite the Wild Coast Sun making a wide range of ethnic wares. Tel (03930) 31785.

Gillian Redpath, Port Shepstone. Sculptures in ceramic, wood, mixed media. Tel (0391) 21213.

Vivienne Zanner, near Port Edward. Sculptural, decorative and domestic pottery. Tel (03930) 32382.

Bellevue Lodge, Ramsgate. Artists' retreat where art holidays and workshops are held throughout the year. Tel (03931) 4240.

Mud Hut Gallery, Margate. African arts and crafts, designer clothing, framed prints by South African artists. Open seven days a week 8am to 5pm. Tel (03931) 21739.

Accommodation KwaZulu-Natal is well supplied with guest beds — Durban alone has 17,000 — and these include graded as well as ungraded hotels from five-star bliss to beach cabanas, and alternatives such as holiday apartments, guesthouses, B&B options and backpacker hostels. In the game parks and reserves run by the Natal Parks Board there is a choice of 16 different types of accommodation, from rustic camps, caves, and mountain eyries to thatched huts and luxury lodges. Numerous smaller, private game parks and nature reserves offer accommodation ranging from eco-friendly lodges to wooden tree-houses. The Parks Board has a reservations office in Durban's Tourist Junction. This is linked to the board's central reservations system and enables you to reserve accommodation, caravan and camp sites, and hiking and horseback trails. Book-a-Bed Ahead makes countrywide reservations for visitors. Contact them at the Tourist Junction, First Floor, Station Building, 160 Pine Street, tel (031) 304-4934, fax (031) 304-3868, e-mail funinsun@iafrica.com

In addition to those mentioned earlier in the chapter, the province has the following **caravan parks and resorts**:

> *Albert Falls Nature Reserve*, tel (03393) 202/3.
> *Amcor Dam Caravan Park*, tel (03431) 91273.
> *Balele Recreation Resort*, tel (03433) 3041.
> *Dundee Municipal Caravan Park*, tel (0341) 22121.
> *Estcourt Municipal Caravan Park*, tel (0363) 23000.
> *Hillside Campsite, Giants Castle Game Reserve*, tel (0363) 24435.
> *Howick Municipal Caravan Park*, tel (0332) 30-6124.
> *Lake Merthley Resort*, tel (0334) 31115.
> *La Mouette Caravan Park*, tel (0324) 22547.
> *Loteni*, tel (033722) 1540.
> *Midmar Nature Resort*, tel (0332) 30-2067.
> *Mountain Splendour*, tel (036) 468-1172.
> *Riverbank Caravan Park*, tel (0333) 32144.
> *Spioenkop Reserve (Parks Board)*, tel (036) 488-1578.
> *Strand*, tel (03930) 92729.

Eating and Drinking

No-one explores the battlefield of KwaZulu-Natal without popping into *Stan's Pub* in Babanango, an unusual watering hole in this tiny hilltop village on the road between Empangeni and Dundee. Mutton chop-whiskered Stan, the entertaining host, is an Englishman who over the years has filled his bar with a vast and varied collection of weapons and uniforms, film props, knick-knacks and novelties pertaining largely to the Anglo-Zulu wars in the area. Stan also has accommodation, tel (0358) 35-0029. Dundee is at the heart of the Battlefields Route and nearby, at Hattingspruit, is the *Farmers' Brewery*, a German restaurant and Bavarian tavern where they brew the real, unadulterated stuff of the stein. There are brewery tours and beer tastings, as well as hearty German fare, tel (0341) 81725/6.

Entertainment

SPORT AND RECREATION

KwaZulu-Natal can cater for almost every type of sport and is home to the world-famous Comrades Marathon, an ultra which has the reputation of being one of the best organised road-running events in the world. In Durban, most facilities are within an 8km/5-mile radius of the city centre. A 60,000-seater rugby stadium is only one element of the King's Park Complex, which also has a soccer stadium, athletics track, a cricket ground, and a heated Olympic-size swimming pool. There are tennis stadiums, bowling greens, numerous golf courses, astro-turf hockey fields, squash courts, facilities for baseball, basketball, canoeing, fishing, judo, cycling, and volleyball and every surfer worthy of a board has heard of the Gunston 500 and the beaches of 'Surf City.' For golfers, the courses are virtual perfection from the North Coast's Mount Edgecombe, through Durban's Country Club, to the South Coast's San Lameer and the Wild Coast.

Sailing. Durban's Point Yacht Club, founded in 1892, is one of the largest in Africa. It is a five-minute walk from Durban's CBD and its central position and spectacular view of Durban Bay, as well as its Marina and excellent facilities, make it the venue for many international and world championships events. PYC beachsite facilities are regarded as among the best in the world for international dinghy sailing. There is organised sailing almost every weekend for most recognised classes.

The club welcomes visitors and offers free visiting membership to international yachtsmen for a week, after which a charge of R20 (£2.65/$4.40) a week is made. If you are arriving in Durban by yacht from a foreign port you must be cleared by immigration at Oswald Pirow Building, 202 Smith Street, Durban, tel (031) 306-2746 Ext 245, or all hours on (031) 305-2886, and Port Health, 18 Stanger Street, Durban, tel (031) 37-2736/7/8. If the yacht's last port of call was a South African port, Port Health clearance is not necessary. Customs are at New Pier, Bayhead Road, Durban, tel (031) 368-2923. On arrival in port yacht skippers must go and see the Port Liaison Officer on the ground floor of the Ocean Terminal Building, tel (031) 361-8759. Yacht must be cleared outwards by immigration and customs, as well as harbour revenue, which is also on the ground floor of the Ocean Terminal Building. Point Yacht Club is at 3 Maritime Place, tel (031) 301-4787, fax (031) 305-1234. The Royal Natal Yacht Club is at 136 Victoria Embankment, tel (031) 301-5421, fax (031) 307-2590. Meridian Sailing School can show you the ropes with sail training on a 12m/39ft yacht, as well as organise day sails, courses and fishing and diving charters. Contact the school at Bay Services, PO Box 62569, Bishopsgate, Durban 4008, tel (031) 304-1500, fax (031) 301-1116.

Diving. KwaZulu-Natal has plenty of dive sites. Some 18 dive spots off Durban and its Bluff are all easily reached either from the shore or by small boat. Durban is Africa's busiest port, so watch out for shipping. In Durban, Simply Scuba runs a PADI 5-Star Dive Centre offering training from entry level openwater diver to instructor level. They will also fill your scuba tanks or rent you anything from a weight belt to a full set of equipment. Contact PO Box 37937, Overport 4067, tel (031) 309-2982, fax (031) 309-2984. The Aliwal Shoal off Umkomaas on the South Coast is recognised as one of the 10 best dives in the world. The shoal, about 5km/3 miles offshore, is renowned for the sharks which gather here between July and December and are docile enough for divers to swim among them in safety. Most of the sharks are Ragged-tooth, which seem to have split personalities as further south in the colder waters of the Cape they can be aggressive. Apart from close encounters with raggies you can sometimes swim among Great Whites, whale sharks, manta rays, bottle-nose dolphins, moray eels, and game-fish. The reef at Aliwal is 4km/2.5 miles long, about 300m/984ft wide, and ranges in depth from 5–35m (16–115ft). About a kilometre north of the shoal lie the wrecks of the 15,000-ton Norwegian bulk carrier *Produce* and the 2000-ton steamship *Nebo*, both popular dives. Contact:

African Watersport Adventures, PO Box 157, Umkomaas 4170, tel (0323) 31609, fax (023) 30923;

Sea Diver, PO Box 245, Umkomaas 4170, tel (0323) 31470, fax (0323) 31509;

Aliwal Cove Hotel & Dive Resort, PO Box 24, Umkomaas 4170, tel (0323) 31002, fax (0323) 30733;

The Whaler, PO Box 1327, Umkomaas 4170, tel (0323) 31562/3, fax (0323) 31564.

Simply Scuba Dive Charters organises dives at Aliwal Shoal with accommodation ranging from camping to five-star hotel level. A dive costs R70 (R100 – £13.35/$22 – for a night dive). Contact PO Box 37938, Overport 4067, tel (0323) 73-2391, fax (0323) 73-2396.

Sodwana Bay is unquestionably South Africa's most popular dive spot, so much so that there are an estimated 100,000 dives a year on its reefs. Despite often heavy underwater traffic the dive areas remain exceptional. The reefs are appropriately named Quarter-Mile, Two, Three, Five, Seven, and Nine-Mile reefs, not for their length, but for their distance from the launch site on the beach. Two-Mile Reef is the most dived, but Nine-Mile has more spectacular coral, the southernmost formations in Africa. Marine life abounds in Sodwana Bay and some moray eels and large fish such as grouper are tame enough to feed by hand. Sodwana Dive Retreat (SDR) operates a dive concession in the area and runs a rustic camp where accommodation varies from a tent, which costs R55 a night per person, to R350 a night for the Lodge House, which sleeps four people. Basic price for a dive on Two-mile reef is R75, with a surcharge for each of the other three reefs. A night dive is R120. SDR also offers packages of two and three night's accommodation with three and five dives for R317 and R478. Contact SDR, Private Bag 317, Mbazwane 3974, tel (035) 571-0117, fax (035) 571-0055, Cell 083 229-0318.

Rafting and Canoeing. The most notable canoe marathon in South Africa is the 138km/86-mile Dusi three-day through the Valley of a Thousand Hills. The Dusi is the country's oldest and without doubt most famous canoe race, starting in Pietermaritzburg and finishing in Durban at the mouth of the beautiful Umgeni River. It takes place in January. Contact the SA Canoe Federation in Pietermaritzburg, tel (0331) 94-0509, and the Natal Canoe Union, tel (0331) 46-0984. Canoeing and rafting rivers are reliant on seasonal rainfall and the best time is between November and May. There is a wide variety of white-water rafting rivers in the province and the narrow-waisted Tugela – known to the Zulus as *Thukela*, 'the startling one' – has shallows and technical rapids that in some respects make it more dangerous than the better known Zambezi. An all-inclusive weekend on the Tugela will cost you R595 per person with River Tours and Safaris, tel (011) 803-9775, who can also organise a Grade 4 run through the awesome Tugela Gorge, a 2.5km/1.6-mile-deep cleft that rivals the Grand Canyon. In Zululand, you can combine rafting in the Tugela Canyon area near Weenen with game-viewing from the tented camp of Zingela Safaris, tel (0363) 41962. If you are a novice, River Ducks runs one-day, 16km/10-mile canoe trails on the Upper Umgeni River; for the more experienced there is the Umkomaas River Adventure through some spectacular wilderness areas. Contact Peter Swinney, 46 Loerie Park, Westville 3630, tel/fax (031) 86-3292.

Road-Running. The Comrades Marathon, run over 87km/54 miles between Durban and Pietermaritzburg, has taken place every year since 1921. International participation is steadily increasing and the field has now reached a total of 13,500 runners, who on the big day consume or use 80,000 litres of cola, half a million sachets of water, 30,000 litres of bottled water, 300,000 litres of sponging and drinking water, and 200,000 sachets and 6250 bottled litres of energy drink. There can't be many road races where you need a passport; one in the Southern Drakensberg is the annual 'Sani Pass Stagger' which is run in summer over 23km/14 miles from the top of Sani Pass in Lesotho to the Sani Pass Hotel and Leisure Resort at the bottom, near Himeville, tel (033) 701-1096. For social road-running in Durban you could enjoy a family outing on Sundays with the Hash House Harriers, tel (031) 305-6729.

Fishing. Catch-and-release saltwater flyfishing is popular in bays and estuaries all along the coast from the sub-tropical beaches of the north to the rocky ledges and reefs of the south. Sodwana Bay and Cape Vidal are good flyfishing spots. The Kosi lakes and estuarine system draining out to sea at Kosi Mouth offers flyfishing that can at times be superb. Crocodiles are scarce but watch out for unpredictable hippos. A permit, available from the Natal Parks Board office at St Lucia, is required to flyfish in the St Lucia estuary mouth. Other river mouths and estuaries worth fishing are Zinkwazi, Tongaat, Umgeni, Illovo, Umkomaas, Umzimkulu, Mpenjati and the Umtamvuna. Flyfishing from a boat is possible all year round in Durban Bay. Between June and November most anglers fish for shad (elf) and nothing else. The open waters of the Indian Ocean are rich with such fighting migratory pelagic species as kingfish, garrick, and king mackerel, as well as bonito, dorado, tuna, and snoek, with billfish such as sailfish and black and striped marlin a possibility the further north you go. A good time for offshore fishing is around the end of June every year when vast shoals of sardines swim up the coast to their spawning grounds, heralded by flocks of gannets. When the sardine run is at its height people flock to the beaches to scoop them up by the bucketful and that is when the sport really begins. The Natal Deep Sea Angling Association in Durban, tel (031) 37-6931, and the Durban Charter Boat Association, tel (031) 301-1115, are useful contacts.

If you are not bewildered by the names Mrs Simpson, Deerhair Poppers, Walkers Killer and Woolly Warms you are probably a trout fisherman, in which case you will be in seventh heaven among the rivers, streams and dams of KwaZulu-Natal in pursuit of *Oncorhyncus mykiss* (rainbow trout) or *Salmo trutta* (brown trout). If you want to chase rainbows in the Southern Drakensberg exciting flyfishing in wild natural waters is available at Goshen, in the Giant's Cup Wilderness Reserve, near Underberg. The perennial Mzimkulwana River flows into Goshen's 25-hectare lake at Giant's Cup. Nature does the stocking here, with the river bringing down wild rainbow and brown for the ultimate flyfishing. The best time for trout is between September and November and from March to May. Record rainbow from Goshen is 4.8kg and for a brown it is 3.9kg. There are serviced, 4-bed self-catering rustic cottages from R250 (£33/$55) a day with the option of meals at the farmhouse. Apart from trout fishing you can hike in the wilderness area, climb or go bird and game-watching. Contact Wolf and Carrie Avni, PO Box 227, Underberg 4590, tel (033) 701-1511. Trout fishing is periodically available at Highmoor, in the Parks Board's Drakensberg area. Licences are available and the daily rod permit fee is R25. The Highmoor camp site offers cold water facilities for R6 per person per night, tel (0333) 37240.

Natal Parks Board staff are stationed along the entire KwaZulu-Natal coastline and in protected areas and you can get information about angling from any of the following:

Port Edward to Uvongo, tel (03931) 30531;
Uvongo to Mtwalume, tel (0391) 51223;
Mtwalume to Umkomaas, tel (0323) 20050;
Umkomaas to Isipingo, tel (031) 904-3201;
Isipingo to Umdloti (including Durban), tel (031) 25-1271;
Umdloti to Tinley Manor, tel (0322) 5796;
Tinley Manor to Amatikhulu, tel (0324) 61574;
Amatikhulu to Umlalazi, tel (0353) 40-1836;
Umlalazi to Mapelane (including Richards Bay), tel (0351) 32330.

Protected areas:

Mpenjati, tel (03931) 30531;
Mapelane, tel (035) 590-1407;
St Lucia, tel (035) 590-1340;
Mission Rocks, tel (035) 590-1233;
Cape Vidal, tel (035) 590-1404;
Sodwana Bay, tel (035) 571-0051.

A good all-round contact in Johannesburg is Garth Brook at the Federation of Southern African Flyfishers, tel (011) 320-0883.

Golf. KwaZulu-Natal has some outstanding courses in breathtaking scenic settings. The Durban Country Club's course is listed among the top 100 in the world. It has hosted more South African Open Championships than any other course and has been rated the number one course in South Africa by *Compleat Golfer*, tel (031) 23-8282.

Three other top-notch courses within the Durban region are:

Royal Durban, located within the Greyville Race Course, tel (031) 309-1373;
Kloof Country Club, 24km/15 miles inland from Durban, tel (031) 764-0555;
Umhlali Country Club, on the Dolphin Coast, 45km/28 miles north of Durban, tel
(0322) 71181/4.

Other courses are:

Glengarry Golf Club, where the Drakensberg mountains provide a background to
the opening hole, tel (03370) 11355;
Maritzburg Country Club, adjacent to Queen Elizabeth Nature Reserve, has an
18-hole championship course, tel (0331) 47-1942;
Prince's Grant, a golf estate in Zululand, 80km/50 miles from Durban, tel (0324)
48-2005;
Mount Edgecombe, in Umhlanga, tel (031) 59-5330;
Kilbarchan Golf Club, in the hills of the Midlands, tel (03431) 6690;
Newcastle Golf Club has a demanding 18-hole course, tel (03431) 87200;
Kokstad Golf Course, tel (037) 727-1244, has many challenging holes.

Kokstad Golf Course is less than a two-hour drive from the 'Golf Coast', the short
scenic stretch of the Hibiscus Coast between Umkomaas and the Wild Coast. This is
the South Coast's famous golf circuit. Within an hour's drive from Margate there are
nine excellent 18-hole courses, two 9-hole, and a driving range.

Umkomaas Golf Club, the first course on the circuit, is just 20 minutes from Durban
International Airport, tel (0323) 31042;
Scottburgh has spectacular views from the 18th tee, tel (0323) 20041;
Selborne Park, is listed in the top 12, tel (0323) 51133;
Port Shepstone Golf Course is on the banks of the Umzimkulu River, tel (0391)
50140;
Southbroom has a fine holiday golf course, tel (039) 376-6026;
Margate Country Club is only 3km/2 miles from the sea, tel (03931) 20571;
San Lameer Country Club has been described as a golfer's dream, tel (039)
373-5141;
St Michaels Golf Course is a 9-hole, 18-tee course, tel (039) 375-1230;
Port Edward Golf Club is reported to have the 'friendliest 19th hole on the Golf
Coast', tel (03931) 51230.

The world-class championship course at the *Wild Coast Country Club* forms part of
the South Coast Golf Circuit, and you can expect to lose a ball or two at the 18th's
enormous dam. The South Coast Publicity Association will organise airport transfers,
accommodation and golf bookings, tel (03931) 22322.

Hiking. Down the eastern side of South Africa is the great escarpment thrown up
more than 150 million years ago and named by the early Dutch trekkers the
Drakensberg ('Dragon Mountain') and known to the Zulus as *Khahlamba* ('Barrier
of Pointed Spears'). The slopes on the western side of the range commonly called the
Berg are fairly gradual, but on the east they are precipitous, and plunge 2743m/9000ft.
With many peaks topping 3200m/10,499ft this is a landscape of soaring buttresses,
splintered gorges and valleys offering climbs and exhilarating trails for hikers and
ramblers in air like champagne. The Drakensberg has the highest concentration of
hiking trails and walks in South Africa and many of them lead to shelters and caves
decorated by some of the finest prehistoric Bushman art in southern Africa. The
whole area is a bird sanctuary and frequented by a variety of species including
Africa's largest eagle, the rare Lammergeyer, as well as martial eagles, jackal
buzzards, Cape vultures, and black eagles.

The Berg falls naturally into northern, central and southern areas. Breaking the
skyline from north to south are Mont-aux-Sources (3282m/10,768ft), the Amphitheatre flanked by the Eastern Buttress (3047m) and the Sentinel (3165m), Cathedral

Peak (3004m), Cathkin Peak (3148m), Champagne Castle (3377m) and, at the easternmost rim of the sweep, Giant's Castle (3316m).

Giant's Cup hiking trail runs for nearly 60km/37 miles along the foothills of the Drakensberg from Sani Pass to Bushman's Nek. The trail has five sections with overnight accommodation at Cobham, Mzimkulwana, Winterhoek, Swiman and Bushman's Nek huts, tel (033) 702-1305.

There are excellent 1:50,000 survey maps of all South Africa's mountain areas. Sign in the Mountain Rescue Register at your point of entry into the Drakensberg. All hotels, forestry and Natal Parks Board offices have registers. Sign off when you come back. Take warm clothing. Even in mid-summer when the valleys can be 28°C/82°F it can be cold enough on top for blizzards. Cold wind can kill above the 3000m/9843ft mark. The internationally recognised mountain distress signal is six whistle blasts or torch flashes a minute, then a minute's pause and repeat.

Some useful contacts:

Mountain Club of South Africa (KwaZulu-Natal Section), tel (031) 72-7844;
Hiking Federation of South Africa (Midlands Section), tel (0331) 63440;
Mountain Backpackers Club, Durban area, tel (031) 86-3970;
Durban Ramblers Hiking Club, tel (031) 701-8996/21-3592;
Midlands Hiking Club, tel (0331) 42-9423 or (03322) 3071;
Sani Hiking Club, Underberg, tel (033) 701-1466.

Wilderness trails in game parks and sanctuaries give you an opportunity of getting close to the wildlife for which KwaZulu-Natal is noted. Since the first one was conducted in the Umfolozi Game Reserve in 1959 trails have been opened in many other areas, including the Drakensberg, Mkuzi and St Lucia, all of which offer you the experience of a lifetime. Contact the Natal Parks Board.

4x4 Trails. For information about off-roading you can contact Halfway Toyota 4x4 Club (Natal), PO Box 15, Park Rynie 4182, tel (0323) 21337; Land Rover Owners Club of SA (Natal), PO Box 3, Pietermaritzburg 3200; and the Zululand 4x4 Club, PO Box 20188, Richards Bay 3900, tel (0351) 53-3375, fax (0351) 90-3484. Advanced and basic courses are held in the Babanango Valley, three hours' drive from Durban. No experience is required. Contact Fred or Terry Cathro, tel (0331) 96-1220, or Graham Slater-Brown at Eagle's View Country House, tel (0358) 35-0054, fax (0358) 35-0010. There is a little-known 4x4 trail at Thangami Safari Spa, on the Black Umfolozi River, 30 minutes' drive from Gluckstadt, near Vryheid, which also offers some excellent bird-watching and a hot mineral spa (41°C/106°F). There are also hiking and horse-riding trails, one to some recently discovered Bushman cave paintings. Camp sites are available. Contact Gert and Santie Uys, tel (03824) 841/852/853.

Hunting. The Natal Parks Board permits hunts in Mkuzi, Spioenkop and Chelmsford Controlled Hunting Areas from March to October. Hunts vary from three to five days, with accommodation in tented bush camps at Mkuzi and Spioenkop and in chalets at Chelmsford. Hunts with accommodation included cost from R1820 (£243/$400) at Chelmsford to R8960 at Mkuzi. Game usually available for hunting at Chelmsford includes blesbok, springbok, and red hartebeest; Spioenkop: blesbok, kudu, impala, black and blue wildebeest, zebra and red hartebeest; and at Mkuzi: nyala, impala, bushpig, warthog, common duiker, zebra, blue wildebeest and red duiker. Contact Natal Parks Board.

Horse-racing. There are three major racecourses in the province — Clairwood and Greyville in Durban and Scottsville in Pietermaritzburg. Clairwood Park, 12km/8 miles from the City Hall, is known as the 'Garden Course,' tel (031) 42-5332. As well as Totalisator facilities the course has a good selection of restaurants and bars, among them the Panoramique Restaurant, which has a stunning view of the track from start to finish. Other popular restaurants are the Tavern on the Park and the Whip & Saddle.

Greyville, 4km/2.5 miles from the City Hall, is the venue for the premier race on the calendar, the July Handicap. The racecourse was the first in South Africa to introduce night racing, tel (031) 309-4545. Scottsville Racecourse, 76km/47 miles from Durban, is regarded as the most picturesque in the country, combining Mediterranean-style architecture and green lawns, tel (0331) 45-3405.

KwaZulu-Natal is the home to innumerable artists and craftspeople, whose traditional skills in wood-carving, beadwork, weaving and basketry produce investment pieces sold in galleries and art centres and colourful, casual handicrafts sold by curio shops and kerbside traders. The province is also home to most of South Africa's 800,000 Indians, so there is also more than a hint of the east, with shops and markets selling spices, silks, ornaments, leatherwork, filigree jewellery and a variety of souvenirs. Larger hotels, resorts and game parks usually have curio shops and craft centres where you can buy mementoes.

On the N2 north into Zululand look out for roadside stalls selling Zulu beadwork and handicrafts. There is also a wealth of ethnic craftwork along the way in quaint shops, galleries and fleamarkets, ranging from pottery, Zulu fabrics, furniture, stained glass windows and lamps, wood carvings, ethnic clothing, and curios. South of Durban the Amanzimtoti Fleamarket, Beach Road, Rogies Park, is held on the first Sunday of every month from 9am; the Illovo River Market features quality arts and crafts as well as the usual fleamarket stalls, tel (031) 916-6251; the Umnini Craft Centre at Umgababa has Zulu curios and souvenirs. On the banks of the Mpambanyoni River at the entrance to Scottburgh, the Aliwal Adventure Craft Market has exquisitely hand-crafted goods, and there is a beer garden with live music. Open from 8.30am to 4pm, tel (0323) 21364 and (0323) 21202; the Sea Shell Museum & Gift Shop on Marine Drive, Shelly Beach, has the biggest display of sea shells in southern Africa and the biggest variety of shells and shell creations in the country. Open daily from 9am to 5pm in season, and on Wednesday to Saturday from 10am to 4pm out of season, tel (03931) 75723. Craftshop *The Barn Owl* has three outlets on the South Coast, in Margate, Southbroom and Ramsgate, where you can also watch Zulu dancing on Sundays at 3pm, tel (03931) 78380; the Wildabout Art and Craft Trail, between Port Shepstone and Margate, gives you a chance to watch artists and craftsmen at work in their studios. In Margate, tel (03931) 22322 for a route map. Basket weavers work and sell their wares on the Margate beachfront. Near the Mtamvuna River bridge, outside Port Edward, is Mzamba Village, which has loads of ethnic arts and crafts.

Watch out for beachfront muggers and pickpockets, particularly street children. Pickpockets find easy pickings in and around the Indian Market. Although Durban's crime rate doesn't quite match Johannesburg's it is getting there. Keep your car windows up and doors locked. Car thieves abound in the CBD, so park in parkades or brightly lit areas. Durban drivers have a tendency to crawl in the fast lane and change lanes without indicating. Tourist Support Unit, tel (031) 32-5923.

In Durban:

Police, tel (031) 306-4422.
Flying Squad, tel 10111.
Ambulance, 10177.
Sea Rescue Services, tel (031) 37-2200.

Fire Brigade, tel (031) 361-0000.
Weather and Tides, tel (031) 307-4135.
Gayline Durban, tel Mike Gordon (031) 37-5784 (o/h), or write to PO Box 11744, Marine Parade 4056, KwaZulu-Natal.
Link – Lesbians in KwaZulu-Natal, PO Box 30890, Mayville 4058.
Natal Gay Community, PO Box 37521, Overport 4067, tel (031) 37-5784.
Colonial Towers, 332 West Street (off Mark Lane), tel (031) 304-6701.

In Pietermaritzburg:

Police, tel (0331) 42-2211.
Fire Brigade, tel (0331) 42-1311.

TOURIST INFORMATION

KwaZulu-Natal Tourism Authority, tel (031) 304-7144, fax (031) 305-6693.
Natal Parks Board, PO Box 662, Pietermaritzburg 3200, tel (0331) 47-1961, fax (0331) 47-3137, e-mail npb@aztec.co.za
Durban Unlimited/Tourist Junction, 160 Pine Street, Central Durban, PO Box 1044, Durban 4000. Open Monday to Friday, 8am–5pm, Saturday and Sunday, 9am–2pm, tel (031) 304-4934, fax (031) 304-3868, e-mail funinsun@iafrica.com. Beach Office (open every day) is on Marine Parade, next to Sea World, tel (031) 32-2595; and the Airport Kiosk is in the Domestic Arrivals Hall at Durban International Airport, tel (031) 42-0400.
Pietermaritzburg Publicity Association, 177 Commercial Road, Central City, PO Box 25, Pietermaritzburg 3200, tel (0331) 45-1348/9, fax (0331) 94-3535.
Amanzimtoti, tel (031) 903-7493, fax (031) 903-7509.
Colenso, tel (03622) 2111, fax (03622) 2469.
Dolphin Coast Publicity, PO Box 534, Ballito 4420, tel (0322) 61997, fax (0322) 62434.
Drakensberg, tel (036) 448-1557, fax (036) 448-1562.
Dundee, tel (0341) 22139, fax (0341) 21664.
Eshowe, tel (0354) 74079, fax (0354) 41908.
Estcourt, tel (0363) 21188, fax (0363) 23077.
Greytown, tel (0334) 32735, fax (0334) 31933.
Hluhluwe, tel/fax (035) 562-0353.
Ladysmith, tel (0361) 22992, fax (0361) 27952.
Margate, tel (03931) 22322, fax (03931) 21886.
Newcastle, tel (03431) 53318, fax (03431) 29815.
Ramsgate, tel (03931) 79411, fax (03931) 44761.
Richards Bay, tel (0351) 31111, fax (0351) 31897.
St Lucia, tel (035) 590-1143.
Southern Drakensberg, tel (0331) 701-1096.
Shelly Beach, tel (03931) 76970, fax (03931) 76443.
South Coast Publicity Association, tel (03931) 22322, fax (03931) 21886.
Umhlanga, tel (031) 561-4257, fax (031) 561-1397.
Vryheid, tel (0381) 81-2133, fax (0381) 80-9637.
Zululand, tel (0351) 27777, fax (0351) 92-1519.

Eastern Cape

The Perfect Wave

The Eastern Cape tends to suffer from the fact that it is neighbour to the Western Cape, whose attractions are more obvious and better known throughout the world. In reality it need fear no comparison as it has so far been spared too great a fame, and its magnificent shoreline has still to be ruined by the sort of development meant to draw tourists but which not surprisingly eventually drives them away. The redrawing of the provincial boundaries returned to the Eastern Cape two under-developed and neglected chunks of territory — the Ciskei and the Transkei — which had laughably 'independent' status under the old apartheid regime, and this has added lots more natural attractions and endless stretches of incomparable coastline to the Eastern Cape. It has also unfortunately added to the province's economic problems. The

Eastern Cape is the country's poorest province and nearly a quarter of its inhabitants live below the bread line — a figure which rises to a staggering 92 per cent in the Transkei — and 7.2 million people give it the highest population density in South Africa. Another addition it could well do without is its nominal capital Bisho, which was the capital of the former Ciskei bantustan. Apart from retaining the necessary legislative apparatus to justify its existence there is little to be said for this sad backwater down the road from historic King William's Town, which is why people generally regard Port Elizabeth, the largest city in the province, and East London as the unofficial pivotal capitals of the Eastern Cape.

The province is one of the country's most diverse areas, bridging the winter rainfall of the Western Cape and the summer rainfall area. The result is the merging of five major types of vegetation, which produce an astonishing variety of plants, animals, birds and other wildlife, conserved in three National Parks and numerous nature reserves. This diversity extends from the lush Tsitsikamma Forest and the 200,000-hectare Baviaanskloof Wilderness Area to the vast dry Karoo region and the southern alpine slopes of the Drakensberg and encompasses a coastline that is a delight. The unparalleled Wild Coast bounding the unexploited Transkei and stretching from the Kei River mouth, 95km/59 miles beyond East London, all the way to the KwaZulu-Natal border, gets its name from the harsh conditions experienced here by early shipwreck survivors. This coast is an irresistible lure for saltwater anglers and summer catches include huge reef fish such as musselcracker, while the annual autumn sardine run brings fighting game-fish to the area. The Wild Coast is dotted with free and easy family resorts and comfortable camp sites. Bear in mind that as roads and bridges are few getting from one resort to another, even if they are only a few kilometres apart, can involve you in a lengthy journey inland and back. Hiking trails abound and southern right whales and their calves are regularly spotted offshore between May and November, while common and bottlenose dolphins are often seen surfing the inshore breakers. Nelson Mandela was born in the Transkei, at Qunu, and East London-based tour operator Kai Safaris runs a trip to this little village which is still a favourite retreat of the president. Port Elizabeth is the largest city on the coast between Cape Town and Durban. It is often called the Windy City and in the old sailing ship days the summer south-easterly gales which flailed Algoa Bay made it a place skippers avoided. Now it is a year-round leisure resort with more days of sunshine than any other place on the coast. Beaches are always alive with sun worshippers and conditions are usually excellent for surfing, sailing, diving and angling, with water temperatures ranging from a maximum of 23°C/73°F in summer to a minimum of 16°C/61°F in winter. Algoa Bay was the place where the 1820 Settlers from Britain first set foot and graceful period homes in the city and its environs reflect the influence of the 4000 men and women originally chosen to act as unsuspecting buffers between the Colony and the Xhosa tribes. Inland are the rolling green hills of what is still known as Settler Country, where most of the towns and villages were founded in the troubled early years of the 19th century and have British names such as Balfour, Bedford, Bathurst and Somerset East. The central historic university town of Grahamstown still reflects the origins of its founders, both in its buildings and its atmosphere. Many of the interior towns, such as Fort Beaufort and King William's Town, were strategic outposts in the 19th century's seemingly endless frontier wars in which Xhosa pastoralists fought with white immigrants for the rich grazing. Further inland, in stark contrast to the verdant coastal belt, are the arid plains of the Karoo where summer months are hot and winter is dry and mild, except in the mountainous areas to the east where snow often falls. East London, at the mouth of the Buffalo River, is a popular seaside holiday destination and the gateway to the Wild Coast. River as well as saltwater sports are popular and regattas are regular events in summer. The area around East London also reflects its British roots, with a leavening German influence which was the result of the settlement of families

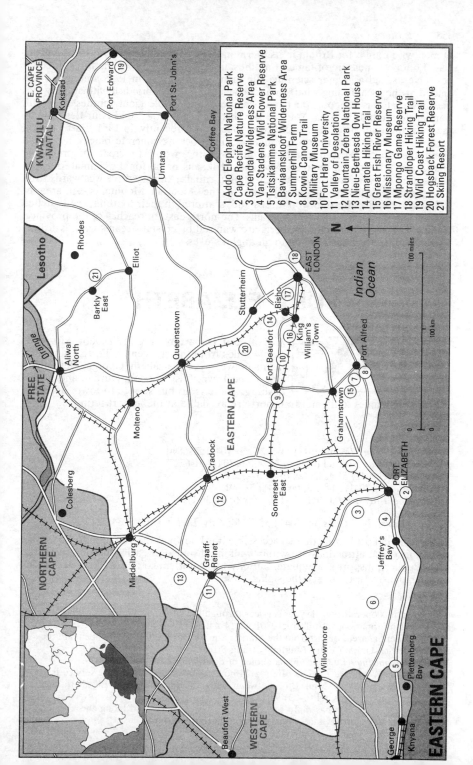

EASTERN CAPE

1 Addo Elephant National Park
2 Cape Recife Nature Reserve
3 Groendal Wilderness Area
4 Van Stadens Wild Flower Reserve
5 Tsitsikamma National Park
6 Baviaanskloof Wilderness Area
7 Summerhill Farm
8 Kowie Canoe Trail
9 Military Museum
10 Fort Hare University
11 Valley of Desolation
12 Mountain Zebra National Park
13 Nieu-Bethesda Owl House
14 Amatola Hiking Trail
15 Great Fish River Reserve
16 Missionary Museum
17 Mpongo Game Reserve
18 Strandloper Hiking Trail
19 Hogsback Hiking Trail
20 Wild Coast Hiking Trail
21 Skiing Resort

of men who fought for Britain in its German Legion. Two marine events have given East London a measure of fame. If a dinosaur had ambled out of the forest it could not have caused a greater scientific stir than the discovery in 1938 among a catch landed at the local fishing wharf of a Coelacanth, a prehistoric fish with stumpy leg-like fins that was supposed to have become extinct while giant reptiles were still wandering around the area. You can see this living fossil — 'Old Four-Legs' — in the local museum. The other event took place more recently. In 1961, East London harbour engineer Eric Merrifields invented interlocking concrete blocks, now used along the South African coast and all over the world to create impregnable breakwaters. He called them *dolosse*, the Afrikaans name for the animal knuckle-bones used by witchdoctors in their divination rituals. An easy drive westwards from East London leads to the escarpment of the Amatola Mountains, an area of yellowwood and white stinkwood trees and, scattered in their foothills, the thatched huts of the Xhosa and their cattle kraals. The north-eastern reaches of the province, leading to the southern Drakensberg, are watered by crystal streams with fly-fishing guaranteed to bring tears of joy to an angler's eyes.

PORT ELIZABETH

Arrival and Departure. Port Elizabeth Airport is 6km/4 miles from the city centre. There are regular flights between Port Elizabeth, George, Plettenberg Bay, Cape Town, East London, Durban and Johannesburg. There is no bus service to town, but taxis, car hire companies and hotel transport are available at the airport terminal.

Car hire:

> *Avis*, tel (041) 51-1306;
> *Economic Car Hire*, tel (041) 51-5826, fax (041) 51-5840;
> *Economy Car Hire*, tel (041) 51-6724, fax (041) 51-6727;
> *Budget*, tel (041) 51-4242, fax (041) 51-5531;
> *Imperial*, tel (041) 51-1268, fax (041) 51-3919;
> *Runabout Rentals*, tel (041) 35-1764, fax (041) 35-1764.

Taxis: *Hunters Taxi Cabs*, tel (041) 55-7344; *City Taxi*, tel (041) 34-2212.

Everything in Port Elizabeth is so accessible it is known as the 'ten-minute city'. Most of the historical attractions are within walking distance of each other in the central area. Public transport is adequate, but city bus shuttle, taxi and walking are all fun and inexpensive ways to see the sights.

Bus services:

> *Algoa Bus* operates regular bus services through the city and suburbs. For timetable and information, tel toll-free 0801 42 14 44. Buses to all parts of the city and residential areas depart from the Market Square Bus Station, located beneath the Norwich Union Centre Building, Strand Street.
> *Greyhound Intercity Coach* has a choice of destinations, tel (041) 56-4879.
> The *J-Bay Sunshine Express* offers a 24-hour, door to door transport service in a 15-Seater Luxury Mini Bus, between Jeffreys Bay and Port Elizabeth and surrounding areas, tel (0423) 93-2221.
> *Intercape Mainliner* has daily coaches from East London and along the Garden Route to Cape Town, tel (041) 56-0055, fax (041) 56-1165.

Translux Express has daily luxury coaches to major destinations, tel (041) 507-2366, fax (041) 507-2299.

The *Garden Route Hopper Bus* operates in both directions along the Garden Route between Port Elizabeth and Mossel Bay, tel (041) 55-4000, fax (041) 55-8402.

Other services include:

Springbok Atlas, tel (041) 51-2555, fax (041) 51-2550;
Bay Tourism, tel (041) 55-2977, fax (041) 55-1979;
Tour De Cape, tel/fax (041) 456-3443;
Silver Line Tours, tel (041) 55-1977, fax (041) 55-1979.

Air Trips. You can take aerial flips over Port Elizabeth with *Algoa Flying Club*, tel (041) 51-3274; *National Airways Corporation*, tel (041) 507-2333; and *John Huddlestone Helicopter Tours & Flips*, which lift off from the Gravy Train Restaurant at King's Beach on holidays and Sunday afternoons (R50 per person), tel (041) 52-2597.

Rail. The mainline railway station is in the centre of the town in Station Street, just off Strand Street, tel (041) 507-2662. Spoornet mainline passenger services run overnight train services between Port Elizabeth and Johannesburg via Bloemfontein on Monday, Wednesday and Friday. An overnight service runs from Port Elizabeth to Cape Town on Sunday, tel (041) 507-2222.

You can get an unusual view of the harbour from The Diaz Express, a steam train that offers a short excursion between Kings Beach and the harbour on the second weekend of every month.

City Tours. *Friendly City Tours* provide a 90-minute orientation tour of the city in a luxury mini-bus, with a running commentary on the historical as well as the latest developments. The tour costs R55 per person, tel (041) 55-1801. For R120 (£16/$26.40) there is also a tour to Addo Elephant National Park, inclusive of park entrance fees, tel (041) 55-1801. *Algoa Tours* has a half-day tour of Port Elizabeth for R85 per person, tel (041) 51-2403. *Bay Tourism* offers a R45 2-hour city tour which takes in, among other sites, the beachfront, the University of Port Elizabeth, the historical Central Hill area, the residential area of Walmer, and the industrial area. There is also a variation which includes a city tour, a tour to the Addo Elephant National Park, back to Port Elizabeth for sundowners at Sardinia Bay, and ends with a township cultural visit, tel (041) 55-1977, fax (041) 55-1979. *Ndlovini Tours* has a R45 per person day and evening tour of Gqebera black township, which began its life in the mid-19th century as Walmer Township and was named after Walmer Castle, home of the Duke of Wellington. The tour includes historical insights, a visit to the *abakwetha* (boys initiation camp) and squatter camp, development projects, as well as a visit to a shebeen to taste traditional food and beer. Contact Wicliff Quza, tel (041) 51-2572.

Accommodation These up-market hotels are at the beachfront, less than 10 minutes' drive from the airport:

Marine Protea Hotel, four-star, tel (041) 53-2101, fax (041) 53-2076;
Beach Hotel, three-star, tel/fax (041) 53-2161;
The Summerstrand Inn, tel (041) 53-3131, fax (041) 53-2505.

One and two-star value-for-money places on the beachfront and in the historical Hill area of the city:

Caboose Budget Hotel, where each room is built like a first-class train compartment, and the *Brookes Hill Bunk House*, tel (041) 56-0088, fax (041) 56-0087;
Edward Hotel, two-stars, a city landmark and a great carvery, tel (041) 56-2056, fax (041) 56-4925.

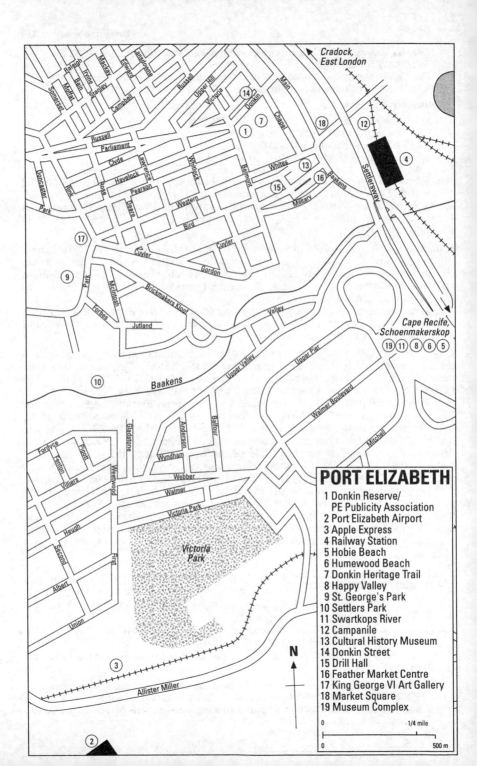

PORT ELIZABETH

1 Donkin Reserve/
  PE Publicity Association
2 Port Elizabeth Airport
3 Apple Express
4 Railway Station
5 Hobie Beach
6 Humewood Beach
7 Donkin Heritage Trail
8 Happy Valley
9 St. George's Park
10 Settlers Park
11 Swartkops River
12 Campanile
13 Cultural History Museum
14 Donkin Street
15 Drill Hall
16 Feather Market Centre
17 King George VI Art Gallery
18 Market Square
19 Museum Complex

Cradock,
East London

Cape Recife,
Schoenmakerskop

Victoria
Park

N

0   1/4 mile

0   500 m

Budget accommodation:

Jikeleza Lodge, 44 Cuyler Street, central city, tel/fax (041) 56-3721;
YMCA, Havelock Street, PO Box 12007, Centrahil, tel (041) 55-9792, fax (041) 55-3026;
Middle Stump B&B, Brickmakerskloof Road, central city, tel (041) 52-2694.

Backpackers:

Kings Beach Backpackers Hostel, 41 Windermere Road, Humewood, Port Elizabeth 6110, tel (041) 55-8113/32-2345;
Global Backpackers, 75 Cape Road, Port Elizabeth 6001, tel (041) 34-3768;
Port Elizabeth Backpackers, 7 Prospect Hill, Port Elizabeth 6001, tel (041) 56-0697, fax (0441) 74-6054;
Port Penguin Backpackers, 67b Russell Road, Central Port Elizabeth 6001, tel (041) 55-4499, fax (041) 56-2714;
Protea Lodge, 17 Prospect Hill Road, Port Elizabeth 6001, tel (041) 55-1721.

Caravans and Camping:

Willows, Marine Drive, Schoenmakerskop, PO Box 13368, Humewood 6013, tel (041) 36-1717, fax (041) 36-1878;
Beachview, Seaview Main Road, Beachview, PO Box 15367, Emerald Hill 6001, tel (041) 74-1884, fax (041) 74-1885;
Highbrae Walking & Camping, PO Box 7954, Newton Park 6055, tel (041) 955-5355;
Sea Acres Holiday Resort (Pty) Ltd, tel (041) 53-3095.

Game Lodges within an hour's drive of the city with accommodation from five-star to self-catering:

Shamwari Game Reserve, tel (042) 851-1196, fax (042) 851-1224;
Addo Elephant National Park, tel (0426) 40-0556, fax (0426) 40-0196;
Shumba Safaris, tel (042) 851-1436;
Kariega Park Game Lodge, tel (0461) 31-1049, fax (0461) 23040.

House That!! Accommodation Agency has a network of **bed-and-breakfasts** from R95 per person, **guest houses** from R100 (£13.35/$22) per night and backpackers from R25 a night. Contact 10 Southway Close, South End, Port Elizabeth 6001, PO Box 5671, Walmer, Port Elizabeth 6065, tel (041) 55-4779, fax (041) 55-3511.

Jeffreys Bay

Accommodation down the coast in 'J Bay' includes *Seashells Beach Hotel*, 45 minutes from Port Elizabeth, with luxury 2, 3 or 4-bed serviced apartments. Da Gama Road, Jeffreys Bay, tel (0423) 93-1143, fax (0423) 93-1104. Others include:

Beach Cabanas, tel (0423) 93-2323;
Sunshine Bay, tel (0423) 93-2582;
Diaz 15, tel (0423) 93-1779.

Backpackers:

Cape St Francis Backpackers, 200m/219 yards from Seal Point, 20 minutes' drive to Jeffreys Bay. R20 (£2.65/$4.40) a night, tel (0423) 94-0420, fax (0423) 94-0409;
Jeffreys Bay Backpackers, 12 Jeffreys Street, Jeffreys Bay 6330, tel (0423) 93-1379, tel (0423) 93-1021;
Koffie's Surf Camp, PO Box 1894, Jeffreys Bay 6330, tel (0423) 93-1530;
Peggy's Place, SA Oribi Street, Jeffreys Bay 6330, tel (0423) 93-2160/1210.

Caravanning. *Jeffreys Bay Caravan Park*, tel (0423) 93-1111.

Eating and Drinking

Port Elizabeth has more restaurants per head of population than anywhere else in South Africa and there is a lively pub and tavern scene which usually erupts into a colourful and lively source of entertainment. Bear these points in mind: cover charges are almost non-existent as locals get pretty peeved if they have to pay to get in anywhere; the best day to party is Wednesday, with Friday and Saturday coming close seconds. The best time to party is from 8pm onwards. If you hate queues, arrive early or after 11pm; don't drink and drive, the police are insomniacs and will pull you over just because; dress is informal, at most you will need to wear a collared shirt and longs after 6pm (in some venues). Check the local press for Happy Hours as these guarantee swinging parties; R100 (£13.35/$22) should see you very, very well through the night. Finally, parking is not a problem, there are few muggers and car thefts are relatively unknown — thanks to the insomniac policemen.

Among restaurants specialising in fresh seafood are:

Nelson's Arm Restaurant & Seafood Grill, at 3 Trinder Square, in the city centre, tel (041) 56-0072;
Blackbeards Lookout & Seafood Restaurant, tel (041) 55-5567;
The Bell Restaurant at the Beach Hotel, Beach Road, in Humewood, tel (041) 53-2161.

Traditional Cape cooking can be found at:

Sir Rufane Donkin, a restaurant in a delightfully renovated Settler's cottage, tel (041) 55-5534;
Cuyler Crescent Diner, tel (041) 55-3672;
Aviemore has provincial cuisine, with lots of game dishes, tel (041) 55-1125;
Sandpiper has traditional home-cooked food, tel (041) 55-8961;
49 Havelock Street is a quaint, homely restaurant with a cosy historical ambience, tel (041) 56-4949.

The *Keg & Fox* English-style pub on the corner of Clyde and Rose Streets, has traditional pub lunches, tel (041) 55-4547; so does *Blinking Owl*, at 306 Cape Road, Newton Park, tel (041) 35-3591, and *Chatters Bar & Grill*, in Grace Street, Central, which is open from Monday to Saturday from 7.30am till late. You can start the day here with a full English breakfast, and there is health food as well as dinner and a fully licensed bar, tel (041) 55-7510.

The British influence is evident in the number of tea-rooms, often in lovely gardens, which offer tempting sweet treats as well as light meals. An alternative eating establishment where you can enjoy a Victorian tea party in a pleasant greenhouse setting is the *Lemon Tree Restaurant and Coffee Shop*, 58 Pearson Street, city centre, tel (041) 56-4782; and another relaxing place is the *Chippendale Tea Garden* at 35 Parliament Street, Central, tel (041) 55-2372. Further afield is the *Kisumu Cheese and Wine Farm*, 14km/9 miles along the Old Cape Road, Rockland Road turn-off, St Albans, tel (041) 955-5503.

Gay Restaurants

Galleri, 95 Parliament Street, Central, tel (041) 55-5223;
Priscilla's Coffee Shop, corner Clyde and Lawrence Street, Central.

Exploring

Port Elizabeth, often known as the Friendly City is the fifth largest city in South Africa and a major industrial centre with lots of beautiful beaches and facilities for indoor and outdoor activities. There are also interesting museums, parks and a Heritage Trail which takes in most of the city sights. Every year thousands of road runners race against the Apple Express, a narrow gauge locomotive, in The Great Train Race. The performing dolphins at the Oceanarium should not be missed.

Beaches. Algoa Bay has 40km/25 miles of clean golden beaches. Hobie Beach, closest to the city at Summerstrand, is the venue for the annual Splash Festival and world boardsailing championships. Humewood Beach, sheltered by the promenade above, is a favourite family beach, with a swimming pool and body surfing. A subway links the beach to Happy Valley, where there are lawns, flower beds, lily ponds and winding paths ideal for family strolls. King's Beach, stretching 1.6km/1 mile from the harbour breakwater to Humewood, is ideal for safe swimming, sunbathing and long walks. There is good surfing near the harbour wall. The McArthur Pool Complex has sea and freshwater pools, change rooms, waterchutes, a mini-golf course, go-karts, and a supertube. Pollock Beach, or the 'Pipe' as it is known locally, is a choice surfing spot because of its excellent waves. Along Marine Drive on the way to the village of Schoenmakerskop, 24km/15 miles away, there are picnic spots, coves, rock pools and holiday resorts with safe bathing. Schools of dolphins are often seen here. Sardinia Bay has a beach that is regarded as one of the best walking beaches around, with miles of unspoilt coastline. Fishing is not permitted as the area is a Marine Reserve, but snorkelling and scuba-diving are popular. The northern beaches, a vast stretch of sand and dunes, includes New Brighton Beach, a large unspoilt stretch just before Bluewater Bay. It has a promenade with a cafeteria and children's playground, change rooms, a lifesaver's tower, and is good for swimming and angling, as is the magnificent stretch of beach at Bluewater Bay. St George's Strand is the closest beach to the St George's Strand and Joorst Park holiday resorts and apart from good swimming has some fine sand dunes, pleasant picnic spots, and a large children's playground. There are chalets and camp sites at the two nearby resorts. Water temperatures are 18–21°C (64–70°F) during summer and 14–19°C (57–66°F) during winter. Sea conditions are generally calm in Algoa Bay, except when the south-easterly wind blows. All popular beaches are patrolled by professional life guards.

Campanile. This bell tower was erected as a memorial to the 1820 Settlers and stands at the entrance to the railway station and docks. Climb 204 steps to the Observation Room for an excellent view from more than 52m/171ft above the city. The tower has a carillon of 23 bells, the country's largest, which rings changes on 10 bells three times a day. It also has a chiming clock.

Cape Recife Nature Reserve. The Roseate Tern Trail, a 9km/6 mile circular walking trail, starts at the entrance to this 366-hectare reserve and takes you through an area of unspoilt beaches, natural dune vegetation, rocky outcrops, a lighthouse built in 1851, and a penguin sanctuary and bird hide. This is regarded as one of the best bird-watching spots close to Port Elizabeth.

No 7 Castle Hill. This restored rectory, built in 1827 by the first Colonial Chaplain, is the oldest surviving private house in Port Elizabeth and is typical of town houses built in the region in the early 1800s. It is a national monument and a museum.

Donkin Heritage Trail. A 5km/3-mile walk linking 47 places of historical interest in the old Hill area of central Port Elizabeth. Maps are available from Tourism Port Elizabeth's Donkin Reserve office. The *Donkin Reserve* was proclaimed in 1820 by Sir Rufane Donkin, founder of Port Elizabeth, who erected the stone pyramid there in memory of his wife, Elizabeth, who gave her name to the city.

Fort Frederick. This stone fort on Belmont Terrace was built in 1799 by the British to defend the entrance to the Baakens River, but it never heard a shot fired in anger. The fort contains a powder magazine and a guardhouse.

Graveyard Tour. A macabre tour taking in the city's oldest graveyards, including St Mary's Churchyard, which was until 1850 the town's only burial place, and St

George's Cemetery. Known as the Scottish cemetery, this has been restored in the tradition of an old English rose garden. Tours cost R50 per person, tel (041) 38-2214.

Haunted Ghost Walk. There are reportedly plenty of ghosts in the city's oldest areas. A local historian conducts spine-chilling evening tours through the haunted areas and their quaint cottages during the Christmas and Easter holidays. Cost is R10 (£1.35/$2.20) per person, tel (041) 52-2515.

Historical Perspective Tour. The chief librarian in the Africana/South African section of the city's main library is an avid historian and in her private capacity conducts small groups of history lovers on tours of the city, tel (041) 55-8133.

Horse Memorial. Monument at the corner of Rink Street and Cape Road erected to the 347,000 horses killed during the Anglo-Boer War. This famous piece of sculpture depicts a kneeling trooper watering his horse and is reputedly one of only two such memorials in the world.

The **King George VI Art Gallery** has collections of South African, British and Oriental art and international printmaking, and some outstanding pottery and sculpture. The gallery faces the top of Western Road, at the entrance to St George's Park, where the Edwardian Pearson Conservatory has collections of water lillies, orchids and other hothouse flowering plants. Open weekdays 8.30am–5.30pm (closed Tuesday mornings), Saturdays 9am–4.30pm, Sundays and public holidays 2–4.30pm, tel (041) 56-1030.

Port Elizabeth Museum Complex and Oceanarium. This is on the beachfront at Humewood and comprises a museum, oceanarium, snake park and tropical house, as well as the No 7 Castle Hill Museum. The main museum blends cultural and natural history. The Maritime Hall exhibits fully-rigged models of early sailing ships, salvaged artefacts, marine animals and fish. Part of the museum exhibits relics and fossils of dinosaurs and early man, as well as a display of ethnic beadwork, costumes, and historical photographs. At the Oceanarium there are dolphin and seal performances daily at 11am and 3pm. You can also see penguins, fish and sharks through underwater observation ports in the aquarium. The Snake Park and Tropical House house about 1000 exotic and indigenous snakes, from tiny adders to monstrous pythons, as well as an impressive variety of Eastern Cape reptiles. The complex is open Monday to Sunday from 9am to 5pm, tel (041) 56-1051.

Settlers Park. A tranquil 54-hectare park in the heart of the city enhanced by indigenous flora, rock pools and grassy areas. The Baakens River, which flows through, attracts about 100 bird species, small buck and other animals. There are lots of walks, including the 8km/5 mile Guinea Fowl Trail through the Baakens River Valley.

Swartkops River. 18km/11 miles of navigable waters for power boating, canoeing, sailing, windsurfing and angling. The Zwartkops Yacht Club has two public launching slipways and upstream you will find the Redhouse Yacht Club and the Redhouse Rowing Club. Amsterdam Hoek at the mouth of the river, is a pleasant little riverside village.

Entertainment

Cinema lovers have a choice of 25 air-conditioned venues in Port Elizabeth: The Bridge Complex, along Cape Road, shows Ster-Kinekor movies, tel (041) 34-4340; Kine Montage, Rink Street, screens foreign films, tel (041) 52-3311; and Walmer Nu-Metro, Sixth Avenue Walmer Shopping Centre, offers four venue options, tel (041) 51-5380. Concerts, musicals, operettas and small productions by various performing groups are staged at the *Opera House and Barn*, half-way down White's Road, which opened in 1892 and is still going strong and is the only surviving example of Victorian Theatre in the country, tel (041) 56-1122; Feather Market Centre, a concert hall on the corner of Baakens Street and Military Road, tel (041) 55-5514; *Mannville Open Air Theatre*, on the south-western side of St George's Park, presents a summer festival of Shakespeare every year; the *Ford Little Theatre*, on the corner of Castle Hill and Belmont Terrace, was built in the 1850s. It is home to the Port Elizabeth Music and Drama Society, which occasionally stages small productions and modern musicals, tel (041) 55-8354; the *Savoy Club Theatre* on the corner of Stirk and Collet streets, Adcockville, is home to the Gilbert & Sullivan Society, tel (041) 33-8417.

There is no shortage of talented local musicians and you will find decent live music all over the city. Try *Galleri*, a stylish and sophisticated wine bar and restaurant in Parliament Street, tel (041) 55-5223. The *Boardwalk* is one of the most popular entertainment centres in Port Elizabeth along Marine Drive and has a number of main venues: *Einstein's* has alternate techno-trance raves and modern rock nights, tel (041) 53-4343; *Barneys* has live entertainment every night and on Saturday and Sunday afternoons on *The Deck*, tel (041) 53-4500; *Cadillac Jacks Rock 'n Roll Diner*, is Port Elizabeth's 'hot spot', with great vibes, sounds and food, tel (041) 53-4500.

Gay Bars and Clubs

Evening Shade, 10 Market Street, North End, Cell 083 654-4144;
Oscar's, above Karieba Batteries, Hancock Street, North End;
Rich's, 3rd Floor Lincoln House, corner Kemp and Strand Streets.

Port Elizabeth's small suburban complexes and massive all-encompassing city malls cater for all shoppers. There are craft and curio shops galore, as well as weekend craft markets and roadside hawkers with everything from fresh fruit and vegetables to ethnic clothing and African crafts. Most popular vending areas are along Main Street and in the City Square. Greenacres and the Bridge Shopping Centre in Cape Road, Newton Park, is an immense shopping centre under one roof. Shops specialising in African arts, crafts and curios include African Curios at 18 Main Street, which specialises in semi-precious stone jewellery, animal charms carved from African wood, verdite and soapstone, as well as wild game skins, mats and cushions. Open Monday to Friday 9am to 5pm, and Saturday from 9am to 1pm, tel (041) 55-4679; Tradebeads, in 39 Newton Street, Newton Park, has ethnic and traditional antique jewellery, as well as colourful beads, tel (041) 35-3852; and the Wezandla Gallery & Craft Centre in Baakens Street, which on request can organise traditional food and African dancing. Open Monday to Friday, 9am–5pm, and Saturday, 9am–1pm, tel (041) 55 1185. The Wildlife Society Shop has a gift shop at 2b Lawrence Street, offering colourful T-shirts, African curios, hand-crafted gifts, wildlife books, cards, videos and tapes. Open Monday to Friday from 8.30am to 4pm, Saturday from 9am to 1pm, tel (041) 55-9606. The Wildlife Museum Shop is a Wildlife Society outlet next to the Port Elizabeth Oceanarium, stocking similar items. Open Monday to Sunday from 8.30am to 4.30pm, tel (041) 55-5040. Memento's of Africa at the Port Elizabeth Airport has items produced by community development projects, such as hand-crafted mohair products, beadwork, pottery and baskets, tel (041) 507-7214.

Port Elizabeth has an art walk which links all the art, antique, and speciality shops in the central area. Most antique and speciality shops can be found along Rink, Parliament, Lawrence, Clyde, and Pearson streets, and on Westbourne Road. Tetbury Antiques is in an historic building at 35 Parliament Street. One of the city's oldest shops, it is a treasure-house of furniture, pictures, porcelain and other interesting items. It also runs a quaint tea-garden which serves hearty breakfasts, light lunches and tea-time treats. Open weekdays from 9am to 5pm, Saturday from 9am to 3pm, tel (041) 55-2372. Flea markets are held at St George's Park on the first Sunday of every month, and at Hobie Beach every Saturday and Sunday. The Beachfront Traders' flea market is strung along the promenade between King's Beach and McArthur's Baths and is open from 8am till late afternoon every Saturday and Sunday, tel (041) 52-2959. The children should enjoy Pier 14 Shopping Centre, at 444 Main Street, North End, which has a fun nautical theme. The centre has three levels and an elevator designed as a submarine. Silvermine Tours has a half-day tour of factory shops where you can buy clothing, knitwear, shoes, underwear, mohair products, and towelling at bargain prices and visit a curio shop, tel (041) 55-1977.

EAST LONDON

GETTING AROUND

East London Airport is 13km/8 miles north-west of the city, tel (0431) 46-2267. Airport transfers: *The Little Red Bus* airport shuttle, Cell 082 569-3599; Kai Safaris, tel (0431) 36-6494.

Car hire:

> *Avis*, tel (0431) 46-1344;
> *Imperial*, tel (0431) 46-2230;
> *Tempest*, tel (0431) 46-1320;
> *Budget*, tel (0431) 46-1084.

Taxis:

> *Herman Taxis*, tel (0431) 43-8076;
> *Komani Taxis*, tel (0431) 33-1175;
> *Moeba Taxis*, tel (0431) 33-8884;
> *Smith Taxis*, tel (0431) 43-9918;
> *Springbok & Leons Taxis*, tel (0431) 31-1567;
> *Taxi Rank*, tel (0431) 27901;
> *Velile Gwavus*, tel (0431) 33-2446.

Bus services:

> *Bus timetables*, tel (0431) 21251;
> *Amatola Regional Council*, 60 Cambridge Street, tel (0431) 21251;
> *Translux* has services to Cape Town, Johannesburg, Durban, Bloemfontein, King William's Town, Port Elizabeth and Kroonstad, departing from the railway station in Station Street, tel (0431) 44-2333, fax (0431) 43-0471;
> *Intercape destinations:* Fish River Sun, Kenton-on-Sea, Port Alfred, Alexandria, Port Elizabeth, Cape Town, Upington, departing from Orient Beach, Fleet Street, tel (0431) 25508;
> *Greyhound destinations:* Johannesburg, Bloemfontein, Pretoria, departing from Kennaway Hotel on the Esplanade, tel (0431) 55327;
> *Minilux destinations:* King William's Town, Grahamstown, Port Alfred, Port Elizabeth, departing from Major Square in Beacon Bay and the Tourism Office, 35 Argyle Street, city centre, tel (0431) 41-3107;
> *Amatola Sun Express*, departs from the Tourism Office, tel (0401) 91111.

Rail. Railway station, Station Street, tel (0431) 44-2020; Spoornet mainline passenger services, tel (0431) 44-2719; Metro commuter trains, tel (0431) 44-2118; suburban stations, tel (0431) 44-2717.

Sea. The *Unicorn Shipping Line* has a limited weekly passenger service between East London and Durban, tel (0431) 31-1818, fax (0431) 31-2308, or Cape Town, tel (021) 25-2280, fax (021) 419-6727.

ACCOMMODATION

Three stars is as high as you go in East London. In this bracket are the *King David Hotel* on Inverleith Terrace, PO Box 1582, East London 5200, tel (0431) 23174, fax (0431) 43-6939; the *Kennaway Protea Hotel*, on the beachfront, tel (0431) 25531, fax (0431) 21326; and the *Osner Hotel*, also on the beachfront, tel (0431) 43-3433.

Bed-and-breakfast and self-catering:

> *BB Lodge*, 14 Clifford Street, beachfront, tel (0431) 43-8827 and at 5 Mashona Terrace, Quigney, tel (0431) 43-1345;
> *Beth's*, on Kidd's Beach, tel/fax (0432) 81-1575;
> *Mike's Guest House*, 22 Clifford Street, Quigney, tel (0431) 43-3647;
> *St Andrews Lodge*, 14 St Andrews Road, Selborne, tel (0431) 43-5131;
> *Abalone Guest House*, 8 Fitzmaurice Road, Baysville, Cell 082 492-5206.

Backpackers:

> *East London Backpackers*, 128 Moore Street, East London 5201, tel (0431) 23423, fax (0441) 74-6054.
> *Sugar Shack*, Esplanade, East London 5201, tel (0431) 21111.

East London YWCA is at 49 St Georges Road, tel (0431) 29819.

Caravan Parks:

> *Nahoon*, tel (0431) 34-2129;
> *Lagoon Valley*, Marine Drive, 10km/6 miles from city, tel (0431) 46-1080;
> *Rocklyffe on Sea*, 17km/11 miles from city, tel (0431) 36-6431;
> *Calgary Museum of Transport*, 10km/6 miles from the city, has caravan sites and self-catering hostel-type accommodation, tel (0431) 38-7244.

Amatola Sun, serves the towns of Bisho and King William's Town, 65km/40 miles from East London. Mashie golf course, jogging trail, tennis, and casino. Contact PO Box 1274, King William's Town 5600, tel (0401) 91111, fax (0401) 91330.

EATING AND DRINKING

East London is big on pub restaurants and popular on this circuit are:

> *Tug & Ferry*, at Latimers Landing, the city's waterfront development on the banks of the Buffalo River, tel (0431) 43-1187/8;
> *Hunter's Jetty*, also at the Landing, tel (0431) 43-8410/9;
> *Buccaneers Sports Pub and Grill*, on the Eastern Beachfront, tel (0431) 43-5171;
> *Keg and Rose*, Patcyn Centre, 44 Frere Road, tel (0431) 56164;
> *O'Hagan's Irish Pub & Grill*, in the Aquarium Complex on the Esplanade, tel (0431) 43-8713;
> *Jekyll & Hyde Pub 'n Grill*, Lock Street Gaol Complex, tel (0431) 24434;
> *Bulldog Pub & Grill*, Devereux Avenue, tel (0431) 56862.

For takeaway fish and chips, *Skippers* is also in Devereux Avenue, tel (0431) 56937, and so is the *Spud Rock Café* for baked murphies.

Gay bars in East London include *Club Byrons*, tel (0431) 726-9449, and *Thumpers*, Recreation Road, tel (0431) 726-9449.

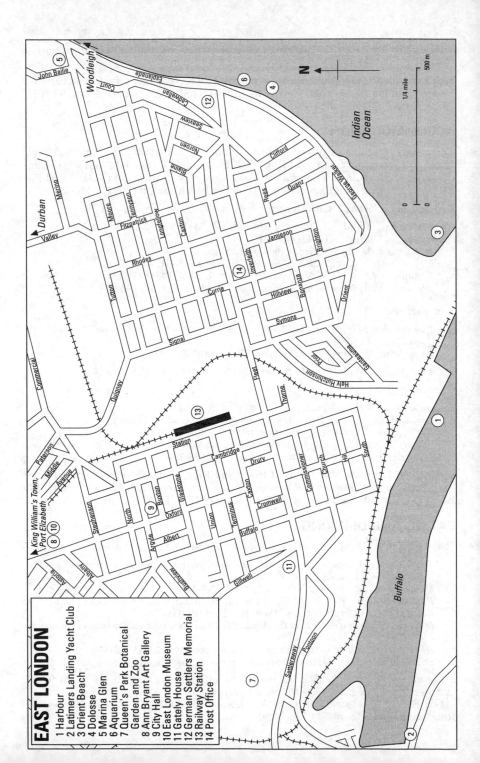

EXPLORING

East London is divided into east and west banks by a river the Khoikhoi and Xhosa called the 'place of buffaloes'. The town was established at the sheltered mouth of the Buffalo River on the Indian Ocean in 1835 and its slow growth only changed tempo in 1858 with the arrival of more than 3000 German settlers, whose legacy can be seen in the region in the names of towns such as Hamburg, Berlin, Stutterheim and Braunschweig. The harbour, South Africa's only river port, handles a considerable quantity of imports, and exports of citrus fruits, mineral ores, wool and pineapples. Three of the many beautiful beaches in the area are within the city limits. Close to the city centre on the east bank, and separated from the harbour by a long pier built over the wreck of Russian vessel *Orient*, is Orient Beach, which is a pay beach popular for its safe swimming and surfing.

There is also good surfing at Eastern Beach, just past the Aquarium and opposite Marina Glen, and still further east at Nahoon Beach, where the waves are spectacular enough for top level surf-ski competitions to be held. Much further east, beyond Beacon Bay, Bonza Bay Beach also offers miles of dazzling sands. There are also popular beaches on the west bank, among them Shelly Beach and Fullers Bay, with its tidal pool and waterworld complex.

The East London Museum is one of the finest and most interesting museums in the country. Not only does it have one of the most comprehensive natural history exhibits in the world, it also has an exhibit for which many museum curators would give their eye teeth — a prehistoric fish, the Coelacanth, except this is not a fossil, but the real thing. In December 1938, the world of science was electrified by the netting off the Chalumna River, west of East London, of an ugly fish which was thought to have been extinct at least 80 million years. This large, blue, oily creature was identified by the late Professor JLB Smith of Rhodes University, Grahamstown, as a Coelacanth. Scientists believe that four-legged land animals developed from these and similar lobe-finned fishes hundreds of millions of years ago.

Ann Bryant Art Gallery is housed in The Gables, a beautiful double-storey Edwardian house on the corner of Oxford Street and St Luke's Road. Its permanent collection is representative of South African art from the 1880s to the present and includes paintings, sculptures, ceramics, graphics, drawings and photographs. There is also a model of the brig *Knysna*, the first known vessel to call at the mouth of the Buffalo River in 1836. Open weekdays 9.30am to 5pm, Saturday 9.30am to midday. The gallery is also open on the third Sunday of each month, tel (0431) 34-2209.

Although fairly small the **Aquarium** on the Esplanade between Orient and Eastern beaches contains about 400 species of marine life. Injured and oil-soaked creatures are often restored to health here before being released. Seals and penguins perform twice a day at 11.30am and 3.30pm and you can watch the fish being fed daily at 10.30am and 3pm. Open daily from 9am to 5pm, tel (0431) 34-2209.

The striking red and white **City Hall** has a beautiful marble staircase, a Victorian hall and quadrangle. The clock tower was built to commemorate the diamond jubilee of Queen Victoria. With its clock faces it rather resembles Big Ben. Tours of the impressive interior can be arranged, tel (0431) 34-2235.

East London Museum. As well as being home to the most famous fish in the world, the Coelacanth *Latimeria chalumnae*, this museum on Upper Oxford Street has an outstanding collection of Nguni beadwork, maritime history displays, and collections of butterflies, sea shells and corals. There is also a reconstruction of the extinct Mauritian dodo, along with the only known dodo egg in the world. Open Monday to Friday from 9.30am and 5pm, Saturday 9.30am to midday; and Sunday 11am to 4pm, tel (0431) 43-0686.

Fort Glamorgan was established in 1848-49, at the same time as the harbour, to provide quarters for troops fighting in the Frontier Wars. The Powder Magazine is now a national monument. For permission to visit, tel (0431) 31-1610.

Gately House, at the bottom of Terminus Street on the east bank near the zoo, dates from 1876 when it was the home of local businessman John Gately, who was the town's first mayor and known as the father of East London. Well preserved family heirlooms are on display and give you a good idea of local lifestyle during the Victorian era, tel (0431) 22141.

The **German Settler Memorial** on the Esplanade near the Aquarium commemorates the 1858–9 arrival of more than 3000 German men, women and children, who helped to expand East London. It is particularly impressive at night when floodlit. There is no memorial to the 157 Irish spinsters who arrived on the *Lady Kennaway* to provide wives for bachelor settlers.

Hood Point Lighthouse, near the West Bank Golf Course, was built in 1895 and is rather picturesque with its traditional 'keyhole' windows, consoled upper gallery, and a steel upper structure topped by a weathervane. Open Monday, Wednesday and Friday, 2–4pm, Saturday 9–11am, tel (0431) 44-3056.

Latimers Landing is a waterfront development project on the banks of the Buffalo River, on the site of the old wooden wharf where trawlers used to land their catches and where the famous Coelacanth, now affectionately nicknamed 'Old Fourlegs,' was unloaded. There is now a collection of pubs, shops and restaurants overlooking the yacht moorings.

At the end of the Esplanade opposite Eastern Beach is **Marina Glen**, a delightful children's playground with a miniature railway, roundabouts, go-karts, trampolines, tea-garden and a kiosk for gooey ice-cream and sticky candy floss. Open weekends, public and school holidays, 9am–1pm and 2–5pm.

Queen's Park Botanical Garden and Zoo on Beaconsfield Road is a natural bowl of 30 hectares holding a variety of indigenous plants and a compact zoo with some 1200 animals and reptiles. It is the only natural habitat in the world of *umtiza listerana*, a small-leafed tree with a distinctive fluted trunk. Rural blacks hang the bark in their huts as protection against evil spirits and lightning. There are pony rides for children and a refreshment kiosk. Open every day, 9am–5pm, tel (0431) 21171.

SHOPPING

The Xhosa people's richly diverse culture is strikingly displayed in their colourful arts and crafts and their beadwork, weaving, basketware and clay pottery can be bought at craft centres throughout the area. Oxford Street is the heart of the shopping and central business district. Here South Africa's first women's prison, Lock Street Gaol, has been transformed into an unusual small shopping centre housing many fascinating home industries, as well as a flea market, arts and crafts stalls and a restaurant. You can inspect the old death cells and the restored original gallows while you are browsing. On the Old Transkei Road, the Floradale Craft Gallery is worth a visit. Popular flea markets are held at Buxton Street and in front of the Gonubie municipal offices on Saturday mornings, Latimers Landing on Saturday and Sunday, Marine Park and the Ann Bryant Art Gallery on Sunday.

WESTERN REGION

Addo Elephant National Park (51,534 hectares) just 72km/45 miles from Port Elizabeth in the Sundays River Valley is a major conservation success story.

By 1920, ruthless hunting has reduced the area's once great herds to only 11 survivors. Since the Addo Park was established in 1931 its elephant population has grown to more than 200. Elephants calve throughout the year and so baby jumbos are a prime attraction. The evergreen Addo bush is among the most impenetrable in South Africa so elephant spotting as you drive along the park's gravel roads is very much a hide-and-seek affair. The Hapoor waterhole, named after a legendary elephant bull, is the best area in the park to see elephant. The park also supports Cape buffalo, black rhino, kudu and other antelope, and more than 185 bird species. Two walking trails have been laid out and there are night drives. The self-guided Spekboom Trail takes you through a fenced-off botanic reserve, safe from elephant, but where you can see buck, monkey and porcupine. You can also watch animals from the comfort of your veranda at night as they drink at the illuminated waterhole. Game watching is complemented by Addo's Big Five — but these are five with a difference. They are the elephant, suricate, flightless dung beetle, black rhino and buffalo. The flightless dung beetle is an endangered species in the region, but thrives in the park, where dung from elephant, buffalo and rhino makes it dung beetle heaven. As they are attracted to dung on the roads they are often killed by cars, so if you see a road sign bearing a beetle silhouette watch out for excited dung beetles. You can enjoy bird-watching from a hide, nature trails, swimming, tennis, and film shows. The park's rest camp has accommodation ranging from 2-bed rondavels at R180 (£24/$39.60) a night (including breakfast) to R550 a night for a 6-bed cottage. There is also caravan and camp site — R33 a night for two with R9 for each additional person — a pleasant restaurant, a swimming pool and a well stocked shop. Contact PO Box 52, Addo 6105, Eastern Cape, tel (0426) 40-0556, fax (0426) 40-0196, or the National Parks Board, tel (012) 343-1991.

Alexandria. In this area, in 1856, a Xhosa teenager called Nonquase told the local Gcaleka people that their ancestral spirits had ordered them to destroy their crops and cattle so that the white settlers would leave the land and the tribe's cattle kraals and grains bins would fill to overflowing. For 10 months the Gcaleka killed their cattle and burnt their crops. They then starved to death in their thousands. Nonquase sought sanctuary with the British in King William's Town. She is buried on the boundary between the farm Glenshaw and the Alexandria State Forest. In the town, site of the largest chicory factory in the world and centre of a chicory, pineapple and dairy farming area, are many restored old houses. The gaol dates back to 1840.

Bathurst. This hamlet lies between Grahamstown and Port Alfred and is best known as the home of the world's biggest artificial pineapple, which is a pity as there are some more noteworthy landmarks. Bathurst is one of the smallest municipalities in South Africa and has the country's oldest pub, the Pig and Whistle. Once you have been to Summerhill Farm to see the 16.7m/55ft-high glass fibre monstrosity (inspired by a similar Australian model) proclaiming Bathurst's status as the pineapple metropolis of southern Africa, you can visit St John's Anglican Church, the oldest unaltered Anglican church in South Africa, which was used as a sanctuary during successive Frontier Wars, a Xhosa village, the Bathurst Agricultural Museum, with its display of more than 2000 farming implement and the circular toposcope, built around the original stone beacon from which many 1820 Settlers were shown their allotments of land. Embedded in the toposcope are 57 bronze plaques recording details of each settler party. The town's distinctly English atmosphere dates from this period. Then you can wet your whistle at the Pig & Whistle, which was built soon after the village was established. The original forge was built by settler Thomas Hartley, a blacksmith from Nottingham, and subsequently turned into the accommodation which remains the heart of the pub. Formerly known as the Bathurst Inn, its present name goes back to World War II, when it was affectionately bestowed by local soldiers. Across the road is the Bathurst Arms. On a hilltop 3km/1.8 miles from the village is Horseshoe Bend Nature Reserve which offers an outstanding view of the valley where the Kowie River makes this bend.

Baviaanskloof Wilderness Area. One of the largest conservation areas in southern Africa, this rugged 200,000-hectare area includes three mountain ranges and two rivers. Peaks, valleys and plateaux characterise the area, and altitudes range from 500m/1640ft to 1700m/5577ft above sea level. Some 58 mammal species live in the park, and 293 bird species have been noted. There are 4x4 and hiking trails. Use the *Baviaanskloof Self-Guided Motor Trail* in conjunction with a 1:50,000 map of Baviaanskloof Wilderness Area. Overnight accommodation is available, tel (041) 390-2179.

Coldstream. Village on the Tsitsikamma coast, in the Joubertina district, which is famous for a burial stone excavated nearby in 1910. This depicts a prehistoric artist holding a brush feather and palette, indicating that rock paintings were being executed here at least 2000 years ago.

Compassberg. Peak 2540m/8333ft high, 55km/34 miles north of Graaff-Reinet, on the watershed between the Orange and Sundays rivers. It was named by RJ Gordon in 1778 because from the summit he could see streams flowing in all directions.

Cradock. The main centre of the Eastern Cape Midlands, this charming Karoo town at the foot of the Banksberg Mountains has an interesting cultural heritage, including a close association with author Olive Schreiner, who lived and worked here for many years. The Mountain Zebra Park is 15 minutes' drive from the town. Just outside Cradock is Egg Rock, a precariously balanced 10m/33ft-high egg-shaped 500-ton dolorite boulder. The Great Fish River Museum, behind the Town Hall, was built in 1849 and depicts local history from 1840 to 1900. Open Tuesday to Friday from 8am to 1pm and 2pm to 4pm, Saturday from 8am to midday, tel (0481) 4509. The Olive Schreiner Museum has a pictorial display of the writer's life in this house in Cross Street, where she lived between 1867 and 1870. Open Monday to Friday from 8am to 12.45pm and 2pm to 4.30pm, tel (0481) 5251. Olive Schreiner's grave is on the summit of Buffelskop, 24km/15 miles from the town on the Mortimer road. For permission to visit the site, tel (0481) 4424 or (0481) 3815. In the old heart of Cradock, 14 typical Karoo townhouses are clustered in Market Street, east of the town square, making it the most authentic period street in the country. At least one of the houses is haunted and guests have smelt coconut biscuits being baked in the middle of the night. Next to the square is the Dutch Reformed Church, built in 1867 as a replica of London's St. Martin's-in-the-Fields. Locals who have long made the novel wire Karoo windmills for tourists are now also turning out wooden sailing ships with paper sails. Cradock Spa's natural sulphur spring waters feed self-contained chalets, an outdoor swimming pool and a heated indoor pool. There are caravan and camping sites on banks of the Great Fish River.

Fort Beaufort. Established in 1822 to keep warring Xhosa tribes in check the town today is the centre of a prosperous citrus farming area. Displays at the Historical Museum, Military Museum and Martello Tower testify to the town's military past.

Grahamstown. 125km/78 miles from Port Elizabeth, is the unofficial capital of the Settler Country. There are fine examples of Georgian and Victorian architecture in its wide, tree-lined streets, as well as restored artisans' cottages, classic town houses and the ornamental facades of the Victorian High Street. More than 40 churches and some fine museums and monuments are among the town's attractions. The Albany Museum has five components: the Natural Sciences Museum, and the History Museum, in Somerset Street; Fort Selwyn, on Gunfire Hill, a restored semaphore station opened only on request; the eccentrically designed Observatory Museum, in Bathurst Street, which has the only camera obscura in the southern hemisphere; and the old Provost Prison in the Botanical Gardens, in Lucas Avenue. The Botanical

Gardens contain flora from around the world, as well as various cycads. Grahamstown's most prominent landmark is the Cathedral of St Michael and St George, which is the seat of the Bishop of Grahamstown and has the tallest spire in South Africa. Rhodes University was founded here at the turn of the century and among its research institutes is the world-renowned JLB Smith Institute of Ichthyology, in Somerset Street. For guided city walks, tel (0461) 31-1049. The stunning 18km/11-mile Mountain Drive through the commonage above the city includes a nature reserve and the Thomas Baines Reserve, 15km/9 miles from the city. Grey Dam outside Grahamstown is a reserve for Kowie River fish and a refuge for the eastern Cape rocky, a fish unique to this region and now endangered.

Once described by an 18th century traveller as 'an assemblage of mud huts' gracious **Graaff-Reinet** is now known as the 'Gem of the Karoo' and lies in a horseshoe bend of the Sundays River, encircled by the 16,000-hectare Karoo Nature Reserve. The town retains much of its 19th century rural character and meticulously restored buildings and monuments make it a town where every house seems to be a museum. If you are interested in history and architecture there is a feast of it here, from simple Karoo-style houses to Cape Dutch, Georgian and Victorian. For some fine examples visit Stretch's Court, the former Residency, the Hester Rupert Art Museum, Urquhart House, and Graaff-Reinet Pharmacy. There are numerous other monuments (more than in any other town in South Africa), particularly military ones, but the most unusual is the monument to Jewish *smouse* (pedlars) recognising their contribution to the economic development of the region. The imposing century-old Dutch Reformed Church at the head of the main street contains valuable ecclesiastical vessels which are fine examples of Cape Silver. Pride of place is Reinet House, once the Murray Pastorie and now a national monument and museum. Livingstone slept here, as did his father-in-law Robert Moffat, and other passing missionaries. The Cape Dutch house is furnished with 18th and 19th century yellowwood and stinkwood pieces and in the garden is a vine planted in 1870 and reputed to be the largest grape vine in the world. The main stem had a circumference of 3.10m/10ft in 1983, but since then fungal rot has reduced it. The museum uses a postmark depicting this vine for anything posted there. Graaff-Reinet's great natural landmark is Spandau Kop, a steep cone rising about 300m/984ft above the town. In the western section of the Karoo Nature Reserve, 14km/9 miles from town, is the weirdly dramatic Valley of Desolation, a geological phenomenon which has over millions of years produced grotesque piles and pinnacles of rock. There are some interesting trails here and in the surrounding Sneeuberg Mountains. You can get maps from the local publicity association, tel (0491) 24248.

Island Nature Reserve. 25km/15 miles from Port Elizabeth, this 480-hectare reserve preserves stands of indigenous Alexandria coastal forest, with tree species such as Outeniqua yellowwood, white and hard pear, and white milkwood which shelter small blue duiker, bushbuck, vervet monkeys and bushpigs. More than 50 species of birds, among them the Knysna lourie, can be seen and the reserve has numerous pleasant walks, as well as picnic sites and a barbecue area. A more strenuous walk is the 16km/10 mile Bushbuck hiking trail, tel (041) 74-1634.

Jeffreys Bay. is a fishing village and seaside resort 72km/45 miles west of Port Elizabeth on the western shore of St Francis Bay and is renowned almost as much for its exquisite shells as it is for surfing. Unusual shells are on display in the little museum. It is one of the world's most famous surfing spots and the site of consistently perfect waves. The world-class Billabong Country Feeling Surf Classic is held here in July.

Maitland Nature Reserve. A small (127 hectares) but interesting reserve with dense indigenous coastal forest, abundant birdlife, an old wagon road which leads to Maitland lead mines, a variety of small animals such as bushbuck and blue duikers, as well as some giant sand dunes. Three nature trails provide easy access into the forest, a 3km/2 mile self-guided trail along the old wagon road; a 9km/6 mile-long trail with a magnificent view of St Francis Bay and the Maitland dunes; and a 4km/2.5 mile walk passing through some of the thickest areas of the forest. Contact tel (041) 55-5213/56-1000.

Mountain Zebra National Park. In the 1930s, the mountain zebra was on the brink of extinction. This 6721-hectare park was established in 1937 to ensure their survival, and today some 200 of these little (1.2m/3.9ft-high) animals roam the sanctuary, 24km/15 miles from Cradock. The scenery is beautiful and varied, encompassing mountains, ravines and high plateaus, with many kinds of aloes, trees and flowering shrubs. The predominantly mountainous terrain becomes carpeted with mesembryanthemums, blue tulips and grasses after the lightest rainfall. Game viewing is rewarding throughout the year and although the park is devoted primarily to the mountain zebra, you can see many of the antelope species that once roamed this region, such as mountain reedbuck, kudu, springbok, duiker, eland, steenbok, black wildebeest, blesbok, red hartebeest, as well as small predators and 200 species of birds, including the magnificent black eagle. Accommodation includes fully equipped chalets, a caravan park and a splendid renovated Victorian guesthouse. A two-bed chalet costs R180 (£24/$39.60) a night, and the guest house, which sleeps six, costs R325 a night. A camp site for one or two people costs R30 (£4/$6.60), with R8 for each additional person. There is a licensed restaurant, a tourist shop, a post office and public telephones in the park.

Temperatures in the park can be quite low in the winter months. The climate is cold with sunny days and cold nights. Snowfall can be expected, especially on the higher ridges which rise to 1957m/6421ft above sea level. During the summer the weather is mild to hot. The three-day Mountain Zebra Hiking Trail in the park costs R60 and covers 26km/16 miles. Comfortable overnight accommodation is available, with showers and toilets. All you need is your sleeping bag, food, cooking and eating utensils. Reservations for the trail can be made up to 12 months in advance. There are also shorter nature trails for the less energetic. Swimming and horse riding are popular. As with other national parks you should book as far in advance as possible. For the off-chance of accommodation within three days of your application, tel (0481) 2427 during office hours, otherwise tel (012) 343-1991, or (021) 22-2810.

Nieu-Bethesda. This tiny village 50km/31 miles north-west of Graaff-Reinet found fame as a result of the work of an eccentric artist, the late Helen Martins. She created scores of bizarre sculptures at her home, which became known as The Owl House for its congregation of concrete owls. Behind the house is the Camel Yard in which a group of men and camels, apparently facing Mecca, are surrounded by mythological birds and animals, mermaids and dancing girls with beer bottle skirts. Helen Martins and her work were the inspiration for Athol Fugard's successful play *The Road to Mecca*.

Schotia Safaris is set in the rolling hills and valleys of the Paterson area, a 35-minute drive from Port Elizabeth, on a 1000-hectare family ranch. There is an abundance of game which can be seen on guided game drives, followed by cocktails round the camp-fire at sunset and a traditional safari-style cuisine, tel (042) 851-1436/1368.

Shamwari Game Reserve. This 11,000-hectare reserve bordering the Addo National Park is the only private one in the Eastern Cape with the Big Five (elephant, black rhino, buffalo, lion and leopard). Individual lodges have been restored in keeping with their original 1800s style. There are early morning and late afternoon game drives with an armed game-ranger as escort. As well as the Big Five you can see eland, gemsbok, white rhino, giraffe, hippo, zebra, black wildebeest and a wide variety of antelope. There are also some of the unusual species such as the white blesbok, red hartebeest and blue hartebeest and the black springbok. On night drives you might spot aardvark, aardwolf, genet, and Cape grysbok. More than 230 species of bird are present, ranging from massive eagles to the tiny greater double-collared sunbird. Eminent traditional healer Credo Mutwa has built a cultural complex at Shamwari, where 14 villages showcase different tribal lifestyles. Tel (042) 851-1196.

Steytlerville on the Groot River is a town to avoid if you are fond of a sundowner. No liquor is ever sold here.

St Francis Bay is another surfer's paradise and great recreational area an hour's drive from Port Elizabeth and next door to Jeffreys Bay. As well as for its surfing, the bay is renowned for its beach, shells, Hobie cat sailing, and windsurfing, as well as some of the finest rock and surf angling on the east coast.

You can't hike many trails in the world where you can watch game, whales, otters and dolphins virtually at the same time, but the **Tsitsikamma National Park** is one of them. Africa's first marine national park comprises a narrow coastal plain bounded by cliffs and beaches and extends 5km/3 miles out to sea. In total, the park covers 66,500 hectares, of which over half is ocean. The park's rocky coastline stretches more than 80km/50 miles between two rivers, both named Groot (big), one in the Eastern Cape and the other in the Western Cape. It is a wonderland of quiet tidal pools, deep gorges, whisky-coloured rivers, exquisite beaches and evergreen forests, populated with small mammals and birds. Nature trails meander through dense forest and along the coast, the most famous being the five-day Otter Trail, which ends — or begins — at Nature's Valley in the Western Cape, and the inland five-day Tsitsikamma Trail, through forest on the northern side of the national N2 road. There is even a snorkelling and scuba underwater trail at Storms River Mouth. There are fully equipped log cabins (R230 a night for two people) self-contained 'oceanettes' for R230 a night for two people, and caravan and camp sites at R50 a night for two. There is a restaurant, shop and a swimming pool, tel (042) 541-1607.

Van Stadens Wild Flower Reserve is a 500ha/1235-acre reserve 35km/22 miles from Port Elizabeth, set up to protect and propagate indigenous flora and visitors are encouraged to explore and enjoy the extraordinary diversity of the natural fynbos, succulents and other plant life. There are picnic sites, as well as a nursery selling indigenous plants. Open daily from 8am to 5pm, tel (041) 955-5649.

EASTERN REGION

Aliwal North. This town on the banks of the Orange River is famed for its hot springs. The spa has large thermal pools, including two for children, as well as saunas, a gym and a treatment block with amenities for invalids. Close to the town, on the Kraai River, is the 1000-hectare Buffelspruit Nature Reserve.

Barkly East. This village in the Witteberg range is 1813m/5948ft above sea level and draws skiers to the slopes in winter. During the summer wild river trout fishing and stillwater fly-fishing are major attractions and there is a Trout Festival every March. There is a novel railway between Barkly East and Lady Grey; to descend, the train negotiates eight steep gradients in reverse. Excursions can be arranged for steam train enthusiasts. Enquire at the Town Clerk's office. In the local cemetery is the grave of Lord Kitchener's horse. There are large caves in the vicinity with well-preserved examples of Bushman rock art and there are several hiking trails in the nearby Drakensberg.

Bisho. Formerly the capital of the Ciskei when it was an independent 'homeland,' it is now the official capital of the Eastern Cape. The town was established in 1981, so there is little of note here and its main attraction is a gambling casino.

Bonza Bay. Some of the best waves on this part of the coast roll on to this broad beach off the lagoon at the Quinera River, which is reached by a paved walkway from the parking area. Two nearby nature reserves, Quinera and Nahoon, are noted for their birdlife.

Calgary Museum of Transport. 10km/6 miles from East London on the Stutterheim-East London road, this farm museum features antique carts and wagons, as well as a blacksmith's and wheelwright's shop. Open Wednesday to Sunday from 9am to 4pm. Caravan sites and hostel-type self-catering accommodation are available.

Coastal Resorts. South-west of East London are a number of coastal resorts popular with anglers, boardsailors and surfers. Not far away, Cove Rock, Fuller's Bay and Shelly Beach are all good fishing spots. Kidd's Beach has a sandy beach and tidal pool. Up the coast to the north-east is a string of coastal resorts set in almost unbelievable scenery. They include Gonubie, Rainbow Valley, Haga-Haga, Morgan's Bay and Kei Mouth. A fine lagoon is a major feature of the holiday resort of Gonubie, which is dominated by massive sand dunes. The river is navigable for small boats and the beach is safe for swimming. Rainbow Valley, on the far side of the Gonubie River has a private beach and all the facilities of a modern holiday resort. Morgan's Bay is one of the most charming and attractive coastal resorts in this area. The gateway to the Wild Coast is the resort of Kei Mouth where bathing, watersports and fishing can be enjoyed throughout the year. A pontoon ferry takes you across the Kei River to the beginning of the Wild Coast. For accommodation at resorts north-east and south-west of East London contact Tourism East London, tel (0431) 26015, fax (0431) 43-5091.

In Algoa Bay, off the mouth of the Coega River, is **Doddington Rock**, some 5km/3 miles south of Bird Island. It is misnamed after the English East Indiaman *Dodington* wrecked nearby on 17 July 1755 with the loss of 247 lives. 23 survivors lived on Bird Island for seven months before reaching the mainland on a vessel built from wreckage. Divers have recovered cannon, coins and many interesting artefacts from the wreck.

Fort Beaufort. Town 147km/91 miles north-west of East London and 80km/50 miles north of Grahamstown. The War of the Axe (1846) started here as a result of a dispute over an axe in a local shop and saw British and Xhosa fighting periodic wars on the frontier until the ninth and last in 1877–8.

West of Bisho, at Alice, is **Fort Hare University**, an institution that has produced not only several renowned South Africans, including Nobel Peace Prize winners President Nelson Mandela, Archbishop Desmond Tutu and the late Albert Luthuli, but several of Africa's other leaders, among them presidents Robert Mugabe of Zimbabwe, Sir Seretse Khama of Botswana, and Ntsu Mokhetle of Lesotho. The campus is today home to nearly 6000 students, and the De Beers Centenary Gallery displays a comprehensive collection of contemporary black South African art, tel (0404) 22011.

Great Fish River Reserve Complex. 34km/21 miles from Grahamstown, this vast 45,000-hectare conservation area incorporates the Andries Vosloo, Sam Knott and Double Drift Nature reserves which allows you to travel a circular route through all three. This is an enjoyable day drive and you can picnic on the banks of the Fish River. Game includes elephant, black and white rhino, buffalo, eland, hippo, leopard and some 2000 kudu. Photographic safaris, bird-watching, hiking and fishing are popular, and hunting is allowed in part of the reserve.

Hogsback, on a spur at the western end of the Amatola Mountain range, is perfect for walks along country lanes and through fragrant forests where arum lilies and other plants flower in the shadow of giant yellowwood, blackwood and wild lemon trees. It is a favourite place for nature lovers, photographers and hikers. Some of the walks take in beautiful waterfalls, the best known being the Madonna and Child, the Swallowtail, the Kettlespout, and the Bridal Veil.

About 28km/17 miles from Port Alfred is the 670-hectare **Kap River Nature Reserve** bounded to the south by the Indian Ocean, to the east by the Great Fish River and to the west by the Kap River. There is a 7km/4-mile nature trail and a canoe trail on the Kap River. There is a self-catering lodge sleeping 10 with swimming pool at R150 (£20/$33) a night, a fisherman's cottage at R50 a night for 4 people, or two camps sites at R25 a night, tel (0464) 25-0631.

King William's Town. 54km/34 miles north-west of East London, was founded as a mission station in 1825. Today it is the commercial centre of a thriving agricultural area. The Kaffrarian Museum in Albert Road concentrates on natural history and on the traditions and culture of the Xhosa and Khoisan people. It houses more than 30,000 specimens of African mammals, but its most famous exhibit is Huberta, a hippo whose wanderings between 1928 and 1931 enthralled the nation; the Missionary Museum in Berkeley Street focuses on the early missionary history of the region.

Lusikisiki is a village 45km/28 miles north of Port St Johns, in East Pondoland. The name is onomatopoeic and derives from the rustling sound made by reeds in the wind. 14km/9 miles to the south-east are the 148m/486ft high *Magwa Falls* which pour through a narrow chasm. The name is Xhosa and means 'wondrous'.

Mpongo Park Game Reserve. The park has more than 40 kinds of large game, including elephant, hippopotamus, rhino and giraffe, and prolific birdlife in its 1619 hectares. You can explore the park by car on a 25km/16-mile circular road, walk, or trot along narrow trails on horseback. Guided trails range from one-hour rambles to full-day hikes. Facilities include a restaurant, caravan and camp sites, picnic spots and a natural history museum, tel (04326) 739-1669.

Port Alfred. Flanked by miles of beaches, the town straddles the banks of the Kowie River and has a picturesque boat harbour and residential marina and offers first-class angling, boating, water-skiing, surfing, scuba-diving and bird-watching, as well as the Royal Port Alfred Golf Course, recognised as the finest on the coast. The 200-hectare Kowie River Nature Reserve starts 8km/5 miles north of the town and preserves rare cycads, rare blue duiker, and many bird species. There are hiking trails along the river bank. The Kowie Game Trail takes canoeists upriver for a night in the Bathurst Nature Reserve, with a hike back next day, and is a popular wilderness experience. Within easy driving distance is the Fish River Sun Casino.

Port Grosvenor is a bay on the Wild Coast near Lusikisiki, in Pondoland, and is named after the English East Indiaman *Grosvenor*, which was wrecked near here on 4 August 1782. Legend says this 729-ton sailing ship was carrying treasure, including the fabled Peacock Throne of the Great Moguls, when she went down but nothing more than a few gold and silver coins have, officially, been recovered by divers over the years. There is no port, though there was a harbour here from 1878 to 1885.

Port St Johns. The beauty and tranquillity of this little resort town's setting at the mouth of the Umzimvubu River has attracted drop-out beachcombers and artists alike, who give the place a restful, laid-back atmosphere. The town probably takes its name from the Portuguese galleon *Sao Joao*, which sank north of here in 1552. Two towering cliffs known as Port St John Gates dominate the town. There are three beaches — one within the Silaka Nature Reserve — where the fishing is excellent. On Second Beach, the only one where swimming is allowed, there are bungalows and camp sites. The subtropical area produces pawpaws, avocado pears, pecan and macadamia nuts, which you can buy from roadside vendors.

Queenstown. One of the odd features of this old frontier town is the hexagonal open square with six streets radiating from it. It was built like this to allow fast access from the central command post to surrounding defence points. The Frontier Museum and the Municipal Art Gallery are worth a visit. The ornamental Everitt Sunken Gardens feature ponds frequented by aquatic birds. Water sports are popular on the Bongola Dam. The J de Lange Game Reserve supports antelope and indigenous plants.

The village of **Rhodes** on the Bell River, 56km/35 miles north-east of Barkly East, draws ski-enthusiasts in winter when the slopes of nearby Ben MacDhui (3000m/9842ft high) are covered in snow. 25km/15 miles from Rhodes is Tiffendell Ski, an Alpine-type resort accessible only by 4x4 vehicle. Tiffendell is sited in the southern Drakensberg at around 2720m/8924ft, where the snow lasts longest. If there is not enough of the natural stuff between 30 May and 31 August Tiffendell makes its own. The slopes can handle 180 skiers a day, and a ski shop hires out gear. To keep rates affordable, the rooms are small but functional, the facilities rustic, and there is a choice between chalets and rooms in the lodge, sharing ablutions. In the evenings you can enjoy schnapps and glühwein in what is claimed to be the highest pub in South Africa — *Ice Station 2720*. Some of the highest fly-fishing in the country is also available on the Bell River. The surrounding district, with its clear mountain streams, is popular with trout fishermen, horse-riders and hikers alike, tel (011) 640-7416, fax (011) 485-2915.

Stutterheim. The first European settlers here were Berlin Missionary Society missionaries. There are walks and trails in the nearby Kologha and Kubusi forests. Rivers in the area are home to fat trout, so fly-fishing is a major recreation. South of the town is the grave of the famous Xhosa chief Sandile, who was killed in 1878 in the last frontier war.

Umngazi Mouth. According to Pondo history, when Faku, their legendary king, executed his enemies at Mlengana (Execution) Rock overlooking the Umngazi River valley, their blood (*igazi*) literally flowed down into the river. In 1842, Dick King watered his horses here during his historic 1000km/621-mile ride from Durban and Grahamstown. It is now the site of a pleasant holiday resort.

Umtata. 235km/146 miles north-east of East London, was the capital of the formerly independent Transkei before this 'homeland' territory was reincorporated into South Africa. It has a couple of worthwhile buildings, including the City Hall, the *Bunga* (Parliament) and the Anglican Cathedral. After you have seen these there is not much to do, apart from visiting the casino and playing golf or bowls. For handicrafts visit Izandla Pottery, Illinge Craft and the Ezibileni Industrial Centre. Luchaba and Nduli nature reserves, on the outskirts of town, are good for game and bird-watching.

The **Wild Coast** is a vast stretch of truly wild and often inaccessible rocky shoreline stretching nearly 300km/186 miles from the Great Kei River to the KwaZulu-Natal border. So few roads traverse this neglected region of the Transkei that wherever the rugged coast is accessible by road there are tiny resorts that are well worth the effort to reach. Heading towards Durban from the Kei Mouth are the resorts of *Trennerys* and *Seagulls*, at the Qolora River mouth, at the Naxo River is *Wavecrest*, and Mazeppa Bay is the location of the *Mazeppa Hotel*, whose palm tree-fringed beaches are popular for fishing, surfing and shell collecting. **Coffee Bay** is named after the coffee trees which once grew from beans from a shipwreck, and is easily accessible and popular with surfers, anglers and shell collectors. 8km/5 miles away is the prominent detached outcrop of pierced rock rising from the sea known as Hole in the Wall. Many ships have come to grief here, the most recent being the Greek cruise ship *Oceanos*, which went down south of here in 1991.

Further afield is the *Happy Haven Inn*, between the Kariega and Bushman rivers, has amenities which include squash, sauna, spa and spitzbath, and a fully equipped gym. Wheelchair-friendly. R125–225 (£16.65–30/$27.50–49.50) per person sharing per night B&B. Contact PO Box 199, Kenton-on-Sea 6191, tel (0464) 31-1802, fax (0464) 31-1803. The *Kowie Grand Hotel* is a two-star, country-style hotel in Port Alfred. Discounts for backpackers. Contact PO Box 1, Kowie West 6171, tel (0464) 41150, fax (0464) 43769.

Midway between East London and Port Elizabeth is the *Fish River Sun*, with an 18-hole Gary Player-designed golf course, a casino and slot machines. Contact PO Box 232, Port Alfred 6170, tel (0405) 66-1101, fax (0405) 66-1115. On the main coastal route between East London and Port Alfred and overlooking the Indian Ocean is the *Mpekweni Sun*. Accessible via a shuttle bus. Contact PO Box 2060, Port Alfred 6170, tel (0405) 66-1026, fax (0405) 66-1040.

Graham Protea Hotel, three-star, near Rhodes University, museums and historical monuments. R279 per person sharing B&B. Contact PO Box 316, Grahamstown 6140, tel (0461) 22324, fax (0461) 22424.

Grahamstown Municipal Caravan Park has caravan and tent sites, as well as rondavels and chalets. Reservations are not necessary, except during the Grahamstown Festival. R25 a day for caravan and camp sites, R60 for rondavels, and R125 for chalets. Contact PO Box 176, Grahamstown 6140, tel (0461) 30-6072. Grahamstown also has at least 50 B&B places ranging from R65 to R150 per person. B&B and self-catering accommodation on game farms, and in hiking huts from R25 to R100 (£13.35/$22) per person. Contact Festnest Accommodation Agency, tel/fax (0461) 29720.

Drostdy Hotel, three-star, R225–325 for an *en-suite* double room. 30 Church Street, Graaff-Reinet, PO Box 400, Graaff-Reinet 6280, tel (0491) 22161, fax (0491) 24582. *Karoopark Guest House*, B&B R219 a double. 81 Caledon Street, central Graaff-Reinet, PO Box 388, Graaff-Reinet 6280, tel (0491) 22557, fax (0491) 25730. The grand dame of Cradock hostelries is the *Victoria Manor* in Voortrekker Street, which has been around for 150 years. R200 (£26.65/$44) per couple sharing, R80 per person single. Contact PO Box 848, Cradock 5880, tel (0481) 71-1650, fax (0481) 71-1164. The *1904 Guest House* has a Victorian atmosphere and is close to town and opposite the Sports Complex and caravan park. R80 per person B&B. Contact 98 Stockenstroom Street, Cradock 5880, tel (0481) 5185 or 2551. The *Municipal Caravan Park* costs R17 a day for the site, plus R7 a day for adults and R4 for children. Contact PO Box 24, Cradock 5880, tel (0481) 3443, fax (0481) 71-1421.

The *Haga-Haga Hotel* and self-catering cabanas is 70km/44 miles from East London on the way to the Wild Coast. The hotel's Saturday night seafood extravaganza is the highlight of the week. DB&B at reasonable rates. Contact Private Bag X610, East London 5200, tel/fax (04372) 6302. *Umngazi River Bungalows* has miles of unspoilt beaches and a meandering river, plus tennis, water-skiing, mountain-biking, and five walking trails. Full board costs R160 per person a day to R205. Contact PO Box 75, Port St Johns 4830, tel (0475) 44-1115/6/8/9. The *Wild Coast Sun* is near the border with KwaZulu-Natal and is set on a glorious stretch of coast, two hour's drive from Durban. The hotel claims to have one of the most modern casino layouts in the world, with 34 tables offering American roulette, blackjack, punto banco, American poker, Sic Bo, a Wheel of Fortune, 800 slot machines and an electronic Bingo lounge with 94 consoles. There is also a magnificent 18-hole championship golf course. Contact central reservations in Johannesburg, tel (011) 780-7800, fax (011) 780-7457.

Backpacker accommodation:

Backpackers Barn, 4 Trollope Street, Grahamstown 6139, tel (0461) 29720, fax (0461) 29720.

Buccaneers Retreat Backpackers, Cintsa West Road, Cintsa 5275, PO Box 14, Cintsa 5275, tel (0481) 38-3012.

Hamburg Oyster Lodge, Main Street, Hamburg 5641, tel (0405) 88-1020, fax (0405) 88-1020.

Port St John's Backpackers, c/o PO Box 1216, Margate 4276.

Four Winds Backpackers, Coffee Bay, PO Box 154, Umtata 5100, tel (0475) 44-2007.

Caravans:

Addo Elephant National Park, tel (0426) 40-0556.
Aliwal Spa Holiday Resort, tel (0551) 2951/3008.
Boesmansriviermond, tel (0464) 81227.
Cannon Rocks Holiday Resort, tel (046) 654-0043.
Medolino, tel (0464) 41651.
Palm Springs Holiday Resort, tel (0432) 81-1901.
Urquhart Park, tel (0491) 22136.
Van Stadens River Mouth Resorts, tel (05332) 776-1059.

If you are in Grahamstown try the alternative coffee shop, *Cosmic Café*, the purple shop in Hill Street, open Monday to Sunday 10am until late. There is pub fare in the *Rat & Parrot*, 59 New Street, open Monday to Saturday midday till late, tel (0461) 25002; and *The Cock House* offers home-cooked fare with a cordon bleu touch, 10 Market Street, tel (0461) 31-1295.

In East London the beachfront Esplanade boasts about 16 restaurants and places of entertainment, including a Health & Racket Club and the *Numbers Dance Club*, which offers the very latest in disco and can jam in 1200 ravers — and often does. July in South Africa has become synonymous with the *Grahamstown National Arts Festival*, which has grown across cultural, social and political borders to become an important influence on South African arts and culture and the country's most prestigious showcase for top creative talent. If you are in Grahamstown for the festival, musts include the flea market at Village Green, which not only has good buys but an astonishing assortment of good food, and the pub at the Settlers' Hotel, where performers and fans mingle.

Dance revues, music extravaganzas, films, and all the Las Vegas-type entertainment usual in gaming complexes goes on virtually non-stop at Sun International's *Amatola Sun Resort*, near King William's Town, tel (0401) 91111, fax (0401) 91330; *Fish River Sun Casino & Resort*, tel (0405) 66-1101, fax (0405) 66-1115, and *Mpekweni Sun Marine Resort*, tel (0405) 66-1026, fax (0405) 66-1040, both at Port Alfred.

SPORT AND RECREATION

Port Elizabeth is a sporting enthusiast's city and is often called 'Sport Elizabeth' because of its excellent facilities. The city has two premier stadiums, St George's Park Cricket Oval and rugby ground Boet Erasmus Stadium. The stadium is the only one in the world with a bar in a steam locomotive perched on top of a stand. East London international venues are the Jan Smuts Athletics Stadium and the Buffalo Park Sports

Ground and there is also a Grand Prix motor racing circuit. There are numerous clubs throughout the province for bowls, golf, tennis, yachting, athletics, cycling and seasonal sports such as hockey, cricket, and soccer, which is played most weekends from March to October. Most clubs welcome visitors. Algoa Bay has 40km/25 miles and the East London area even more stretches of magnificent beaches which, with their wonderful warm water and fair breezes, are excellent for sailing, surfing, fishing, diving, and all beach and watersports.

Sailing. Algoa Bay is world renowned in sailing circles. There are predominantly two prevailing winds — the south-westerly, which represents 60 per cent of the prevailing winds in the bay, and the south easterly. Both the Port Elizabeth Beach Yacht Club, tel (041) 53-3449, and the Algoa Bay Yacht Club, tel (041) 55-4058, welcome visiting saltwater enthusiasts, as does the East London Yacht Club, the finishing line for the annual Vasco da Gama Yacht Race between Durban and East London, tel (0431) 22278.

Fishing. The concrete dolosse around the Port Elizabeth bay area and the harbour breakwater offer good novice angling. You can get a permit to fish from the harbour wall from Portnet for R2 (25p/45 cents), tel (041) 507-2663. More experienced anglers should try Cape Recife Nature Reserve. Other fishing spots are the Swartkops, Sundays, Maitland — for the prized white steenbras — Van Stadens and Gamtoos rivers, which are all within an hour's drive. Seal Point, the western extremity of Cape St Francis, is claimed by locals to be the best fishing spot in South Africa, and this certainly holds true for yellowtail game-fish, which arrive in huge shoals in summer. Deep sea, rock and surf and river fishing are all excellent and estuary fishing in particular is considered to be the finest in the country. Contact the *Eastern Province Herald* angling correspondent for more information on fishing spots and permits, tel (041) 504-7911/55-5556. For deep-sea game fishing, tel (041) 53-3050/43-2403. The dream destination for wildwater fly fishermen is the north-eastern area of the province around Barkly East, Rhodes, and Maclear, where fish grow to record size in the pristine headwaters of the trout rivers and streams. Many anglers compare Barkly East to Jackson Hole in Wyoming, Cressy in Tasmania, and Smithers in British Columbia. Contact the Barkly Wild Trout Association, PO Box 291, Rhodes 5582, tel (04542), ask for 9203.

Diving. Both Port Elizabeth and East London have good shore and wreck diving, with beautiful reefs, wrecks, and a colourful variety of sea life. Large schools of dolphins sport virtually daily in this area. In the protected warm waters of Algoa Bay reefs and pinnacles range in depth from 10m/33ft to 30m/99ft, especially around Cape Recife. Vis is usually good and up to 30m has been recorded. Diving sites are full of variety. Devil's Reef, St Croix Islands, Thunderbolt Reef, Philips Reef, and the Holland Reef, in the Sardinia Bay Nature Reserve, are popular dives and the area is a graveyard of wrecks. Contact Stingray Divers, tel (041) 53-1619; Ocean Divers, tel (041) 55-6536; and Scubadventures, tel (041) 51-5328. At East London about 150 ships have been wrecked within a 5km/3 mile radius of Buffalo Harbour in the past 150 years. The only visible wreck is the *Orient*, which grounded in 1907 off the beach that now bears its name. There are plenty of wrecks along the spectacular 64km/40 mile Shipwreck Trail stretching along glorious white beaches and unspoilt Ciskei coastline from Kiwane to Mpekweni, between Port Alfred and East London. You can camp on the beach, fish, boardsail, surf, canoe, spearfish and scuba dive along the way. If you would like to do some wreck diving contact Pollock's Sports Shop (you will need to show a certificate of competency), tel (0431) 58586 or Wayne's Diving World, tel (0431) 54194. Turquoise Horizon offers Great White Shark cage diving, tel (0431) 47-2476.

Surfing. Surf's up at many spots along the coast, but if you like hanging 10 you will want to hit the spots which American Bruce Brown immortalised in his cult surfing film *Endless Summer.* These are St Francis Bay and Jeffreys Bay, an easy hour's drive from Port Elizabeth and a magnet for surfers from around the world looking for the perfect wave. The best time of the year to find these waves is between May and August. That is when winter low-pressure systems create a groundswell around Seal Point and Shark Point at Cape St Francis, before rolling round the headland into St Francis Bay and Jeffreys Bay where the prevailing off-shore south-westerly wind sculpts the waves into perfect surfing formations. The eight top surfing spots at Jeffreys Bay, in geographical order, are Kitchen Windows, Magnatubes, Boneyards, Supertubes, Impossibles, Tubes, Point and Albatross. If you are not all that experienced, try the Point; waves on Supertubes can top 4m/13ft, so you need confidence and experience to ride them. None of the others is recommended for beginners. J-Bay has been pulling in board riders for more than 30 years and at Surf Camp, just across the road from Supers, you'll find surfers who look as though they have no plans to return home.

Windsurfing. You have three windsurfing options in Port Elizabeth: flat water river windsurfing at Dufour Park, on the Swartkops River, and in the bay at Hobie Beach, just off Marine Drive, and wilder windsurfing at Noordhoek, 8km/5 miles from Hobie Beach, which is a venue exposed to ocean swells and usually described as 'awesome.'

Golf. Golf clubs in Port Elizabeth and East London welcome visitors. Contact the Humewood Golf Club, along Marine Drive, Summerstrand, tel (041) 53-1016, or the Walmer Country Club, along Victoria Drive, Walmer, tel (041) 51-1613 for a game. Golfers say Humewood's challenging course is on a par with top championship links in Britain. Crowned plovers are residents and their nests are thoughtfully tagged with red flags so that you can avoid them. The Eagles Golf Driving Range, in Perrot Avenue, Humewood, caters for all golfers, from beginners to professionals. The range is open Monday to Sunday from 8am to 8pm, tel (041) 33-4743. The East London Golf Club, dates back to 1893 and is one of South Africa's oldest, tel (0431) 35-1365. Others include the Alexander Golf Club, tel (0431) 46-3646, and the West Bank Golf Club, tel (0431) 31-1523. The magnificent 18-hole course at the Wild Coast Sun, the only one in Africa designed by Robert Trent-Jones Junior, is internationally renowned as one of the most challenging and scenically beautiful in the world.

Hiking. You do not have to go far to enjoy a walk or short hike. There are lots of trails within the city limits in coastal and valley surroundings. They are well marked and range from the 2km Aloe Hiking Trail, in the Swartkops Aloe Reserve, between Amsterdamhoek and Bluewater Bay, three short trails in the 127-hectare Maitland Nature Reserve, to the 8km/5-mile Sacramento Hiking Trail, which is a round trip coastal walk through the Schoemakerskop-Sardinia Bay Nature Reserve. The Eastern Cape branch of the Wilderness Leadership School will take you where there are no footprints or worn footpaths to follow and give you a rare opportunity to experience nature as the Bushmen saw it when the region was a vast, unspoilt wilderness. No hiking experience or special equipment is necessary. Transport, equipment and food are provided. The cost is R375 (£50/$82.50) per person for the weekend, or R125 per day, tel (041) 36-1224.

The *Strandloper Hiking Trail* is a three-day, 65km/40 mile hike along the beach between Kei Mouth and East London, retracing the footsteps of the primitive strandlopers (beachcombers), the early inhabitants of this coast. Hutted accommodation is available. Contact The Wildlife Society, tel (0431) 43-9409.

Otter Trail. This is *the* trail as far as South African hikers are concerned, so much so that it is booked up at least a year in advance. The trail is a five-day hike in the Tsitsikamma National Park, on the rugged Indian Ocean coastline. Make sure you are fit if you take on this incredible trail, which hugs an often precipitous coast most of the way. It weaves through beautiful indigenous forests, crossing ravines, fords, rivers and streams. The furthest you will walk in a day is about 14km/9 miles; other days are shorter but usually much steeper. You have to carry everything you need — food and clothes — so take the bare necessities. Book as far in advance as possible, certainly more than a year. The trail costs R200 (£26.65/$44) per person. Contact the National Parks Board, tel (012) 343-1991 or (021) 22-2810. The 57km/35 miles Tsitsikamma and the 46km/29 miles Otter Trails form a loop between Storms River Mouth and Nature's Valley, with the Otter running along the coast and the Tsitsikamma taking you inland through subtropical forest. The entire loop takes 10 days, but you can hike each trail separately. For permits for the Tsitsikamma Trail, tel (0423) 51180.

The *Amatola Hiking Trail* is one of the toughest trails in the country. It traverses a wild scenic area of primaeval forests, waterfalls, valleys and mountains, rich in Xhosa and Settler history. It takes six days to complete the 105km/65-miles — although there are shorter options — so attempt it only if you are a fit and experienced hiker. An astounding diversity of wildlife and birds adds to the attractions of this trail. Lodges, log cabins and Xhosa huts provide basic accommodation, tel (0401) 92171.

The *Compassberg Hiking Trails* are in the Sneeuberg mountains on a farm of 6000 hectares in the Middelburg district. The two, three, or four-day routes take you over the foothills of Compassberg (2502m/8209ft). Overnight in a base camp, a rustic cottage in the shadows of the Compassberg; a stone-built shed; or a big farmhouse, for R25 a night per person. Contact The Valley, PO Box 205, Middelburg 5900, tel (04924) 22418.

The *Gonaqua Hiking Trail* is 65km/40 miles west of Port Elizabeth, in the Longmore plantation, and follows the ancient footpaths of the Gonaqua tribe in the Elandsberg. There is a two-day circular route of 30km/19 miles or 20km/12 miles. The *Hogsback Hiking Trail* is 35km/22 miles north-west of King William's Town, in the Hogsback plantation. The trail follows the grassy slopes of Hogsback Mountain and is a two-day circular route of 36km/22 miles. For organised hikes around the Port Elizabeth area, with all equipment provided, and sleepovers in mountain log cabins contact Nomads Adventures, tel (041) 53-1387.

Mountain Biking. Port Elizabeth has an active Fat Tracks Mountain Bicycle Club, tel (041) 33-1921, which with the Municipality has marked out riding tracks within the city limits, as well as in the surrounding forests. Trails vary in difficulty from beginners to advanced. Among them are the *Longmore Forest Mountain Bike Trail* in an area covering 20,000 hectares of forestry land about 63km/39 miles from Port Elizabeth. Three trails suitable for intermediate-level riders can be ridden separately or together as one big loop. *Baakens River Mountain Bike Trail* is 12km/7.5 miles long and most of it is suitable for beginners. The 22km/14 mile circular *Zwartkops Mountain Bike Trail* traverses the 850-hectare Zwartkops Valley Nature Reserve, with technical sections up and down the escarpment where beginners are advised to walk. Mountain bikers are welcome to explore the plateau section of Van Stadens Wild Flower Reserve, 35km/22 miles from Port Elizabeth. Flat gravel roads and jeep tracks perfect for mountain bike exploration make the area as a whole ideal for novice bikers and family cycling outings.

Hunting. Various wildlife conservation farms in the Eastern Cape offer hunting packages. Accommodation varies from comfortable thatched chalets and hunting lodges to tented safari camps with outdoor boma dining areas. Bow-hunting, trophy hunts, game-bird shooting and photographic and bird-watching safaris are also available. Contact Cambedoo Safaris, tel (0491) 91-0503; Patrick Grewar Safaris, tel (041) 33-1580; Karoo Fun Safaris, tel (0536612) ask for 1122; Shumba Safaris, tel (041) 51-6516; and Schotia Safaris, tel (042) 851-1436. Southern Cross Safaris has an easily accessible hunting area offering more than 30 species of game, including bontebok, blesbok, bushbuck, grysbok, Vaal rhebok, kudu, springbok, and black wildebeest. There is also good bird hunting. Accommodation is provided in a traditional East African-style tented safari camp. The best hunting is from March to November, although there is hunting throughout the year. Contact PO Box 12, Mortimer 5870, Eastern Cape, tel (0486) 606, fax (0486) 787.

The Eastern Cape has some of the best grey-wing partridge shooting in the world. Dave Walker runs Gateshead shoots over high altitude rough country in the southern Drakensberg, near Rhodes. Greywing numbers here are larger than normal and coveys of up to 32 birds are not unknown. Horseback shoots are organised for up to six guns in the hunting season from June to the end of August. Only over-and-under and side-by-side 12-bore shotguns are permitted and you must have a valid hunting licence, which can be arranged through your hosts. Contact Gateshead Lodges, PO Box 14, Barkly East 5580, tel (04542) 7211 or 7502, fax (04542) 322.

Canoeing. The Eastern Cape branch of the Wilderness Leadership School runs three-day wilderness canoeing trails led by experienced guides. No experience or special equipment is necessary. Transport, backpacks, camping equipment and food are provided by the school and the all-in cost for the three days is R300 (£40/$66) per person, tel (041) 36-1224. The Great Fish River Canoe Trail is a two-day trip above Cradock. The Great Fish River has fast-flowing water, making paddling easy, with mostly easy Grade 1 and 2 rapids. A moderate level of fitness is required. Accommodation is in either chalets or tents. Typical African river birdlife, Karoo countryside and natural history. Contact Honey Guide, PO Box 5452, Walmer 6070, tel (041) 33-1391, fax (041) 51-1357.

Bird-watching. Port Elizabeth has abundant birdlife which you can see in places such as Settlers Park, Cape Recife Nature Reserve, and the Zwartkops Estuary, where you will see large flocks of flamingoes. The Eastern Cape Wild Bird Society welcomes you to join them on their outings to Settlers Park on the first Saturday of each month at 8.30am. Daybreak early-bird and sunset bird-watching tours are also available, tel (041) 55-7715.

Horse Racing. Port Elizabeth's major racecourses are Arlington, home of the St Andrew's Racing Club, and Fairview, headquarters of the Turf Club. Racing takes place every Friday afternoon. East Cape Racing Club, tel (041) 72-1859, fax (041) 72-1032.

About 90km/56 miles along the coastal road to Port Alfred, is the village of Wesley where a single complex contains Kei Carpets, Wesley Crafts, and Bira Crafts and is well worth a detour, tel (0405) 77-1024. At Alicedale, 52km/32 miles west of Grahamstown, you can visit the Jan Paul Barnard mohair factory where spinning and weaving in the age-old way are still practised, tel (042) 831-1015.

In Port Elizabeth:

Ambulance, 10177.
Fire Brigade, (041) 55-1555.
Police, (041) 34-3434.
National Sea Rescue Institute (NSRI), (041) 55-6011.
Weather Forecast, Eastern Cape Region, tel (041) 52-4242.
Gay and Lesbian Organisation of the Cape, tel (041) 52-2921.
Gay Helpline, tel (041) 335-6426.
Gay Men's Social Group, tel (041) 55-7661.
PR Gay and Lesbian Organisation, tel Dawn (041) 55-8287.

In East London:

Police Flying Squad, (0431) 10111.
Ambulance, 10177.
Sea Rescue Services, (0431) 22555.
Fire Brigade, (0431) 21212.
Life Line, (0431) 22000.

TOURIST INFORMATION

Tourism Port Elizabeth, Donkin Lighthouse Building, Donkin Hill, Port Elizabeth 6001. PO Box 357, Port Elizabeth 6006, tel (041) 52-1315, fax (041) 55-2564, 24-hour tourist information on Voice Mail, tel (041) 56-0773, e-mail pepa@iafrica.com, web page http://www.pecc.gov.za

Tourism East London, Old Library Building, 35 Argyle Street, East London 5201. PO Box 533, East London 5200, tel (0431) 26015, fax (0431) 43-5091.

Eastern Cape Tourism Board, Bisho, tel (0401) 95-2115, fax (0401) 92756; Western Region, tel (041) 55-7761; Central Region, tel (0431) 47-4730; Wild Coast Region, tel (0471) 31-2885.

Aliwal North, tel (0551) 2951, fax (0551) 41307.

Amatola Region, tel (0431) 21251, fax (0431) 43-9050.

Barkly East, tel (04542) ask for 73, fax (04542) ask for 350.

Bathurst, tel (0464) 25-0832.

Cradock, tel (0481) 2383, fax (0481) 71-1421.

Fort Beaufort, tel (04634) 32094, fax (04634) 31841.

Graaff-Reinet, tel (0491) 24248, fax (0491) 24319.

Grahamstown, tel (0461) 23241, fax (0461) 23266.

Hogsback, tel (045) 962-1024, fax (045) 962-1058.

Jeffreys Bay, tel (0423) 93-2588, fax (0423) 93-2227.

Kei Mouth/Haga Hagu/Morgan's Bay, tel (043272) ask for 4, fax (043272) ask for 180.

King William's Town, tel (0433) 23391, fax (0433) 22646.

Nieu-Bethesda, tel (04923) 712.

Port Alfred, tel (0464) 41235, fax (0464) 24-4139.

Rhodes, tel (04542) ask for Rhodes 9002.

St Francis Bay/Cape St Francis, tel/fax (0423) 94-0675.

Somerset East, tel/fax (0424) 31333/32079.

Umtata, tel (0471) 31-2885, fax (0471) 31-2887.

Wild Coast, tel (0471) 31-2785/6.

National Hotel Association, fax (041) 55-2779.

Western Cape

Table Mountain

The Western Cape is a province of rugged mountain ranges and broad, fertile valleys watered by fountains and rivers giving bright life to verdant pastures and bountiful vineyards — a region with more than a hint of the Mediterranean about it. The entire coastline from Tiekiesbaai on the West Coast to the eastern boundary beyond Plettenberg Bay and Nature's Valley is characterised by splendid rocky promontories, sheltered bays, and crisp, clean, uncrowded beaches. The province covers an area of 129,386sq km/49,956sq miles and supports a population of more than 4 million people — a figure that annually swells by at least a million as hordes of upcountry holiday-makers descend in the South African summer to enjoy the Winelands, the wild West Coast, and the scenic Garden Route, last haven of both dense indigenous forest and

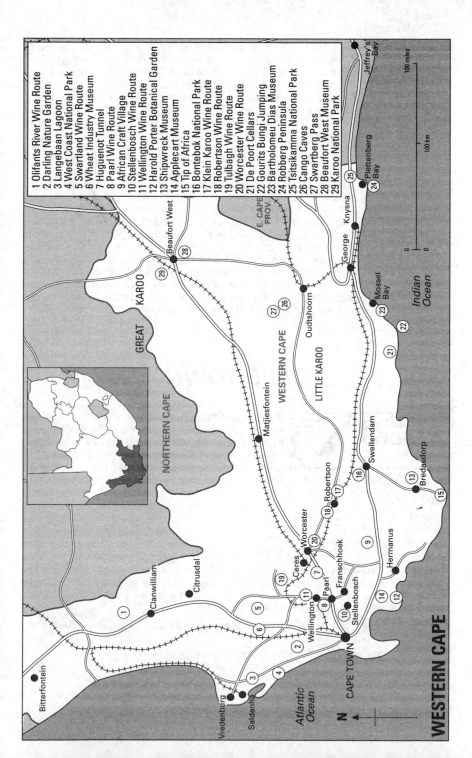

WESTERN CAPE

1 Olifants River Wine Route
2 Darling Nature Garden
3 Langebaan Lagoon
4 West Coast National Park
5 Swartland Wine Route
6 Wheat Industry Museum
7 Huguenot Tunnel
8 Paarl Wine Route
9 African Craft Village
10 Stellenbosch Wine Route
11 Wellington Wine Route
12 Harold Porter Botanical Garden
13 Shipwreck Museum
14 Applecart Museum
15 Tip of Africa
16 Bontebok National Park
17 Klein Karoo Wine Route
18 Robertson Wine Route
19 Tulbagh Wine Route
20 Worcester Wine Route
21 De Poort Cellars
22 Gourits Bungi Jumping
23 Bartholomeu Dias Museum
24 Robberg Peninsula
25 Tsitsikamma National Park
26 Cango Caves
27 Swartberg Pass
28 Beaufort West Museum
29 Karoo National Park

an uncurbed African elephant herd. Cape Town, the province's capital, is fondly known as the Mother City and is a major tourist centre in its own right, with its overlooming Table Mountain, the Victoria & Alfred Waterfront complex on its doorstep and the, literally, 101 beaches that surround the Peninsula on which this halfway house to India has sat for more than three centuries as the renowned 'Tavern of the Seas'. It is an area nonpareil,and everyone who visits falls in love with its charms. *Harper's Travel Magazine* rates Cape Town the world's third best tourist destination after San Francisco and Vancouver.

Certainly, few cities in the world enjoy such a dramatic setting between mountain and two flanking oceans. The Peninsula, which stretches 51km/32 miles south of the city to towering Cape Point, is about 10km/6 miles wide, yet within this tiny area is a spectacular floral kingdom whose plant life delights and draws botanists from all over the world. The region up the West Coast in spring is an even greater magnet when the veld is garlanded by wild flowers. The Western Cape is the only province with a largely white National Party (NP) majority in its provincial parliament, a situation that is something of a political anachronism in the new South Africa. Even so, it has a stable administration that has seen the province emerge as an economic front-runner, with a better track record than most of the other regions of the country. Tourism is the best performer as both a revenue generator and a job creator, and has grown by more than 50% in two years. The natural beauty of the Western Cape and the astonishing diversity of its ecology has made the area a prime destination for, among others, increasing numbers of the world's eco-tourists. For the rest — enjoy.

CAPE TOWN

Getting Around

Arrival and Departure. Cape Town International Airport is 22km/14 miles from the city centre, on the Cape Flats, south of Parow, tel (021) 934-0407. Bus services: *Airport Shuttle Service*, tel (021) 794-2772; *Intercape Shuttle Service* departs from inner court Cape Town Station, tel (021) 386-4444.

Taxis:

> *Rikki's Taxis*, tel (021) 23-4888;
> *Bantry Taxis*, tel 082 770-1000;
> *Marine Taxi Hire*, tel (021) 434-0430;
> Unicab Radio Taxis, tel (021) 448-1720.

Some Cape Town taxi drivers are masters of the art of the 'broken meter'. By law you have a right to insist on the driver's name and identification being displayed; the number allotted to the taxis being clearly visible; and a working meter that is clearly visible. You can also demand a detailed receipt.

Car hire. There are dozens of car hire companies operating in the Cape Town area, among them:

> *ACE Car Hire*, tel (021) 782-6804, fax (021) 782-3316;
> *Adelphi Rent a Car*, tel (021) 439-6144, fax (021) 439-5093;
> *Atlantic Car Hire*, tel (021) 439-1698;
> *Avis*, tel (021) 24-1177, fax (021) 23-3601;
> *Budget*, tel (021) 439-9670, fax (021) 439-9822;
> *Cape Car Hire*, tel (021) 683-2441, fax (021) 683-2443;

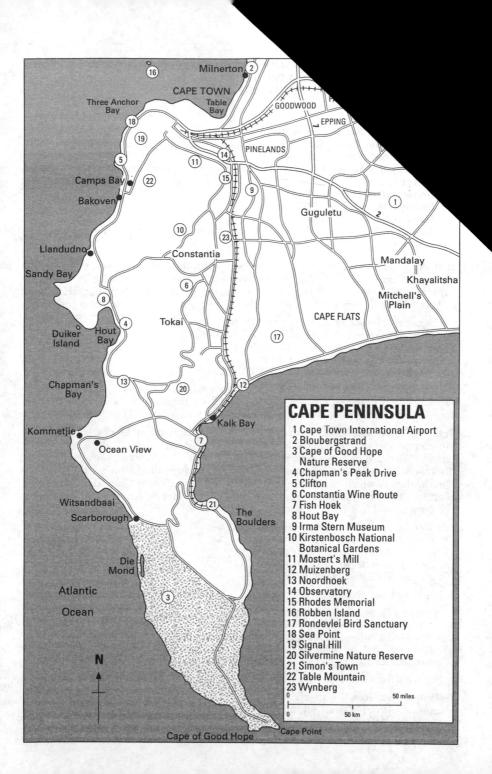

CAPE PENINSULA

1 Cape Town International Airport
2 Bloubergstrand
3 Cape of Good Hope
  Nature Reserve
4 Chapman's Peak Drive
5 Clifton
6 Constantia Wine Route
7 Fish Hoek
8 Hout Bay
9 Irma Stern Museum
10 Kirstenbosch National
   Botanical Gardens
11 Mostert's Mill
12 Muizenberg
13 Noordhoek
14 Observatory
15 Rhodes Memorial
16 Robben Island
17 Rondevlei Bird Sanctuary
18 Sea Point
19 Signal Hill
20 Silvermine Nature Reserve
21 Simon's Town
22 Table Mountain
23 Wynberg

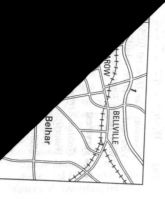

(021) 434-5560;
021) 64-2696;
fax (02211) 28354.

4365;
y quarter of an hour, and from Sea Point

, departures from Mitchell's Plain Town

leparturers from inner court at Cape Town

Rail. An excellent rail system links the city with other towns in the Peninsula, the Western Cape, and the rest of the country. Express trains take 25 hours to Johannesburg from Cape Town, 36 hours from Cape Town to Durban, and 21 hours to Port Elizabeth. Timetables and tickets in the main hall of Cape Town station.

Mainline reservations, tel (021) 405-3871/3581.
Mainline passenger services, tel (021) 405-4033/4213.
Blue Train reservations, tel (021) 405-2672.
Rovos Rail, tel (021) 21-4020, fax (021) 21-4022.
Union Limited Steam Rail Tours, tel (021) 405-4391.

Fun train rides: Epping Market Choo-Choo, tel (021) 64-2447. Train rides every second Sunday of the month at 11am, 1pm and 3pm. Biggsy's, breakfast train between Cape Town and Simon's Town station five times a day, tel (021) 683-6020.

Sea. The Ben Schoeman, Sturrock, Robinson and Duncan Docks in Table Bay Harbour are built on reclaimed land and berth small ships daily. There is a container terminal at the Ben Schoeman Dock, and Sturrock and Robinson are modern dry docks which handle ships under repair. Large cargo ships and passenger liners use the Duncan Dock, which is also home to the Royal Cape Yacht Club. Boat and yacht charters: Daily trips, including sunset cruises, are operated by several boat companies. For trips from Table Bay:

Teachers Spirit of Adventure, tel (021) 418-2989;
Condor Charters, tel (021) 448-5612;
Le Tigre Charters, tel (021) 419-7746;
Sealink Tours, tel (021) 25-4480;
Waterfront Charters, tel (021) 25-4292.

For trips from Hout Bay Harbour:

Bahari Charters, tel (021) 689-1504;
Circe Launches, tel (021) 790-1040;
Drumbeat Charters, tel (021) 438-9208;
Illusive Misty Pearl, tel (021) 64-2203;
Neptunes, tel (021) 782-3889.

For trips from Kalk Bay try Captain Rob's Tours, tel (021) 788-5261.

Helicopter Services. Civair Helicopters, scenic tours and general charter from the Victoria & Alfred Waterfront, tel (021) 419-5182; Court Helicopters have helicopter tours of the Atlantic Coast and the Peninsula, and they can also take you to wine tastings, and on visits to the Bushmen of Kagga Kamma. Flights depart and land at the V&A Waterfront seven days a week during daylight hours and, depending on availability, you can choose your own timetable, tel (021) 25-2966/75.

Other air flips and trips:

Atlantic Air Services, tel (021) 934-6619;
Chart Air, tel (0226) 72327;
Flamingo Flights, tel (021) 790-1010;
Sport Helicopters, tel (021) 434-4444;
Waterfront Heli-Pad, tel (021) 419-5907.

Bikes. If you want to do your sight-seeing on two wheels, *Rent-A-Bike* (part of Rikki's Taxis) hires out at R6 an hour, R30 (£4/$6.60) a day and R55 a weekend, tel (021) 786-2136; *Rent 'n Ride* in Mouille Point hires out bikes for R30 for 4 hours, R50 a day, or R40 a day if you take it for a week, tel (021) 434-1122; and *Bikeabout Cycle Tours*, tel (021) 531-3274, will take you on a full day's tour of the Peninsula down to Cape Point for R140 (£18.65/$30.80), including lunch, and a 3-day ride through the Cedarberg Wilderness Area for R750.

 Accommodation can be difficult to find during the South African summer holiday months, especially in December and January. Captour has an emergency booking service for personal callers at the Tourist Rendezvous Travel Centre, Adderley Street, Cape Town, tel (021) 418-5214, fax (021) 418-5227. Open seven days a week. The Guest House Hotline at Cape Town International Airport will also reserve accommodation for you. The further you go from the city centre the more budget-friendly the prices become and most caravan and camping grounds are on the outskirts of the city.

Orient-Express Hotels runs what is undoubtedly one of the great hotels of the world, the five-star *Mount Nelson*, 76 Orange Street, Gardens 8000. Central Reservations, tel (021) 23-1050, fax (021) 23-1060.

Excellent hotels with a wide range of facilities in medium to upper price brackets make the V&A Waterfront a good base for trips throughout the Peninsula and surrounding area. The *Cape Grace Hotel* is inspired by such great European hotels as the Amstel Inter-Continental, Amsterdam, and The Gritti Palace, Venice. All 92 rooms have views of Table Mountain, the yacht basin, or the working harbour. With the rand-dollar/pound exchange rate being what it is even the most financially pinched budget traveller can afford at least one night of luxury at this hotel — or any of the other up-market hotels for that matter. You can get a double or twin bedroom for R650 per person sharing a night or a three-bedroomed suite for R2000 (£267/$440) per person. Children under the age of 12 sharing with adults stay free. You also get a bountiful breakfast for R45 per person. Contact PO Box 51387, Waterfront 8002, tel (021) 410-7100, fax (021) 419-7622. Central reservations, PO Box 2536, Parklands 2121, Gauteng, tel (011) 880-1675, fax (011) 880-3282.

The *Table Bay* is a Sun International five-star, seven-storey Victorian-style hotel. Each room has a sea or Table Mountain view, from R1300 (£173/$286) per double. As well as all the usual up-market amenities there are even boats for residents, tel (021) 419-8291, fax (021) 21-6042.

Others at V&A include:

Breakwater Lodge, which is close to 15 bars, 10 cinemas, 28 restaurants and more than 200 shops, from R115 per night. Portswood Road, tel (021) 406-1911, fax (021) 406-1070, toll-free 0800 23 32 55;

City Lodge, corner of Alfred and Dock roads, two-star, from R125 (£16.65/$27.50) a night, tel (021) 419-9450;

Portswood Hotel, four-star with a nautical flavour, R145 per person a night sharing.

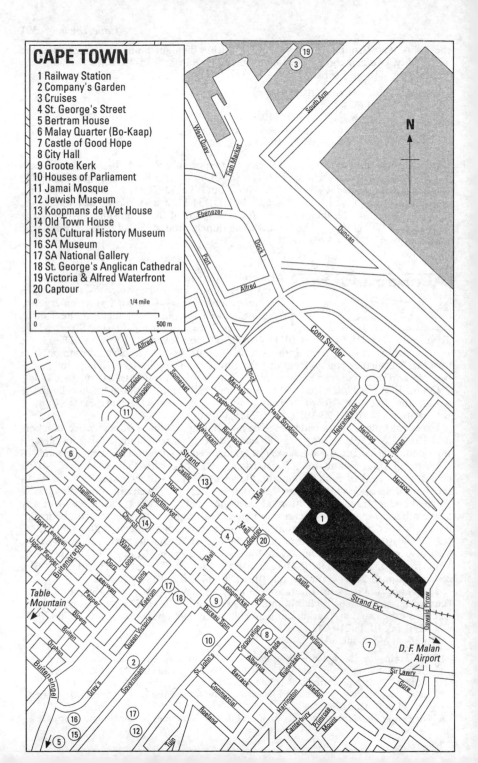

CAPE TOWN

1 Railway Station
2 Company's Garden
3 Cruises
4 St. George's Street
5 Bertram House
6 Malay Quarter (Bo-Kaap)
7 Castle of Good Hope
8 City Hall
9 Groote Kerk
10 Houses of Parliament
11 Jamai Mosque
12 Jewish Museum
13 Koopmans de Wet House
14 Old Town House
15 SA Cultural History Museum
16 SA Museum
17 SA National Gallery
18 St. George's Anglican Cathedral
19 Victoria & Alfred Waterfront
20 Captour

0   1/4 mile
0   500 m

N

Table
Mountain

D. F. Malan
Airport

The Quarterdeck restaurant is housed in the Old Convict Station building, and is a national monument. Contact PO Box 50028, Waterfront 8002, tel (021) 418-3281, fax (021) 419-7570;

Victoria & Alfred Hotel, Pier Head, four-star, rates on application, tel (021) 419-6677.

In Sea Point, the *Ritz Inn* offers affordable, comfortable rooms from R110 per person a night, and Cape Town's only revolving restaurant, the *Top of the Ritz*, gives 360-degree views of Table Bay, the Atlantic Ocean, Robben Island, and the coastline to Bloubergstrand, tel (021) 439-6010. *Cape Manor Hotel*, 1 Marais Road, Sea Point, from R110 per person a night sharing, tel (021) 434-9559, fax (021) 439-6896.

Satour B&B of the year 1996 was *Olaf's Guesthouse,* also in Sea Point, where pampering has been elevated to a fine art. The breakfast nook has a continental spread every day where guests can try typical South African jams such as marula, quince and mango with their muffins and croissants, tel (021) 439-8943, fax (021) 439-5057.

Several other places around Cape Town were highly commended in the most recent Satour awards. *Miramar Guest House*, in Muizenberg, tel (021) 788-4571, fax (021) 788-3695, was runner-up for 'Guesthouse of the Year', and the self-catering *Monkey Valley*, in Noordhoek, with thatched cottages set among milkwood trees on the slopes of Chapman's Peak was similarly highly rated, tel (021) 789-1391, fax (021) 789-1143. 'Newcomer of the Year' was *Kirstenberry Lodge*, Bishopscourt, a private home offering accommodation just a stone's throw from Kirstenbosch National Botanical Garden. Three of the five guest suites have self-catering facilities for longer stays, tel (021) 797-1501, fax (021) 797-2027.

For something entirely different near the V&A are the *Harbour View Cottages*, 16 picturesque houses on Loader and Waterkant streets which have been renovated and refurbished to take guests. There is a shuttle bus service to ferry you around or take you on excursions and transport to and from the airport is free. Most of the serviced cottages sleep four in two bedrooms, but larger ones are available, tel (021) 418-6081, fax (021) 418-6082. Also in Loader Street is *De Waterkant Lodge*, B&B, tel (021) 419-1097.

The *Lord Nelson Inn* overlooks historic Simon's Town harbour. Rates are from R250 for a double room including breakfast. Children under 12 sharing stay free. 58 George's Street, Simon's Town, tel (021) 786-1386, fax (021) 786-1009. *Beach & Bay Accommodation* offers B&B or self-catering in private homes in Simon's Town or Glencairn. Contact 32 Glen Road, Glencairn, Simon's Town 7995, tel (021) 782-2301/1254/2627. Camping is available at *Miller's Point Caravan Park* in Simon's Town, R31 to R65 for a site, tel (021) 786-1142; and in Fish Hoek at *Fish Hoek Beach Caravan Park*, Foreshore, from R65 a site, tel (021) 782-5503. Close by in Kalk Bay is *Harbour Side Backpackers*. Rustic with timber bunks, maximum 8 people a room, and double beds mounted high on the wall so you can lie in bed, check out the surf or watch the whales. 136 Main Road, Kalk Bay, tel (021) 788-2943, fax (021) 788-6452, e-mail backpack@iafrica.com

Makapa Lodge, on the mountainside between Chapman's Peak and Kommetjie, has self-catering accommodation or B&B in self-contained units. R80 (£10.65/$17.60) per person, breakfast R15 per person. 18 Java Close, Fish Hoek, tel (021) 785-3512, fax (021) 785-3416.

Budget accommodation, all around R70 a night, includes:

City Slickers Accommodation, 25 Rose Street, central, tel (021) 22-2357;
Shanti Lodge, 17 Prince Street, Gardens, 8001, tel/fax (021) 461-1408;
Berghof Guest House, 1 Faure Street, Gardens, tel (021) 23-7229, fax (021) 23-7779;

St Paul's German Guest House, 182 Bree Street, Tamboerskloof, tel (021) 23-4420, fax (021) 23-7580;

Saasveld Lodge, 73 Kloof Street, Gardens, tel (021) 24-6169, fax (021) 24-5397;

13 Gull Road, 13 Gull Road, Bloubergstrand, tel (021) 554-3593;

Vesperdene Lodge, 7 Vesperdene Road, Green Point, tel (021) 439-0807, fax (021) 439-8068;

Syringa Cottage, 28 Sluysken Road, Hout Bay, tel (021) 790-4570, fax (021) 24-5532;

Zonnekus Holiday Resort, 13 Morningstar Drive, Milnerton, tel (021) 972-1833;

Globe Trotter, 17 Queens Road, Sea Point, tel/fax (021) 434-1539;

Villa Flamingo, 12 Grey Avenue, Table View, tel/fax (021) 557-4642;

Seaforth Beach Bungalows, Corner Main and Seaforth Roads, Simon's Town, tel (021) 786-1463;

Christel's Guest House, 30 Prince's Road, Claremont, tel (021) 61-7969;

Fairways, Rhodes Drive, Constantia, tel (021) 25-4613, fax (021) 419-4354;

Canterbury and Dunderry Cottages, 5 and 6 La Cases Road, Newlands, tel (021) 64-2808;

Jo Orpen Bed & Breakfast, 12 Stirling Road, Newlands, tel (021) 61-5334;

Willows, 4 Bucksburn Road, Newlands, tel/fax (021) 64-2556;

Catnap, 4 White Road, Newlands, tel (021) 685-2821, fax (021) 23-9079;

Alpha House, 6A Kromboom Road, Rondebosch, tel (021) 75-1667.

Other **backpacker accommodation** includes:

Albergo for Backpackers, 5 Beckham Street, Gardens 8001, tel (021) 22-1849, fax (021) 23-0515.

Ashanti Lodge, 11 Hof Street, Gardens 8001, tel (021) 23-8721, fax (021) 23-8790. e-mail ashanti@iafrica.com

The Backpack, 74 New Church Street, Tamboerskloof 8001, tel (021) 23-4530, fax (021) 23-0065, e-mail backpack@gem.co.za

Belvidere Accommodation Centre, Higgo Crescent, off Bellevue Road, Higgovale 8001, tel (021) 23-1316, fax (021) 24-2909.

Bird's Eye View, 55 High Level Road, Green Point 8001, tel (021) 434-4143, fax (021) 439-9788.

Bob's Backpack, 187 Long Street, Central, tel (021) 24-3584, fax (021) 24-8223.

The Bunkhouse, 23 Antrim Road, Three Anchor Bay 8001, tel/fax (021) 434-5695.

Bunkers, 15 Graham Road, Sea Point 8001, tel (021) 434-0549, fax (021) 434-7899.

Cloudbreak Travellers Lodge, 219 Buitenkant Street, Central, tel (021) 461-6892, fax (021) 461-6892, e-mail: cloudbreak@gem.co.za

The Green Elephant, 57 Milton Road, Newlands 7700, tel (021) 448-6359.

Hip Hop Travellers Stop, 11 Vesperdene Road, Green Point 8001, tel (021) 439-2104, fax (021) 439-2104.

Kings Backpackers, 17 Scott Street, Gardens 8001, tel (021) 461-4722.

Long Street Backpackers, 209 Long Street, Gardens 8001, tel (021) 23-0615, fax (021) 23-1362.

Oak Lodge, 21 Breda Street, Gardens 8001, tel (021) 45-6182, fax (021) 45-6308.

Overseas Visitors Club, 230 Upper Long Street, Central, tel (021) 24-6800, fax (021) 23-4870.

Rolling Stones, 39 Milner Road, Woodstock 7915, tel (021) 448-1124, fax (021) 448-1124.

SA's Guesthouse, 84 St Michael's Road, Claremont 8001, tel (021) 84-2396.

Stan's Halt Youth Hostel, The Glen, Camps Bay 8001, tel (021) 438-9037, fax (021) 438-9037.

St John's Lodge, 5 St John's Road, Sea Point 8001, tel (021) 439-9028, fax (021) 439-4875.

St John's Waterfront Lodge, 4/6 Braemar Road, Green Point 8001, tel (021) 439-1404, fax (021) 439-1404.

Table Mountain Retreat, 13 Union Street, Gardens 8001, tel (021) 24-2110, fax (021) 26-1350.
The Globetrotter, 17 Queens Road, Sea Point 8001, tel (021) 434-1539.
The Lion's Den Backpacker's Lodge, 255 Long Street, Central, tel (021) 23-9003.
The Lodge, 49 Napier Street, Central, tel (021) 21-1106, fax (021) 21-2397.
The Pink Backpack, 116 New Church Street, Central, tel (021) 23-6992.
Zebra Crossing, 82 New Church Street, Central, tel (021) 22-1265, fax (021) 22-1265.

Cape Town has both a *YMCA*, at Burham Drive, Observatory, tel (021) 47-6217, fax (021) 47-6275, and a *YWCA*, 20 Bellevue Street, tel (021) 23-3711.

Further Afield. Backpacker accommodation throughout the Peninsula includes:

Abe Bailey Youth Hostel, 11 Maynard Road, Muizenberg 7951, tel (021) 788-2301, fax (021) 788-2301.
Boulders Beach Backpack, 4 Boulders Beach, Simonstown 7995, tel (021) 786-1758, e-mail stumble@iafrica.com
Harbourside Backpacker, 136 Main Road, Kalk Bay 7975, tel (021) 788-2943, fax (021) 788-6452, e-mail backpackin@iafrica.co.za
Putu Place, Muizenberg Beach, Muizenberg 7951, tel (021) 788-6084.

Caravan and camping further away from the city and suburbs are:

Imhoff Caravan Park, 1 Wireless Road, Kommetjie, R30 (£4/$6.60) a site and R10 per person, tel (021) 783-1634, fax (021) 783-2871;
Chapman's Peak Caravan Farm, Dassenheuwel, R20 (£2.65/$4.40) a person, tel (021) 789-1225;
Ou Skip Park, 3-star, Otto du Plessis Drive, Melkbosstrand, from R60 to R100 (£13.35/$22) a site, tel (021) 553-2058.

Eating and Drinking

The Western Cape is first and foremost the home of traditional South African country food, glorious seafood, and the delicious and subtly spiced dishes of the Cape Malays — in fact, the rainbow cuisine. Fast-food outlets serve favourites such as American hot dogs and hamburgers along with their local equivalents, such as boerewors roll, the Gatsby — a French loaf stuffed with a mixture of hot chips, cold meats and salads dressed in a sauce of your choice — and a variety of roadhouse-style but distinctively Malay-inspired foods, ranging from one-bite samoosa snacks to spiced meat rotis and seafood platters.

For good value city pub lunches try:

Perseverance Tavern, 83 Buitenkant Street, Gardens, tel (021) 461-2440;
Artie's Underground Pub & Grill, 34 Riebeeck Street, central, tel (021) 419-5768;
Townhouse Hotel, 60 Corporation Street, central, tel (021) 45-7050;
The Stag's Head, 7 Hope Street, Gardens; Kimberley Hotel, 48 Roeland Street, Gardens, tel (021) 461-5572;
The Crowbar, 43 Waterkant Street, tel (021) 419-3660;
Helmsley Hotel, 16 Hof Street, Gardens, tel (021) 23-7200;
Metropole Hotel, 38 Long Street, tel (021) 23-6363;
Junction Hotel, 32 Foundry Road, Salt River, tel (021) 448-1778;
Fireman's Arms, 25 Mechau Street, central, tel (021) 419-1513;
Diaz Tavern, corner Harrington and Longmarket streets, central, tel (021) 45-7547.

To sample local specialities such as waterblommetjie bredie, bobotie, snoek, perlemoen, crayfish, and galjoen in Cape Town try *The Kaapse Tafel*, 90 Queen Victoria Street, tel (021) 23-1651; and the *Cape Manna Restaurant*, 34 Napier Street, central, tel (021) 419-2181. For authentic Malay food start with the *Biesmiellah Malay* restaurant (no alcohol), Upper Wale Street, in the Malay Quarter. Although cutlery is provided they say you can eat with 'the tools of mankind.' Closed Sunday. Open for lunch and dinner from 6.30pm to 10.30pm. Wheelchair friendly, tel (021) 23-0850. For take away rotis and other Malay delights try the unpretentious *Café Zorina*, a local secret, at 172 Loop Street, central, tel (021) 24-9301. *Africa Café*, 213 Lower Main Road, Observatory, says it is the only restaurant serving cuisine from all over Africa, tel (021) 47-9553.

For seafood try:

> *The Brass Bell*, Railway Station, Kalk Bay, tel (021) 788-5456;
> *Black Marlin Restaurant*, Main Road, Miller's Point, Simon's Town, tel (021) 786-1621;
> *Camel Rock Restaurant*, Main Road, Scarborough, tel (021) 780-1122;
> *Ons Huisie Restaurant*, Stadler Road, Bloubergstrand, tel (021) 56-1553;
> *Wharfside Grill*, Hout Bay Harbour, tel (021) 790-1100;
> *Fish on the Rocks*, Harbour Road, Hout Bay, for inexpensive English fish and chips and delicious calamari, tel (021) 790-1153.

Bertie's Big Easy at Bertie's Landing, V&A Waterfront, is one of the most popular restaurants in the dock area. Inexpensive, giant portions, fresh seafood and meat, best view on the Waterfront, tel (021) 419-2727. Other choice restaurants at the Waterfront are:

> *Ferryman's Tavern*, traditional pub/restaurant, tel (021) 419-7748;
> *Morton's on the Wharf*, Cajun/Creole, tel (021) 418-3633;
> *St Elmo's*, pasta, pizza, tel (021) 21-7005;
> *The Musselcracker*, seafood buffet, tel (021) 419-4300;
> *The Sports Café*, American, tel (021) 419-5558;
> *Dock Road Café*, Halaal food, live music, tel (021) 419-7722.

The US-inspired Mugg & Bean is an in-spot on the Waterfront, offering four blends of drink-as-much-as-you-like coffee. Breakfasts include flapjacks, hash browns and eggs easy-over. For something stronger with your food there is Mitchell's Waterfront Brewery and Scottish Ale House, next to the Ferrymans Tavern in the harbour, tel (021) 419-5074.

Some nooks and crannies: The Crypt, in St George's Cathedral, Wale Street, a favourite with down-and-outs, is good for affordable light meals. Open 7.30am to 4.30pm Monday to Friday only, tel (021) 23-1936; the Homestead Restaurant, in the Cape of Good Hope Nature Reserve at Cape Point, has inexpensive, good quality food, tel (021) 780-1040. Cream and chocolate lovers should try the confections at Zerban's Restaurant, Gardens Centre, Mill Street, Cape Town, tel (021) 461-4060, and Zerban's Cake and Coffee Shop, Galleria Centre, Sea Point, tel (021) 439-3953. Capetonians usually beat a path to the door of Rieses Delicatessen at 367 Main Road, Sea Point, when they want something special for a summer lunch or picnic. Not cheap, but the selection is mind-boggling, tel (021) 434-1938. The Old Cape Farm Stall, on Groot Constantia Road, Constantia, has a bakery and bistro that are definitely worth a halt, tel (021) 794-7062.

Gay Restaurants

> *108 Loop Street Restaurant*, 108 Loop Street, Cape Town, tel (021) 24-0888.
> *Aladdin Coffee Shop*, Nedbank Centre Shop 7, Kloof Road, Sea Point, tel (021) 439-4428.
> *Café Erte*, Astria Building, 265A Main Road, Seapoint, tel (021) 434-6624.
> *Carte Blanche*, Trill Road, Observatory, tel (021) 448-2266.
> *Castro's*, 72 Upper Waterkant Street, Greenpoint.
> *Clementines*, Wolfe Street, Chelsea Village, Wynberg, tel (021) 797-6168.

Don Pedro's, 113 Roodebloem Road, Woodstock, tel (021) 47-4493.
Elaine's Curry Bistro, 105 Lower Main Road, Observatory, tel (021) 47-2616.
Heaven, Napier Street, Greenpoint.
L'Orient, 50 Main Road, Three Anchor Bay, tel (021) 439-6572.
Le Petit Paris, Green Market Square, Cape Town, tel (021) 23-7648.
The Africa Café, 213 Lower Main Road, Observatory, tel (021) 47-9553.

Captour has planned a *Route of Many Cultures* so that visitors can see Cape Town in its social and cultural entirety and to experience all facets of the Mother City. Of special interest to Muslim visitors, for instance, is the Malay Quarter Tour, which introduces the people of the inner-city enclave called the Bo-Kaap, home to nearly 10,000 people, most of whom worship at the seven mosques in the immediate surroundings. The **Bo-Kaap Museum**, at 71 Wale Street, tel (021) 24-3846, is housed in a late 18th-century Cape Malay home fitted with artefacts and beautiful furniture representative of the quarter that is home to the descendants of slaves and political dissidents brought by Dutch settlers from Malaysia and Indonesia. The first Muslim community was established in 1694 by Javanese exile Sheikh Yusuf, and the first mosque was founded 200 years ago during the first British occupation of the Cape.

For an insight into South African history, and particularly its apartheid years, there is a wealth of information at the **District Six Museum**, tel (021) 461-8745, at the Methodist Church, 25A Buitenkant Street, central city. The museum, comprising a collection of memorabilia and artefacts that bring home the disruptions caused by the forced removal of thousands of Capetonians from the heart of the city and their resettlement in soulless townships on the Cape Flats.

Complementing the District Six collection is the **Mayibuye Centre** of the University of the Western Cape, about 25km/16 miles from the city centre. The centre, on Modderdam Road, Bellville, has a large collection of apartheid memorabilia, ranging from 'Whites Only' signs to letters and other writings by former Robben Island prisoners, among them President Nelson Mandela. Cape Town also houses Parliament and daily tours enable you to watch politicians at work. For visits and tickets, free of charge, to debates in the two Houses of Assembly call Parliament, tel (021) 403-2911.

A 15-minute drive from the city centre is **Langa** ('The Sun'), Cape Town's oldest black township, where dormitory-style hostels share the neighbourhood with the stylish homes of an emergent black middle-class. In the area you can also visit **Gugulethu** ('Our Hope'), **Nyanga** ('The Moon') and the squatter township of **Khayelitsha**, where nearly half a million people live, and which is the first area in the Western Cape whose squatter shacks have been given electricity. Khayelitsha stretches southward from the N2 freeway and is, at its southernmost point, a few minutes' drive from the False Bay resort of Monwabisi, where a barbecue area, bungalows, camping facilities and the largest man-made tidal pool in the southern hemisphere provide a welcome break after the township tour. Adjoining is **Mitchell's Plain**, established in 1974 to provide housing for the thousands relocated from other areas in terms of the infamous Group Areas Act. Today, Mitchell's Plain has a population of more than 250,000. Another centre of coloured community life is to be found in **Athlone**, once known as West London and now a thriving business centre with a buzzing nightlife and clubs playing some of the best music around (try Club Lenin on the Klipfontein Road).

Since the repeal of the apartheid legislation which created them, each of these areas has gradually assumed a new, multi-cultural face and tour operators and residents themselves will introduce you to artists, craftsmen, traditional healers, sporting personalities and others who have made the Cape Flats the vibrant place it is today. Tour operators include:

Arnoni Tours, tel (021) 762-3262;
Bo-Kaap Community Guided Tours, tel (021) 24-0014;
Legend Tours, tel/fax (021) 461-2952;
One City Tours, tel (021) 387-5351;
Ubuntu Tours, tel 083 250-1193.

Cape Town is the Mother City of South Africa, nestling between Table Mountain and Table Bay. The settlement was established by Jan van Riebeeck in 1652. It became a municipality in 1839. The city's Afrikaans name is Kaapstad, the Khoikhoi name *Huigais* means 'Stone Place' and its Koranna name *Ikxab* means the same. The city's main thoroughfare is **Adderley Street**, which is named after Sir Charles Adderley, the man responsible for representative government at the Cape in 1884. Near the bottom is the **Golden Acre**, which contains one of the city's major shopping centres.

Beaches. There are literally scores of beaches along the Peninsula's 150km/93 miles of coastline — family beaches, beaches for sunbathing, snorkelling, scuba diving, boardsailing, surfing, fishing and swimming. There is also an unofficial beach for nudists at Sandy Bay. The waters of False Bay are generally 5°C/41°F warmer than those of the Atlantic, but the Atlantic beaches are more sheltered from the south-easter wind which blows in summer between November and February. This is the wind that puts the famous 'tablecloth' of cloud on Table Mountain and is known as the Cape Doctor because it is believed to clear the city of germs. The longer and harder the south-easter blows the calmer, and colder, the Atlantic waters become.

False Bay Beaches. *Muizenberg* (Surfer's Corner) is the start of a long beach that runs for 40km/25 miles to Gordon's Bay. It is regarded as the finest and safest beach in the Peninsula and is popular with families and surfers. There is a pavilion for fun activities and entertainment. Colourful Victorian changing booths line the beach.

Strand Beach. Less than an hour's drive from Cape Town, the beach is a long wide stretch of sand backed by a promenade and is popular for its safe swimming. There is a wide variety of shops, cafés and accommodation.

Gordon's Bay. Bikini Beach is well-sheltered and Main Beach is popular for watersports. A path links the two. Numerous cafés and restaurants are close by.

St James. A large tidal pool ideal for toddlers. Change-rooms in the old brightly coloured bathing boxes. Close to the main road and cafés. There is a boardwalk between Muizenberg and St James, a walk of about 1.5km/1 mile.

Clovelly. Sand dunes and a long beach stretching to Fish Hoek. Popular with kite flyers.

Fish Hoek. At its southern end is Jager's Walkway, a path winding along the rocky coastline. Popular Hobie Cat launching spot, where regattas are regularly held.

Glencairn. Safe swimming in a tidal pool and a good whale-watching spot in season.

Seaforth Beach. The nearest bathing resort for Simon's Town and like the other beaches in the area, Boulders, Windmill Beach and Froggy Pond, it is sheltered and offers safe swimming. A water slide and wooden raft make this an enjoyable spot for youngsters.

Boulders. Coves among gigantic boulders offer shelter and safe swimming for children. Within walking distance of Simon's Town. There is a resident colony of 700 Jackass penguins — and a heavy fine for disturbing them.

Miller's Point. There is a popular caravan park nearby, as well as the Black Marlin restaurant. Beyond here to Cape Point the coast becomes more rocky and precipitous and is more popular with scuba divers and anglers than swimmers and sunbathers.

There are a number of small beaches in the Cape of Good Hope Nature Reserve, but bathing can be dangerous.

Atlantic Seaboard. Rounding the Point and heading back to Cape Town are *Scarborough* and *Witsands*, with steeply shelving beaches, good for surfing and angling, but not for swimming.

Kommetjie. Known as 'the Kom' to surfers, who favour the south end of the beach. Gravel walkways give access to picnic spots and rocky coves. There is a channel for launching boats. Kelp beds off nearby Slangkop lighthouse are good crayfishing spots. Noordhoek *Long Beach* is a favourite spot for surfing, windsurfing, paddle-skiing and crayfish diving. The surf is powerful and the facilities are basic. The movie *Ryan's Daughter* was filmed here because it looks like Ireland, with sunshine. The beach is aptly named and is good for walks and horse-riding. It is part of the Kakapo Trail, a two-hour ride through dunes and lagoons. From Noordhoek there is a spectacular mountainside drive above the sea all the way to Hout Bay, down winding Chapman's Peak Drive.

Hout Bay. The beach (just over half a mile) is flanked by the picturesque 800m-high Sentinel and Chapman's Peak and is a popular place for windsurfing, sailing, paddle-skiing and surfing. Ideal for small children. Numerous shops and restaurants nearby, and Mariners Wharf is a short drive away.

Llandudno. One of the Peninsula's prettiest beaches and popular for sunset picnics. Powerful surf and swimming can be dangerous. Offshore, near Sunset Rocks, is the wreck of the tanker *Romelia* which grounded here in 1977. A 10-minute walk will take you to the unofficial nudist beach at *Sandy Bay*. The path starts at the Llandudno parking area.

Oudekraal. More rocks than sand. A popular diving spot. The Dutch East Indiaman *Het Huise te Kraaienstein*, carrying 19 chests of silver coins sank here in 1698. Three chests remain to be discovered.

Camps Bay. Table Mountain and its Twelve Apostles look down on this spacious and usually uncrowded palm-lined beach. The surf is strong and freak waves make bathing dangerous. Best for walks and sunbathing. Shops, restaurants, and a police station line a Miami-like beachfront. Nearby *Glen Beach* is frequented only by picknickers and anglers.

Clifton. Cape Town's most packed and popular beach, primarily for the body beautiful show, not the sea. Huge granite boulders divide the sands into four separate beaches, all sheltered from the south-easter. In summer you can oil up and sunbathe until 8pm. If you take children, go to *Fourth Beach*. La Med is a trendy tapas bar nearby.

Sea Point. All along this stretch running into Table Bay by way of Three Anchor Bay, Green Point and Mouille Point are pretty but rocky beaches. In the middle of this densely populated high-rise flatland, only 50m/55 yards from the promenade is Graaff's Pool, for men-only nude bathing.

Bertram House. This late Georgian red-brick house is typical of early 19th century Cape British architecture and the last local example of its kind. The Anna Lidderdale Collection has some fine examples of furniture, ceramics, and silver. Open Tuesday to Saturday from 9.30am to 4.30pm. Corner Orange Street and Government Avenue, central, tel (021) 24-9381.

Bloubergstrand. Major national and international windsurfing competitions are held here at Big Bay. Little Bay is for family outings. From the beach on the shore of Table Bay, you can see one of the best and most photographed views of Table Mountain and Lion's Head and the low outline of Robben Island.

Breakwater Prison. This was built in 1895 to house convicts who were set to work cutting stone for the breakwater to protect the harbour from fierce north-west gales.

A treadmill installed in 1890 is on show. The old prison now houses the University of Cape Town's Graduate School of Business and the Breakwater Lodge Hotel.

Cape Flats. This region linking the Cape Peninsula with the mainland was used during the apartheid years to accommodate relocated coloured (mixed race) communities. The area includes Athlone, Elsies River, Gugulethu, Khayelitsha, Lansdowne, Manenberg, Mitchell's Plain, Monwabisi, Rylands, and Wetton. The Cape Flats Nature Reserve protects 30 hectares of indigenous flora (21 different species) as well as a variety of small mammals. Open Monday to Friday from 9am to 3.30pm.

The 7750-hectare **Cape of Good Hope Nature Reserve** conserves a priceless wilderness area at the very tip of the Peninsula, where the Indian and Atlantic oceans meet. The reserve covers 40km/25 miles of coastline, and is a floral wonderland, with more than 1200 indigenous plant species, 160 species of birds and a variety of wildlife ranging from Cape mountain zebra, springbok, steenbok, grysbok, and grey rhebok to caracal, Cape fox and some rather irksome baboons. At Olifantsboschbaai lies the bones of the *Thomas T Tucker*, which broke up here in 1942. The Cape Point lighthouse — the most powerful in the southern hemisphere — beams an electric light of 19 million candle-power across the ocean. About 3km/2 miles offshore is Bellows Rock, where the *Lusitania* sank in 1911. A monument to Vasco da Gama in the shape of a cross commemorates his voyage around the Cape in 1497. From a lookout platform you can see forever. Open November to January 6am to 10pm, February to April 7am to 7pm and from May to October 8am to 6pm, tel (021) 78-1100.

The **Castle of Good Hope**, at the corner of Buitenkant and Darling streets, was built between 1666–1679, and is the oldest building in South Africa. The fortification has bastions at each corner of its five-pointed star named after the titles of the Prince of Orange: Buren, Nassau, Catzenellenbogen, Oranje and Leerdam. Carved above the main gateway are the arms of the cities of Amsterdam, Rotterdam, Delft, Hoorn, Middleburg and Enkhuizen, where the various chambers of the Dutch East India Company were established. The Castle contains priceless historical objects and the William Fehr Collection of paintings, porcelain, carpets, and furniture. Anton Anreith, South Africa's finest sculptor, had a workshop in the Castle and the Kat Balcony (originally dating from 1695) was rebuilt by him between 1785-1790. The military museum links the military histories of the Castle, the Cape and various Cape regiments. Cetshwayo, King of the Zulus, and his wives were detained at the Castle after his banishment in 1879 at the end of the Anglo-Zulu War. Guided tours Monday to Sunday, 10am, 11am, midday, 1pm, 2pm, 3pm. Castle Street, tel (021) 469-1111, and (021) 469-1249/50.

Round Cape Town is a ring of *kramats*, or tombs, of Muslim holy men, known as '**Circle of Islam.**' One is on Signal Hill, close to the Malay Quarter. It is the tomb of Towang Guru (Kuroo), who wrote the Koran, which he knew by heart, for the Malays of Cape Town and built the Dorp Street mosque. On the edge of Signal Hill quarry is the grave of Hadji Shahmohammed who, it is said, walked through locked doors at night to convert slaves to Islam.

The **City Hall** (1905) overlooks the Grand Parade and houses the City Library and the Cape Town Symphony Orchestra, tel (021) 400-2230.

The oldest garden in South Africa is the **Company's Garden**, at the top of Adderley Street, established in 1652 by Jan van Riebeeck to supply Dutch East India Company ships with fresh vegetables and fruit. Today it contains a wide variety of indigenous and exotic plants, shrubs and trees, an aviary and a restaurant. Below the restaurant is a Saffren Pear Tree, the oldest cultivated tree in South Africa and believed to have been planted soon after Jan van Riebeeck established his settlement here. The Sun Dial dates from 1787 and The Bell Tower from 1855.

Constantia, 24km/15 miles from Cape Town, was originally a farm given to Governor Simon van der Stel in 1685. Constantia is a wine-producing valley and Groot Constantia Estate is probably the oldest wine estate in the country. The house, a superb example of Cape-Dutch architecture, is now a museum, with collections of Cape furniture and Chinese, Japanese, Rhenish and Delft porcelain. The Wine Museum has wine drinking and storage vessels in glass, silver, copper and stoneware from 500BC to the 19th century. Open daily from 10am to 5pm. Off Constantia Road, Wynberg, tel (021) 794-5067. The Constantia Wine Route includes the famous wine estates of Groot Constantia, Buitenverwachting and Klein Constantia.

The **Cultural History Museum**, at 49 Adderley Street, was originally built as a slave lodge for the Dutch East India Company in 1679 and later used at the Cape Supreme Court. It houses early Post Office stones, furniture, glass, ceramics, weapons, musical instruments and toys from many countries. The reconstructed tombstone of Jan van Riebeeck can also be seen in the courtyard. Open Monday to Saturday from 9.30am to 4.30pm, tel (021) 461-8280.

Devil's Peak is 1002m/3287ft high north-east peak of Table Mountain. Said to have got its name from a pirate called Van Hunks who lived on the slopes and spent his days smoking and drinking rum. Van Hunks met a stranger and said he could smoke any man under the table. The stranger accepted the challenge and they smoked until the stranger collapsed. Van Hunks bent down to help him and saw that it was the Devil. That is when the mountain became Devil's Peak and whenever the clouds roll down they say Van Hunk and the Devil are at it again.

Fish Hoek, 35km/22 miles from Cape Town, is a holiday resort on the western coast of False Bay that is well-known for fossilised skeletons of Fish Hoek Man, some 10,000 years old. False Bay Fire Museum has a large display of fire equipment, old and new, technical data and uniforms.

The **Grand Parade** in front of the City Hall was one of the city's main squares and a military parade during the 18th and 19th centuries. There is a daily flower and fruit market and on Wednesday and Saturday morning a flea market. Red lines painted on the ground from the fruit stalls to the King Edward Statue show the location of the original fort.

Cobbled **Greenmarket Square**, bordered by Shortmarket, Longmarket and Burg streets, is the site of a daily flea market, and a national monument.

Green Point, 3km/2 miles from the city, is the site of South Africa's first lighthouse. It has one of the largest sports stadiums in the Peninsula. On the city side lies Granger Bay with the old Breakwater and the old General Botha Nautical Academy Building, which is now the Cape Technikon School for Hotel Management.

The lovely old Dutch Cape homestead **Groote Schuur** (Big Barn) was restored for Cecil John Rhodes by the well-known architect Sir Herbert Baker. Rhodes bequeathed his home to the nation. Rhodes died on 26 March 1902 in a little thatched cottage in Muizenberg. On his deathbed he is said to have uttered the sentence 'So little done, so much to do.' In reality his last words were, 'Turn me over, Jack.' In 1967, the world's first human heart transplant was performed by Professor Chris Barnard at the University of Cape Town's teaching hospital, also called Groote Schuur.

Houses of Parliament. When Parliament is in session, gallery tickets are available for the public. Overseas visitors must show their passports. During parliamentary recess guided tours are conducted on Monday to Thursday at 11am and 2pm, and on Friday at 11am, tel (021) 403-2460/1.

Hout Bay, literally 'Wood Bay,' is a sheltered bay on the west coast of the Cape Peninsula, 25km/16 miles from Cape Town. A picturesque fishing harbour, a wide sandy beach, a quaint village, and numerous mountain walks make this valley a delightful place. Hout Bay Museum is open Tuesday to Saturday, 10am–12.30pm and 2–4.30pm at 4 St Andrews Road, tel (021) 790-3270. Mariners Wharf is a harbour-front complex of live lobster and fish markets, seafood restaurants and bistros, and a cluster of souvenir and nautical shops. There are sunset cruises from the harbour to the V&A Waterfront from October to April, as well as trips to Seal Island, where huge herds of Cape fur seals and flocks of rare Bank cormorants and black-backed gulls congregate in summer. Seal Island Cruises, tel (021) 438-9208; Circe Launches, tel (021) 790-1040.

The **Irma Stern Museum** is in the former home of this internationally acclaimed artist. Many of her finest works are displayed, as well as antique furniture, art treasures, and Congolese artefacts. Open Tuesday to Saturday from 10am to 5pm, UCT, Cecil Road, Rosebank, tel (021) 685-5686.

The **Jewish Museum** at 84 Hatfield Street, Gardens, is the oldest synagogue in South Africa and contains items of Jewish historical and ceremonial significance. Open December to February, Tuesday and Thursday 10am–5pm, Wednesday and Sunday 10am–12.30pm; March to November, Tuesday and Thursday 2–5pm, Sunday 10am–12.30pm, tel (021) 434-6605.

Kalk Bay, 33km/21 miles from Cape Town, is a seaside village and holiday resort on the western shore of False Bay, between St James and Fish Hoek. Snoek catches are brought in to the harbour throughout the year, peaking during June and July. For snoek catches, Seal Island trips and trips to Fish Hoek, Glencairn and Simon's Town, tel Captain Rob's Tours, tel (021) 788-5261.

On the eastern slopes of Table Mountain are the world-renowned **Kirstenbosch National Botanical Gardens**, dedicated to the preservation of the indigenous plants of southern Africa. Some 6000 of South Africa's 20,000 different species of flora are grown here. It was established in 1913 with about 1500 plant specimens from all over southern Africa, and later gifted to the nation by Cecil John Rhodes.

The setting of the garden below Castle Rock is ideal because of the diversity of terrain and plentiful water (Newlands is Cape Town's wettest suburb). Part of a hedge of wild almonds planted by Jan van Riebeeck to protect the settlement's cattle and sheep can still be seen at Kirstenbosch and there are some well signposted walks. The Fynbos Walk takes in all the major plants of the fabulous Cape Floral Kingdom. Leading off the walk are paths through the *Protea* and *Erica* gardens. The route is hard-surfaced with no steps, and runs along a contour with no severe gradients, which makes it ideal for family groups with push-chairs or prams, and for the disabled with wheelchairs. There is also a Braille Trail and an aromatic plant garden. Details of walks are available at the information kiosk. The Silver Tree, Stinkwood and Yellowwood trails lead through various sections of the cultivated garden and the indigenous forests on the mountain slopes. Guided walks take place on Tuesdays and Saturdays, starting at 11am at the Information Office. A Happy Tractor service to enable the elderly and disabled to view the upper parts at the garden operates on Saturdays 2–4pm, Sundays 10am–1pm and 2–4pm. Children must be accompanied by an adult. Tel (021) 726-1166.

To reach the garden from Cape Town, travel along De Waal Drive (M3) in the direction of Muizenberg, past the University of Cape Town. At the first traffic light intersection turn right (southwards) into Rhodes Drive (M63) and follow the signs. There is a second entrance through the Rycroft Gate at the upper, south side of the garden. A bus service links the garden with Mowbray and Claremont stations. Details from the Information Officer at Kirstenbosch, tel (021) 765-4916, or City Tramways, tel toll-free 080 121 2111. Kirstenbosch is open every day of the year (8am–7pm September to March, 8am–6pm April to August). The Information Office is open 8am–4.45pm every day of the week. There is an entrance fee of R4 (55p/90 cents) for adults and R1 for students and scholars (free for pensioners on Tuesdays). The Kirstenbosch Garden Shop offers a wide range of indigenous plants, books on natural history, plants and gardening, as well as gifts and mementos. It is open daily 9am–5pm, tel (021) 762-1621. The tea house is open daily (Monday to Friday 9am–5pm, Saturdays and Sundays 8.30am–5pm), for breakfasts, teas and lunches, tel (021) 797-7614.

Koopmans de Wet House, 35 Strand Street, central city, was built in 1701 and is an excellent example of a typical Cape townhouse. Exhibits portray the lifestyle of a successful businessman of the late 18th century and include a collection of Cape and European furniture, Cape silver, European glass and blue and white porcelain bearing the VOC monogram. Open Tuesday to Saturday from 9.30am to 4.30pm, tel (021) 24-2473. Up the road is the Lutheran Church (1774); the Sexton's House, now the Netherlands Embassy (1787); and the Martin Melck House (1781), now an interior decorators' shop.

Melkbosstrand, 28km/17 miles from Cape Town, is named after its milkwood (melkbos) trees. Excellent fishing and skin-diving. Rock lobsters are protected south of Melkbosstrand, but north of the resort you can dive out four a day during the season. Permits are obtainable from Magistrates and the Receiver of Revenue, tel (021) 460-2035.

The **Old Townhouse** (1755) on Greenmarket Square, central city, houses the Michaelis Collection, a permanent exhibition of 17th century Dutch and Flemish paintings. Open Monday to Sunday 10am to 5pm, tel (021) 24-6367.

Milnerton is the gateway to the West Coast and also gives you a breathtaking view 10km/6 miles across the Bay to Table Mountain, Devil's Peak and Lion's Head. You can look around the Milnerton Lighthouse and the nearby Rietvlei Nature Reserve is the haunt of wading birds.

On Rhodes Drive **Mostert's Mill** dates back to 1796 and is the only wind-operated mill still in existence in the Western Cape. It has been restored to full working order and is open daily from 9am to 3pm. Another mill, water-driven, is the Josephine Mill on the Liesbeek River, between Rondebosch and Newlands. It was built in 1840 by a Swedish businessman and brewer and named in honour of Swedish Crown Princess Josephine. It is Cape Town's only surviving and operational watermill and has an 1840 waterwheel. The mill is open 9.30am to 4pm daily throughout the summer, tel (021) 686-4939.

Muizenberg, 28km/17 miles from Cape Town, is famous for its excellent bathing and surfing beach. The beachfront has a pavilion, esplanade, and an amusement park. The Muizenberg-St James' Historical Walk is a 15-minute amble along the coast to St James, starting out at the end of the car park next to the Muizenberg pavilion. Muizenberg Museum Complex, Main Road, Muizenberg, tel (021) 788-7035. Muizenberg Toy Museum and Collectors Shop, display of toys from 1900 to 1960, including cars, trains, rocking horses, boats, Dinky toys and pedal cars. Open Tuesday to Sunday from 10am to 5pm at 8 Beach Road, tel (021) 788-1569. Natale Labia Museum, is a satellite museum of the SA National Gallery and has art exhibitions, concerts, and poetry readings. Open Tuesday to Sunday from 10am to 5pm. 192 Main Road, tel (021) 788-4106. Rhodes Cottage was a seaside retreat of Cecil John Rhodes, Prime Minister of the Cape from 1890-1895. He died here in 1902. Open Tuesday to Sunday from 10am to 1pm and 2pm to 5pm. Main Road, tel (021) 788-1816. Die Posthuys, probably built late in the 18th century, is the oldest structure along the False Bay coast. It was built from stone on the site as a lookout post for the Dutch East India Company. The Railway Station, built in 1912-13, is a fine example of the Edwardian era, with a noteworthy spiral staircase. It now houses shops and a restaurant.

Newlands. The graceful Vineyard Hotel in this upmarket suburb of Cape Town was once the home of indefatigable letter-writer Lady Anne Barnard, who lived here in 1800. Nearby are the grounds for provincial and international rugby and cricket matches. The South African Rugby Board Museum in the mill complex, is said to be the largest of its kind in the world. Its collection of rugby memorabilia dates back to 1891. It is open daily on weekdays from 9.30am to 4pm and also on Saturdays when matches are being played, tel (021) 686-4532. Across the road is South Africa's oldest brewery, Ohlsson's, which has conducted tours on Tuesday and Thursday at 2.30pm, tel (021) 658-7511.

Observatory. Apart from a visit to the South African Astronomical Observatory, off Liesbeek Parkway, tel (021) 47-2005, after which this suburb is named, a visit to Lower Main Road is worthwhile. In addition to some good restaurants there is a fascinating range of speciality shops. Stepping into Dominion hardware store, for instance, is like stepping back in time. The shop was established at the turn of the century and has remained in the same state, and apparently with the same stock, ever since. Many other interesting Victorian buildings remain intact, despite neglect.

Potteries. The Hymie Rabinowitz pottery is in the Eagle's Nest forest at Constantia, only 20 minutes from Cape Town. He is one of the country's best known potters, tel (021) 794-5458. For pottery with a Japanese flavour, visit Steve Shapiro down the road at Watersound Pottery, Turkeyberry Lane, Hout Bay, tel (021) 790-3125.

The **Railway Station** is the bottom of Adderley Street. In the concourse stands South Africa's very first locomotive, built by Hawthorne and Leith of Scotland and shipped out in 1859, along with driver William Dabbs, who drove it until the day of his death.

Made of Table Mountain granite and bronze as a tribute to the memory of Cecil John Rhodes, **Rhodes Memorial** looks out over the city from the mountain slopes of Devil's Peak above Rhodes Drive, Rondebosch. There are magnificent panoramic view of the Cape Flats, False Bay and the Drakenstein Mountains. Behind the monument is a delightful thatch and stone tea-room, tel (021) 689-9151.

Robben Island, South Africa's own Alcatraz, is now a national monument and museum and best known as the place where Nelson Mandela was imprisoned for nearly two decades, 11km/7 miles offshore. Visitors are restricted to 300 a day in groups of up to 30 people at a time. The little kidney-shaped island is reached by ferry, which leaves the V&A Waterfront three times a day. The trip costs R80 a person, tel (021) 411-1006 and (021) 25-4292.

Rondebosch, 10km/6 miles from Cape Town, is best known for its resident population of students from the nearby University of Cape Town whose 10 faculties has more than 14,000 students to help to make this one of the more livewire suburbs of the city. For visits to the university contact UCT Public Relations Department, tel (021) 650-9111.

Rondevlei Bird Sanctuary, 21km/13 miles from Cape Town, is one of the most important waterfowl wetlands in the Peninsula. This 12070-hectare reserve gives sanctuary to more than 200 species, with flamingoes, storks, herons and pelicans among the more spectacular. There are observation towers and thatched hides for serious twitchers. Open daily from 8am and 5pm, tel (021) 706-2404. Bordering Rondevlei is Zeekoevlei (Hippopotamus Lake), the largest freshwater lake on the Cape Flats, where yachting and boating are popular.

The road from Cape Town that climbs the slopes of Lion's Head runs past the domed kramat (tomb) of a Muslim holy man to the summit of **Signal Hill.** The view of the city's twinkling lights at night is unforgettable, and even better at weekends and every night from December to April when adjoining Table Mountain is floodlit. The 350m/1148ft hill gets its name from the old days when a cannon was fired to signal the approach of a ship. The city's time-keeping noonday gun here is fired electrically every day except Sunday from Observatory.

Silvermine Nature Reserve encompasses a wild area from Muizenberg and Kalk Bay in the east to Noordhoek Peak in the west and is accessible from the Ou KaapseWeg (Old Cape Road), Tokai. Hiking trails give fine views across False Bay and as far as Hout Bay. There is a network of paths and a mountain bike route, which is signposted from the main gate on the Kalk Bay side. Open daily in summer from 8am to 7pm, and in winter from 8am to 5pm, tel (021) 75-3040.

A scenic 38km/24-mile rail trip from Cape Town to **Simon's Town** on one of the country's oldest railway lines with ocean waves literally splashing the coach windows has got to be one of the cheapest and most spectacular outings in South Africa. Simon's Town is known as the Gibraltar of South Africa and from 1814 to 1957 was the Royal Navy's main South Atlantic base. There are 21 buildings along the main street, all more than 160 years old, which have been restored to their Victorian splendour. The cylindrical stone Martello Tower built in 1796 is the oldest surviving British building in South Africa and houses the *SA Naval Museum*, tel (021) 787-4635, while the *Simon's Town Museum* highlights the history of the town, tel (021) 786-3046. The *Warrior Toy Museum* in St George's Street has a permanent exhibition of Dinky toys, dolls, Meccano model cars, boats, trains and other toys, tel (021) 786-1395. In Jubilee Square is the statue of Able Seaman Just Nuisance, a Great Dane who was formally enrolled in the Royal Navy during the Second World War and on his death received a military funeral and this memorial.

Topstones is a large tumble-polish gemstone factory in Dido Valley Road, where you can see the various manufacturing and polishing processes and fossick in the scratch-patch, tel (021) 786-2020.

The **South African Fisheries Museum** on West Quay Road at the V&A Waterfront has, besides a small seawater aquarium, a DIY computerised encyclopedia that provides useful information, ranging from where to obtain a fishing licence for snoek, to find a good seafood restaurant. Open Tuesday to Sunday from 10am to 4pm, tel (021) 418-2312. On Dock Road is the **South African Maritime Museum**, which contains information about the fishing industry, shipwrecks, shipping lines, Table Bay harbour, ship modelling, and the Union Castle Company. It also has a shipwright's workshop and a discovery cove for children. The museum incorporates two floating exhibitions, the old boom defence vessel *SAS Somerset* and the steam tug *Alwyn Vintcent*. They are moored in the Alfred Basin. Open Monday to Sunday from 10am to 5pm, tel (021) 419-2506.

Founded in 1825, the **South African Museum** in Queen Victoria Street, central city, is the oldest and largest museum in the country. Its exhibits include a fossil gallery which traces the evolution of life in the Karoo, a Whale Well dominated by the 20m/66ft skeleton of a blue whale and resonant with recorded whale songs, the only example of a quagga foal, Bushman rock paintings, and the mysterious Lydenburg Heads, which rank among the earliest expressions of African art. Natural history videos are also shown. Presentations at the Planetarium take place daily. The museum is open daily from 10am to 5pm. Queen Victoria Street, city centre, tel (021) 24-3330.

The **South African National Gallery** in Government Avenue, Cape Town, has a permanent collection of European paintings, with some magnificent examples of landscape and portraiture from the Dutch, English and French schools of the 17th to 19th centuries. The gallery also has a small but growing collection of leading local artists, and is developing a name for displays of non-Eurocentric, indigenous as well as what in conservative South Africa is regarded as controversial art. Makhoba's award-winning painting *Azibuye Emasisweni*, which features an old man herding his cattle and is seen as an allegory for President Mandela, hangs in the gallery. The gallery is open on Monday from 1pm to 5.30pm, Tuesday to Saturday from 10am to 5.30pm, and on Sunday from 10am to 5pm, tel (021) 45-1628.

Flat-topped **Table Mountain** looming 1086m/3562ft above Cape Town and flanked by Devil's Peak, Lion's Head and Signal Hill, is a world-famous landmark visible at sea from as far away as 150km/93 miles. It is a magnet for the eye wherever you are in the city and the weekend playground of thousands, who climb it, skim it in helicopters, micro-lights, and hang-gliders, or simply ramble on its 3km/2-mile-long table-top and around its craggy slopes to admire its plants and flowers — 2620 different kinds — its 140 species of bird and the odd-looking shaggy thars, Himalayan mountain goats descended from a bunch which once escaped from nearby Groote Schuur Zoo and now share the slopes with troops of chacma baboons, rock rabbits, porcupines, mongoose, fallow deer and other smallish mammals. You can't say you have really been to Cape Town unless you have stood on top of this sandstone mass. It is a 3-hour climb to the top (the easiest route starts at the Kirstenbosch Botanical Gardens), but the majority of visitors use the handy cable car from Kloof Nek for a 6-minute aerial ride to the summit, where you can admire the truly spectacular view, peer through one of the mounted telescopes, refresh yourself in the restaurant, buy souvenirs at the Cableway kiosk and post letters or postcards which will carry a special Table Mountain postmark. Stretching away towards Hout Bay you can see the peaks of the Twelve Apostles. The first recorded climb was made in 1503 by Portuguese navigator Antonio da Saldanha who wanted to find out where he was. The cable car service started in 1929 and has since carried more than 10 million people to the top without a single accident. More than 450,000 now use the cableway every year, so queues are frequent in the holiday season and it is best to get to the station early. Check times with the Table Mountain Aerial Cableway Company, Lower Station, tel (021) 24-5148, or its city office, tel (021) 24-8409. If you are planning a hike or a climb they will advise you on weather conditions, and the Mountain Club of SA, tel (021) 45-3412, will also give helpful advice.

Tygerberg Nature Reserve. A nature reserve of 67 hectares containing indigenous plants, a variety of small game, birds, numerous walking trails and picnic spots. Permits at the gate. Open weekdays from 8.30am to 4.30pm and Saturday and Sunday from 9am to 6pm. Totius Street, Welgemoed, tel (021) 913-5695.

San Francisco has its Fisherman's Wharf, Ghirardelli Square and The Cannery, Sydney has The Rocks, and London has its Dockland Canary Wharf area. Cape Town's answer is the **Victoria & Alfred Waterfront**, where South Africa's formerly neglected dockland has been transformed from a waterfront slum to one of the country's leading tourist attractions, attracting up to 60,000 visitors a day. In the old days you went to Cape Town docks to catch fish, a ship or trawl for ladies of the night. Now the attractions include more than 30 top-class restaurants, first-class accommodation, and 240 up and down-market shops, as well as, pubs, bistros, taverns, live music venues, craft markets, museums, tours, ferry boats, cruises, airflips and other diversions. There is also plenty to amuse children, from the *Two Oceans Aquarium* with its 50,000 marine creatures, including penguins, sharks, crayfish, abalone, and endangered Knysna seahorses, the *Telkom Exploratorium* in the Union Castle Building, where fun and communications technology meet, to harbour rides on a steam tug and the Penny Ferry (no longer a penny), and the Shipwreck Playground near the Market Plaza. The Waterfront Visitor's Centre will give you maps and details of events planned for the day; tel (021) 418-2369, or contact the 24-hour information hotline, tel (021) 418-4644.

In Valley Road, the **World of Birds**, is one of the largest bird parks in the world, with

3000 birds of 450 different species from all over the world in 100 walk-through, landscaped aviaries. Open daily from 9am to 5pm, tel (021) 790-2730/4838.

As South Africa's oldest city, Cape Town regards itself as the country's cultural capital. Its first theatre was built in 1800 and museums and art galleries dot the Peninsula. Appreciation of the performing arts is widespread and generates year-round productions of theatre, music, opera, ballet and modern dance. The Cape Town Symphony Orchestra performs on Thursdays at 8pm in the City Hall, opposite the Grand Parade, and there are often free lunchtime organ recitals. There are also lots of good movie houses, pubs and clubs with live jazz, pop, rock and rave in Cape Town and its suburbs. To find out what's on check the local newspapers or the monthly *Going Out in the Cape* for details. The majority of the city's clubs and night spots are in Sea Point, at the Waterfront, and in the suburb of Rondebosch, where a strong student population supports anything far-out and late-night.

There are more than 30 cinemas in Cape Town and its suburbs, including three drive-ins (open-air cinemas). Most of them are part of the usual national Ster-Kinekor (tel (021) 25-1106) and Nu Metro (tel (021) 23-0478) circuits, although there are a couple of movie houses dedicated to art and experimental films, such as The Labia, in Orange Street, Gardens, tel (021) 24-5927, the Baxter Cinema, in Main Road, Rondebosch, tel (021) 689-1069, and the Imax Cinema, V&A Waterfront, tel (021) 419-7364/5.

There are around a dozen theatres in and around the city. The main ones are the Nico Malan Theatre Centre, on DF Malan Street, Foreshore, which regularly hosts international stars, and the University of Cape Town's Baxter Theatre Complex, on Main Road, Rondebosch. The Nico is a complete performing arts centre and features a 1188-seat opera house, a 541-seat theatre, a 100-seat arena theatre, and a coffee shop, tel (021) 21-5470, or make credit card telephone bookings through Nico Dial-a-Seat at (021) 21-7695. The Baxter contains a 665-seat theatre, a concert hall for 638, the Studio Theatre seating 150, and a restaurant, tel (021) 685-7880. Other venues are The UCT Arena, Orange Street, a theatre belonging to the University of Cape Town, tel (021) 24-2340; Dock Road Café and Theatre, V&A Waterfront, tel (021) 25-4334; Herschel Theatre, 21 Herschel Road, Claremont, tel (021) 64-4010, a school groups and amateur theatre seating 299; Long Street Theatre, Waterkant Street, an alternative arts, culture and experimental theatre with a resident band playing a fusion of rock 'n roll and African rhythms, tel (021) 418-3496; Masque Theatre, Main Road, Muizenberg, amateur theatre, tel (021) 788-1898; Maynardville Open-Air Theatre, corner Church and Wolfe streets, Wynberg, performances of Shakespeare and ballet during the summer season, tel (021) 21-4715; Milnerton Playhouse, Pienaar Road, amateur theatre seating 100, tel (021) 557-3206; Theatre on the Bay, Link Street, Camps Bay, top quality work in 396-seater theatre, tel (021) 438-3301; V&A Theatre, V&A Waterfront, performances by professionals in a 266-seat theatre, tel (021) 419-4767.

At venues that consistently feature live jazz you might come across South African jazz legends such as saxmen Basil 'Manenberg' Coetzee, Winston 'Mankunku' Ngozi, and Robbie Jansen. Since 1990, jazz pianist Abdullah Ibrahim has also re-established himself in Cape Town. You can listen to jazz, jazz fusion, funk and various other types of music at:

Baker Street Jazz Club, corner of Halt Road and 28th Avenue, Elsies River, tel (021) 932-2170;
Blue Note (Galaxy), Cine 400, College Road, Rylands;
Café Blue Moon, corner of Shortmarket and Long streets, central city, tel (021) 24-5100;

Club Montreal, York Street, Sherwood Park, Manenberg, tel (021) 694-1780;
Club Palazzo, Shop 615, Upper level, North Mall, Tyger Valley Centre, tel (021) 948-3029;
Club Montreal, York Street, Sherwood Park, tel (021) 694-1780;
Dizzy's Jazz Café, The Drive, Camps Bay, tel (021) 438-2686;
Gershwin's Karaoke and Jazz Club, Strawberry Mall, Church Way, Strandfontein, tel (021) 33-1831;
Goodfellow's Jazz Club, 13 Halt Road, Elsies River, tel (021) 591-7379;
—*Green Dolphin*, Pierhead, V&A Waterfront, tel (021) 21-7471;
Heatwave, Victoria Road, Grassy Park Centre, Zeekoevlei, tel (021) 706-5019;
Manenberg's Jazz Café, 2nd Floor, Dumbarton House, corner Adderley and Church streets, central, tel (021) 23-8304;
Riff's Jazz Pub, 139 Wetton Road, Wetton, tel (021) 73-2676;
The Jol & Gimba's Restaurant, 7 Bree Street, central, tel (021) 418-1148;
— *The Pumphouse*, V&A Waterfront, Sunday afternoons for Dixieland jazz, tel (021) 419-7722.

Laid-back jazz cruises are run by Teacher's Cruising Venue every Sunday evening in season at the V&A Waterfront. The three-hour cruise costs R35 (£4.65/$7.70), or R125 with dinner. Cast-off in their 24m/79ft catamaran from Quay 6. They also do breakfast (R85), lunch (140), cocktail (R60) and dinner R155) cruises in season, tel (021) 419-3122. For Eurosounds try The Purple Turtle, Shortmarket Street, central; Take Four Bistro, Longkloof Studios, Kloof Street; River Club, Liesbeeck Park, Observatory; The Planet, Station Road, Observatory; Ruby in the Dust, Lower Main Road, Observatory; Hard Rock Café, one on Beach Road in Sea Point, and another on Main Road, Rondebosch; Cygnet, Modderdam Road, Bellville South; Taboo, Main Road, Claremont; and Fat Boys, off Somerset Road, Green Point.

City and suburban hotels and pubs with live music include the Canterbury Inn, Blue Danube, Hohenhort Hotel, Inn on the Square, Kommetjie Hotel, the Palace Hotel, Chelsea Arms, Coach House Pub, Pig & Whistle, Forester's Arms, Rompies Pub at the New Regency Hotel, Regent Road, Sea Point, the London Pub at the Century Hotel, The Gaiety Bar at the New Kimberley Hotel, Kings Hotel, Lady Diana's Bar at the Fairmead Hotel, the Killarney Hotel in Koeberg Road, Milnerton, and Dirty Dick's Tavern, Harbour Road, Hout Bay.

Gay Bars and Clubs

Angels/Detour/Bronx, 27 Somerset Road, Greenpoint, tel (021) 419-9216.
Brunswick Tavern, 17 Bree Street, tel (021) 25-2739.
Café Carte Blanche, Trill Road, Observatory, tel (021) 419-9798/705-3659.
Club Welgelegen, 51 William Street, Mowbray, tel (021) 448-6202/2014.
Owens 'Gat' Party, Temple of Israel Hall, corner Main and Upper Portswood Road, Green Point, tel (021) 930-3399.
Steamers Health and Leisure Club, Old Creda Press Building, corner Wembly and Solan Roads, Gardens, tel (021) 419-9216.
Café Manhattan, Waterkant Street, is a gay institution in Cape Town. Next door is The Empire Lounge, done out in Afro-Camp.

FLOWER SHOWS AND GARDENS

Unless you are a keen botanist, gardener or flower lover you might not have the week to spare that is regarded as the minimum needed really to enjoy the floral spectacle. Every year a number of country **wildflower shows** are held to celebrate the bounty of particular regions. The *Darling Wildflower Show* is popular in September, especially as it is only 70km/44 miles from Cape Town. Some local farmers also allow you into their fields to see the flowers in their natural state. More than 420 species of flowering plant have been recorded in the Darling area. Contact tel (02241) 2422 or (02241) 3361.

The following flower shows are also in September:

Caledon Wild Flower Show, tel (0286) 937;
Cape Town Botanical Society Wildflower Show, Kirstenbosch, tel (021) 797-2090;
Clanwilliam Wild Flower Show, tel (027) 482-2024;
Hopefield Fynbos Show, tel (02288) 30856;
Hermanus Flower Show, tel (0283) 77-0919/70-0300;
Villiersdorp Flower Show, tel (0225) 3-1130 and (0225) 32374.

In October, Porterville stages its agricultural and wild flower show, tel (02623) 2900; and the Ceres Show takes place, tel (0233) 61287. To find out where the best displays are on any given spring day you should contact *Flower Line,* tel (021) 418-3705, during July and October. Flower Line is a seven-day-a-week hotline number that can also give you details of accommodation, tours and special attractions in the flower regions.

As well as flower shows there are also some wonderful **flower reserves and gardens** in the Western Cape:

Akkerendam. In Calvinia, 421km/262 miles from Cape Town. Take the N7 to Vanrhynsdorp, then the turn off to Nieuwoudtville, which leads to Calvinia. Proclaimed bird sanctuary. Two hiking trails. Open all year round. Tel (0273) 41-1011.

Caledon Garden. About 112km/70 miles from Cape Town. Take N2 from Cape Town over Sir Lowry's Pass. Garden lies to the left of the main road approaching town. Open 7am to 6pm daily. Tel (0281) 21511.

Cape of Good Hope Nature Reserve. Cape Point, 7750 hectares of indigenous flora and fauna. Reserve open 7am to 6pm (1 October to 31 March) and 7am to 5pm (1 April to 30 September). Tel (021) 780-9100.

Cedarberg Wilderness Area. About 225km/140 miles from the city. Follow the N7 from Cape Town. Turn off right 28km/17 miles after Citrusdal on the Algeria–Cedarberg road. Continue 18km/11 miles in this direction over the Nieuwoudt Pass, till the entrance of the reserve is reached. Contact Nature Conservation for information on camping and hiking. Office hours 8am to 4.30pm, tel (022) 921-2289.

Ceres Mountain Fynbos Reserve. 127km/79 miles from Cape Town. Follow R303 of the N1 from Paarl to Ceres. The nature reserve is situated on the left at the entrance to the town opposite the golf course. Rock art and Cape fynbos can be seen. Open daily, tel (0233) 21177 x 259 or 21437.

Darling. 76km/47 miles from Cape Town. Contreberg: on the Darling/Mamre Road. Waylands: 6km/3.8 miles from Darling (R307). Oudepost: Some 3km/1.9 miles from Darling at the T-junction to Malmesbury. Tel (02241) 3361.

Dassieshoek. 173km/108 miles from Cape Town. Take N1, Du Toit's Kloof, Worcester to Robertson. Saturday and Sunday 8am to 6pm, tel (02351) 4035.

De Hoop Nature Reserve. 260km/162 miles from Cape Town on the N2 and R319. 50km/31 miles from either Bredasdorp or Swellendam along gravel road. Access to the reserve is via Wydgeleë (Ouplaas) on the Bredasdorp-Malgas road. Open daily 7am to 6pm, tel (028) 542-1126.

Fernkloof. 119km/74 miles from Cape Town, near Hermanus. Open daily. Guided walks on request. Enquiries through Hermanus Publicity Association, 105 Main Street, Hermanus, Western Cape, tel (0283) 22629.

Goegap. 571km/355 miles from Cape Town. Follow N7 from Cape Town. The reserve is situated 14km/9 miles north-east of Springbok. A 6km walking trail, mountain bike trail, and a 4x4 route as well as a 17km/11 miles drive are available. Great variety of succulents. Open daily 8am to 4.15pm, tel (0251) 21880.

Helderberg. 48km/30 miles from Cape Town, at Somerset West. Open 7am to 8pm (November to April), 7am to 6pm (May to October). Reached via Main Street and Lourensford Road in the town. Reserve is indicated by signboard. Open daily, tel (024) 51-4022.

Hortus Botanicus. Corner Neethling and Van Riebeeck Streets, Stellenbosch. Open 8.30am to 4.30pm Monday to Friday and 8.30am to 10.30am on Saturday, tel (021) 808-3054.

Klein Karoo. Many different species of wild flowers can be viewed throughout the year. For details of the seven reserves contact Cape Nature Conservation, tel (0443) 29-1739 or 22-5955.

Montagu. 198km/123 miles from Cape Town. Follow N1 from Cape Town via Du Toit's Kloof, Worcester and Robertson. The garden is in Van Riebeeck Street, 15 minutes' walk from the centre of town. Open 9am to 6pm, tel (0234) 42471 or 41426.

Nieuwoudtville. 3km from the town on the R27. The flora of this 115-hectare reserve is particularly rich, with 306 species. Tel (02726) 81316/81363/81223.

Oorlogskloof. Some of the most unspoilt *fynbos* in existence covers the 4000 hectares of this reserve. 46km/29 miles of trails: three to four days of hiking with camping, spring flowers, mammals and birds. Tel (022) 921-2289.

Paarl Mountain Flower Reserve. 56km/35 miles from Cape Town, on the slopes of Paarl Mountain. Turn off Main Road into Jan Phillips Mountain Drive to its end. Open daily, tel (021) 872-3829.

Ramskop. 225km from city on the N7. Just outside Clanwilliam, next to the Municipal Holiday Resort. Open daily 7am to sunset, mid-July to October, tel (027) 482-2133 or 482-2024.

Rocherpan. 25km/16 miles north of Velddrif. Follow the R27 to Velddrif. 1000 hectares comprising a water pan and wetlands with a large variety of waterbirds and West Coast flora. Open daily 7am to 6pm, tel (02625) 727.

Salmonsdam. 152km/94 miles from Cape Town on the N2 and R43 to Hermanus and Stanford. 10km/6 miles from Stanford. Accommodation available. Open daily 7am to 7pm, tel (0283) 77-0062.

Silvermine. On the Ou Kaapseweg, M64 near Tokai, Cape Town. Picnic sites, barbecue, hiking trails. Open daily 8am to 7pm, tel (021) 75-3040/1/2/3.

Steenbras Dam. 64km/40 miles from Cape Town, N2 on Sir Lowry's Pass. Admission by permit from Civic Amenities, Civic Centre, Cape Town, or Strand Municipal Offices, tel (021) 400-2507 or (024) 51-4022.

Villiersdorp. 106km/66 miles from Cape Town. N2 and R43, Villiersdorp. 1km from town past the caravan park. Open daily 8am to 5pm, tel (0225) 31130.

West Coast National Park. 120km/75 miles from Cape Town off the R27, West Coast road. Open 9am to 5pm (August and September), tel (02287) 22144.

WINELANDS

The Winelands encompass a variety of regions, each different in terrain and each producing distinctly different wines. What the areas do have in common is breathtaking scenery, gracious homesteads, generous, friendly people and, running like red and white threads through the whole tapestry, the stuff that caused an exultant Jan van Riebeeck to jot in his diary on 2 February 1659: 'Today, praise be to God, wine was made for the first time from Cape grapes...' A variety of routes have been established throughout the wine-growing areas, from the Olifants River area in the north, the prime routes of Stellenbosch, Paarl and Franschhoek, to the Breede River Valley and the little towns of the Klein Karoo in the east. Towns and villages

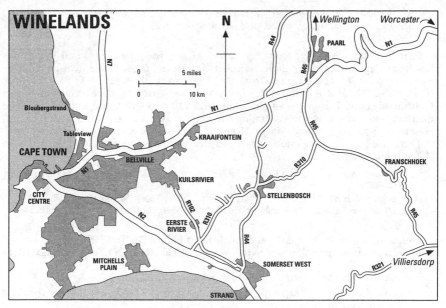

throughout the Winelands are linked to the Cape metropolitan area and the rest of the province by a first-rate network of national and provincial roads. There are also rail services to the major centres. There is little to beat a day on one or other of the wine routes, sampling the products of the vine along the way and lunching on a vintner's platter on the dappled stoep of an ancient gabled farmhouse. The most instructive time to visit the Winelands is during the pressing season, roughly mid-February to mid-April, although every other month has something to offer. The Stumble Inn Youth Hostel in Stellenbosch has a special package offer of two nights' accommodation and a full wine tour which is a snip at R170 (a normal day tour costs R150 per person), tel/fax (021) 887-4049. e-mail stumble@iafrica.com

ACCOMMODATION

Stellenbosch has luxury hotels and guest houses, affordable B&Bs and self-catering cottages and youth hostels, as well as a caravan park within easy reach of the wine estates.

> The three-star *D'Ouwe Werf*, 30 Church Street, dates back to 1802 and is the oldest existing country inn in South Africa, R215 per person B&B, tel (021) 887-4608, fax (021) 887-4626.
> *Stellenbosch Hotel*, three-star, old-world charm in the centre of town. R160 (£21.35/$35.20) per person B&B. Contact PO Box 500, Stellenbosch 7599, tel (021) 887-3644, fax (021) 887-3673.
> *Lanzerac Hotel*, PO Box 4, Stellenbosch 7599, tel (021) 887-1132, fax (021) 887-2310.
> *Devon Valley Protea Hotel*, three-star, Devon Valley Road, from R180 a night, tel (021) 882-2012, fax (021) 882-2610.
> *Zandberg Farm*, guest cottages, R125 per person a night B&B, PO Box 5337, Helderberg 7135, tel (024) 842-2945.
> *De Goue Druif*, 3-star guest house at 110 Dorp Street, tel (021) 883-3555, fax (021) 883-3588.

Rust & Vrede, Strand Road, from R70 per person B&B, tel (024) 55-4068.
Stumble Inn, dormitory and double rooms from R25 per person, tel/fax (021) 887-4049.

Paarl is 30 minutes' drive from the centre of Cape Town on the N1 and 10 minutes less from Cape Town International Airport. Top of the range is the five-star *Grande Roche Hotel* in Plantasie Street, from R610 a person B&B, tel (021) 863-2727, fax (021) 863-2220. This is one of the few hotels in Africa to have achieved Relais Gourmand status. It is set on an old estate with suites in a restored wine cellar, slave quarters and stables, as well as among the vineyards. Its award-winning restaurant, Bosman's, is in the restored Manor House. There is even a helicopter landing pad.

There are also intimate guesthouses and B&Bs; budget accommodation, at about R70 a night, includes:

Safariland, Wemmershoek Road, Suider-Paarl, tel (021) 864-0064, fax (021) 864-0065;
Berg River Resort, PO Box 552, Paarl 7646, tel (021) 863-1650, fax (021) 863-2583;
Boschenmeer Resort, Wemmershoek Road, Paarl 7646, tel (021) 863-1250, fax (021) 863-3082.

Mountain Shadows, in Paarl, on a small farm below Du Toit's Kloof, was one of Satour's runner-up guesthouses of the year in 1996, tel (021) 862-3192, fax (021) 862-6796.

Among the quainter places in Franschhoek are:

The *Auberge Bligny*, 28 Van Wijk Street, from R150 per person sharing, tel (021) 876-3767, fax (021) 876-3483;
Rodeberg Lodge, 74 Main Street, R135 per person B&B, tel (02211) 63-3202, fax (02211) 63-3203;
La Provence — Jonkershuis, R150 per person a night sharing, PO Box 393, Franschhoek 7690, tel (02212) 2163, fax (02212) 2616;
Franschhoek Mountain Manor, 3-star, R110 a night, tel (02212) 2071, fax (02212) 2177.

Farms that rent out cottages are:

Dassenberg, R90 and R110, tel (02212) 2107;
Dieu Donné, R180, tel (02212) 2131;
Boven La Motte, R90, tel (02212) 2312.

All rates are per night, per person sharing B&B.

In Tulbagh, *Hunter's Retreat* is a mile out of town on Ruimte farm. Converted labourer's cottages at R120 per person a night. Fully equipped kitchens for the self-catering traveller, although you can eat in the farmhouse. PO Box 248, Tulbagh 6820, tel (0236) 30-0582, fax (0236) 30-0101; *De Oude Herberg*, 6 Church Street, R90 per person B&B, tel (0236) 30-0260; and *Witzenberg Hotel*, in Piet Retief Street, has rooms from R75 a night, tel/fax (0236) 30-0159.

Accommodation in Worcester includes:

Cumberland Hotel, 3-star, in the centre of town, with a spa bath, pool, gym, tennis and squash courts, from R140 per person a night B&B. PO Box 8, Worcester 6850, tel (0231) 72641, fax (0231) 73613.
Church Street Lodge and Table Talk Café, 36 Church Street, R125 (£16.65/$27.50) per person a night B&B, tel (0231) 25194, fax (0231) 28859.
ATKV Goudini Spa and Holiday Resort, 22km/14 miles from Worcester, off the N1 on the R101 in the Rawsonville area, has self-catering rondavels and flats at R97 a night, and caravan sites for R51 a night. It also has one of the hottest mineral springs in the country, tel (0231) 91100, fax (0231) 91903.
Rustig Holiday Resort, chalets from R120 (£16/$26.40) a night, caravan sites R30 a night. PO Box 958, Worcester 6850, tel (0231) 27245, fax (0231) 24681.

Du Toitskloof Resort, from R110 B&B. Catch your own dinner on the trout farm.
Camp sites from R50 a night, tel (0231) 91092/91153, fax (0231) 91813.
Burger Caravan Park, in the town, sites at R21 a night, tel (0231) 71992.
Nekkies Caravan Park, sites R22 a night, tel (0231) 23461.

Montagu is world-famous for its healing hot mineral springs. Try the *Avalon
Springs*, 3-star hotel, hot spa and holiday resort. Accommodation in luxury hotel
rooms or self-catering holiday flats. PO Box 110, Montagu 6720, tel (0234) 41150, fax
(0234) 41906; or the *Montagu Springs*, fully-equipped chalets from R210 a night, and
villas at R300 a night, tel (0234) 41050. At the gateway to the Klein Karoo is the
Montagu Country Inn, 2-star, R190 per person a night DB&B, PO Box 338, Montagu
6720, tel (0234) 41115, fax (0234) 41905. *Montagu Caravan Park*, PO Box 273,
Montagu 6720, tel (0234) 42675.

Also in Montagu are *Mimosa Lodge,* Church Street, tel (0234) 42351, fax (0234)
41408, and *Kingna Lodge,* a charming Victorian house in Bath Street, tel (0234)
41066, fax (0234) 42405; both of these were runners-up for Satour 'Guesthouse of the
Year' in 1996.

Budget Accommodation, at about R70 a night:

> *Pat Busch Nature Reserve*, PO Box 579, Robertson 6705, tel (02351) 2033;
> *Mountain View Holiday Home*, 10 Steynsrust Road, Braeview, Somerset West 7130,
> tel/fax (024) 55-2435;
> *Kliprivier Park Holiday Resort*, Van Der Stel Street, Tulbagh 6820, tel (0236) 30-0506,
> fax (0236) 30-1250.

Backpacker accommodation includes:

> *The Wave*, 288 Main Road, Clovelly 7975, tel (021) 782-3659.
> *Cluver Lodge*, 12 Cluver Street, PO Box 7248, Stellenbosch 7599, tel (021) 887-2123,
> fax (021) 887-2397.
> *Hillbillies Haven*, 24 Dennesig Street, Stellenbosch 7600, tel (021) 887-8475.
> *Stumble Inn*, 12 Market Street, Stellenbosch 7600, tel (021) 887-4049, fax (021)
> 887-4049.
> *Wicked West Backpacker and Campground*, off N2 Highway in vineyards, Somerset
> West, tel (024) 852-1976.

EATING AND DRINKING

Stellenbosch and its surrounding countryside is noted for its wines and good food,
usually of the traditional variety — tasty, filling and inexpensive. Restaurants are
often in historic homesteads, and many farms offer a wide variety of meals, ranging
from a single bowl of thick soup, a vintner's or coachman's platter or picnic lunch to
the works. There are numerous pubs and taverns, some with live music and some
which stay open into the wee small hours. *De Volkskombuis* specialises in Cape
cooking. Open Monday to Saturday for lunch, dinner and teas, Ou Strandweg, tel
(021) 887-2121; *Lanzerac Restaurant* looks out over vineyards that are more than 200
years old, and there is a legendary cheese buffet at the Vinkel en Koljander in the
parent Lanzerac Hotel, tel (021) 887-1132. The *Van Ryn Brandy Cellar*, near
Stellenbosch, has cellar tours Monday to Thursday at 10.30am and 3pm and Friday at
10.30am, tel (021) 881-3875. *KWV Brandy Cellar,* Worcester, with 120 copper potstills
is the largest of its kind in the world. Daily guided tours on weekdays at 11am and
3.30pm and Saturday at 11am, tel (0231) 20255.

In Paarl, the top (expensive) restaurant — with the awards to prove it — is
Bosman's Restaurant at Grande Roche Hotel, Plantasie Street, tel (021) 863-2727.
Other gourmet fare at *Rhebokskloof Estate Victorian Restaurant*, Noorder Paarl, tel
(021) 863-8606, and *Laborie Restaurant and Wine House*, in Taillefert Street, tel (021)
807-3095.

Franschhoek lives up to the cuisine of its original French settler families. Try:

Chez Michel, Huguenot Road, tel (021) 876-2671;
La Maison de Chamonix, 1 Uitkyk Street, tel (021) 876-2393;
La Petite Ferme, Franschhoek Pass, tel (021) 876-3016;
Le Quartier Francais, 16 Huguenot Road, tel (021) 876-2151;
Le Ballon Rouge, 7 Reservoir Street, tel (021) 876-2651.

These are all fairly pricey. *Brinjals* at 18 Huguenot Road is a great value-for-money bistro and delicatessen, tel (021) 876-2151.

In Tulbagh's historic Church Street, the *Paddagang Restaurant and Wine House* (1809) serves traditional Cape country food. The restaurant got its unusual name from the frogs (paddas) that cross the nearby river bridge during mating season. Try the Padda wines sporting amusing froggy labels and names like Brulpadda, Platanna and Paddarotti, tel (0236) 30-0242.

EXPLORING

The **Cedarberg** is a mountain range roughly 100km/62 miles from Cape Town. At the northern end is the town of Clanwilliam and at the southern end is the village of Citrusdal, both used as gateways to the beautiful Cedarberg Wilderness Area. Citrusdal is the hub of the vast citrus estates of the Olifants River Valley, while Clanwilliam is best known as the centre of the *rooibos* ('red bush') tea industry.

Named after the Roman goddess of agriculture **Ceres** lies in the country's most important deciduous fruit-growing district, 130km/81 miles north-east of Cape Town. The Ceres Bergfynbos Reserve has a large variety of indigenous flora, dramatic rock formations and Bushman rock paintings, tel (0233) 22301. From mid-November to January, you can pick your own cherries at Klondyke Cherry Farm, tel (0233) 22085. For advice on fruit tours, fishing spots and hiking and 4x4 trails, tel (0233) 61287. At Kagga Kamma ('The Place of the Bushmen') you can get a glimpse of San lifestyle through the Bushman clan that still lives there, tel (02211) 63-8334.

Citrusdal is one of the province's major eco-tourism destinations. The surrounding Cedarberg, Olifants River and Koue Bokkeveld mountains offer excellent hiking, mountain biking and rugged 4x4 trails. The Ramskop Nature Reserve in **Clanwilliam** is the place to go between July and September to see wild flowers in bloom, and the Clanwilliam district as a whole can be rewarding in the wild flower season, even when there has been a bad season in the prime floral area of Namaqualand. 70km/44 miles south-east of Clanwilliam is the Rhenish Missionary Society village of **Wuppertal**, which is a neat little settlement seemingly left behind by time. The village is noted for the leather velskoen made there. An old Bushman trail goes through the mountains from Wuppertal to Clanwilliam and is a magnificent but testing hike.

Franschhoek is a little corner of France in the Cape and gets its names ('French Corner') from the Huguenot refugees who settled there between 1688 and 1690 after fleeing religious persecution in France for their Calvinist beliefs. The town is 25km/16 miles south-east of Paarl and is the heart of a wine route (see page 439), the Vignerons de Franschhoek, and a cluster of some of the best nouvelle cuisine restaurants in the Winelands.

Gordon's Bay is a resort and harbour at the foot of the Hottentots Holland mountains in the north-east corner of False Bay. This is the home of the annual International Broadbill Classic deep-sea angling competition. Nearby, the Steenbras Dam, and its gardens and forests, offer a variety of recreational options. Permits obtainable from the Cape Town Civic Centre, tel (021) 400-2607.

Goudini is a region with Rawsonville as its principal town. Its Khoikhoi name means 'bitter honey.' Goudini Spa is a noted health resort with a hot spring that reaches a surface temperature of 40°C/104°F and is said to have therapeutic properties (and also good for hangovers), tel (0231) 91100.

The town of **Montagu** was founded in 1851 and named after John Montagu, then Colonial Secretary of the Cape. The Klein Karoo Wine Route (see page 440) starts in the town. The Montagu Museum in Long Street depicts local history and has a collection of Africana well worth seeing. Montagu's radioactive hot springs have made the town a well known health resort. Montagu is noted for its sweet wines and its annual Muscadet Wine Festival in March. Outside the town is Cogman's Kloof, a vivid and colourful example of the earth's buckling which has the oldest road tunnel still in use in the country. This was constructed in 1877 by Thomas Bain.

Olifants River ('Elephants River') Wine Route encompasses vineyards that have been tended along the river banks for the past 150 years. The Wine Route stretches from Citrusdal to Lutzville, and takes in six co-operative wine cellars and one estate (see page 441).

The pretty Boland town of **Paarl** ('Pearl') was named by the early Dutch settlers after the huge, rounded, granite rock outside the town that glistens after rain (it is the largest granite rock form in the world after the Rock of Gibraltar, and one of three that make up Paarl Mountain). Vying with it are the twin pinnacles of the *Taalmonument* ('Language Monument'), which can be seen for miles around and commemorate the birth of Afrikaans as a recognised language.

Oak trees and graceful old buildings line Paarl's 12km/8-mile long Main Street, claimed to be the longest street in the country. The town is the imposing headquarters of the KWV (Ko-operatiewe Wijnbouwers Vereeniging Van Zuid Afrika Beperkt) or the Co-operative Wine Farmer's Association of South Africa, which has some of the largest wine cellars in the world. There are nearly 1000 underground tanks for storing wine, each tank containing 12,700 gallons, and all told there is storage for more than 12 million gallons. Each big vat in the cellars can hold 45,000 gallons of wine — enough to last a bottle-a-day man for 750 years. Tel (021) 807-3007/8, e-mail dekockm@kwv.co.za.

The Oude Pastorie (1714) and Paarl Museum exhibit Cape Dutch antiques and items of Huguenot and early Afrikaner culture. The collection of Cape silver in particular is superb. Open Monday to Friday from 8am to 1pm and 2pm to 5pm, Saturday from 10am to midday, and Sunday from 3pm to 5pm. The Afrikaans Taalmuseum is a cultural museum dedicated to the language of the Afrikaner people, which first came to flower in this area around 1875. It is open on weekdays from 9am to 4.30pm on Saturday from 9am to midday and on Sunday from 3.30pm to 5.30pm, tel (021) 872-3441.

Paarlberg Nature Reserve has fine displays of disas and proteas. Open sunrise to sunset. The Huguenot Tunnel provides access to the Breede River Valley shortening the distance between Paarl and Worcester by 11km/7 miles.

Robertson lies in the valley watered by the Breede River, below the Langeberg Mountains, which stretch 200km/124 miles from Worcester to the vicinity of George. The local wine route starts here (see page 440). The Robertson Museum in Paul Kruger Street has an interesting collection of lace and lace-making tools, tel (02351) 3681. Most of the country's champion racehorses come from this district.

In the foothills of the Hottentots Holland Mountains, 45km/28 miles south-east of Cape Town, **Somerset West** retains the village atmosphere of its early years. Vergelegen ('Far Away') Wine Estate is one of the finest and most historic of the Cape Dutch stately homes, and was established in 1700 by Governor Willem van der

Stel. The estate is open daily from 9.30am to 6pm. Cellar tours are conducted at 10.30am, 11.30am and 2.30pm, tel (024) 51-7060.

After Cape Town, **Stellenbosch** is the oldest town in the country. It was founded in 1679 and is one of South Africa's best preserved and best loved towns. Lying in the Eerste River Valley, 48km/30 miles east of Cape Town, it is well known for its university, its oak trees, and the surrounding wine farms, which comprise the most popular of all the wine routes (see page 432). No fewer than 60 buildings have been proclaimed national monuments. Five museums display the local furniture, arts, crafts and clothing of the 17th and 18th centuries. Dorp Street is the most picturesque and certainly the oldest thoroughfare in Stellenbosch. Once the wagon road to Cape Town, it is bordered by mature oaks, water furrows and one of the longest rows of old buildings in the country. The Village Museum complex on Ryneveld Street covers two street blocks and encompasses some of the oldest houses and gardens in Stellenbosch, among them Schreuder House, which was built before 1709 and is the oldest town house in South Africa. Of particular interest to American visitors is the neo-classical-style house La Gratitude at 95 Dorp Street, which features an all-seeing 'Eye of God' on its central gable. La Gratitude was once the home of enterprising William Charles Winshaw, a Kentuckian who arrived at the Cape in 1900 with 4000 mules and stayed to make wine. Winshaw established Stellenbosch Farmers' Winery (SFW) in 1924 to encourage the development and sale of South African wine. SFW is still in Stellenbosch and has grown to be the largest winery in the country. Open Monday to Saturday from 9.30am to 5pm, Sunday 2pm to 5pm, tel (021) 887-2902. For an interesting and pleasant introduction to the many features of this historical town, join local guides on a leisurely 50-minute walk from the Stellenbosch Tourist Bureau at 36 Market Street, Monday to Saturday at 10am, midday and 3pm, or contact Stellenbosch Historical Walks, tel (021) 883-9633. Cycling is an excellent way of getting around Stellenbosch and the surrounding countryside. You can hire a bike from Village Cycles at 3 Victoria Street, for R10 (£1.35/$2.20) an hour, or R40 a day, tel (021) 883-8593, and from the Stumble Inn Youth Hostel at 12–14 Market Street, for R5 an hour or R30 a day, tel (021) 887-4049.

For nature lovers there are mountains close to town, among them the Jonkershoek and Papegaaiberg ('Parrot Mountain'), whose slopes are clothed in leucadendrons, ericas, pincushions and proteas. Among the reserves, parks and gardens are the university's Botanical Garden in Van Riebeeck Street, where ferns, bonsai trees, orchids, proteas and succulents grow, as well as specimens of the weird *Welwitschia mirabilis*, indigenous to the Namibian desert, and the most complete collection of pelargoniums in the world. Open Monday to Friday from 8am to 4.30pm, Saturday from 8.30am to 10.30am, tel (021) 808-9111. Near the university is the Jan Marais Nature Reserve which has a wealth of flora once indigenous to the area. Open daily from 7.30am to 6pm (1 April to 30 September) and 7.30am to 7.30pm (1 October to 31 March), tel (021) 883-2111. The Jonkershoek Forestry Reserve is open all year round, although it might be closed without warning during the hot summer months (November to March) because of the danger of fire. There are a number of hiking trails of which the 8-hour Panorama Route is the most strenuous, tel (021) 886-5715. Although the Jonkershoek Trout Hatchery can be visited only by appointment, the aquarium is open to visitors on weekdays from 8am to 4.15pm, tel (021) 887-0184. 16km/10 miles south-west of Stellenbosch is **Faure**, whose nearby kramat, or tomb, of Islamic expatriate priest Sheikh Yusuf (1626-1699) is a place of pilgrimage for local Muslims.

The picturesque Boland town of **Tulbagh** is one of the best known towns in South Africa. It achieved its fame in September 1969 when an earthquake measuring 6.5 on the Richter Scale, the most powerful ever recorded in South Africa, devastated the town (a quake registering 6 is the equivalent of 6 kilotons, or one-third of an atomic bomb). The 32 dazzling white buildings which line Church Street today are a perfect representation of an 18th century village. They were rebuilt after the earthquake and now form the only street in South Africa where every single building is an historical monument. No 4 Church Street should be the first port of call as it outlines the history of the settlement from 1700 as well as the details of the quake that brought about such a faithful architectural restoration. Nos 14 and 22 house collections of furnishings and costumes. The three buildings together comprise the Town Museum. De Oude Drostdy, 4km/2.5 miles from Tulbagh, was completed in 1806, and displays early Cape furniture and utensils, and a fun collection of gramophones. The Oude Kerk Museum (1743), near the end of Church Street, has a collection of furniture, among which are some fine Cape chairs. The Tulbagh valley, originally known as Het Land van Waveren in honour of an 18th century prominent Dutch family, is an hour and a half's drive from Cape Town and has a wine route among scenery that is stunning, even for the Cape (see page 440). Tulbagh Wine Association, tel (0236) 30-0242.

Wellington had several names before it was renamed in 1840 in honour of Napoleon's conqueror. The town lies on the banks of the Kromme River, 70km/44 miles from Cape Town. Wellington is known for its leather products and dried fruit, which find their way all over the world. The Wellington Museum, tel (021) 873-4710, showcases the town's archaeological, agricultural and cultural history. Spectacular Bain's Kloof Pass is Wellington's 16km/10 miles link with the interior, and was built in 1853 by South Africa's renowned road engineer, Andrew Geddes Bain. The Wellington Wine Route is small and compact with five members, all open to the public for tastings and sales (see page 443).

In the Breede River Valley, 121km/75 miles from Cape Town, is **Worcester**, famous for its winter sports, including skiing, and for its schools for the blind and deaf. Kleinplasie Open-air Museum complex on the Robertson Road comprises the agricultural showgrounds, an Open-Air Living Museum, restaurant and wine cellar, as well as Reptile World. The open-air museum depicts the lifestyle of the Cape's early pioneer farmers, and you can see tobacco-twisting, donkeys rotating bucket pumps to irrigate land, witblits-distilling, candle-making, wheat-milling, bread-baking, and lots of other rustic arts. Reptile World houses more than 30 species of snake and has daily reptile demonstrations in the snake, leguaan and crocodile enclosures. Open daily from 9am to 5pm, tel (0231) 26480. The Kleinplasie Restaurant specialises in traditional Western Cape cuisine.

The Karoo National Botanic Garden, 3km/2 miles outside town, has the largest collection of succulents in South Africa, and is particularly lovely in spring. The garden covers 154 hectares, ten of which are landscaped, and has nearly 6000 species of plants under cultivation, 250 of them rare and endangered. A traditional Namaqualand *kookskerm*, or cooking shelter, marks the start of the Karoo Trail, which takes you through different areas of the garden, each depicting a different part of the Karoo. There are walkways suitable for wheelchairs and pushchairs, and a trail for the blind with labels in braille. Open daily 8am–4.30pm. Entrance is R3 (40p/65 cents) for adults and children and senior citizens R1 from 1 August to 30 November. Tel (0231) 70785.

The KWV Brandy Cellar in Worcester is the largest brandy distillery of its kind in the world, where 120 copper potstills produce KWV's award-winning matured brandies. Tours of the distillery and its working cooperage are conducted from Monday to Saturday, tel (0231) 20255.

WEST COAST

Stretching north from Cape Town lies what was once known as the Great Desolate Plain (*De Groote Woeste Vlakte*). Today the rugged edge of the coastal plain is dotted with such quaint fishing villages as Paternoster, St Helena Bay, Laaiplek, Elands Bay, Lambert's Bay, and Doringbaai, where you can tuck into abundant fresh seafood, enjoy clean, uncrowded beaches and get really close to unspoilt nature. Inland for much of the year the terrain as it ranges into Namaqualand proper is unrelentingly arid. Then, from July until the end of September, the whole area northwards from Darling is a riot of colour as the wild spring flowers — some 2600 different kinds — burst from the veld after the winter rains. You do not have to be a botanist or a gardener to enjoy this floral spectacle. If you would like a specialist guide contact Penny Mustart or Stephen Townley Bassett at Cape Specialist Eco Tours, tel/fax (021) 689-2978. There are also lots of local wildflower shows, and you can get details about these and also information about what is blooming where, from Flowerline, tel (021) 418-3705, 7 days a week between July and October.

ACCOMMODATION

Langebaan Country Club has accommodation in well equipped lodges, a private beach on the 15km/9 mile-long lagoon, and plenty of sports facilities. R230 (£30.65/$50.60) per person a night, tel (02287) 22112/3, fax (02287) 22460. Also at Langebaan are *Die Strandloper*, B&B from R30 (£4/$6.60) per person a night. 46 Oostewal Street, tel (02287) 22490; *The Farmhouse*, overlooking the lagoon, from R280 a night B&B. Contact PO Box 160, Langebaan 7357, tel (02287) 22062, fax (02287) 21980; and for couples who want to get away from it all you can rent a houseboat on the lagoon at Kraalbaai. You're taken there by a motorboat and can either remain on the houseboat for your entire stay, of you can take a canoe. Take your own food and drink. There is a barbecue area on the foredeck and a fully equipped galley. It costs R400 a night for two. Contact National Parks Board, tel (021) 22-2810.

Other hotels include *Strassberger's Hotel Clanwilliam*, a 2-star hotel in Main Street, from R130 per person B&B, tel (027) 482-1101, fax (027) 482-2678; and *Cedarberg Lodge*, 67 Voortrekker Street, R215 per person B&B, tel (022) 921-2221, fax (022) 921-2704.

Budget accommodation, at about R70 (£9.35/$15.40) a night:

  The Baths, natural hot springs. PO Box 133, Citrusdal 7340, tel/fax (022) 921-3609;
  Old Buffers, 9 Station Road, Darling 7345, tel/fax (02241) 3008;
  Noupoort Guest Farm, PO Box 101, Piketberg 7320, tel (0261) 5754, fax (0261) 5834.

EATING AND DRINKING

Four novel informal open-air seafood restaurants are: *Die Strandloper*, on the beach at Langebaan, 125km/78 miles from Cape Town, flat R70 a head, tel (02287) 22490; *Die Muisbosskerm*, tel (027) 432-1017, and *Bosduifklip Restaurant*, tel (027) 432-2735, both at Lambert's Bay; and the *Soverby Lapa*, at Dwarskersbos, 8km/5 miles from Laaiplek, Cell 082 492-3852.

The Lambert's Bay restaurants are outstanding. Imagine you have had an invigorating day at the beach and your appetite has been sharpened by the sea air. Could you now tackle an outdoor buffet that groaned with smoked snoek paté and wholemeal bread, mussel kebabs, crayfish barbecued with butter sauce, marinated mussels, snoek smoked to perfection or herbed and barbecued, home-made pickled fish, seafood bouillabaisse, freshly baked *potbrood* (pot-bread), *roosterkoekies,* or scones, crisply grilled on the fire, potatoes with bacon, onions, green beans and cream, sweet potatoes in raisin and orange sauce, lemon rice, lamb on the spit, *souskluitjies* (dumplings) in a cinnamon sauce, washed down with steaming *rooibos* (red bush) tea or coffee? This is what is dished up at the Bosduifklip. All this costs R75 a head — R55 without the crayfish, children 7 to 15, R30. The restaurant is 4km/2.5 miles from Lambert's Bay, on the farm Albina, and it has a reputation for some of the best veld-dining along the coast. When you have finished tucking in you can listen to the concertina and guitar playing old South African melodies and perhaps try a quick-step or two in the old stone kraal before you head back to your luxury suite or sleeping bag.

The Muisboskerm serves a similarly novel open-air cook-up, also a short distance out of Lambert's Bay. You can try *bokkoms,* a local wind-dried mullet, or pickled herrings as starters. Fish for your main meal is filleted and grilled while you wait, or there is a choice of curried tripe, *kreef* (rock lobster), paella, pig roasted over a pit, and fat crayfish tails.

If you are in this area in December, you will be able to enjoy the Lambert's Bay annual Crayfish Festival and see more crayfish grilling in one spot than anywhere else on the coast. On the way back to Cape Town you can fill any gaps at the *Breakwater Open-Air Fish Braai Boma,* just 135km/84 miles from the Mother City, in Saldanha Bay, tel (02281) 42547. Closer to the city (25km/16 miles) there is *Die Melkbosskerm* fish and seafood outdoor restaurant, on the R27 (West Coast road), tel (021) 553-2583.

Snoek barbecues are worth checking out at the Paternoster Hotel, Paternoster, near Cape Columbine, tel (02281) 752-2703.

EXPLORING

The town of **Darling**, 75km/47 miles from Cape Town, falls in the southern section of the Cape Flower Route and stages a popular wildflower show every year in September, tel (02241) 2422/3361. The Duckitt Nurseries September Orchid Show, tel (02241) 2606, and the wild flower reserves near the town are also well worth visiting. Darling's Museum and Art Gallery in Pastorie Street are housed in the old Town Hall and exhibits include a collection of artefacts from the local butter-making industry, for which the area was noted. The information centre is also in the museum. Local art walks start here. 18km/11 miles south-east of Darling is **Mamre** village and mission station with an old church built by Moravian missionaries in 1808, and an old watermill, which has been converted into a museum. The old Mission Store has been renovated and turned into a restaurant. A small reserve and a number of trails enable walkers to see Cape fynbos in its natural habitat. The old-world atmosphere of the village makes it a favourite with artists and photographers.

The fishing village of **Dwarskersbos** in the Piketberg district is 11km/7 miles north of Laaiplek (loading place), near where on 7 November 1497 Portuguese navigator Vasco da Gama first set foot on South African soil. **Piketberg** itself is noted for its striking Gothic-style stone Dutch Reformed Church (1882) and its protea farms. The town takes its name from the Piquet Berg, or Piketberg, at the foot of which it sits. The name refers to the 17th century practice of posting a military guard (piquet) against marauding Khoikhoi.

Lambert's Bay is a fishing village on the Atlantic seaboard, 64km/40 miles north of Clanwilliam and 290km/180 miles north of Cape Town. Its crayfish (rock lobster) feasts and open-air restaurants have made it a popular attraction. Bird Island is a must for twitchers. From a lookout platform you can watch a host of Cape cormorants, gannets, and other sea birds. Further south along the coast is **Paternoster**, another sleepy fishing village of quaint whitewashed cottages at Cape Columbine, between Saldanha Bay and St Helena Bay. Paternoster, of course, is Latin for 'Our Father' and is allegedly associated with the fervent prayers of Portuguese sailors shipwrecked here. Cape Columbine Nature Reserve conserves coastal fynbos and Karoo succulents and is frequented by sacred ibis, seagulls, cormorants and many other seabirds. There are caravan and camp sites in the reserve, at **Tieties Bay**, 6km/4 miles from Paternoster. Main activities are hiking, angling, and diving for crayfish and perlemoen, tel (02281) 75-2718. **Saldanha** is a peaceful town, 150km/93 miles north of Cape Town, set on an attractive bay, the only natural harbour along the coastline. Saldanha Bay is named after Portuguese mariner Antonio da Saldanha, who took on fresh water here in 1601. Over the centuries the bay area has seen numerous conflicts — Dutch and French, Dutch and local Khoikhoi, Dutch and English. In 1781 British men o' war penned a Dutch fleet in the bay. The Dutch fired their ships to prevent them falling into enemy hands, but the English captured them all except the *Middelburg*, whose charred timbers are periodically picked over by scuba divers. Another wreck in Saldanha which over the years has yielded a bounty of ducatoons and silver riders is that of the 826-ton Dutch pinnace *Meeresteijn*, which broke up in 1702 on Jutten Island, at the entrance to the bay. On the farm Kliprug stands the only US Confederate monument in Africa. It marks the spot where, in July 1863, Simeon Cummings of the Confederate raider *Alabama* accidentally shot himself dead while returning from a day's hunting. Closer to Cape Town is Langebaan Lagoon, a wetland of international importance which, with the coastal waters and four offshore islands attracts more water birds than any other wetland in the country and makes up the West Coast National Park. The lagoon, 18.5km/11.5 miles north of Darling, is 16km/ 10 miles and 4.5km/2.8 miles across at its widest point. On its shores are some picturesque and tranquil little villages and settlements. On the western shores are the settlements of Skrywershoek and Churchhaven while at the tip of a narrow isthmus is the old whaling station of **Donkergat.** On the eastern shore of the lagoon is the village of **Langebaan**.

Malmesbury, 66km/41 miles north-east of Cape Town, is the principal town of the Swartland, one of the country's main wheat granaries and a wine-producing area on the Swartland Wine Route (see page 441). Of the other five wine route members three are in the area around Malmesbury, at Darling, Riebeeck-Kasteel and Riebeek West. The others are at Porterville and Piketberg. Swartland Wine Cellars press and bottle a range of wines from the vineyards covering the hills around the town and you can sample full-bodied reds and the famous hanepoot of the winery, tel (0224) 21134/5/6. You can also visit the local Cimalat Italian cheese factory and taste their products, tel (0224) 77024. As well as its wine and wheat the town is known to South Africans for a peculiar local rolling of the letter 'R' in speech.

Moorreesburg is situated in the heart of the Swartland wheat area, 100km/62 miles from Cape Town. The Wheat Industry Museum is one of only three in the world and is well worth a visit. Several dioramas depict old harvesting and milling methods and three large sheds contain harvesting machinery, including two large steam engines, tel (0264) 31093.

On the slopes of 946m/3 104ft-high Kasteelberg mountain, 4km/2 miles apart, lie the twin towns of **Riebeek-Kasteel** and **Riebeeck West.** The latter is the birthplace of General Jan Christiaan Smuts, arguably South Africa's most famous statesman. The farmhouse in which he was born in May 1870 has been preserved as a museum and is open to the public Tuesday to Sunday from 10am to 5pm, tel (02246) 445. In the scenic valley is the Riebeeck Wine Cellar, noted for its white wines, particularly chenin blanc and chardonnay, tel (022) 448-1213.

South Africa has relatively few marine parks along its 3000km/1864-mile coastline and because of this the 30,000-hectare **West Coast National Park** in the Langebaan-Saldanha Bay area occupies an important position among the country's national parks and is of international importance because of the birds migrating there from the northern hemisphere. During the year, this region harbours 50 per cent of the world's total population of a sub-species of the swift tern, 25 per cent of the global gannet population, 15 per cent of the breeding population of crowned cormorants, and about 12 per cent of all African black oyster catchers. It is also the feeding ground of thousands of waders that breed in the higher latitudes of the Arctic. Vast areas in Siberia and Greenland are designated breeding grounds for these birds and they would be pointless if these birds' natural southern habitat were not protected. More colourful are the flamingoes, which are resident on Langebaan Lagoon's 5500 hectares in great numbers in winter and can most easily be seen from the road south of Churchhaven. In and around Saldanha Bay are penguin colonies on the islands of Marcus, Jutten, Vondeling and Malgas, as well as cormorants, gulls, gannets, and swift terns. The system is classified as a wetland of international importance in terms of the Ramsar Convention of 1975, supporting more birdlife than any other wetland in South Africa. The birdlist of the Langebaan Lagoon area tops 200 species, nearly a quarter of all the species in South Africa. Among the park's mammals are the big-eared steenbok, along with grysbok and duiker. Mongoose, genets, caracal and jackals are around, but more difficult to spot, although bat-eared foxes are frequently seen. There is no accommodation at the park, but on the doorstep are beach bungalows, caravan and camp sites provided by the Langebaan Municipality, tel (02287) 22115/22752 and 21921 (a/h). To contact the park, tel (02287) 22144.

KAROO

The Central Karoo, better known as the Great Karoo, is one of the world's oldest regions and is famous for ancient fossils of creatures that roamed here even before dinosaurs came on the scene. The Karoo has a fascinating range of plants, animals, reptiles and insects that have adapted to harsh thirstland conditions. More species of tortoise are found here than anywhere else on earth, and it is home to South Africa's most endangered mammal, the riverine rabbit. The region is sparsely dotted with quiet little towns and villages, isolated whitewashed farmsteads, and large flocks of dorper and merino sheep, which are the mainstay of local agriculture. The semi-desert Klein ('Little') Karoo is a long narrow plain some 250km/155 miles long and 60km/37 miles wide, sandwiched between the Outeniqua and Langeberg mountains to the south and the Swartberg in the north, a range which is traversed by some of the most spectacular road and rail passes in Africa. Despite its meagre rainfall it is a scenic area with diverse farming activities and well known for its dried fruit, wine and cheese. Main town of the Klein Karoo is Oudsthoorn, which is the centre of the ostrich farming industry and often referred to as 'the feather capital of the world.' The Cango Caves in the foothills of the Swartberg are a major attraction and famous for their spectacular limestone formations. The Little Karoo was once known as Gannaland because of its proliferation of succulent ganna plants, whose leaves contain a substance related to cocaine. When dried and chewed the leaves induce intoxication and dreamy hallucinations.

ACCOMMODATION

Royal Hotel, two-star, R195 (£26/$43) a double room and R28 for breakfast. PO Box 33, Beaufort West 6970, tel (0201) 3241; *Oasis Hotel*, two-star, R220 a double room, breakfast R20. PO Box 115, Beaufort West 6970, tel (0201) 3221; *Wagon Wheel Protea*, two-star, R195 a double, breakfast R18. PO Box 111, Beaufort West 6970, tel (0201) 2145.

Oue Werf Guest House, halfway between Oudsthoorn and the Cango Caves, tel/fax (0443) 22-8712; *Cango Mountain Resort*, chalets, caravans and tents, tel (0443) 22-4506, fax (0443) 22-6075.

Outlap Country House, on the slopes of the Swartberg in the Klein Karoo, was awarded the title of runner-up 'Guesthouse of the Year' in the Satour Tourism awards, 1996, tel (04439) 2250, fax (04439) 2298.

Budget accommodation:

Donkin House, R50 (£6.65/$11) per person a night, tel (0201) 4287;

McGregor Country Cottages, 1 Voortekker Street, McGregor 6708, tel (02353) 816, fax (02353) 840;

The Oaks, Koo Valley, Montagu 6720, tel (0234) 42194, fax (0234) 42800;

Montagu Country Inn, Bath Street, Montagu 6720, tel (0234) 41115, fax (0234) 41905.

Caravan Parks:

Beaufort West Caravan Park, sites cost R33 (£4.40/$7.25) and R17 per person. Contact PO Box 352, Beaufort West 6970, tel (0201) 2800;

Laingsburg Caravan Park, tel (02372) ask for 124.

EXPLORING

In the heart of the Central Karoo, at the foot of the Nuweveld Mountains and in the centre of the world's largest plateau outside Asia is **Beaufort West.** The Beaufort West Museum has an impressive collection of awards made to pioneer human heart transplant surgeon Professor Chris Barnard, who was born here. The town also has a collection of silver and glassware used by Napoleon Bonaparte during his years of exile on the island of St Helena. An Anglo-Boer War blockhouse built in 1901 to guard the railway bridge still stands. Near the town is the **Karoo National Park.** Dominated by the Nuweveld Mountains, the 43,325-hectare park lies at their foot in a rugged, arid area transformed in spring by carpets of veld flowers. Whether you explore the plains and mountains of the park by car, 4x4, or on foot, you are likely to see Cape mountain zebra, gemsbok, springbok, red hartebeest, kudu, black wildebeest, and even black rhino, as well as the black eagle, one of 180 bird species in the park, which has one of the largest known concentrations of this majestic raptor. Among the park's many walks and hiking trails is the world's first fossil trail for the blind, and especially designed for the adventurous is the strenuous three-day Springbok Hiking Trail, which leads to the highest point of the Nuweveld Mountains. A 4x4 trail also traverses the park. There is a licensed à la carte restaurant. A cottage for 4 costs R400 (£53.35/$88) a night. A chalet for 2 is R220 a night, and a camp site costs R33 a night for up to 2 people, plus R9 for each additional person, tel (021) 22-2810.

Die Hel is the colloquial name for **Gamkaskloof**, a 22km/14-mile valley in the Swartberg Mountains, near Oudsthoorn. There was no road into this isolated valley until 1963 and the pass leading into it drops 579m/1900ft in just over 3km/2 miles, almost a 1 in 3 gradient. The valley was once the home of Bushmen, who have left their artistic trademark on rock faces. They were followed by trekboers who lived in inbred isolation until the road brought contact with the outside world. It is now a wilderness area with hiking and 4x4 trails. For more information contact Cape Nature Conservation, tel (021) 483-4051/4227.

The town of **Laingsburg** on the main Cape Town-Johannesburg road was almost completely destroyed by flood in 1981 and pictures of the widespread devastation, as well as the Wolfaard Historical Collection, are displayed at the local library. The town is less interesting than the Karoo geological area in which it lies. Sunsets, though, are usually spectacular. 27km/17 miles from Laingsburg on the road to Cape Town is the beguiling Victorian Karoo hamlet of **Matjiesfontein** ('Fountain of Rushes'), established in 1884 by ailing Scottish railway employee James Douglas Logan, who found the crisp, dry air good for his lung complaint. It became a fashionable halt and was popular with Cecil John Rhodes, Lord Randolph Churchill, Olive Schreiner, and the Sultan of Zanzibar. During the Anglo-Boer War some of Britain's most famous soldiers were billeted here, among them Haig, Roberts, Ironside and French. Well-known hotelier David Rawdon bought and restored the entire village in 1968 and it was declared a national monument in 1975. The old railway station houses the Railway Museum and the Marie Rawdon Museum, the largest privately owned museum in South Africa. The turreted Lord Milner Hotel is the focal point of the hamlet, tel (023) 551-3011.

Oudsthoorn is the capital of the Little Karoo and the hub of a flourishing ostrich industry. The town's main attractions are three show farms — Highgate, tel (0443) 22-7115; Safari, tel (0443) 22-7311; and Cango Ostrich Farm, which also has a butterfly farm, the only one in southern Africa, tel (0443) 22-4623. The **Cango Caves**, 30km/19 miles from Oudsthoorn, are justifiably regarded as one of the world's natural underground wonders. A variety of tours can be taken through the calcite caves, where naturally sculptured formations are enhanced by clever lighting. The total system stretches 5.3km/3.3 miles underground, but only 1km/0.6 miles is used as a tourist route.

If you are fit and do not suffer from claustrophobia there is a 1½-hour adventure tour which involves wriggling through confined crawlways. Open every day of the year, except Christmas Day, tel (0443) 22-7410 (caves), or (0443) 22-6643 (information office). Ornate palatial houses known as 'feather palaces,' built during the boom years when fashion decreed feathers, are a quirky feature of the area. A section of the CP Nel Museum in Baron van Rheede Street, tel (0443) 22-7306, tells the story of this remarkable bird. The Cango Crocodile Ranch and Cheetahland, on the road to the Cango Caves, is open daily from 8am. More than 400 crocodiles and alligators of up to 4m/13ft are stocked by the ranch, tel (0443) 22-5593.

One of the many twisting passes in the region is the **Swartberg Pass**, which yields magnificent views on the road linking the Klein Karoo with the Central Karoo. A circular drive from Oudsthoorn to the picturesque little town of Prince Albert and back by way of Klaarstroom and Meiringspoort is a rewarding day trip. The 20km/12-mile gorge of **Meiringspoort** carves through the Swartberg Mountains and is worth visiting to see its convoluted sandstone folding, which is clearly visible in the brilliantly coloured sandstone cliffs and precipices along the road through this natural gateway between the Great and Little Karoo. Between Prince Albert and Ladismith is another fantastic pass, **Seven Weeks Poort**, along the 17km/11-mile ravine cut by the Seweweekspoort River through the Swartberg.

GARDEN ROUTE

The Garden Route links a chain of atmospheric little towns and resorts punctuated by spacious beaches, dense indigenous forests, lakes, lagoons and meandering rivers along the rugged coastline of the southern Cape coast. The route area is bordered in the north by a series of impressive mountain ranges, broached by a number of scenic passes to the interior uplands. As tourist numbers increase the Garden Route seems to grow in length by the year. It is currently said to run from Swellendam to Humansdorp, near Port Elizabeth in the Eastern Cape. In reality, the true garden part stretches from Mossel Bay to Storms River and the Tsitsikamma Forest, taking in the main Western Cape route towns of George, Sedgefield, Knysna, and Plettenberg Bay, with three commercial airports at George, Plettenberg Bay and Oudsthoorn providing easy access to the region. The N2 highway between Cape Town and Port Elizabeth runs along the route and provides road access and a link with major attractions of the Little Karoo.

From Mossel Bay the road follows the coastline to Plettenberg Bay, and on past Storms River, in the Eastern Cape. Luxury inter-city coaches operate regularly between the major cities of the country and the towns of the Garden Route and Karoo. Intercape Mainliner Ferreira Coaches, tel (021) 419-8888; Translux Express, tel (021) 405-3333. Intercity trains run from Cape Town (via Mossel Bay) and from Gauteng and Port Elizabeth (via Oudsthoorn) to George, tel (021) 405-2200 and (0444) 73-8202. The Outeniqua Choo-Tjoe steam train runs between George and Knysna from Monday to Saturday and may be boarded at a number of stops along the route, tel (0441) 73-8288 and (0445) 21361. National and regional airlines serve George Airport which is 8km/5 miles from town. Scheduled flights link the town with all the major centres of the country, tel (0441) 76-9310. There is no bus service to town from the airport, but you can hire a car there. An airport transfer service operates between George, Wilderness, Sedgefield, Knysna, Plettenberg Bay and Oudsthoorn, tel (0445) 23522. Taxis are also available. Regional airlines fly to Plettenberg Bay and Oudsthoorn.

The **Overberg** region stretches east from the Hottentots Holland mountains in the Cape Winelands to the Breede River, and includes the southernmost tip of Africa at Cape Agulhas, where the Indian and Atlantic oceans meet, and the towns of Caledon, Hermanus, Bredasdorp, and Swellendam. The superb coastal area stretches from Betty's Bay to the mouth of the Breede River and from the sea the plain runs back to the foot of the Langeberg Mountains.

ACCOMMODATION

Hunter's Country House in Plettenberg Bay was chosen South Africa's hotel of the year in the 1996 Satour Tourism Awards. Situated in the heart of the Garden Route the hotel has thatched *en-suite* chalets, superb cuisine and a cellar with an award-winning wine list. Hunter's has won numerous awards including Gallivanter's Guide UK's best family-run hotel worldwide. Tel (04457) 7818, fax (04457) 7878.

Windsor Hotel, 49 Marine Drive, on the edge of the sea, from R75 to R110 a night, tel (0283) 23727, fax (0283) 22181; *Marine Hotel*, Main Road, 3-star, overlooking Walker Bay. From R181 a night, tel (0283) 70-1000, fax (0283) 70-0160.

Arniston Hotel, Beach Road, 3-star, R180 a night, tel (02847) 59000, fax (02847) 59633; *Die Herberg*, Waenhuiskrans Road, R110 a night, tel (02847) 59240, fax (02847) 59254; *Arniston Seaside Cottages*, self-contained thatch cottages in Waenhui-skrans, tel (02847) 59772, fax (02847) 59125.

Budget accommodation: *Peter's Place*, Wallers Way, Betty's Bay 7141, tel/fax (02823) 29527; *Fir Tree Park*, Breede River 6858, tel/fax (021) 434-6166; *Mike's Guest House*, 67 Main Street, Knysna 6570, tel (0445) 21728.

Several places around Knysna have been recognised in the most recent Satour awards as being particularly good; these include *Leisure Isle Lodge,* on Leisure Isle, overlooking Knysna Lagoon, tel/fax (0445) 23923; *Old Drift Forest Lodge,* in a forest setting on the banks of the Knysna River, tel (0445) 21994; and the newly established *Knysna River Club,* a resort with 35 log chalets on the Knysna Lagoon, where there are a jetty, slipway and moorings, tel (0445) 82-6483, fax (0445) 82-6484.

Cottage Pie, off Robberg Beach, Plettenberg Bay, was a runner-up for the title of Satour 'B&B of the Year' 1996, tel/fax (04457) 30369.

The *Overberger*, is in Caledon, which has the country's most historic hot spring spa. From R182 per person sharing a double room. Contact PO Box 480, Caledon 7230, tel (0281) 41271, fax (0281) 41270. The *Swellengrebel Hotel*, 3-star, on the main road through Swellendam, PO Box 9, Swellendam 6740, tel (0291) 41144, fax (0291) 42453; *Klippe Rivier Homestead*, a luxurious 1820s Cape country guest house, tel (0291) 43341, fax (0291) 43337.

In Mossel Bay, *Santos Express* offers holiday accommodation on rails, at Santos Beach, 30m/33 yards from the sea. Two and four-berth first-class compartments, showers, toilets and a kitchen on the train. R125 (£16.65/$27.50) per compartment a day, sleeps four people, tel (0444) 91-1995. Other interesting places in Mossel Bay include *Cape St Blaize Hotel*, centrally situated. Contact PO Box 302, Mossel Bay 6500, tel (0444) 91-1069, fax (0444) 91-1426; the *Old Post Office Tree Guest House*, one of the oldest buildings in Mossel Bay, is part of the Bartolomeu Dias Museum Complex. R180 a night B&B. Contact PO Box 349, Mossel Bay 6500, tel (0444) 91-3738, fax (0444) 91-3104. *Park Backpackers* has dormitory accommodation for R25 per person a night. Walking distance from town and beach activities. Contact PO Box 615, Mossel Bay 6500, tel (0444) 91-1800, fax (0444) 91-3815.

In George, *Oakhurst* is a Cape-style manor house, R225 per person. Contact PO Box 9416, George 6530, tel (0441) 74-7130, fax (0441) 74-7131. The *King George III Hotel* overlooks the George Golf Course. The distinctive green and white Cape-styled buildings offer luxurious accommodation. Contact PO Box 9292, George 6530, tel (0441) 74-7659, fax (0441) 74-7664.

In the heart of the Garden Route, Caboose, made from timber and designed to look like first-class train compartments are popular with budgeteers. Single, double and triple rooms are wood-panelled with private showers, toilets and washhand basins. Single R69, Double R108, and triple R127, includes breakfast. Self-catering *Caboose Knysna*, corner Gray and Trotter Streets, Knysna, tel (0445) 82-5850, fax (0445) 82-5224. Contact PO Box 2044 Knysna 6570.

Formosa Bay, self-catering villas. One-bedroomed villa (sleeps up to 4) R225 (£30/$49.50) a villa a night, two-bedroomed villas (sleep up to 6) R325 per villa per night. Breakfast R26 per person. Contact PO Box 121, Plettenberg Bay 6600, tel (04457) 32060, fax (04457) 33343. *Crescent Hotel*, a stone's throw from Plett's beaches, 2-star, R110 per person B&B. PO Box 191, Plettenberg Bay 6600, tel (04457) 34490, fax (04457) 34491. *Four Seasons Guest House*, 33 Cutty Sark, panoramic views, R110 per person, tel (04457) 32619, fax (04457) 34066.

Backpacker accommodation:

Kiwi Extreme, PO Box 1850, Mossel Bay 6500, tel (0444) 7448.

Mossel Bay Backpackers, 1 Marsh Street, Mossel Bay 6500, tel (0444) 91-3182, fax (0444) 91-3182.

George Backpackers, 29 York Street, George 6530, tel (0441) 74-7807, fax (0441) 74-6054.

Hiker's Home, 17 Tide Street, Knysna 6570, tel (0445) 24362.

Knysna Backpackers, 42 Queen Street, Knysna 6570, tel (0445) 22554, fax (0441) 74-6054.

Overlander's Lodge, 11 Nelson Street, Knysna 6570, tel (0445) 82-5920.

Peregrin Backpackers, 37 Queen Street, Knysna 6570, tel (0445) 23747.

Albergo, 8 Church Street, Plettenberg Bay 6600, tel (04457) 34434, fax (021) 23-0515.

Hog Hollow, Askop Road, The Crags 6602, tel (04457) 8879.

Woodgate Farm ITH, Redford Road, The Crags, Plettenberg Bay 6600, PO Box 146, The Crags 6602, tel (04457) 48690.

Camping:

In Mossel Bay:

Point Caravan Park, end of Point Street, R29 to R80 a night, tel (0444) 3501;

George Tourist Resort, York Street, R30 (£4/$6.60) to R65 a night, tel (0441) 74-5205;
Sea Glimpse, Victoria Bay, R24 to R75, tel (0441) 71-1583;
Lake Brenton Holiday Resort, Capt WA Duthie Avenue, R20 to R58 a night, tel (0445) 81-0060.

In the Knysna area:

Buffalo Bay Caravan Park, Buffalo Bay, R25 to R62 a night, tel (0445) 83-0045.

Plettenberg Bay:

Dune Park Caravan Park, Keurboomstrand, 8km/5 miles from Plettenberg Bay, R12 to R27 a night, tel (04457) 32567;
Robberg Holiday Resort, R16 to R72 a night, Robberg Road, tel (04457) 32571;
Aventura Plettenberg is 6km/4 miles east of Plettenberg Bay on the mouth of the Keurbooms River. Chalets are fully-equipped and the camp sites cost R15 to R45 a night, central reservations, tel (012) 346-2277;
Tsitsikamma National Park, Storms River Mouth, R24 to R50 a night, tel (042) 541-1607.

EATING AND DRINKING

With more than 60 restaurants, Knysna offers as wide a selection as anywhere along the Garden Route. Mossel Bay sole, coastal oysters and black mussels are specialities of this seaside town and look for the yellow-belly rock cod, red steenbras, kob, red stumpnose and red roman which are often on the menu.

For seafood pub lunches and local Mitchell's beer try the Jetty Tapas Bar, at Thesens Jetty, on the lagoon, tel (0445) 21927; Crabs Creek, pub lunches and suppers daily, tel (0445) 87-1043; Pelican Restaurant and pub, seafood, Cajun, Tex-Mex, great long bar, music and choice of beers, Woodmill Lane Shopping Centre, Main Street, Knysna, tel (0445) 82-5711; Cranzgot's Restaurant, on the water at the Knysna Heads, tel (0445) 23629; Tin Roof Blues, pub and restaurant with live music, 17 Main Street, tel (04457) 82-6009.

Fresh Knysna oysters and mussels are available at the Knysna Oyster Company. You can take them away, or eat them on the spot in their tasting tavern, which is open Monday to Thursday from 8am to 5pm, Friday 8am to 4pm, Saturday 9am to 3pm, and Sunday at 9am to 3pm. Long Street jetty, tel (0445) 22168/9. If you want to try the local beer at source it is worth the hassle to find Mitchell's Brewery, Arend Street, in the industrial area not far from the centre of town. You can take a brewery tour and taste all the beers before deciding on takeaways. The beer comes in 2-litre bottles only, tel (0445) 24685 and (0445) 82-5530.

The Islander, 8km/5 miles from Plettenberg Bay puts on a seafood buffet like you've seldom seen before — virtually everything that comes out of the sea. Don't go if you are not ravenous, tel (04457) 7776.

EXPLORING

The tiny coastal village resort of **Agulhas** is at the southernmost tip of Africa, near Cape Agulhas, some 32km/20 miles south of Bredasdorp. It gets its name from the Portuguese for 'needle' because it was here the compass needle of the old navigators was seen to point due north, with no magnetic deviation. The L'Agulhas lighthouse is designed in the style of the Pharos Lighthouse in Alexandria, Egypt, and was built in 1848. The lighthouse and museum are open Monday to Friday from 9am to 4.30pm and on Sundays between 9.30am and 11.30am, tel (02846) 56078. More than 120 wrecks have been recorded on the coast here, dating back to 1673. In **Bredasdorp** is a superb Shipwreck Museum which is a treasure trove of salvaged artefacts. Open weekdays from 9am to 4.45pm, Saturday 9am to 1pm, and Sunday from 11am to 12.30pm, tel (02841) 41240. On the coast to the east of Bredasdorp is **De Hoop Nature Reserve**, with its amazing seven ecosystems. The reserve is visited by the southern right whale and the rare African oystercatcher. Rare and endangered animals species in the reserve include the bontebok, Cape mountain zebra and Cape vulture. The reserve conserves a major wetland, Die Hoop Vlei, which is home to nearly 100 waterbirds. There is a walking trail on the nearby Potberg Mountain. Prior booking and a permit are necessary for the mountain bike trail. Open daily from 7am to 6pm, tel (028) 542-1126. 48km/30 miles inland from Cape Agulhas is **Elim**, which was founded as a mission station in 1824 by the Moravian Church. Today it is known for its impressive architectural heritage and its Moravian cultural traditions. There is a thatched-roof church in the heart of the village, with a 200-year-old clock from Germany still keeping good time. In mid-August the church is decorated with veld flowers for the annual Love Festival. The village also has one of the last of the old Cape water-mills, built in 1828. The mill has been restored and now grinds wheat flour for sale, tel (02841) 42584.

Albertinia is the site of the only aloe factory in South Africa. The juice and gel from the aloe ferox plant are used to make medicine and skin-care products, tel (02934) 51454. It is also the jumping off point for bungi jumps at the nearby Gourits River Gorge. 35km/22 miles north of Albertinia is Die Poort Wine Cellars, the only wine farm on the Garden Route, tel (02952) 52406.

Arniston, officially known as Waenhuiskrans, was named after a British troopship wrecked in the bay here 40km/25 miles north-east of Cape Agulhas on 30 May 1815, with the loss of 372 lives. There were only 6 survivors. This 200-year-old cluster of fishermen's cottages is a picture postcard village. Nearby is Waenhuiskrans ('Wagon House Cliff') cave, a giant sea cavern that could easily house several ox-wagons. It is accessible only at low tide.

Betty's Bay is not much to look at, but it is the navel of the Cape Floral Kingdom, and the Harold Porter Botanical Garden here is famous for its *Ericas*, *Proteas*, and bulbous plants such as *Gladioli* and *Watsonias*. There are several guided scenic trails up to the kloofs and waterfalls, where you can swim. The flowering season is from October to February. Open daily from 8am to 6pm, tel (02823) 29311. The colony of jackass penguins at nearby Stony Point, near the old whaling station is worth a visit.

George, the main town on the Garden Route, was declared a town in 1811 and named after King George III. The museum in the Drostdy at the end of York Street is a must for those interested in history. Open Monday to Friday from 9am to 4.30pm, Saturday from 9am to 12.30pm, tel (0441) 73-5343. The gnarled oak known as the Slave Tree is one of George's most famous landmarks. It has an old iron chain embedded in its trunk, attached to the remains of a heavy lock. St Mark's Cathedral, built in 1850, is one of the smallest Anglican cathedrals in South Africa. It gives George its unlikely city status. From George you can catch the Outeniqua Choo-Tjoe for a steam-train ride through magnificent scenery to Knysna. The Moederkerk with its superb yellowwood pillars and domes and carved stinkwood pulpit was built in 1842. The George area was known to the Khoikhoi people as Outeniqua ('Man laden with honey') because of the bee-hives on the nearby mountain slopes. The tranquillity of the region beneath these mountains along the Garden Route gradually seeps into the bones and you become a victim of what locals call 'Outeniqua rust.'

Some 65 per cent of South Africa's export apples are produced in the **Grabouw** area of the Overberg and the story of the industry is well documented at the Applecart Museum. Conducted tours of apple farms can be arranged, tel (024) 59-2042, and (024) 859-9302.

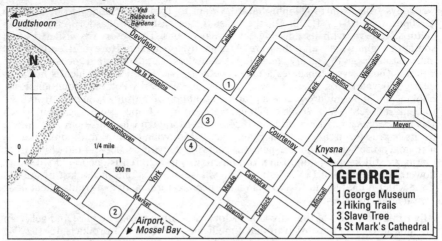

In 1995, State President Nelson Mandela decided to drop 'Westbrooke' as the name of his official Cape Town residence and call it 'Genadendal' instead. The original **Genadendal** is a half-forgotten town which had its beginnings back in 1738 when Moravian missionary Georg Schmidt came from Germany to work among the Khoi below the Zonderend mountains. Tourists are now trickling in and hikers come to trek the 25km/16-mile mountain trail that starts and ends here at the old mill. There is a simple hostel, often used by hikers, and meals can be arranged. Call Pat Johannes, tel (02822) 8140 (daytime) and 8132 (evenings).

The Langeberg Mountains are the backdrop to the village of **Heidelberg.** At the Grootvadersbosch Nature Reserve and Boosmansbos Wilderness Area more than 170 bird species have been recorded, adding to the pleasure of the Bushbuck Hiking Trail through the Langeberg. There is also a wilderness trail, two mountain bike trails, and a camping ground, tel (02934) 21917, and 22412. At Malgas is the only remaining working pont in the country, ferrying vehicles and livestock across the Breede River.

The people who live in **Hermanus**, 121km/75 miles from Cape Town, believe it is one of the most beautiful seaside villages in the world. With its impressive setting — a backcloth of high mountains, a rugged coastline in front and a beautiful lagoon with long white beaches stretching to the east — they could be right. A whale crier walks the streets of Hermanus, calling out information about viewing sites. Nearby Walker Bay is one of the best spots for whale-watching. Whale programmes are presented at the Old Harbour Museum, where a whale listening sonar buoy enables you to hear whales singing offshore while you watch them through the windows. Open Monday to Friday 9am–4pm, Saturday 9am–1pm, tel (0283) 21475. If you are in Hermanus in September that is when it stages its annual Whale Festival; details from the Hermanus Publicity Association, tel (0283) 22629.

There are day walks at Fernkloof Nature Reserve, where overnight huts are available. The reserve has about 1000 plant species and more than 100 bird species, tel (0283) 70-0300. A Whale Coast Art Route has been established and a free map covering the area from Rooi Els to Stanford is available from the *Whale Cottage Guest House*, 20 Main Road, Hermanus. The map has details of more than 100 artists, art galleries and crafters in the area as well as restaurants, hotels, guest houses and B&B establishments in each town or village listed, tel (021) 438-3838 or (02823) 3398.

Gansbaai is a fishing village on the opposite side of Walker Bay from Hermanus. It is known for rock and boat angling, diving and excellent whale watching. The wrecks of the *Birkenhead* (1852), *Johanna* (1692), *Nicobar* (1783) and many others are nearby scuba dives. *De Kelders* is the only freshwater cave on the coast to have its mineral-rich water converted into a swimming pool. The 7km/4-mile Duiwelsgat hiking trail goes from Gansbaai to De Kelders. For a map tel (02834) 41439. 3km/2 miles offshore is Dyers Island, named after an American negro who was there in 1806, which has a breeding colony of jackass penguins. Neighbouring Geyser Island supports a rookery of seals and both attract Great White sharks in considerable numbers. You can view these predators in their natural environment; contact White Shark Tour, tel (02834) 41380, and White Shark Ecoventures, Cell 082 658-0185.

Southcoast Seafaris specialises in cage dives, although they will also take you whale-watching in Walker Bay between June and December every year when the whales calve. You can also join one of their crayfish and abalone diving outings or go on a hike to the mussel banks where you can gather (25 per person a day) these succulent shellfish where the ancient *strandlopers* and Khoikhoi collected lunch 90,000 years ago.

Contact Southcoast Seafaris at 124 Cliff Street, De Kelders. Accommodation is available, ranging from self-catering to a guest house, *Mooiuitsig*, which has a magnificent view over Walker Bay, tel (02834) 41380, fax (02834) 41381, Cell 082 553-0999, e-mail seafaris@iafrica.com

Knysna, one of the most popular resorts on the Garden Route, is situated on the northern bank of the Knysna Lagoon, surrounded by indigenous forest. Knysna's legendary founder, George Rex, is popularly believed to have been the illegitimate son of King George III of England. The Knysna Estuary, or lagoon as it is popularly known, is a protected marine reserve of a 21sq km/8sq miles where the threatened Knysna seahorse breeds. At the entrance to the lagoon are two large sandstone cliffs, The Heads, forming the gateway to the old harbour, now known as Thesens Jetty. Cabin cruisers can be hired for novel overnight accommodation on the lagoon, tel (0445) 87-1026. For daily cruises, tel (0445) 87-1026 or (0445) 21693. The town is famous for both its beer and its oysters. Mitchell's Brewery welcome visitors and you can sample oysters at the Knysna Oyster Company, tel (0445) 22168. Millwood House Museum records the history of the area and the Angling Museum (with a real coelacanth specimen) is housed in the Old Gaol Complex in Queen Street, along with the Maritime Museum and the Knysna Art Gallery. The Featherbed Nature Reserve, Buffalo Valley Game Farm, and Noetzie with its five seaside brick castles, are additional attractions. Opposite the turn-off to Noetzie on the N2, a road turns northwards to Uniondale, where, 17km/11 miles away, lies Diepwalle forest, with its 40m/131ft-high yellowwood tree, aged about 600 years and named the King Edward VII tree. The Knysna Forest is a haven for South Africa's last few surviving free-range elephants. Knysna Tuk-Tuk is a shuttle service that meets the Outeniqua Choo-Tjoe, and does airport transfers and mini tours, tel (0445) 82-5878, fax (0445) 82-5879.

Halfway between Cape Town and Port Elizabeth is **Mossel Bay**, where Portuguese navigator Bartolomeu Dias landed more than 500 years ago, The town's history is recounted by displays at the Bartolomeu Dias Museum Complex, on Museum Square, tel (0444) 91-1067. The complex also includes the Shell Museum, and its most popular attraction, the Maritime Museum, which displays a full-size replica of the caravel in which the famous Portuguese navigator sailed to South Africa in 1488. Open weekdays, 9am–4.45pm, Saturday and Sunday 10am–4pm. Entry is free, although a charge of R4 is made if you want to board the ship, tel (0444) 91-1342.

The many historical and natural attractions in Mossel Bay include the Post Office Tree, where passing mariners used to leave letters in a boot hung in the still-standing ancient milkwood tree in the hope a passing ship would carry them to Europe. You can still post letters here; they will be franked 'Old Post Office Tree'. The stream that supplied ships with fresh water from 1488 still runs nearby. Other features are the Khoi-San (strandloper) Cave where many artefacts dating back 80,000 years have been discovered; a replica of the Brighton's famous Pavilion; and Seal Island, which is home territory to Great White sharks and the colonies of Cape fur seals they feed on. Shark-watching trips out in the bay are increasingly popular, Cell 082 455-2438. JJ Moorcraft takes divers out to the shark grounds and organises sail, dive and accommodation packages; contact him at The Old Post Office, Tree Manor, PO Box 349, Mossel Bay 6500, Western Cape, tel (0444) 91378, fax (0444) 91-3104. For a pleasure cruise to Seal Island, tel (0444) 3101. The St Blaise Hiking Trail follows untrammelled coastline, tel (0444) 91-2202.

Plettenberg Bay is so lovely it was called *Bahia Formosa* ('Beautiful Bay') by the first Portuguese explorers in 1576. Its most prominent landmark is the Robberg Peninsula, projecting into the sea to the south-west of the town and the site of a wild, unspoilt nature reserve, covered in proteas and fynbos. Southern right whales migrate to the bay to calve and can often be seen close inshore.

The reserve is open 7am–5pm daily. Some 50,000 people visit the reserve every year so the footpaths have been upgraded and boardwalks and concrete steps installed. There is an information centre next to the car park with exhibits on the flora, fauna, geology and archaeology.

Nelson Bay Cave, in the Reserve, is one of many Stone Age sites in the vicinity and is now an archaeological museum. The cave is a large cavern about 30m/98ft long and 15m/49ft wide. It was occupied for much of the last 125,000 years by Middle Stone Age people and those of the Later Stone Age from about 18,000 years ago, and finally Khoikhoi herders until a few hundred years ago when Europeans arrived in the area.

About 20 caves, rock shelters and open sites on Robberg and the adjacent mainland show signs of occupation by Stone Age people. The coast between Robberg and Humansdorp is regarded as the capital of Later Stone Age culture, and prehistoric beachcombers called *strandlopers* have left evidence of their existence in the shape of often huge kitchen middens of sea shells, bones and other discarded inedibles. These ancient rubbish heaps are found all along the coastline and are protected by law. For more information contact the *South African Archaeological Society*, PO Box 15700, Vlaeberg 8018, Western Cape.

During the holidays the town itself and its lovely beaches can get irritatingly crowded. If you can get through the throng, the swimming, surfing, angling and sailing are excellent. Plettenberg Bay Country Club welcomes visitors and has an attractive golf course, tel (04457) 32132. In Piesang Valley is the Global Craft Village, which echoes past days of flower-power, love, beads and peace. A short drive away is the village of The Crags, the little settlement of Nature's Valley, and the small resort of Keurboomstrand. Atlantic Air operates a regular service from Cape Town to Plettenberg Bay Airport via Oudtshoorn, tel (021) 934-6619, and Airlink operates a service between Johannesburg and Plettenberg Bay via Port Elizabeth, tel (011) 394-2430. Plettenberg Bay Airport, tel (04457) 31293.

While it might seem to be peopled by Rip van Winkles **Sedgefield** has plenty to offer. There are trails through forests full of wildlife in the Goukamma Nature Reserve, where the Groenvlei bushcamp offers accommodation in wooden chalets, tel (0441) 74-2160. Swartvlei, the largest natural inland saltwater lake in South Africa, is popular for swimming, boating, windsurfing, water-skiing and fishing. Groenvlei, the only natural freshwater lake in the area, can produce handsome catches of black bass. The Town Clerk will give you more information, tel (04455) 31635.

Swellendam, at the foot of the Langeberg Mountains retains some of its graceful mid-18th century origins. Game viewing, bird-watching and hiking are popular pursuits, as well as swimming and fishing in the Breede ('broad') River. The Drostdy Museum and Ambagswerf in the museum complex are worth a visit, tel (0291) 41138. Nearby are the Marloth Nature Reserve, which offers day walks and overnight hiking trails, and *Bontebok National Park*. The park, 6km/4 miles south-east of Swellendam, was established in 1931 when fewer than 30 bontebok were left of the vast herds that once roamed the Cape interior. Distinctive markings, coupled with a nosy nature, had made the buck an easy target. The park now provides sanctuary for more than 300, as well as other antelope species, Cape mountain zebra and smaller mammals. The 2786ha/6884-acre park is host to more than 470 plant species, among them, erica, gladiolus and protea. Birdlife includes the secretarybird, fish eagles and francolin. The camping ground on the lawned banks of the river has panoramic views of the Langeberg mountains. Sites cost R30 (£4/$6.60) a night for two people. There is also accommodation in fully equipped 6-berth 'chalavans' which costs a basic R77 a night, plus R12 per adult and R6 for each child, tel (0291) 42735.

Wilderness, 15km/9 miles east of George, is renowned for its vast stretches of beach, although a strong backwash can make swimming dangerous at some beaches. It is a favourite retirement village for South African businessmen and politicians of the old order. The 2612-hectare *Wilderness National Park* encompasses five rivers and five lakes, two estuaries and 18km/11 miles of coastline. It is surrounded by a 10,000-hectare national lake area, administered by the National Parks Board. This sensitive eco-system is home to a wealth of waterbirds, and the elusive long-tailed Knysna loerie. Water sports are a major feature and there is a selection of day trails. Among the ferns and orchids there is always a chance of spotting a buck or even a playful Cape clawless otter. The Wilderness restcamp has accommodation in 4-bed log cabins and 6-bed cottages at R300 (£40/$66) a night; Ebb and Flow is a small rustic restcamp providing only basic accommodation in 2-bed chalets at R110 a night. There is also a caravan and camp ground on the banks of the Touw River at R45 a site for 2 people. Contact PO Box 35, Wilderness 6560, tel (0441) 877-1197, fax (0441) 877-0111.

WINE ROUTES

CONSTANTIA WINE ROUTE

The nearest wine route to Cape Town is on the city's doorstep, 20 minutes' drive away in the beautiful Constantia Valley, the country's first wine-producing area. The Constantia Wine Route is the shortest of them all; there are only three estates on it and you can cover them all in half a day, in time for lunch at *Groot (Great) Constantia*, the most famous estate of them all.

The other estates on the route are *Klein (Small) Constantia* and *Buitenverwachting* (Beyond Expectation). Together these made up the original farm granted to Cape Governor Simon van der Stel in 1685. It was the luscious wine from this valley that conquered the courts and chancelleries of Europe in the 19th century and earned praise from poets and monarchs alike.

Groot Constantia is one of the finest examples of Cape Dutch architecture in the winelands. The homestead is furnished with exquisite antiques. Exhibits at the Wine Museum include stoneware from 500BC. The estate is open for sales and wine tasting all week, 10am–5pm, and guided tours of the cellars start on the hour, 10am–4pm. Groot Constantia's Jonkerhuis restaurant is nothing to shout about, but gives plain, fresh fare at reasonable prices. For rollicking revelry the estate tavern is a good bet, with Student Prince-type wooden benches and tables, free-flowing wine and unfussy pub grub, hot and cold.

Near the entrance to the estate on Groot Constantia Road is a farmstall that is a local institution, the Old Cape Farm Stall, with every conceivable kind of traditional and delicatessen food to take away for later. Particularly good are the wholewheat bread, chicken pies and quiches. There is also a bakery and a bistro. Tel (021) 794-7062. Groot Constantia Estate, tel (021) 794-5128. Restaurant, tel (021) 794-6255. Tavern, tel (021) 794-1144. Museum complex, tel (021) 794-5067.

Klein Constantia Estate is open for sales and tastings Monday to Friday 9am–1pm and 2–5pm. Saturdays, 9am–1pm. Cellar tours are by appointment only. Tel (021) 794-5188.

Buitenverwachting is open for sales and tastings Monday to Friday, 9am–5pm, and on Saturday, 9am–1pm. Cellar tours are at 11am and 3pm, Monday to Friday, or by appointment. With every justification, Buitenverwachting boasts the finest restaurant cuisine in the Peninsula and if you can afford to splurge — or if the exchange rate has been particularly kind to you that day — indulge yourself and enjoy the best fare the winelands and the nearby sea can proffer. As they say in Cape Town, to die for. Tel (021) 794-5190, restaurant (021) 794-3522.

Another old wine farm in the Constantia Valley is the 203ha/502 acre *Steenberg* Estate in Tokai, which has been developed recently as a premier wine estate, golf course and restaurant. The winery was completed only in January 1996 to produce a range of high quality white and red wines for the top end of the market. Steenberg was bought by a large industrial corporation in 1990 and neither money nor effort has been spared to restore the property to its former glory. Development includes an 18-hole championship golf course, clubhouse and residential property.

The Steenberg hotel opened in November 1996 and comprises 19 luxury bedrooms all with *en suite* (separate shower and bath) bathrooms. An upmarket restaurant in the old winery can serve up to 30 guests.

Steenberg Estate is open weekdays only, 8am–4.30pm. Wine tastings are by appointment only, but no wine is sold from the cellar. Contact (021) 713-2211.

STELLENBOSCH WINE ROUTE

To enjoy an unforgettable (if at times hazy) day explore the Cape's winelands, a seemingly never-ending patchwork of enchantingly gabled old Cape Dutch farm-steads dotting lush vineyards in sweet-watered valleys and sheltered by benign mountains. Over the years the number of official wine routes in the Western Cape has grown to 13 (other routes are at Paarl, Wellington, Franschhoek, Worcester, Robertson, Olifants River, Swartland, Klein Karoo and Tulbagh, the micro-wine routes of Constantia and Durbanville, and the latest addition at Somerset West) as shrewd estate owners and co-operatives alike have recognised the benefits of opening their doors to visitors keen to taste and buy. Even so, the Stellenbosch Wine Route, the oldest and first to be organised along French *Routes du Vin* and German *Weinstrassen* lines — it opened to the public in 1971 — remains for most the premier attraction, blending as it does some of the country's premier wines and one of its most picturesque regions. The route is loosely cruciform and any one of the four major roads out of the university town of Stellenbosch will take you to a number of the 23 private estates and five co-operative wineries which all surround it within a radius of 12km/7.5 miles. Stellenbosch itself is the heart of the wine industry and the headquarters of major producing wholesalers Stellenbosch Farmers' Winery, the Bergkelder and Gilbeys, along with two of the leading viticultural research institutes. A guided tour of SFW, the biggest winery in South Africa, is a must for any wine lover. The tour includes a video presentation on wine, an informative walkabout through the winery and its cooperage and winds up with the tasting of some SFW wines. SFW distributes wines in more than 40 countries. Hours: Monday to Friday, 9am–5pm, and Saturday, 9.30am–12.30pm. Booking for tours essential, tel (021) 808-7911. There is a moderate charge for the tour and tasting. A selection of award-winning wines is available for sale at the SFW Wine Shop, and its famous Oude Libertas Cellar Restaurant is open to the public. Bookings, tel (021) 808-7429. The Oude Libertas Amphitheatre is the venue for concerts, ballet and other entertainment from December to March. Libertas Parvas, an old gabled homestead, houses a wine museum and the Rembrandt van Rijn Art Gallery, where works by Irma Stern, Pierneef and Anton von Wouw, among others, are on display.

A good place to start the route is at the Stellenbosch Tourist Bureau and Wine Route Office at 36 Market Street where you can pick up a copy of the official guide to the route and its surrounds before deciding in which direction to drive first. If you do not have your own transport the Stellenbosch Tourist Bureau can arrange private tours for both small and large groups. It is possible to visit most of the estates within the space of a day, but it is not advisable if you want to remember where you have been, and get home in one piece. The entrances to the cellars and co-ops are easy to spot; each is clearly signposted and carries the official Wine Route symbol of a winding path leading to a bunch of grapes. Almost all the estates and wineries are happy to organise tastings and tours if you contact them in advance. All sell wine on the premises and will arrange delivery both locally and internationally. Some provide picnic lunches and you can have a vintner's platter (smoked chicken, selected cheeses, paté and salads at Morgenhof, Hartenberg or Delheim, a Swiss country lunch at Eikendal Vineyards; or a five-star meal in an old slave house that is now known as Spier Restaurant (on the Spier Estate). Mix 'n match your own route among the following — listed alphabetically, not in order of importance — to sample the best the region has to offer in red, white, sparkling, fortified wines, and even non-alcoholic grape juice. Some make a small charge for tastings. All are closed on Christmas Day, New Year's Day and Good Fridays; some close on Sundays and public holidays. Check before you go.

Blaauwklippen: The estate, 4km/2.5 miles from Stellenbosch along the Strand Road (R44), is on the lower slopes of Stellenbosch Mountain and is planted with 15 cultivars from which award-winning wines are produced. Weinwurst, chutney and relish products are also available on the estate and sold during wine sales hours. You can see an extensive collection of antique Cape furniture, kitchen utensils and coaches in the estate museum. Sales and tastings Monday to Friday 9am–5pm, Saturday 9am–1pm. Cellar tours Monday to Friday 11am–3pm, Saturday 11am. Coachman's lunch Monday to Saturday 12–2pm (1 October to 30 April). Coach rides Monday to Friday, 10am–midday and 2–3.45pm (1 October to 30 April). Saturday, 10am–midday weather permitting. PO Box 54, Stellenbosch 7599, tel (021) 880-0133/4.

Bottelary: This co-op has been serving around 40 farmers for more than 50 years. Its vineyards range from Devon Valley through to Durbanville and along to Bottelary Road to Kuilsrivier and provide it with a wide range of cultivar wines, mainly white. An annual Harvest Day on the last Saturday of February gives you the opportunity of joining in the picking and pressing of grapes. Tickets are available from 3 January. Bottelary Wines are sold from the cellar. Sales and tastings Monday to Friday, 8.30am–6pm, Saturday 8.30am–1pm. Cellar tours by appointment. You can order lunch picnic baskets. PO Box 16, Koelenhof 7605, tel (021) 882-2204.

Clos Malverne: Situated on Devon Valley Road, Devon Valley, in a prime red wine area. Clos Malverne is one of the few specialist pinotage producers and has won numerous international awards. Sales and tastings Monday to Friday 8.30am–5.30pm, Saturday 9am–1pm. Informal cellar tours all day. PO Box 187, Stellenbosch 7599, tel (021) 882-2022.

De Helderberg: Close to Somerset West, this is the region's oldest co-operative

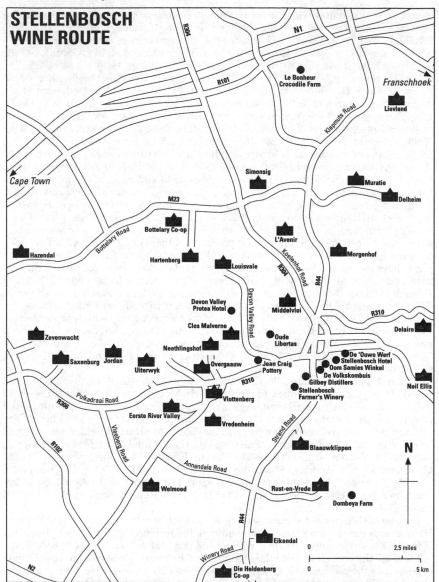

STELLENBOSCH WINE ROUTE

R304

N1

R101

Le Bonheur
Crocodile Farm

Franschhoek

Lievland

Klapmuts Road

Cape Town

M23

Simonsig

Muratie

Delheim

Bottelary Co-op

Bottelary Road

L'Avenir

Hazendal

Hartenberg

Louisvale

Morgenhof

Koelenhof Road

R304

R44

Devon Valley
Protea Hotel

Devon Valley Road

Middelvlei

R310

Clos Malverne

Delaire

Zevenwacht

Neethlingshof

Oude
Libertas

De 'Ouwe Werf
Stellenbosch Hotel
Oom Samies Winkel

Saxenburg Jordan

Uiterwyk

Overgaauw

Jean Craig
Pottery

De Volkskombuis

Gilbey Distillers

R310

Stellenbosch
Farmer's Winery

Neil Ellis

R306

Polkadraai Road

Vlottenberg

Vlaeberg Road

Eerste River Valley

R102

Vredenheim

Annandale Road

Strand Road

Blaauwklippen

N

Welmoed

Rust-en-Vrede

Dombeya Farm

N2

Eikendal

Winery Road

R44

Die Heldenberg
Co-op

0   2.5 miles

0   5 km

wine cellar, *De Helderberg Ko-operatiewe Wijnmakerij Beperkt*. In its early years it exported port in barrels to Britain and is still well known for its port. In 1993 the port received a gold Veritas Award and in 1994 the Chenin Blanc (off dry) won a double gold. The co-op offers white wines, red wines, sparkling wines, fortified wines and grape juice. Sales and tastings Monday to Friday, 9am–5.30pm, Saturday, 9am–3pm. Cellar tours by appointment. Light lunches are served, 12–2pm. Contact PO Box 71, Firgrove 7110, tel (024) 842-2370/1/2.

Delaire: Situated at the top of Helshoogte Pass the vineyards of Delaire are known locally as the 'Vineyards in the Sky.' The view from the tasting room encompasses a sweeping panorama of the Simonsberg, Drakenstein and Helderberg mountains. Two mountain chalets are available to rent. The estate makes mainly white wines with three reds. Sales and tastings Monday to Saturday, 10am–5pm. Cellar tours on request between April and September only. Lunches available throughout the year from Tuesday to Saturday 12–2pm. Picnics (October to April) available from Tuesday to Saturday. Booking is essential. PO Box 3058, Stellenbosch 7602, tel (021) 885-1756.

Delheim: The vineyards are high up on the slopes of the Simonsberg, offering views of the Peninsula and Table Mountain. Sales and tastings Monday to Friday, 8.30am– 5pm, Saturday 9am–3pm, Sunday 11.30am–3pm (November to February). Cellar tours Monday to Friday (1 October to 30 April) 10.30am–2.30pm. Saturday (all year) 10.30am. Vintner's Platter lunch (1 October to 30 April) Monday to Saturday 11.30am–2pm. Sunday 11.30am–2pm (November to February). Light lunch Monday to Saturday, 11.30am–2pm (May to September). Contact PO Box 10, Koelenhof 7605, tel (021) 882-2033.

Eersterivier: This winery is on the Lynedoch Road (R310), opposite the Van Ryn Brandy Cellar, at Vlottenburg. You can taste award-winning white wines and learn something about them, as well as the winery's red wines and its port, hanepoot, jerepigo and demi-sec sparkling wine. A playpark is available for tots. Sales and tastings Monday to Friday, 8.30am–5pm (tastings till 4.30pm), Saturday 9am–1pm. Cellar tours by appointment. Light lunches during the December holidays. Picnic and barbecue facilities are available all year round. Contact PO Box 2, Vlottenburg 7604, tel (021) 881-3870/1.

Eikendal: These Swiss-owned vineyards are on the slopes of the Helderberg Mountains and enjoy a micro-climate ideally suited to the production of red and white wines. On Friday evenings (June–September) the Swiss cheese fondue with live entertainment is a bonus. Booking is essential. Gifts and Cape kitchen products are on sale. Sales and tastings Monday to Friday, 9am–5pm, Saturday 9am–12.30pm (October to April 9am–3pm), and Sunday 10.30am–3pm. Cellar tours Monday to Friday, 11.30am–2.30pm (December to February). Groups by appointment. Lunches Sunday to Friday, 12–2pm. Contact PO Box 2261, Stellenbosch 7601, tel (024) 55-1422.

Hartenberg: Founded in 1692, Hartenberg Estate produces quality red and white wines from 16 different grape cultivars. Apart from the usual Hartenberg range, a selected range of house wines is available from the estate only. Sales and tastings Monday to Friday, 9am–5pm, Saturday 9am–2pm, and Sunday 10am–3pm (December to January). Cellar tours Monday to Friday 10am–3pm, Saturday 10am only. Lunches 12–2pm every day except Sunday and religious holidays. Contact PO Box 69, Koelenhof 7605, tel (021) 882-2541.

Hazendal: This estate lies between Stellenbosch and Kuilsrivier and dates back to 1704. The farm is regarded as one of the oldest and most beautiful in South Africa and is a national monument. The main homestead is a museum. Major renovations and building works have kept Hazendal closed to visitors, but check to see whether this has changed. Contact PO Box 336, Stellenbosch 7600, tel (021) 903-5034/5.

Jordan: From the vineyards on the hillside at the upper end of Stellenbosch Kloof you can raise your glass to a spectacular view of Table Mountain, False Bay and Stellenbosch. This is state-of-the-art winery, with an underground maturation cellar which can hold 180,000 bottles. Noble red and white wines are made in limited quantities. Sales and tastings Monday to Friday, 10am–4.30pm, Saturday 9.30am– 2.30pm (November to April), Saturday 9.30am–12.30pm (May to October). Cellar tours by appointment. Contact PO Box 94, Vlottenburg 7604, tel (021) 881-3441.

L'Avenir: The aptly named estate ('The Future') is 5km/3 miles out of Stellenbosch on the road to Paarl. It produces fine red and white wines. L'Avenir exhibited eight wines and won eight medals at the 1995 South African National Wine Show. The homestead has been converted into four-star accommodation. The estate also produces and preserves its own olives. Sales and tastings Monday to Saturday, 10am–4pm. Cellar tours by appointment. Contact PO Box 1135, Stellenbosch 7599, tel (021) 889-5001.

Lievland: Some of the finest wines of the Cape are made on the slopes of the Simonsberg, where the Lievland Estate is situated. Some of these red and white wines can be tasted in the attractive gabled tasting centre dating back to 1823. Sales and tastings Monday to Friday, 9am–5pm, Saturday, 9am–1pm. Cellar tours by appointment. Contact PO Box 66, Klapmuts 7625, tel (021) 875-5226.

Louisvale: This wine farm high on the slopes of Devon Valley has earned a reputation as an internationally recognised specialist producer of chardonnay. The restored homestead sits in a small but delightful garden and has an intimate wine-tasting centre. Louisvale's chardonnays are complemented by a range of elegant red wines. Wine gift packs are for sale at the farm on the Devon Valley Road. Sales and tastings Monday to Friday, 10am–5pm, Saturday, 10am–1pm. Contact PO Box 542, Stellenbosch 7599, tel (021) 882-2422.

Middelvlei: This estate is on the slopes of the Papegaaiberg (Parrot mountain), in the suburbs of Stellenbosch. The vineyards are unusual in that they are not irrigated and only natural fertilisers are used. Many of Middelvlei's red and white wines have won medals and trophies. Sales and tastings Monday to Friday, 10am–4.30pm, Saturday, 10am–1pm. Cellar tours Monday to Friday (1 February to 21 March) and lunches by appointment. Contact PO Box 66, Stellenbosch 7599, tel (021) 883-2565.

Morgenhof: This farm's history dates back more than 300 years. You can enjoy a picnic lunch served with home-baked breads under the oaks or in the gazebo, in summer, or lunches during winter next to the open fireplace, while sipping the estate's white and red wines and mellow ruby port. Sales and tastings Monday to Friday, 9am–4.30pm, Saturday 10am–3pm, and Sunday 10am–3pm (October to May). Cellar tours by appointment. Lunches Monday to Saturday, 12–2.30pm (June to September), Monday to Sunday, 12–2.30pm (October to May). Picnics (October to April). Contacts PO Box 365, Stellenbosch 7599, tel (021) 889-5510.

Muratie: This is one of the oldest privately owned wine estates in the Cape (established 1685). While Muratie is best known for its outstanding port, its reds will also make you sit up and take notice. Sales and tastings Monday to Thursday, 9.30am–5pm, Friday, 9.30am–4pm, and Saturday, 9am–3pm. Cellar tours by appointment. Contact PO Box 133, Koelenhof 7605, tel (021) 882-2330/6.

Neetlingshof: A half-mile long avenue of palms leads you to this estate, which has produced notable wines since 1692. Book a seat on the guided vineyard tour, Monday to Sunday at 11am, midday and 1pm (October to April), featuring a typical South African *braai* (barbecue) in the vineyards. Sales and tastings Monday to Friday, 9am–5pm, Saturday and Sunday, 10am–4pm. Lunches at Lord Neethling Restaurant and Palm Terrace. For reservations, tel (021) 883-8966. Contact PO Box 104, Stellenbosch 7599, tel (021) 883-8988.

Neil Ellis: The picturesque Jonkershoek Valley, above the Eerste River, is home to vineyards which produce white and red wines with an excellent reputation. Sales and tastings Monday to Friday, 9am–4.30pm, Saturday, 9am–12.30pm (November to March), Monday to Friday, 9am–1pm and 2–4.30pm (April to October). Contact PO Box 917, Stellenbosch 7599, tel (021) 887-0649.

Overgaauw: This estate, established in 1905, is a relative newcomer in South African terms, comprising 130 hectares on the hillside west of Stellenbosch. The sloping vineyards face south towards False Bay on the Atlantic Ocean. Try the white and red wines and the excellent vintage port. Contact PO Box 3, Vlottenburg 7604, tel (021) 881-3815.

Rust-en-Vrede: This historical wine farm is one of the jewels of the Stellenbosch wine route. The buildings, dating back to 1780, are fine examples of Cape Dutch architecture. The farmstead is reminiscent of a Bordeaux chateau and is one of few wineries specialising exclusively in red wine. The exclusive use of French Nevers oak barrels gives the estate wines their distinctive identity. Sales and tastings Monday to Friday, 8.30am–5pm, Saturday, 9.30am–1pm. Cellar tours on request.Contact PO Box 473, Stellenbosch 7599, tel (021) 881-3881/3757.

Saxenburg: This wine farm dates back to 1693. It is on the slopes of the Bottelary Hill, above Kuils Rivier. The Guinea Fowl Restaurant is a great place for lunch and dinner (and brunch on Saturday and Sunday). Booking is essential, tel (021) 903-4308. Sales and tastings of classic Cape red and white wines Monday to Friday, 9am–5pm, Saturday, 9am–4pm, and Sunday in season. Contact PO Box 171, Kuils Rivier 7580, tel (021) 903-6113.

Simonsberg: Frans Malan of Simonsig is a pioneer winemaker who, with Neil Joubert of Spier Estate, founded the Stellenbosch Wine Route. The estate comprises De Hoop and Simonsig, two farms dating back to 1692, and lies about 9km/5.6 miles north of Stellenbosch. It produces red and white wines, but is best known for its *Kaapse Vonkel,* which was the first South African sparkling wine made using the *Cap Classique* method. You can taste award-winning wines and tour the cellars while the children romp in the playground. Sales and tastings Monday to Friday, 8.30am–5pm, Saturday, 8.30am–5pm. Cellar tours Monday to Friday, 10am–3pm, and Saturday at 10am. Contact PO Box 6, Koelenhof 7605, tel (021) 882-2044.

Uiterwyk: More than 200 years ago Uiterwyk homestead looked very much as it does today. Built in 1791 and now a national monument, this is one of the finest examples of early Cape Dutch architecture in the region; with the original hand-hewn yellowwood floors and ceilings, darkened by time to rich honey, still in place. In the tasting room of the new cellar you can savour red and white wines. Sales and tastings Saturday, 10am–4.30pm all year round, Monday to Friday, 10am–4.30pm (November to April), and 10am–12.30pm and 2–4.30pm (May to October). Cellar tours on Saturday at 11am by the winemaker (Monday to Saturday during harvest time). Contact PO Box 15, Vlottenburg 7604, tel (021) 881-3711.

Vlottenburg: This co-operative cellar, 5km south of Stellenbosch on the airport road opposite Vlottenburg Station, presses 12,000 tons of grapes a year from which about 10 million litres of wine are produced. The co-op produces white, red, and dessert wines, as well as white and red grape juice. Sales and tastings Monday to Friday, 8.30am–5pm, Saturday, 9am–12.30pm. Cellar tours by appointment. Contact PO Box 40, Vlottenburg 7604, tel (021) 881-3828/9.

Vredenheim: This estate is unusual in that it has a female winemaker. The manor house, which is more than 200 years old, is a national monument. Spend some time in the lovely rose and miniature herb garden. Ostriches, donkeys, horses, cattle, sheep, birds and bunnies should keep the children entertained. You can choose from a selection of gifts and home-made preservatives. The tasting room, as well as the cellar and toilets, are accessible to wheelchairs. White, red, sweet and sparkling wines as well as grape juice can be tasted and bought Monday to Friday, 8.30am–5pm, Saturday, 9am–2pm. Cellar tours by appointment and light lunches available. Contact PO Box 369, Stellenbosch 7599, tel (021) 881-3878.

Welmoed: This is the first winery on the route when you wander off from the N2 along the R310. A range of 10 white and five red wines, two fortifieds, three sparkling wines and a red and white grape juice should be enough for all tastes. Bookings essential, tel (021) 881-3310, for the restaurant – Brad's Original Kitchen. Open Sundays. Sales and tastings Monday to Saturday, 8.30am–5pm, Sunday, 10am–4pm. Cellar tours in season by appointment. Contact PO Box 465, Stellenbosch 7599, tel (021) 881-3800.

Zevenwacht: This estate produces some commendable red and white wines and its main restaurant, the Zevenwacht Pride, in the historic manor house, has a reputation as one of the finest in the Western Cape. You can enjoy a light lunch, barbecue or tea in the beautiful gardens. Two mouthwatering picnic baskets are also available which should appeal to both vegetarians and meat eaters alike. Childrens' menus are also available, as well as a secure playground, small animals and an aviary to keep tots occupied. You can take a ride through the vineyards in a tractor-drawn surrey or explore them on foot. The estate includes a country inn with 14 luxury suites. Sales and tastings daily, 8am–5pm. Cellar tours by appointment. Contact PO Box 387, Kuils River 7580, tel (021) 903-5123.

The Stumble Inn, in Stellenbosch, offers an all-day excursion into the local vineyards for R45. Tel (021) 887-4049.

PAARL WINE ROUTE

The Paarl Wine Route has 20 members, most of whom arrange cellar tours, wine tastings and sales. Contact Paarl Wine Route, PO Box 46, Paarl 7622, tel (021) 872-3605.

Paarl lies in the Berg River Valley between the second largest granite rock in the world, which gave Paarl (Pearl) its name, and Du Toit's Kloof Mountains. South Africa's best-known wine farm, *Nederburg,* 60km/37 miles north-east of Cape Town is one of the highlights of the route, and although wine is not sold to visitors there are cheese and wine tastings, light lunches in summer, soup and home-baked breads in winter. The Nouveau Wine Festival, to celebrate the first vintage of the year, is held in April every year.

Backsberg: Has a reputation for fine wines and also produces an excellent brandy. Open Monday to Friday, 8.30am–5pm, and Saturday, 8.30am–1pm. Contact PO Box 1, Klapmuts 7625, tel (021) 875-5141.

Berg & Brook: Monday to Friday, 8.30am–5pm, and Saturday 9am–12.30pm. PO Box 19, Simondium 7670, tel (021) 874-1659.

Boland: Monday to Friday, 8am–5pm, and Saturday 8.30am–midday. Contact PO Box 7007, Noorder-Paarl 7623, tel (021) 862-6190.

De Leuwen Jagt: Quality wines and cellar lunches served on weekdays throughout the year. Open Monday to Friday, 8.30am–5pm, and Saturday, 9am–1pm. PO Box 505, Suider-Paarl 7624, tel (021) 863-3595/6.

De Zoete Inval: Monday to Saturday, 9am–5pm. PO Box 591, Suider-Paarl 7624, tel (021) 863-2375.

Fairview: Monday to Friday, 8am–5pm, and Saturday, 8am–1pm. PO Box 583, Suider-Paarl 7624, tel (021) 863-2450.

Fredericksburg: Monday to Friday, 9am–4.30pm. Private Bag X6001, Suider-Paarl 7624, tel (021) 874-1497.

KWV Cellar Complex: The largest in the world, covering 22 ha. More than 100 different natural wines, as well as brandies and fortified wines, are produced here. Monday to Friday, 8am–4.30pm, and Saturday, 8am–1pm. Contact PO Box 528, Suider-Paarl 7624, tel (021) 807-3007/8.

Laborie: Monday to Friday, 9am–5pm, and Saturday, 9am–1pm. PO Box 528, Suider-Paarl 7624, tel (021) 807-3390.

Landskroon: Monday to Friday, 8.30am–5pm, and Saturday, 8.30am–12.30pm. Contact PO Box 519, Suider-Paarl 7620, tel (021) 863-1039.

Nederburg: Open Monday to Friday, 8.30am–5pm, and Saturdays, 9am–1pm. For a tour of the cellar, an audio-visual programme and a tasting of five of Nederburg's best-known wines, tel (021) 862-3104. A light lunch under the oak trees costs R37.50 (£5/$8.25) per person. By appointment only. Contact Private Bag X3006, Paarl 7630.

Nelson's Creek: Wines and picnics on the estate. Open Monday to Friday, 8am–5pm, and Saturday, 8am–2pm. PO Box 2009, Windmeul 7630, tel (021) 863-8453.

Paarl Rock: Monday to Friday, 8am–5pm. Contact PO Box 63, Huguenot 7645, tel (021) 862-6159.

Perdeberg: Monday to Friday, 8am–12.30pm and 2–5pm. Contact PO Box 214, Paarl 7620, tel (021) 863-8112.

Ruitersvlei: Monday to Friday, 8.30am–5pm, and Saturday, 8.30am–1pm. Contact PO Box 532, Suider-Paarl 7624, tel (021) 863-1517.

Simonsvlei: Monday to Friday, 8am–5pm, and Saturday, 8.30am–4.30pm. PO Box 584, Suider-Paarl 7624, tel (021) 863-3040.

Villiera: Renowned for its fine wines and *Cap Classique* sparkling wine. Open Monday to Friday, 8.30am–5pm, and Saturday, 8.30am–1pm. Contact PO Box 66, Koelenhof 7630, tel (021) 882-2002/3.

Windmeul: Speciality wines direct from the cellar. Open Monday to Friday, 8am–12.30pm and 1.30–5pm. Contact PO Box 2013, Windmeul 7630, tel (021) 863-8043.

Zanddrift: Monday to Sunday, 9.30am–5pm. PO Box 541, Suider-Paarl 7624, tel (021) 863-2076.

Zandwijk: An historic farm at the foot of the Afrikaans Language Monument. Open Monday to Friday, 8am–12.30pm and 1.30–5pm. Closed on Jewish holidays. Contact PO Box 2674, Paarl 7620, tel (021) 863-2368/70.

FRANSCHHOEK WINE ROUTE

The rich cultural and historical heritage of Franschhoek (French Corner) and its tradition of viniculture date back to 1688 when some 200 French Huguenots escaping persecution in their homeland were given land in the district. Finding the cool climate similar to that of France, they introduced vinicultural refinements which have resulted in the wide range of quality wines now produced by the 20 members of the Vignerons de Franschhoek. Most of them offer tastings and sales.

Bellingham, tel (021) 874-1011;
Boschendal, tel (021) 874-1031;
Cabriére Estate, tel (021) 876-2630;
Chamonix, tel (021) 876-3241;
De Lucque and *Dieu Donné,* tel (021) 876-2493;
Franschhoek Vineyards Co-op, tel (021) 876-2086;
Haute Provence, tel (021) 876-3195;
La Bourgogne, tel (021) 876-2115;
La Bri, tel (021) 876-2593;
La Motte, tel (021) 876-3119;
Landau du Val, tel (021) 876-2317;
L'Ormarins, tel (021) 876-1026;
La Provence, tel (021) 876-2163;
Mont Rochelle, tel (021) 876-3000;
Môreson, tel (021) 876-3112;
Mouton-Excelsior, tel (021) 876-3316;
Oude Kelder, tel (021) 876-3666;
Plaisir de Merle, tel (021) 874-1071;
Rickety Bridge, tel (021) 876-2129;
Stoney Brook, tel and fax (021) 876-2182.

Contact Vignerons de Franschhoek, 66 Huguenot Road, Franschhoek, Western Cape. PO Box 280, Franschhoek 7690, tel (021) 876-3062.

Franschhoek is well known for its excellent restaurants, and it is delightful to browse through its galleries and antique shops and boutiques selling arts and crafts. The Huguenot Monument, at the foot of the Franschhoek Pass, commemorates the arrival of the Huguenots in South Africa and reflects the genealogy of many local families. Open Monday to Saturday, 9am–5pm, and Sunday, 2–5pm.

TULBAGH WINE ROUTE

Most of the wine estates and co-operatives on this route offer wine tastings and sales.
Book through Tulbagh Wine Association, tel (0236) 30-0242.

Drostdy Wine Cellars, tel (0236) 30-1086;
Kloofzicht, tel (0236) 30-0658;
Lemberg, tel (0236) 30-0659;
Paddagang Vignerons, tel (0236) 30-0242;
Theuniskraal, tel (0236) 30-0690;
Tulbagh Co-op, tel (0236) 30-1001;
Twee Jonge Gezellen, tel (0236) 30-0680.

Tulbagh Winery, established 1906, is the oldest co-op winery in South Africa.
Tasting Monday to Friday, 8am–12.30pm and 1.30–5pm, and Saturday, 8.30am–
midday, tel (0236) 30-1001.

Historic Church Street forms the largest concentration of national monuments in
the country. The Paddagang Restaurant, renowned for its delicious Western Cape
cuisine, and De Oude Drostdy Museum are also worth a visit.

KLEIN KAROO WINE ROUTE

This route starts at Montagu and winds through Barrydale, Ladismith and Calitzdorp,
ending in Oudtshoorn and De Rust and covers an enormous area, with member
wineries widely scattered throughout a long, narrow valley between the Outeniqua-
Langeberg and the Swartberg ranges. It is a semi-desert area as well-known for its
dried fruit and cheese as it is for excellent sweet wines. You can taste and buy wines
at most estates and co-operatives. You can get information on the route from the
Klein Karoo Wine Trust, tel (04439) 6715.

Montagu: Montagu Co-op Winery, tel (0234) 41125; Rietrivier Co-op Winery, tel
(0234) 41705; Cogmans Boere Co-op Winery, tel (0234) 41340.

Barrydale: Barrydale Co-op Winery for Chardonnay, tel (028) 572-1012.

Ladismith: Ladismith Co-op Winery has some excellent white wines, tel (02324)
740. The Towerkop Dairy for good cheese and dairy products.

Albertinia: Die Poort Winery, a private cellar where you taste wine and eat at the
restaurant. It is between Albertinia and Herbertsdale, near Mossel Bay, tel (02952)
2030.

Calitzdorp: The town looks out over the wine and fruit-producing Gamka River
Valley. Port capital of South Africa, 50km/31 miles west of Oudsthoorn, it has three
port producers in the country. Boplaas Estate, tel (04437) 33326; Calitzdorp Co-op
Winery, tel (04437) 33328; try the port, sparkling wines and merlot at Die Krans, tel
(04437) 33314. On the road to Calitzdorp. Taste white muscadel, liqueurs and the
bottled dynamite called *Witblits* (white lightning).

De Rust: Domein Doornkraal Wynhuis, tel (044391) 6715.

Oudsthoorn: Kango Co-op Winery has a shop in the middle of town selling their
range. Try the popular Herfsgoud semi-sweet wine. Tel (0443) 22-6065.

ROBERTSON WINE ROUTE

Robertson is the largest wine-producing area in the Western Cape where vines are
grown under irrigation. The Robertson Wine Trust comprises Ashton, Bonnievale,
McGregor and Robertson, and represents 11 co-operatives, nine estates and private
producers. Most have tastings and sales. Tours can be arranged, tel (02351) 3167 for
details. Robertson produces some superior wines and also breeds most of the
country's top race horses.

Agterkliphoogte Co-op, tel (02351) 61103;

Ashton Co-op, tel (0234) 51135;
Bon Courage Estate, tel (02351) 4178;
Bonnievale Co-op, tel (02346) 2795;
Clairvaux Wines, tel (02351) 3842;
De Wetshof Estate, tel (0234) 51857/53;
Goedverwacht Estate, tel (02346) 3430;
Graham Beck Wines, tel (02351) 61214;
Langeberg Winery, tel (02351) 2212;
Langverwacht Co-op, tel (02346) 2815;
Merwespont Co-op, tel (02346) 2800;
McGregor Winery, tel (02353) 741;
Nordale Co-op, tel (02346) 2050/1;
Robertson Winery, tel (02351) 3059;
Roodezandt Winery, tel (02351) 2912;
Rooiberg Winery, tel (02351) 61663;
Springfield Estate, tel (02351) 3661;
Van Loveren, tel (0234) 51505;
Van Zylshof Estate, tel (02346) 2940;
Weltevrede Estate, tel (02346) 2141;
Zandvliet Estate, tel (0234) 51146.

OLIFANTS RIVER WINE ROUTE

This route threads an area which stretches over 300km/186 miles from Citrusdal in the south to Bitterfontein in the north, and from the Atlantic Ocean in the west to the natural eastern boundary formed by part of the Cape Fold Belt, comprising the Cedarberg, Bifberg, Matsikamma and Bokkeveld Mountains. The fertile Olifants River Valley is cultivated intensively, with the emphasis being on citrus, fruit, vegetables and vineyards. The wine route, from Citrusdal to Lutzville, produces a wide selection of wines and includes the Cape's two single largest co-operatives.

Cederberg Estate: Open Monday to Saturday, 8am–12.30pm and 1.30–6pm, tel (027) 482-2825/27.

Goue Vallei Co-op: Open Monday to Friday, 8am–12.40pm and 2–5pm, and Saturday, 9am–12.30pm, tel (022) 921-2233.

Klawer Co-op: Open Monday to Friday, 8am–5pm, and Saturday, 9am–midday, tel (02724) 61530.

Lutzville: Open Monday to Friday, 8am–12.30pm and 2–5pm, and Saturday, 8.30am–midday, tel (02725) 71516.

Spruitdrift Co-op: Open Monday to Friday, 8am–5.30pm, and Saturday, 8am–midday, tel (0271) 33086.

Trawal Co-op: Open Monday to Friday, 7.30am–5.30pm, and Saturday, 8am–1pm, tel (02724) 61616.

Vredendal Co-op: Open Monday to Friday, 8am–12.30pm and 2–5.30pm, and Saturday, 8am–midday, tel (0271) 31080.

Wines can be tasted and bought from all the cellars and most have conducted tours and serve light meals. Contact Olifants River Wine Trust, tel (0271) 33126, or Olifants River Tourist Information.

SWARTLAND WINE ROUTE

A bare 20-minute drive to the north of Cape Town, the rolling wheatfields of the Swartland begin, dotted by the vineyards of five cellars and one estate (Allesverloren) which make up this route. You can usually sample their products before buying. Contact:

Allesverloren, tel (02246) 320;

Mamreweg, tel (02241) 2276/7;
Porterville, tel (02623) 2170;
Riebeeck, tel (02244) 213/632;
Swartland, tel (0224) 21134/5/6;
Winkelshoek, tel (02624) 830.

WORCESTER WINE ROUTE

Worcester's winelands lie in the Breede River valley, an hour's drive from Cape Town through some spectacular scenery, and include the Worcester district as far as Wolseley, the picturesque Slanghoek and Hex River valleys, and stretch as far south as Villiersdorp and Wildekrans, with the Nuy cellar to the east. The district is the largest wine-making area in the country, producing nearly 25% of South Africa's total volume. Apart from the sweet dessert wines for which the area is renowned the winelands also produce good quality white and red wines. The region is also the country's most important brandy producing area and Worcester has the world's largest brandy cellar, with 120 copper stills under one roof. KWV Brandy Cellar, tel (0231) 20255 for conducted tours. Two private estates and 22 co-operative cellars on the route are open to visitors for wine tastings, cellar tours, and sales and offer an extensive range of white and red, dessert, and sparkling wines. Cellars and routes are clearly signposted. Contact:

Aan-de-Doorns, tel (0231) 72301;
Aufwaerts, tel (0231) 91202;
Badsberg Co-op, tel (0231) 91120;
Bergsig Estate, tel (02324) 603/721;
Botha Co-op Cellar, tel (02324) 740;
Brandvlei Co-op, tel (0231) 349-4215;
De Doorns Co-op, tel (02322) 2100;
De Wet Co-op, tel (0231) 92710;
Du Toitskloof Co-op, tel (0231) 91601;
Goudini, tel (0231) 91090;
Groot-Eiland Co-op, tel (0231) 91140;
Lategans Co-op, tel (02324) 719;
Lebensraum, tel (0231) 91137;
Louwshoek-Voorsorg Co-op, tel (0231) 91110;
Merwida Co-op, tel (0231) 91144;
Nuy Co-op, tel (0231) 70272;
Opstal Estate, tel (0231) 91066;
Overhex Co-op, tel (0231) 71057/75012;
Romansrivier Co-op, tel (0236) 31-1070;
Slanghoek Co-op, tel (0231) 91130;
Villiersdorp Co-op, tel (0225) 31151;
Waboomsrivier Co-op, tel (02324) 730;
Wildekrans, tel (02824) 49829;
KWV Brandy Cellar, tel (0231) 20255;
Kleinplasie Wine Cellar, tel (0231) 28710;
Breëvallei-wyne, tel (0231) 22335.

If you are passing through Worcester without enough time to explore the Wine Route, regional wines can be bought by the bottle or case at the *Kleinplasie Wine Cellar,* which forms part of the Kleinplasie Complex. Contact PO Box 59, Worcester 6849, tel (0231) 28710.

DURBANVILLE WINE ROUTE

Durbanville is one of the oldest municipalities in the Western Cape. In the 18th century it was a public outspan (resting place) originally and subsequently the town was renamed after Sir Benjamin D'Urban, Cape Governor from 1834 to 1838. Most members offer wine tastings and sales:

Altydgedacht, tel (021) 96-1295;
Bloemendal, tel (021) 96-6050;
Diemersdal, tel (021) 96-3361;
Meerendal, tel (021) 96-1915.

Contact Durbanville Wine Route for more information, tel (021) 96-3453/3020.

HELDERBERG WINE ROUTE

In the Somerset West area between the Helderberg and False Bay is where some of the estates are steeped in history and others are modern developments. Villagey Somerset West lies at the foot of the Hottentots Holland Mountains, and was named after Lord Charles Somerset in 1819. Most members offer wine tastings and sales:

Avontuur, tel (024) 55-3450;
JP Bredell, tel (024) 842-2478;
De Helderberg Co-op, tel (024) 842-2370;
Eikendal, tel (024) 55-1422;
Longridge, tel (024) 55-2004;
Yonder Hill, tel (024) 55-1008;
Grangehurst, tel (024) 55-3625;
Vergelegen, tel (024) 51-7060;
Helderbrau Brewery, tel (024) 55-4626.

WELLINGTON WINE ROUTE

Wine farms in this area produce fortified, as well as red and white wines. There are no estates on the route, but there are four co-operatives producing mainly muscadel dessert wines, which go down well on a hot day when iced. Most members offer tastings and sales.

Bovlei Co-op, tel (021) 873-1567;
Jacaranda, tel (021) 864-1235;
Retief Family Cellar, tel (021) 864-1238;
Wagenmakersvallei Co-op, tel (021) 873-1582;
Wellington Winery, tel (021) 873-1163.

Contact Wellington Wine Route, tel (021) 873-4604.

ORANJERIVIER

This is not a wine route but a co-operative, Oranjerivier Wine Cellars, whose five cellars combined make it the largest wine-co-operative in South Africa and in the southern hemisphere, as well as the second largest in the world. There is a cellar and head office in Upington, on the banks of the Orange River, supplied by four other cellars, at Groblershoop, Grootdrink, Keimos and Kakamas, with about 750 members farming along 300km of the Orange River. They delivered 109,000 tons of grapes to Upington in 1996 for pressing. Tastings are arranged on request and wines are sold Monday to Friday, 8am–12.45pm and 2–5pm and on Saturday, 8am–midday. Contact Upington, tel (054) 25651; Kakamas, tel (054) 431-0830; Keimos, tel (054) 461-1006; Grootdrink, tel (0020) and ask for 1; and Groblershoop, tel (05472) 47.

Automobile Association (AA) maps covering the wine routes are available at all their branches.

OTHER VINEYARDS

Hamilton Russell Vineyards. While this estate is not part of a formally registered wine route, it is located on a route that makes a visit logical along with the other wineries in the Hemel-en-Aarde Valley, Hermanus, such as *WhaleHaven* at the turn-off to the valley, and *Bouchard Finlayson*. Wines are available for sale. There are no facilities for lunch or dinner, though you can picnic in the vineyards if you make arrangements beforehand. The estate also makes a fine extra virgin olive oil which is on sale at the tasting room in 375ml bottles. PO Box 158, Hermanus 7200, Western Cape, tel (0283) 23595/23441.

Bouchard Finlayson. The vineyard known as Klein Hemel-en-Aarde is set snugly on the slopes of the Glen Vauloch mountains 9km from Hermanus in the Hemel-en-Aarde Valley. The wines are unashamedly pitched at the top end of the market and include Blanc de Mer, Sauvignon, two Chardonnays and Pinot Noir. Tastings are available in small groups of not more than eight to ten because of the small tasting room. Wines can be bought on the farm. Visiting hours on Monday to Friday, 10am–5pm, and Saturday 9.30am–12.30pm. Contact Bouchard Finlayson Vineyard and Winery, Klein Hemel-en-Aarde Winery. PO Box 303, Hermanus 7200, Western Cape, tel (0283) 23515.

Backpacker accommodation throughout the Western Cape:

Vine Lodge, 23 Meintjies Street, Beaufort West 6970, tel (0201) 51055.

Doncan House, 14 Doncan Street, Beaufort West 6970, tel (0201) 4287.

De Bos Farm, Brown Street, Montagu 6720, tel (0234) 42532.

Swellendam Backpackers, 5 Lichtenstein Street, Swellendam 6740, tel (0291) 42648. Adrenalin junkies ask for Stephanie.

Waenhuis Backpackers, 29 Berg Street, Swellendam 6740, tel (0291) 43350.

Tradouw Guest House, 48 van Riebeck Street, Barrydale 6750, tel (028) 572-1434.

Betty's Bay Backpack, 2939 Clarence Drive, Betty's Bay 7141, tel (02823) 29240, e-mail emmuller@ilink.nis.za

Hermanus Traveller's Lodge, PO Box 383, Hermanus 7200, tel (0283) 22820.

Zoete Inval, 23 Main Road, Hermanus 7200, tel (0283) 21242, fax (0283) 21242.

Oudsthoorn Backpackers Oasis, 3 Church Street, Oudsthoorn 6620, tel (0443) 29-1163.

Solar Power Backpacker, off Robinson Pass, between Oudsthoorn and Mossel Bay, tel (0444) 95-2688.

Camping and caravanning:

ATKV, tel (0444) 95-0110/1.

Berg Rivier, tel (02211) 61750/2.

Boschenmeer Oord, tel (02211) 63-1250.

Fish Hoek Beach Caravan Park, tel (021) 782-5503.

Hendon Park, tel (024) 56-2321.

Island Lake Holiday Resort (Pty) Ltd, tel (0441) 1194.

Keurbooms (Aventura), tel (04457) 9309.

Kuils Rivier Caravan Park, tel (021) 903-3111.

Lake Brenton Holiday Resort, tel (0445) 81-0060.

Lake Pleasant Holiday Resort, tel (04455) 31985.

Millers Point, tel (021) 786-1142.

Oatlands Holiday Village, tel (021) 786-1410.

Palmiet Caravan Park, tel (02823) 4010.

Panorama Park, tel (024) 56-1730.

Pine Forest Holiday Resort, tel (0233) 21170.
Pinnie Joubert Woonwapark, tel (02211) 32603.
Riverside Holiday Resort, tel (0444) 96-6061.
Saldanha Holiday Resort, tel (02281) 32231.
San Marino, tel (04457) 9700.
Sea Breeze Holiday Resort, tel (024) 56-1400.
Voortrekker Park, tel (024) 853-7316.
Yzerfontein Caravan Park, tel (02245) 211.
Zandvlei, tel (021) 788-5215.

 In the Winelands the Oude Libertas Amphitheatre in Stellenbosch is a delightful setting where you can relax and enjoy an evening of entertainment under the stars. There is a summer festival of music, theatre and dance from November to March and you can picnic in the extensive gardens, tel (021) 808-7911. Endler Hall in Stellenbosch has regular music concerts, tel (021) 808-2334. Among the local theatres are the HB Thom Theatre University Students Theatre, tel (021) 808-3216; and Breughel Amateur Theatre, tel (021) 889-5765. The Hugo Naude Theatre in Russel Street, Worcester, is the Boland's regional theatre. All the actors are amateurs, tel (0231) 25881 and (0231) 21299. Symphony concerts, choirs, choral groups, and brass band performances are regularly held on wine estates and other venues in and around Paarl. Contact Paarl Publicity, tel (021) 812-3829. You can watch gumboot dancing and traditional dancing in Paarl at the Khutehele and Mbekwini Cultural Centre, tel (021) 863-2043 and (021) 868-1707.

SPORT AND RECREATION

A unique blend of sea, sand, mountains and veld combine to make the Western Cape the ideal playground — and testing ground — for anyone with a penchant for outdoor activity. It is all here, from yachting, surfing, scuba diving and big game fishing to hiking, climbing, bungi-jumping, hang-gliding, and white-water rafting. For spectators the province offers international standard rugby, cricket, soccer, volley ball, tennis and a host of other sports where your most strenuous movement is to reach for another cold drink. Almost as undemanding are hot-air ballooning jaunts over the winelands — Wineland Ballooning, tel (021) 863-3192 — helicopter flips around the Peninsula — Court Helicopters, tel (021) 25-2966/7 — and whale-watching by seaplane — Flamingo Flights, tel/fax (021) 790-1010.

Hiking and Climbing. There are spectacular walks and trails in every part of the province and in their understandable eagerness to get to these visitors often miss an area right on Cape Town's doorstep, which is a pleasant introduction to the geography of the Peninsula and its truly incredible plant life. Stretching virtually unbroken from Table Mountain to Cape Point is a wilderness area with a spinal range of sandstone holding some fascinating nooks and crannies. Between Constantia Nek and the Noordhoek-Fish Hoek Valley skirted by Chapman's Peak Drive, Ou Kaapseweg and Boyes Drive, this small section of mountain chain is crammed with indigenous plant species, many of which are considered rare, threatened or endemic. Above the valley, in the Silvermine Nature Reserve, the Kalk Bay mountains are honeycombed by caverns and passages. About 3km/2 miles up the valley from Fish Hoek is Peer's Cave where prehistoric man left wall paintings, the only known example of rock art within 100km/62 miles of the Peninsula. In 1927 an Australian named Victor Peer discovered a prehistoric human skeleton in this cave and there is still a great deal of argument about the age (16,000 to 30,000 years) and the genealogy of 'Fish Hoek Man.' A good introduction to trails on the Table Mountain range from Lion's Head to Cape Point is *Table Mountain Walks*, by Colin Paterson-Jones, which details 25 of the best rambles. For guided walks contact Cape Eco Trails, tel (021) 785-4018/82, Greencape, tel (021) 797-0166, or Mountain Guide, tel (021) 438-7206. The amphitheatre above the Silvermine naval base of Simon's Town offers some good rock climbing and there is a variety of climbs all the way round the mountains back to the frontal face of Table Mountain above Cape Town where, below the upper cableway station, are some truly challenging routes. An introductory rock climbing course, covering abseiling, belaying and multi-pitch climbing with qualified instructors is available for R605 (includes all gear), with climbs done on faces around the Peninsula. Contact Simon Larsen, Cape Town School of Mountaineering in Claremont, tel/fax (021) 61-9604. The Mountain Club of South Africa, 97 Hatfield Street, Gardens, tel (021) 45-3412, fax (021) 461-8456, and the Camp & Climb shop, 6 Pepper Street, central city, tel (021) 23-2175, fax (021) 23-2177, are good contact points for hikers and climbers.

Cedarberg Wilderness Area, a magnificent pristine mountainous region of 71,000 hectares, 200km/124 miles north of Cape Town, is generally rated as the finest hiking and climbing area in the Western Cape, with rock climbs of world-class standard and trails among beautiful valleys and peaks eroded into the most fantastic shapes, with such names as the Maltese Cross and the Wolfberg Arch. The Cedarberg is a sanctuary for leopard, and also supports animals such as klipspringer, caracal, aardwolf, baboons and porcupine. Other striking features of the area are the pure white snow protea that grows only above the snowline, the elephant's foot plant, which was the original source of cortisone, and some of the finest examples of Bushman rock art in the Western Cape. In the reserve at the Algeria Forestry Station there are six chalets, as well as caravan and camp sites along the banks of the Rondegat River. There are also patrol shelters, camp sites and forest refuges throughout the reserve, tel (022) 921-2289. Other useful contacts are Cedarberg Adventure Tours and Trails, tel (027) 482-1558, and for day hikes, mountain bike routes and horse trails, tel (022) 921-3210.

Cape Nature Conservation administers 27 reserves in the Western Cape from the Cedarberg to Plettenberg Bay. Most of them have trails, ranging from an easy day to a 7-day hike. Contact Cape Nature Conservation, Private Bag X9086, Cape Town 8000, tel (021) 483-4051/4227, fax (021) 23-0939. For information on West Coast hiking trails, tel (02281) 42088/42058, fax (02281) 44240, and for trails in the reserves run by the National Parks Board, tel (021) 22-2810, fax (021) 24-6211.

There are numerous hiking trails along the Garden Route and the Regional Tourist Information Centre puts out a handy pamphlet on 72 of the more interesting and better known ones. These cater for everyone — experienced hikers, beginners, the fit, the not-so-fit and the disabled hiker. Trails vary from day to overnight hikes on routes taking in cliffs, beaches and forests. Contact RTIC, PO Box 1514, George 6530, Western Cape, tel (0441) 73-6314/55, fax (0441) 74-6840. Walks suited to families with small children are conducted around the Peninsula by Marine Environmental Education Trust, of Scarborough, who will take you on tours of exploration to meet jackass penguins, call the whales (July to November), discover rock pools, and trek the Floral Kingdom Trail. Prices range from R7 to R15 for children and R10 to R20 (£2.65/$4.40) for adults, tel/fax (021) 780-1353/83.

There are some pleasant, undemanding walks in the winelands around Stellenbosch, as well as a Vineyard Trail of 24km/15 miles. The full route stretches from Stellenbosch to Kuils River, although there are shorter 12km/8 miles and 16km/10 mile alternatives. All start at the Stellenbosch Farmers' Winery Oude Libertas Amphitheatre complex. Contact the Stellenbosch Tourist Bureau, or the Stellenbosch Hiking Club, tel (021) 887-3138.

Abseiling is a great way of seeing the Cape from a different angle, whether is its from the top of Table Mountain, the granite rocks of Chapman's Peak, or Kamikaze Canyon at Gordon's Bay, where you can abseil down a waterfall. Contact Abseil Africa, tel (021) 23-1646, and WildThing Adventures, tel/fax (021) 461-1653. Another unusual variation on plain old hiking and climbing is called kloofing. A kloof is a ravine or canyon in the mountains and the sport of kloofing calls for you to hike into a gorge then follow a river down its rocky bed, jumping into pools on the way down from heights of 2m/7ft to 15m/49ft and even higher, and swimming for stretches. It is all the rage with adrenalin junkies tired of bungi-jumping. The people to give you this new perspective on hiking are Day Trippers of Cape Town. They will guide you while you kloof down Suicide Gorge for R120, or you can choose the gentler option of Steenbras for R140. Price includes picnic lunches and a beer to calm your nerves, tel (021) 531-3274.

4x4 Trails. In 1992 the National Parks Board chose the Karoo National Park to launch its first 4x4 trail. You can tackle the 80km/50 miles as a day or overnight trail in your own vehicle or in one provided by the Parks Board. The trail is not recommended for inexperienced 4x4 drivers. You are likely to see wildebeest, zebra, gemsbok, hartebeest, duiker, springbok, kudu, jackal, bat-eared foxes and South Africa's most endangered animal, the riverine rabbit, as well as other small mammals and more than 180 species of birds, including large numbers of black eagles. The 43,325ha/ 107,058-acre park is 470km/292 miles north of Cape Town and the entrance is on the outskirts of Beaufort West. The Parks Board publishes a booklet *Karoo 4x4 Trail* which you can pick up on arrival. Book through the National Parks Board in Cape Town or Pretoria, tel (021) 22-2810, fax (021) 24-6211 or (012) 343-1991, fax (012) 343-0905.

Some useful 4x4 contacts are:

Land Rover Owners Club of SA (Cape), PO Box 22173, Fish Hoek 7975, Western Cape;

Hex River 4x4 Trail, De Doorns, contact Faan Therblanche, tel (02322) 2114, or Niel de Kock, Cell 082 891-9034;

Waboomsberg 4x4 Trail, Montagu, tel (0234) 42209, or contact Montagu Information;

Hillandale Farm 4x4 Trail, Beaufort West, tel (0201) 51050 or (02024) 714;

Karoo 4x4 Trails, contact Rose Willis, tel (0201) 3001/51160;

Calitzdorp, tel (04437) 33312;

Oudsthoorn, tel (04436) 736;

Riversdale, tel (02933) 33214;

Sedgefield, tel (04455) 31313/32628;

Sedgefield 4x4 Club, tel (04455) 31737;

Uniondale, tel (04942) 6102.

Bungi-jumping. If you feel the need to stretch your legs on the Garden Route you can dive headfirst off the Gourits River Bridge, assisted by a group of Australians, New Zealanders and South Africans who call themselves Kiwi Extreme. They have set up a bungi-jump on the bridge, 30km/19 miles from Mossel Bay. You pay before you jump (R100; £13.35/$22), after being weighed and strapped into two harnesses. Total time for the jump is less than three minutes. No one under 14 is allowed to jump, and if you are under 18 you need parental consent. Kiwi Extreme has a fatality-free record and more than 30,000 people have taken the plunge since Kiwi Extreme began in 1990. Contact Kiwi Extreme, tel (0444) 7448, and (021) 72-4516, or Chris Upton on Cell 083 264-5221. Others who can arrange for you to jump off a bridge are WildThing Adventures in Cape Town, tel/fax (021) 461-1653, and Hellswing on Cell 083 675-3537.

Sailing. There is challenging sailing in all the Cape waters and yacht clubs abound all along the coast. The first Cape to Rio Yacht race started in Table Bay in 1971 and has now resumed, with the next planned for the year 2000. Rothmans Week Regatta is a colourful feature of the Cape Town calendar every December. The Royal Cape Yacht Club is the premier yacht club in the province and hosts leading international events and is the usual port of call for round-the-worlders. The club is a popular dining and drinking venue, but you must be a member of a yacht club to enjoy the facilities, unless you are a guest. RCYC has reciprocity with 35 other yacht clubs, among the overseas clubs are Associaciao Naval de Lisboa; Clube Naval, Departamento Nautico, Niteroi, Brazil; Fremantle Sailing Club; Noordeutscher Regatta Verein, Germany; Royal Hong Kong Yacht Club; Royal Northern and Clyde Yacht Club, Scotland; Royal Solent Yacht Club, Isle of Wight; Royal Thames Yacht Club, England; Royal Vancouver Yacht Club, Canada; Royal Victoria Yacht Club, British Columbia; Seattle Yacht Club, USA; Yacht Club de France, Chatou, France; and Yacht Club de Monaco. Contact the club at PO Box 772, Cape Town 8000, tel (021) 21-1354/5, fax (021) 21-6028.

Schaafsma Charters of Saldanha Bay — 90 minutes drive from Cape Town — will take you sailing in the exhilarating waters off the West Coast. They also run daily boat trips (R25) and sundowner cruises (R45). For R65 you can join the yachts *Sailfisher* or *Sailtrader* for a three-hour cruise to Malgas (Mad Goose) Island to see jackass penguins and other sea birds. Schaafsma also run the Slipway Waterfront restaurant at Saldanha Bay where, if the seafood was any fresher, it would still be swimming or scuttling in the bay. Contact Schaafsma Charters and the restaurant at PO Box 172, Vredenburg 7380, tel (02281) 44235, fax (02281) 43896.

Useful contacts:

WP Sailing Association, Cape Town, tel (021) 439-7976;
Mossel Bay Sailing Club, tel (0444) 91-2202;
Seven Seas Club, Simon's Town, tel (021) 786-2729;
Zeekoevlei Yacht Club, tel (021) 705-3373;
Knysna Yacht Club, tel (0445) 82-5724;
Hermanus Yacht Club, tel (0283) 77-1420.

For dinghy sailing, powerboating, windsurfing and other watersports contact the Milnerton Aquatic Club in Cape Town, tel (021) 557-7090.

Surfing. Popular surfing spots on the Cape Peninsula are Kommetjie ('the Kom') and Long Beach south of Cape Town and Big Bay at nearby Bloubergstrand, all on the Atlantic coast. Western Province Surfing Association, tel (021) 64-2972, will fill you in on surfing spots both local and further afield, and so will any local surf shop. Big Bay is also the place for boardsailing (windsurfing) when the south-easter is blowing, but only the experienced should hit the waves. In December, the Gunston Boardsailing Championships are held at Bloubergstrand, tel (021) 788-3920. At Langebaan about an hour's drive from Cape Town along the West Coast road, the Cape Windsurf Centre rents out good up-to-date Mistral boards and Naish sails. The wind is measured four times a day and although the wind blows year-round it is more regular from September to mid-April. Windsurfing is on the 25km-long (16 miles) and 2km-wide lagoon. Accommodation packages are available, tel (02287) 21114, fax (02287) 21115.

Diving. The most popular diving options in the Western Cape are snorkel diving for crayfish (rock lobster) and perlemoen (abalone), or wreck diving with scuba gear. Whether you dive the cold Atlantic side or the warmer Indian Ocean side you need a full neoprene wetsuit, one of at least 5mm/0.19 inch thickness is usual, although 7mm/0.28 inch is preferable. Over the past five centuries or so at least a thousand ships have gone down off the Cape coast, many of them in the waters of the Atlantic. Some of the wrecks, especially the later ones, are accessible to scuba divers, although wreck diving is not for the inexperienced on this high-energy coastline. Get *The Shipwreck and Lighthouse Guide* brochure from Captour. Contact:

Atlantic Underwater Club, Cape Town's largest and oldest diving club, tel (021) 49-7147;
False Bay Underwater Club, 24-hour Diveline, tel (021) 761-2763;
South African Underwater Union, tel (021) 930-6549, fax (021) 930-6541;
Mossel Bay Divers, tel (0444) 91-1441;
Waterfront Divers, Knysna Heads, tel (0445) 82-6737, fax (0445) 22938.

You are allowed to dive out four rock lobsters a day in Western Cape waters, but not with scuba gear. Your legal perlemoen quota is also four a day. Good spots within an hour's drive of Cape Town — excluding the forbidden marine reserves — are Cape Point, Buffels Bay, Kommetjie, Melkbostrand, Hangklip, Kleinmond and Hermanus. A rock lobster licence costs R25 (£3.35/$5.50) and a perlemoen licence the same. You can get them at any revenue or magistrate's office. There are stiff fines for ignoring regulations regarding size and season. Copies of regulations applying to angling and diving are available from Sea Fisheries, Private Bag X2, Roggebaai 8012, tel (021) 439-6160, in the form of a handy pamphlet listing the do's and dont's of marine conservation. This includes a map and details of marine reserves and restricted areas from St Helena on the West Coast to the Maputaland reserve and sanctuary in northern Zululand. It also gives details of permits, restrictions on shellfish, bait, and fish species, as well as closed seasons (West Coast rock lobster cannot be caught between 1 May and 15 November, East Coast rock lobster between 1 November and 31 January, and perlemoen between 1 May and 31 October). Buy a measuring ring from any sports shop to check that any perlemoen and crayfish you catch are legal size. False Bay, on the east side of the Peninsula, is an area of about 1000sq km/386sq miles of sheltered warmish water. It is a popular and pleasant dive, but beware of the Great Whites which cruise the bay for the easy pickings among the seal colonies which also favour the area. One of these predators is so big it is often spotted by SAA pilots flying into Cape Town International Airport. They call it 'The Submarine.' For safer Great White watching, contact *Adventure Safaris and Sports Tours* in Cape Town, tel (021) 438-5201.

Canoeing. There is not a great deal of wild white water around but there are several notable events. In June there is a canoe marathon on the Olifants River, Citrusdal, tel (022) 921-3544. The Berg River Canoe Marathon is held every July, a four-day event over 232km/144 miles between the Boland wine town of Paarl to the mouth of the river at Port Owen, near Velddrif. Contact Western Province Canoe Union, tel (021) 23-2120, or Charles Melck, tel (021) 551-1770. In August there is the Breede River Canoe Marathon, Swellendam. Contact Swellendam Publicity, tel (0291) 42770. For more information on river rafting, kayaking and canoeing, contact the South African River Rafters Association in Cape Town, tel (021) 762-2350.

There are weekend trips in the Western Cape as close as 70km/44 miles from Cape Town and generally within 250km/155 miles. Cape Town operators include:

Orange River Adventures, tel (021) 419-1705;
Adventures Unlimited, tel (021) 790-3980;
Aquatrails, tel (021) 794-5808;
Cape Canoe Trails, tel (021) 789-2040;
Felix Unite River Adventures, tel (021) 762-6935 for Orange, Doring and Berg Rivers,
   and tel (021) 762-5602 for the Breede River, fax for both is (021) 761-9259;
River Rafters, tel (021) 72-5094, fax (021) 72-5241;
River Runners, tel (021) 762-6935;
River Drifters, tel (021) 790-4902.

Seal Island, just over an hour's easy paddle from Hout Bay, is home to hundreds of Cape fur seals. Coastal Kayak Trails offers sea kayak trips along the Cape coast. Contact Leon or Estelle, tel/fax (021) 551-8739, e-mail ctrail@gem.co.za

Angling. The meeting of two ocean currents — one warm, the other cold — add spice and variety to sea angling off the Western Cape coast; for trout there are rivers and mountain streams, with vleis and dams for carp, bass and other freshwater species, while tidal rivers give you the best of both worlds, with garrick, white steenbras, kob and spotted grunter haunting the estuaries, and rock and surf spots offering galjoen, musselcracker, shad, white stumpnose and the fighting yellowtail.

Salt water fishing spots. Cape Point to Hangklip encompasses False Bay and includes most of the recognised major surf angling spots. From Muizenberg to Cape Point there are kob and steenbras, especially when the south-easter blows. Kalk Bay is good for steenbras, white stumpnose, kob and mackerel and the ledges of Rooikranz, inside the Cape of Good Hope Nature Reserve, are the most famous spots of all, producing spectacular catches of yellowtail and even the odd tunny. Along the coast from Cape Hangklip to Gansbaai the Hermanus area provides good angling in the Bot River lagoon at Fisherhaven and nearby Hermanus lagoon. Beyond Gansbaai the coastline from Agulhas, the southernmost tip of Africa, to Mossel Bay offers some of the province's prime rock and beach angling, and along the Garden Route from Mossel Bay to Plettenberg Bay the national road runs close to the coastline, so most of the best known fishing spots are easy to reach. The little holiday resort of Buffels Bay is one of the most accessible and safest spots and is known for its musselcracker and galjoen. Inside the majestic Knysna Heads, one of the best known landmarks along this coast, is the Knysna lagoon, one of the best lagoon fishing spots on this section of coast, and known for white steenbras, leervis and kob. The famed Robberg Peninsula at Plettenberg Bay offers really deep-water angling. Plettenberg Bay itself, one of the most fashionable and trendy resorts on the coast, is famous for its elf (shad) and leervis and just beyond the town, at Keurboomstrand, is some of the best steenbras angling the province has to offer.

Heading up the West Coast there is good fishing from the Cape of Good Hope Nature Reserve at Cape Point up to Melkbos and beyond. The Blouberg area not far from Cape Town is good for galjoen and the white mussels you need for bait can be dug up there on the beach. Along the coastal road towards Saldanha Bay the seaside village of Yzerfontein is worth a cast. Nearby Langebaan Lagoon is an angler's and nature lover's paradise. Part of the lagoon, which is open to the sea, is a National Park but most of it is still open to angling. From 32 to 48km/20 to 30 miles out from Cape Point broadbill challenge big game fishermen with their weight and fighting spirit. The South African record billfish, caught in these waters, tops 246.5kg/543.4lb. Every year around the end of April local and overseas deep-sea anglers gather at Gordon's Bay for the annual 3-day International Broadbill Classic. The event is organised by the Gordon's Bay Boat Angling Club. Contact Dave Melley, tel (021) 856-1250 or (021) 511-1636.

Contacts: WP Deep Sea Angling Association, Martin Botha, tel (021) 52-4967 and 92-4386; WP Shore Angling Association, John Cunningham, tel (021) 551-2045 or (021) 557-8428; Southern Cape Beach Angling Association, J Saayman, tel (0444) 95-1602; Southern Cape Deep Sea Angling Association, Knysna, J Engelbrecht, tel (0445) 22011.

Charters for game fish or deep-sea bottom fishing: Cape Town — Big Game Fishing Safaris, tel (021) 64-2203; Bluefin Charters, tel (021) 783-1756/786-1463; Game Fish Charters, tel (021) 790-4550; Neptune Deep Sea Angling, R. Davis, tel (021) 782-3889; Pommery Charters, tel (021) 25-4277. Knysna — Kelsea Fishing Charters, tel (0445) 82-5577, or Colleen, tel (0445) 22062; Knysna Fishing Charters, Peter Baker, tel (0445) 21548, Cell 082 569-7835. Plettenberg Bay — Crecy Charters, Boet Lourens, tel (04457) 30748.

Freshwater Angling. There are 19 species of freshwater fish in the Western Cape, of which 12 are found nowhere else in the world. You don't need to go much further than the suburbs of Cape Town for some satisfying fishing. For the carp angler there are three main easily accessible areas: Sandvlei at Muizenberg, Princessvlei and Zeekoevlei. Sandvlei is great for saltwater flyfishing, as well as for giant carp. Catches of 10kg/22lb carp are not unusual. Princessvlei, a smaller body of water, and its neighbour Zeekoevlei, hold plenty of carp, although not as big as the Sandvlei beauties. At the top of Sir Lowry's Pass heading out of Cape Town is Steenbras Dam, which contains brown and rainbow trout. On the West Coast is the Clanwilliam Dam, which is one of the Western Cape's top smallmouth bass areas. Outside the Boland town of Villiersdorp is the Theewaterskloof Dam offering some of the best largemouth bass fishing anywhere. The Breede River is also a fine freshwater area in its upper reaches where it flows past the towns of Robertson, Bonnievale and Swellendam. For trout, go to the Witte River, near Wellington, and the Elandspad and Smalblaar rivers, in the Du Toit's Kloof Pass area.

Contacts:

Cape Piscatorial Society, tel (021) 24-7725;
Hermanus Trout Fishing Club, tel (0283) 21409/21235;
Trout Adventures Africa, tel (021) 26-1057;
WP Artlure Angling Association, tel (02212) 3783/2437;
WP Freshwater Angling Association, tel (021) 981-5205/886-4234;
Adventure Safaris and Sport Tours, tel (021) 438-5201, fax (021) 438-4807;
Budget Angling, tel (021) 72-3558/406-8180.

Horse-riding. Ride the Stellenbosch Wine Route on horseback. A half-day ride with wine tasting costs R125 (£16.65/$27.50); full day R190, plus lunch or overnight in a mountain chalet with wine, lunch, supper and breakfast for R400. Contact:

Wine Valley Horse Trails, tel (021) 981-6331, Cell 083 226-8735;
Vineyard Horse Trails, tel (021) 981-2480;
Valley Trails, tel (021) 790-6601;
The Dunes Horse Trails, tel (021) 789-1723.

You can take to the air at the Stellenbosch Flying Club, where the Cape Parachute Club has its headquarters, tel (021) 58-8514, (021) 880-1264, and (021) 880-0294. The Cape Gliding Club takes passengers up every weekend at the Worcester airfield, between Rawsonville and Worcester. Contact Barry, tel (021) 531-9203 (h) or (021) 448-3811 (w). Cape Albatross Hang-gliding Club, tel (021) 21-1802 (w), (021) 438-9093 (h).

Horse-racing.

Kenilworth Racecourse, 11km/7 miles from Cape Town on Lansdowne Road, Kenilworth, tel (021) 762-7777;
Milnerton Racecourse, 13km/8 miles from Cape Town, off Koeberg Road and Otto du Plessis Drive, tel (021) 551-2110;
Durbanville Racecourse, 27km/17 miles from Cape Town on Racecourse Road, Durbanville, tel (021) 96-8239;
Western Province Racing Club, tel (021) 762-7777, fax (021) 762-1919.

 The Western Cape has many indigenous arts and crafts, but as it was not historically a region of black settlement 'traditional' wood and soapstone carvings of animals and ceremonial masks will probably come from some other part of Africa. More interesting are figures and items crafted locally from tin cans, wire and string and sold along the road. The Western Cape, and particularly Cape Town and the Peninsula, are repositories of European collectables, such as fine silver, porcelain, furniture, paintings and jewellery, which you will find principally in Longmarket Street, Cape Town, and in the suburbs of Wynberg and Claremont.

Craft markets are popular throughout the Cape and are mostly held over weekends. Everything from yellowwood furniture to rugs, clothing and jewellery attuned to ethnic designs can be found. You can get an Arts and Crafts Map and an Antique Route brochure from Captour. Four of the most popular Cape Town flea markets are at Green Point (Sundays), Greenmarket Square (Monday to Friday all day, as well as Saturday mornings), the Grand Parade (Wednesdays and Saturdays) and the V&A Waterfront Arts and Crafts Market (Saturdays and Sundays). Other markets are: Station Market at the Cape Town Station, Monday to Friday; Constantia Sunday Craft Market, tel (021) 531-2653; Durbanville Craft Market, every Saturday at Rust-en-Vrede, Wellington Road (try the Boy Scouts' famous hamburgers and bacon rolls), tel (021) 96-2937; Craft in the Park, Campground Road, Rondebosch, tel (021) 531-4236; Pinelands Craft Market, tel (021) 531-4236; Kirstenbosch Craft Market, tel (021) 61-5468; the Red Shed Craft Workshop, next to the Victoria shopping centre at the V&A Waterfront, features crafters at work 9am to 6pm daily, tel (021) 419-2885; the Church Street market, central city, is open daily, tel (021) 438-8566. Petticoat Lane craft market is open daily at the old jail, Bellville, Tyger Valley Road (below Tyger Valley Centre); there is an antique and craft market at Muizenberg every Sunday and public holiday at Shoprite Centre, tel (021) 782-7031 or (021) 761-9620; Hout Bay has a market every Sunday featuring 80 crafters, tel (021) 790-3474. Do not miss the flower market in Trafalgar Place off Adderley Street, in the city centre; a chat with the colourful flower sellers is an education.

For curios and souvenirs try:

African Image, tel (021) 23-8385;
African Market Curios, tel (021) 25-3537;
African Memories, tel (021) 23-8866;
Afrogem, tel (021) 24-8048;
Bundu Art & Craft Curios, tel (021) 21-5383;
Gemstone Paradise, tel (021) 883-9542;
Indaba Curios, tel (021) 25-3639;
Out of Africa, tel (021) 24-2362;
Zinkomo, tel (021) 419-1837.

There are many antique and bric-a-brac shops and art galleries in Stellenbosch and a Winelands Craft Market is held every Sunday in summer. On Devon Valley Road, Jean Craig Pottery makes and sells ethnic pottery based on Xhosa, Zulu and Ndebele traditional motifs. Open Monday to Thursday from 8.15am to 5pm, Friday from 8.15am to 4.30pm and Saturday from 9am to 1pm, tel (021) 883-2998. Dombeya Farm beneath the Helderberg Mountains has a handspinning, dyeing, weaving and knitting workshop where you can watch the women making the wide variety of wool and yarn, hand-knitted jerseys and soft furnishings they sell. Open Monday to Saturday from 8.30am to 5pm, tel (021) 881-2746. A variety of farm stalls sell fresh local produce and a factory shop at Simonsberg offers cheeses and dairy products. In summer you can pick your own strawberries on some of the local farms. A visit to Oom Samie se Winkel in Dorp Street, a general dealer with a difference, is a novel experience.

Paarl has a flea market in the central shopping area on Saturdays and an Art and Craft Market in Victoria Park on the first Saturday of every month.

Shopping in Hermanus is a delight with fascinating little shops tucked away in unexpected places. Visit the speciality shops and boutiques in Warrington's Arcade, Astoria Village, Oudehof Mall, Victoria Square, Royal Centre, Long Street, Aberdeen Centre, Cope's Centre, Mitchell Street and High Street.

De Oude Pastorie in Oudtshoorn has a wonderful variety of arts and crafts. The Klein Karoo, and in particular Oudtshoorn, the 'feather capital of the world,' is renowned for its ostrich products. Try the ostrich biltong while you are looking at the feather dusters.

Knysna's oaklined streets are crammed with tiny shops. Pieces crafted from indigenous yellowwood, stinkwood and wild olive are good buys. Street markets and antique shops abound, stained glass and leather artists, painters and sculptors have one-of-a-kind creations for sale. Quaint shops with interesting names and contents are found along Main Road and in its main shopping centres. The Knysna Arts and Crafts Society in the Old Gaol in Queen Street has regular exhibitions.

Plettenberg Bay Arts and Crafts Route:

The Gift Estate. Delightful functional pottery. Fynbos-protea trail. Open Monday to Saturday 9am to 5pm. Tel (04457) 33451.

Bokkie Farm and Craft Shop. Farm fare, hand-made leather fashion bags and belts. Bauern Malerea/Folk Art articles, pottery. Open seven days a week. Tel (04457) 7676.

The Potter. An extensive range of functional and decorative clayware for home and garden. Open seven days a week. Tel/fax (04457) 7735.

The Islander. Nesting sculptured bowls from local woods for salads, dips and other food. Open Wednesday to Saturday from 9am to 11pm, except in August and September. Tel (04457) 7776.

Graines Gallery. Watch artists at work in most mediums from miniatures to very big. Open Monday to Saturday from 10am to 4pm. Tel (04457) 32134.

Simran Batik. Fine art and batik murals by artists in this unique community. Open during business hours. Tel (04457) 32115/31297.

Global Craft Village. A mini-village of eight shops selling folk art, yellowwood crafts, gifts, curios, fabrics and clothing. Open from 9am to 5pm. Open every day during the holiday season. Tel (04457) 33743.

Old Valley Yellowwood. Handcrafted yellowwood coffee tables, dining tables, chests and furniture in both old and new wood. Open Monday to Friday from 8am to 6pm. Tel (04457) 32997.

Arts Association Gallery. The Plettenberg Bay Arts Association displays local artists' work. Open between 10am and 4pm. Tel (04457) 32350.

Christos Pottery. Decorated, functional pottery and modern porcelain dolls. Open seven days a week, tel (04457) 34160.

Old Nick. A shop, workshop, tea garden and gallery. Pottery, mohair blankets, and woodwork. Open seven days a week (December to April). Tel (04457) 31395.

Porcupine Art Studio. A presentation of inventive and provoking art forms as ceramics, textiles and woodcarvings, blending traditional folklore art with contemporary materials and concepts. Open six days a week from 10am to 5pm. Tel (04457) 9868.

Langa Lapu. Hand-dyed fabrics, pottery, jewellery, beadwork, baskets and clothing. Open Monday to Sunday from 9am to 5pm in season. Tel (04457) 48827.

Woodgate Farm. Handcrafted jewellery in brass and copper, crafts and curios. Backpackers' and travellers' retreat. Open seven days a week from 8am to 5pm. Tel/fax (04457) 48690.

Crime and Safety

In spite of what Princess Diana's former journalist brother Earl Spencer says in British glossy *Harpers and Queen*, the level of crime in Cape Town is dropping. Spencer, who lives in Cape Town with his family, talks of a newspaper advertisement offering anti-personnel mines for readers' gardens. Good, gruesome stuff but statistics reveal a downward trend in criminal activities. Police say Cape Town's city centre is not as dangerous as many think. They report about a dozen cases a month of crimes against tourists, mostly by pickpockets. Muggings involving violence are minimal. Even so, you should take the same precautions as you would in any other city and carry keys and valuables on your person; keep handbags firmly grasped under your arm; remain calm and co-operative if you are robbed; do not carry large sums of money with you;

do not keep your wallet in your back pocket — and do not enter or cross dark and deserted areas. Contact the Tourist Assistance Police Unit in Tulbagh Square, in the city centre, or tel (021) 418-2853 if you need help.

In Cape Town:

Flying Squad, tel 10111.
Police, tel (021) 418-2853 and (021) 461-7282.
Ambulance, 10177.
Sea Rescue Services, tel (021) 405-3500.

Poison Centre, tel (021) 689-5227/931-6129.
Fire Brigade, tel (021) 535-1100.
Waterfront Security, tel (021) 418-2340.
Waterfront Visitor's Centre, tel (021) 418-2369.
Table Bay Harbour Detective Branch, tel (021) 419-0919.
Weather (for the coastal region), tel (021) 40881.
Cape Nature Conservation, Private Bag X9086, Cape Town 8000, tel (021) 483-4051/4227, fax (021) 23-0939, for information about hiking in the Western Cape.
Gay travel information and accommodation, tel (021) 23-9001.
Gay Cape Town information, fax Lars Schwinges at (021) 21-1383, e-mail lars@forward.co.za
Cape Organisation for Gay Sport (Cogs), Free post CB0860, Bloubergrant 7443, tel (021) 557-7195, e-mail ro@global.co.za
Gay Counselling Service, tel (021) 21-5420.
Gay esCape Travel Consultant, 10th Floor, Guarantee House, Burg Street, tel (021) 23-9001.
Out in Africa Film Festival is an annual event, tel Festival Office (021) 24-1532.
Listen to *In the Pink* on 89.5FM every Thursday night from 8.30pm for an in-depth round up of what's happening in gay Cape Town.

TOURIST INFORMATION

Satour has a regional office in Cape Town on the 10th Floor of the Golden Acre Shopping Centre in Adderley Street, city centre. Contact Private Bag X9108, Cape Town 8000, tel (021) 21-6274.
Captour (Cape Tourism Authority) Information Bureau, Tourist Rendezvous Travel Centre, Adderley Street, central city. PO Box 1403, Cape Town 8000, tel (021) 418-5214, fax (021) 418-5227. 1 May to 20 September: Monday to Friday, 8am–5pm, Saturday, 8am–1pm, Sunday, 10am–1pm; 1 October to 30 April: Monday to Friday, 8am–6pm, Saturday, 8.30am–3pm, Sunday 10am–1pm. e-mail captour@iafrica.com
Western Cape Tourism Board, PO Box 1403, Welgemoed 7538, tel (021) 418-3705/6, fax (021) 21-4875.
Bredasdorp Publicity, PO Box 51, Bredasdorp 7280, tel (02841) 42584.
Breede River Valley, PO Box 91 Worcester 6850, tel (0231) 76411/2.
Caledon Publicity, PO Box 258, Caledon 7230, tel (0281) 21511.
Central Karoo, PO Box 56, Beaufort West 6970, tel (0201) 51160, fax (0201) 3675.
Ceres Publicity Association, PO Box 563, Ceres 6835, tel (0233) 61287.
Clanwilliam Tourism Association, PO Box 5, Clanwilliam 8135, tel (027) 482-2024.
Darling Information, PO Box 5, Darling 7345, tel (02241) 2237.
False Bay Publicity Association, PO Box 302, Muizenberg 7951, tel (021) 788-8048.
Franschhoek, PO Box 37, Franschhoek 7690, tel (021) 876-3603.
Gansbaai, PO Box 399, Gansbaai 7220, tel/fax (02834) 41439.
Garden Route, PO Box 1514, George 6530, tel (0441) 73-6314, fax (0441) 74-6840.

George Tourism Association, PO Box 1109, George 6530, tel (0441) 863-9295/6, fax (0441) 73-5228.

Great Karoo, PO Box 56, Beaufort West 6970, tel (0201) 51160, fax (0201) 3675.

Greater Hermanus, PO Box 117, Hermanus 7200, tel (0283) 22629.

Klein Karoo, PO Box 1234, Oudsthoorn 6620, tel (0443) 22-6643.

Knysna Publicity Association, PO Box 87, Knysna 6570, tel (0445) 21610.

Lambert's Bay Information, PO Box 245, Lambert's Bay 8130, tel (027) 432-2335.

Langebaan, PO Box 11, Langebaan 7357, tel (02287) 22115.

Matjiesfontein, Lord Milner Hotel, Matjiesfontein 6901, tel (02372) 5203.

Muizenberg Publicity Association, tel/fax (021) 788-7673.

Montagu Publicity, PO Box 24, Montagu 6720, tel (0234) 42471.

Mossel Bay Marketing Association, PO Box 25, Mossel Bay 6500, tel (0444) 91-2202.

Olifants River Valley, PO Box 351, Clanwilliam 8135, tel (027) 482-2029.

Overberg, PO Box 250, Caledon 7230, tel (0281) 22090.

Paarl Publicity, PO Box 47, Paarl 7622, tel (02211) 23829.

Plettenberg Bay Publicity Association, PO Box 894, Plettenberg Bay 6600, tel (04457) 34065.

Robertson Publicity Association, PO Box 52, Robertson 6705, tel (02351) 4437.

Simon's Town Information Centre, PO Box 56, Simon's Town 7995, tel (021) 786-3046.

Stellenbosch Tourist Information, PO Box 368, Stellenbosch 7600, tel (021) 883-3584.

Stilbaai Publicity Association, PO Box 245, Stilbaai 6785, tel (02934) 42602.

Strand Publicity Association, PO Box 3, Strand 7140, tel (021) 853-6796.

Swartland/Sandveld, Private Bag X52, Malmesbury 7300, tel (0224)-22996.

Swellendam Publicity Association, PO Box 369, Swellendam 6740, tel (0291) 42770.

Tulbagh Valley Publicity Association, PO Box 277, Tulbagh 6820, tel (0236) 30-1348.

Wellington Publicity Association, PO Box 695, Wellington 7655, tel (02211) 34604.

West Coast Publicity, PO Box 139, Saldanha 7395, tel (02281) 42058/88, fax (02281) 44240.

Wilderness Eco-Tourism Association, PO Box 188, Wilderness 6560, tel (0441) 877-0045.

Winelands Tourism Association, PO Box 19, Somerset West 7129, tel (021) 851-1497.

Worcester Publicity, 75 Church Street, Worcester 6850, tel (0231)-71408.

INDEX

Vacation Work publish:

	Paperback	Hardback
The Directory of Summer Jobs Abroad	£7.99	£12.99
The Directory of Summer Jobs in Britain	£7.99	£12.99
Adventure Holidays	£6.99	£11.99
The Teenager's Vacation Guide to Work, Study & Adventure ..	£6.95	£9.95
Work Your Way Around the World	£10.99	£16.99
Working in Tourism — The UK, Europe & Beyond	£9.99	£15.99
Kibbutz Volunteer	£7.99	£12.99
Working on Cruise Ships	£8.99	£12.99
Teaching English Abroad	£10.99	£15.99
The Au Pair & Nanny's Guide to Working Abroad	£9.99	£14.99
Working in Ski Resorts — Europe & North America	£8.95	£14.95
Working with the Environment	£9.99	£15.99
Health Professionals Abroad	£9.99	£15.99
The Directory of Jobs and Careers Abroad	£10.99	£16.99
The International Directory of Voluntary Work	£9.99	£15.99
The Directory of Work & Study in Developing Countries	£8.99	£10.99
Live & Work in France	£8.95	£14.95
Live & Work in Australia & New Zealand	£8.95	£14.95
Live & Work in Scandinavia	£8.95	£14.95
Live & Work in USA & Canada	£8.95	£14.95
Live & Work in Spain & Portugal	£8.95	£11.95
Live & Work in Belgium, The Netherlands & Luxembourg	£8.95	–
Live & Work in Germany	£8.95	–
Live & Work in Italy	£7.95	–
Travellers Survival Kit: Lebanon	£9.99	–
Travellers Survival Kit: South Africa	£9.99	–
Travellers Survival Kit: India	£9.99	–
Travellers Survival Kit: Russia & the Republics	£9.95	–
Travellers Survival Kit: Western Europe	£8.95	–
Travellers Survival Kit: Eastern Europe	£9.95	–
Travellers Survival Kit: South America	£12.95	–
Travellers Survival Kit: Central America	£8.95	–
Travellers Survival Kit: Cuba	£9.99	–
Travellers Survival Kit: USA & Canada	£9.95	–
Travellers Survival Kit to the East	£6.95	–
Travellers Survival Kit: Australia & New Zealand	£9.99	–
Hitch-hikers' Manual Britain	£3.95	–
Europe — Manual for Hitch-hikers	£4.95	–

Distributors of:

Summer Jobs USA	£10.99	–
Internships (On-the-Job Training Opportunities in the USA)	£15.99	–
Sports Scholarships in the USA	£12.99	–
The Directory of College Accommodations USA	£5.95	–
Making it in Japan	£8.95	–

Vacation Work Publications, 9 Park End Street, Oxford OX1 1HJ
(Tel 01865-241978. Fax 01865-790885)